CASES AND MATERIAL

BEYOND RATIONAL CHOICE:
ALTERNATIVE PERSPECTIVES ON ECONOMICS

by

EMMA COLEMAN JORDAN
Professor of Law
Georgetown University Law Center

ANGELA P. HARRIS
Professor of Law
Boalt Hall—School of Law, University of California, Berkeley

FOUNDATION PRESS

NEW YORK, NEW YORK

2006

© 2006 By FOUNDATION PRESS

       395 Hudson Street
       New York, NY 10014
       Phone Toll Free 1–877–888–1330
       Fax (212) 367–6799
       fdpress.com

Printed in the United States of America

ISBN–13: 978–1–58778–958–8
ISBN–10: 1–58778–958–2

 *TEXT IS PRINTED ON 10% POST CONSUMER RECYCLED PAPER*

For the late E. W. Coleman and M. H. Coleman,
my daughters Kristen and Allison and my sisters Betty, Jean and Earlene

*

INTRODUCTION

Today, the discipline of Economics is in transition. Ironically, the transition returns to some of the original insights of the first Economist Adam Smith, albeit with Twenty–first Century tools. It was Smith who first directed our attention to the role of human beings in the development of markets and how these markets function to solve the basic problems that every society must address. These problems are: what goods to produce, how to produce them, and to whom they should be distributed. Smith's focus on people was pioneering, and defined the classical school of Economics. When Smith created the discipline of economics, the discipline of human psychology did not exist. So, Smith's central speculation about human motivation was derived from his training as a moral philosopher. Economics was built on the assumption that people make choices based upon self interest. Over time as the discipline of economics matured, this insight became imbedded in the notion of rational choice. Gradually, almost imperceptibly, the rational choice assumption became rigid, and out of touch with the developments into human judgment coming from psychology.

A major recognition that the rigid assumptions of human rationality that have dominated economics were incomplete, if not totally wrong, came in 2002 when the Nobel Prize in Economics was awarded to Daniel Kahneman, a psychologist. Kahneman's website summarizes his influence by noting that "although he never took an economics course, Princeton psychologist Daniel Kahneman received the Nobel Prize in economic sciences ... [t]he award recognized [his] life-long work in integrating psychological research and economic science. His work showed economists how people don't always make reasoned choices, over-turning long held views and opening up a new field of research"

This book is designed to provide materials for faculty and students who want to explore the basic intellectual history of modern economics and its turn away from rigid rationality assumptions. We have chosen material that would be useful in courses and seminars taught in economics departments. at all levels, law school courses and seminars. We expect that both traditionalists and contrarians who subscribe to the views of the newly developed field of behavioral economics will find this material stimulating.

The major questions that frame our work here are: Does traditional legal analysis play a role in reinforcing the rational choice, efficiency and wealth maximization rationales of conventional market theory? Can psychology, sociology, and anthropology contribute to more robust accounts of human decisionmaking, and thus provide more accurate accounts of the environment in which legal rules operate. How do race, gender, or sexual identity and class status operate in market transactions?

In order to pursue these questions we have focused our attention on the problem of economic inequality. We believe that the problem of social inequality and systematic race, gender, and sexual orientation subordination lead to predictably unequal economic distributions for members of the subordinated groups. Chapter 5 provides an opportunity to discuss the meaning of "class" in America. Chapter 6 looks at the portrait of class difference, and subordination from the bottom up.

In Chapter 5 we look at the role of educational opportunity in shaping our class structure. Affirmative action, long a hotly contested remedy for past racial discrimination, serves as a vehicle for discussing the consequences of the development of vastly different economic opportunity structure based on race. We ask whether the U.S. Constitution has played an important role in facilitating market-driven inequality in primary and secondary education. Chapter 5 also provides materials to discuss the economic history of subordination of women and Native Americans, their wealth and participation in our economy.

Stagnant, and declining economic mobility is the most challenging problem that defies rationality assumptions of conventional economic theory. As we explore in what follows, conventional theory assumes that market competition will drive out the structural impact of individual preferences for harmful discrimination. Recent data shows that contrary to what many traditional economists have always assumed, the myth of Horatio Alger, is just that, a myth. Individual movement up the economic ladder is tightly linked to the economic status that one's parents and siblings held.

The famous line attributed to Andrew Carnegie that hard working Americans can go from "shirt sleeves to shirt sleeves in three generations" is not true now, if it ever was. As Princeton economist, Alan B. Krueger argues: [f]ive or six generations is probably required, on average to erase the advantages or disadvantages of one's economic origins. We conclude the investigation in Chapter 5 of the data showing increasing economic inequality, leading to increasing social inequality, with a proposal from two Yale law professors who want to give every American, regardless of wealth, a "stake", provided by the government of a sum of money that would be a birthright that could be collected at the age of 18 and financed by an annual "wealth tax".

We end this book with a look from the bottom. We bring the stories of the lives of desperately poor people such as Rosa Lee, the central personality of Washington Post Reporter Leon Dash's book about one black family's poverty in the neighborhoods of Washington, DC. We call on the poetry of the rap artist Mos Def to express the texture of life at the bottom, in his song "Mathematics". This final chapter also explores the deeper question of the role that materialism plays in fostering a hunger for consumption in the lives of the poorest Americans. Advertising, popular music, and other features of popular culture create an ineluctable allure for those with the least economic resources who are seeking to restore a sense of belonging to America through consumption that depletes their resources today and cramps their economic futures. The discussion of consumption ends with a view of a wealthy, celebrity shoplifter.

This book is our contribution to stimulating a conversation about wealth and inequality and its impact on the strength of democratic participation. We invite you to join this conversation with your own experiences and perceptions strongly in mind.

*

ACKNOWLEDGEMENTS

The idea for creating teaching materials to introduce law students to a systematic examination of the interdisciplinary dimensions of increasing economic inequality and the role of identity in the distribution of wealth first occurred to me more than ten years ago. My decision to create this casebook arose from my mounting frustration with the conceptual limitations of the consumer protection features of commercial law and banking, the two traditional areas in which I had been working over the course of my career. I deeply appreciate the contributions of Nancy Ota who came to Georgetown Law Center in 1992–93 as a graduate Fellow in the Future Law Professor Program to work with me. She invested her unique imagination and commitment to assist me in creating the first set of teaching materials for the first course on Economic Justice.

This casebook owes much to the confidence and support I enjoyed from my publisher, Steven Errick. His enthusiasm and shared vision for the innovations of this effort and his never-failing generosity in responding to and initiating additional publishing opportunities for the Economic Justice topic were important at critical points in the process. Steve's departure in the weeks before this book went to press was a real personal loss. I look forward to working with the new publisher, John Bloomquist in future editions.

I especially want to thank the many Georgetown University Law Center students who enrolled in the early courses in Economic Justice, and who became my most enthusiastic cheering section (offering rap and pop lyrics, African proverbs, Equal Access to Justice/E.A.T. Justice, a socially conscious business venture and strong counterarguments) as this project moved forward to completion. I learned so much from our intense classroom investigations of some of my then forming hypotheses about educational capital, wealth and income inequalities, intergenerational economic effects, linguistic differences, the relationship of the Constitution to economic outcomes, and the limits of conventional market theory. The richness and complexity of this project owe much to my students.

From my Georgetown law students, I chose outstanding research assistants who worked with passion and conviction on the research for this book. They found many truly important additions to the materials. They designed the critical copyright accounting system, chased elusive copyright holders with the zeal of a "repo" man/woman. They kept me laughing when I might have otherwise turned grouchy. They discussed this newly emerging field with me with intelligence and energy. My special thanks go to Angela

Ahern '05, Rashida Baskerville '06, Katherine Buell '04, Cassandra Charles '05, Kenneth Leichter '06, William Morriss '05, Michael Radolinski '06, and Joshua Soszynski '07.

Shaping the boundaries of this project required many hours of conversation with colleagues. Steven Salop was exceptionally generous with his time and the contents of his library on economics. The time we spent talking about economics and shuttling from my office to his across the hall, undoubtedly accelerated my understanding of the intellectual framework of modern economics. I benefited greatly from the expertise and gentle prodding of several colleagues: Alex Aleinikoff, William Braxton, Jerry Kang (during his visit in 2004–5), Carrie Menkel-Meadow, Michael Seidman, Gerry Spann, Rebecca Tushnet, Kathy Zeiler and the colleagues who participated in the Georgetown Law Center Summer Faculty Workshop in 2004. If there are any errors in what follows, it must be because I didn't listen to their sage advice.

This project could not have been finished without the superb institutional arrangements in place at Georgetown University Law Center to support faculty manuscripts. Georgetown enjoys an organizational structure that would be the envy of most casebook writers. I received several summer research grants to allow me to devote time to developing and completing the project. In their capacities as lead manuscript editor and faculty services librarian for this book, Zinta Saulkans and Jennifer Locke and her staff were truly indispensable to achieving a high technical quality for the final manuscript. Diane McDonald, my faculty assistant, Derreck Brown, Sylvia Johnson, Toni Patterson, Ronnie Reese, and Anna Selden in the Office of Faculty Support were always optimistic in the face of frustrations and the unexpected nightmares of formatting, and other technical meltdowns. They were responsive to my many requests during the development of this book. Finally, the Office of Information Systems and Technology introduced me to new equipment and software for managing the project. My special thanks go to Dianne H. Ferro Mesarch, Dimo Michailov, Pablo Molina and Barry Wileman.

In 2001, Angela Harris visited at Georgetown from Boalt Hall at the Univ. of California at Berkeley. As we discussed her work on class and race, it became clear that I could benefit from working with her on this casebook. When she agreed to join the project, I could not know then what a terrific contributor she would be. Her intelligence and humor made the work flow effortlessly to conclusion. We truly had fun doing this work; my only regret is that I didn't think to ask her to join me sooner.

Finally, I want to thank my dear friends Gail, Audrey, Fay and Marta for their support, as well as my two daughters Kristen and Allison for their patience and understanding during the many hours I devoted to completing this project.

EMMA COLEMAN JORDAN

Washington, D.C. August, 2005

I would like to thank my students at Boalt and at Georgetown (Wealth and Class Relations, fall 2000; Wealth and Class Relations, fall 2001; and Law, Markets, and Culture, fall 2004) for their excitement, hard work, and insight as we tried to think through the complicated mutual entanglements of "fairness," "efficiency," "markets," "culture," and "law," and as we struggled toward an institutional theory of human flourishing.

I would like to thank my assistant, Ayn Lowry, for her skill and dedication at tracking down copyright holders across the globe, and for her enthusiasm for this project despite the many last-minute headaches it caused.

I owe a huge debt to my co-author, Emma Coleman Jordan, for talking me into joining and then sticking with the project, and for her wonderful combination of brilliant vision, sisterly solidarity, and can-do spirit.

Last, but not least, I would like to thank my amazing research assistants, Tucker Bolt Culbertson and Naomi Ruth Tsu, for everything: research, pep talks, proofreading, formatting, article suggestions, critical feedback, and, of course, cookies.

ANGELA HARRIS

Berkeley, California

August 2005

*

SUMMARY OF CONTENTS

TABLE OF CONTENTS

*

TABLE OF CASES

Principal cases are in bold type. Non-principal cases are in roman type. References are to Pages.

*

CASES AND MATERIALS

BEYOND RATIONAL CHOICE:
ALTERNATIVE PERSPECTIVES ON ECONOMICS

*

CHAPTER 1

RACE, MARKETS AND NEUTRALITY IN TWO DISCIPLINES

Introduction and Overview

Almost fifty years ago, Charles P. Snow, the British novelist and physicist, identified an important communications gap between the literary and scientific cultures. In a now famous lecture, he used the metaphor of "two cultures" to represent the often incompatible world views of science and literature. He worried that the progress of knowledge in the western world would be compromised by the incomprehension then existing between scientists on one hand, and scholars in the humanities on the other. For Snow, science embodied a culture of objectivity, neutrality, and detached factual inquiry. Literary intellectuals, on the other hand were concerned with questions of meaning, identity, and history.

We conclude that an analogous gap exists today between two groups of legal scholars who think seriously about markets. On one hand, traditional law and economics scholars, like economists, are interested in questions of rational choice, efficiency, wealth maximization, and production and transactions costs. On the other hand, legal scholars concerned with questions of identity, including race, gender and sexual orientation have focused their scholarly investigations on issues of subordination, identity, cultural context, and legal indeterminacy. These two groups of scholars might have much to learn from each other. However, these "two cultures" of law, with few exceptions, remain in separate conversations, with separate world views and separate, even antagonistic, operating assumptions about how to evaluate market phenomena.

In this book, we investigate the problems of the market domain with respect for both cultures. We suspect that the economics perspective, with its reliance on scientific measurement and numerical representation of experience, offers much that can be useful. Our vantage point as scholars who have been active in anti-subordination theory, however, also leads us to be attentive to questions of identity, culture, context, history, and dominance.

Central to the tension between the two cultures of law is the question of method. Is legal analysis (or should it be) a science? Or is legal reasoning inherently interpretive, more art than science? Is the law a neutral and objective forum for conflict resolution, or is it a tool of the powerful? Scholars concerned with the problem of subordination—especially subordination based on race and gender identity—have challenged the claims of neutrality of traditional legal theory. This challenge has brought to the surface the conflict between the two cultures of law. In this book we extend the anti-subordination critique to classic market economics and to law and economics. We believe that the question of method—whether there is an objective science of society, or whether knowledge is inherently perspectival—is of such central importance to understanding the structure of economic inequality that it provides a promising field upon which to begin the three-way conversation between the traditionalists in economics, the traditionalists in law, and the anti-subordination-oriented legal theorists.

As legal scholars concerned with the impact of subordination in law and in markets, we want to examine the role that traditional legal analysis plays in reinforcing the rational choice, efficiency, and wealth maximization assumptions of traditional economic views of the operation of markets. It is not surprising to find that claims of neutrality play as central a role in traditional legal theory as they do in traditional economic analysis.

We turn now to the central organizing question of this first chapter: what methods and normative assumptions are most useful in evaluating the complex landscape of law, markets, and culture? What tools are best suited to sort truth from ideology and myth? What would "truth" look like if we found it? We begin with these questions because we believe that unless these intensely contested, yet often invisible, first premises of analysis are explored, it will be impossible to make sense of the claims and arguments of the traditionalists in economics and in law or the contradictory positions of critical race, feminist and other scholars concerned with the problem of intertwined structures of subordination. Throughout this book we will use a variety of tools to pursue our interest in fostering a conversation between economics and the critical perspectives. We will use methodologies and insights from sociology, psychology, and behavioral economics, as well as the various schools of modern legal thought.

To begin our discussion we have chosen a now-famous narrative account by Professor Patricia Williams. Williams is a part of the critical race theory movement, described below. Our choice to begin with a narrative reflects our view about neutrality and truth. Stories can provide a potent starting point for identifying and examining buried assumptions. As you work through this material keep in mind the structure and sources of the neutrality claims identified above. See if you can detect them on your own.

A.   CRITICAL RACE THEORY: NARRATIVE, NEUTRALITY, AND THE MARKETPLACE

The Death of the Profane

THE ALCHEMY OF RACE AND RIGHTS 44–51 (1991).

■ PATRICIA J. WILLIAMS

Buzzers are big in New York City. Favored particularly by smaller stores and boutiques, merchants throughout the city have installed them as screening devices to reduce the incidence of robbery: if the face at the door looks desirable, the buzzer is pressed and the door is unlocked. If the face is that of an undesirable, the door stays locked. Predictably, the issue of undesirability has revealed itself to be a racial determination. While controversial enough at first, even civil-rights organizations backed down eventually in the face of arguments that the buzzer system is a "necessary evil," that it is a "mere inconvenience" in comparison to the risks of being murdered, that suffering discrimination is not as bad as being assaulted, and that in any event it is not all blacks who are barred, just "17-year-old black males wearing running shoes and hooded sweatshirts."

The installation of these buzzers happened swiftly in New York; stores that had always had their doors wide open suddenly became exclusive or received people by appointment only. I discovered them and their meaning one Saturday in 1986. I was shopping in Soho and saw in a store window a sweater that I wanted to buy for my mother. I pressed my round brown face to the window and my finger to the buzzer, seeking admittance. A narrow-eyed, white teenager wearing running shoes and feasting on bubble gum glared out, evaluating me for signs that would pit me against the limits of his social understanding. After about five seconds, he mouthed "We're closed," and blew pink rubber at me. It was two Saturdays before Christmas, at one o'clock in the afternoon; there were several white people in the store who appeared to be shopping for things for *their* mothers.

I was enraged. At that moment I literally wanted to break all the windows of the store and *take* lots of sweaters for my mother. In the flicker of his judgmental gray eyes, that saleschild had transformed my brightly sentimental, joy-to-the-world, pre-Christmas spree to a shambles. He snuffed my sense of humanitarian catholicity, and there was nothing I could do to snuff his, without making a spectacle of myself.

I am still struck by the structure of power that drove me into such a blizzard of rage. There was almost nothing I could do, short of physically intruding upon him, that would humiliate him the way he humiliated me. No words, no gestures, no prejudices of my own would make a bit of difference to him; his refusal to let me into the store—it was Benetton's, whose colorfully punish ad campaign is premised on wrapping every one of the world's peoples in its cottons and woolens—was an outward manifestation of his never having let someone like me into the realm of his reality. He had no compassion, no remorse, no reference to me; and no desire to acknowledge me even at the estranged level of arm's-length transactor. He saw me only as one who would take his money and therefore could not conceive that I was there to give him money.

In this weird ontological imbalance, I realized that buying something in that store was like bestowing a gift, the gift of my commerce, the lucre of my patronage. In the wake of my outrage, I wanted to take back the gift of appreciation that my peering in the window must have appeared to be. I wanted to take it back in the form of unappreciation, disrespect, defilement. I wanted to work so hard at wishing he could feel what I felt that he would never again mistake my hatred for some sort of plaintive wish to be included. I was quite willing to disenfranchise myself, in the heat of my need to revoke the flattery of my purchasing power. I was willing to boycott Benetton's, random white-owned businesses, and anyone who ever blew bubble gum in my face again.

My rage was admittedly diffuse, even self-destructive, but it was symmetrical. The perhaps loose-ended but utter propriety of that rage is no doubt lost not just to the young man who actually barred me, but to those who would appreciate my being barred only as an abstract precaution, who approve of those who would bar even as they deny that they would bar *me*.

The violence of my desire to burst into Benetton's is probably quite apparent. I often wonder if the violence, the exclusionary hatred, is equally apparent in the repeated public urgings that blacks understand the buzzer system by putting themselves in the shoes of white storeowners—that, in effect, blacks look into the mirror of frightened white faces for the reality of their undesirability; and that then blacks would "just as surely conclude that they would not let themselves in under similar circumstances." (That some blacks might agree merely shows that some of us have learned too well the lessons of privatized intimacies of self-hatred and rationalized away the fullness of our public, participatory selves.)

On the same day I was barred from Benetton's, I went home and wrote the above impassioned account in my journal. On the day after that, I found I was still brooding, so I turned to a form of catharsis I have always found healing. I typed up as much of the story as I have just told, made a big poster of it, put a nice colorful border around it, and, after Benetton's was truly closed, stuck it to their big sweater-filled window. I exercised my first amendment right to place my business with them right out in the street.

So that was the first telling of this story. The second telling came a few months later, for a symposium on Excluded Voices sponsored by a law review. I wrote an essay summing up my feelings about being excluded from Benetton's and analyzing "how the rhetoric of increased privatization, in response to racial issues, functions as the rationalizing agent of public unaccountability and, ultimately, irresponsibility." Weeks later, I received the first edit. From the first page to the last, my fury had been carefully cut out. My rushing, run-on-rage had been reduced to simple declarative sentences. The active personal had been inverted in favor of the passive impersonal. My words were different; they spoke to me upside down. I was afraid to read too much of it at a time—meanings rose up at me oddly, stolen and strange.

A week and a half later, I received the second edit. All reference to Benetton's had been deleted because, according to the editors and the faculty adviser, it was defamatory; they feared harassment and liability; they said printing it would be irresponsible. I called them and offered to supply a footnote attesting to this as my personal experience at one particular location and of a buzzer system not limited to Benetton's; the editors told me that they were not in the habit of publishing things that were unverifiable. I could not but wonder, in this refusal even to let me file an affidavit, what it would take to make my experience verifiable. The testimony of an independent white bystander? (a requirement in fact imposed in U.S. Supreme Court holdings through the first part of the century).

Two days *after* the piece was sent to press, I received copies of the final page proofs. All reference to my race had been eliminated because it was against "editorial policy" to permit descriptions of physiognomy. "I realize," wrote one editor, "that this was a very personal experience, but any reader will know what you must have looked like when standing at that window." In a telephone conversation to them, I ranted wildly about the significance of such an omission. "It's irrelevant," another editor explained in a voice gummy with soothing and patience; "It's nice and poetic" but it doesn't "advance the discussion of any principle.... This is a law review, after all." Frustrated, I accused him of censorship; calmly he assured me it was not. "This is just a matter of style," he said with firmness and finality.

Ultimately I did convince the editors that mention of my race was central to the whole sense of the subsequent text; that my story became one of extreme paranoia without the information that I am black; or that it became one in which the reader had to fill in the gap by assumption, presumption, prejudgment, or prejudice. What was most interesting to me in this experience was how the blind application of principles of neutrality, through the device of omission, acted either to make me look crazy or to make the reader participate in old habits of cultural bias.

That was the second telling of my story. The third telling came last April, when I was invited to participate in a law-school conference on Equality and Difference. I retold my sad tale of exclusion from Soho's most glitzy boutique, focusing in this version on the law-review editing process as a consequence of an ideology of style rooted in a social text of neutrality, I opined:

> Law and legal writing aspire to formalized, color-blind, liberal ideals. Neutrality is the standard for assuring these ideals; yet the adherence to it is often determined by reference to an aesthetic of uniformity, in which difference is simply omitted. For example, when segregation was eradicated from the American lexicon, its omission led many to actually believe that racism therefore no longer existed. Race-neutrality in law has become the presumed antidote for race bias in real life. With the entrenchment of the notion of race-neutrality came attacks on the concept of affirmative action and the rise of reverse discrimination suits. Blacks, for so many generations deprived of jobs based on the color of our skin, are now told that we ought to find it demeaning to be hired, based on the color of our skin. Such is the silliness of simplistic either-or inversions as remedies to complex problems.

What is truly demeaning in this era of double-speak-no-evil is going on interviews and not getting hired because someone doesn't think we'll be comfortable. It is demeaning not to get promoted because we're judged "too weak," then putting in a lot of energy the next time and getting fired because we're "too strong." It is demeaning to be told what we find demeaning. It is very demeaning to stand on street corners unemployed and begging. It is downright demeaning to have to explain why we haven't been employed for months and then watch the job go to someone who is "more experienced." It is outrageously demeaning that none of this can be called racism, even if it happens only to, or to large numbers of, black people; as long is it's done with a smile, a handshake and a shrug; as long as the phantom-word "race" is never used.

The image of race as a phantom-word came to me after I moved into my late godmother's home. In an attempt to make it my own, I cleared the bedroom for painting. The following morning the room asserted itself, came rushing and raging at me through the emptiness, exactly as it had been for twenty-five years. One day filled with profuse and overwhelming complexity, the next day filled with persistently recurring memories. The shape of the past came to haunt me, the shape of the emptiness confronted me each time I was about to enter the room. The force of its spirit still drifts like an odor throughout the house.

The power of that room, I have thought since, is very like the power of racism as status quo: it is deep, angry, eradicated from view, but strong enough to make everyone who enters the room walk around the bed that isn't there, avoiding the phantom as they did the substance, for fear of bodily harm. They do not even know they are avoiding; they defer to the unseen shapes of things with subtle responsiveness, guided by an impulsive awareness of nothingness, and the deep knowledge and denial of witchcraft at work.

The phantom room to me is symbolic of the emptiness of formal equal opportunity, particularly as propounded by President Reagan, the Reagan Civil Rights Commission and the Reagan Supreme Court. Blindly formalized constructions of equal opportunity are the creation of a space that is filled in by a meandering stream of unguided hopes, dreams, fantasies, fears, recollections. They are the presence of the past imaginary, imagistic form—the phantom-roomed exile of our longing.

> It is thus that I strongly believe in the efficacy of programs and paradigms like affirmative action. Blacks are the objects of constitutional omission which has been incorporated into a theory of neutrality. It is thus that omission is really a form of expression, as oxymoronic as that sounds: racial omission is a literal part of original intent; it is the fixed, reiterated prophecy of the Founding Fathers. It is thus that affirmative action is an affirmation; the affirmative act of hiring—or hearing—blacks is a recognition of individuality that replaces blacks as a social statistic that is profoundly interconnective to the fate of blacks and whites either as sub-groups or as one group. In this sense, affirmative action is as mystical and beyond-the-self as an initiation ceremony. It is an

act of verification and of vision. It is an act of social as well as professional responsibility.

The following morning I opened the local newspaper, to find that the event of my speech had commanded two columns on the front page of the Metro section. I quote only the opening lines: "Affirmative action promotes prejudice by denying the status of women and blacks, instead of affirming them as its name suggests. So said New York City attorney Patricia Williams to an audience Wednesday."

I clipped out the article and put it in my journal. In the margin there is a note to myself: eventually, it says, I should try to pull all these threads together into yet another law-review article. The problem, of course, will be that in the hierarchy of law-review citation, the article in the newspaper will have more authoritative weight about me, as a so-called "primary resource," than I will have; it will take precedence over my own citation of the unverifiable testimony of my speech.

I have used the Benetton's story a lot, in speaking engagements at various schools. I tell it whenever I am too tired to whip up an original speech from scratch. Here are some of the questions I have been asked in the wake of its telling:

Am I not privileging a racial perspective, by considering only the black point of view? Don't I have an obligation to include the "salesman's side" of the story?

Am I not putting the salesman on trial and finding him guilty of racism without giving him a chance to respond to or cross-examine me?

Am I not using the store window as a "metaphorical fence" against the potential of his explanation in order to represent my side as "authentic"?

How can I be sure I'm right?

What makes my experience the real black one anyway?

Isn't it possible that another black person would disagree with my experience? If so, doesn't that render my story too unempirical and subjective to pay any attention to?

Always a major objection is to my having put the poster on Benetton's window. As one law professor put it: "It's one thing to publish this in a law review, where no one can take it personally, but it's another thing altogether to put your own interpretation right out there, just like that, uncontested, I mean, with nothing to counter it."

———

NOTES AND QUESTIONS

1. Shared claims of neutrality: legal neutrality and economic neutrality. In their declarations of "truth," legal opinions are presented as objective, indifferent, and neutral. Similarly, the market is based on the notion that a willing buyer and a willing seller will participate in an arm's-length transaction according to their preferences. The sum total of these discrete transactions is a market expressing cumulative preferences that are neutral, in that they do not reflect central government control. It was Adam Smith, one of the founding fathers of modern economics, who asserted that the greater good for all could be best achieved through such a market of free exchanges, guided by the invisible hand. But, what happens when only one party is willing to participate in a transaction? How do individual preferences and choices affect the market? What role does legal neutrality play in weakening or reinforcing these preferences?

2.   Wechslerian principles of neutrality. Lawyer and legal scholar Herbert Wechsler promoted constitutional interpretation based on neutral principles, not the immediate results of particular cases. He described the "ad hoc evaluation" based on individual outcome as "the deepest problem of our constitutionalism." Herbert Wechsler, *Toward Neutral Principles of Constitutional Law*, 73 HARV. L. REV. 1 (1959).

> A principled decision, in the sense I have in mind, is one that rests on reasons with respect to all the issues in the case, reasons that in their generality and their neutrality transcend any immediate result that is involved. When no sufficient reasons of this kind can be assigned for overturning value choices of the other branches of the Government or of a state, those choices must, of course, survive. Otherwise, as Holmes said in his first opinion for the Court, "a constitution, instead of embodying only relatively fundamental rules of right, as generally understood by all English-speaking communities, would become the partisan of a particular set of ethical or economical opinions...." *Id.* at 19.

Wechsler recognizes the potential for constitutional decisions that do not reflect personal views of justice, and he points to use of the Fourteenth Amendment to remedy racial discrimination as "the hardest test." *Id.* at 26. Though he claimed to be in favor of desegregated schools, he says:

> I find it hard to think the judgment [in *Brown v. Board of Education*] really turned upon the facts. Rather, it seems to me, it must have rested on the view that racial segregation is, in principle, a denial of equality to the minority against whom it is directed; that is, the group that is not dominant politically and, therefore, does not make the choice involved. For many who support the Court's decision this assuredly is the decisive ground. But this position also presents problems. Does it not involve an inquiry into the motive of the legislature, which is generally foreclosed to the courts? Is it alternatively defensible to make the measure of validity of legislation the way it is interpreted by those who are affected by it? In the context of a charge that segregation *with equal facilities* is a denial of equality, is there not a point in *Plessy* in the statement that if "enforced separation stamps the colored race with a badge of inferiority" it is solely because its members choose "to put that construction upon it"? ...

> For me, assuming equal facilities, the question posed by state-enforced segregation is not one of discrimination at all. Its human and its

constitutional dimensions lie entirely elsewhere, in the denial by the state of freedom to associate, a denial that impinges in the same way on any groups or races that may be involved.

* * *

But if the freedom of association is denied by segregation, integration forces an association upon those for whom it is unpleasant or repugnant.... Given a situation where the state must practically choose between denying the association to those individuals who wish it or imposing it on those who would avoid it, is there a basis in neutral principles for holding that the Constitution demands that the claims for association should prevail? (I should like to think there is, but I confess that I have not yet written the opinion. To write it is for me the challenge of the school-segregation cases.)

Id. at 33–34.

The requirement of neutrality in law, as described by Wechsler, limits the judiciary's ability to make law based on value judgments. Is it more important for the legal system to make decisions based on neutral principles or outcomes? Are "neutral" principles really neutral, or do they promote value judgments as well? Is the refusal of the courts to inquire into the motive of the legislature a neutral principle or one which upholds the power of the political majority? In what ways has this philosophy influenced the development of the common law? We return to the question of motive in *Washington v. Davis* infra at 44.

Williams challenges the "blind application of principles of neutrality," claiming, "[b]lacks are the objects of a constitutional omission which has been incorporated into a theory of neutrality." WILLIAMS, *supra* at 50. How would Williams respond to Wechsler's question whether there is a neutral principle upon which *Brown v. Board of Education* could have, or should have, been decided?

3. **Neutrality of facts** in appellate opinions. Courts use the law as a screen through which certain facts emerge as relevant while other facts are sifted out as irrelevant. *See* Richard Delgado, *Storytelling for Oppositionists and Others: A Plea for Narrative*, 87 MICH. L. REV. 2411, 2428 (1989). Sometimes the facts after they pass through this screen are startlingly dissimilar to the experiences of the parties involved.

For example, the Supreme Court's opinion in *United States v. Cruikshank*, 92 U.S. 542 (1875) did not include any significant discussion of the facts, only stating the indictments at issue:

The general charge ... that of "banding," and ... that of "conspiring" together to injure, oppress, threaten, and intimidate Levi Nelson and Alexander Tillman, citizens of the United States, of African descent and persons of color, with the intent thereby to hinder and prevent them in their free exercise and enjoyment of rights and privileges "granted and secured" to them "in common with all other good citizens of the United States by the constitution and law of the United States." United States v. Cruikshank, 92 U.S. 542, 548 (1875).

omission of facts

The Court found that the charges were insufficiently specific under the Civil Rights Enforcement Act of 1870, and the convictions were overturned. *id.* at 559. The Court failed to mention that the charges stemmed from the "bloodiest violence of the Reconstruction." ENCYCLOPEDIA OF AFRICAN AMERICAN CIVIL RIGHTS: FROM EMANCIPATION TO THE PRESENT 541 (Charles D. Lowery & John F. Marszalek, eds., 1992). On Easter Sunday of 1873 in Colfax, Louisiana, 280 African Americans were massacred. *id.* at 541. In *Cruikshank*, the Court overturned the only convictions among scores of federal prosecutions for the Colfax Riot, but the significance of the opinion's blow to the post-Civil War civil rights movement is lost without a factual setting.

invention o. facts

Rather than failing to include significant facts, Justice Cardozo seems to have invented his own version of what took place in the famous torts case *Palsgraf v. Long Island Railroad*. After reading Cardozo's impossible account of Mrs. Palsgraf being injured from across the station platform after a small package exploded, her attorney requested a rehearing because "there was an apparent error in the understanding of the facts of the case." Manz, *Palsgraf, Cardozo's Urban Legend?*, 107 DICK. L. REV. 785, at 818 (Spring 2003). Manz asserts that the importance of this case, despite its questionable fact pattern, does not indicate disregard for the truth so much as academic interest in the opinion itself, not the underlying event. Manz, *supra* at 789. As Wechsler advocated, principled reasoning, not the immediate outcome, is important. *See* Wechsler, *supra* text at note 2. Perhaps the outcome of this case is relevant, however. Mrs. Palsgraf was reportedly upset by the lost case for the rest of her life. Manz, *supra* at 840. Additionally, Cardozo's version of the facts has raised questions about his attitudes toward women and the poor. *Id.* at 786. For more on the Palsgraf case factual history, see JOHN T. NOONAN, JR., PERSONS AND MASKS OF THE LAW (1976).

The law review board attempted to screen references to Williams's race as irrelevant and the role of Benetton's as unverifiable. Is Williams correct in asserting that these facts were relevant to her story?

> Questioning the neutrality of law, Richard Delgado observed:
>
> Traditional legal writing purports to be neutral and dispassionately analytical, but too often it is not. In part, this is so because legal writers rarely focus on their own mindsets, the received wisdoms that serve as their starting points, themselves no more than stories, that lie behind their quasi-scientific string of deductions. The supposedly objective point of view often mischaracterizes, minimizes, dismisses, or derides without fully understanding opposing viewpoints. Implying that objective, correct answers can be given to legal questions also obscures the moral and political value judgments that lie at the heart of any legal inquiry. Delgado, *supra* at 2440–41.

Delgado is describing the indeterminacy of the law and challenging the notion of neutral application—central themes in the critical legal studies movement. *See* RICHARD W. BAUMAN, CRITICAL LEGAL STUDIES: A GUIDE TO THE LITERATURE 3 (1996). Although "[n]o single manifesto" can summarize the diversity of critical legal thought, "[t]he critique of law, its theories, and its institutions is meant to break down hierarchies of gender, race, class, or so-called merit." *Id.* at 3–4.

4. Challenging neutrality in practice. Law students generally learn the language of law through legal writing courses, which teach the tone, culture, factual analysis, and reasoning of the practice of law. Kathryn M. Stanchi, *Resistance is Futile: How Legal Writing Pedagogy Contributes to the Law's Marginalization of the Outsider*, 103 DICK. L. REV. 1, 11 (1998).

In addition to internalizing the labels of "relevant" and "irrelevant" facts, students learn how to write objectively. The dominant perspective is described as neutral and objective, and the subjective is disregarded as personal, as opposed to professional. *id.* at 40. "[O]bjectivity is a hallmark of legal language, of the professional voice." *id.* at 35.

To counteract the negative effects of objectivity, instructors must incorporate critical legal theory into teaching lawyering skills, but critical writing has generally been focused on legal scholarship instead of the practice of law. Stanchi, *supra* at 56; Brook K. Baker, *Transcending Legacies of Literacy and Transforming the Traditional Repertoire: Critical Discourse Strategies for Practice*, 23 WM. MITCHELL L. REV. 491, 516 (1997).

> Developing a critical discourse is fraught with contradictions arising from lawyers' competing obligations to act and write zealously on behalf of clients on the one hand, and to resist dogma and write transformatively in furtherance of community interests and social justice on the other. Nonetheless, legal writing specialists might consider the efficacy of increased reliance on: (1) using subversive outsider-narratives; (2) confronting and avoiding appeals to bias; and (3) using a more dialogic, less adversarial, more feminist discourse. *Id.* at 517.

Narratives, when subversive instead of hegemonic, use an individual story to reveal a collective wrong. *Id.* at 528–29, 532. The adversarial nature of legal representation allows lawyers to use almost any relevant tactic and prevents only the most blatant appeals to biases. The backlash of color-blind jurisprudence restricts the means to counteract stereotypes, employing biases as well. *Id.* at 543. Using feminist ideals to counteract the male ideology of legal representation as combat, "a nonadversarial advocacy might tone down excessive rhetoric, decrease competitive posturing, and instead engage in a more serious legal, moral, and political dialogue with opponents and legal decision-makers." *Id.* at 555–56.

How might Williams have used her experience in a discrimination suit against Benetton's? Could she find a role for her narrative in the formality of legal documents, thereby avoiding appeals to biases and creating a dialogue about retailers' use of buzzers? *See* Williams at 48, in which she claims omission of her race would make the reader participate in old habits of cultural bias.

5. Narratives in legal discourse. Narratives are a powerful means of constructing moral and social realities, which are indeterminate and therefore subject to interpretation. Richard Delgado, *Storytelling for Opposition-*

ists and Others: A Plea for Narrative, 87 MICH. L. REV. 2411, 2415–16 (1989) (illustrating how the reality of a single event changes with the perspective of five different stories).

The stories of the dominant ingroup are used to construct a "shared reality in which its own superior position is seen as natural," by picking and choosing facts to justify the world as it is. But " 'neutrality' can feel [different] from the perspective of an outsider." *Id.* at 2412, 2421, 2425.

Members of outgroups use counterstories, which directly challenge the stories of the ingroup, as (1) a means of self-preservation and (2) a means of lessening their own subordination. *Id.* at 2436.

> [S]tories about oppression, about victimization, about one's own bru-talization—far from deepening the despair of the oppressed, lead to healing, liberation, mental health. They also promote group solidarity. Storytelling emboldens the hearer, who may have had the same thoughts and experiences the storyteller describes, but hesitated to give them voice. Having heard another express them, he or she realizes, I am not alone.
>
> Yet, stories help oppressed groups in a second way—through their effect on the oppressor. Most oppression ... does not seem like oppression to those perpetrating it. It is rationalized, causing few pangs of conscience. The dominant group justifies its privileged posi-tion by means of stories, stock explanations that construct reality in ways favorable to it. . . .
>
> This story is drastically at odds with the way most people of color would describe their condition. . . . Counterstories can attack that complacency.
>
> What is more, they can do so in ways that promise at least the possibility of success. Most civil rights strategies confront the obstacle of blacks' otherness. The dominant group, noticing that a particular effort is waged on behalf of blacks, increases its resistance. Stories at times can overcome that otherness, hold that instinctive resistance in abeyance. Stories are the oldest, most primordial meeting ground in human experience. Their allure will often provide the most effective means of overcoming otherness, of forming a new collectivity based on the shared story.

Id. at 2436–38.

Listeners asked Patricia Williams why she did not feel obligated to include the salesman's side of the story and why her individual experience was worth their attention. How could Williams, had she chosen to answer the questions, have defended putting "[her] own interpretation right out there"?

6. Significance of Williams's self description. While describing her face in a manner that reinforces connections with this country's segregated history, is Williams giving short shrift to descriptive accuracy? What relationship should the accuracy of Williams's self description have with her publication of the Benetton's story in a law review? If the law review editors believe Williams's description was wholly inaccurate, should they refuse to publish her work? Would the answer change if Williams's piece were written in the traditional, "objective" law review style? For an especially heated exchange between two critical legal scholars about exactly the point raised in the notes above, and the credibility of Patricia Williams's Benetton story, see Mark Tushnet, *The Degradation of Constitutional Discourse*, 81 Geo. L.J. 251, 265–78 (1992) and Gary Peller, *The Discourse of Constitutional Degradation*, 81 Geo. L.J. 313 (1992). *See generally* Richard Posner, *The Skin Trade*, The New Republic, Oct. 13, 1997, at 40; Daniel A. Farber and Suzanna Sherry, Beyond All Reason (1997).

One possible criticism that can be made of Williams's decision to describe her face as round and brown is that it paints a much more familiar picture of racism. Discrimination against Patricia Williams implies a difficult problem which can not be solved simply by assimilation or affirmative action. Law review readers who believe in marketplace neutrality will not want to believe in discrimination against Patricia Williams because it may raise issues of their own culpability for not finding ways of combating prejudice beyond assimilation.

Does Williams's article lose some of its effectiveness by perpetuating a comforting picture of racism? *See also* Devon W. Carbado & Mitu Gulati, *The Law and Economics of Critical Race Theory: Crossroads, Directions, and a New Critical Race Theory*, 112 Yale L.J. 1757, 1817 (2003) (book review).

7. Williams and anonymous clerk. In *Death of the Profane*, Williams describes not one, but two transactions. First, there is the actual transaction between her and the clerk: the gift of her commerce in exchange for his permission to enter Benetton's. Second, there is the hypothetical exchange which never took place: Williams's money in exchange for Benetton's sweater. When analyzing the situation in this way, doesn't it seem simply as though Williams didn't meet the clerk's asking price for admittance? Obviously, the clerk undervalued Williams's cultural capital. Since the clerk did not open the door, should Williams have pressed a twenty dollar bill against the window in order to sweeten her offer? Would it indicate that the market was functioning properly, at least in the first exchange, if the clerk who refused Williams entry was fired because of bringing bad publicity to Benetton's?

8. Note on Williams's "marketplace." Williams's poignant personal account details her exclusion from participating in the marketplace, an environment where, theoretically, a willing buyer and a willing seller make a connection based on each of their preferences and enter into agreements to buy and sell products and services. The marketplace is fundamentally associated with freedom, functional objectivity, and deference to personal preference. Deborah Waire Post et al., Contracting Law 1 (1996). In making exchanges for goods and services, willing buyers and sellers usually engage in single transactions or once-only interactions. Craig Calhoun et al.,

STRUCTURES OF POWER AND CONSTRAINT: PAPERS IN HONOR OF PETER M. BLAU 134 (1990). These transactions are not based on personal trust between these buying and selling actors; rather, individuals depend on the independent system of law, official contracts, courts, and enforcement agencies to regulate interaction and exchange in the marketplace. *Id.* In this case, Williams requesting to enter Benetton's was an offer to participate in the marketplace, a manifestation of intent to enter into an exchange of her money for a Benetton's product. POST, *supra* at 196. However, Williams's offer created the power of acceptance in the sales associate—the "narrow-eyed, white teenager"—and in denying her admittance into the store, the young clerk abruptly ended a potential exchange in the retail market. *Id.* Therefore, economists may claim that there was no acceptance on the part of the sales clerk, thereby making no obligation on the part of Benetton's to sell Williams any goods or services. The absence of an acceptance failed to complete the formation of a contract between Benetton's to sell goods and Williams to grant "the gift of her commerce."

Though the marketplace paradigm explicates exchanges between buying and selling actors in a straightforward, ostensibly neutral model, it largely ignores several ideological, cultural, and social implications of everyday human interaction. The simple paradigm assumes that actors voluntarily enter into these transactions and that these buyers and sellers do not consider salient issues, such as the other actor's race, class, gender, or ethnicity. *Id.* at 2. As societal norms, citizens' biases, and the nation's socioeconomic hierarchy play a large role in social life, economic models of exchange in the marketplace fail to consider the varied rule systems that constitute and control social transactions. CALHOUN, *supra* at 142.

Williams challenges the simple economic model by asserting that the market is not an impartial setting, but a partial milieu where market players are significantly influenced by their own prejudices and self-indulgence to exclude certain actors from participating in the process of exchange. Williams claims the white clerk's rejection of her admittance into the store was an overt "manifestation of his never having let someone like me into the realm of his reality"; this clerk was only a willing seller to certain willing buyers, not buyers like Williams. Rather than a simple economic transaction, where two players are interested in generating an efficient exchange with one another, negotiating, and creating bilateral decisions, Williams is not given a chance to enter into the bargain; she is on the receiving end of a unilateral decision. According to Williams, a critical race scholar, the marketplace is not an environment where players are on equal footing and make decisions based on individual preferences, but a place where her "round brown face" banishes her from creating stable economic relationships.

9. *Death of the Profane* as demonstrating market power. At first glance, Professor Williams's experience seems to imply a market failure. However, market economics does not say that businesses (like Benetton's) always make correct decisions; it says that when businesses make bad decisions, they are punished by lost profits which provide an incentive to make better decisions in the future. According to this model, if a business does not stop making bad decisions, its competitors will eventually drive it out of business. With this in mind, is Williams's story an example of the market in action? Benetton's has certainly suffered for its bad decision. Not only did Professor Williams not patronize Benetton's, she also posted a sign in Benetton's window and immortalized the episode in a law review article. Will the loss of business and bad publicity generated by this incident lead Benetton's to change its ways, demonstrating that there wasn't a market failure after all?

10.   *Death of the Profane* as demonstrating market impotence. If Williams's experience was not a market failure, does that mean that the market provides no means of dealing with any particular act of injustice, and that it can only (theoretically) work to minimize possible future injustice? However, if the market can not deal with actual acts of injustice, does that argue strongly for legislative solutions?

11.   Does a famous black face make any difference? In the summer of 2005, Oprah Winfrey, the billionare entertainer and entrepreneur, went shopping in Paris. Just fifteen minutes after closing, Oprah approached the very exclusive Hermes store, accompanied by a small party of friends. She noticed a group of people still milling about in the store, and she tried to enter. She was firmly turned away by a clerk. Oprah's best friend, Gayle King, who witnessed the incident reports that: " 'People were in the store and they were shopping. **Oprah** was at the door and she was not allowed into the store.' **Oprah** describes it herself as "one of the most humillating moments of her life." ' "

King said it's unlikely that Winfrey will shop there again. *Store Sorry for Closed Door Policy*, CHI. TRIB., June 24, 2005, at p. 23.

Oprah was as enraged as Patricia Williams at this shopping slight. Oprah turned her considerable publicity apparatus to respond to the store's refusal. Although she received an apology, she has promised to devote an entire show to the episode when she begins taping for the new season in the fall of 2005.

Does the Oprah incident reinforce, undercut, or complicate the racial explanation of Patricia Williams story? Like Williams, Oprah concluded that this was an example of racism. What weight should we give the store's explanation that it refused entry to Oprah because it was preparing for a special promotional event? Does it matter that the store did not fire or demote the clerk who denied entry to Oprah and friends?

12.   Buzzer's role in market model. Does the buzzer fit into the conventional model of the market discussed above? Rather than a traditional negotiation between a willing buyer and a willing seller, the buzzer creates a unilateral decision made by an unwilling seller to exclude a willing buyer from the market. What factors might have influenced the clerk's decision to exclude Williams?

13.   Buzzer and racism in marketplace. Williams notes that some deemed the buzzer system to be a "necessary evil" to mitigate the risk of crime in retail establishments. Another possible interpretation of the cultural and social context of the buzzer is that it symbolizes an elevated economic status or a means to establish economic segregation, utilized to prevent theft by excluding people who do not look as if they could afford the merchandise.

If the buzzer system was created to serve this purpose, why did the sales clerk choose to exclude Williams from the store? What is the basis of his belief that a black woman like Williams cannot afford clothes from Benetton's? Did the clerk exclude Williams based on the pervasive cultural representations of African Americans' socioeconomic background in the media or in the courts? Teun A. Van Dijk's study of racism and prejudice at a micro level observed interpersonal communication in everyday life. Van Dijk asserts that the media and the law are major vehicles that create ethnic prejudices in society. TEUN A. VAN DIJK, COMMUNICATING RACISM: ETHNIC PREJUDICE IN THOUGHT AND TALK 361 (1987). These representations of minorities may have a deleterious effect on interpersonal relations in the marketplace:

> Prejudices about aggression and crime of ethic groups largely derive from biased media stories that mention the ethnic backgrounds of suspects, which are again based on police reports or court trials, as well as on media articles about crime statistics or crime "waves" that are also partly derived from information supplied by the authorities. This is one of the most socially destructive ethnic prejudices, and there is much empirical evidence that the law and the media together help construct public attitudes about crime, deviance, or similar negative properties attributed to ethnic minority groups. *Id.* at 364.

Do you share Van Dijk's view? Do court trials aid in creating derogatory beliefs about the socioeconomic status of minorities and thus reinforce the legitimacy of the buzzer system?

An article in the *Washington Post Magazine* created heated debate concerning the buzzer system when it ran a column that supported the use of locks and buzzers as a security measure to discriminatorily screen young black male customers entering retail shops.

> As for me, I'm with the store owners, although I was not at first. . . . Young black males commit an inordinate amount of urban crime. . . . [R]ace is only one factor in their admissions policy. Age and sex count, too. And while race is clearly the most compelling factor, ask yourself what their policies would be if young white males were responsible for most urban crime.

> A nation with our history is entitled to be sensitive to race and racism—and we are all wary of behavior that would bring a charge of racism. But the mere recognition of race as a factor—especially if those of the same race recognize the same factor—is not in itself racism. This may apply as much to some opponents of busing or public housing in their own neighborhood as it does to who gets admitted to jewelry stores. Let he who would open the door throw the first stone.

Richard Cohen, *Closing the Door on Crime*, WASH. POST, Sept. 7, 1986 (magazine), at W13; *see also* Jane Gross, *When "By Appointment" Means Keep Out*, N.Y. TIMES, Dec. 17, 1986, at B1.

Was race "only one factor" in the exclusion of Williams, a successful female law professor? How does race as a factor in exclusion affect the model of the market described above? Is using race as a factor in excluding a willing buyer from the market racist? If not, what would meet the commentator's definition of racism?

14.   More screening based on race. Discriminatory screening practices are not an isolated occurrence. In New York, small shops on the Upper Eastside have used, in addition to locks and buzzers, signs that read, "Men by appointment only." *Fear of Blacks, Fear of Crime*, N.Y. Times, Dec. 28, 1986, at § 4, 10. In addition, an African American man in Philadelphia filed a complaint with the Human Rights Commission after he was denied entrance to Mums & Pops Confectionary, which employs a lock and buzzer system. *See* Tamar Charry, *Bitter Sweets Battle*, Philadelphia City Paper, Dec. 7–14, 1995.

The retailers employing such security measures seem to equate blackness with criminality, and the *New York Times* editorial board warned, "discrimination, cumulatively, can be as poisonous as mugging or burglary." *Fear of Blacks, supra.* "Fearful whites need to put themselves in the shoes of innocent blacks. Doing so will not dissipate fear, but it can steadily inspire the understanding and reason that keep fear in its place." *Id.* A letter to the editor disagreed "that a society in which prejudice is rampant is as bad as one in which violent crime is rampant." Michael Levin and Margarita Levin, *Howard Beach Turns a Beam on Racial Tension*, N.Y. Times, Jan. 11, 1987, at § 4, 30. The letter concluded that an innocent black person would not let himself into the shop if standing in the owner's shoes. After reading Williams's description of the humiliation and rage she felt, do you think she would agree with the letter's conclusion? For an array of responses to a hypothetical involving decisions to screen customers based on race, see *The Jeweler's Dilemma* in The New Republic, November 10, 1986, at 18.

15.   Law and economics criticisms of critical race narrative methodology. Judge Richard Posner, a leading law and economics scholar, faults the critical race narrative methodology as non scientific, selective, and unreliable when compared to economic methodology. Posner, Overcoming Law, 368–384, "Nuance, Narrative and Empathy in Critical Race Theory." This argument is discussed in the next section of this chapter.

B.   A Law and Economics Challenge to the Neutrality of the Critical Race Narrative Methodology

Nuance, Narrative, and Empathy in Critical Race Theory

Overcoming Law 368–84 (1995).

■ Richard Posner

The Alchemy of Race and Rights describes its author, Patricia Williams, as a young black female law professor of contracts and commercial law whose abiding interest is the plight of the American black. Or plights, for she is particularly concerned with the lack of fit that her condition of being a black professional woman makes with the attitudes and expectations of the predominantly white community in which, as a professor in an academic field that has relatively few women, very few blacks, and therefore almost no black women, she mainly circulates. The lack of fit induces in her at times a sense of disorientation that is almost vertiginous. So it is a book about both "privileged" blacks like herself and her underprivileged coracialists at the bottom of the social totem pole.

The book offers a black feminist perspective on a variety of practices and institutions: law's pretense to objectivity and impersonality, surrogate motherhood, consumerism, constitutional protection of hate speech and condemnation of governmental efforts at affirmative action, the inept and insensitive behavior of well-meaning white liberal academics, and above all white racism in what she considers its hydra-headed manifestations. There is little that is new in the paraphrasable content of her criticisms. The novelty is the form, which can aptly be described as literary, in which Williams has cast her discussion of these legal and social issues. She is not unique in employing literary methods in legal scholarship; earlier and essentially isolated examples of this genre to one side, it is the methodological signature of critical race theory. But she is one of the most skillful practitioners of the genre.

The subtitle of the book—"Diary of a Law Professor"—is a clue to her technique. The book is not literally a diary, although it contains some excerpts from the author's diary. But it is like a diary in presenting the author's analyses of legal and social issues in the form of reactions to her daily experiences, whether as consumer, law professor, television viewer, or daughter. The reader comes to understand that Williams's way of coping with the many stresses of her life is to write down her reactions to stressful or arresting events as soon after they occur as she can. Writing in a diary-like format is thus a form of therapy. But it also gives scope for her powerful gift for narration. * * *

The rhetorical highlight of the book, however, is the description of an episode at a Benetton clothing store. "Buzzers are big in New York City. Favored particularly by smaller stores and boutiques, merchants throughout the city have installed them as screening devices to reduce the incidence of robbery: if the face at the door looks desirable, the buzzer is pressed and the door is unlocked. If the face is that of an undesirable, the door stays locked. Predictably, the issue of undesirability has revealed itself to be a racial determination," as Williams discovers one Saturday afternoon when she

> was shopping in Soho and saw in a store window a sweater that I wanted to buy for my mother. * * *

The power of this sketch lies in its compression, its vivid contrasting of the round brown face with the sales clerk's narrow eyes and pink bubble gum, its use of physical exclusion as a metaphor for social exclusion, its suggestion that the least significant of whites (this gum-chewing bubble-blowing teenage sales clerk) is utterly comfortable with exercising power over an older and more accomplished black, and its elegant summation of the clerk's reaction to her ("evaluating me for signs that would pit me against the limits of his social understanding"). Yet here at the very pinnacle of Williams's art the careful reader will begin to feel a sense of disquiet. Did Williams really press her face against the window—that is, did her face actually touch the glass? Or is she embroidering the facts for dramatic effect—making the insult to her seem even graver than it was because it shattered a childlike eagerness and innocence? Also, how does she know that the sales clerk refused to let her in the store because she's black? The only evidence she cites is that, since Christmas was approaching, it was unlikely that the store had closed, and that there were other shoppers in the store. The second point has no force. Stores normally stop admitting customers before all the customers already in the store have left—otherwise the store might never be able to close. The first point has greater force. Although many stores close early on Saturday, the likelihood that a Benetton store in New York City during the Christmas shopping season would be one of them is slight. Yet Williams does not suggest that she has tried to find out whether the store was open. She does not suggest that she saw any customers admitted after she was turned away. The absence of a sign indicating that the store was closed would be some evidence that it was not, but she doesn't say anything about the presence or absence of a sign. Many stores list their hours on the front door. She makes no mention of this either. In all likelihood the store was open, but I am surprised that she—a lawyer—did not attempt to verify the point.

But of course the attempt might have been futile. And it is even possible, though I find no clues to this in the text, that her anger at the episode reflects in part a pervasive, debilitating uncertainty that confronts blacks in their encounters with whites. Not every disappointment that a black person encounters is a result of discrimination, and yet it may be impossible to determine which is and which is not. We like to know where we stand with other people, and this may be difficult for blacks in their dealings with whites.

Yet she had told us at the outset, in defense of doing legal scholarship in the form of story telling, "that one of the most important results of reconceptualizing from 'objective truth' to rhetorical event will be a more nuanced sense of legal and social responsibility" (p. 11). Unless "nuanced" is a euphemism for fictive, Williams has promised to get the particulars of an event or situation right, rather than submerging them in a generality, such as that whites hate blacks. That promise implies an effort to find out what *really* was going on in that white teenager's mind when he told her the store was closed. Maybe, as I said, it was closed; or maybe it wasn't but the clerk had his hands full with the customers inside. Maybe he was a disloyal employee who wanted to get his employer in trouble; maybe he was lazy, mischievous, rude, irresponsible, or just plain dumb.

The Alchemy of Race and Rights suppresses every perspective other than that of the suffering, oppressed black. * * *

This is a pattern. In discussing the case of Bernhard Goetz, who shot four black youths in a subway car and was acquitted of all but an illegal weapons charge even though he could not have been acting in *reasonable* self-defense, Williams disparages white fear of black crime by characterizing the criminal records of Goetz's victims as mere "allegations" by asking rhetorically how the community would have reacted to Goetz's action if he had been black and his victims white *and the crime had occurred in a department store rather than in the subway*—an added fictive touch that magnifies the malignant irrationality of Goetz's action—and by reciting irrelevant statistics showing that whites commit more crimes than blacks. What is omitted is that the prison population is almost half black, although blacks are only 12 percent of the population, and that urban street (and subway) crime is committed mostly by blacks. Black criminality is a serious social problem. To pretend otherwise is an evasion. AIDS, drug addiction, homophobia, neglect of children, anti-Semitism, and poor political leadership are other problems of the black community that Williams ignores. * * *

Mention of black anti-Semitism brings me back to the question of Beethoven's color. That Beethoven was black is a typical and recurrent claim of the Afrocentrist movement, members of which have also asserted that melanin is positively correlated with intelligence, that the ancient Greeks stole philosophy from black Egyptians and, specifically, that Alexander the Great pillaged the library at Alexandria to steal Egyptian philosophical ideas for his old tutor, Aristotle (never mind that Alexander *founded* Alexandria and that the library was built long after his death), that Napoleon shot off the sphinx's nose so that no one would know that the sphinx had Negroid features, that not only Beethoven but also Haydn, Cleopatra, and Lincoln were black, that Beethoven's blackness is shown by (among other things) his confidence in his abilities, a confidence similar to that of Mohammed Ali, that Dwight Eisenhower's mother was black, that America was first discovered by Africans, that AIDS was invented by whites to exterminate the black race, that the telephone and carbon steel were invented in Africa along with science, medicine, and mathematics, that "the [African] Blacks' conception of God was on a scale too grand to be acceptable to Western minds"—and that Jews controlled the African slave trade and today are plotting with the Mafia the financial destruction of the black race. *Not all Afrocentrists are anti-Semitic; but irresponsible claims appear to be the hallmark of the movement* [emphasis added], and I should have thought that Williams, as a lawyer and an academic, would have wanted to place as much distance as possible between herself and it rather than to embrace uncritically one of its representative wild claims.

Could it be—despite Martha Nussbaum's argument that imaginative literature in general and the novel in particular renders social reality with a degree of balance, nuance, and concreteness that provides a needed antidote to the partial visions furnished by abstract, generalizing social-scientific approaches, such as that of economics—that one-sidedness is an endemic risk of the literary depiction of reality, rather than a particular characteristic of Patricia Williams? * * *

We accept one-sidedness in literature, moreover, because we make allowance for *autres temps*, *autres moeurs* and because factual accuracy and scholarly detachment are not rules of the literature game. But they are rules of the scholarly game, and Williams is writing as a scholar. If my criticisms of her in this chapter should turn out to be one-sided, misleading, and tendentious, she would not be impressed by my rejoining that mine is only one voice in an ongoing conversation and I can leave it to others to rectify any omissions or imbalance in my contribution.

If one-sidedness is the other side of literature's empathetic concreteness, empathetic awareness of strangers' pains and pleasures is the unexpected other side of the economist's Gradgrindian detachment. Consider rent control. The beneficiaries are plain to see: they are the tenants when the rent-control law is adopted. The victims are invisible: they are the future would-be tenants, who will face a restricted supply of rental housing because landowners will have a diminished incentive to build rental housing and owners of existing apartment buildings will prefer to sell rather than to rent the apartments in them. Economics brings these victims before the analyst's eye; literature, and the type of legal scholarship that imitates literature, does not.

Maybe economic scholarship is not *really* empathetic. The economist does not enter imaginatively into the distress of the disappointed quester for rental housing; all he does is tote up some additional costs. But that may be a sounder way of doing policy than by cultivating empathy. A jurisprudence of empathy can foster short-sighted substantive justice because the power to enter imaginatively into another person's outlook, emotions, and experiences diminishes with physical, social, and temporal distance.[30] Compare the maxims *tout comprendre c'est tout pardoner* and no man is a villain in his own eyes (an actor's adage). The second maxim should remind us that when we succeed in looking at the world through another's eyes, we lose the perspective necessary for judgment. We find ourselves in a stew of rationalization, warped perception, and overmastering emotion. (Any lawyer knows the risk of overidentification with his client.) The *tout comprendre* maxim expresses a different point: To understand another person completely· is to understand the causality of his behavior, to see that behavior as the end of a chain of causes and thus as determined rather than responsible. It is to understand the person as completely as a scientist understands an animal, which is to say as a phenomenon of nature rather than as a free agent. If we understand a criminal's behavior as well as we understand a rattlesnake's behavior, we are unlikely to accord him much dignity and respect.

---

30.   A more basic point is that the internal perspective—the putting oneself in the other person's shoes—that is achieved by the exercise of empathetic imagination lacks normative significance *[Emphasis added]*.

The project of empathetic jurisprudence invites us to choose between achieving a warped internal perspective and an inhumanly clinical detachment: between becoming too hot and too cold. The affective dimension of empathy leads to identification with the person whose fate or welfare is at stake; the intellectual dimension leads to embedding the person in a web of causes that transforms him from a free human being into (in Nietzsche's phrase) an irresponsible piece of fate. I take back nothing I said in discussing the German judges about the importance of remembering that other human beings are—human. That does not require us to be able to crawl into their minds. Indeed, a lively awareness that other people are in an important sense closed to us—that they have their own plans and perspectives, into which we can enter imperfectly if at all—is one of the planks of the liberal platform. It is a presupposition of individuality.

Another problem with Williams's method is a <u>lack of clarity</u>. Here is the ending of the chapter in which Williams stands up for rights against the critical legal studies movement: "Give [rights] to trees. Give them to cows. Give them to history. Give them to rivers and rocks. Give to all of society's objects and untouchables the rights of privacy, integrity, and self-assertion; give them distance and respect" (p. 165). "What does it *mean* to give rights to history, or to entitle cows to privacy, integrity, and self-assertion? Is the reference to cows meant to put us in mind of Hindu doctrine regarding the sacredness of animals? Is Williams an animist, a 'Green'? Is she the second coming of Walt Whitman? (likely Carl Sandburg.) How can all this be squared with her being a fashion-conscious shopper." * * *

Narrative has two aspects, Narrative in the sense of the telling of a story is the way we make sense of a sequence of events unfolding in history. Black scholars like it because they believe that the current condition of the American black population cannot be understood without reference to the history of Negro slavery. But despite Williams's references to her great-great-grandmother, a slave, her book does not employ historical narration.

Narration is also a literary technique. To present an issue, such as the clash between critical legal studies and critical race theory, in the form of a story, * * * is to reinforce or replace abstract argument with a portrait. Portraits, including the verbal portraits that we call literature—works that depict rather than overtly argue—can change minds. This role of verbal portraiture, as also of photographs, is especially valuable in situations in which we have difficulty *seeing* important aspects of a problem because it involves people whose experiences are remote from ours. In education and occupation Patricia Williams is like other establishment legal figures, but in race and all that that connotes in this country (at least when the race is black) she is not, and maybe one has to learn to see the world through her eyes as well as one's own before one can fully evaluate the arguments pro and con various racial policies. On this view the <u>very one-sidedness of her presentation, however questionable by the conventional standards of schol-</u>arship and even by the professed standards of critical race theory (which promised us, remember, nuance), <u>has value in providing insight into the</u>

psychology and rhetoric of many blacks. But if whites must acquire a stereoscopic biracial perspective in order to cope effectively with our society's racial problems, blacks must too.

———

NOTES AND QUESTIONS

1. **Standards of proof and burden of persuasion in narrative**. What standards of proof and persuasion does Judge Posner rely upon to assess the Williams narrative? *See* Richard H. Gaskins, Burdens of Proof in Modern Discourse (1993) (New Haven, Yale University Press).

2. **Throwing rhetorical stones from glass houses?** Does Posner's essay exhibit any of the problems that he sees in Williams work? Lack of clarity, exaggeration for rhetorical effect, manipulation of empathy, one-sidedness?

3. **Difference between legal and economic standards of proof.** Is the Posner essay structured by the standards of economic proof, or legal proof?

4. **Finding "truth" in law or economics**. What would persuade Judge Posner that a report of racism or microaggression is "true"?

5. **Valuing collective experience.** What place does group experience with subordination have in the Posnerian schema? *But see* Charles R. Lawrence, III, *The Id, the Ego, and Equal Protection: Reckoning with Unconscious Racism*, 39 Stan. L. Rev. 317 (1987) (arguing for "cultural meaning test" based on a community's collective experience as the targets of racism).

6. **Statistics as a scientific form of collective experience.** In economics, collective experience is represented in statistical forms of aggregate data, including the mode, mean, average, and regression analysis. *Mode* is the value or item occurring most frequently in a series of observations or statistical data. *Mean* is the sum of all the members of the set divided by the number of items in the set. *Average* is something, as a type, number, quantity, or degree, that represents a midpoint between points on a scale of valuation. In statistics, *regression analysis* is a mathematical method of modeling the relationships among three or more variables. It is used to predict the value of one variable given the values of the others.

———

C. The Narrative of Post-Modern Racism: The "Microaggressions"

Popular Legal Culture: Law as Microaggression
98 Yale L.J. 1559 (1989).

■ Peggy C. Davis

[*The scene is a courthouse in Bronx, New York. A white assistant city attorney "takes the court elevator up to the ninth floor. At the fifth floor, the doors open. A black woman asks: 'Going down?' 'Up,' says [the city attorney]. And then, as the doors close: 'You see? They can't even tell up from down. I'm sorry, but it's true.' "]*

The black woman's words are subject to a variety of interpretations. She may have thought it efficient, appropriate, or congenial to ask the direction of the elevator rather than to search for the indicator. The indicator may have been broken. Or, the woman may have been incapable of competent elevator travel. The city attorney is led, by cognitive habit and by personal and cultural history, to seize upon the pejorative interpretation.

The city attorney lives in a society in which blacks are commonly regarded as incompetent. The traditional stereotype of blacks includes inferior mentality, primitive morality, emotional instability, laziness, boisterousness, closeness to anthropoid ancestors, occupational instability, superstition, care-free attitude, and ignorance. Common culture reinforces the belief in black incompetence in that the black is "less often depicted as a thinking being." If, for example, the city attorney watches television, she has observed that whites, but not blacks, are likely to exert authority or display superior knowledge; that whites, but not blacks, dispense goods and favors; and that blacks are disproportionately likely to be dependent and subservient. Cognitive psychologists tell us that the city attorney shares with all human beings a need to "categorize in order to make sense of experience. Too many events occur daily for us to deal successfully with each one on an individual basis; we must categorize in order to cope." In a world in which sidewalk grates routinely collapsed under the weight of an average person, we would walk around sidewalk grates. We would not stop to inspect them and distinguish secure ones from loose ones: It is more efficient to act on the basis of a stereotyping heuristic. In a world in which blacks are commonly thought to be incompetent (or dangerous, or musical, or highly sexed), it is more efficient for the city attorney to rely on the generalization than to make individuating judgments.

It is likely that the city attorney assimilated negative stereotypes about blacks before she reached the age of judgment. She will, therefore, have accepted them as truth rather than opinion. Having assimilated the stereotypes, the city attorney will have developed a pattern of interpreting and remembering ambiguous events in ways that confirm, rather than unsettle, her stereotyped beliefs. If she sees or hears of two people on a subway, one white, one black, and one holding a knife, she is predisposed to form an impression that the black person held the knife, regardless of the truth of the matter. She will remember examples of black incompetence and may fail to remember examples of black competence.

Psychoanalysts tell us that the stereotype serves the city attorney as a mental repository for traits and impulses that she senses within herself and dislikes or fears. According to this view, people manage normal developmental conflicts involving impulse control by projecting forbidden impulses onto an outgroup. This defense mechanism allows the city attorney to distance herself psychologically from threatening traits and thoughts. In this respect, the pejorative outgroup stereotype serves to reduce her level of stress and anxiety.

Historians tell us of the rootedness of the city attorney's views. During the early seventeenth century, the circumstances of blacks living in what was to become the United States were consistent with principles of open, although not equal, opportunity. African–Americans lived both as indentured servants and as free people. This early potential for egalitarianism was destroyed by the creation of a color-caste system. Colonial legislatures enacted slavery laws that transformed black servitude from a temporary status, under which both blacks and whites labored, to a lifelong status that was hereditary and racially defined. Slavery required a system of beliefs that would rationalize white domination, and laws and customs that would assure control of the slave population.

The beliefs that served to rationalize white domination are documented in an 1858 treatise. In many respects, they echo the beliefs identified one hundred years later as constitutive of the twentieth century black stereotype:

> [T]he negro, ... whether in a state of bondage or in his native wilds, exhibits such a weakness of intellect that ... 'when he has the fortune to live in subjection to a wise director, he is, without doubt, fixed in such a state of life as is most agreeable to his genius and capacity.' ...
>
> ... So debased is their [moral] condition generally, that their humanity has been even doubted.... [T]he negro race is habitually indolent and indisposed to exertion.... * * *
>
> The negro is naturally mendacious, and as a concomitant, thievish....
>
> ... Lust is his strongest passion; and hence, rape is an offence of too frequent occurrence.

The laws and customs that assured control of the slave population reinforced the image of blacks as incompetent and in need of white governance. The master was afforded ownership, the right to command labor, and the virtually absolute right of discipline. Social controls extending beyond the master-slave relationship served to exclude the slave—and in some respects to exclude free blacks—from independent, self-defining activity. * * * Social relationships between whites and blacks were regulated on the basis of caste hierarchy: Breaches of the social order, such as "insolence" of a slave towards a white person, were criminally punishable.

This history is part of the cultural heritage of the city attorney. The system of legal segregation, which maintained caste distinctions after abolition, is part of her life experience. This "new system continued to place all Negroes in inferior positions and all whites in superior positions." The city attorney is among the

> two-thirds of the current population [that] lived during a time when it was legal and customary in some parts of this country to require that

blacks sit in the back of a bus, give up their seats to whites, use different rest rooms and drinking fountains, and eat at different restaurants.

The civil rights movement and post–1954 desegregation efforts are also part of the city attorney's cultural heritage. As an educated woman in the 1980s, she understands racial prejudice to be socially and morally unacceptable. Psychological research that targets her contemporaries reveals an expressed commitment to egalitarian ideals along with lingering negative beliefs and aversive feelings about blacks. "Prejudiced thinking and discrimination still exist, but the contemporary forms are more subtle, more indirect, and less overtly negative than are more traditional forms."

Recent research also suggests that the city attorney can be expected to conceal her anti-black feelings except in private, homoracial settings. Many of her white contemporaries will suppress such feelings from their conscious thoughts. White Americans of the city attorney's generation do not wish to appear prejudiced. "[T]he contemporary form[ ] of prejudice is expressed [at least in testing situations] in ways that protect and perpetuate a nonprejudiced, nondiscriminating self-image." Americans of the city attorney's generation live under the combined influence of egalitarian ideology and "cultural forces and cognitive processes that ... promote prejudice and racism." Anti-black attitudes persist in a climate of denial.

The denial and the persistence are related. It is difficult to change an attitude that is unacknowledged. Thus, "like a virus that mutates into new forms, old-fashioned prejudice seems to have evolved into a new type that is, at least temporarily, resistant to traditional ... remedies."

II. THE VIEW FROM THE OTHER SIDE OF THE LENS: MICROAGGRESSION

Return to the fifth floor and to the moment at which the elevator door opened. The black woman sees two white passengers. She inquires and perceives the response to her inquiry. She sees and hears, or thinks she sees and hears, condescension. It is in the tone and body language that surround the word, "Up." Perhaps the tone is flat, the head turns slowly in the direction of the second passenger and the eyes roll upward in apparent exasperation. Perhaps the head remains lowered, and the word is uttered as the eyes are raised to a stare that suggests mock disbelief. The woman does not hear the words spoken behind the closed elevator doors. Yet she feels that she has been branded incompetent, even for elevator travel. This feeling produces anger, frustration, and a need to be hypervigilant against subsequent, similar brandings.

The elevator encounter is a microaggression. "These are subtle, stunning, often automatic, and non-verbal exchanges which are 'put downs' of blacks by offenders." Psychiatrists who have studied black populations view them as "incessant and cumulative" assaults on black self-esteem.

Microaggressions simultaneously sustain defensive-deferential

thinking and erode self confidence in Blacks. . . . [B]y monopolizing ... perception and action through regularly irregular disruptions, they contribute to relative paralysis of action, planning and self-esteem. They seem to be the principal foundation for the verification of Black inferiority for both whites and Blacks.

The management of these assaults is a preoccupying activity, simultaneously necessary to and disruptive of black adaptation.

[The black person's] self-esteem suffers ... because he is constantly receiving an unpleasant image of himself from the behavior of others to him. This is the subjective impact of social discrimination.... It seems to be an ever-present and unrelieved irritant. Its influence is not alone due to the fact that it is painful in its intensity, but also because the individual, in order to maintain internal balance and to protect himself from being overwhelmed by it, must initiate restitutive maneuvers ... —all quite automatic and unconscious. In addition to maintaining an internal balance, the individual must continue to maintain a social facade and some kind of adaptation to the offending stimuli so that he can preserve some social effectiveness. All of this requires a constant preoccupation, notwithstanding ... that these adaptational processes ... take place on a low order of awareness.

Vigilance and psychic energy are required not only to marshall adaptational techniques, but also to distinguish microaggressions from differently motivated actions and to determine "which of many daily microaggressions one must undercut."

The microaggressive acts that characterize interracial encounters are carried out in "automatic, preconscious, or unconscious fashion" and "stem from the mental attitude of presumed superiority." They are the product of the factors described in Part I. The elevator incident represents their least insidious form. This is so for three reasons. First, the black woman at the elevator initiated an interaction, thereby providing social cues that would predictably result in an expressed judgment. The microaggression she suffered was avoidable. The black woman can in the future decline to initiate an exchange with a white stranger. To the extent that she minimizes such exchanges, she can protect against further insult. Moreover, the microaggression was arguably content-based. The reaction of the city attorney can be interpreted as a response to the woman's question—to the data gathered in the interaction—rather than a response to the person. Susceptibility to content-based microaggression can be minimized or controlled, not only by avoiding interactions, but also by avoiding ambiguity when interactions occur: The black woman might have said, "The indicator is broken. Is this elevator going up or down?" The more frequent and more insidious microaggressions, however, are unavoidable in that they are neither initiated by blacks nor based in any apparent way on the behavior of blacks. Finally, the elevator incident is benign among microaggressions because the white woman's implicit assertion of superiority did not culminate in an achievement of subordination. A fictitious continuation of the elevator incident illustrates microaggressions that are not only unprovoked in the sense described above but also complete in their achievement of subordination:

[The city attorney decides to leave the elevator. She is standing at the right side of the car—directly opposite, but several feet away from, the black woman. Although she might easily exit by walking a path angled toward the center of the car, she takes a step directly forward. After a moment's hesitation, the black woman steps aside.]

This is microaggression in its most potent form. It is the direct descendent of an aspect of color-caste behavior described fifty years ago as "deference":

> The most striking form of ... "caste behavior" is deference, the respectful yielding exhibited by the Negroes in their contacts with whites. According to the dogma and to a large extent actually, the behavior of both Negroes and white people must be such as to indicate that the two are socially distinct and that the Negro is subordinate. Thus ... [i]n places of business the Negro should stand back and wait until the white has been served before receiving any attention, and in entering or leaving he should not precede a white but should stand back and hold the door for him. On the streets and sidewalks the Negro should "give way" to the white person.

The wordless interchange was not initiated by the black woman. It was not based upon any action taken by her. It was a natural manifestation of an imbedded interactive pattern in which "skin color determines whether or not one is expected to operate from an inferior or superior vantage point. Both races have come to expect and accept as unremarkable that the blacks' time, energy, space, and mobility will be at the service of the white." The inferiority of the black is more than an implicit assertion; it is a background assumption that supports the seizure of a prerogative.

* * *

NOTES AND QUESTIONS

1. Neutrality in law: its sources. In the public law debates over constitutional principle, the once well-accepted idea that legal rules are neutral, formal, and even scientific has been a vigorously contested terrain. In the 1980s, critical legal scholars mounted a broad challenge to the neutrality of legal rules. They argued that legal rules are indeterminate, lacking in objective neutrality, controlled instead by context, politics, and discretionary incorporation of the decision maker's perspective. However, when we turn to the debates about the rules that control outcomes in the market, skepticism about neutrality and rationality has emerged among legal scholars more recently.

In what follows we offer a preliminary map, tracing the role of the neutrality claim in legal theory. We start with the formalism of Christopher C. Langdell, a late 19th century dean of Harvard Law School, who introduced the study of appellate cases and the classification of legal subjects into categories that he defined as based upon a scientifically rigorous organization of legal thought, derived from provable "principles" of law. Langdell's formalism thus served to introduce the early framework of the neutrality claim through its assertion that legal reasoning was based upon "scientifically provable premises."

In the practice of law, legal neutrality is featured in several professional norms. First, we have the expectation of professional detachment in which the lawyer serves as a vigorous advocate on behalf of the client, without becoming so identified with the client as to lose perspective on sound professional assessments of what best serves the client's interest. Second, in litigation, neutrality expectations are on display in the rules that govern judicial conduct. Judges are expected to maintain an even temperament. Our chosen garb for judges, black robes, strips them of their ordinary clothing and the signifiers of class status that are a part of ordinary "street" clothing. Thus, the black robe is chosen to signal to participants in the legal process that judges have left behind personal identity in the service of their professional obligation of fair treatment and neutrality for every litigant.

In the dynamics of the courtroom, we can see the contest model of truth-seeking neutrality at work. In the contest model opposing lawyers may introduce palpably false testimony, misleading evidence, and they may use harsh tactics to destroy the credibility of witnesses who speak the objective truth. However, in the contest model, neutrality does not depend upon the truth or unbiased participation of litigants, but depends instead upon the dynamics of contested assertions. Neutrality emerges from the competing vectors of truth introduced by the interested parties. The contest model is also carried over into our expectations for jury deliberation. Juries are expected to rely upon their diverse identities, experience, and preferences to arrive at a verdict in both the criminal and civil cases. The verdict is the product of a contest of competing points of view, ultimately produces a compromise that represents a fair and neutral adjudication of the disputed claims.

In constitutional frameworks, the ideal of neutrality finds its home in the Equal Protection Clause. The equality norm has, at least since Wechsler (see note 2, supra at page 8), merged with legal formalism to insist on the application of "neutral principles." The concept of legal neutrality therefore can be traced to many complex and mutually reinforcing structures in legal theory, legal practice, and doctrine.

2. Neutrality in economics: its sources. In the market domain, belief in the insights of the first modern economist, Adam Smith, is still very firmly entrenched. Smith's central argument, in the 1759 classic the *Theory of Moral Sentiments*, was that private markets operate on the self-interested decisions of each individual participant. He argued that society achieved its maximum productivity when individuals were left alone to figure out from whom they wanted to buy and to whom they wanted to sell. Smith's famous metaphor for the social good that would arise from the cumulative impact of these buyer-seller decisions is the "invisible hand." In the centuries since Smith wrote, the argument that individuals are "led by an invisible hand to promote" what was good for society by choosing what was good for themselves has been enormously influential across all social-science disciplines, such as law, sociology, psychology, and economics.

Traditional economic analysis does not incorporate variables for either culture or identity. The language of economic analysis is built upon the implicit assumption that economic activity is natural and pre-political, and that economic actors possess abstract, identity-free preferences, devoid of the influences of culture or the dynamics of social groups. We adopt an opposing view that economic institutions are suffused with cultural power. We know that identity matters, and that economic subordination is not an abstract preference to those excluded from participation in the material comforts of our wealthy economic system.

As in traditional models of legal practice, traditional economic method-ologies are framed with the claim of neutrality in seeking truth. Truth seeking in the hard sciences, like mathematics, physics, and chemistry depends upon the use of the scientific method, in which researchers do not have a normative stake in the outcome of the investigations. So, empiri-cism, and experimental procedures that can be duplicated by any trained scientist, insure that the "truth" is not subject to manipulation. Economics associates itself with the scientific culture. This association plays a role in advancing the neutrality premises, as well. In this culture, professional detachment is a prerequisite. There is a preference for laboratory experi-ments over *in vivo* (life), in which variables can be controlled, unlike the messy multivariate environments of real human interaction.

Despite the association of economics with the physical sciences and mathematics, we notice that contemporary economics imposes crucial limi-tations upon its fields of inquiry. For example, questions of distribution—who has how much wealth—have been defined as outside the scope of research for the discipline. The problems of economic inequality and the structures of identity-based subordination have no place in the equations featuring wealth maximization, zero transactions costs, rational choice, and perfect competition.

3. Critical race theory objections to neutrality frameworks: sources and central themes. Critical race theory rejects the neutrality and objectivity of law, elevating a personal, subjective, outsider experience to the center of jurisprudence, and demanding non-neutral laws to eradi-cate the ramifications of oppression. In addition to its anti-neutrality position, critical race theory explores other themes, including the following characteristic viewpoints:

> a. **Race as a social construction.** Critical race theorists deem the notion of race developed as a function of communal needs, econom-ics, and politics. This belief aids in explaining the simplicity and prevalence of race as a social category (the mere existence of race) and the derogatory and positive connotations related to particular racial identities.

Because race is a social construct, it does not exist a priori; rather, it is created by discourses in politics, law, and science. In addition, the constructs that support race formation are mutable and volatile. The meaning of race, the number of racial groupings, and the cultural definition of particular racial personalities have all changed over time.

b. **Narrative.** Critical race scholars write narratives to liberate themselves from the constraining effects of conformity. With narratives, scholars can choose from a range of techniques—autobiographies, parables, and self-portraits—to communicate race and equality issues. Narrative provides a framework about the character of discrimination from the view of those who experience it and also challenges the "truth" (the objective reasoning) of American jurisprudence. Carbado & Gulati, *supra* at 1784–86. Though there is some "storytelling" in the legal world—in the courtroom and in legal documents—stories told through a detached lens fail to capture central experiences.

c. **Color-blind society.** Critical race theorists reject the notion of colorblindness and embrace race consciousness. According to these scholars, colorblindness promotes nonwhites to assimilate and to deny their racial background because association with that group would cause these nonwhites to appear to be different. Critical race theory scholars argue that one simply cannot be "blind" to race because it is impossible not to notice an individual's attributes without having first thought about such traits at least once before. Neil Gotanda elaborates on this notion as he discusses the difference between medical colorblindness and liberal theorists' "nonrecognition" of race:

> A medically color-blind person is someone who cannot see what others can. It is a partial nonperception of what is "really" there. To be racially color-blind, on the other hand, is to ignore what one has already noticed. The medically color-blind individual never perceives color in the first place; the racially color-blind individual perceives race and then ignores it. . . . The characteristics of race that are noticed . . . are situated within an already existing understanding of race. . . . This preexisting race consciousness makes it impossible for an individual to be truly nonconscious of race.

Neil Gotanda, *A Critique of "Our Constitution is Color–Blind,"* 44 Stan. L. Rev. 1, 18–19 (1991).

d. **Race as performative identity.** Legal scholars Devon Carbado and Mitu Gulati argue that the social definition of an individual's racial identity is a function of the way that person "performs" his or her race—for example, how an Asian person presents her "Asianness." In everyday encounters, people create or project specific images of race. This implies that the simplicity of an African American's racial identity partly originates from (1) the image of blackness he presents, and (2) how that racial projection is interpreted. Carbado and Gulati argue that they often have to suppress their racial or ethnic attributes in speech, clothing, and hair in order to dispel derogatory stereotypes about their demographic groups. This implies that racial minorities have some power to configure the parameters upon which they are experienced.

The racial "performance" an individual exhibits can span a wide range, and that individual's susceptibility to racism largely depends on where he falls on the racial spectrum:

> On one side of the spectrum are "conventional" black people. They are black prototypes—that is, people who are perceived to be stereotypically black. Their performance of blackness is consistent with society's understanding of who black people really are. On the other side are "unconventional" black people—people who are not stereotypically black. Their performance of blackness is outside of what society perceives to be conventional black behavior. A black person's vulnerability to discrimination is shaped in part by her racial position on this spectrum. The less stereotypically black she is, the more palatable her identity is. The more palatable her identity is, the less vulnerable she is to discrimination. The relationship among black unconventionality, racial palatability, and vulnerability to discrimination creates an incentive for black people to signal—through identity performances—that they are unconventionally black. These signals convey the idea that the sender is black in a phenotypic but not a social sense. Put another way, the signals function as a marketing device. They brand the black person so as to make clear that she is not a black prototype.

Devon W. Carbado & Mitu Gulati, *The Law and Economics of Critical Race Theory*, 112 YALE L.J. 1757, 1769 (2003) (book review).

e. **Essentialism.** To "essentialize" about race is to assume that a specific racial or gender personality has a singular and particular essence, isolated from other parts of identity. Some critical race scholars choose not to follow this essentialized methodology and are instead committed to intersectionality, a theory that insinuates that people's identities are intersectional—that is raced, gendered, sexually oriented, etc.—and that people's susceptibility to racism is a function of their specific intersectional identities. *Id. See* Kimberlé W. Crenshaw, *Mapping the Margins: Intersectionality, Identity Politics, and Violence Against Women of Color*, 43 STAN. L. REV. 1241 (1991); Angela P. Harris, *Race and Essentialism in Feminist Legal Theory*, 42 STAN. L. REV. 581 (1990).

f. **Identity privilege.** Critical race theorists argue that because racial discrimination is an enduring social predicament, there will be victims and recipients of this discrimination.

g. **Multiracialism.** A primary premise of critical race theory is a multiracial concept. This implies that the effects of racism are larger than any particular racial group. Certain critical race scholars condemn the black/white paradigm, asserting that most legal and political discussions concerning race focus on black and white experiences, failing to consider or marginalizing the experiences of nonblack minorities.

D.   Economics and Law: Two Cultures in Tension

Economics and Law: Two Cultures in Tension

54 Tenn. L. Rev. 161 (1986).

■ James Boyd White

* * *

Many people think of economics solely as a scientific, conceptual, and cognitive system, apparently unaware that there are any other dimensions of meaning in economic talk. But all expression is loaded with values, ethical and otherwise; all expression defines a self and another and proposes a relation between them; all expression remakes its language; in these senses all expression proposes the creation of a community and a culture. All expression, in short, is ethical, cultural, and political, and it can be analyzed and judged as such. To claim that economics is a science is perhaps to claim that it cannot be judged in such terms. But "sciences" are cultures too, with their own created worlds and values. One way to describe my aim in this talk, then, is to say that it reverses the usual flow: we are used to economic analyses of this or that aspect of our common life—voting, the family, war, etc. I propose here to begin what I would call a rhetorical or cultural analysis of a certain kind of economics.

* * *

III.   Economics as a Language of Theory

Neoclassical microeconomics proceeds upon certain assumptions that can be summarized this way. The universe is populated by a number of discrete human actors, each of whom is competent, rational, and motivated solely by self-interest. External to the human actors is a natural universe that affords what are called "resources," which are acted upon by human actors to create something called "wealth." Partly for reasons of practicality, this kind of economics defines economic activity, and hence wealth, in terms of the process of exchange by which one actor exchanges some item within his dominion for an item within the dominion of another, or, far more commonly, for money which is the medium of exchange. To look at everything from the point of view of exchange is, naturally enough, to regard the universe as a collection of items for potential exchange, and in this sense to itemize it. When an exchange takes place these items enter the economic system and become part of what we mean by productivity. Where no exchange actually takes place—as where wealth is created and consumed by the same person, or where leisure is chosen over work—the economic effect of the actor's decision is not disregarded by professional economics, as it often is in popular economic thought, but it is still measured by the value of an imagined exchange, the one the actor has forgone. The central principle of the system is that everything is at least hypothetically interchangeable and thus of necessity quantifiable in ways that permit meaningful commensuration, at any rate by the actors who are faced with the choices to which economics speaks.

As the natural universe is itemized by these real or imagined exchanges, the social world is atomized, conceived of as a set of actors of equal competence, without race, gender, age, or culture. Each actor is assumed to be motivated by an unlimited desire to acquire or consume. Since each is interested only in its own welfare, each is in structural competition with all the others. This in turn creates a severe scarcity with respect to the resources. Where there is no scarcity, as there once was not with respect to clean air or water, there can be no economics of this kind. The final ingredient is money, a medium in which surplus can be accumulated with convenience and, in principle, without limit. So far as possible, all human interaction is reduced to the single model of exchange. Economics is the study of what life would be like on such assumptions.

Exchange is a method of determining value, which, tautologically, is said to be the price for which items are sold. This is the value that is put upon them by the economic system, and the only kind of value that economics can express. Obviously individuals may put different values on different items—indeed, this is ordinarily necessary for the exchange to occur in the first place—but although these private values drive the economic system, they are not directly expressible in its terms.

In the world of economics individual actors function according to what economists call "rationality." This is a reasoning process that consists of identifying items of potential consumption or dominion in the world, calculating their value in dollar or other common terms, and then estimating various kinds of positive and negative risks. Reason is thus reducible to calculation and risk assessment. * * *

       * * *

IV.   ECONOMICS AS A SYSTEM OF VALUES

We can start with the question of value. In its purest form economics claims to be a value-free social science. But as I suggested earlier I think it in fact enacts a set of values, including political ones, values to which the speaker of the language cannot avoid finding himself at least in part committed.

A.   In the World

Think, for example, of the way in which economics defines the economic actor and the processes by which he functions. He is for the most part assumed to be an individual of indeterminate age, sex, race and cultural background, but of adequate competence at manipulating economic relations. He acts as one who is both perfectly aware of his own wishes and wholly rational—in the special sense in which that term is used, to mean "calculating"—in his pursuit of them. He exists as an individual, not as part of a community, except insofar as he establishes contractual or exchange relations with others. He is assumed to be motivated by self-interest, which in turn is defined in terms of competition, acquisition, and dominion, at least in relation to resources and other actors, for in the process of exchange the self is reduced to those desires.

Of course a particular individual may have other values—indeed the economist insists that he must, calling them "tastes" or "preferences"—perhaps including a "taste" for altruism, for peace and quiet, for heavy metal music, for appreciating nature unspoiled, for beautiful or ugly art, and so forth. These values will drive his participation in the exchange process, or his decision to withdraw from it. But in either case they are themselves valued by the method of exchange: either by an actual exchange that takes place or by a hypothetical or imagined exchange that is forgone (or in a more complicated case by a combination of exchanges made and forgone). In both cases these external values are converted by the discourse into the acquisitive or instrumental values—the desire to extend the dominion of the will—that all economic actors are assumed to have, for this is the only kind of value about which economics can directly talk.

With respect to the external values in their original form, the system is purportedly "value neutral." That is, it regards individual values as simply exogenous to the system itself. Economics of course recognizes that these values exist, but it demeans them by calling them "tastes" or "preferences," names that imply that no serious conversation can proceed on such subjects. And economics itself is by definition not about those values, but about the process by which they are reflected in the activity of exchange. This means that economics cannot, in principle, talk about any value other than the acquisitive or instrumental one that it universalizes. (Indeed it does not talk about this value either, but merely assumes and acts upon it.) This is not to be "value free," as its apologists claim, but to make self-interest the central, indeed almost the only, value, for it is the only one that can be talked about in these terms. To come at it the other way, it is to claim that all values can be talked about, at least for some purposes, as if they were selfish, quantifiable, and interchangeable.

* * *

Yet economics is troubling not only for the self-interested values it directly asserts, but also for the very neutrality, the "value freedom," that it claims. It is in principle neutral on all questions of value that are external to the acquisitive and competitive ones enacted in the exchange game, which it lumps together as "tastes" or "preferences" among which no distinctions can be drawn. But this is to be silent on all the great questions of human life: questions of beauty and ugliness in art and music, sincerity and falsity in human relations, wisdom and folly in conduct and judgment, and the greatest of all questions, which is how we ought to lead our lives. Economic analysis assumes as a given the existence of "tastes" or "preferences" which drive the system, but economics as a language can provide no way of talking about these values, whether in oneself or another, no way of thinking about which to prefer and which not. To the extent that economics does reach out for these questions it may be worse than silent, for silence after all can be a mode of controlling a discourse. When economics tries to speak about these matters it does so in the only way it knows how to speak, in purely quantitative terms and on the assumption that all human transactions can be reduced to the model of exchange.

* * *

For the purposes of economic analysis all human wishes and desires are thus reduced to the same level, as though no principled choices could be made among them, as though it didn't matter what choices one made. This in turn means that it is impossible to talk in these terms about our most important choices as individuals and communities, or about the education of mind or heart, for any impulse that we or others may happen to have is as good, valid, and entitled to respect as any other.

* * * We must and do have preferences, as the economist knows; and these necessarily commit those who have them to the inquiry of better and worse, as well as to that of greater and less. To refuse to engage in this inquiry—to privatize it—as economics in its neutral phase necessarily does, is to deny an essential and necessary aspect of human life. To reduce all value to self-interest, as it does the rest of the time, is intellectually and ethically intolerable. How could one educate one's children or oneself to live in a world that was neutral on all the great questions of life, except that it reduced them to acquisition, competition, and calculation?

B. Among Economists

There is another dimension to economics, as a discourse among economists. Here too, in the discourse, values are of necessity enacted. For example, economics necessarily values the reduction of life to terms such as I describe, for this is what it achieves. It values linear reasoning and competition for dominance. This last is especially so among economists, for it is ostensibly a premise of economic discourse, as a rule of proof appropriate to a science, that we will believe only what we are forced by logic and fact to believe. This means that economic conversations—like certain other academic discussions—are often attempts to compel others to submit to one's views, or to resist such submission. In doing so they necessarily perform a claim that this is the most appropriate and valuable way to converse on these subjects, itself a most dubious position.

* * *

The claim that microeconomics is a value-free science is thus false in at least two ways. First, even as a science it is not value-free, for no science can be. It values the positivist and behaviorist premises from which it functions, the reduction of reason to calculation, the performed conversion of the world into quantifiable units, and so on. Second, economics attributes motives and values to its actors, those of acquisitiveness and self-interest, and invests itself in these attributions, which it assumes to be universal. This assumption is qualified by the recognition that one actor may choose to act for others, but in the end economics always reduces motive to self-interest, the only kind of motive it can conceive of and speak about. The reduction of all human interaction to the model of exchange, actual or imagined, simply erases whole fields of life and thought, from art to morals, for economics recognizes no ground, other than competitive survivability, upon which one can choose one form of life or one work of art over another, or even upon which one can choose to favor the market and its methods of analysis over others.

In saying that "value-free" economics is actually committed to certain values, both in the assumptions it makes about the world and in the conventions by which its own discourse operates, I do not mean to suggest that the field is in this respect peculiar. Quite the contrary. As I say above I think that all systems of discourse commit their users to values and do so in both domains, that is in one's account of the "other world" one talks about and in the here-and-now world one creates by talking. Science does this, and so do law and literary criticism too. Economics is not to be blamed, then, for having values. But no one should be allowed to claim value-neutrality where it does not exist, and economics, like other disciplines, can be praised or blamed for the values it has. All of us, economists and lawyers and lecturers among the rest, should be held responsible for the values we enact in our talking.

All this is not to say that economics is wrong to do what it does, namely, to isolate the practices of exchange for study, especially when its results are applied to spheres of life that are in fact characterized by exchanges that take place on conditions roughly matching the assumptions of the discourse. This is, after all, a good deal of the economic life of the investor or entrepreneur in a capitalist economy. But it is to say that this study would lead to insanity unless it were premised on a recognition that these activities, and the culture they and their study together create, require subordination to other activities and cultures, both at the level of the individual and of the polity.

V.   Economics as a Political System

An economist might agree with most of this and say that the language and practices in which he engages as an economist must somehow be put together with the languages and practices that make up the rest of his life, both public and private. This would raise the wonderfully interesting and important question, how this might be done, and with what effect on economics itself, a question to which I shall return below.

But another line of justification is possible as well, one that neither denies the political character of this discourse nor seeks to subordinate it to other languages and practices, but affirmatively celebrates the politics and ethics that this kind of economics entails, mainly on the ground that the market is affirmatively desirable both as a model of life and as a political and social institution. The premises of the analytic method, in other words, can be regarded as the proper premises upon which to build our collective life. In talking this way the economist moves off the ground of purportedly pure science. He begins to use his language not as a "filing system" but as a way of expressing overt social and political attitudes, largely in support of the institution of the market. I should stress that not all economists would take this step. But some would. They are of course perfectly entitled to do so, but only to the extent that their politics and ethics, not their economics, persuade us of the rightness of their vision.

A.   Justifying the Market as a Model of Life

The institution of the market is celebrated by its proponents because in their view it is democratic—each person brings to the market his own values and can "maximize" them his own way—and because it is creative and open, leaving the widest room for individual choice and action. The market establishes a community based upon a competitive process that allows each person freedom to choose what to do with what is his. These merits mean, for some economists at least, that all social institutions ought to be modified to approximate the market—to conform to the analytic model of life as exchange—or at least to be analyzed and judged on that presumption.

The market is further justified, when such justification is thought necessary, in either of two rather conflicting ways. The first is to say that the market is good because it promotes efficiency, that is to say it maximizes the "welfare" of all participants in the process. It does this by definition, because each person participates in the process only because he thinks he gets more that way than he would any other way, and who are we to tell him differently? In maximizing the welfare of all participants it does the same for society as a whole, which is nothing more or less than the sum of all the participants in the market. The obvious trouble with this is that it takes for granted not only the existing values (or "tastes") of the actors, but also the existing distributions among them of wealth, capacity, and entitlement, which it has no way of criticizing. Yet these may of course be eminently criticizable.

The "welfare" defense of the market would justify all transactions—including the sale of oneself into slavery or prostitution—that are not in an obvious sense "coerced" by another because they are marginal improvements for the actors involved. But an economy might provide a different set of starting points for its actors, so that such degrading activities would no longer be "improvements" for anyone. We would all benefit from living in such a world. But the economist has no way of saying this. On the premises I have described he cannot deny the desirability of redistribution, but he cannot affirm it either. Even to discuss the question requires a shift of discourse, to ways of talking that economics of the sort I have been discussing excludes.

The second ground upon which the market is justified is that not of its gross effects but of its fairness. In one version this justification rests upon the ethical standing of voluntary action and holds that the results of the market process are justified with respect to every actor because the choices by which the market works are voluntary. In another version, it becomes the affirmative celebration of autonomy or liberty: whether or not it is efficient, the market is good because it gives the widest possible range to freedom of choice and action. Here the claim moves beyond justifying market results by the voluntary character of the choices upon which they rest to the point of asserting autonomy as the central social and political value. The obvious trouble with this line of defense, in both of its forms, is that it assumes that all exchanges are for all actors equally voluntary and equally expressive of autonomy, a position that common sense denies.

* * *

The market purports to rest upon an assumption of the equality of all the actors in the system. In fact, it rests upon a different assumption, namely, the equality of every dollar in the system. Since some players have many more dollars, and through this fact are at a competitive advantage, it is a system that actively supports inequality among its actors.

It is not too much to say, I think, that the modern celebration of the market as the central social institution—the most fair, the most respecting of autonomy, and the most efficient—threatens to destroy the single greatest achievement of Western political culture: the discovery that a community can govern itself through a rule of law that attempts to create a fundamental moral and political equality among human beings. The great phrase in the Declaration of Independence—"all men are created equal"— is partly a theological statement about the conditions under which we are created and partly a political statement about the obligation of the government to acknowledge, indeed to create or recreate, that equality. This value is the heart of what is meant both by equality under law and by our democratic institutions more generally, resting as they do on the premise that each person's vote is worth exactly what everyone else's is. The ideology of the market, if it prevailed in its desire to convert all institutions into markets, would destroy this set of political relations and would create another in its stead, based upon the dollar.

* * *

The market ideology claims to be radically democratic and egalitarian because it leaves every person free to do with her own what she will. But this freedom of choice is not equally distributed among all people. The market is democratic not on the principle of one person one vote, but on the far different principle of one dollar, one vote. One could hardly make a greater mistake than to equate, as so much modern public talk carelessly does, the "free market" with democracy.

There are two distinct points here. First, the exchange transactions that the market celebrates are not entitled to the special respect claimed for them as free and voluntary, and hence fair, unless each person has roughly the same amount of money and the same competence and freedom in its use, which is demonstrably not the case. The accumulations of wealth it permits thus cannot be justified by the fairness of the transactions by which the accumulation occurs. Second, if the advocates of the market succeeded in converting other institutions into markets, the result would be to transfer to those who have wealth not only the economic power that inescapably follows it but also the political power that in our democratic tradition the people have claimed for themselves and have exercised through the institutions of self-government. This would validate and institutionalize private economic power held by one person over another, of the rich over the poor. If we were to yield entirely to its claims, we would gradually find our traditional government, which operates by collective deliberation on a premise of fundamental equality of citizens, replaced by a private-sector government of the few over the many, wholly unregulated by collective judgment.

VI.   ECONOMICS AS A SYSTEM OF ECONOMIC ANALYSIS

But it is not only as a system of value and politics that this kind of economics, and the ways of thought it encourages, are troubling. I think that it is distorted and unrealistic as a way of imagining, thinking about, and shaping the processes of production and exchange that we think of as the economy itself.

A.   *The Social and Natural Matrix*

The first distortion I wish to consider has to do with the relationship between the exchange system and the cultural and natural world that it necessarily presupposes. What I mean is this. The economic activity of exchange takes place under natural and cultural conditions that are absolutely essential to it, but about which economics has no way of talking except by itemization, quantification, and conversion into the material of actual or hypothetical exchange. All talk about exchanges, that is, necessarily presupposes that the exchangers live in the natural world of sun, air, and water, subject to the powers of growth and health and disease, a world the organization of which is complex far beyond our understanding. Each of the exchangers is part of that world in another sense as well, for each is himself an organism, and one that incompletely understands both himself and his relation to the natural world upon which he absolutely depends for his existence. The language of economics similarly assumes the existence of a society and culture, a set of human understandings and expectations upon which each exchanger can rely: that promises will normally be kept, that one can get one's money home without being robbed, that it is worth thinking about the future, for oneself or for one's children, and so on. What is more, the actor's motives or values (what the economists call his "preferences") are themselves formed by interactions both with his culture and with nature. This is how we are made as individuals, how we cohere as a community, and how we connect ourselves to the past and to the future.

But on all this economics is silent, for it begins to speak only when an actor has, at least in his mind, identified some item in the world and begun to think of exchanging it for something else. It is his judgment of its worth, in exchanging it or in declining to do so, that is for the economist its value. But what confidence can we have in such judgments of worth, by actors necessarily imperfectly aware both of themselves and of the cultural and natural worlds they inhabit? To put it in epistemological terms, the economist assumes that there is nothing to be known about the natural or cultural world that cannot be known through the process of exchange itself. But in order to judge the value of an item now, or to predict one for the future (which is very much the same thing), one must make estimates about possible changes in the social, cultural, and natural matrix in which all exchange takes place, and about the effect of this and similar exchanges upon that matrix. There is no reason to be especially confident in anyone's capacity to make such estimates.

* * *

This is to talk about it in terms of knowledge, the knowledge that the economist assumes we have. But it can be cast in terms of value as well, for the language of economics assumes that the relation between humanity and nature should be one of dominion, that the expanded assertion of control by individual actors over nature—called "natural resources"—is inherently a good thing. But why should one grant such an assumption? As Wendell Berry repeatedly points out in his works on agricultural economics, modern agriculture can be considered a great technological success only if one uses the measure of present-day output per man-hour, disregarding both the destructive effects of modern farming on soil and water and the costs, natural and economic, of the fossil fuels used for both fertilizer and power. If productivity over decades or per acre is the test, as in a world of five billion perhaps it should be, our agriculture falls well below that of many more "primitive" peoples. If one includes the meaning of the work the farmer does, its rhythms and its harmonies or disharmonies with nature, the picture is complicated further; still further if one asks how important it is in a nuclear age for a particular polity, or for humanity, that the capacity for fruitful and stable survival on a small scale be maintained. Economic language assumes, with what a theologian like James Gustafson might call a foolish pride, that man's wants and wishes are the ultimate measure of value; it then claims that these wishes are constrained only in ways that traders can see and account for. These are assumptions of fact and value that one might generously regard as dubious.

The only kind of meaning economics can reflect is one that can be expressed in the medium of exchange, that is, quantifiable and comparative. This is in turn to give the world itself a meaning of a new kind, reflected in the Japanese phrase for the blue sky that can rarely be seen over Tokyo these days: it is called a "recession sky."

* * *

D. Erasing Community

For similar reasons this kind of economics has the greatest difficulty in reflecting the reality of human community and the value of communal institutions. Its necessary tendency seems to be to destroy the idea of public action, indeed the idea of community itself. This is partly because this methodology tends to resolve all communities and organizations into the individual human actors who constitute them, partly because commitment to the market system leads one to think that everything that can be made the subject of the market should be. The idea is that every economic actor should pay for what he wants, and should not have to pay for what he doesn't want. But this tends to destroy our public institutions, all of which extend benefits far beyond those who would pay (if they were reduced to markets) or who do pay (when they are supported by taxes). Such institutions reflect a communal judgment that we need to educate ourselves and each other, that our "tastes" are not all of equal value but need to be formed, and formed well rather than badly. Public universities, libraries, orchestras, museums, parks—all these would fall before the ideology that denies the existence and reality of community and reduces all institutions, all human production, to the language of the market.

Think here of the way economists explain why people who will probably never visit, say, the Everglades or an art museum are happy to have their taxes used to maintain them. The economist says it is because the actor wants to maintain the option of visiting them some day, and calls this an "option demand." But may it not be that the voter simply takes pleasure in what other people have and in what other people can do, in belonging to a community that is good for all its members? Or that he respects their desires and wants a community based on that kind of mutual respect? This possibility is systematically denied by the assumption of economic talk, that individuals and communities are in principle incapable of generosity, or more precisely, that "altruism" can adequately be talked about as a species of selfishness.

The language of self and self-interest not only fails to reflect the reality of community and of shared interests, it draws attention away from those aspects of life and devalues them. To continue to talk on these assumptions, even hypothetically, is to encourage "self-interest" in an ethical sense and to erode the commitments we have to each other that underlie such essential practices of citizenship as the willingness to pay taxes, to work for the local school, or to serve in the army, upon which everything depends. To adopt the economic view would in fact threaten the very existence of community, for on these premises no one would conceivably die or seriously risk his life for his community: at the point of danger one's self-interest in survival would outweigh all other self-interests. And to speak of all "tastes" as if they were equivalent is to invite oneself and others to think that they are, and to confirm the premises of our culture, already drummed into the mind by the consumer economy, that the consumer is king, that whatever you happen to want is a good that you should seek to satisfy, that no distinction can be drawn between the beautiful and ugly, the wise and foolish, and so on. It is to confirm a vulgar view of democracy that makes the preference or will supreme, as if we functioned by instant referendum. It erases the sense that a democracy is a mode of communal self-constitution and self-education that may have higher ends than the satisfaction of wants, namely the creation of a community of a certain sort, at once based upon a set of responsibilities and offering us a set of opportunities for civic and social action.

————

NOTES AND QUESTIONS

1.   Effect of terminology on White's critique. White states that "all systems of discourse commit their users to values . . . [and that] economics is [not] wrong to do what it does." James Boyd White, *Economics and Law: Two Cultures in Tension*, 54 Tenn. L. Rev. 161, 176 (1986). If all White wishes is for economics to acknowledge that it is no different from other systems of discourse, does his critique of law and economics have any value? Would the problems White identifies with law and economics be solved by acknowledging that law and economics has values without making any substantive changes to the discipline? Would White be satisfied with this solution?

2.   Pernicious nature of law and economics. At the close of his article, White states that "to continue to talk on . . . [law and economics'] assumptions, even hypothetically, is to encourage 'self interest' in an ethical sense and to erode the commitments we have to each other that underlie such essential practices of citizenship as the willingness to pay taxes, to work for the local school, or to serve in the army, upon which everything depends. To adopt the economic view would in fact threaten the very existence of community. . . ." *Id.* at 192. If White is correct about the dire consequences of even hypothesizing in an economic framework, how can he assert that economics is not wrong to "do what it does"? *Id.* at 176.

E.   Judging Race: The Doctrine of Discriminatory Intent

Note About Neutrality in Form, Discriminatory Impact and the Paradox of Statistical Correlation vs. Motivation

The debate about race, neutrality, and markets has not been limited to economic theories of rationality contesting the subjective narratives of critical race scholars. Conflicting perspectives about neutrality also extend to disputes about what evidence can trigger a constitutional violation of the Equal Protection Clause. In this debate, the liberal and conservative positions have been reversed. Civil rights advocates sought to rely upon scientific measures of statistical racial disparity to show that the impact of a facially neutral policy violated the Equal Protection standard. The Court rejected statistical measures of the disparate impact of the employment screening test on black applicants.

For "facially neutral" policies, such as this employment screening test, the Court introduced a motive-focused standard that required evidence of intentional racial discrimination to establish a violation of the Fourteenth Amendment. The demise of disparate impact theory to prove an Equal Protection violation was a major setback for the use of civil rights legal theory seeking to challenge government policies and practices, even though such policies did not contain a race-specific classification.

Consider how this case contributes to our understanding of the uses of the concept of neutrality. Does the fact that scientific tools, such as statistical proof of disproportionate harm to racial minority groups, were rejected in this case turn the conservative (scientific) vs. liberal (empathetic, seeking to enter the subjective experience of another) on its head? As you read the case that follows, recall that it was Judge Posner who said:

> Maybe economic scholarship is not *really* empathetic. The economist does not enter imaginatively into the distress of the disappointed quester for rental housing; all he does is tote up some additional costs. But that may be a sounder way of doing policy than by cultivating empathy. A jurisprudence of empathy can foster short-sighted substantive justice . . . [1]

Posner, OVERCOMING LAW, *supra* at 381.

On the basis of the observations above, had he been a Justice, do you think Judge Posner would have dissented in the following case?

Washington v. Davis

426 U.S. 229 (1976).

■ MR. JUSTICE WHITE DELIVERED THE OPINION OF THE COURT.

This case involves the validity of a qualifying test administered to applicants for positions as police officers in the District of Columbia Metropolitan Police Department. The test was sustained by the District Court, but invalidated by the Court of Appeals. We are in agreement with the District Court and hence reverse the judgment of the Court of Appeals.

[The action was filed by black applicants to become police officers in the District of Columbia. The claimants were unsuccessful in passing a test that was designed to measure verbal skills, vocabulary and reading. They introduced evidence in the District Court showing that a greater percentage of blacks failed, than did whites. In addition, the claimants alleged that the

---

1. A more basic point is that the internal perspective—putting oneself in the other person's shoes—that is achieved by the exercise of empathic imagination lacks normative significance.

test had not been validated, by accepted test measurement methodology, to provide reliable test results for predicting future job performance.]

The central purpose of the Equal Protection Clause of the Fourteenth Amendment is the prevention of official conduct discriminating on the basis of race. It is also true that the Due Process Clause of the Fifth Amendment contains an equal protection component prohibiting the United States from invidiously discriminating between individuals or groups. *Bolling* v. *Sharpe,* 347 U.S. 497 (1954). But our cases have not embraced the proposition that a law or other official act, without regard to whether it reflects a racially discriminatory purpose, is unconstitutional *solely* because it has a racially disproportionate impact.

Almost 100 years ago, *Strauder* v. *West Virginia,* 100 U.S. 303 (1879), established that the exclusion of Negroes from grand and petit juries in criminal proceedings violated the Equal Protection Clause, but the fact that a particular jury or a series of juries does not statistically reflect the racial composition of the community does not in itself make out an invidious discrimination forbidden by the Clause. "A purpose to discriminate must be present which may be proven by systematic exclusion of eligible jurymen of the proscribed race or by unequal application of the law to such an extent as to show intentional discrimination." A defendant in a criminal case is entitled "to require that the State not deliberately and systematically deny to members of his race the right to participate as jurors in the administration of justice."

The rule is the same in other contexts [a 1964 case] upheld a New York congressional apportionment statute against claims that district lines had been racially gerrymandered. The challenged districts were made up predominantly of whites or of minority races and their boundaries were irregularly drawn. The challengers did not prevail because they failed to prove that the New York Legislature "was either motivated by racial considerations or in fact drew the districts on racial lines"; the plaintiffs had not shown that the statute "was the product of a state contrivance to segregate on the basis of race or place of origin." * * *

The school desegregation cases have also adhered to the basic equal protection principle that the invidious quality of a law claimed to be racially discriminatory must ultimately be traced to a racially discriminatory purpose. That there are both predominantly black and predominantly white schools in a community is not alone violative of the Equal Protection Clause. The essential element of *de jure* segregation is "a current condition of segregation resulting from intentional state action." *Keyes* v. *School Dist. No. 1,* 413 U.S. 189, 205 (1973). "The differentiating factor between *de jure* segregation and so-called *de facto* segregation ... is *purpose* or *intent* to *segregate*." *Id.,* at 208. See also *id.,* at 199, 211, and 213. The Court has also recently rejected allegations of racial discrimination based solely on the statistically disproportionate racial impact of various provisions of the Social Security Act because "[t]he acceptance of appellants' constitutional theory would render suspect each difference in treatment among the grant classes, however lacking in racial motivation and however otherwise rational the treatment might be.''

This is not to say that the necessary discriminatory racial purpose must be express or appear on the face of the statute, or that a law's disproportionate impact is irrelevant in cases involving Constitution-based claims of racial discrimination. A statute, otherwise neutral on its face, must not be applied so as invidiously to discriminate on the basis of race. *Yick Wo v. Hopkins,* 118 U.S. 356 (1886). It is also clear from the cases dealing with racial discrimination in the selection of juries that the systematic exclusion of Negroes is itself such an ''unequal application of the law ... as to show intentional discrimination.'' A prima facie case of discriminatory purpose may be proved as well by the absence of Negroes on a particular jury combined with the failure of the jury commissioners to be informed of eligible Negro jurors in a community, or with racially nonneutral selection procedures. With a prima facie case made out, ''the burden of proof shifts to the State to rebut the presumption of unconstitutional action by showing that permissible racially neutral selection criteria and procedures have produced the monochromatic result.''

Necessarily, an invidious discriminatory purpose may often be inferred from the totality of the relevant facts, including the fact, if it is true, that the law bears more heavily on one race than another. It is also not infrequently true that the discriminatory impact—in the jury cases for example, the total or seriously disproportionate exclusion of Negroes from jury venires—may for all practical purposes demonstrate unconstitutionality because in various circumstances the discrimination is very difficult to explain on nonracial grounds. Nevertheless, we have not held that a law, neutral on its face and serving ends otherwise within the power of government to pursue, is invalid under the Equal Protection Clause simply because it may affect a greater proportion of one race than of another. Disproportionate impact is not irrelevant, but it is not the sole touchstone of an invidious racial discrimination forbidden by the Constitution. Standing alone, it does not trigger the rule, that racial classifications are to be subjected to the strictest scrutiny and are justifiable only by the weightiest of considerations. * * *

As an initial matter, we have difficulty understanding how a law establishing a racially neutral qualification for employment is nevertheless racially discriminatory and denies ''any person ... equal protection of the laws'' simply because a greater proportion of Negroes fail to qualify than members of other racial or ethnic groups. Had respondents, along with all others who had failed Test 21, whether white or black, brought an action claiming that the test denied each of them equal protection of the laws as compared with those who had passed with high enough scores to qualify them as police recruits, it is most unlikely that their challenge would have been sustained. Test 21, which is administered generally to prospective Government employees, concededly seeks to ascertain whether those who take it have acquired a particular level of verbal skill; and it is untenable that the Constitution prevents the Government from seeking modestly to upgrade the communicative abilities of its employees rather than to be satisfied with some lower level of competence, particularly where the job requires special ability to communicate orally and in writing. Respondents, as Negroes, could no more successfully claim that the test denied them equal protection than could white applicants who also failed. The conclusion would not be different in the face of proof that more Negroes than whites had been disqualified by Test 21. That other Negroes also failed to score well would, alone, not demonstrate that respondents individually were being denied equal protection of the laws by the application of an otherwise valid qualifying test being administered to prospective police recruits.

Nor on the facts of the case before us would the disproportionate impact of Test 21 warrant the conclusion that it is a purposeful device to discriminate against Negroes and hence an infringement of the constitutional rights of respondents as well as other black applicants. As we have said, the test is neutral on its face and rationally may be said to serve a purpose the Government is constitutionally empowered to pursue. Even agreeing with the District Court that the differential racial effect of Test 21 called for further inquiry, we think the District Court correctly held that the affirmative efforts of the Metropolitan Police Department to recruit black officers, the changing racial composition of the recruit classes and of the force in general, and the relationship of the test to the training program negated any inference that the Department discriminated on the basis of race or that "a police officer qualifies on the color of his skin rather than ability."[13] * * *

A rule that a statute designed to serve neutral ends is nevertheless invalid, absent compelling justification, if in practice it benefits or burdens one race more than another would be far reaching and would raise serious questions about, and perhaps invalidate, a whole range of tax, welfare, public service, regulatory, and licensing statutes that may be more burdensome to the poor and to the average black than to the more affluent white. . . .

We also hold that the Court of Appeals should have affirmed the judgment of the District Court granting the motions for summary judgment

---

13. It appears beyond doubt by now that there is no single method for appropriately validating employment tests for their relationship to job performance. Professional standards developed by the American Psychological Association in its Standards for Educational and Psychological Tests and Manuals (1966), accept three basic methods of validation: "empirical" or "criterion" validity (demonstrated by identifying criteria that indicate successful job performance and then correlating test scores and the criteria so identified); "construct" validity (demonstrated by examinations structured to measure the degree to which job applicants have identifiable characteristics that have been determined to be important in successful job performance); and "content" validity (demonstrated by tests whose content closely approximates tasks to be performed on the job by the applicant). These standards have been relied upon by the Equal Employment Opportunity Commission in fashioning its Guidelines on Employee Selection Procedures, 29 CFR pt. 1607 (1975), and have been judicially noted in cases where validation of employment tests has been in issue.

filed by petitioners and the federal parties. Respondents were entitled to relief on neither constitutional nor statutory grounds. * * *

■ MR. JUSTICE STEVENS concurring. . .

While I agree with the Court's disposition of this case, I add these comments on the constitutional issue discussed. . . .

The requirement of purposeful discrimination is a common thread running through the cases summarized in Part II. These cases include criminal convictions which were set aside because blacks were excluded from the grand jury, a reapportionment case in which political boundaries were obviously influenced to some extent by racial considerations, a school desegregation case, and a case involving the unequal administration of an ordinance purporting to prohibit the operation of laundries in frame buildings. Although it may be proper to use the same language to describe the constitutional claim in each of these contexts, the burden of proving a prima facie case may well involve differing evidentiary considerations. The extent of deference that one pays to the trial court's determination of the factual issue, and indeed, the extent to which one characterizes the intent issue as a question of fact or a question of law, will vary in different contexts.

Frequently the most probative evidence of intent will be objective evidence of what actually happened rather than evidence describing the subjective state of mind of the actor. For normally the actor is presumed to have intended the natural consequences of his deeds. This is particularly true in the case of governmental action which is frequently the product of compromise, of collective decision-making, and of mixed motivation. It is unrealistic, on the one hand, to require the victim of alleged discrimination to uncover the actual subjective intent of the decision-maker or, conversely, to invalidate otherwise legitimate action simply because an improper motive affected the deliberation of a participant in the decisional process. A law conscripting clerics should not be invalidated because an atheist voted for it.

My point in making this observation is to suggest that the line between discriminatory purpose and discriminatory impact is not nearly as bright, and perhaps not quite as critical, as the reader of the Court's opinion might assume. I agree, of course, that a constitutional issue does not arise every time some disproportionate impact is shown. On the other hand, when the disproportion is as dramatic as in *Gomillion* v. *Lightfoot,* 364 U.S. 339, or *Yick Wo* v. *Hopkins,* 118 U.S. 356, it really does not matter whether the standard is phrased in terms of purpose or effect. Therefore, although I accept the statement of the general rule in the Court's opinion, I am not yet prepared to indicate how that standard should be applied in the many cases which have formulated the governing standard in different language. * * *

My agreement . . . rests on a ground narrower than the Court describes. I do not rely at all on the evidence of good-faith efforts to recruit black police officers. In my judgment, neither those efforts nor the subjective good faith of the District administration, would save Test 21 if it were otherwise invalid.

There are two reasons why I am convinced that the challenge to Test 21 is insufficient. First, the test serves the neutral and legitimate purpose of requiring all applicants to meet a uniform minimum standard of literacy. Reading ability is manifestly relevant to the police function, there is no evidence that the required passing grade was set at an arbitrarily high level, and there is sufficient disparity among high schools and high school graduates to justify the use of a separate uniform test. Second, the same test is used throughout the federal service. The applicants for employment in the District Columbia Police Department represent such a small fraction of the total number of persons who have taken the test that their experience is of minimal probative value in assessing the neutrality of the test itself. That evidence, without more, is not sufficient to overcome the presumption that a test which is this widely used by the Federal Government is in fact neutral in its effect as well as its "purpose" as that term is used in constitutional adjudication. * * *

■ MR. JUSTICE BRENNAN and MR. JUSTICE MARSHALL dissent

[I]t should be observed that every federal court, except the District Court in this case, presented with proof identical to that offered to validate Test 21 has reached a conclusion directly opposite to that of the Court today. * * *

———

Empirical Evidence

PERVASIVE PREJUDICE, UNCONVENTIONAL EVIDENCE OF RACE AND GENDER DISCRIMINATION 3–8 (2001).

■ IAN AYRES

Indeed, there seems to be a widespread, implicit belief (at least among white males) that race and gender discrimination is not a serious problem in retail markets. The civil rights laws of the 1960s focused on only a handful of non-retail markets-chiefly concerning employment, housing, and public accommodation services. Indeed, the most gaping hole in our civil rights law concerns retail gender discrimination. No federal law prohibits gender discrimination in the sale of goods or services. A seller could flatly refuse to deal with a potential buyer of a car or a paperclip because of her gender. And while the civil rights laws of the 1860s prohibited race discrimination in contracting, the civil rights laws a century later only prohibited sex discrimination in a narrow range of "titled" markets. The thousands of other markets that make up our economy are completely unregulated with regard to gender (as well as to religion and national origin) discrimination and only somewhat more regulated with regard to race. And only a handful of cities and states (chief among them California) make up for this failing by prohibiting gender discrimination in contracting generally.

The non-regulation of retail discrimination seems to be premised on a vague coterie of assumptions: (1) retail discrimination does not exist because retailers have no motive to discriminate; (2) retail discrimination does not exist because competition forces retailers not to discriminate; and (3) any retail discrimination that does occur does not have serious consequences because of effective counterstrategies by potential victims. It is also argued that any discrimination in the sale of goods or services is less important than the potential effects of discrimination in the markets for employment and housing. But without denying the primacy of employment, the current regulatory regime leaves approximately 66 percent of the dollars we spend-and 35 percent of the dollars we earn-unregulated (with respect to gender discrimination) or less regulated (with respect to race discrimination).

In this book, I contest the idea that race and gender discrimination in the retail sale of goods is nonexistent or unimportant. My thesis is that race and gender discrimination is neither a thing of the past nor is it limited to the narrow set of "titled" markets regulated by the civil rights legislation of the 1960s (Title VII, Title II, and so on). The book's primary contribution is empirical, but let me begin with a few theoretical reasons why we should take the possibility of retail discrimination seriously.

RETAILERS MAY HAVE A MOTIVE TO DISCRIMINATE

The argument that discrimination in the sale of goods and services does not exist because retailers lack any disparate treatment motive is itself premised on the twin ideas that discriminating against economically marginal groups would not be profitable and that racial animus would not manifest itself in discrete retail transactions.

The latter idea is that while animus might cause race discrimination in the more relational settings employment, apartment rental, and restaurants-which civil rights laws regulate, regulated retail transactions are sufficiently discrete that seller and/or customer prejudice would not induce disparate treatment. There are, however, several problems with this theory. First, as pointed out by Ian MacNeil, contractual arrangements are not as discrete as initially appear. Barbers may have much more tactile and repeated contact with their customers than one-time sellers of a house, but the law much more vigorously regulates the latter transaction. Second, the thought that prejudice is less likely to be acted upon in discrete transactions is premised on a narrow theory of what might be called "associational" animus-that is, that bigots don't like associating with particular groups. But, * * * there are other types of animus that might persist even in discrete markets. For example, if sellers enjoy extracting an extra dollar of profit from people of color more than from whites, we might expect to see disparate racial treatment in pricing or quality of service. Finally, appreciating the pervasive discretion given to employees as agents open up the possibility that even profit-maximizing principals will by necessity countenance some disparate treatment by their subordinates.

Discriminating retailers may also be actuated by profit. Sellers may have a profit-maximizing incentive to price discriminate against minorities and women-even if sellers believe that members of these groups are on average poorer. It has long been known that "statistical discrimination" might cause rational, profit-maximizing sellers to charge more to groups that on average cause sellers to incur higher costs. Thus, as a theoretical matter, the drivers of taxis might discriminate against African American men if the drivers perceive a higher chance of being robbed by such passengers. But, more provocatively, focusing on the example of new car sales, I argue that profit-maximizing sellers may engage in "revenue-based" race and gender disparate treatment. Dealerships may discriminate not because they expect higher costs but because they expect to be able to extract higher revenues. This is a surprising possibility because, as an empirical matter, people of color have a substantially lower ability to pay for new cars. But profit-maximizing sellers care far more about the variability in willingness to pay than in the mean willingness. The presence of a few minority members who are willing to pay a large markup can make it rational for the dealership to offer higher prices to all members of the group-even if group members are on average poorer.

It is correct and useful to ask whether sellers would plausibly be motivated to engage in a particular type of discrimination. But treating this issue seriously opens up a variety of dimensions where discrimination in the retail sale of goods and services could be a plausible seller strategy for either profit or non-profit-based reasons.

COMPETITION MAY NOT DRIVE OUT RETAIL DISCRIMINATION

Nobel-prize winning economist Gary Becker emphasized how competition could provide a much-needed antidote for the disease of discrimination. Non-discriminating sellers could earn higher profits by picking up the sales of those minorities and/or women excluded from equal access to the discriminating sellers. One problem with this theory is that it focuses on the ability of competition to drive out discriminating sellers, but competition may not be as effective at driving out the preferences of discriminating customers. If fixed costs of production limit the number of firms selling and if a substantial number of, say, white customers prefer dealing with a firm that discriminates against (by excluding or offering inferior service to) people of color, then firms may decide that it is more profitable to exclude minorities than to lose the patronage of whites.

As an empirical matter, however, my guess is that most firms would not find overt race or gender discrimination to be a profit-maximizing strategy. While Lester Maddox may have increased his sales by excluding African Americans, in most markets a "whites only" or "males only" policy or overtly charging higher prices to particular demographic groups would lead to a general negative consumer reaction-by both minorities and progressive white consumers.

A more important limitation on competition is consumer information. In order for discrimination to cause the competitive shift of consumers toward nondiscriminatory sellers, consumers must know which sellers are discriminating and which are not. There is thus an important informational prerequisite for competition to have the predicted Beckerian effect. But as described above, there are many aspects of treatment where consumers may not be able to compare how sellers treat similarly situated counterparts. Retail discrimination is most likely to persist where consumers do not learn the benchmark treatment of fellow consumers. Thus, while there is little opportunity for a single fast food franchise to charge different prices for hamburgers, it is possible for a dealership to charge different prices to potential buyers of cars. Since bargained prices diverge from the list price, it is very difficult for a consumer to know whether she has received a nondiscriminatory price. And it will be more difficult for a nondiscriminatory seller to credibly market itself on the basis that the race or gender of customers do not influence its bargaining strategy.

Markets in which price or other terms of trade are individually bargained for provide much greater opportunities for race or gender discrimination than markets with homogeneous product attributes and posted prices. However, even retailers that sell standardized products at posted prices might discriminate on the basis of race or gender with regard to discretionary aspects of service. Anyone watching the *Prime Time* segment could vividly see that record and department stores could substantially increase the "transaction costs" of minority customers. This is not just an issue of whether the retailer provides "service with a smile" but, as in the *Prime Time Live* testing, whether the retailers make minority customers wait substantially longer before being served (or whether the minority customers are conspicuously shadowed to scrutinize whether they are shoplifting).

Retailers may also discriminate in their willingness to accommodate private and somewhat idiosyncratic consumer requests. For example, Jane Connor is currently testing retailers in Binghamton, New York, to see whether there are racial differences in their willingness to accede to a request to use a restroom or a request to return a sweater without a receipt. Economists (and others) tend to ignore or downplay the harms of such discrimination. But nontrivial injury may be visited on people of color in terms of both higher transactions costs and taking more precaution to comply strictly with retailer policies. One audit study showed that African Americans in Washington, D.C., had to wait 27 percent longer to hail a cab If this seems a minor inconvenience, white readers should try to imagine what their life would be like if *every* (or even just many) transactions took 27 percent longer. Even a single incident can impose real psychological costs. Consider, for example, Patricia Williams's story of being denied entrance to an open Benneton store by a gum-chewing, buzzerwielding store clerk.

———

NOTES AND QUESTIONS

1.   Statistical discrimination. Statistical discrimination exists when a seller or provider of services or property owner treats two equally suitable persons differently, solely on the basis of the average characteristics of members of a race, gender, or other subordinated group.

2.   References for statistical discrimination. For more extensive discussion of statistical discrimination, see D.J. Aigner & G.C. Cain, *Statistical Theories of Discrimination in the Labor Market,* 30 INDUS. & LAB. REL. REV. 175 (1977); K.J. Arrow, *The Theory of Discrimination; in* DISCRIMINATION IN LABOR MARKETS (Ashenfelter and Rees eds.) (1973); A. Moro & P. Norman, *A General Equilibrium Model of Statistical Discrimination,* 114 J. OF ECON. THEORY 1 (2004); S. Schwab, *Is Statistical Discrimination Efficient?,* 76 AMER. ECON. REV. 228 (1986); P. Norman, *Statistical Discrimination and Efficiency,* 70 REV. OF ECON. STUDIES 615 (2003).

3.   Does statistical discrimination account for the proliferation of stereotypes and the presence of negative cognitive associations for subordinated groups whose average characteristics are the product of a societal history of exclusion from opportunity?

F.   NEUTRALITY CHALLENGES FROM OTHER SOCIAL SCIENCE METHODOLOGIES:

1.   COGNITIVE PSYCHOLOGY—SCIENTIFIC EVIDENCE OF COGNITIVE BIAS?

Racism lost its explicit social endorsement in the aftermath of the civil rights revolution that followed in the more than half-century since the 1954 Supreme Court decision in *Brown v. Board of Education.* Hostile racial attitudes and prejudicial belief systems gradually went underground, flourishing in the subterranean world of personal cognition, family norms, and private conversations in racially homogeneous settings. Until recently, this bias was undetectable by scientifically reliable assessment tools. Moreover, both economic theory and legal theory operated on heuristics that assumed that significant racial bias no longer existed.

As Ian Ayres has shown, with a series of empirical research studies of racial discrimination in retail markets, this assumption is probably false. *See* Ayres, PERVASIVE PREJUDICE? UNCONVENTIONAL EVIDENCE OF RACE AND GENDER DISCRIMINATION, *infra* at ___. However, notwithstanding Ayres path-breaking empirical research, the difficulty for those seeking to challenge the neutrality heuristics of economics and law has been to find ways to identify individual biases, and more importantly to link those biases to racially harmful behavior.

Note on the Implicit Association Test (I.A.T.)

The development of the Implicit Association Test has provided a method to penetrate the web of latent individual bias. The test, in its most widely used version, is administered to individuals who choose to take it on the internet. Test takers are asked to sort a randomly shown series of faces into two categories: black American or white American. The test instructions encourage speedy responses using two keys on the computer keyboard that require the use of either the left or right hand. In the second stage of the test, a sequence of value-laden words, such as "joy" and "failure" appear on the screen. The test taker is asked to associate these words with a random distribution of the same set of faces representing the two racial groups. In the final step, the words and faces are reversed, and the test taker is asked again to associate the words with the, now racialized faces. The existence of bias is measured by the time difference between the length of time it takes to match the faces to words that are consistent with the racial stereotype, and the length of time required to match the faces with words associated with the other group, so that matching blacks with joy takes longer than matching blacks with "failure." The test is built on the psychological phenomenon of cognitive dissonance, in which there is discrepancy between beliefs, and new facts require more mental effort to process. The test results, from tens of thousands of self-selected test takers who described themselves as liberal, identified 88 percent of white test takers as having an anti-black bias. Perhaps even more interesting than the bias of whites against blacks, were the results of black bias against other blacks, revealing an internalization of the cultural tilt against all blacks. A startling 48 percent of blacks showed an anti-black bias.

The test is not without its critics who charge that even if it accurately measures interior states of mind, it should not be the basis for policymaking, or legal intervention by government, because it only reveals "thoughts". Psychologist, Hal Arkes, argues that the problem with the test is "where we are going to set our threshold of proof for saying something represents prejudice. My view is the implicit prejudice program sets the threshold at a historical low." Quoted in, Shankar Vedantam, "See No Bias", *The Washington Post Magazine*, 12, at 40, January 23, 2005.

Taking the I.A.T. We encourage you to take a moment to take the test for yourself. The website is https://implicit.harvard.edu. A full explanation of the research design can be found at https://implicit.harvard.edu/implicit/demo/faqs.html.

Pro–Black Bias. Courtland Milloy, a black columnist for the *Washington Post*, took the Implict Association Test. He reports that his results told him that: "your data suggest a strong automatic preference for Black relative to White." White notes:

> For some readers, no doubt, this is confirmation that I am a reverse racist ... The last thing I wanted [was] to end up in that group of African Americans who showed a pro-white or anti-black bias [48 percent]. ... A conscious effort is what it has taken for me not to absorb the worst of white society's stereotypes about blacks.

Courtland Milloy, "Out From Under the Thumb of White Bias", *Washington Post*, B1, January 26, 2005.

———

Civil Rights Perestroika: Intergroup Relations After Affirmative Action

86 CAL. L. REV. 1251 (1998).

■ LINDA HAMILTON KRIEGER

Here at the University of California at Berkeley, there was a surreal quality to November 6, 1996, the day after voters, in enacting Proposition 209, elected to end affirmative action in California state hiring, contracting, and education. The few protests that had been organized ended quickly and quietly. At the law school, students seemed uncharacteristically subdued: quietly resigned—or quietly pleased. In the newspapers that morning and on the mornings that followed, articles about Texaco executives referring to their African–American employees as "niggers" and "black jelly beans" were oddly juxtaposed against others in which Proposition 209's triumphant sponsors heralded a glorious new era of truly equal opportunity and the long-awaited dawning of a colorblind society.

Now, many months later and well into the first of Berkeley's "post-affirmative action" years, the atmosphere here is no less strange. On the first day of classes in 1997, the halls and courtyards swarmed with television cameras and reporters, attempting, I noted with a sense of irony, to identify the lone African–American member of Boalt Hall's first "colorblind" class. We were no longer supposed to consider race, but race was everywhere in these halls on that first morning of the new school year. * * *

If history is any guide, the trend started in California will spread to other states and to the national stage in the months ahead. The 105th Congress witnessed the introduction of three separate bills that would have "nationalized" Proposition 209, and, events in Houston notwithstanding, many States are contemplating similar legislation.

But before proceeding further down this road, it might be wise to pause and ask some hard questions. * * * What can we expect to occur with respect to intergroup relations, and with race relations in particular, in a post-affirmative action environment? If affirmative action is eliminated, will remaining policy tools prove adequate to effectuate racial and gender equity and to prevent the resegregation of American society? Will the idea of "colorblindness" suffice as a theoretical model for understanding what it means not to discriminate? Or will we find instead that affirmative action actually served to mask a "multiplicity of sins"—critical failings in our approach to intergroup relations and serious defects in the tools available to make the equal opportunity society a reality instead of a hazy, unattainable dream? * * *

[This article] inquires whether, absent preferential forms of affirmative action, remaining policy tools would prove adequate to control discrimination and prevent the further segregation of American society. It concludes that these remaining tools, which include a colorblindness model of nondiscrimination, an objective concept of merit, and individualized adjudication as a primary policy enforcement tool, are unequal to the task. In short, we still lack adequate tools for coping successfully with the problems of intergroup competition and cooperation in a pluralistic society.

This failure, which I will argue has been masked to a certain extent by preferential forms of affirmative action, derives from a misunderstanding of the nature and sources of intergroup bias, from a failure to recognize its tendency to persist over time, and from over-reliance on limited adjudicatory and regulatory approaches to address what is fundamentally a complex cultural problem. Accordingly, I argue that unless we develop a broadened understanding of intergroup bias and new approaches to reducing it, the problems of discrimination and inequality of opportunity will worsen in a post-affirmative action environment.

[D]iscrimination does not solely derive from stable, dispositional traits internal to actors we call "discriminators." Rather, intergroup bias increases or decreases in response to contextual, environmental factors which shape how social actors perceive, judge, and make decisions about members of their own and other social reference groups. Accordingly, an anti-discrimination policy grounded in an individualized search for discriminatory intent cannot be expected to succeed either in identifying and preventing intergroup bias or in managing social tendencies toward intergroup conflict. If we are to solve the problem of intergroup discrimination, we must attend more closely to the ecology of intergroup relations. Eliminating affirmative action before we have developed an effective alternative theoretical and doctrinal approach to managing intergroup bias is a strategy more risky than many might assume. * * *

II

AFTER AFFIRMATIVE ACTION: RECOGNIZING DISCRIMINATION
IN THE LAND OF THE COLORBLIND

What might we expect if every institution in the nation—every college and university, every corporation, every state and local public agency, and every arm and organ of the federal government—suddenly prohibited its employees from considering the race, sex, or national origin of applicants or employees in hiring, contracting, promotion, or admission to educational programs? What would happen if every employment and admissions decision maker was told simply to "be colorblind," to base his or her decisions only on "considerations of merit"? Would they do it? Could they do it? Could we identify those who did not do it, whose decisions were tainted by intergroup bias?

The answers to these questions are, quite simply, "no," "no," and "no." Perhaps constitutions can be colorblind. Perhaps official government or corporate policies can be colorblind. But human beings living in a society in which history, ideology, law, and patterns of social, economic, and political distribution have made race, sex, and ethnicity salient, cannot be colorblind. The "colorblindness" approach to nondiscrimination will prove ineffective because it provides neither a framework for enabling people to recognize the effects of race, gender, or national origin on their perceptions and judgments, nor the tools required to help them counteract those effects. Indeed, a color blindness-centered interpretation of the nondiscrimination principle, coupled with well-meaning people's awareness that they do categorize along racial and ethnic lines, <u>may exacerbate the very intergroup anxiety and ambivalence that lead to what social psychologists refer to as aversive racism.</u>

Furthermore, decision makers cannot base selection decisions only on colorblind considerations of merit for the simple reason that <u>merit has a color.</u> Conceptions of merit are socially and politically constructed and are shaped by the same ingroup preferences that give rise to other subtle forms of intergroup bias. Affirmative action preferences have, in many ways, diverted our attention from the biases inherent in the construction of merit. But if preferences are eliminated, this problem and the inequities it generates will soon rise into sharp relief.

Finally, there is substantial reason to doubt that remaining law enforcement tools, particularly the adjudication of individual disparate treatment cases, will prove effective in identifying and remedying subtle but pervasive forms of intergroup bias. For a variety of reasons, <u>reliance on individual disparate treatment adjudication can be expected to result in the serious underidentification of discrimination</u> by judicial decision makers, victims, and private fact finders.

A. *The Inefficacy of Colorblindness as a Normative Construct*

[E]xisting antidiscrimination law constructs intergroup bias as something that occurs when a "discriminatory purpose" motivates a decision. In other words, in order for a decision to be considered "discriminatory" under a statute such as Title VII, the <u>disparate treatment plaintiff must show that the employer chose to take the negative action against him because of his membership in a particular protected class.</u> Thus, to say that discrimination is intentional means that the decision stands in a particular sort of close relation to the target person's group status. Specifically, in the decision maker's mental process, there must be some syllogistic connection between the two.

So, for example, existing antidiscrimination law understands cognitive stereotypes as causing discrimination through the <u>operation of a conscious, syllogistic reasoning process,</u> through which the decision maker uses a person's group status in the following sort of way:

Major Premise: Women with young children are preoccupied with family responsibilities and do not put their jobs first;

Minor Premise: This applicant is a woman with young children;

Conclusion: This applicant cannot be expected to put the job first.

Current antidiscrimination law further conceives gender role expectations, or normative stereotypes, as causing discrimination through the operation of a similar sort of syllogistic reasoning:

Major Premise: Women with young children should be preoccupied with family responsibilities and should not hold jobs that will compete with the responsibilities associated with raising children;

Minor Premise (1) The rigors of this job can be expected to conflict with family responsibilities associated with raising young children;

Minor Premise (2) This applicant is a mother with young children;

Conclusion: This applicant should not hold this job.

According to the existing jurisprudential model of discrimination, personal animosity may also lead to discrimination through the operation of implicit syllogistic reasoning:

Major Premise: Working with black coworkers makes me feel uncomfortable;

Minor Premise: This applicant is black;

Conclusion: Working with him would make me feel uncomfortable.

In each of these contexts, the decision maker's thinking moves directly through the target person's group status. So long as we understand discrimination as operating in this way, we can rely on a color-blindness model of nondiscrimination to function as an effective normative principle. A social decision maker can refrain from discriminating simply by refraining from any syllogistic use of the target person's group status, in other words, by being "colorblind."

unconscious effects ↓ automatic

But as I have also attempted to demonstrate, not all discrimination is of this sort. Much discrimination has little connection with discriminatory motive or intent. This sort of discrimination occurs when an individual's group status subtly, even unconsciously, affects a decision makers' subjective perception of relevant traits, on which ostensibly non-discriminatory decision are subsequently based. This form of discrimination results from a variety of categorization-related cognitive biases, and can result in disparate treatment based on race, sex, national origin, or other factors, even among the well-intentioned.

I do not wish to rehash the evidence supporting this proposition described at length elsewhere. Rather, using related but more recent research, I wish to demonstrate that only "color-consciousness" can control these cognitive forms of intergroup bias. This research strongly suggests that cognitive biases in social judgment operate automatically, without intention or awareness, and can be controlled only through subsequent, deliberate "mental correction" that takes group status squarely into account.

1. Automatic Processes in Intergroup Judgment

In his early work on perceptual readiness, Jerome Bruner observed that when a person receives information with the goal of forming an impression, his or her first cognitive task is to fit that information into some existing knowledge structure. As Bruner described, only when behavioral information is encoded in this way does it becomes useful, or even meaningful.

Of course, in many situations incoming information is ambiguous in that it is susceptible to varied interpretations. A student's volunteered but halting response to a question can be interpreted as reflecting dull-wittedness—or courageous engagement with a difficult subject. An employee's hesitancy in the face of an important decision may evince timidity—or prudence. As Bruner suggested, "All perception is generic," meaning that observed actions, like objects, take on meaning only when they are assigned to a particular trait construct—a preexisting knowledge structure residing in the observer's mind.

In their attempts to understand this process more fully, cognitive psychologists originally assumed that assigning an action to a particular trait construct depended primarily on the extent of the "match" between the features of the action and those of the construct. Then in the late 1970s through the early 1980s, encouraged no doubt by Amos Tversky and Daniel Kahneman's seminal work on the availability heuristic, various researchers began investigating the role of trait construct accessibility in social perception. Their work showed that the readiness with which a person will characterize a particular behavior in terms of any given trait construct is a function of that construct's availability in memory at the time the behavior is perceived. Any activity, conscious or unconscious, that "primes" a particular trait construct will tend to increase its accessibility and the corresponding likelihood that ambiguous information will be assimilated or encoded in a manner consistent with that trait.

Social stereotypes bias perception in this general manner. As numerous researchers have demonstrated, one learns at an early age stereotypes of the major social groups in the United States. These stereotypes have a long history of activation, and are likely to be highly accessible, regardless of whether they are believed. They are invoked automatically when people encounter members of a stereotyped outgroup. Once activated, stereotypes serve to "prime" the trait constructs with which they are associated. Incoming behavioral information, especially if capable of various interpretations, is accordingly assimilated into those traits associated with the stereotype.

This tendency to assimilate ambiguous information into stereotypic trait constructs might not be so serious if people were aware that they were doing it. To understand the significance of this process and its implications for the debate over affirmative action, it is useful to understand a phenomenon which attribution theorists refer to as spontaneous trait inference.

People are highly concerned with understanding why things happen in their social environments. Rightly or wrongly, we assume that understanding why something has happened will improve our power to predict or even control what will happen in the future. To the extent that personality traits play an important role in understanding people's actions, one might expect the process of translating observed behaviors into trait-related meanings to occur with great frequency. Given that social perception and judgment processes become increasingly efficient with repeated execution, one might further hypothesize that trait inference processes could become so overlearned as to operate without intention or awareness, much like the processes involved in recognizing a word or a face.

This hypothesis appears to be correct. In a number of studies replicated in a variety of contexts by other researchers, New York University psychologist James S. Uleman and his colleagues demonstrated that European-American subjects spontaneously encode behaviors into stable trait constructs without intention or awareness. Thus, there is a strong tendency, at least among European Americans, to attribute stable dispositional qualities spontaneously, as part of the process of perceiving and encoding information about another person's behavior. To say that trait inference is "spontaneous" however is not quite the same as saying it is "automatic," and the difference is critical to equal opportunity policy.

Through the early-1980s, it was generally believed that a particular mental process was either entirely automatic or entirely deliberate. Over time, however, cognitive processes came to be understood as falling along a continuum. On one side of that continuum lie "controlled processes," which require substantial processing capacity and occur with greater levels of focus and awareness. On the other side lie fully automatic processes, which occur without intention or awareness, are difficult if not impossible to control once triggered, and interfere little with other ongoing mental activity. Eventually, it became apparent that complex mental processes such as causal attribution and other forms of social inference were neither exclusively automatic nor exclusively controlled, but rather combined aspects of both. Specifically, social inference came to be understood as comprising a chain of three sequential subprocesses: "categorization," in which the person perceived is identified and placed within an existing categorical structure; "characterization," in which spontaneous dispositional inferences are drawn from the observed behavior; and "correction," in which those dispositional inferences are adjusted to account for situational factors. While categorization and characterization are automatic, correction is controlled. It requires deliberate, effortful mental processing and will compete for cognitive resources with other information processing demands. * * *

The significance of these processes and their implications for the colorblindness approach to nondiscrimination can hardly be overemphasized. Very little information shapes a social perceiver's impression of a target person. Rather, it is the perceiver's interpretation of the raw information that influences social judgment. If the target's social group membership influences these interpretations, and if one is unaware of the effect of such status on those interpretations, how can we expect a colorblindness approach to nondiscrimination to function successfully as a normative principle? Given the realities of social perception, we can anticipate that similarly situated people will be treated differently based on their group membership, because decision makers, influenced by these subtle forms of intergroup bias, will not perceive them as similarly situated at all.

Nothing in the colorblindness approach to nondiscrimination provides social decision makers with the tools required to recognize or to correct for biases of this sort.

According to spontaneous trait inference theory, only the application of deliberate, controlled, corrective processes can prevent stereotypes and subtle ingroup priming valences from biasing interpersonal judgment. As social cognition researchers Patricia Devine and Susan Fiske observe, it is neither that nonprejudiced individuals "do not notice" such traits as gender or ethnicity nor that the presence of a member of another group does not "prime" the stereotypes associated with those groups. Rather, insofar as cognitive sources of bias are concerned, the difference between people who discriminate and those who do not is that members of the latter group notice the influences of stereotypes on their thinking and counteract those influences by consciously adjusting responses in a nonprejudiced direction. This process, however, is effortful: it requires both strong motivation and a great deal of capacity, attention, and practice. In short, controlling the biases stemming from such processes as spontaneous trait inference is substantially more complicated than it might at first seem.

2. Controlled Processes and Nondiscrimination: Taming the Beast of Automaticity

The major sources of error in human judgment divide into two broad types. Errors of the first type stem from a failure to know or apply normative rules of inference. Errors of the second type result from a phenomenon which Timothy Wilson and Nancy Brekke refer to as "mental contamination." Mental contamination occurs when a person's judgment or behavior is corrupted by unconscious or uncontrollable mental processes which she would rather not have influence her behavior or decisions. Judgment errors deriving from rule ignorance or incorrect rule application are easier to remedy than those resulting from mental contamination. Normative rules of inference, like the rule of regression to the mean, supply specific procedures for solving the problems to which they pertain and can be consciously learned and deliberately applied.

Correcting judgmental errors resulting from mental contamination is more difficult, in large part because simply teaching people a particular decision rule is unlikely to control biases of which they are unaware. This will be particularly true if the biases in question are difficult to recognize, or easily mistaken for valid, decision-relevant considerations. A supervisor evaluating employees for promotion, or a professor considering which student to hire as a research assistant, may know the rule, "don't discriminate against the black guy." But that kind of rule, in this case the colorblindness rule, cannot be applied in the same way as cost-benefit analysis or the rule of regression to the mean. It can be applied to eliminate facial discrimination—that is, a conscious, explicit policy of excluding a certain group of persons from consideration. It might even be applied to eliminate the conscious, deliberate use of group status as a proxy for decision-relevant traits like initiative or writing ability. But it cannot be applied to prevent or correct biases caused by emotional discomfort, the subconscious effects of stereotypes, causal attribution, or spontaneous trait inference, because it fails to provide a specific set of procedures or techniques which can be applied to the evaluation or decision task at hand. A normative decision rule, such as one prohibiting discrimination on the basis of race, cannot be applied to eliminate a source of bias if the decision maker is unaware that her judgment might be biased or is unable to control the effects of such bias for lack of applicable remedial tools.

As Wilson and Brekke explain, four discrete conditions must be satisfied if people are to control the effects of nonconscious biases. First, one must become aware of the nature of the particular mental process which threatens to bias one's judgment. Second, one must be motivated to correct its unwanted influence once it has been recognized. Third, one must be able to discern the direction and magnitude of the bias, lest it be "overcorrected" and judgment skewed in the opposite direction. And finally, one must have sufficient control over his or her mental processes to correct the effect of the unwanted influences. While it is beyond the scope of this Article to review all of the problems encountered at each of these four stages, those with the most serious implications for the colorblindness model of nondiscrimination warrant attention here.

a.   Unawareness of Mental Process

During the fall of 1996, while the campaign on Proposition 209 swirled around the University, I was teaching a class on employment discrimination law. Every day, I called on a different student to respond to questions about the cases prepared for that day's class. Most of my students were Caucasian; only three of sixty-five were African American. Let us assume for purposes of illustration, that one day I had called on one of these three African–American students, and that he experienced a certain amount of difficulty answering various questions. He was not unprepared, but many of his answers were halting and somewhat confused, leaving me with the initial impression that he was not particularly capable.

I flatly reject the belief that African–American law students are less intelligent than others. If asked at the beginning of the semester to predict how any one of my three African–American students would perform relative to their classmates, I would have vigorously objected to making a prediction in the absence of individuating information. Given that I am familiar with certain normative rules of inference such as the principle of regression to the mean, I would probably, if pushed, have predicted that his or her performance would be about average.

But it is also true that, although I reject them as untrue, I am aware of the stereotypes associated with intelligence, academic achievement, and African–American males. I too was exposed to those stereotypes at a very early age, before I developed my own powers of critical and moral intelligence and made a conscious decision to reject these stereotypes as inaccurate and unfair. But my nonprejudiced beliefs did not displace the stereotypes, which exist alongside and function independently of these beliefs.

The stereotypes are triggered whether I believe in them or not. And, once triggered, those stereotypes prime the trait constructs associated with them, constructs like "not too bright" or "underachieving," rather than "grappling courageously with a difficult subject."

So, what should one conclude if I had taken from this hypothetical encounter the initial impression that the student in question was "not particularly capable?" His performance had not been very good. Why then, should I even question whether the student's race had anything to do with my judgment?

If such a situation were to arise, I would likely question my initial impression only if: (1) I was aware of the possibility that negative stereotypes of African–American males, or some other aspects of the situation had subtly influenced my judgment; and (2) I was motivated to do something about it.

Of course, other subtle cognitive sources of bias besides racial stereotypes could have "contaminated" my judgment as well. If I approached the issue mindfully, I would probably have noticed that over the course of the semester, a number of students I had called on had performed relatively poorly, some just as poorly as the student in question. But try as I might, if I had not made contemporaneous notes, I probably could not now remember just who those students were. I would remember the African–American student, but I would most likely have forgotten the others.

This scenario illustrates a common unconscious source of bias—the polarized evaluation of distinctive members of an otherwise largely homogeneous group. It is well-established that people pay particularly close attention to distinctive stimulus objects, such as a "token" woman or minority group member. And the more attention we pay to something, the more about it we perceive, encode, and store in memory. Indeed, under conditions of high attention, we are more likely to encode an event visually, which makes it more readily available in memory and more influential in the formation of subsequent judgments. Accordingly, the poor performance of a distinctive minority student is more likely to be remembered, and will tend to be charged with a more powerful negative valence, than the poor performance of a majority white student.

[handwritten margin note: bad or poor things re: minority are more likely to be remembered]

If I were unschooled in these sorts of salience or expectancy-related biases, I would likely remain unaware that the student's race had played any role in the formation of my initial impression that he was "not particularly capable." But could I fairly deny that he had been negatively judged, at least in part, because of his race?

The colorblindness approach to nondiscrimination is dangerous because it leads a decision maker to believe that, so long as she is not consciously thinking about race, she is not discriminating. But social cognition theory teaches that, in a culture pervaded by racial stereotypes, or where persons of one race constitute a small minority in an otherwise homogeneous group, one must think about race in order not to discrimi-

[handwritten margin note: One must think about race not to discriminate]

nate. In short, the colorblindness principle discourages the first step prerequisite to controlling cognitive sources of intergroup bias.

b.   The Role of Motivation

All "dual process" models of social inference posit that in order to correct errors caused by an automatic mental process, people must not only be aware of the process, but must also be motivated to control its biasing effects. Of course, the development of awareness itself requires motivation. Despite early controversy on particular issues, it is now relatively well-accepted that people lack awareness of a large proportion of mental processing, including the processes comprising impression formation.

Developing self-awareness of such processes and correcting for the various biases inherent in them is in any context objectively difficult. Even after they are activated, the controlled processes required for mental correction require a great deal of capacity and attention and will compete for cognitive resources with other mental demands. But in the context of intergroup discrimination, the order is taller still. Increasing awareness of and sustained attention to the biasing effects of racial, ethnic, or gender stereotypes on one's social judgments is apt to engender fear of moral opprobrium and substantial psychological discomfort. Thus, especially in the context of reducing intergroup bias, there is little reason to assume that people will expend the effort or bear the psychological discomfort associated with mental correction unless they have strong motivations for so doing. Thus, the colorblindness approach not only fails to provide incentives for developing an awareness of mental contamination, but the model itself and the rhetoric that often accompanies it actually establish disincentives for so doing. * * *

c.   The Limits of Mental Correction

As Timothy Wilson and Nancy Brekke observe, even if a person becomes aware that some unwanted mental process has tainted her judgment, she may not be able to determine the magnitude of the resulting bias. For example, in my hypothetical interaction with my African–American student, I might have become aware that stereotype or salience-related biases had influenced my assessment of his performance. But assuming that I were eventually required to formulate an evaluation, how far, if at all, should I adjust it? There is really no way for me to assess how much of my impression is fairly attributable to bias and how much to the student's flawed performance.

Even more troubling is the question whether "correction" is feasible at all. Once the initial impression that the student was "not particularly capable" had been formed, would I be able to erase it from my mind, or prevent it from influencing my impressions of him in connection with future interactions?

There is ample reason to fear that I would not. In a series of now classic studies, Stanford psychologist Lee Ross and his colleagues demonstrated that, even after a belief is discredited, the causal explanations generated to support it persist, giving the discredited belief a kind of cognitive life after death. More recently, University of Texas psychologists Daniel Gilbert and Randall Osborne extended these observations to the process of spontaneous trait inference. Their work demonstrates that once a trait inference is made, subsequent efforts to adjust it may prove ineffective. As they observed, misperceptions are "metastatic." Controlled processing may correct the original misperception, but it often fails to eliminate subsidiary changes that the original misperception engendered. These endure and influence subsequent judgments of the person perceived. It is easier to forbear from action based on a biased impression than to eliminate the impression itself.

Assuming I realized that my impression formation process was potentially biased, I might have decided to reject the view that the student was not particularly capable. I might even have decided not to take action based on my initial impression of his in-class performance, for example, deciding not to use it in calculating his grade. But I would probably not be able to erase the impression from my mind. Given its enduring presence, I would likely experience any adjustments in my subsequent behavior toward or expressed beliefs about the student as a form of racial preferencing. "After all," I might tell myself, "if the student weren't African–American, I wouldn't be bending over backwards like this." What the colorblindness perspective would allow me to forget, or never teach me in the first place, is that if the student were not African–American, I probably would not have remembered his performance at all. * * *

[Krieger's discussion of how conceptions of "merit" are "defined and assessed through the same complex, largely unconscious cognitive processes which subtly bias social judgment in other contexts and give rise to more easily recognizable forms of discrimination" is omitted.]

b.   Schematic Expectancies and the Problem of Ingroup Favoritism * * *

   iii.   Ingroup Helping Discrimination and the Leniency Effect

Patterns of modern discrimination turn in large measure on the answer to one simple question: Who gets cut slack, and who does not? What happens when an employee violates a rule? Is she subjected to discipline under established policies, or are her transgressions overlooked, or attributed to factors beyond her control? When an ambiguous aspect of a person's background can be interpreted in various ways, one negative, one neutral, which attribution is made? And when a person simply needs help, does she receive it?

Type II bias in large measure shapes people's tendencies to assist or ignore, to excuse others' transgressions or hold them accountable under objective standards of conduct. The earliest, and perhaps still the most vivid of the studies illustrating this effect, was conducted in the early 1970s, in front of a Kansas supermarket. In this study, one black woman and one white woman, whom researchers matched for age and social class-related appearance, dropped a bag of groceries while leaving a supermarket, right in the path of oncoming shoppers. Researchers investigated whether white shoppers would help a white "bag dropper" more frequently than a black bag dropper.

The results were complex and intriguing. Overall, the experimenters found no significant effect of race on the provision of help per se: approximately the same percentage of incoming white shoppers in either condition stopped to help. Subsequent analysis of the data however, revealed an important, if more subtle, phenomenon. When the bag dropper was white, sixty three percent of those who stopped continued to provide assistance until the job was done. When the bag dropper was black, helpers tended to pick up one or two items and then leave, providing complete assistance only thirty percent of the time.

Additional studies provide further evidence of an ingroup helping bias. In 1977, Samuel Gaertner and John Dovidio conducted an experiment in which white subjects were led to believe that they were participating in an investigation of extrasensory perception (ESP). Researchers assigned subjects to serve as either a "sender" or a "receiver," and paired each with a partner/confederate, who was either white or black. Senders and receivers sat in different rooms. Researchers told some subjects that a second person was sitting with their partner in the other room, and told other subjects that the partner was alone.

During the course of the "ESP" experiment, researchers staged an emergency. Subjects heard the sound of falling chairs and the screams of the partner in the other room, followed by prolonged silence. Researchers investigated whether the partner's race would effect the rates at which subjects would go to the aid of their partner.

When subjects believed that their partner was alone in the other room, the partner's race had no significant effect on responses. However, when subjects believed that there was another person in the room with the partner, race made a dramatic difference. Where the apparently imperiled partner was white, seventy-five percent of subjects offered aid, but where the partner was black, the rate dropped to thirty-seven percent. Perhaps even more significantly, subjects showed greater physiological arousal, measured by change in heart rate, when the partner/confederate was white than when he was black.

Gaertner and Dovidio interpreted these results as indicating that whites do not deliberately avoid providing assistance to blacks. However, when features of the situation are ambiguous, when it is unclear whether help is called for, they tend to resolve uncertainty in favor of helping whites and against helping blacks. * * *

As the tendency to assist is biased, so is the tendency to overlook or excuse transgression. For example, in a 1974 field study of whites' reactions to apparent shoplifting, Max Dertke and his colleagues demonstrated that when the shoplifter/confederate was black, white shoppers spontaneously reported and followed up on an observed shoplifting incident at a much higher rate than when the shoplifter/confederate was white. * * *

One can easily see how over time, these subtle forms of ingroup favoritism would result in markedly different outcomes for ingroup and outgroup members. If decision makers react to members of their own social reference groups with more positive associations, a quicker willingness to help, and a stronger inclination to ignore or excuse shortcomings, it is easy to predict who will be systematically advantaged in hiring and promotion decisions. Disparities will develop even absent hostile animus or negative actions directed towards the outgroup. * * *

[Krieger's discussion of how current anti-discrimination law is poorly equipped to control Type II discrimination is omitted.]

D.   Individualized Adjudication, Hypothesis Testing, and Causal Attribution: The Effects of Intergroup Bias

Consider for a moment the judgment task involved in adjudicating an individual employment discrimination suit. Determining in any given case whether discrimination has occurred is fundamentally an exercise in causal attribution. The employer has taken some negative action, most frequently a termination of employment, against the plaintiff. The jury's role is to determine why that negative action was taken. Was it, as the plaintiff alleges, because the decision maker discriminated against her because of her membership in a protected group? Or was it, as the defendant argues, because of some legitimate, nondiscriminatory reason, usually some malfeasance or deficiency on the plaintiff's part? In a hiring case, did the plaintiff fail to get the job because the decision maker took her group status into account in making the challenged decision? Or did the decision maker believe that some other candidate would do a better job? The trial of such a case will essentially entail a battle between two competing causal theories. Seeking to convince the jury that discrimination is to blame, the plaintiff will portray the decision makers as discriminators. Seeking to convince the jury that the plaintiff is to blame, the defendant will do everything possible to make his or her deficiencies salient.

Why should we expect a jury to approach this social decision task free from the various forms of intergroup bias that distort intergroup perception and judgment in other contexts? As we have seen, unconscious stereotypes about members of different social groups create implicit expectancies in the minds of social perceivers. These expectancies in turn distort the perception, interpretation, and recall of information about members of the targeted groups, pulling subsequent social judgments in a stereotype-consistent direction. Stereotypic expectancies and other forms of intergroup bias also affect causal attribution, causing unconscious distortions in the interpretation and perceived predictiveness of past behavior.

Attributing the causes of employment decisions implicates the very processes of social perception and judgment bound up in the challenged employment decisions themselves. Unless the demographic characteristics of fact finders vary in some dramatic way from those of the decision makers, we cannot reasonably expect that the level of intergroup discrimination reflected in employment decisions will vary in any meaningful way from the level reflected in discrimination verdicts. Indeed, the analytical structure and content of disparate treatment adjudications, focusing as it does on the plausibility of defendant's proffered legitimate nondiscriminatory reasons for a challenged employment decision, can be expected to potentiate those forms of intergroup bias caused by stereotypic expectancies. Discrimination adjudications therefore may be even more vulnerable to cognitive forms of intergroup bias than the decision tasks which give rise to them.

An employer's determination, for example, whether a particular employee should be terminated is not much different from a court's determination whether an employer believed in good faith that a particular employee deserved to be terminated. Similarly, an employer judging whether a particular candidate is best qualified for a position is not particularly different from a court judging whether a particular candidate would reasonably have been viewed by a well-intentioned employer as the best qualified person for a position. Expectancy confirmation effects, such as those illustrated in Darley's and Gross's study discussed above, will distort both types of judgments. Thus, there is no reason to believe that the incidence of stereotype-induced judgment error in discrimination adjudications will differ in any significant way from its incidence in employment or educational decision making. Indeed, if as Darley and Gross suggest, exposure to ambiguous but ostensibly diagnostic collections of information potentiates expectancy confirmation bias, we can expect disparate treatment adjudications, with their "information rich texture," to suffer even more from such biases than hiring or educational admissions decisions, where relatively little diagnostic information is available and decision makers may be more on guard against making stereotypic judgments.

In short, from a cognitive process standpoint we cannot expect disparate treatment adjudications to be any less subject to subtle forms of intergroup bias than the decisions which give rise to them. Correspondingly, we cannot expect individualized adjudication of disparate treatment claims to be particularly effective in identifying or redressing cognitive discrimination. For this reason as for others, disparate treatment adjudication, like the colorblindness model of nondiscrimination and reliance on an objective concept of merit, is an extremely weak tool for combating cognitive forms of intergroup bias. We cannot expect these policies to do the work once accomplished by disparate impact theory, numerical standards, and the systematic, self-critical analysis of selection procedures. Unfortunately, when a person is color-blind, there is simply much he will not see.
* * *

_____

What is the explanation for the stubborn persistence of pervasive discrimination today? In what follows, R.A. Lenhardt draws on sociological research to argue that the focus should be on the racial harm, including citizenship harms arising from exclusion, instead of either disparate impact, or intent.

2. Sociology and Law: Stigma Theory

Understanding the Mark: Race, Stigma, and Equality in Context

79 N.Y.U. L. Rev. 803 (2005).

■ R.A. Lenhardt

* * *

* * * In fact, we are approaching a state in which many minority youths arguably stand a greater chance of being incarcerated than of obtaining a college degree and entering the economic mainstream. According to a recent study, of the approximately two million people in adult correctional facilities in the United States, an astounding 1.2 million, or 63%, are African–American or Latino, even though these groups together comprise only 25% of the total population.

These statistics paint a devastating picture of increasing racial separation and inequality along several fundamental life axes and demonstrate how far away we actually are from remedying the problem of racial disadvantage. The truth is that, in many ways, we are as racially divided a society today as we were before the Supreme Court's landmark decision in *Brown v. Board of Education* and the enactment of the Civil Rights Act of 1964. Where we live, go to school, and work are all still greatly determined by race. The question we must ask is: Why? What accounts for the stubborn persistence of the color line DuBois identified so many years ago? Why do racial disparities still exist?

For some time, the only legal framework available for understanding questions of racial inequity and disadvantage, reflected in cases such as *Washington v. Davis*, was that of intentional discrimination. Then, more than fifteen years ago, Professor Charles Lawrence revolutionized legal scholarship by arguing that the source of racial harm lay principally in unconsciously racist acts. Drawing on psychoanalytic theory and cognitive psychology, Lawrence's article, *The Id, The Ego, and Equal Protection: Reckoning with Unconscious Racism*, challenged the view that only intentionally discriminatory conduct ran the risk of imposing racial harm. Because of the cognitive processes and meanings associated with race in this country, Lawrence argued, racial motive was most often reflected in unconscious conduct bearing a disparate racial impact. He maintained that the messages communicated by facially neutral governmental actions were the best indicator of racist motive, and he therefore advocated greater judicial attention to the cultural or racial meaning of policy choices and initiatives.

This Article seeks to advance the conversation about the nature and contours of racial harm by asserting that we should be concerned, not with the meanings associated with conduct, but rather with the meanings associated with race itself. My argument is that racial stigma, not intentional discrimination or unconscious racism, is the true source of racial injury in the United States. This theory accounts for the persistence of racial disparities that mark the color line, as well as the incidence of intentionally discriminatory or racialized behavior. It conceives of these problems as a function of racial stigma, not vice versa. In this respect, it is perhaps the most comprehensive theory of racial harm advanced thus far.

[Lenhardt defines racial stigma as consisting of the following 4 characteristics:]

I.   WHAT IS RACIAL STIGMA?

* * * Brands were used as a way of identifying African slaves as human property up until the latter part of the eighteenth century and as a method of punishment well into the nineteenth century. When we talk about racial stigma today, however, we are almost never referring directly to the brands and cuts that were used to demarcate slave or outsider status. We plainly mean something different, something less physical and perhaps more cognitive in nature. The question is: What?

Even as the term racial stigma has become part of common parlance, it has escaped clear definition. An informal survey of individuals on the street likely would generate as many definitions as people interviewed. For some, it refers to demeaning racial insults or stereotypes. For others, it is synonymous with the concept of racial inferiority. Still others see it principally as a by-product of discriminatory treatment that excludes or denies a benefit on the basis of race. The connotation given the term seems to vary by individual and even by context.

Significantly, this holds true even among courts and legal scholars, who ordinarily might be expected to have a more uniform understanding of a concept that has been embraced as a key constitutional principle in the race context. The legal approach to racial stigma, for the most part, has mirrored the strategy that former Justice Potter Stewart infamously adopted in obscenity cases: "I know it when I see it." By contrast, with only a few refinements, social scientists seem to have employed the same basic understanding of stigma for some time. In this Section, I thus look principally outside the legal arena to social science for direction in defining what racial stigma is and how it functions.

1.   DEHUMANIZATION AND THE IMPOSITION OF VIRTUAL IDENTITY

Most lawyers are probably familiar with the social research on racial stigma that Dr. Kenneth Clark completed nearly fifty years ago as an expert in the litigation surrounding *Brown v. Board of Education*. In the social science world, however, the work of another social scientist—Erving Goffman—is most often cited in connection with questions surrounding the problem of racial stigma. Nearly forty years after it was first published, Goffman's book, STIGMA: NOTES ON THE MANAGEMENT OF SPOILED IDENTITY, continues to be regarded as one of the definitive texts in this area.

In Stigma, Goffman concerned himself with a single purpose: defining the problem of stigma. Looking to a variety of psychological, sociological, and historical studies and texts, he explored a range of stigma-inducing conditions and situations, including the so-called "tribal" or group-based stigmas such as "race, nation, and religion." Although Goffman also studied the etiology and function of stigmas relating to physical deformities and character "blemishes" attributed to a variety of conditions, the many insights he garnered through his research are extremely relevant to the race-focused inquiry that I take up here. Even today, virtually all social scientists accept the broad definition of stigma developed through his work, namely that "stigmatized persons possess an attribute that is deeply *Stigma* discrediting and that they are viewed as less than fully human because of it." * * *

2. SHARED NEGATIVE MEANINGS ABOUT THE RACIALLY STIGMATIZED

* * * Racial stigma, at bottom, concerns the relationship between a group of individuals perceived as essentially similar and shared community beliefs about that group and the attributes they possess. While racist attitudes are held at an individual level as well, the group-level responses to racial difference are most important here. Part of the strength of the "societal devaluations" associated with race in this country is that "they cannot be dismissed as the ravings of some idiosyncratic bigot." They are shared and consensual, which means that they cannot easily be ignored. This, perhaps even more than the precise character of the messages conveyed about race, is what makes racial stigma such a powerful social force. The meanings ascribed to an attribute—i.e., that dark skin or an accent provide meaningful evidence of intellectual or moral inferiority— begin to form what constitutes "a socially shared sense of 'reality.'" * * *

3. THE AUTOMATIC NATURE OF RESPONSES TO THE RACIALLY STIGMATIZED

The next stigma factor that contributes to broad-scale racial inequality relates to the automatic or unconscious nature of the responses the no stigmatized—and sometimes even minorities themselves—have to the racially stigmatized. The prevailing constitutional paradigm in the race context is, of course, the discrimination model discussed earlier. Under that model, embodied in cases such as Washington v. Davis, only conduct and policies that reflect discriminatory intent or motive can be actionable. No remedies exist for racialized, unconsciously committed behavior or policies that have merely a discriminatory impact. * * *

4. THE REINFORCING NATURE OF RACIAL STIGMA AND STEREOTYPES

As previously noted, when asked to define racial stigma, people often confuse it with the problem of racial stereotypes, which have historically been defined as inaccurate or overbroad generalizations, but have more recently come to be understood as "cognitive categories" employed in processing information. Most "profoundly stigmatized social identities" have a myriad of well-accepted stereotypes associated with them: "Blacks are dumb"; "Latinos are lazy"; "Asians are smart, but conniving." The terms racial stigma and racial stereotype are, however, two analytically distinct concepts. Whereas racial stigma provides the negative meanings associated with race and accounts for the initial affective reactions individuals often have toward racial minorities, racial stereotypes help to explain the persistence of certain attitudes about and responses toward race and the racially stigmatized. In this way, they also are directly related not just to discrimination but to the broader problem of racial inequality.

Racial stigma and stereotypes, in some sense, play mutually reinforcing roles in the dehumanization and marginalization—social, as well as economic and political—of minority groups. On the one hand, racial stigma contributes to the development of negative racial stereotypes about stigmatized groups. It is thought that the social meanings conveyed by racial stigma actually influence the cognitive processes that lead to stereotype formation. As Glenn Loury notes, "The 'social meaning of race'—that is, the tacit understanding associated with 'blackness' [or dark skin] in the public's imagination, especially the negative connotations—biases the social cognitions and distorts the specifications of observing agents, inducing them to make causal misattributions [or categorizations] detrimental to" racial minorities.

CHAPTER 2

CLASSIC MARKET THEORY AND LAW AND ECONOMICS

A. CLASSIC MARKET THEORY

Economics is the study of how scarce resources—land, capital, and labor—can best be allocated to satisfy human wants. Although it would be impossible to cover the whole of economic theory in a single chapter, this section describes some basic assumptions about human nature, the organization of society, and the role of government that have influenced the development of our modern economic and legal systems.

Economic analyses can be divided into two types: *positive* and *normative.* Positive economics attempts to describe in a rigorous way how markets operate, without judging whether the outcomes are good or bad. Normative economics takes the pursuit of greater efficiency as the primary good in governance, and frequently argues that governance through markets is superior to governance by direct state regulation. As you read the excerpts below, ask yourself which arguments are positive and which are normative, and why it makes a difference. Ask yourself, also, in what ways contemporary economic analysis has diverged from the work of Adam Smith.

Both strands of economic analysis—positive and normative—owe a central debt to the work of Adam Smith (1723–1790). Smith was a popular, absent-minded professor of moral philosophy—a field that at the time incorporated theology, ethics, justice, and political economy—at Scotland's University of Glasgow. Smith is called the "father of modern economics" because "[he] was the first to explain in detail the role of human beings in the development of markets and how these markets function to solve the basic economic problems that confront any society: what goods to produce, how to produce them, and to whom they should be distributed."

From the sixteenth through the nineteenth centuries, European nations generally solved these problems through mercantilism, an economic system in which the government regulated and dictated economic activity. Mercantilism used tools such as monopolies, subsidies, tariffs, and restrictive labor policies to build up a nation's gold and silver reserves, the theoretical source of economic power. Despite the restrictive regulations mercantilism involved, the English economy was expanding, in part through illegal market activities.

Smith's emphasis on the role of people in economic development was pioneering. His work defined the classical school of economics, which explains the economy in the context of human behavior. *The Theory of Moral Sentiments* (1759) explored the ethics and principles motivating human behavior and argued that people are mainly driven by self-interest, tempered by an "impartial spectator," or conscience. In the *Wealth of Nations* (1776), his most famous work, Smith used his theory of human nature to show how individuals acting in their own self-interest, unregulated by the state, could nevertheless collectively maximize the wealth of all. Smith argued that "[s]elf interest leads to market exchange, which fosters the division of labor, which leads in turn to specialization, expertise, dexterity, and improved machinery and ultimately creates greater wealth." Most famously, Smith described the results of this system of undirected market exchange as "the invisible hand": even purely self-interested behavior can result in a better life for all, as if an invisible hand had ordered the result.

Smith's assumption, shared by most contemporary economists, that people are chiefly motivated by self-interest is a controversial one. The following excerpt examines in more detail Smith's beliefs about human nature.

Adam Smith's View of Man

19 J.L. & ECON. 529 (1976).

■ R. H. COASE

* * * It is sometimes said that Adam Smith assumes that human beings are motivated solely by self-interest. Self-interest is certainly, in Adam Smith's view, a powerful motive in human behaviour, but it is by no means the only motive. I think it is important to recognise this since the inclusion of other motives in his analysis does not weaken but rather strengthens Adam Smith's argument for the use of the market and the limitation of government action in economic affairs.

* * * In *The Theory of Moral Sentiments*, man's actions are influenced by benevolence. In the *Wealth of Nations*, this motive is apparently absent. This view is supported by a much-quoted passage: "It is not from the benevolence of the butcher, the brewer, or the baker, that we expect our dinner, but from their regard to their own interest. We address ourselves, not to their humanity but to their self-love, and never talk to them of our own necessities but of their advantages." What is not quoted is something which Adam Smith says earlier in the same paragraph: "In civilized society [man] stands at all times in need of the co-operation and assistance of great multitudes, while his whole life is scarce sufficient to gain the friendship of a few persons." This puts a completely different complexion on the matter. For that extensive division of labour required to maintain a civilized standard of living, we need to have the co-operation of great multitudes, scattered all over the world. There is no way in which this co-operation could be secured through the exercise of benevolence. Benevolence, or love, may be the dominant or, at any rate, an important factor within the family or in our relations with colleagues or friends, but as Adam Smith indicates,

it operates weakly or not at all when we deal with strangers. Benevolence is highly personal and most of those who benefit from the economic activities in which we engage are unknown to us. * * *

Looked at in this way, Adam Smith's argument for the use of the market for the organisation of economic activity is much stronger than it is usually thought to be. The market is not simply an ingenious mechanism, fueled by self-interest, for securing the co-operation of individuals in the production of goods and services. In most circumstances it is the only way in which this could be done. Nor does government regulation or operation represent a satisfactory way out. A politician, when motivated by benevolence, will tend to favour his family, his friends, members of his party, inhabitants of his region or country (and this whether or not he is democratically elected). Such benevolence will not necessarily redound to the general good. And when politicians are motivated by self-interest unalloyed by benevolence, it is easy to see that the results may be even less satisfactory.

The great advantage of the market is that it is able to use the strength of self-interest to offset the weakness and partiality of benevolence, so that those who are unknown, unattractive, or unimportant, will have their wants served. But this should not lead us to ignore the part which benevolence and moral sentiments do play in making possible a market system. Consider, for example, the care and training of the young, largely carried out within the family and sustained by parental devotion. If love were absent and the task of training the young was therefore placed on other institutions, run presumably by people following their own self-interest, it seems likely that this task, on which the successful working of human societies depends, would be worse performed. At least, that was Adam Smith's opinion: "Domestic education is the institution of nature—public education the contrivance of man. It is surely unnecessary to say which is likely to be the wisest." Again, the observance of moral codes must very greatly reduce the costs of doing business with others and must therefore facilitate market transactions. As Adam Smith observes, "Society ... cannot subsist among those who are at all times ready to hurt and injure one another...."

Adam Smith allows for a good deal of folly in human behaviour. But this does not lead him to advocate an extensive role for government. Politicians and government officials are also men. Private individuals are constrained in their folly because they personally suffer its consequences: "Bankruptcy is perhaps the greatest and most humiliating calamity which can befall an innocent man. The greater part of men, therefore, are sufficiently careful to avoid it." But, of course, men who bankrupt a city or a nation are not necessarily themselves made bankrupt. Adam Smith, therefore, continues: "Great nations are never impoverished by private, though they sometimes are by public prodigality and misconduct." As he later observes: "[Kings are and ministers] are themselves, always, and without any exception, the greatest spend thrifts in the society. Let them look well after their own expence, and they may safely trust private people with theirs. If their own extravagance does not ruin the state, that of their subjects never will.''

* * *

It is wrong to believe, as is commonly done, that Adam Smith had as his view of man an abstraction, an "economic man," rationally pursuing his self-interest in a single-minded way. Adam Smith would not have thought it sensible to treat man as a rational utility-maximiser. He thinks of man as he actually is—dominated, it is true, by self-love but not without some concern for others, able to reason but not necessarily in such a way as to reach the right conclusion, seeing the outcomes of his actions but through a veil of self-delusion. No doubt modern psychologists have added a great deal, some of it correct, to this eighteenth-century view of human nature. But if one is willing to accept Adam Smith's view of man as containing, if not the whole truth, at least a large part of it, realisation that his thought has a much broader foundation than is commonly assumed makes his argument for economic freedom more powerful and his conclusions more persuasive.

———

As the Coase excerpt above suggests, Smith's theory was influential in part because it sought to provide a better policy solution than mercantilism to the problem of production and exchange in a mass society. Smith showed how a system of competition, under which producers competed to offer the highest quality goods at the lowest possible prices, could encourage the efficient allocation of resources without the need to resort to government coercion. The excerpt that follows updates Smith's basic insight.

———

The Advantages of a Free–Enterprise Price System

INVISIBLE HAND 64–68 (Adrian Klaasen ed., 1965).

■ W. ALLEN WALLIS

* * *

Suppose you were asked how to organize [the population of the United States] to utilize the resources available to them for their material satisfactions. You can imagine you have a fairly detailed inventory of the natural resources of the country, of the people and their knowledge, energies and abilities and of their wants. Imagine that all these resources are as unorganized as a set of chessmen just poured out of their box and awaiting organization on the chessboard. [The next issue concerns deciding how to organize the supply to meet the demand.]

[O]ne of the first things you are going to need is some way of establishing goals and measuring achievement. Which of the many things wanted are going to be produced, in what quantities, and with what priorities?

After you establish these goals and priorities, you will need a method of assigning the various pieces of capital, the various natural resources and the various people to particular activities. Each will have several alternative uses; you will need a method of deciding which use to assign it or him to, and of coordinating the resources assigned to cooperate in each task.

Then, third, you will have to have some system for dividing the product among the people: who gets how much of what, and when?

Fourth, you will probably realize that for one reason or another your system [will create mismatches between supply and demand]. You will need some system of adjustment to [account for these mismatches], until your method of measuring achievement and your method of allocating resources can get the basic situation corrected.

A fifth kind of problem you may worry about is that of providing for the expansion and improvement of your capital, equipment and technological knowledge.

These five functions have to be provided for when you establish any organization, even a small and relatively simple one. When we consider the large and complex organization of an entire economy, what are some of the alternative ways of arranging for them?

The most obvious way to arrange things is the way an army does. You set up a commander or a general staff. They decide on goals, they decide who shall do what to attain them, they decide how to apportion the product; and they issue orders accordingly. Another method is that used in beehives and ant colonies, in which caste and custom determine who does what. Things go on in the same way, generation after generation.

A third way is to introduce money and let each person decide what activities that others will pay for he will engage in, and what things that others offer for money he will buy. This is a method that no one really invented. It requires careful and sometimes complicated analysis to discover how it will really work. Indeed, it was only with the recognition that this is in fact a method of organizing society that the scientific study of economics began, back in 1776.

Under this system, goals are set by the money offers of individuals for goods and services. Resources are allocated to one activity or another by the desires of their owners for money income. Goods are distributed to individuals according to their willingness and ability to pay the prices. Thus prices become the crucial organizing element in such an economy. Indeed, this system is often called the "price system."

The price system has two outstanding features. First, it is by all odds the most efficient system of social organization ever conceived. It makes it possible for huge multitudes to cooperate effectively, multitudes who may hardly know of each other's existence, or whose personal attitudes toward one another may be indifference or hostility. Second, it affords a maximum of individual freedom and a minimum of coercion. And since people can cooperate effectively in production even when their attitudes on other issues are hostile, there is no need for unity and conformity in religion, politics, recreation and language—or even in patriotism and goodwill, except in the very broadest senses.

* * *

———

NOTES AND QUESTIONS

1. Markets, price theory, and the invisible hand. Are there times when price theory fails to adequately serve the communication function Wallis identifies? Are there technical obstacles in some situations to using the price system for the allocation of goods? Theories of "market failure," discussed in the next chapter, take up these questions.

2. Smith and professional economists. For many modern economists, Smith was a great economist, perhaps the greatest ever. Adam Smith was not truly an economist as we understand that discipline today. Smith laid many of the foundations of modern economics with the *Wealth of Nations*, "but not for another century did economics truly become established as . . . a separate discipline." Skousen, *supra* at 195. As an academic, Smith was appointed professor of Logic at the University of Glasgow in 1751, and transferred to the chair of moral philosophy in 1752. ROBIN PAUL MALLOY & JERRY EVENSKY, ADAM SMITH AND THE PHILOSOPHY OF LAW AND ECONOMICS 34 (1994). As a moral philosopher, Smith drew on the work of contemporary thinkers such as Hume, Franklin, and Montesquieu when writing both *The Theory of Moral Sentiments* and the *Wealth of Nations*. SKOUSEN, *supra* at 38, 41–42.

3. Economic analysis and the rational actor. Although Adam Smith's understanding of "economic man" incorporated benevolence, altruism, and sympathy, the tradition of "neoclassical" economics that followed in his footsteps focused on modeling self-interested behavior rather than other-directed behavior. In contemporary terms, economic analysis adopts some version of "rational choice" theory: individuals enter a market with specific preferences, and they act so as to satisfy those preferences to the greatest extent possible at the lowest possible cost. Rational actor theory has been much criticized; these critiques will be taken up in the next chapter.

4. Modern evolution of classic market theory: victory of neoclassi-cal theory. Historian Michael Bernstein notes that an important debate within the discipline of economics took place around the turn of the twentieth century. On the one hand were:

> those determined to preserve for economics a pride of place, grounded in rigorous theory, among the social sciences. For these scholars it was clear that, in the words of the eminent Alfred Marshall, "the raison d'être of economics as a separate science [wa]s that it deal[t] chiefly with the part of [people's] action which [wa]s most under the control of

measurable motives." It was necessarily the case, therefore, that economists had to employ "selective principles" in order to understand human behavior. Utilizing "a series of deductions from the fundamental concept of scarcity," the discipline's practitioners were thus in a position to engage in truly "analytical" studies that were, given a "correspondence [between] original assumptions and the facts," realistic approximations of social conduct. While history, institutions, law, and ideology could provide more detailed and nuanced explanations of actual economic events, the core analytical principles of economic explanation remained distinct.

Michael A. Bernstein, A Perilous Progress: Economists and Public Purpose in Twentieth-Century America 45–46 (2001).

For these scholars, the discipline of economics could provide an "objective science of society." *id.* at 45. These "neoclassical" economists were drawn to rigorous mathematical models of economic behavior.

On the other side of the debate were the "institutionalists," a group of economists, many of them involved in public policy work for the federal government, who sought a broader scope for economics. Institutionalist economics was rooted in the work of Thorstein Veblen, who in the late 1890s and early 1900s attacked neoclassical theory for its excessive abstraction from the real world of economic behavior and posited that the search for social "status"—not just the desire for financial profit—motivated much of economic production, by spurring the desire for conspicuous consumption. According to Bernstein:

> [T]he institutionalists conceived of economics as a far more catholic field in which any claims to realism rested perforce on broadly construed disciplinary boundaries. Indeed, both [Wesley] Mitchell and Veblen themselves had aggressively attacked the manner in which neoclassical investigators ignored human activity that could not be understood simply as the "rational" and calculating response of individuals to the constraints of the market. To their minds "such institutions as the market, trade, contract, property, and competition" were themselves the product of political, cultural, and historical circumstances all of which were worthy of the economist's attention.

id., at 46.

Accordingly, the institutionalists were empiricist rather than theoretical and mathematical in their bent. Ultimately, however, it was the neoclassicists who won the battle and ascended to power over the institutionalists.

5. Cold War and discipline of economics. Michael Bernstein argues that "[i]n its theoretical and methodological trajectory, the American economics profession was decisively affected by the pressures, constraints, and opportunities afforded by the Cold War preoccupations of the federal government, colleges and universities, and private foundations and 'think tanks.' " *id.* at 94. During World War II, mathematically-driven developments in economics such as "activity analysis" and "linear programming" made it possible for economists to help the War Department plan resource allocation and distribution plans (for example, to calculate the most efficient supply shipments). During the Cold War, the federal government, both directly and through organizations such as the RAND Corporation (originally Project RAND under the supervision of the Air Force) and the National Science Foundation, generously supported research into "game theory" and other mathematical approaches to the problem of modeling competitive behavior. Game theory, for example, demonstrated how strategic behavior could be modeled mathematically, and these models could be applied to problems such as nuclear deterrence. Macroeconomic theory was also appealing to government funders, because of the promise that it could be directly applied to the project of sustaining the American economy and preserving and protecting the nation's security. For example, in 1954, the staff of the Council of Economic Advisers initiated "a series of wide-ranging discussions on the matter of 'emergency economic stabilization' in the event of a nuclear exchange." *id.* at 104. The idea was that "in the event of a nuclear attack civil defense authorities should be given the power to set wages, prices, and rents—as well as to ration goods and services. To be effective, plans for such a contingency would need to be set up in advance." *Id.*

The issues of national security and national prosperity were intertwined, and both of them seemed uniquely suited to economists' strengths. Bernstein observes:

> High rates of growth, robust levels of employment, and stable prices were the standards by which a capitalist society could demonstrate its advantages over command economies premised upon socialist or communist designs. As the emblematic "Kitchen Debate" between Soviet premier Nikita Khrushchev and Vice President Richard Nixon had suggested in 1959, winning the Cold War involved more than husbanding a credible nuclear deterrent, deploying fleets, garrisons, and air wings around the world, and utilizing special forces in counterinsurgency campaigns. It also required that an economic system deliver the goods to the people. Prosperity was an essential weapon in the struggle for the hearts and minds of any society.

id. at 107.

By the 1950s, argues Bernstein, "No longer the study of 'the nature and causes of the wealth of nations' (as Adam Smith had claimed), or 'a critical analysis of capitalist production' (as Karl Marx suggested), economics had become the formal study of 'the adaptation of scarce means to given ends.'" *id.* at 95. The means to this study should be apolitical and objective. Thus, "[g]one from a rising number of nationally ranked graduate programs in economics, by the late 1950s, were agendas that acquainted the student with the work of a Thorstein Veblen, a Joseph Schumpeter, or a Karl Polanyi—not to mention a Karl Marx. In their place were 'core' course sequences that emphasized neoclassical theory, most often in its mathematical representations," *id.* at 123. Although the 1960s and 1970s saw a challenge by a "New Left" within the economics profession—which formed organizations such as the Union for Radical Political Economics (URPE), and identified and attacked logical inconsistencies at the heart of neoclassical economics—neoclassical economics continued to define the discipline up to the end of the twentieth century.

6. Economic theory and the rise and fall of Keynesian macroeconomics. As we have seen, Adam Smith wrote primarily against the "mercantilism" of his time, a system in which the state heavily controlled economic behavior, often by granting monopolies in crucial trading industries to particular organizations and individuals. Smith's metaphor of the invisible hand suggested that a market free of such government intervention would provide more prosperity for everyone, and that such a market would be self-regulating. In 1936, however, an Englander named John Maynard Keynes [1883–1946], published a book called *The General Theory of Employment, Interest, and Money* [hereafter the *General Theory*] that paved the way for a new discipline of "macroeconomics." Keynes was many things during his illustrious career: "a brilliant student at England's most famous prep school; an equally brilliant student and then professor at Kings College in Cambridge; a financier who made a fortune for himself, and, later for Kings College by overseeing its endowment fund; president of a life-insurance company; patron of the arts; husband of a famous Russian ballerina; member of the influential 'Bloomsbury set' of intellectuals; esteemed official of the British Treasury; board member of the Bank of England; and the principal designer of the international financial system after World War II." CHARLES SACKREY & GEOFFREY SCHNEIDER, INTRODUCTION TO POLITICAL ECONOMY 80–81 (3d ed. 2002).

Keynes's innovation begins with the "business cycle": over time, national economies tend to experience periods of growth, followed by periods of seeming economic collapse, involving sudden drops in wages, mass unemployment, and drastically reduced spending power (known as recessions). The most famous of these in the United States was, of course, the Great Depression, which followed the stock crash of 1929. Classical economists argued that during these depressions, falling wages would lower costs and prices and invite a greater demand for goods and services. Thus, downturns in the business cycle are always self-correcting. Keynes argued, however, that "a *general* fall in wages ... would likely cause an eventual *decline* in the demand for goods and services that workers buy, rather than an increase encouraged by the lower prices." *id.* at 92. Moreover, falling wages could reduce the optimism of capitalists and encourage them to reduce investment in new equipment. The result would be a downward spiral for the economy rather than a self-correcting equilibrium. As a policy matter, then, Keynes argued that an active rather than passive government response to recessions and depressions was required:

> "[A]s investment and consumption spending fell, the government should take up the slack in demand by borrowing money to increase its own expenditures * * * And it didn't matter for what those expenditures were made. As this spending worked its way through the economy, it would ultimately produce a better outlook for businesses, which

meant more investment on capital goods. * * * [T]his would start the whole process moving back upward to recovery and economic growth.

id. at 97.

Keynesian theory and policy quickly became mainstream. The massive government spending involved in the United States' participation in World War II appeared to prove Keynes right about the ability of governments to take action against economic recessions, and the Cold War period saw the adoption of Keynesian macroeconomic policy on a broad scale. Sackrey and Schneider observe:

> A symbolic highpoint of the influence of Keynes occurred in 1963, when in a speech at Yale University John Kennedy used the idea of the Keynesian multiplier to justify the cut in personal income taxes he was urging on the Congress as a way to cause a sluggish economy to grow faster. The essentially Keynesian basis of domestic U.S. economic policy remained in place for about 25 years, and, in 1971, an economic conservative, Richard Nixon, argued that "we are all Keynesians now."

id. at 98.

Nevertheless, the rise of Keynesian macroeconomics was followed by a fall. Beginning in the late 1960s, the American national economy began to experience persistent and growing inflation. In the early 1970s, the Organization of Petroleum Exporting Countries (OPEC) announced a plan to dramatically cut petroleum production, setting off a series of global economic shocks. Soon the American economy was experiencing high inflation and high unemployment at the same time—a situation, nicknamed "stagflation," thought to be impossible by professional economists. Real incomes fell dramatically and capital investments stagnated, and Keynesian theorists seemed helpless to address the problem. Into the breach stepped new macroeconomic theories. The "new classical" economists argued that government interventions in the market were futile because economic actors would always be able to anticipate and adjust their behavior to such interventions. "Supply-side" economists argued that the country's economic woes were caused by

> high levels of government spending, high taxation of income, and extensive governmental regulation of economic affairs. Excessive income taxation, it was argued, stifled productive effort, for example, by discouraging overtime work. It robbed individuals of the fruits of enterprise and risk-bearing. Finally, it distorted economic decision making so as to slow growth and create the very fiscal pressure that contributed to the problems of "stagflation" in the first instance. The solution would involve a radical reduction in taxes, a systematic shrinking of government spending programs and, thus, federal agency budgets, and the elimination of costly regulatory measures.

MICHAEL A. BERNSTEIN, A PERILOUS PROGRESS, *supra* at 164.

These scholarly arguments were supported by a new turn in electoral politics against "big government." Ronald Reagan's decisive 1980 victory over Jimmy Carter for the presidency symbolized a new consensus in the electorate that government did not work, that private businesses should be as free of regulation as possible, and that taxes should be cut in order to reward individual initiative and let the "invisible hand" do its work. Although few professional economists agreed with the excesses of "Reaganomics," a general mood in favor of laissez-faire economics, deregulation, and "privatization" now characterized the electorate and dominated thought in the Beltway.

B. LIBERTARIANISM

Created Equal

FREE TO CHOOSE: A PERSONAL STATEMENT 128–49 (1980).

■ MILTON FRIEDMAN & ROSE FRIEDMAN

"Equality," "liberty"—what precisely do these words from the Declaration of Independence mean? Can the ideals they express be realized in practice? Are equality and liberty consistent one with the other, or are they in conflict?

Since well before the Declaration of Independence, these questions have played a central role in the history of the United States. The attempt to answer them has shaped the intellectual climate of opinion, led to bloody war, and produced major changes in economic and political institutions. This attempt continues to dominate our political debate. It will shape our future as it has our past.

In the early decades of the Republic, equality meant equality before God; liberty meant the liberty to shape one's own life. The obvious conflict between the Declaration of Independence and the institution of slavery occupied the center of the stage. That conflict was finally resolved by the Civil War. The debate then moved to a different level. Equality came more and more to be interpreted as "equality of opportunity" in the sense that no one should be prevented by arbitrary obstacles from using his capacities to pursue his own objectives. That is still its dominant meaning to most citizens of the United States.

Neither equality before God nor equality of opportunity presented any conflict with liberty to shape one's own life. Quite the opposite. Equality and liberty were two faces of the same basic value—that every individual should be regarded as an end in himself.

A very different meaning of equality has emerged in the United States in recent decades—equality of outcome. Everyone should have the same level of living or of income, should finish the race at the same time. Equality of outcome is in clear conflict with liberty. The attempt to promote it has been a major source of bigger and bigger government, and of government-imposed restrictions on our liberty.

EQUALITY BEFORE GOD

When Thomas Jefferson, at the age of thirty-three, wrote "all men are created equal," he and his contemporaries did not take these words literally. They did not regard "men"—or as we would say today, "persons"—as equal in physical characteristics, emotional reactions, mechanical and intellectual abilities. * * *

The clue to what Thomas Jefferson and his contemporaries meant by equal is in the next phrase of the Declaration—"endowed by their Creator with certain unalienable rights; that among these are Life, Liberty, and the pursuit of Happiness." Men were equal before God. Each person is precious in and of himself. He has unalienable rights, rights that no one else is entitled to invade. He is entitled to serve his own purposes and not to be treated simply as an instrument to promote someone else's purposes. "Liberty" is part of the definition of equality, not in conflict with it.

Equality before God—personal equality—is important precisely because people are not identical. Their different values, their different tastes, their different capacities will lead them to want to lead very different lives. Personal equality requires respect for their right to do so, not the imposition on them of someone else's values or judgment. Jefferson had no doubt that some men were superior to others, that there was an elite. But that did not give them the right to rule others.

If an elite did not have the right to impose its will on others, neither did any other group, even a majority. Every person was to be his own ruler—provided that he did not interfere with the similar right of others. Government was established to protect that right—from fellow citizens and from external threat—not to give a majority unbridled rule. * * *

Similarly, Alexis de Tocqueville, the famous French political philosopher and sociologist, in his classic *Democracy in America*, written after a lengthy visit in the 1830s, saw equality, not majority rule, as the outstanding characteristic of America. "In America," he wrote,

> the aristocratic element has always been feeble from its birth; and if at the present day it is not actually destroyed, it is at any rate so completely disabled, that we can scarcely assign to it any degree of influence on the course of affairs. The democratic principle, on the contrary, has gained so much strength by time, by events, and by legislation, as to have become not only predominant but all-powerful. There is no family or corporate authority....

> America, then, exhibits in her social state a most extraordinary phenomenon. Men are there seen on a greater equality in point of fortune and intellect, or, in other words, more equal in their strength, than in any other country of the world, or in any age of which history has preserved the remembrance.

> * * *

It is striking testimony to the changing meaning of words that in recent decades the Democratic party of the United States has been the chief instrument for strengthening that government power which Jefferson and many of his contemporaries viewed as the greatest threat to democracy. And it has striven to increase government power in the name of a concept of "equality" that is almost the opposite of the concept of equality Jefferson identified with liberty and Tocqueville with democracy.

* * *

Equality of Opportunity

Once the Civil War abolished slavery and the concept of personal equality—equality before God and the law—came closer to realization, emphasis shifted, in intellectual discussion and in government and private policy, to a different concept—equality of opportunity.

Literal equality of opportunity—in the sense of "identity"—is impossible. One child is born blind, another with sight. One child has parents deeply concerned about his welfare who provide a background of culture and understanding; another has dissolute, improvident parents. One child is born in the United States, another in India, or China, or Russia. They clearly do not have identical opportunities open to them at birth, and there is no way that their opportunities can be made identical.

Like personal equality, equality of opportunity is not to be interpreted literally. Its real meaning is perhaps best expressed by the French expression dating from the French Revolution: *Une carriere ouverte aux les talents*—a career open to the talents. No arbitrary obstacles should prevent people from achieving those positions for which their talents fit them and which their values lead them to seek. Not birth, nationality, color, religion, sex, nor any other irrelevant characteristic should determine the opportunities that are open to a person—only his abilities.

On this interpretation, equality of opportunity simply spells out in more detail the meaning of personal equality, of equality before the law. And like personal equality, it has meaning and importance precisely because people are different in their genetic and cultural characteristics, and hence both want to and can pursue different careers.

Equality of opportunity, like personal equality, is not inconsistent with liberty; on the contrary, it is an essential component of liberty. If some people are denied access to particular positions in life for which they are qualified simply because of their ethnic background, color, or religion, that is an interference with their right to "Life, Liberty, and the pursuit of Happiness." It denies equality of opportunity and, by the same token, sacrifices the freedom of some for the advantage of others.

Like every ideal, equality of opportunity is incapable of being fully realized. The most serious departure was undoubtedly with respect to the blacks, particularly in the South but in the North as well. Yet there was also tremendous progress—for blacks and for other groups. The very concept of a "melting pot" reflected the goal of equality of opportunity. So also did the expansion of "free" education at elementary, secondary, and higher levels—though, as we shall see in the next chapter, this development has not been an unmixed blessing.

The priority given to equality of opportunity in the hierarchy of values generally accepted by the public after the Civil War is manifested particularly in economic policy. The catchwords were free enterprise, competition, laissez-faire. Everyone was to be free to go into any business, follow any occupation, buy any property, subject only to the agreement of the other parties to the transaction. Each was to have the opportunity to reap the benefits if he succeeded, to suffer the costs if he failed. There were to be no arbitrary obstacles. Performance, not birth, religion, or nationality, was the touchstone.

One corollary was the development of what many who regarded themselves as the cultural elite sneered at as vulgar materialism—an emphasis on the almighty dollar, on wealth as both the symbol and the seal of success.

* * *

Another corollary, of course, was an enormous release of human energy that made America an increasingly productive and dynamic society in which social mobility was an everyday reality. Still another, perhaps surprisingly, was an explosion in charitable activity. This explosion was made possible by the rapid growth in wealth. It took the form it did—of nonprofit hospitals, privately endowed colleges and universities, a plethora of charitable organizations directed to helping the poor—because of the dominant values of the society, including, especially, promotion of equality of opportunity.

Of course, in the economic sphere as elsewhere, practice did not always conform to the ideal. Government *was* kept to a minor role; no major obstacles to enterprise were erected, and by the end of the nineteenth century, positive government measures, especially the Sherman Anti-Trust Law, were adopted to eliminate private barriers to competition. But extralegal arrangements continued to interfere with the freedom of individuals to enter various businesses or professions, and social practices unquestionably gave special advantages to persons born in the "right" families, of the "right" color, and practicing the "right" religion. However, the rapid rise in the economic and social position of various less privileged groups demonstrates that these obstacles were by no means insurmountable.

In respect of government measures, one major deviation from free markets was in foreign trade, where Alexander Hamilton's *Report on Manufactures* had enshrined tariff protection for domestic industries as part of the American way. Tariff protection was inconsistent with thoroughgoing equality of opportunity * * * and, indeed, with the free immigration of persons, which was the rule until World War I, except only for Orientals. Yet it could be rationalized both by the needs of national defense and on the very different ground that equality stops at the water's edge—an illogical rationalization that is adopted also by most of today's proponents of a very different concept of equality.

EQUALITY OF OUTCOME

That different concept, equality of outcome, has been gaining ground in this century. It first affected government policy in Great Britain and on the European continent. Over the past half-century it has increasingly affected government policy in the United States as well. In some intellectual circles the desirability of equality of outcome has become an article of religious faith: everyone should finish the race at the same time. As the Dodo said in *Alice in Wonderland*, "*Everybody* has won, and *all* must have prizes."

For this concept, as for the other two, "equal" is not to be interpreted literally as "identical." No one really maintains that everyone, regardless of age or sex or other physical qualities should have identical rations of each separate item of food, clothing, and so on. The goal is rather "fairness," a much vaguer notion—indeed, one that it is difficult, if not impossible, to define precisely. "Fair shares for all" is the modern slogan that has replaced Karl Marx's, "To each according to his needs, from each according to his ability."

This concept of equality differs radically from the other two. Government measures that promote personal equality or equality of opportunity enhanced liberty; government measures to achieve "fair shares for all" reduce liberty. If what people get is to be determined by "fairness," who is to decide what is "fair"? As a chorus of voices asked the Dodo, "But who is to give the prizes?" "Fairness" is not an objectively determined concept once it departs from identity. "Fairness," like "needs," is in the eye of the beholder. If all are to have "fair shares," someone or some group of people must decide what shares are fair—and they must be able to impose their decisions on others, taking from those who have more than their "fair" share and giving to those who have less. Are those who make and impose such decisions equal to those for whom they decide? Are we not in George Orwell's *Animal Farm*, where "all animals are equal, but some animals are more equal than others"?

In addition, if what people get is determined by "fairness" and not by what they produce, where are the "prizes" to come from? What incentive is there to work and produce? How is it to be decided who is to be the doctor, who the lawyer, who the garbage collector, who the street sweeper? What assures that people will accept the roles assigned to them and perform those roles in accordance with their abilities? Clearly, only force or the threat of force will do.

The key point is not merely that practice will depart from the ideal. Of course it will, as it does with respect to the other two concepts of equality as well. The point is rather that there is a fundamental conflict between the *ideal* of "fair shares" or of its precursor, "to each according to his needs," and the *ideal* of personal liberty. This conflict has plagued every attempt to make equality of outcome the overriding principle of social organization. The end result has invariably been a state of terror: Russia, China, and, more recently, Cambodia offer clear and convincing evidence.

* * *

The far less extreme measures taken in Western countries in the name of equality of outcome have shared the same fate to a lesser extent. They, too, have restricted individual liberty. They, too, have failed to achieve their objective. It has proved impossible to define "fair shares" in a way that is generally acceptable, or to satisfy the members of the community that they are being treated "fairly." On the contrary, dissatisfaction has mounted with every additional attempt to implement equality of outcome.

Much of the moral fervor behind the drive for equality of outcome comes from the widespread belief that it is not fair that some children should have a great advantage over others simply because they happen to have wealthy parents. Of course it is not fair. However, unfairness can take many forms. It can take the form of the inheritance of property—bonds and stocks, houses, factories; it can also take the form of the inheritance of talent—musical ability, strength, mathematical genius. The inheritance of property can be interfered with more readily than the inheritance of talent. But from an ethical point of view, is there any difference between the two? Yet many people resent the inheritance of property but not the inheritance of talent.

Look at the same issue from the point of view of the parent. If you want to assure your child a higher income in life, you can do so in various ways. You can buy him (or her) an education that will equip him to pursue an occupation yielding a high income; or you can set him up in a business that will yield a higher income than he could earn as a salaried employee; or you can leave him property, the income from which will enable him to live better. Is there any ethical difference among these three ways of using your property? Or again, if the state leaves you any money to spend over and above taxes, should the state permit you to spend it on riotous living but not to leave it to your children?

The ethical issues involved are subtle and complex. They are not to be resolved by such simplistic formulas as "fair shares for all." Indeed, if we took that seriously, youngsters with less musical skill should be given the greatest amount of musical training in order to compensate for their inherited disadvantage, and those with greater musical aptitude should be prevented from having access to good musical training; and similarly with all other categories of inherited personal qualities. That might be "fair" to the youngsters lacking in talent, but would it be "fair" to the talented, let alone to those who had to work to pay for training the youngsters lacking talent, or to the persons deprived of the benefits that might have come from the cultivation of the talents of the gifted?

* * *

Still another facet of this complex issue of fairness can be illustrated by considering a game of chance, for example, an evening at baccarat. The people who choose to play may start the evening with equal piles of chips, but as the play progresses, those piles will become unequal. By the end of the evening, some will be big winners, others big losers. In the name of the ideal of equality, should the winners be required to repay the losers? That would take all the fun out of the game. Not even the losers would like that.

They might like it for the one evening, but would they come back again to play if they knew that whatever happened, they'd end up exactly where they started?

This example has a great deal more to do with the real world than one might at first suppose. Every day each of us makes decisions that involve taking a chance. Occasionally it's a big chance as when we decide what occupation to pursue, whom to marry, whether to buy a house or make a major investment. More often it's a small chance, as when we decide what movie to go to, whether to cross the street against the traffic, whether to buy one security rather than another. Each time the question is, who is to decide what chances we take? That in turn depends on who bears the consequences of the decision. If we bear the consequences, we can make the decision. But if someone else bears the consequences, should we or will we be permitted to make the decision? * * *

The system under which people make their own choices—and bear most of the consequences of their decisions—is the system that has prevailed for most of our history. It is the system that gave the Henry Fords, the Thomas Alva Edisons, the George Eastmans, the John D. Rockefellers, the James Cash Penneys the incentive to transform our society over the past two centuries. It is the system that gave other people an incentive to furnish venture capital to finance the risky enterprises that these ambitious inventors and captains of industry undertook. Of course, there were many losers along the way—probably more losers than winners. We don't remember their names. But for the most part they went in with their eyes open. They knew they were taking chances. And win or lose, society as a whole benefited from their willingness to take a chance.

The fortunes that this system produced came overwhelmingly from developing new products or services, or new ways of producing products or services, or of distributing them widely. The resulting addition to the wealth of the community as a whole, to the well-being of the masses of the people, amounted to many times the wealth accumulated by the innovators. Henry Ford acquired a great fortune. The country acquired a cheap and reliable means of transportation and the techniques of mass production. Moreover, in many cases the private fortunes were largely devoted in the end to the benefit of society. The Rockefeller, Ford, and Carnegie foundations are only the most prominent of the numerous private benefactions which are so outstanding a consequence of the operation of a system that corresponded to "equality of opportunity" and "liberty" as these terms were understood until recently.

     * * *

There is no inconsistency between a free market system and the pursuit of broad social and cultural goals, or between a free market system and compassion for the less fortunate, whether that compassion takes the form, as it did in the nineteenth century, of private charitable activity, or, as it has done increasingly in the twentieth, of assistance through government—provided that in both cases it is an expression of a desire to help others. There is all the difference in the world, however, between two kinds of assistance through government that seem superficially similar: first, 90 percent of us agreeing to impose taxes on ourselves in order to help the bottom 10 percent, and second, 80 percent voting to impose taxes on the top 10 percent to help the bottom 10 percent—William Graham Sumner's famous example of B and C deciding what D shall do for A. The first may be wise or unwise, an effective or an ineffective way to help the disadvantaged—but it is consistent with belief in both equality of opportunity and liberty. The second seeks equality of outcome and is entirely antithetical to liberty.

WHO FAVORS EQUALITY OF OUTCOME?

There is little support for the goal of equality of outcome despite the extent to which it has become almost an article of religious faith among intellectuals and despite its prominence in the speeches of politicians and the preambles of legislation. The talk is belied alike by the behavior of government, of the intellectuals who most ardently espouse egalitarian sentiments, and of the public at large.

* * *

For intellectuals, the clearest evidence is their failure to practice what so many of them preach. Equality of outcome can be promoted on a do-it-yourself basis. First, decide exactly what you mean by equality. Do you want to achieve equality within the United States? In a selected group of countries as a whole? In the world as a whole? Is equality to be judged in terms of income per person? Per family? Per year? Per decade? Per lifetime? Income in the form of money alone? Or including such nonmonetary items as the rental value of an owned home; food grown for one's own use; services rendered by members of the family not employed for money, notably the housewife? How are physical and mental handicaps or advantages to be allowed for?

However you decide these issues, you can, if you are an egalitarian, estimate what money income would correspond to your concept of equality. If your actual income is higher than that, you can keep that amount and distribute the rest to people who are below that level. If your criterion were to encompass the world—as most egalitarian rhetoric suggests it should—something less than, say, $200 a year (in 1979 dollars) per person would be an amount that would correspond to the conception of equality that seems implicit in most egalitarian rhetoric. That is about the average income per person worldwide.

What Irving Kristol has called the "new class"—government bureaucrats, academics whose research is supported by government funds or who are employed in government financed "think tanks," staffs of the many so-called "general interest" or "public policy" groups, journalists and others in the communications industry—are among the most ardent preachers of the doctrine of equality. Yet they remind us very much of the old, if unfair, saw about the Quakers: "They came to the New World to do good, and ended up doing well." The members of the new class are in general among the highest paid persons in the community. And for many among them, preaching equality and promoting or administering the resulting legislation has proved an effective means of achieving such high incomes. All of us find it easy to identify our own welfare with the welfare of the community.

Of course, an egalitarian may protest that he is but a drop in the ocean, that he would be willing to redistribute the excess of his income over his concept of an equal income if everyone else were compelled to do the same. On one level this contention that compulsion would change matters is wrong—even if everyone else did the same, his specific contribution to the income of others would still be a drop in the ocean. His individual contribution would be just as large if he were the only contributor as if he were one of many. Indeed, it would be more valuable because he could target his contribution to go to the very worst off among those he regards as appropriate recipients. On another level compulsion would change matters drastically: the kind of society that would emerge if such acts of redistribution were voluntary is altogether different—and, by our standards, infinitely preferable—to the kind that would emerge if redistribution were compulsory.

Persons who believe that a society of enforced equality is preferable can also practice what they preach. They can join one of the many communes in this country and elsewhere, or establish new ones. And, of course, it is entirely consistent with a belief in personal equality or equality of opportunity and liberty that any group of individuals who wish to live in that way should be free to do so. Our thesis that support for equality of outcome is word-deep receives strong support from the small number of persons who have wished to join such communes and from the fragility of the communes that have been established.

* * *

CONSEQUENCES OF EGALITARIAN POLICIES

In shaping our own policy, we can learn from the experience of Western countries with which we share a common intellectual and cultural background, and from which we derive many of our values. Perhaps the most instructive example is Great Britain, which led the way in the nineteenth century toward implementing equality of opportunity and in the twentieth toward implementing equality of outcome.

Since the end of World War II, British domestic policy has been dominated by the search for greater equality of outcome. Measure after measure has been adopted designed to take from the rich and give to the poor. Taxes were raised on income until they reached a top rate of 98 percent on property income and 83 percent on "earned" income, and were supplemented by ever heavier taxes on inheritances. State-provided medical, housing, and other welfare services were greatly expanded, along with payments to the unemployed and the aged. Unfortunately, the results have been very different from those that were intended by the people who were quite properly offended by the class structure that dominated Britain for centuries. There has been a vast redistribution of wealth, but the end result is not an equitable distribution.

Instead, new classes of privileged have been created to replace or supplement the old: the bureaucrats, secure in their jobs, protected against inflation both when they work and when they retire; the trade unions that profess to represent the most downtrodden workers but in fact consist of the highest paid laborers in the land—the aristocrats of the labor movement; and the new millionaires—people who have been cleverest at finding ways around the laws, the rules, the regulations that have poured from Parliament and the bureaucracy, who have found ways to avoid paying taxes on their income and to get their wealth overseas beyond the grasp of the tax collectors. A vast reshuffling of income and wealth, yes; greater equity, hardly.

The drive for equality in Britain failed, not because the wrong measures were adopted—though some no doubt were; not because they were badly administered—though some no doubt were; not because the wrong people administered them—though no doubt some did. The drive for equality failed for a much more fundamental reason. It went against one of the most basic instincts of all human beings. In the words of Adam Smith, "The uniform, constant, and uninterrupted effort of every man to better his condition"—and, one may add, the condition of his children and his children's children. Smith, of course, meant by "condition" not merely material well-being, though certainly that was one component. He had a much broader concept in mind, one that included all of the values by which men judge their success—in particular the kind of social values that gave rise to the outpouring of philanthropic activities in the nineteenth century.

When the law interferes with people's pursuit of their own values, they will try to find a way around. They will evade the law, they will break the law, or they will leave the country. Few of us believe in a moral code that justifies forcing people to give up much of what they produce to finance payments to persons they do not know for purposes they may not approve of. When the law contradicts what most people regard as moral and proper, they will break the law—whether the law is enacted in the name of a noble ideal such as equality or in the naked interest of one group at the expense of another. Only fear of punishment, not a sense of justice and morality, will lead people to obey the law.

When people start to break one set of laws, the lack of respect for the law inevitably spreads to all laws, even those that everyone regards as moral and proper—laws against violence, theft, and vandalism. Hard as it may be to believe, the growth of crude criminality in Britain in recent decades may well be one consequence of the drive for equality.

* * *

We in the United States have not gone as far as Britain in promoting the goal of equality of outcome. Yet many of the same consequences are already evident—from a failure of egalitarian measures to achieve their objectives, to a reshuffling of wealth that by no standards can be regarded as equitable; to a rise in criminality, to a depressing effect on productivity and efficiency.

Capitalism and Equality

Everywhere in the world there are gross inequities of income and wealth. They offend most of us. Few can fail to be moved by the contrast between the luxury enjoyed by some and the grinding poverty suffered by others.

In the past century a myth has grown up that free market capitalism—equality of opportunity as we have interpreted that term—increases such inequalities, that it is a system under which the rich exploit the poor.

Nothing could be further from the truth. Wherever the free market has been permitted to operate, wherever anything approaching equality of opportunity has existed, the ordinary man has been able to attain levels of living never dreamed of before. Nowhere is the gap between rich and poor wider, nowhere are the rich richer and the poor poorer, than in those societies that do not permit the free market to operate. That is true of feudal societies like medieval Europe, India before independence, and much of modern South America, where inherited status determines position. It is equally true of centrally planned societies, like Russia or China or India since independence, where access to government determines position. It is true even where central planning was introduced, as in all three of these countries, in the name of equality.

* * *

In 1848 John Stuart Mill wrote: "Hitherto it is questionable if all the mechanical inventions yet made have lightened the day's toil of any human being. They have enabled a greater population to live the same life of drudgery and imprisonment, and an increased number of manufacturers and others to make fortunes. They have increased the comforts of the middle classes. But they have not yet begun to effect those great changes in human destiny, which it is in their nature and in their futurity to accomplish."

No one could say that today. You can travel from one end of the industrialized world to the other and almost the only people you will find engaging in backbreaking toil are people who are doing it for sport. To find people whose day's toil has not been lightened by mechanical invention, you must go to the non-capitalist world: to Russia, China, India or Bangladesh, parts of Yugoslavia; or to the more backward capitalist countries—in Africa, the Mideast, South America; and until recently, Spain or Italy.

Conclusion

A society that puts equality—in the sense of equality of outcome—ahead of freedom will end up with neither equality nor freedom. The use of force to achieve equality will destroy freedom, and the force, introduced for good purposes, will end up in the hands of people who use it to promote their own interests.

On the other hand, a society that puts freedom first will, as a happy by-product, end up with both greater freedom and greater equality. Though a by-product of freedom, greater equality is not an accident. A free society releases the energies and abilities of people to pursue their own objectives. It prevents some people from arbitrarily suppressing others. It does not prevent some people from achieving positions of privilege, but so long as freedom is maintained, it prevents those positions of privilege from becoming institutionalized; they are subject to continued attack by other able, ambitious people. Freedom means diversity but also mobility. It preserves the opportunity for today's disadvantaged to become tomorrow's privileged and, in the process, enables almost everyone, from top to bottom, to enjoy a fuller and richer life.

———

NOTES AND QUESTIONS

1. Operation of government and market in Wealth of Nations. In his second book, the *Wealth of Nations*, Adam Smith advocated a limited role for government in economic life. Nevertheless, Smith advocated government authority to ensure the provision of four basic necessities:

1. The need for a well-financed militia for national defense

2. A legal system to protect liberty, property rights, and to enforce contracts and payment of debts

3. Public works—roads, canals, bridges, harbors, and other infrastructure projects

4. Universal public education to counter the alienating and mentally degrading effects of specialization (division of labor) under capitalism

MARK SKOUSEN, THE MAKING OF MODERN ECONOMICS 33 (2001).

Additionally, Smith identifies three characteristics necessary for a self-regulating economics system:

1. Freedom: the right to produce and exchange products, labor, and capital

2. Self-interest: the right to pursue one's own business and to appeal to the self interest of others

3. Competition: the right to compete in the production and exchange of goods and services

Id. at 22.

2. Friedman's political philosophy. Milton Friedman is associated with the libertarian school of political philosophy. According to this school, the best government is the smallest, least intrusive government possible, "consistent with the maximum freedom for each individual to follow his own ways, his own values, as long as he doesn't interfere with anybody else who's doing the same." *Uncommon Knowledge, Take it to the Limits: Milton Friedman on Libertarianism* (American Public Television broadcast, Feb. 10, 1999), *available at* http://www.uncommonknowledge.org/99winter/324.html.

Friedman does not justify his advocacy of a free market society by some external referent like wealth maximization. Instead he says that:

> A free society, I believe, is a more productive society than any other.... But that is not why I am in favor of a free society. I believe and hope that I would favor a free society even if it were less productive than some alternative.... I favor a free society because my basic value is freedom itself.

Rubin Paul Malloy & Jerry Evensky, Adam Smith and the Philosophy of Law and Economics 160 (1994).

3. Libertarianism and law and economics. Friedman's libertarian political philosophy is often associated with the law and economics movement discussed *infra* at 83. As one commentator put it "law and economics scholars will—with only rare exceptions—take positions comparable with libertarian conservatives." Michael McConnell, *The Counter–Revolution in Legal Thought,* 41 Pol'y Rev. 18, 24 (1987). For more on libertarianism, especially as it relates to law and economics see this text, *infra* at 84, note 7 & 8 at 122, 225.

4. Friedman's equality.

   a. Friedman's negative definitions of equality. Friedman, when introducing what he asserts are distinct stages in the progression of equality, defines what each stage was not. For example, Friedman states that Thomas Jefferson "did not regard men ... as equal in physical characteristics, emotional reactions, mechanical and intellectual abilities." Friedman, *supra* at 84. Why does Friedman do this? Does he mean to imply that the only alternative interpretation of equality to the one he ascribes to the founding fathers is literal physical equality? If there are other possible interpretations of the Declaration of Independence, why should we choose Friedman's? For example, Charles Black asserts that the Declaration of Independence can be read as guaranteeing every person a right to a livelihood. Charles Black, *Further Reflections on the Constitutional Justice of Livelihood,* 86 Colum. L. Rev. 1103 (1986) (arguing that the right to pursuit of happiness and the elimination of poverty are not simply matters of compassion. Black argues that these rights can be derived from the preamble to, and Ninth Amendment of, the Constitution and the Declaration of Independence). Given that there are alternative readings of the Declaration of Independence that are vastly more persuasive than the literal equality Friedman addresses, should his refusal to address those alternatives make us skeptical about his main claims?

   b. Friedman's use of straw-men when discussing equality of outcome. When discussing personal equality and equality of opportunity, Friedman cites admired historical and cultural figures such as Jefferson, de Tocqueville, and Lincoln. When discussing equality of outcome, Friedman cites the Dodo from *Alice in Wonderland* and Karl Marx. If, as Friedman claims is the case, "equality of outcome

... has become almost an article of religious faith among intellectuals," why did Friedman not cite a supporter of equality of outcome who is both nonfictional and non-discredited? FRIEDMAN, *supra* at 157. A possible example of an individual who believed in equality of outcome would be Martin Luther King, Jr. who stated that a political alliance between organized labor and African Americans could bring about the American dream which King interpreted as "a dream of equality of opportunity, of privilege and property widely distributed, a dream of a nation where all our gifts and resources are held not for ourselves but as instruments of service for the rest of humanity...." STEPHEN B. OATES, LET THE TRUMPET SOUND: A LIFE OF MARTIN LUTHER KING, JR. 187 (1994). Does the fact that Friedman chose to attribute equality of outcome to a fictional dodo rather than the infinitely more persuasive Dr. King detract from the persuasiveness of his conclusions?

c. Effect of Dr. King on Friedman's piece. Including the views of Dr. King would have had three effects on Friedman's piece. First, because Dr. King believed that his dream was the realization of the American dream, including his views would have demonstrated that Friedman's assertion that equality of outcome is a radical departure from traditions of liberty is highly questionable. Second, including the voice of Dr. King, or any minority leader, would have drawn attention to the fact that, to minorities, formal equality is inadequate because it ignores the handicaps placed upon them by private discrimination, both past and present. *See* MARTIN LUTHER KING, JR., WHY WE CAN'T WAIT 134 (1964); T. Alexander Aleinikoff, *A Case for Race–Consciousness*, 91 COLUM. L. REV. 1060 (1991). This insufficiency of formal equality would have led to the third effect of including Dr. King, tying wealth redistribution to Friedman's second duty of government, "establishing an exact administration of justice." MILTON FRIEDMAN & ROSE FRIEDMAN, *The Role of Government, in* FREE TO CHOOSE: A PERSONAL STATEMENT 27, 29 (1980). Dr. King stated that American society had done "something special *against* the Negro for hundreds of years [and] must ... do something special *for* him, in order to equip him to compete on a just and equal basis." WHERE DO WE GO FROM HERE (quoted in OATES, *supra* note 2b, at 426). Linking wealth redistribution to justice would have been anathema to a libertarian like Friedman. For a history of the development of affirmative action, including its origins as a compensatory measure, *see* Erin E. Byrnes, *Unmasking White Privilege to Expose the Fallacy of White Innocence: Using a Theory of Moral Correlativity to Make the Case for Affirmative Action Programs in Education*, 41 ARIZ. L. REV. 535 (1999).

5. Equality and liberty. Friedman sees equality of outcome as antithetical to liberty, but he claims equality of opportunity to be a companion to liberty. How do barriers to equality interfere with liberty? What can be done to remove those barriers?

a. Private barriers. In *Capitalism and Freedom*, Friedman said, "[T]he preserves of discrimination in any society are the areas that are most monopolistic in character, whereas discrimination against groups of particular color or religion is least in those areas where there is the greatest freedom of competition." MILTON FRIEDMAN (WITH THE ASSISTANCE OF ROSE D. FRIEDMAN), CAPITALISM AND FREEDOM 109 (1962). The invisible hand of the market ideally promotes society's welfare through competition and self-interest, and equality of opportunity ideally allows such competition by rendering characteristics such as birth, race, and sex irrelevant. Friedman resigns himself to the fact that equality of opportunity is an ideal which cannot be fully realized while he applauds government efforts to legally reinforce the ideal of competition. If supposedly irrelevant characteristics in reality impede equality of income, and therefore its partner liberty, what justifies government intervention to remove some private barriers to competition but not others? What similarities and differences exist between the concentration of wealth and monopolistic trade practices?

> The Sherman Anti–Trust Act is a "positive government measure ... adopted to eliminate private barriers to competition." The Act outlaws monopolies and contracts, combinations, or conspiracies to restrain trade. Sherman Antitrust Act, 15 U.S.C. §§ 1–7 (2000). At common law, contracts in restraint of trade were void and unenforceable, but in 1890 Congress deemed such contracts illegal and created a civil action for damages. Denison Mattress Factory v. Spring-Air Co., 308 F.2d 403, 407 (5th Cir. 1962). In 1910, the Supreme Court affirmed the dissolution of the Rockefellers' Standard Oil Company, which controlled approximately ninety percent of the petroleum trade, and stock was transferred back to the many subsidiary companies. Standard Oil Co. v. United States, 221 U.S. 1 (1911). By controlling the petroleum trade, Standard Oil had been able to fix prices and restrain trade, violating the principles of the price system. Antitrust law gave the Court the tools to promote a competitive oil market. *Id.* at 33. If the triumphs of antitrust law over obstacles to competition are favorable in this situation, can we ignore other private obstacles to competition, such as race and gender inequality, because they are "not insurmountable"? If measures such as the Fourteenth Amendment and the Civil Rights Acts have not completely eliminated such barriers, what else can be done to improve competition?

b. Equality of access. Friedman compares the unfairness of inherited property to inherited talent, and he uses access to musical training for an untalented child instead of a musically gifted child to illustrate the impossibility of fairness. But suppose that the talented child was too poor to afford private music lessons and lived in an impoverished school district that had cut the music program for financial reasons, as so many schools have been forced to do, and his musical talent was never developed. And suppose the untalented child, whose family was wealthy, had unlimited access to music lessons, which did little to improve her skill. While we cannot, and probably would not want to, evenly distribute talents and interests throughout the population, it is at least possible that resources could be distributed in such a manner that makes them available to all. Perhaps equality of outcome is not possible or desirable, but meaningful freedom to choose demands true equality of access.

C. LAW AND ECONOMICS

The Uses of History in Law and Economics
4 THEORETICAL INQUIRIES L. 659 (2003).

Ron Harris

    * * *

The debate over the intellectual origins of the law and economics field is still at a very preliminary stage. Some outside observers suggest a peculiar connection between the law and economics movement and either institutional economics or else legal realism, or a combination of the two in the form of the "first great law & economics movement." Insiders disdainfully repudiate such intellectual origins. They point to Chicago (not Yale, Columbia, or Wisconsin), to economics (not law), and to the neo-classical (not institutional or historical) school of economics as the bedrock of the field. Thus, the official, internal history of the field begins in Chicago. The questions that then arise are, When and who? * * * But most stress as the immediate origins, both in terms of time and substance, the contributions of two economists: Ronald Coase and Gary Becker, circa 1960. Coase, in his seminal 1960 article [*The Problem of Social Cost*, 3 J.L. & ECON. 1 (1960)], reintroduced transaction costs (after doing so for the first, relatively unnoticed, time twenty-three years earlier in the context of his *The Nature of the Firm*), but this time with direct reference to the relevance of legal liability rules in a world with transaction costs. Becker, after completing his doctoral dissertation in 1955 (published in 1957), extended the realm of neo-classical theory by employing it in the analysis of non-market behavior. His starting point was racial discrimination; he then proceeded to the family (until then a black box for economists), and, by the late 1960s, arrived at crime and punishment. Thus the work of Coase and Becker planted the roots of the modern incarnation of law and economics in Chicago and in the neo-classical tradition.

    * * *

Both Coase and Becker, the intellectual founders of law and economics, were economists by training and much more interested in the study of economics than law. Ironically, the new field of law and economics that their work launched focused mainly on the law. Both noted this a few years ago at a [University of] Chicago Law School round table on the future of law and economics. Becker noted, "I am certainly not an expert in law and economics.... [A] relatively small fraction of my time over the years has been spent on this subject." Coase confessed, "[N]ow an economist isn't really interested in this part of Law and Economics—the use of economics to analyze the law—at least this economist isn't." Despite the fact that Coase and Becker laid the theoretical foundations of law and economics and occupy a mythical position in its official history, they were not awarded the Nobel Prize for their contribution to this field, but, rather, for their work in economics in general. Nor did they operate in the field of law and economics as later defined by Posner, and they failed to shift the field's research agenda to studying the effects of the law on the economy or the economy on the law.

It was Richard Posner who, in fact, set and shaped the boundaries of the Chicago School of Law and Economics, limiting them to the economic analysis of the law. This school of thought marginalized and may even have prevented other potential connections between law and economics. The boundaries set by Posner and his colleagues held strong for at least three decades. A discussion of the reasons for this is beyond the scope of this article. I believe that it is related to Posner's personal interest and eminent position in the field. Limiting the boundaries of law and economics made sense for a newly formed field, as it enabled concentrating on research resources and rapidly advancing learning on a narrow front. Moreover, law and economics was institutionalized as a discipline in law schools rather than in economics departments. By analyzing legal rules and providing prescriptions for legal reforms, law and economics scholars could participate in the major areas of discourse within legal academia. They could even demonstrate the power of their coherent and rigorous theory over the confused intuitions of other legal scholars. This further expanded their sphere of activity within the law schools. Only in the last decade has research transgressing these boundaries begun to appear.

In sum, on the assumption that law has no methodology of its own to contribute to the study of economics, three potential outcomes of the interaction between the disciplines of economics and law appeared around 1960: 1) the study of the effects of law on the economy; 2) the study of the effects of the economy on legal change; and 3) the application of economic methodology to the analysis of law. Until recently, only the third of these possible research agendas was considerably advanced within the field of law and economics. The narrow scope of the newly created field partly explains its a-historical nature and its lack of interaction with economic and legal history.

In addition to developing a normatively-based policy analysis, Posner and colleagues developed a positive branch of law and economics. The two were unified in the framework of the theory of the common law's tendency toward efficiency. This theory deals with the effects of law on economic growth or the effects of economic growth on the law. It also can be understood as encompassing both the positive and normative research agendas by creating identification between them, at least insofar as the common law is concerned. * * * [R]efining and defending this general theory of the common law's tendency toward efficiency consumed a great deal of the time and energy of law and economics scholars and impinged on their interest in positive theories. Instead, they were occupied with proposing and examining theoretical mechanisms that might explain the tendency toward efficiency in the common law. * * * This weak start at positive research further removed law and economics scholars from engaging in the first two research agendas, which seemed important to both Coase and Becker. The interest in these two agendas was developed outside law and economics in fields such as New Institutional Economics, Historical New Institutional Economics, and the Wisconsin School of Legal History. Only recently has law and economics expanded its agenda to include these two issues.

More specifically, Chicago law and economics scholars claimed to be interested not only in legal rules but also in how legal incentives affect individuals' behavior. However, their research did not focus on studying the behavior of individuals, and the behavior of societies and basic social structures and trends was entirely beyond the scope of their research agenda. The behavior of individuals was assumed to be affected by changes in legal rules that affected individual incentives. Law and economics aimed at changing behavior but, in fact, studied rules and their change. As its other name, economic analysis of the law, implies, law and economics mainly aspired to normatively evaluate legal rules and prescribe their modification. Only rarely, when legal rules functioned within a market setting, as in the case of anti-trust and securities regulation, did Chicago law and economics scholars inquire into the behavior of individual agents more closely. It was more often the case that the legal rules were analyzed in non-market settings and the behavior of individuals was assumed rather than studied. * * *

From its inception, Chicago law and economics involved the application of neo-classical tools, which reached a powerful phase in the 1950s and 1960s in the Chicago School of Economics. Neo-classical economics at [the University of Chicago] was remarkably a-historical. The detachment of economics from change over real time, and thus from history, began with the marginalist revolution and [Alfred Marshall], continued with Keynes, and culminated in Chicago in the 1950s.

For economics, the 1950s was a decade of high theory. It was one of markets, allocation, and equilibrium; of abstraction and deduction; of marginalism and incremental change; of optimization and mathematization. It was one in which the basic assumptions of neo-classical theory still held strong. This decade was a low point in economic theory in terms of interest in history and change over real time. Theory was mainly static, not dynamic. Insofar as dynamic elements played a role in economic theory, they were reflected in shifts of curves, moves from point to point along curves, or leaps from one equilibrium to the next, over a single time period.

Time was not discussed in terms of months or years or decades; the flow of time was not treated differently for different historical eras. Not only was change over time neglected, but there was also a perception that the past of any given system had no bearing on its present and certainly not on its future. Since any given current regime of functions, allocations, and equilibria is not burdened by its past, it can serve as a good starting point for future predictions. An economic theoretician thus did not have to reconstruct the passage of time, as did historians—and some sociologists, anthropologists, political scientists, lawyers, literary critics, and philosophers. Imagining change was confined to the two-dimensional classroom world of blackboard curves and to figures in books. This static state of economic theory thus hindered the development of a history-conscious law and economics.

This was the economic theory applied in the late 1960s and early 1970s by Richard Posner and his colleagues at the University of Chicago Law School. By that point, law and economics had acquired all its familiar characteristics: reliance on the neo-classical assumption that individuals are rational maximizers; equating change in legal rules with change in relative prices; and adoption of Kaldor–Hicks efficiency ("potential Pareto efficiency," in more obscure terms) in the sense of wealth maximization as a standard of evaluation.

The a-historical neoclassical characteristics of law and economics dominated the field. Well into the 1980s and beyond, law and economics was still engaged in adapting price theory to non-market legal behavior as part of a wider project of the expansion of economics. It focused on the application of price theory to the specific contours of the law: judge-made law and legislation; property, contracts, and torts; liability rules; and remedies. Law and economics scholars were engaged in intense normative and policy debates with critics from rival jurisprudential and doctrinal schools. These debates revolved around the imperialistic tendencies of economics, its unrealistic assumptions (e.g., of rationality), and its ideological bias in favor of efficiency considerations at the expense of distributive considerations. As long as the debates at the normative and policy level were intense, law and economics scholars were not likely to find much time or motivation to turn to the study of history.

     * * *

In the first edition of *Economic Analysis of Law* (1972), what Posner termed "the economic logic of the common law" was the first theoretical argument in law and economics to draw the attention of scholars in the emerging field of the history of law. * * * Posner based his thesis that common law exhibits a tendency toward efficiency on a few historical examples from nineteenth-century America, including: enterprise liability for faulty products; industrial accidents; railroad-crossing accidents; damage caused by train engine sparks; and the impossibility doctrine in contracts. He claimed that these examples, when viewed in the framework of his positive theory of common law, confirm his thesis. These examples also serve to counter arguments that common law is either irrelevant to economic growth or encourages economic growth by subsidizing big business and increasing social inequality.

Posner did not base his claims on thorough historical research, but he most decidedly challenged historians. His positive theory of the law was historical in nature. It purported to explain how law changes over time. This explanation was too deterministic for most legal historians. It subjected their micro-historical interpretations to his macro theory and, in a sense, made them secondary to it. Furthermore, he used concrete examples rooted in time and place that are central to the work of many American legal historians. In doing so, he called into dispute concrete historical studies. It is not surprising that several legal historians, in response to this challenge, criticized Posner for misunderstanding the history of legal doctrines and their social and economic effects. In each of the editions of *Economic Analysis of Law*, Posner's discussion of the positive theory of common law's tendency toward efficiency grew in length, increasing from the four-and-a-half pages in the first edition to six-and-a-half pages in the 1977 second edition to nine-and-a-half pages in the 1986 third edition. * * * These increases in length were not the result of more historical studies conducted to test or confirm the theory. Rather, greater space was devoted to criticizing legal historians for not understanding economic theory, including the theory of the common law's tendency toward efficiency and the concept of efficiency. Legal historians became more critical of Posner, and Posner became more critical of legal historians, particularly those who viewed the law as subsidizing business, redistributing wealth, and oppressing the weak.

Posner had to answer not only to legal historians, but also to other legal scholars, even some with an economic orientation. These legal scholars questioned his thesis on a theoretical rather than empirical-historical level. What in the common law, they asked, could lead it to produce efficient rules? Some law and economics scholars tried to support Posner's claim and counter the growing criticism against it, by explaining its theoretical logic. Some suggested that judges are the agents who steer the common law toward efficiency; even if they are not aware that they maximize efficiency, they behave as if they are doing so. Justice and common sense considerations lead to efficient judgments. Other scholars saw litigants in general (losing litigants or repeat litigants) as the agents of the drive toward efficiency: inefficient rules will be rooted out by ongoing litigation. By the mid–1980s, the debate over the tendency of the common law toward efficiency, both on the historical and theoretical levels, had exhausted itself.

* * *

Though not one of the first fields within economics to apply theoretical novelties, over time, law and economics adopted extensions and modifications of the basic models of price theory to account for, among other things, transaction costs, risk sensitivity, and information a-symmetry. A main new feature of research in the 1980s and early 1990s was the addition of game theory tools to the law and economics analysis. Another was the

gradual opening up of law and economics to public choice analysis. * * *
Law and economics has become more empirical and more comparative in
recent years. * * *

Contrary to these trends in economic theory and the research agenda
of law and economics, some Chicago law and economics scholars still view
price theory as the sole economic tool for analyzing the law. They believe
that despite its imperfections, it cannot be successfully replaced by any
other theoretical framework. Moreover, they argue that the use of multiple
theoretical frameworks will cause incoherence and complications, which
would result in less rigorous tools, more limited applicability, and less
insightful conclusions. They view the future of their field as developing
along three main trajectories: first, sophistication within the neo-classical
price theory paradigm, by employing heavier mathematical, game theoretic,
and micro tools; second, expansion into the relatively neglected areas of
public law; and third, the filling in of the remaining gaps in the analysis of
private law. * * *

The Economic Approach to Law

THE PROBLEMS OF JURISPRUDENCE 353–92 (1990).

■ RICHARD A. POSNER

* * *

THE APPROACH

The basic assumption of economics that guides the version of economic
analysis of law that I shall be presenting is that people are rational
maximizers of their satisfactions—*all* people (with the exception of small
children and the profoundly retarded) in all of their activities (except when
under the influence of psychosis or similarly deranged through drug or
alcohol abuse) that involve choice. Because this definition embraces the
criminal deciding whether to commit another crime, the litigant deciding
whether to settle or litigate a case, the legislator deciding whether to vote
for or against a bill, the judge deciding how to cast his vote in a case, the
party to a contract deciding whether to break it, the driver deciding how
fast to drive, and the pedestrian deciding how boldly to cross the street, as
well as the usual economic actors, such as businessmen and consumers, it is
apparent that most activities either regulated by or occurring within the
legal system are grist for the economic analyst's mill. It should go without
saying that nonmonetary as well as monetary satisfactions enter into the
individual's calculus of maximizing (indeed, money for most people is a
means rather than an end) and that decisions, to be rational, need not be
well thought out at the conscious level—indeed, need not be conscious at
all. Recall that "rational" denotes suiting means to ends, rather than
mulling things over, and that much of our knowledge is tacit.

Since my interest is in legal doctrines and institutions, it will be best to
begin at the legislative (including the constitutional) level. I assume that

legislators are rational maximizers of their satisfactions just like everyone else. Thus nothing they do is motivated by the public interest as such. But they want to be elected and reelected, and they need money to wage an effective campaign. This money is more likely to be forthcoming from well-organized groups than from unorganized individuals. The rational individual knows that his contribution is unlikely to make a difference; for this reason and also because voters in most elections are voting for candidates rather than policies, which further weakens the link between casting one's vote and obtaining one's preferred policy. The rational individual will have little incentive to invest time and effort in deciding whom to vote for. Only an organized group of individuals (or firms or other organizations—but these are just conduits for individuals) will be able to overcome the informational and free-rider problems that plague collective action. But such a group will not organize and act effectively unless its members have much to gain or much to lose from specific policies, as tobacco farmers, for example, have much to gain from federal subsidies for growing tobacco and much to lose from the withdrawal of those subsidies. The basic tactic of an interest group is to trade the votes of its members and its financial support to candidates in exchange for an implied promise of favorable legislation. Such legislation will normally take the form of a statute transferring wealth from unorganized taxpayers (for example, consumers) to the interest group. If the target were another interest group, the legislative transfer might be effectively opposed. The unorganized are unlikely to mount effective opposition, and it is their wealth, therefore, that typically is transferred to interest groups.

* * * [B]ecause of the costs of transactions within a multi-headed legislative body, and the costs of effective communication through time, legislation does not spring full-grown from the head of the legislature; it needs interpretation and application, and this is the role of the courts. They are agents of the legislature. But to impart credibility and durability to the deals the legislature strikes with interest groups, courts must be able to resist the wishes of current legislators who want to undo their predecessors' deals yet cannot do so through repeal because the costs of passing legislation (whether original or amended) are so high, and who might therefore look to the courts for a repealing "interpretation." The impediments to legislation actually facilitate rather than retard the striking of deals, by giving interest groups some assurance that a deal struck with the legislature will not promptly be undone by repeal. An independent judiciary is one of the impediments.

Judicial independence makes the judges imperfect agents of the legislature. This is tolerable not only for the reason just mentioned but also because an independent judiciary is necessary for the resolution of ordinary disputes in a way that will encourage trade, travel, freedom of action, and other highly valued activities or conditions and will minimize the expenditure of resources on influencing governmental action. Legislators might appear to have little to gain from these widely diffused rule-of-law virtues. But if the aggregate benefits from a particular social policy are very large and no interest group's ox is gored, legislators may find it in their own interest to support the policy. Voters understand in a rough way the benefits to them of national defense, crime control, dispute settlement, and the other elements of the night watchman state, and they will not vote for legislators who refuse to provide these basic public services. It is only when those services are in place, and when (usually later) effective means of taxation and redistribution develop, that the formation of narrow interest groups and the extraction by them of transfers from unorganized groups become feasible.

The judges thus have a dual role: to interpret the interest-group deals embodied in legislation and to provide the basic public service of authoritative dispute resolution. They perform the latter function not only by deciding cases in accordance with preexisting norms, but also—especially in the Anglo–American legal system—by elaborating those norms. They fashioned the common law out of customary practices, out of ideas borrowed from statutes and from other legal systems (for example, Roman law), and out of their own conceptions of public policy. The law they created exhibits, according to the economic theory that I am expounding, a remarkable (although not total—remember the extension of the rule of capture to oil and gas) substantive consistency. It is as if the judges wanted to adopt the rules, procedures, and case outcomes that would maximize society's wealth.

I must pause to define "wealth maximization," a term often misunderstood. The "wealth" in "wealth maximization" refers to the sum of all tangible and intangible goods and services, weighted by prices of two sorts: offer prices (what people are willing to pay for goods they do not already own); and asking prices (what people demand to sell what they do own). If A would be willing to pay up to $100 for B's stamp collection, it is worth $100 to A. If B would be willing to sell the stamp collection for any price above $90, it is worth $90 to B. So if B sells the stamp collection to A (say for $100, but the analysis is qualitatively unaffected at any price between $90 and $100—and it is only in that range that a transaction will occur), the wealth of society will rise by $10. Before the transaction A had $100 in cash and B had a stamp collection worth $90 (a total of $190); after the transaction A has a stamp collection worth $100 and B has $100 in cash (a total of $200). The transaction will not raise measured wealth—gross national product, national income, or whatever—by $10; it will not raise it at all unless the transaction is recorded, and if it is recorded it is likely to raise measured wealth by the full $100 purchase price. But the real addition to social wealth consists of the $10 increment in *nonpecuniary* satisfaction that A derives from the purchase, compared with that of B. This shows that "wealth" in the economist's sense is not a simple monetary measure, and explains why it is a fallacy (the Earl of Lauderdale's fallacy) to think that wealth would be maximized by encouraging the charging of monopoly prices. The wealth of producers would increase but that of consumers would diminish—and actually by a greater amount, since monopoly pricing will induce some consumers to switch to goods that cost society more to produce but, being priced at a competitive rather than a monopoly price, appear to the consumer to be cheaper. The fallacy thus lies in equating business income to social wealth.

Similarly, if I am given a choice between remaining in a job in which I work forty hours a week for $1,000 and switching to a job in which I would work thirty hours for $500, and I decide to make the switch, the extra ten hours of leisure must be worth at least $500 to me, yet GNP will fall when I reduce my hours of work. Suppose the extra hours of leisure are worth $600 to me, so that my full income rises from $1,000 to $1,100 when I reduce my hours. My former employer presumably is made worse off by my leaving (else why did he employ me?), but not more than $100 worse off, for if he were, he would offer to pay me a shade over $1,100 a week to stay—and I would stay. (The example abstracts from income tax.)

Wealth is *related* to money, in that a desire not backed by ability to pay has no standing—such a desire is neither an offer price nor an asking price. I may desperately desire a BMW, but if I am unwilling or unable to pay its purchase price, society's wealth would not be increased by transferring the BMW from its present owner to me. Abandon this essential constraint (an important distinction, also, between wealth maximization and utilitarianism—for I might derive greater utility from the BMW than its present owner or anyone else to whom he might sell the car), and the way is open to tolerating the crimes committed by the passionate and the avaricious against the cold and the frugal.

The common law facilitates wealth-maximizing transactions in a variety of ways. It recognizes property rights, and these facilitate exchange. It also protects property rights, through tort and criminal law. (Although today criminal law is almost entirely statutory, the basic criminal protections—for example, those against murder, assault, rape, and theft—have, as one might expect, common law origins.) Through contract law it protects the process of exchange. And it establishes procedural rules for resolving disputes in these various fields as efficiently as possible.

The illustrations given thus far of wealth-maximizing transactions have been of transactions that are voluntary in the strict sense of making everyone affected by them better off, or at least no worse off. Every transaction has been assumed to affect just two parties, each of whom has been made better off by it. Such a transaction is said to be Pareto superior, but Pareto superiority is not a necessary condition for a transaction to be wealth maximizing. Consider an accident that inflicts a cost of $100 with a probability of .01 and that would have cost $3 to avoid. The accident is a wealth-maximizing "transaction" (recall Aristotle's distinction between voluntary and involuntary transactions) because the expected accident cost ($1) is less than the cost of avoidance. (I am assuming risk neutrality. Risk aversion would complicate the analysis but not change it fundamentally.) It is wealth maximizing even if the victim is not compensated. The result is consistent with Learned Hand's formula, which defines negligence as the failure to take cost-justified precautions. If the only precaution that would have averted the accident is not cost-justified, the failure to take it is not negligent and the injurer will not have to compensate the victim for the costs of the accident.

* * *

The wealth-maximizing properties of common law rules have been elucidated at considerable length in the literature of the economic analysis of law. Such doctrines as conspiracy, general average (admiralty), contributory negligence, equitable servitudes, employment at will, the standard for granting preliminary injunctions, entrapment, the contract defense of impossibility, the collateral-benefits rule, the expectation measure of damages, assumption of risk, attempt, invasion of privacy, wrongful interference with contract rights, the availability of punitive damages in some cases but not others, privilege in the law of evidence, official immunity, and the doctrine of moral consideration have been found—at least by some contributors to this literature—to conform to the dictates of wealth maximization. * * * It has even been argued that the system of precedent itself has an economic equilibrium. Precedents are created as a by-product of litigation. The greater the number of recent precedents in an area, the lower the rate of litigation will be. In particular, cases involving disputes over legal as distinct from purely factual issues will be settled. The existence of abundant, highly informative (in part because recent) precedents will enable the parties to legal disputes to form more convergent estimates of the likely outcome of a trial, and as noted in previous chapters, if both parties agree on the outcome of trial they will settle beforehand because a trial is more costly than a settlement. But with less litigation, fewer new precedents will be produced, and the existing precedents will obsolesce as changing circumstances render them less apt and informative. So the rate of litigation will rise, producing more precedents and thereby causing the rate of litigation again to fall.

This analysis does not explain what drives judges to decide common law cases in accordance with the dictates of wealth maximization. Prosperity, however, which wealth maximization measures more sensitively than purely monetary measures such as GNP, is a relatively uncontroversial policy, and most judges try to steer clear of controversy: their age, method of compensation, and relative weakness vis-a-vis the other branches of government make the avoidance of controversy attractive. It probably is no accident, therefore, that many common law doctrines assumed their modern form in the nineteenth century, when laissez-faire ideology, which resembles wealth maximization, had a strong hold on the Anglo–American judicial imagination * * *.

It may be objected that in assigning ideology as a cause of judicial behavior, the economist strays outside the boundaries of his discipline; but he need not rest on ideology. The economic analysis of legislation implies that fields of law left to the judges to elaborate, such as the common law fields, must be the ones in which interest-group pressures are too weak to deflect the legislature from pursuing goals that are in the general interest. Prosperity is one of these goals, and one that judges are especially well equipped to promote. The rules of the common law that they promulgate attach prices to socially undesirable conduct, whether free riding or imposing social costs without corresponding benefits. By doing this the rules create incentives to avoid such conduct, and these incentives foster prosperity. In contrast, judges can, despite appearances, do little to redistribute wealth. A rule that makes it easy for poor tenants to break leases with rich landlords, for example, will induce landlords to raise rents in order to offset the costs that such a rule imposes, and tenants will bear the brunt of these higher costs. Indeed, the principal redistribution accomplished by such a rule may be from the prudent, responsible tenant, who may derive little or no benefit from having additional legal rights to use against landlords—rights that enable a tenant to avoid or postpone eviction for nonpayment of rental—to the feckless tenant. That is a capricious redistribution. Legislatures, however, have by virtue of their taxing and spending powers powerful tools for redistributing wealth. So an efficient division of labor between the legislative and judicial branches has the legislative branch concentrate on catering to interest-group demands for wealth distribution and the judicial branch on meeting the broad-based social demand for efficient rules governing safety, property, and transactions. Although there are other possible goals of judicial action besides efficiency and redistribution, many of these (various conceptions of "fairness" and "justice") are labels for wealth maximization,[1] or for redistribution in favor of powerful interest groups; or else they are too controversial in a heterogeneous society, too ad hoc, or insufficiently developed to provide judges who desire a reputation for objectivity and disinterest with adequate grounds for their decisions.

Finally, even if judges have little commitment to efficiency, their inefficient decisions will, by definition, impose greater social costs than their efficient ones will. As a result, losers of cases decided mistakenly from an economic standpoint will have a greater incentive, on average, to press for correction through appeal, new litigation, or legislative action than losers of cases decided soundly from an economic standpoint—so there will be a steady pressure for efficient results. Moreover, cases litigated under inefficient rules tend to involve larger stakes than cases litigated under efficient rules (for the inefficient rules, by definition, generate social waste), and the larger the stakes in a dispute the likelier it is to be litigated rather than settled; so judges will have a chance to reconsider the inefficient rule.

Thus we should not be surprised to see the common law tending to become efficient, although since the incentives to judges to perform well along any dimension are weak (this is a by-product of judicial independence), we cannot expect the law ever to achieve perfect efficiency. Since wealth maximization is not only a guide in fact to common law judging but also a genuine social value and the only one judges are in a good position to promote, it provides not only the key to an accurate description of what the judges are up to but also the right benchmark for criticism and reform. If judges are failing to maximize wealth, the economic analyst of law will urge them to alter practice or doctrine accordingly. In addition, the analyst will urge—on any legislator sufficiently free of interest-group pressures to be

1. EDWARD W. RYAN, IN THE WORDS OF ADAM SMITH: THE FIRST CONSUMER ADVOCATE 1 (1990). For example, it is unclear whether Weinrib's Kantian theory of tort law has different substantive implications from the economic theory; the differences may be in vocabulary only.

able to legislate in the public interest—a program of enacting only legislation that conforms to the dictates of wealth maximization.

Besides generating both predictions and prescriptions, the economic approach enables the common law to be reconceived in simple, coherent terms and to be applied more objectively than traditional lawyers would think possible. From the premise that the common law does and should seek to maximize society's wealth, the economic analyst can deduce in logical—if you will, formalist—fashion (economic theory is formulated nowadays largely in mathematical terms) the set of legal doctrines that will express and perfect the inner nature of the common law, and can compare these doctrines with the actual doctrines of common law. After translating from the economic vocabulary back into the legal one, the analyst will find that most of the actual doctrines are tolerable approximations to the implications of economic theory and so are formalistically valid. * * *

The project of reducing the common law—with its many separate fields, its thousands of separate doctrines, its hundreds of thousands of reported decisions—to a handful of mathematical formulas may seem quixotic, but the economic analyst can give reasons for doubting this assessment. Much of the doctrinal luxuriance of common law is seen to be superficial once the essentially economic nature of the common law is understood. A few principles, such as cost-benefit analysis, the prevention of free riding, decision under uncertainty, risk aversion, and the promotion of mutually beneficial-exchanges, can explain most doctrines and decisions. Tort cases can be translated into contract cases by re-characterizing the tort issue as finding the implied pre-accident contract that the parties would have chosen had transaction costs not been prohibitive, and contract cases can be translated into tort cases by asking what remedy if any would maximize the expected benefits of the contractual undertaking considered ex ante. The criminal's decision whether to commit a crime is no different in principle from the prosecutor's decision whether to prosecute; a plea bargain is a contract; crimes are in effect torts by insolvent defendants because if all criminals could pay the full social costs of their crimes, the task of deterring antisocial behavior could be left to tort law. Such examples suggest not only that the logic of the common law really is economics but also that the teaching of law could be simplified by exposing students to the clean and simple economic structure beneath the garb of legal doctrine.

If all this seems reminiscent of Langdell; it differs fundamentally in being empirically verifiable. The ultimate test of a rule derived from economic theory is not the elegance or logicality of the derivation but the rule's effect on social wealth. The extension of the rule of capture to oil and gas was subjected to such a test, flunked, and was replaced (albeit through legislative rather than judicial action) by efficient rules. The other rules of the common law can and should be tested likewise.

* * *

CRITICISMS OF THE NORMATIVE THEORY

The question whether wealth maximization *should* guide legal policy, either in general or just in common law fields (plus those statutory fields where the legislative intent is to promote efficiency—antitrust law being a possible example), is ordinarily treated as separate from the question whether it *has* guided legal policy, except insofar as the positive theory may be undermined by the inadequacies of the normative theory. Actually the two theories are not as separable as this, illustrating again the lack of a clear boundary between "is" and "ought" propositions. One of the things judges ought to do is follow precedent, although not inflexibly; so if efficiency is the animating principle of much common law doctrine, judges have some obligation to make decisions that will be consistent with efficiency. This is one reason why the positive economic theory of the common law is so contentious.

The normative theory has been highly contentious in its own right. Most contributors to the debate over it conclude that it is a bad theory, and although many of the criticisms can be answered, several cannot be, and it is those I shall focus on.

The first is that wealth maximization is inherently incomplete as a guide to social action because it has nothing to say about the distribution of rights—or at least nothing we want to hear. Given the distribution of rights (whatever it is), wealth maximization can be used to derive the policies that will maximize the value of those rights. But this does not go far enough, because naturally we are curious about whether it would be just to start off with a society in which, say, one member owned all the others. If wealth maximization is indifferent to the initial distribution of rights, it is a truncated concept of justice.

Since the initial distribution may dissipate rapidly, this point may have little practical significance. Nor is wealth maximization completely silent on the initial distribution. If we could compare two otherwise identical nascent societies, in one of which one person owned all the others and in the other of which slavery was forbidden, and could repeat the comparison a century later, almost certainly we would find that the second society was wealthier and the first had abolished slavery (if so, this would further illustrate the limited effect of the initial distribution on the current distribution). Although it has not always and everywhere been true, under modern conditions of production slavery is an inefficient method of organizing production. The extensive use of slave labor by the Nazis during World War II may seem an exception—but only if we disregard the welfare of the slave laborers.

This response to the demand that wealth maximization tell us something about the justice of the initial distribution of rights is incomplete. Suppose it were the case—it almost surely *is* the case—that some people in modern American society would be more productive as slaves than as free persons. These are not antisocial people whom we want to punish by imprisoning (a form of slavery that is tolerated); they are not psychotic or profoundly retarded; they just are lazy, feckless, poorly organized, undisciplined people—people incompetent to manage their own lives in a way that will maximize their output, even though the relevant output is not market output alone but also leisure, family associations, and any other sources of satisfaction to these people as well as to others. Wealth would be maximized by enslaving these people, provided the costs of supervision were not too high—but the assumption that they would not be too high is built into the proposition that their output would be greater as slaves than as free persons, for it is net output that we are interested in. Yet no one thinks it would be right to enslave such people, even if there were no evidentiary problems in identifying them, the slave masters could be trusted to be benign, and so on; and these conditions, too, may be implicit in the proposition that the net social output of some people would be greater if they were slaves.

It is no answer that it would be inefficient to enslave such people unless they consented to be enslaved, that is, unless the would-be slave-master met the asking price for their freedom. The term *"their* freedom" assumes they have the property right in their persons, and the assumption is arbitrary. We can imagine assigning the property rights in persons (perhaps only persons who appeared likely to be unproductive) to the state to auction them to the highest bidder. The putative slave could bid against the putative master, but would lose. His expected earnings, net of consumption, would be smaller than the expected profits to the master, otherwise enslavement would not be efficient. Therefore he could not borrow enough—even if capital markets worked without any friction (in the present setting, even if the lender could enslave the borrower if the latter defaulted!)—to outbid his master-to-be.

This example points to a deeper criticism of wealth maximization as a norm or value: like utilitarianism, which it closely resembles, or nationalism, or Social Darwinism, or racialism, or organic theories of the state, it treats people as if they were the cells of a single organism; the welfare of the cell is important only insofar as it promotes the welfare of the organism. Wealth maximization implies that if the prosperity of the society can be promoted by enslaving its least productive citizens, the sacrifice of their freedom is worthwhile. But this implication is contrary to the unshakable moral intuitions of Americans, and . . . conformity to intuition is the ultimate test of a moral (indeed of any) theory.

* * *

[S]uppose it were the case—it may be the case—that some religious faiths are particularly effective in producing law-abiding, productive, healthy citizens. Mormonism is a plausible example. Would it not make sense on purely secular grounds, indeed on purely wealth-maximizing grounds, for government to subsidize these faiths? Practitioners of other religious faiths would be greatly offended, but from the standpoint of wealth maximization the only question would be whether the cost to them was greater than the benefits to the country as a whole.

Consider now a faith that both has few adherents in the United States and is feared or despised by the rest of the population. (The Rastafarian faith is a plausible example.) Such a faith will by assumption be imposing costs on the rest of the community, and given the fewness of its adherents, the benefits conferred by the faith may, even when aggregated across all its adherents, be smaller than the costs. It could then be argued that wealth maximization warranted or even required the suppression of the faith. This example suggests another objection to wealth maximization, one alluded to in the discussion of slavery: its results are sensitive to assumptions about the initial distribution of rights—a distribution that is distinct from the initial distribution of wealth (which is unlikely to remain stable over time), but about which wealth maximization may again have relatively little to say. If Rastafarians are conceived to have a property right in their religion, so that the state or anyone else who wants to acquire that right and suppress the religion must meet their asking price, probably the right will not be sold. Asking prices can be very high—in principle, infinite: how much would the average person sell his life for, if the sale had to be completed immediately? But if rights over religious practices are given to the part of the populace that is not Rastafarian, the Rastafarians may find it impossible to buy the right back; their offer price will be limited to their net wealth, which may be slight.

No doubt in this country, in this day and age, religious liberty is the cost-justified policy. The broader point is that a system of rights—perhaps the system we have—may well be required by a *realistic* conception of utilitarianism, that is, one that understands that given the realities of human nature a society dedicated to utilitarianism requires rules and institutions that place checks on utility-maximizing behavior in particular cases. For example, although one can imagine specific cases in which deliberately punishing an innocent person as a criminal would increase aggregate utility, one has trouble imagining a system in which government officials could be trusted to make such decisions. "Wealth maximizing" can be substituted for "utilitarian" without affecting the analysis. Religious liberty may well be both utility maximizing and wealth maximizing, and this may even be why we have it. And if it became *too* costly, probably it would be abandoned; and so with the prohibition of torture, and the other civilized political amenities of a wealthy society. If our crime rate were much lower than it is, we probably would not have capital punishment—and if it gets much higher, we surely will have fewer civil liberties.

But at least in the present relatively comfortable conditions of our society, the regard for individual freedom appears to transcend instrumental considerations; freedom appears to be valued for itself rather than just for its contribution to prosperity—or at least to be valued for reasons that escape the economic calculus. Is society really better off in a utilitarian or wealth-maximizing sense as a result of the extraordinarily elaborate procedural safeguards that the Bill of Rights gives criminal defendants? This is by no means clear. Are minority rights welfare maximizing—when the minority in question is a small one? That is not clear either, as the Rastafarian example showed. The main reasons these institutions are valued seem not to be utilitarian or even instrumental in character. *What* those reasons are is far from clear; indeed, "noninstrumental reason" is almost an oxymoron. And as I have suggested, we surely are not willing to pay an infinite price, perhaps not even a very high price, for freedom. * * *

Still, hypocritical and incoherent as our political ethics may frequently be, we do not permit degrading invasions of individual autonomy merely on a judgment that, on balance, the invasion would make a net addition to the social wealth. And whatever the philosophical grounding of this sentiment, it is too deeply entrenched in our society at present for wealth maximization to be given a free rein. The same may be true of the residue of corrective-justice sentiment.

I have said nothing about the conflict between wealth maximization and equality of wealth, because I am less sure of the extent of egalitarian sentiment in our society than that of individualistic sentiment (by "individualism" I mean simply the rivals to aggregative philosophies, such as utilitarianism and wealth maximization). Conflict there is, however, and it points to another important criticism of wealth maximization even if the critic is not an egalitarian. Imagine that a limited supply of growth hormone, privately manufactured and sold, must be allocated. A wealthy parent wants the hormone so that his child of average height will grow tall; a poor parent wants the hormone so that his child of dwarfish height can grow to normal height. In a system of wealth maximization the wealthy parent might outbid the poor parent and get the hormone. This is not certain. Amount of wealth is only one factor in willingness to pay. The poor parent might offer his entire wealth for the hormone, and that wealth, although meager, might exceed the amount of money the wealthy parent was willing to pay, given alternative uses to which he could put his money. Also, altruists might help the poor parent bid more than he could with only his own resources. The poor might actually be better off in a system in which the distribution of the hormone were left to the private market, even if there were no altruism. Such a system would create incentives to produce and sell the hormone sooner, and perhaps at a lower price, than if the government controlled its distribution; for the costs of production would probably be lower under private rather than public production, and even a monopolist will charge less when his costs fall.

But what seems impossible to maintain convincingly in the present ethical climate is that the wealthy parent has the *right* to the hormone by virtue of being willing to pay the supplier more than the poor parent can; more broadly, that consumers have a right to purchase in free markets. These propositions cannot be derived from wealth maximization. Indeed, they look like propositions about transactional freedom rather than about distribution only because I have assumed that the growth hormone is produced and distributed exclusively through the free market. An alternative possibility would be for the state to own the property right in the hormone and to allocate it on the basis of need rather than willingness to pay. To argue against this alternative (socialist medicine writ small) would require an appeal either to the deeply controversial idea of a natural right to private property, or to purely instrumental considerations, such as the possibility that in the long run the poor will be better off with a free market in growth hormone—but to put the question *this* way is to assume that the poor have some sort of social claim by virtue of being poor, and thus to admit the relevance of egalitarian considerations and thereby break out of the limits of wealth maximization.

A stronger-seeming argument for the free-enterprise solution is that the inventor of the hormone should have a right to use it as he wishes, which includes the right to sell it to the highest bidder. But this argument seems stronger only because we are inclined to suppose that what has happened is that *after* the inventor invented it the government decided to rob him of the reward for which he had labored. If instead we assume that Congress passes a law in 1989 which provides that after the year 2000 the right to patent new drugs will be conditioned on the patentee's agreeing to limit the price he charges, we shall have difficulty objecting to the law on ethical, as distinct from practical, grounds. It would be just one more restriction on free markets.

* * * Although the advocate of wealth maximization can argue that to the productive should belong the fruits of their labor, the argument can be countered along the lines [that] production is really a social rather than individual effort[] to which it can be added that wealth may often be due more to luck (and not the luck of the genetic lottery, either) than to skill or effort. Furthermore, if altruism is so greatly admired, as it is by conservatives as well as by liberals, why should not its spirit inform legislation? Why should government protect only our selfish instincts? To this it can be replied that the spirit of altruism is voluntary giving. But the reply is weak. The biggest reason we value altruism is that we *desire* some redistribution—we may admire the altruist for his self-sacrifice but we would not admire him as much if he destroyed his wealth rather than giving it to others—and we think that voluntary redistribution is less costly than involuntary. If redistribution is desirable, some involuntary redistribution may be justifiable, depending on the costs, of course, but not on the principle of the thing.

There is a still deeper problem with founding wealth maximization on a notion of natural rights. The economic perspective is thoroughly (and fruitfully) behaviorist. "Economic man" is not, as vulgarly supposed, a person driven by purely pecuniary incentives, but he is a person whose behavior is completely determined by incentives; his rationality is no different from that of a pigeon or a rat. The economic task from the perspective of wealth maximization is to influence his incentives so as to maximize his output. How a person so conceived could be thought to have a *moral* entitlement to a particular distribution of the world's goods—an entitlement, say, to the share proportional to his contribution to the world's wealth—is unclear. Have marmots moral entitlements? Two levels of discourse are being mixed.

* * *

The strongest argument for wealth maximization is not moral, but pragmatic. Such classic defenses of the free market as chapter 4 of Mill's *On Liberty* can easily be given a pragmatic reading. We look around the world and see that in general people who live in societies in which markets are allowed to function more or less freely not only are wealthier than people in other societies but have more political rights, more liberty and dignity, are more content (as evidenced, for example, by their being less prone to emigrate)—so that wealth maximization may be the most direct route to a variety of moral ends. The recent history of England, France, and Turkey, of Japan and Southeast Asia, of East versus West Germany and North versus South Korea, of China and Taiwan, of Chile, of the Soviet Union, Poland, and Hungary, and of Cuba and Argentina provides striking support for this thesis.

Writing in the early 1970s, the English political philosopher Brian Barry doubted the importance of incentives. "My own guess," he said, "is that enough people with professional and managerial jobs really like them (and enough others who would enjoy them and have sufficient ability to do them are waiting to replace those who do not) to enable the pay of these jobs to be brought down considerably ... I would suggest that the pay levels in Britain of schoolteachers and social workers seem to offer net rewards which recruit and maintain just enough people, and that this provides a guideline to the pay levels that could be sustained generally among professionals and managers." He rejected the "assumption that a sufficient supply of highly educated people will be forthcoming only if lured by the anticipation of a higher income afterwards as a result," adding that "it would also be rash to assume that it would be an economic loss if fewer sought higher education." He discussed with approval the Swedish experiment at redistributing income and wealth but thought it hampered by the fact that "Sweden still has a privately owned economy." He worried about "brain drain" but concluded that it was a serious problem only with regard to airline pilots and physicians; and a nation can do without airlines and may be able to replace general practitioners "with people having a lower (and less marketable) qualification." (Yet Barry himself was soon to join the brain drain, and he is neither a physician nor an airline pilot.) He proposed "to spread the nastiest jobs around by requiring everyone, before entering higher education or entering a profession, to do, say, three years of work wherever he or she was directed. (This would also have educational advantages.) To supplement this there could be a call-up of say a month every year, as with the Swiss and Israeli armed forces but directed towards peaceful occupations."

At least with the benefit of hindsight we can see that Barry wrote a prescription for economic disaster. It may be impossible to lay solid philosophical foundations under wealth maximization, just as it may be impossible to lay solid philosophical foundations under the natural sciences, but this would be a poor reason for abandoning wealth maximization, just as the existence of intractable problems in the philosophy of science would be a poor reason for abandoning science. We have reason to believe that markets work—that capitalism delivers the goods, if not the Good—and it would be a mistake to allow philosophy to deflect us from the implications, just as it would be a mistake to allow philosophy to alter our views of infanticide.

A sensible pragmatism does not ignore theory. The mounting evidence that capitalism is more efficient than socialism gives us an additional reason for believing economic theory (not every application of it, to be sure). The theory in turn gives us greater confidence in the evidence. Theory and evidence are mutually supporting. From the perspective of economic theory, brain drain is not the mysterious disease that Barry supposes it to be; it is the rational response to leveling policies by those whose incomes are being leveled downward.

> * * *

My pragmatic judgment is, moreover, a qualified one. All societies depart from the precepts of wealth maximization. The unanswered question is how the conditions in these societies would change if the public sector could somehow be cut all the way down to the modest dimensions of the night watchman state that the precepts of wealth maximization seem to imply. That is a difficult counterfactual question (it seems that no society's leadership has both the will and the power to play the guinea pig in an experiment with full-fledged wealth maximization) * * *. Until it is answered, we should be cautious in pushing wealth maximization; incrementalism should be our watchword.

The fact that wealth maximization, pragmatically construed, is instrumental rather than foundational is not an objection to its use in guiding law and public policy. It may be the right principle for that purpose even though it is right only in virtue of ends that are not solely economic. At least it may be the right default principle, placing on the proponent of departures from wealth maximization the burden of demonstrating their desirability.

Even if my observations on comparative economic performance in the Third World and elsewhere are correct, do such matters belong in a book on jurisprudence? They do. The object of pragmatic analysis is to lead discussion away from issues semantic and metaphysical and toward issues factual and empirical. Jurisprudence is greatly in need of such a shift in direction. Jurisprudence needs to become more pragmatic.

COMMON LAW REVISITED

The case for using wealth maximization as a guiding principle in common law adjudication is particularly strong. The common law judge operates within a framework established by the Constitution, which, by virtue of a number of the amendments, not only rules out of bounds the ethically most questionable applications of wealth maximization but largely eliminates the problems of incompleteness and indeterminacy that result from the uncertain relationship between wealth maximization and the initial distribution of rights. That initial distribution is more or less a given for the common law judge. A related point is that such a judge operates in a domain where distributive or egalitarian considerations can play at best only a small role. The judge whose business is enforcing tort, contract, and property law lacks effective tools for bringing about an equitable distribution of wealth, even if he thinks he knows what such a distribution would be. He would be further handicapped in such an endeavor by the absence of consensus in our society on the nature of a just distribution, an absence that undermines the social acceptability of attempts to use the judicial office to achieve distributive goals. A sensible division of labor has the judge making rules and deciding cases in the areas regulated by the common law in such a way as to maximize the size of the social pie, and the legislature attending to the sizes of the slices.

The case is strongest in those common law areas where the relevant policies are admitted to be economic. Suppose the idea of an implied warranty of habitability—which entitles a tenant to sue his landlord if the premises fall below the standards of safety and comfort specified in the local housing code—is defended, as normally it is defended, on the ground that it is needed to protect tenants from deception and over reaching by landlords and will not lead to a reduction in the stock of housing available to poor people or to higher rentals than the poor are willing and able to pay. If research demonstrates that these assumptions are incorrect, the proponent, if fair-minded, will have to withdraw the proposal. In this example, in principle (for the necessary research is difficult to conduct), legal questions can be made determinate by the translation of a legal question into a social-scientific one in a setting of common ends, and therefore the valid Benthamite project of placing law on a more scientific basis can be advanced without injury to competing values.

If it could be shown or if it is conceded that common law decision making is indeed not an apt field for efforts to redistribute wealth, then it may be possible to ground wealth maximization (as used to guide such decision making) in a more powerful normative principle of economics, the Pareto principle. A transaction is Pareto superior when it makes at least one person better off and no one worse off. A simple contract approximates a Pareto-superior transaction. Neither party would sign the contract unless he thought he would be better off as a result. So, assuming adequate information (which does not mean assuming omniscience) and no adverse effects on third parties, the contract will be Pareto superior. At least this will be so on an ex ante basis, for as things turn out one of the parties (perhaps both) may be made worse off by the contract. This possibility is inevitable if there is uncertainty, and uncertainty is inevitable.

The ethical appeal of the Pareto principle is similar to that of unanimity. If everyone affected by a transaction is better off, how can the transaction be socially or ethically bad? There are answers to this question, yet a Pareto-superior transaction makes a powerful claim for ethical respect because it draws on intuitions that are fundamental to both utilitarianism and Kantian individualism-respect for preferences, and for persons, respectively. It may seem paradoxical to derive a norm of wealth maximization from the principle of Pareto superiority, when the hallmark of the latter is compensation of all potential losers (for remember that no one must be made worse off by the transaction if it is to be Pareto superior), while wealth maximization requires only that the winners' gains exceed the losers' losses. But if, as in the contract example, compensation is permitted to be ex ante, the paradox disappears.

The difference between the ex ante and ex post perspectives is fundamental, and failure to attend to it underlies much confused thinking about markets and transactional competence. Because many choices are made, unavoidably, under conditions of uncertainty, a fair number must turn out badly. Ex post, they are regarded as mistaken and engender regret, yet ex ante they may have been perfectly sensible. Suppose I have a choice between two jobs. One would pay me $50,000 every year with certainty the other either $500,000 a year (with a 90 percent probability) or nothing (with a 10 percent probability). The expected income in the first job is $50,000 and in the second $450,000. (Notice the use of Bayesian probability, mentioned in Chapter 5.) The second, however, involves uncertainty. If I am risk averse—and let us assume I am—I will value an uncertain expectation at less than its actual equivalent. Hence the second job will not really be worth $450,000 to me, and let us suppose it will be worth only one-third as much—$150,000. Still, that is more than $50,000, so I will take the second job. But I am unlucky, the 10 percent chance materializes, and my income is zero. I would be less (or more) than human if I did not regret my choice, rail against my fate, berate myself for having chosen stupidly. But in fact I made the right choice—and would make it again, given the same uncertainty as before.

Consider now the case where negligence is the more efficient principle, in a wealth-maximizing sense, than strict liability because when all the costs and benefits are toted up the negligence regime turns out to produce the greater excess of benefits over costs. If so, the sum of liability and accident insurance premiums will be lower in the negligence regime and all drivers will be better off ex ante, although ex post, of course, some may do better in a regime of strict liability. Actually, not all will be better off even ex ante. Some people who are more prone to be injured than to injure will be worse off, since negligence favors injurers relative to strict liability, and some who are more prone to injure than to be injured will be better off. The "losers" will lose little, though—a matter of slightly higher insurance premiums. And both the "winners" and the vast majority of drivers who are neither disproportionately likely to injure than to be injured nor vice versa will be better off. Complete unanimity will be unattainable, but near unanimity can be presumed and the few losers will hardly be degraded, their autonomy wrecked, or their rights destroyed by having to pay a few dollars a month more in automobile insurance premiums.

I am painting with slightly too rosy a palette. Some people will lack the knowledge, intelligence, and foresight to buy insurance (I am putting to one side the deliberate risk takers); some may not be able to afford adequate insurance; and insurance that pays off as generously as common law damages may not be available in the market. When a person becomes a victim of a serious accident in which the injurer is not at fault, it may spell a financial disaster not attributable to the choices or the deserts of the victim—a disaster that strict liability could have avoided. An alternative, of course, is social insurance—the famous safety net. If cases of catastrophic uninsured nonnegligent accidental injury are rare, social insurance may be a better solution than a strict liability system that would require compensation through the tort system in all accident cases.

The essential point is that the availability of insurance, private or social, is necessary to back wealth maximization with the ethical weight of the Pareto principle. Once it is so backed, however, wealth maximization provides an ethically adequate guide to common law decision making— indeed a superior guide to any other that has been suggested. And the adequacy of private and public insurance markets, on which this conclusion depends, is an empirical, a studiable, issue.

No doubt most judges (and lawyers) think that the guiding light for common law decision making should be either an intuitive sense of justice or reasonableness, or a casual utilitarianism. But these may all be the same thing, and if pressed such a judge would probably have to admit that what he called utilitarianism was what I am calling wealth maximization. Consider whether a thief should be permitted to defend himself at trial on the ground that he derived greater pleasure from the stolen item than the pain suffered by the owner. The answer obviously is no, but it is offered more confidently by the wealth maximizer than by the pure utilitarian. The former can point out that the thief is bypassing the market system of exchange and that the pleasure he derives from the good he has stolen has no social standing because his desire for the good is not backed by willingness to pay. These are separate points. The thief might be willing to pay if he had to—that is, he might value the good more than its owner—yet prefer theft because it is a cheaper way for him to acquire the good. So theft might be utility maximizing, although this is unlikely because a practice of theft would result in enormous, utility-reducing expenditures on protection of property.

Since utility is more difficult to estimate than wealth, a system of wealth maximization may seem a proxy for a utilitarian system, but it is more; its spirit is different. Wealth maximization is an ethic of productivity and social cooperation—to have a claim on society's goods and services you must be able to offer something that other people value—while utilitarianism is a hedonistic, unsocial ethic, as the last example showed. And an ethic of productivity and cooperation is more congruent with the values of the dominant groups in our society than the pure utilitarian ethic would be. Unfortunately, wealth maximization is not a pure ethic of productivity and cooperation, not only because even lawful efforts at maximizing wealth often make some other people worse off, but more fundamentally because luck plays a big role in the returns to market activities. What is worse, it is always possible to argue that the distribution of productivity among a population is itself the luck of the genetic draw, or of upbringing, or of where one happens to have been born, and that these forms of luck have no ethical charge. There are counterarguments, of course, but they are not decisive. So, once again, the foundations of an overarching principle for resolving legal disputes are rotten, and one is driven back to the pragmatic ramparts.

* * *

———

NOTES AND QUESTIONS

1. Increase of wealth through theft. Posner claims that society's wealth will not be increased by transferring a BMW to an individual who can not pay for it, even if that individual would enjoy the BMW more than anyone who could pay for it. However, is this why this is true? If, for example, the BMW is worth $50,000 to A and $60,000 to B, then transferring the BMW from A to B will increase society's wealth by $10,000, regardless of whether B pays for the BMW or not. If B pays nothing, then A will be $50,000 worse off from having his car stolen, but B will be $60,000 better off for having stolen the car, a net gain to society of $10,000. This transfer, in which society's wealth is maximized even though one party to the transfer is left worse off, is based on the idea of Kaldor–Hicks efficiency which states that a transaction is efficient if "the winners win more than the losers lose." Guido Calabresi, *The Pointlessness of Pareto: Carrying Coase Further*, 100 YALE L.J. 1211, 1221 (1991).

2. Place of poor in law and economics. In Posner's view, society's wealth is generated not through money but through individual preferences. *See* the stamp collection example discussed *supra* at note 2. However, Posner distinguishes law and economics from utilitarianism by stating that only those preferences backed by money should "count." Does this reliance on money, which admittedly does not increase society's wealth not have the effect of simply shutting the poor out of the law and economics equation? Is Posner explicitly calling on the law to treat the rich (who have the money to back up their preferences in the market) differently from the poor (who, under Posner's framework, can only have preferences for the necessities of life, and sometimes not even those)? Additionally, Posner states that slavery is inefficient and that Nazi use of slave labor only looks efficient when the welfare of the slaves is ignored. POSNER, *supra* at 375–76. But, since slave laborers in Nazi Germany had no money, do we not have to ignore their preferences? How can Posner's statement about paying attention to the welfare of slaves be squared with his assertion that "a desire not backed by ability to pay has no standing?"

3. Relationship between price and wealth. Under Posner's analysis, the price of a commodity actually has no relationship to the wealth generated by its exchange. To use his stamp collection example from page 105, if B paid $1,000,000 for A's stamp collection, then society would be better off because A would have gained $1,000,000 and lost $90.00, while B would have lost $1,000,000 and gained $100. In all cases, because B values the stamp collection more highly than A and money is fungible, society's wealth is maximized by the exchange, even if it is blatantly unfair to either

A or B. This is a direct result of the wealth maximizing properties of Kaldor–Hicks efficiency, discussed in Calabresi, *supra*.

4. Inefficiency of tort. Posner claims that the common law "establishes procedural rules for resolving disputes . . . as efficiently as possible." THE PROBLEMS OF JURISPRUDENCE, *supra* at 357. However, tort law is notoriously inefficient at resolving disputes and several alternative statutory systems such as no-fault insurance and worker's compensation might provide better methods of adjudication. In particular, no-fault auto insurance might return over 90 percent of premium dollars in the form of benefits, compared with only 50 percent for liability insurance. DAN B. DOBBS & PAUL T. HAYDEN, TORTS AND COMPENSATION: PERSONAL ACCOUNTABILITY AND SOCIAL RESPONSIBILITY FOR INJURY 898 (4th ed. 2001). How can such inefficiency in the tort system be squared with Posner's claims about the procedural benefits of the common law?

5. Effect of family privilege.

   a. Intergenerational persistence of wealth. Posner's claim that the initial distribution of wealth will dissipate within three generations is almost certainly incorrect. The study by Becker and Tomes on which he based his statements on has since been criticized for, among other things, estimating an individual's lifetime income from one year's income. Gary Solon, *Intergenerational Income Mobility in the United States*, 82 AM. ECON. REV. 393, 395 (1992); *see also* BHASHKAR MAZUMDER, FEDERAL RESERVE BANK OF CHICAGO, THE MIS-MEASUREMENT OF PERMANENT EARNINGS: NEW EVIDENCE FROM SOCIAL SECURITY EARNINGS DATA (2001), *available at* http://www.chicagofed.org/publications/workingpapers/papers/Wp2001–24.pdf (critiquing the use of short-term averages of earnings as a proxy for permanent earnings). Newer research indicates that the actual requirement for regression to the mean is between four and six generations. Alan B. Krueger, *The Apple Falls Close to the Tree, Even in the Land of Opportunity*, N.Y. TIMES, Nov. 14, 2002, at C2.

   b. Effect of legacy on meritocracy. In 1998, nine students from Groton boarding school in Massachusetts applied for admission to Stanford University; only one was admitted. Her SAT score was lower than seven of the eight other Groton grads who applied to Stanford and both her SAT scores and class rank were significantly lower than the class ranks and test scores of the vast majority of students admitted to Stanford. However, she had something other students' didn't have: a father who was chairman of Stanford's board and who had given $25,000,000 to Stanford in 1992. Does the policy of preferential admission of the children of alumnae and donors cast doubt on Posner's arguments about the rapid dissipation of the initial distribution of wealth? Even if a free market would lead to dissipation of the initial wealth distribution, do policies like legacy admissions serve to maintain the initial distribution of wealth, perhaps indefinitely? For more, see Daniel Gold-

> en, *College Ties: For Groton Grads, Academics Aren't Only Keys to Ivy Schools*, WALL ST. J., Apr. 25, 2003, at A1.

6. Morality in law and economics. Is law and economics amoral? Judge Posner notes that "it would be possible in a system unflinchingly dedicated to wealth maximization to come up with results that would be deeply, perhaps universally, offensive." Richard Posner, *Law and Economics is Moral, in* ADAM SMITH AND THE PHILOSOPHY OF LAW AND ECONOMICS 174 (Rubin Paul Malloy & Jerry Evensky eds., 1994). One such specific proposal is child trafficking which Posner believes

> is a form of transaction that would be wealth maximizing and would repair a serious imbalance in the supply and demand for babies for adoption. We have in this country an enormous production of illegitimate births and, on the other hand, a terrible shortage of babies for adoption. This is clearly a disequilibrium, and it results in part from refusing to allow an explicit trade in babies.

id. at 173.

Should the fact that law and economics can justify such schemes which even Posner admits are "deeply, perhaps universally, offensive" undermine the persuasive authority of law and economics?

7. Libertarianism and persuasive power of law and economics. In its statement of principles, the Libertarian party of the United States declares that:

> People should not be forced to sacrifice their lives and property for the benefit of others. They should be left free by government to deal with one another as free traders; and the resultant economic system, the only one compatible with the protection of individual rights, is the free market.

LIBERTARIAN PARTY, STATEMENT OF PRINCIPALS, *available at* http://www.lp.org/issues/platform_all.shtml#sop.

This economic position seems to mirror the law and economics of Judge Posner which recommends that the legal system act as much like the free market as possible when resolving disputes. Indeed, many of the thinkers most closely associated with law and economics, including Judge Posner himself, identify as libertarians. Given the conservative nature of libertarianism, does this association undermine claims of Law and Economics as a value-neutral method of jurisprudence?

8. Contradictions between libertarianism and utilitarianism. Ayn Rand, an influential libertarian thinker, stated:

> Parasites, moochers, looters, brutes and thugs can be of no value to a human being—nor can he gain any benefit from living in a society geared to their needs, demands and protection, a society that treats him as a sacrificial animal and penalizes him for his virtues in order to reward them for their vices, which means: a society based on the ethics of altruism.

AYN RAND, THE VIRTUE OF SELFISHNESS 32 (1964).

Such sentiments are very similar to the consequence of the money requirement in law and economics which results in the preferences of the destitute having zero weight. Thus, it seems that libertarianism and law and economics are a perfect match for one another. However, on closer examination, is there not a contradiction between libertarianism, which focuses on the primacy of the individual, and law and economics, which bases its normative appeal on the good of the community? Some libertarians, like Posner, support economic individualism only to the extent that it is the most effective way of providing for the well-being of everyone. Others, like Rand, seem to favor a devil take the hindmost approach to the marketplace. For more on this tension, see Gary Lawson, *Efficiency and Individualism*, 42 DUKE L.J. 53 (1992) (explaining difficulties relating to interpersonal comparisons of utility and addresses the tension between individualism and social wealth); Larry Alexander & Maimon Schwarzschild, *The Uncertain Relationship Between Libertarianism and Utilitarianism*, 19 QUINNIPIAC L. REV. 657 (2000) (tracing the development of the jurisprudence of Epstein and noting the contradiction between his early libertarian philosophy and his later utilitarian bent.); Heidi Li Feldman, *Law and Economics: Libertarianism with a Twist*, 94 MICH. L. REV. 1883 (1996) (questioning Epstein's attempt to justify a libertarian state through rule utilitarianism).

1. LAW AND ECONOMICS IN JUDICIAL REASONING

A. An Early Precursor

Learned Hand's opinion in *U.S. v. Carroll Towing Co.* is a classic of tort law. It is recognized for introducing an algebraic representation (negligence $=PL > B$) of the economic cost benefit test to replace the more vague and general common law standard of "reasonable care." In the arguments of the law and economics movement, the Hand formulation is taken as an expression of the goal of economic efficiency. The Hand formulation fits neatly into both the positive and normative claims of law and economics. The positive argument is that the common law has been constructed so as to pursue efficiency as its goal. This argument has been vigorously contested by torts scholars who have argued that many nineteenth-century tort cases are quite inconsistent with the efficiency interpretation. *See* Gary T. Schwartz, *The Character of Early American Tort Law*, 36 UCLA L. REV. 641 (1989); Gary T. Schwartz, *Tort Law and the Economy in Nineteenth–Century America: A Reinterpretation*, 90 YALE L.J. 1717 (1981).

Other scholars have disputed the normative claim, that tort law *should* pursue efficiency and wealth maximization as primary goals. *Carroll Towing Company*, is often used to support the normative position as well. The cost benefit approach to personal injury rules is designed to allow the party whose activities will inflict injury to continue to do so, as long as the burden of taking precaution exceeds the combined probability of injury multiplied by the gravity of injury should it occur. Legal philosopher Jules Coleman argued that corrective justice, rather than economic efficiency, explains the arc of tort common law developments. JULES COLEMAN, RISK AND WRONGS, 374–382 (1992).

Now, read this familiar case and decide whether it supports either the Posnerian positive or normative efficiency claims.

———

United States v. Carroll Towing Co.

159 F.2d 169 (2d Cir.1947).

■ L. HAND, Circuit Judge.

* * *

On June 20, 1943, the Conners Company chartered the barge, "Anna C." to the Pennsylvania Railroad Company at a stated hire per diem, by a charter of the kind usual in the Harbor, which included the services of a bargee, apparently limited to the hours 8 A.M. to 4 P.M. On January 2, 1944, the barge, which had lifted the cargo of flour, was made fast off the end of Pier 58 on the Manhattan side of the North River, whence she was later shifted to Pier 52. At some time not disclosed, five other barges were moored outside her, extending into the river; her lines to the pier were not then strengthened. At the end of the next pier north (called the Public Pier), lay four barges; and a line had been made fast from the outermost of these to the fourth barge of the tier hanging to Pier 52. The purpose of this line is not entirely apparent, and in any event it obstructed entrance into the slip between the two piers of barges. The Grace Line, which had chartered the tug, "Carroll," sent her down to the locus in quo to "drill" out one of the barges which lay at the end of the Public Pier; and in order to do so it was necessary to throw off the line between the two tiers. On board the "Carroll" at the time were not only her master, but a "harbormaster" employed by the Grace Line. Before throwing off the line between the two tiers, the "Carroll" nosed up against the outer barge of the tier lying off Pier 52, ran a line from her own stem to the middle bit of that barge, and kept working her engines "slow ahead" against the ebb tide which was making at that time. The captain of the "Carroll" put a deckhand and the "harbormaster" on the barges, told them to throw off the line which barred the entrance to the slip; but, before doing so, to make sure that the tier on Pier 52 was safely moored, as there was a strong northerly wind blowing down the river. The "harbormaster" and the deckhand went aboard the barges and readjusted all the fasts to their satisfaction, including those from the "Anna C." to the pier.

After doing so, they threw off the line between the two tiers and again boarded the "Carroll," which backed away from the outside barge, preparatory to "drilling" out the barge she was after in the tier off the Public Pier. She had only got about seventy-five feet away when the tier off Pier 52 broke adrift because the fasts from the "Anna C," either rendered, or carried away. The tide and wind carried down the six barges, still holding together, until the "Anna C" fetched up against a tanker, lying on the north side of the pier below—Pier 51—whose propeller broke a hole in her at or near her bottom. Shortly thereafter: i.e., at about 2:15 P.M., she careened, dumped her cargo of flour and sank. The tug, "Grace," owned by the Grace Line, and the "Carroll," came to the help of the flotilla after it broke loose; and, as both had syphon pumps on board, they could have kept the "Anna C" afloat, had they learned of her condition; but the bargee had left her on the evening before, and nobody was on board to observe that she was leaking. The Grace Line wishes to exonerate itself from all liability because the "harbormaster" was not authorized to pass on the sufficiency of the fasts of the "Anna C" which held the tier to Pier 52; the Carroll Company wishes to charge the Grace Line with the entire liability because the "harbormaster" was given an over-all authority. Both wish to charge the "Anna C" with a share of all her damages, or at least with so much as resulted from her sinking. The Pennsylvania Railroad Company also wishes to hold the barge liable. The Conners Company wishes the decrees to be affirmed.

The first question is whether the Grace Line should be held liable at all for any part of the damages. The answer depends first upon how far the "harbormaster's" authority went, for concededly he was an employee of some sort. Although the judge made no other finding of fact than that he was an "employee," in his second conclusion of law he held that the Grace Line was "responsible for his negligence." Since the facts on which he based this liability do not appear, we cannot give that weight to the conclusion which we should to a finding of fact; but it so happens that on cross-examination the "harbormaster" showed that he was authorized to pass on the sufficiency of the facts of the "Anna C." He said that it was part of his job to tie up barges; that when he came "to tie up a barge" he had "to go in and look at the barges that are inside the barge" he was "handling"; that in such cases "most of the time" he went in "to see that the lines to the inside barges are strong enough to hold these barges"; and that "if they are not" he "put out sufficient other lines as are necessary." That does not, however, determine the other question: i.e., whether, when the master of the "Carroll" told him and the deckhand to go aboard the tier and look at the fasts, preparatory to casting off the line between the tiers, the tug master meant the "harbormaster" to exercise a joint authority with the deckhand. As to this the judge in his tenth finding said: "The captain of the Carroll then put the deckhand of the tug and the harbor master aboard the boats at the end of Pier 52 to throw off the line between the two tiers of boats after first ascertaining if it would be safe to do so." Whatever doubts the testimony of the "harbormaster" might raise, this finding settles it for us that the master of the "Carroll" deputed the deckhand and the "harbormaster," jointly to pass upon the sufficiency of the "Anna C's" fasts to the pier. The case is stronger against the Grace Line than Rice v. The Marion A. C. Meseck, was against the tug there held liable, because the tug had only acted under the express orders of the "harbormaster." Here, although the relations were reversed, that makes no difference in principle; and the "harbormaster" was not instructed what he should do about the fast, but was allowed to use his own judgment. The fact that the deckhand shared in this decision, did not exonerate him, and there is no reason why both should not be held equally liable, as the judge held them.

We cannot, however, excuse the Conners Company for the bargee's failure to care for the barge, and we think that this prevents full recovery. * * * As we have said, the deckhand and the "harbormaster" jointly undertook to pass upon the "Anna C's" fasts to the pier; and even though we assume that the bargee was responsible for his fasts after the other barges were added outside, there is not the slightest ground for saying that the deckhand and the "harbormaster" would have paid any attention to any protest which he might have made, had he been there. We do not therefore attribute it as in any degree a fault of the "Anna C" that the flotilla broke adrift. Hence she may recover in full against the Carroll Company and the Grace Line for any injury she suffered from the contact with the tanker's propeller, which we shall speak of as the "collision damages." On the other hand, if the bargee had been on board, and had done his duty to his employer, he would have gone below at once, examined the injury, and called for help from the "Carroll" and the Grace Line tug. Moreover, it is clear that these tugs could have kept the barge afloat, until they had safely beached her, and saved her cargo. This would have avoided what we shall call the "sinking damages." Thus, if it was a failure in the Conner Company's proper care of its own barge, for the bargee to be absent, the company can recover only one third of the "sinking" damages from the Carroll Company and one third from the Grace Line. For this reason the question arises whether a barge owner is slack in the care of his barge if the bargee is absent.

* * *

It appears from the foregoing review that there is no general rule to determine when the absence of a bargee or other attendant will make the owner of the barge liable for injuries to other vessels if she breaks away from her moorings. However, in any cases where he would be so liable for injuries to others obviously he must reduce his damages proportionately, if the injury is to his own barge. It becomes apparent why there can be no such general rule, when we consider the grounds for such a liability. Since there are occasions when every vessel will break from her moorings, and since, if she does, she becomes a menace to those about her; the owner's duty, as in other similar situations, to provide against resulting injuries is a function of three variables: (1) The probability that she will break away; (2) the gravity of the resulting injury, if she does; (3) the burden of adequate precautions. Possibly it serves to bring this notion into relief to state it in algebraic terms: if the probability be called P; the injury, L; and the burden, B; liability depends upon whether B is less than L multiplied by P: i.e., whether $B < PL$. Applied to the situation at bar, the likelihood that a barge will break from her fasts and the damage she will do, vary with the place and time; for example, if a storm threatens, the danger is greater; so it is, if she is in a crowded harbor where moored barges are constantly being shifted about. On the other hand, the barge must not be the bargee's prison, even though he lives aboard; he must go ashore at times. We need not say whether, even in such crowded waters as New York Harbor a bargee must be aboard at night at all; it may be that the custom is otherwise, as Ward, J., supposed in "The Kathryn B. Guinan," supra; and that, if so, the situation is one where custom should control. We leave that question open; but we hold that it is not in all cases a sufficient answer to a bargee's absence without excuse, during working hours, that he has properly made fast his barge to a pier, when he leaves her. In the case at bar the bargee left at five o'clock in the afternoon of January 3rd, and the flotilla broke away at about two o'clock in the afternoon of the following day, twenty-one hours afterwards. The bargee had been away all the time, and we hold that his fabricated story was affirmative evidence that he had no excuse for his absence. At the locus in quo-especially during the short January days and in the full tide of war activity-barges were being constantly "drilled" in and out. Certainly it was not beyond reasonable expectation that, with the inevitable haste and bustle, the work might not be done with adequate care. In such circumstances we hold—and it is all that we do hold—that it was a fair requirement that the Conners Company should have a bargee aboard (unless he had some excuse for his absence), during the working hours of daylight.

* * *

B. Modern Cases

It is easy to forget that Professor Posner is also a judge whose views on law and economics extend beyond the realm of theory into the judicial arena. In this Seventh Circuit opinion, we see two University of Chicago law and economics scholars, Judges Easterbrook and Posner, carve out a separate rationale in a concurrence in a case in which they agree with the holding. Can you identify the tenets of law and economics legal theory upon which their opinion is based? What is the difference between the views of Judges Cudahy and Posner and Easterbrook? Do you agree with the Posner/Easterbrook analysis of the disparate impact of the rent control ordinance on the "poor" and the "middle class"?

In the second case in this section, Judge Posner is using law and economics reasoning to define the standard applicable under the common law as restated in the American Law Institute Restatement of the Law of Torts section 520 on strict liability for ultrahazardous activity liability. Like *Chicago Board of Realtors, Indiana Harbor* is strictly a question of law for the judge to decide what legal standard is applicable to resolve the dispute. In *Indiana Harbor*, Posner explores the relationship between two tort liability regimes: negligence, as we have discussed in *U.S. v. Carroll Towing Company* above, and strict liability. He decides that strict liability is inappropriate for the shipper/manufacturer of a highly flammable chemi-cal that leaked while in a Chicago railyard near occupied homes. One component of the Restatement test for whether an activity is abnormally dangerous or ultrahazardous is whether the activity is unusual or inappro-priate in the area in which the accident occurred. Consider Posner's opinion, that:

> ... It is no more realistic to propose to reroute the shipment of all hazardous materials around Chicago than it is to propose the reloca-tion of homes adjacent to the Blue Island switching yard to more distant suburbs. It may be less realistic. Brutal though it may seem to say it, *the inappropriate use* to which land *is* being put in the Blue Island yard and neighborhood may be, not the transportation of hazardous chemicals, but *residential living*. The analogy is to building your home between the runways at O'Hare.

Indiana Harbor Belt R.R. Co. v. American Cyanamid Co., 916 F.2d 1174, 1181 (7th Cir. 1990) (emphasis added).

————

Chicago Board of Realtors, Inc. v. City of Chicago

United States Court of Appeals, Seventh Circuit, 819 F.2d 732 (1987).

■ POSNER, CIRCUIT JUDGE, concurring.

[In 1986, the Chicago City Council passed a Residential Landlord and Tenant ordinance. It codified the "implied warrant of habitability," which is a doctrine of property law that requires landlords to provide a baseline of quality in the housing they let, a duty which is independent of the tenant's obligation to pay rent. The ordinance was upheld against a challenge by property owners who questioned its constitutionality. In his opinion for the court, Judge Cudahy ruled that the ordinance was sufficiently specific and reasonable under the government's police power.

In the concurrence that follows, Judge Posner, joined by Judge Easter-brook, laid out a policy analysis of the ordinance.]

We agree with Judge Cudahy's opinion as far as it goes, and we therefore join it. But in our view it does not go far enough. It makes the rejection of the appeal seem easier than it is, by refusing to acknowledge the strong case that can be made for the unreasonableness of the ordi-nance. It does not explain how the district judge's denial of a preliminary injunction against such an interference with contract rights and economic freedom can be affirmed without violating the contract clause and the due process clause of the Constitution. So we are led to write separately, and since this separate opinion commands the support of two members of this panel, it is also a majority opinion.

The new ordinance rewrites present and future leases of apartments in Chicago to give tenants more legal rights than they would have without the ordinance. It requires the payment of interest on security deposits; requires that those deposits be held in Illinois banks; allows (with some limitations) a tenant to withhold rent in an amount reflecting the cost to him of the landlord's violating a term in the lease; allows a tenant to make minor repairs and subtract the reasonable cost of the repair from his rent; forbids a landlord to charge a tenant more than $10 a month for late payment of rent (regardless of how much is owing); and creates a presumption (albeit rebuttable) that a landlord who seeks to evict a tenant after the tenant has exercised rights conferred by the ordinance is retaliating against the tenant for the exercise of those rights.

The stated purpose of the ordinance is to promote public health, safety, and welfare and the quality of housing in Chicago. It is unlikely that this is the real purpose, and it is not the likely effect. Forbidding landlords to charge interest at market rates on late payment of rent could hardly be thought calculated to improve the health, safety, and welfare of Chicagoans or to improve the quality of the housing stock. But it may have the opposite effect. The initial consequence of the rule will be to reduce the resources that landlords devote to improving the quality of housing, by making the provision of rental housing more costly. Landlords will try to offset the higher cost (in time value of money, less predictable cash flow, and, probably, higher rate of default) by raising rents. To the extent they succeed, tenants will be worse off, or at least no better off. Landlords will also screen applicants more carefully, because the cost of renting to a deadbeat will now be higher; so marginal tenants will find it harder to persuade landlords to rent to them.

Those who do find apartments but then are slow to pay will be subsidized by responsible tenants (some of them marginal too), who will be paying higher rents, assuming the landlord cannot determine in advance who is likely to pay rent on time. Insofar as these efforts to offset the ordinance fail, the cost of rental housing will be higher to landlords and therefore less will be supplied—more of the existing stock than would otherwise be the case will be converted to condominia and cooperatives and less rental housing will be built.

The provisions of the ordinance requiring that interest on security deposits be paid and that those deposits be kept in Illinois banks are as remote as the provision on late payment from any concern with the health or safety of Chicagoans, the quality of housing in Chicago, or the welfare of Chicago as a whole. Their only apparent rationale is to transfer wealth from landlords and out-of-state banks to tenants and local banks—making this an unedifying example of class legislation and economic protectionism rolled into one. However, to the extent the ordinance seeks to transfer wealth from landlords to tenants it could readily be undone by a rent increase; the ordinance puts no cap on rents. Cf. Coase, *The Problem of Social Cost*, 3 J. Law & Econ. 1 (1960).

The provisions that authorize rent withholding, whether directly or by subtracting repair costs, may seem more closely related to the stated objectives of the ordinance; but the relation is tenuous. The right to withhold rent is not limited to cases of hazardous or unhealthy conditions.

And any benefits in safer or healthier housing from exercise of the right are likely to be offset by the higher costs to landlords, resulting in higher rents and less rental housing.

The ordinance is not in the interest of poor people. As is frequently the case with legislation ostensibly designed to promote the welfare of the poor, the principal beneficiaries will be middle-class people. They will be people who buy rather than rent housing (the conversion of rental to owner housing will reduce the price of the latter by increasing its supply); people willing to pay a higher rental for better-quality housing; and (a largely overlapping group) more affluent tenants, who will become more attractive to landlords because such tenants are less likely to be late with the rent or to abuse the right of withholding rent—a right that is more attractive, the poorer the tenant. The losers from the ordinance will be some landlords, some out-of-state banks, the poorest class of tenants, and future tenants. * * *

A growing body of empirical literature deals with the effects of governmental regulation of the market for rental housing. The regulations that have been studied, such as rent control in New York City and Los Angeles, are not identical to the new Chicago ordinance, though some—regulations which require that rental housing be "habitable"—are close. The significance of this literature is not in proving that the Chicago ordinance is unsound, but in showing that the market for rental housing behaves as economic theory predicts: if price is artificially depressed, or the costs of landlords artificially increased, supply falls and many tenants, usually the poorer and the newer tenants, are hurt. * * * The single proposition in economics from which there is the least dissent among American economists is that "a ceiling on rents reduces the quantity and quality of housing available." * * *

Indiana Harbor Belt R.R. Co. v. American Cyanamid Co.

916 F.2d 1174 (7th Cir. 1990).

■ POSNER, CIRCUIT JUDGE.

American Cyanamid Company * * * is a major manufacturer of chemicals, including acrylonitrile, a chemical used in large quantities in making acrylic fibers, plastics, dyes, pharmaceutical chemicals, and other intermediate and final goods. On January 2, 1979, at its manufacturing plant in Louisiana, Cyanamid loaded 20,000 gallons of liquid acrylonitrile into a railroad tank car that it had leased from the North American Car Corporation. * * * [The car was brought to] the Blue Island railroad yard * * * in the Village of Riverdale, which is just south of Chicago and part of the Chicago metropolitan area.

* * * Several hours after it arrived, employees of the switching line noticed fluid gushing from the bottom outlet of the car. The lid on the

outlet was broken. After two hours, the line's supervisor of equipment was able to stop the leak by closing a shut-off valve controlled from the top of the car. No one was sure at the time just how much of the contents of the car had leaked, but it was feared that all 20,000 gallons had, and since acrylonitrile is flammable at a temperature of 30° Fahrenheit or above, highly toxic, and possibly carcinogenic (*Acrylonitrile*, 9 International Toxicity Update, no. 3, May–June 1989, at 2, 4), the local authorities ordered the homes near the yard evacuated. * * *

[The plaintiff] asserts that the transportation of acrylonitrile in bulk through the Chicago metropolitan area is an abnormally dangerous activity, for the consequences of which the shipper (Cyanamid) is strictly liable to the switching line, which bore the financial brunt of those consequences because of the decontamination measures that it was forced to take. * * *

The question whether the shipper of a hazardous chemical by rail should be strictly liable for the consequences of a spill or other accident to the shipment en route is a novel one in Illinois, despite the switching line's contention that the question has been answered in its favor by two decisions of the Illinois Appellate Court that the district judge cited in granting summary judgment. * * *

The parties agree that the question whether placing acrylonitrile in a rail shipment that will pass through a metropolitan area subjects the shipper to strict liability is, as recommended in Restatement (Second) of Torts § 520, comment *l* (1977), a question of law, so that we owe no particular deference to the conclusion of the district court. They also agree * * * that the Supreme Court of Illinois would treat as authoritative the provisions of the Restatement governing abnormally dangerous activities. The key provision is section 520, which sets forth six factors to be considered in deciding whether an activity is abnormally dangerous and the actor therefore strictly liable.

The roots of section 520 are in nineteenth-century cases. [In *Guille v. Swan*, 19 Johns. (N.Y.) 381 (1822) a] man took off in a hot-air balloon and landed, without intending to, in a vegetable garden in New York City. A crowd that had been anxiously watching his involuntary descent trampled the vegetables in their endeavor to rescue him when he landed. The owner of the garden sued the balloonist for the resulting damage, and won. Yet the balloonist had not been careless. In the then state of ballooning it was impossible to make a pinpoint landing.

Guille is a paradigmatic case for strict liability. (a) The risk (probability) of harm was great, and (b) the harm that would ensue if the risk materialized could be, although luckily was not, great (the balloonist could have crashed into the crowd rather than into the vegetables). The confluence of these two factors established the urgency of seeking to prevent such accidents. (c) Yet such accidents could not be prevented by the exercise of due care; the technology of care in ballooning was insufficiently developed. (d) The activity was not a matter of common usage, so there was no presumption that it was a highly valuable activity despite its unavoidable riskiness. (e) The activity was inappropriate to the place in which it took place—densely populated New York City. The risk of serious harm to others (other than the balloonist himself, that is) could have been reduced by shifting the activity to the sparsely inhabited areas that surrounded the city in those days. (f) Reinforcing (d), the value to the community of the activity of recreational ballooning did not appear to be great enough to offset its unavoidable risks.

* * * The baseline common law regime of tort liability is negligence. When it is a workable regime, because the hazards of an activity can be avoided by being careful (which is to say, nonnegligent), there is no need to switch to strict liability. Sometimes, however, a particular type of accident cannot be prevented by taking care but can be avoided, or its consequences minimized, by shifting the activity in which the accident occurs to another locale, where the risk or harm of an accident will be less ((e)), or by reducing the scale of the activity in order to minimize the number of accidents caused by it ((f)). * * * By making the actor strictly liable—by denying him in other words an excuse based on his inability to avoid accidents by being more careful—we give him an incentive, missing in a negligence regime, to experiment with methods of preventing accidents that involve not greater exertions of care, assumed to be futile, but instead relocating, changing, or reducing (perhaps to the vanishing point) the activity giving rise to the accident. * * * The greater the risk of an accident ((a)) and the costs of an accident if one occurs ((b)), the more we want the actor to consider the possibility of making accident-reducing activity changes; the stronger, therefore, is the case for strict liability. Finally, if an activity is extremely common ((d)), like driving an automobile, it is unlikely either that its hazards are perceived as great or that there is no technology of care available to minimize them; so the case for strict liability is weakened.

The largest class of cases in which strict liability has been imposed under the standard codified in the Second Restatement of Torts involves the use of dynamite and other explosives for demolition in residential or urban areas. * * *

Against this background we turn to the particulars of acrylonitrile. Acrylonitrile is one of a large number of chemicals that are hazardous in the sense of being flammable, toxic, or both; acrylonitrile is both, as are many others. * * *

[W]e can get little help from precedent, and might as well apply section 520 to the acrylonitrile problem from the ground up. To begin with, we have been given no reason * * * for believing that a negligence regime is not perfectly adequate to remedy and deter, at reasonable cost, the accidental spillage of acrylonitrile from rail cars * * * More important, although acrylonitrile is flammable even at relatively low temperatures, and toxic, it is not so corrosive or otherwise destructive that it will eat through or otherwise damage or weaken a tank car's valves although they are maintained with due (which essentially means, with average) care. No one suggests, therefore, that the leak in this case was caused by the *inherent* properties of acrylonitrile. It was caused by carelessness—whether that of the North American Car Corporation in failing to maintain or inspect the car properly, or that of Cyanamid in failing to maintain or inspect it, or that of the Missouri Pacific when it had custody of the car, or that of the switching line itself in failing to notice the ruptured lid, or some combination of these possible failures of care. Accidents that are due to a lack of care can be prevented by taking care; and when a lack of care can * * * be shown in court, such accidents are adequately deterred by the threat of liability for negligence.

It is true that the district court purported to find as a fact that there is an inevitable risk of derailment or other calamity in transporting "large quantities of anything." 662 F.Supp. at 642. This is not a finding of fact, but a truism: anything can happen. The question is, how likely is this type of accident if the actor uses due care? For all that appears from the record of the case or any other sources of information that we have found, if a tank car is carefully maintained the danger of a spill of acrylonitrile is negligible. If this is right, there is no compelling reason to move to a regime of strict liability, especially one that might embrace all other hazardous materials shipped by rail as well. This also means, however, that the amici curiae who have filed briefs in support of Cyanamid cry wolf in predicting "devastating" effects on the chemical industry if the district court's decision is affirmed. If the vast majority of chemical spills by railroads are preventable by due care, the imposition of strict liability should cause only a slight, not as they argue a substantial, rise in liability insurance rates, because the incremental liability should be slight. The amici have momentarily lost sight of the fact that the feasibility of avoiding accidents simply by being careful is an argument against strict liability.

* * *

The district judge and the plaintiff's lawyer make much of the fact that the spill occurred in a densely inhabited metropolitan area. Only 4,000 gallons spilled; what if all 20,000 had done so? Isn't the risk that this might happen even if everybody were careful sufficient to warrant giving the shipper an incentive to explore alternative routes? Strict liability would supply that incentive. But this argument overlooks the fact that, like other transportation networks, the railroad network is a hub-and-spoke system. And the hubs are in metropolitan areas. Chicago is one of the nation's largest railroad hubs. In 1983, the latest year for which we have figures, Chicago's railroad yards handled the third highest volume of hazardous-material shipments in the nation. East St. Louis, which is also in Illinois, handled the second highest volume. * * * With most hazardous chemicals (by volume of shipments) being at least as hazardous as acrylonitrile, it is unlikely—and certainly not demonstrated by the plaintiff—that they can be rerouted around all the metropolitan areas in the country, except at prohibitive cost. Even if it were feasible to reroute them one would hardly expect shippers, as distinct from carriers, to be the firms best situated to do the rerouting. * * *

The difference between shipper and carrier points to a deep flaw in the plaintiff's case. * * * [H]ere it is not the actors—that is, the transporters of acrylonitrile and other chemicals—but the manufacturers, who are sought to be held strictly liable. * * * A shipper can in the bill of lading designate the route of his shipment if he likes, 49 U.S.C. § 11710(a)(1), but is it realistic to suppose that shippers will become students of railroading in order to lay out the safest route by which to ship their goods? Anyway, rerouting is no panacea. Often it will increase the length of the journey, or compel the use of poorer track, or both. When this happens, the probability of an accident is increased, even if the consequences of an accident if one occurs are reduced; so the expected accident cost, being the product of the probability of an accident and the harm if the accident occurs, may rise. * * * It is easy to see how the accident in this case might have been prevented at reasonable cost by greater care on the part of those who handled the tank car of acrylonitrile. It is difficult to see how it might have been prevented at reasonable cost by a change in the activity of transporting the chemical. This is therefore not an apt case for strict liability.

We said earlier that Cyanamid, because of the role it played in the transportation of the acrylonitrile—leasing, and especially loading, and also it appears undertaking by contract with North American Car Corporation to maintain, the tank car in which the railroad carried Cyanamid's acrylonitrile to Riverdale—might be viewed as a special type of shipper (call it a "shipper-transporter"), rather than as a passive shipper. But neither the district judge nor the plaintiff's counsel has attempted to distinguish Cyanamid from an ordinary manufacturer of chemicals on this ground, and we consider it waived. Which is not to say that had it not been waived it would have changed the outcome of the case. The very fact that Cyanamid participated actively in the transportation of the acrylonitrile imposed upon it a duty of due care and by doing so brought into play a threat of negligence liability that, for all we know, may provide an adequate regime of accident control in the transportation of this particular chemical.

In emphasizing the flammability and toxicity of acrylonitrile rather than the hazards of transporting it, as in failing to distinguish between the active and the passive shipper, the plaintiff overlooks the fact that ultrahazardousness or abnormal dangerousness is, in the contemplation of the law at least, a property not of substances, but of activities: not of acrylonitrile, but of the transportation of acrylonitrile by rail through populated areas. * * * Natural gas is both flammable and poisonous, but the operation of a natural gas well is not an ultrahazardous activity. * * * Whatever the situation under products liability law (section 402A of the Restatement), the manufacturer of a product is not considered to be engaged in an abnormally dangerous activity merely because the product becomes dangerous when it is handled or used in some way after it leaves his premises, even if the danger is foreseeable. * * * The plaintiff does not suggest that Cyanamid should switch to making some less hazardous chemical that would substitute for acrylonitrile in the textiles and other goods in which acrylonitrile is used. Were this a feasible method of accident avoidance, there would be an argument for making manufacturers strictly liable for accidents that occur during the shipment of their products (how strong an argument we need not decide). Apparently it is not a feasible method.

The relevant activity is transportation, not manufacturing and shipping. This essential distinction the plaintiff ignores. But even if the [defendant] is treated as a transporter and not merely a shipper, [the plaintiff] has not shown that the transportation of acrylonitrile in bulk by rail through populated areas is so hazardous an activity, even when due care is exercised, that the law should seek to create—perhaps quixotically—incentives to relocate the activity to nonpopulated areas, or to reduce the scale of the activity, or to switch to transporting acrylonitrile by road rather than by rail. * * * It is no more realistic to propose to reroute the shipment of all hazardous materials around Chicago than it is to propose the relocation of homes adjacent to the Blue Island switching yard to more distant suburbs. It may be less realistic. Brutal though it may seem to say it, the inappropriate use to which land is being put in the Blue Island yard and neighborhood may be, not the transportation of hazardous chemicals, but residential living. The analogy is to building your home between the runways at O'Hare.

* * *

The case for strict liability has not been made. Not in this suit in any event. We need not speculate on the possibility of imposing strict liability on shippers of more hazardous materials, such as [bombs], any more than we need differentiate (given how the plaintiff has shaped its case) between active and passive shippers. We noted earlier that acrylonitrile is far from being the most hazardous among hazardous materials shipped by rail in highest volume. Or among materials shipped, period. * * *

The judgment is reversed (with no award of costs in this court) and the case remanded for further proceedings, consistent with this opinion, on the plaintiff's claim for negligence.

———

90–Day Hazmat Ban Is Passed; Measure Will Bar Shipments in D.C.

WASHINGTON POST, Feb. 2, 2005, at B01.

■ ERIC M. WEISS AND SPENCER S. HSU

The D.C. Council yesterday approved a temporary ban on shipments of hazardous materials through the nation's capital, becoming the first jurisdiction in the nation to halt such cargo in response to the threat of terrorism. Council members, who approved the 90–day emergency legislation 10 to 1, said reassurances from federal officials were not enough to safeguard residents. Mayor Anthony A. Williams (D) said through a spokesman that he will sign the bill as soon as possible.

Although the legislation does not require congressional review, the council is also considering a bill for a permanent ban, which would be subject to review by Congress.

The D.C. action sets up a potential legal battle with rail giant CSX Corp., which owns and operates the major freight line that runs through the city, passing within four blocks of the U.S. Capitol. Senior federal officials opposed the action, noting that they have pushed CSX to voluntarily reroute dangerous materials. But the officials have declined to make public exactly what safeguards are being taken.

"This is the nation's capital, and we need the toxics out," said council member Kathy Patterson (D–Ward 3), the measure's chief sponsor.

A CSX rail line in the District moves 8,500 chemical cars a year through the city, though only a fraction of those chemicals are toxic when inhaled. The legislation bans the most dangerous types of material, including certain classes of explosives, flammable gases and poisonous gases and materials. It also requires all rail and truck firms carrying other hazardous materials to obtain permits from the city's Transportation Department. Ban advocates say they expect about 5 to 10 percent of rail shipments to fall under the prohibition.

A chief U.S. Naval Research Laboratory scientist projected that in a worst-case scenario, a release of chlorine from a 90–ton tanker car during a Fourth of July celebration on the Mall could kill 100 people a second and 100,000 in 30 minutes.

Council member Carol Schwartz (R–At Large) cast the only vote against the measure. Marion Barry (D–Ward 8) was at a funeral and did not vote.

Schwartz, who is chairman of the council's public works committee, said CSX officials privately assured her that the company has been rerouting the most dangerous cargo since the Madrid train bombing in March. Therefore, she said, the legislation is unnecessary and would trigger a legal battle.

"We are better served by cooperating with the feds rather than by confronting them," Schwartz said.

The U.S. Department of Homeland Security and the U.S. Department of Transportation issued separate statements suggesting that federal and industry officials have taken safety measures that go beyond the D.C. ban but declined to say what material is being rerouted.

"We will also continue to explore other options that might be available with regards to routes for transporting hazardous materials through the national Capital region," the Department of Transportation said.

The Transportation Security Administration last year conducted a security study and hazardous material response plan for 42 miles of rail corridor in the Washington area. It is implementing a $7 million long-term plan for low-tech measures such as fencing and added patrols as well as more sophisticated safeguards, including intrusion detection systems and video surveillance.

The rail industry and transportation lawyers have closely watched the D.C. legislation. Although the consensus of legal analysts is that the law would not pass a federal court challenge, it feeds a national debate about the power of communities to control the flow of toxic shipments, spurred by the Sept. 11, 2001, terrorist attacks and by recent rail accidents.

Spokesman Robert T. Sullivan said CSX had grave reservations about the bill but stopped short of promising a legal challenge.

"We will review it again and make a determination about exactly what to do," Sullivan said. "But when you get into cities dictating how commodities can move, it frustrates interstate commerce."

Industry groups reiterated that shipping hazardous materials by rail is generally safer than using trucks. They noted that chemicals such as chlorine are used to purify half of the nation's water systems and predicted that a D.C. ban would set off a series of prohibitions that would cripple the U.S. rail system.

A coalition of environmental, labor and civic groups, mobilized to pass the ban, called it a landmark.

"This is probably the most important vote D.C. Council members will ever take," said Rick Hind, legislative director of the Greenpeace Toxics Campaign, which mounted a two-year lobbying effort to pass the ban with Friends of the Earth and the local Sierra Club.

Ultimately, whether the city will be allowed to implement a permanent ban may be decided by Congress, which has been reluctant to impose new restrictions on the rail industry since 2001, analysts said.

"Congress may feel compelled to say there are certain circumstances where we shouldn't let materials like this go close to particular sites," said James B. Reed, transportation program director for the National Council of State Legislatures. "But under existing law, it would probably be preempted under a court challenge." On May 3, 2005, the District of Columbia Court of Appeals ruled in favor of the railway, granting an injunction enforcing the HazMat ban. The court found that although under the Federal Rail Safety Act a city could adopt a more protective standard than the Federal Rule, the action must however be limited to eliminating "an essentially local safety or security hazard." In addition the local provision must not "burden interstate commerce." The court found that protecting the Capitol building was not an "essentially local hazard" and that the city ordinance burdened interstate commerce. The injunction sought by the CSX Railway Co. was therefore granted. CSX Transportation, Inc. v. Anthony Williams, 406 F.3d 667 (D.C.Cir.2005).

NOTES AND QUESTIONS

1. Role for judges in deciding economic common law cases. In *The Economic Approach to Law*, THE PROBLEMS OF JURISPRUDENCE 353–92 (1990), Posner argues that:

The judge whose business is enforcing tort, contract, and property law lacks effective tools for bringing about an equitable distribution of wealth, even if he thinks he knows what such a distribution would be. He would be further handicapped in such an endeavor by the absence of consensus in our society on the nature of a just distribution, an absence that undermines the social acceptability of attempts to use the judicial office to achieve distributive goals. *A sensible division of labor has the judge making rules and deciding cases in the areas regulated by the common law in such a way as to maximize the size of the social pie*, and the legislature attending to the sizes of the slices.

RICHARD A. POSNER, *The Economic Approach to Law, in* THE PROBLEMS OF JURISPRUDENCE 353, 388 (1990) (emphasis added).

Does this decision upholding the landlord tenant ordinance "increase the size of the social pie?"

2.   Importance of empirical support for economic assumptions. In the following excerpt *Posner* next takes up a hypothetical, not unlike the *Chicago Board of Realtors* case above, in which a common law judge is asked to rule on the validity of a landlord-tenant ordinance:

The case is strongest in those common law areas where the relevant policies are admitted to be economic. Suppose the idea of an implied warranty of habitability—which entitles a tenant to sue his landlord if the premises fall below the standards of safety and comfort specified in the local housing code—is defended, as normally it is defended, on the ground that it is needed to protect tenants from deception and over reaching by landlords and will not lead to a reduction in the stock of housing available to poor people or to higher rentals than the poor are willing and able to pay. If research demonstrates that these assumptions are incorrect, the proponent, if fair-minded, will have to withdraw the proposal.

Posner, *supra* at 388.

Posner argues that "[a] growing body of empirical literature deals with the effects of governmental regulation of the market for rental housing." *Chicago Bd. of Realtors*, 819 F.2d at 742. However, does Posner base his majority opinion in *Chicago Board of Realtors* on the existence of empirical research showing the characteristics of the rental housing market in Chicago in response to a housing ordinance with the features of the Chicago ordinance? Does comparing Chicago with New York and Los Angeles, where studies were done but the ordinances are different, meet a judge's burden of persuasion to develop the empirical basis for economic reasoning in an action seeking an injunction?

3.   Is economic reasoning precedent? What is the basis for Posner's agreement with the holding of the Cudahy opinion, if he disagrees with Cudahy's conclusion that the ordinance is Constitutional? Consider this passage from the Posner/Easterbrook concurrence:

It does not explain how the district judge's denial of a preliminary injunction against such an interference with contract rights and eco-

nomic freedom can be affirmed without violating the contract clause
and the due process clause of the Constitution. So we are led to write
separately.

id. at 741.

Since the ordinance was ultimately upheld, is the economic reasoning
just a rhetorical flourish in the case—an "advisory opinion"—not a common law precedent based upon economic reasoning, even though it is a
"majority opinion?"

Is the key piece of economic reasoning that might qualify as precedent
found in this passage of the Posner opinion?:

> Their only apparent rationale is to transfer wealth from landlords and
> out-of-state banks to tenants and local banks—making this an unedify-
> ing example of class legislation and economic protectionism rolled into
> one. However, to the extent the ordinance seeks to transfer wealth
> from landlords to tenants it could readily be undone by a rent increase;
> the ordinance puts no cap on rents. Cf. Coase, *The Problem of Social
> Cost*, 3 J. LAW & ECON. 1 (1960).

id. at 742.

Thus, Posner can support the legislation despite his misgivings about
its constitutionality or efficiency because landlords retain wealth-maximizing options to control the price of rental housing in response to any of the
intrusive features of the ordinance.

---

2. THE PROBLEM OF INCOMPATIBLE PROPERTY USES: THE ROLES FOR PRIVATE BARGAINING AND JUDICIAL INJUNCTIONS

A central tenet of the law and economics approach to legal reasoning
has been the Coase Theorem. The theorem asserts that when there are no
barriers to transactions between parties, the affected parties will bargain so
as to obtain an efficient allocation of resources regardless of how the legal
rule or decision would assign the rights initially. The major assumption of
this theorem is that there are no transactions costs. What happens when
transactions costs are substantial—does that change the assessment of
whether the bargaining has produced an efficient outcome?

We now examine the problem of how to structure the remedies for
property owners whose uses are incompatible. Where one owner's use
presents continuing invasions of the rights of others, either because of
pollution, noise, particulate discharge, or because the adjoining structure
blocks the light or view of the other property owner. The question in law
and economic terms is: for the efficient distribution of property value, does
it ultimately matter whether the court grants the injunction or not? Will
the parties seek to bargain in the shadow of the court decision, so that the
party who values the right the most will buy the right to engage in the
incompatible use from the party who values it less?

Boomer v. Atlantic Cement Co.

309 N.Y.S.2d 312, 257 N.E.2d 870 (N.Y. 1970).

■ BERGAN, JUDGE.

Defendant operates a large cement plant near Albany. These are actions for injunction and damages by neighboring land owners alleging injury to property from dirt, smoke and vibration emanating from the plant. A nuisance has been found after trial, temporary damages have been allowed; but an injunction has been denied.

The public concern with air pollution arising from many sources in industry and in transportation is currently accorded ever wider recognition accompanied by a growing sense of responsibility in State and Federal Governments to control it. Cement plants are obvious sources of air pollution in the neighborhoods where they operate.

But there is now before the court private litigation in which individual property owners have sought specific relief from a single plant operation. The threshold question raised by the division of view on this appeal is whether the court should resolve the litigation between the parties now before it as equitably as seems possible; or whether, seeking promotion of the general public welfare, it should channel private litigation into broad public objectives.

* * *

It seems apparent that the amelioration of air pollution will depend on technical research in great depth; on a carefully balanced consideration of the economic impact of close regulation; and of the actual effect on public health. It is likely to require massive public expenditure and to demand more than any local community can accomplish and to depend on regional and interstate controls.

A court should not try to do this on its own as a by-product of private litigation and it seems manifest that the judicial establishment is neither equipped in the limited nature of any judgment it can pronounce nor prepared to lay down and implement an effective policy for the elimination of air pollution. This is an area beyond the circumference of one private lawsuit. It is a direct responsibility for government and should not thus be undertaken as an incident to solving a dispute between property owners and a single cement plant—one of many—in the Hudson River valley.

The cement making operations of defendant have been found by the court at Special Term to have damaged the nearby properties of plaintiffs in these two actions. That court, as it has been noted, accordingly found defendant maintained a nuisance and this has been affirmed at the Appellate Division. The total damage to plaintiffs' properties is, however, relatively small in comparison with the value of defendant's operation and with the consequences of the injunction which plaintiffs seek.

The ground for the denial of injunction, notwithstanding the finding both that there is a nuisance and that plaintiffs have been damaged substantially, is the large disparity in economic consequences of the nuisance and of the injunction. This theory cannot, however, be sustained without overruling a doctrine which has been consistently reaffirmed in several leading cases in this court and which has never been disavowed here, namely that where a nuisance has been found and where there has been any substantial damage shown by the party complaining an injunction will be granted.

The rule in New York has been that such a nuisance will be enjoined although marked disparity be shown in economic consequence between the effect of the injunction and the effect of the nuisance.

* * *

Although the court at Special Term and the Appellate Division held that injunction should be denied, it was found that plaintiffs had been damaged in various specific amounts up to the time of the trial and damages to the respective plaintiffs were awarded for those amounts. The effect of this was, injunction having been denied, plaintiffs could maintain successive actions at law for damages thereafter as further damage was incurred.

The court at Special Term also found the amount of permanent damage attributable to each plaintiff, for the guidance of the parties in the event both sides stipulated to the payment and acceptance of such permanent damage as a settlement of all the controversies among the parties. The total of permanent damages to all plaintiffs thus found was $185,000. This basis of adjustment has not resulted in any stipulation by the parties.

This result at Special Term and at the Appellate Division is a departure from a rule that has become settled; but to follow the rule literally in these cases would be to close down the plant at once. This court is fully agreed to avoid that immediately drastic remedy; the difference in view is how best to avoid it.

One alternative is to grant the injunction but postpone its effect to a specified future date to give opportunity for technical advances to permit defendant to eliminate the nuisance; another is to grant the injunction conditioned on the payment of permanent damages to plaintiffs which would compensate them for the total economic loss to their property present and future caused by defendant's operations. For reasons which will be developed the court chooses the latter alternative.

If the injunction were to be granted unless within a short period—e.g., 18 months—the nuisance be abated by improved methods, there would be no assurance that any significant technical improvement would occur.

The parties could settle this private litigation at any time if defendant paid enough money and the imminent threat of closing the plant would build up the pressure on defendant. If there were no improved techniques found, there would inevitably be applications to the court at Special Term for extensions of time to perform on showing of good faith efforts to find such techniques.

Moreover, techniques to eliminate dust and other annoying by-products of cement making are unlikely to be developed by any research the defendant can undertake within any short period, but will depend on the total resources of the cement industry Nationwide and throughout the world. The problem is universal wherever cement is made.

* * *

On the other hand, to grant the injunction unless defendant pays plaintiffs such permanent damages as may be fixed by the court seems to do justice between the contending parties. All of the attributions of economic loss to the properties on which plaintiffs' complaints are based will have been redressed.

The nuisance complained of by these plaintiffs may have other public or private consequences, but these particular parties are the only ones who have sought remedies and the judgment proposed will fully redress them. The limitation of relief granted is a limitation only within the four corners of these actions and does not foreclose public health or other public agencies from seeking proper relief in a proper court.

It seems reasonable to think that the risk of being required to pay permanent damages to injured property owners by cement plant owners would itself be a reasonable effective spur to research for improved techniques to minimize nuisance.

* * *

JASEN, JUDGE (dissenting).

I agree with the majority that a reversal is required here, but I do not subscribe to the newly enunciated doctrine of assessment of permanent damages, in lieu of an injunction, where substantial property rights have been impaired by the creation of a nuisance.

It has long been the rule in this State, as the majority acknowledges, that a nuisance which results in substantial continuing damage to neighbors must be enjoined. * * * To now change the rule to permit the cement company to continue polluting the air indefinitely upon the payment of permanent damages is, in my opinion, compounding the magnitude of a very serious problem in our State and Nation today.

* * *

The harmful nature and widespread occurrence of air pollution have been extensively documented. Congressional hearings have revealed that air pollution causes substantial property damage, as well as being a contributing factor to a rising incidence of lung cancer, emphysema, bronchitis and asthma.

* * *

I see grave dangers in overruling our long-established rule of granting an injunction where a nuisance results in substantial continuing damage. In permitting the injunction to become inoperative upon the payment of permanent damages, the majority is, in effect, licensing a continuing wrong. It is the same as saying to the cement company, you may continue to do harm to your neighbors so long as you pay a fee for it. Furthermore, once such permanent damages are assessed and paid, the incentive to alleviate the wrong would be eliminated, thereby continuing air pollution of an area without abatement.

* * *

It is not my intention to cause the removal of the cement plant from the Albany area, but to recognize the urgency of the problem stemming from this stationary source of air pollution, and to allow the company a specified period of time to develop a means to alleviate this nuisance.

* * *

Fontainebleau Hotel Corp. v. Forty–Five Twenty–Five, Inc.

114 So.2d 357 (Fla. Dist. Ct. App. 1959).

PER CURIAM

This is an interlocutory appeal from an order temporarily enjoining the appellants from continuing with the construction of a fourteen-story addition to the Fontainebleau Hotel, owned and operated by the appellants. Appellee, plaintiff below, owns the Eden Roc Hotel, which was constructed in 1955, about a year after the Fontainebleau, and adjoins the Fontainebleau on the north. Both are luxury hotels, facing the Atlantic Ocean. The proposed addition to Fontainebleau is being constructed twenty feet from its north property line, 130 feet from the mean high water mark of the Atlantic Ocean, and 76 feet 8 inches from the ocean bulkhead line. The 14–story tower will extend 160 feet above grade in height and is 416 feet long from east to west. During the winter months, from around two o'clock in the afternoon for the remainder of the day, the shadow of the addition will extend over the cabana, swimming pool, and sunbathing areas of the Eden Roc, which are located in the southern portion of its property.

In this action, plaintiff-appellee sought to enjoin the defendants-appellants from proceeding with the construction of the addition to the Fontainebleau (it appears to have been roughly eight stories high at the time suit was filed), alleging that the construction would interfere with the light and air on the beach in front of the Eden Roc and cast a shadow of such size as to render the beach wholly unfitted for the use and enjoyment of its guests, to the irreparable injury of the plaintiff; further, that the construction of such addition on the north side of defendants' property, rather than the south side, was actuated by malice and ill will on the part of the defendants' president toward the plaintiff's president; and that the construction was in violation of a building ordinance requiring a 100–foot setback from the ocean. * * *

The defendants' answer denied the material allegations of the complaint, pleaded laches and estoppel by judgment.

The chancellor heard considerable testimony on the issues made by the complaint and the answer and, as noted, entered a temporary injunction restraining the defendants from continuing with the construction of the addition. His reason for so doing was stated by him, in a memorandum opinion, as follows:

> "In granting the temporary injunction in this case the Court wishes to make several things very clear. The ruling is not based on any alleged presumptive title nor prescriptive right of the plaintiff to light and air nor is it based on any deed restrictions nor recorded plats in the title of the plaintiff nor of the defendant nor of any plat of record. It is not based on any zoning ordinance nor on any provision of the building code of the City of Miami Beach nor on the decision of any court, nisi prius or appellate. It is based solely on the proposition that no one has a right to use his property to the injury of another. In this case it is clear from the evidence that the proposed use by the Fontainebleau will materially damage the Eden Roc. There is evidence indicating that the construction of the proposed annex by the Fontainebleau is malicious or deliberate for the purpose of injuring the Eden Roc, but it is scarcely sufficient, standing alone, to afford a basis for equitable relief."

This is indeed a novel application of the maxim *sic utere tuo ut alienum non laedas*. This maxim does not mean that one must never use his own property in such a way as to do any injury to his neighbor. * * * In Reaver v. Martin Theatres, 52 So.2d 682, under this maxim, it was stated that "it is well settled that a property owner may put his own property to any reasonable and lawful use, so long as he does not thereby deprive the adjoining landowner of any right of enjoyment of his property *which* is *recognized and protected by law, and so long as his use is not such a one as the law will pronounce a nuisance.*" [Emphasis supplied.]

No American decision has been cited, and independent research has revealed none, in which it has been held that—in the absence of some contractual or statutory obligation—a landowner has a legal right to the free flow of light and air across the adjoining land of his neighbor. Even at common law, the landowner had no legal right, in the absence of an easement or uninterrupted use and enjoyment for a period of 20 years, to unobstructed light and air from the adjoining land. * * *

There being, then, no legal right to the free flow of light and air from the adjoining land, it is universally held that where a structure serves a useful and beneficial purpose, it does not give rise to a cause of action, either for damages or for an injunction under the maxim *sic utere tuo ut alienum non laedas*, even though it causes injury to another by cutting off the light and air and interfering with the view that would otherwise be available over adjoining land in its natural state, regardless of the fact that the structure may have been erected partly for spite. * * *

We see no reason for departing from this universal rule. If, as contended on behalf of plaintiff, public policy demands that a landowner in the Miami Beach area refrain from constructing buildings on his premises that will cast a shadow on the adjoining premises, an amendment of its comprehensive planning and zoning ordinance, applicable to the public as a whole, is the means by which such purpose should be achieved. (No opinion is expressed here as to the validity of such an ordinance, if one should be enacted pursuant to the requirements of law. Cf. City of Miami Beach v. State ex rel. Fontainebleau Hotel Corp., Fla.App.1959, 108 So.2d 614, 619; certiorari denied, Fla.1959, 111 So.2d 437.) But to change the universal rule—and the custom followed in this state since its inception—that adjoining landowners have an equal right under the law to build to the line of their respective tracts and to such a height as is desired by them (in the absence, of course, of building restrictions or regulations) amounts, in our opinion, to judicial legislation. * * *

　　* * *

The record affirmatively shows that no statutory basis for the right sought to be enforced by plaintiff exists. The so-called Shadow Ordinance enacted by the City of Miami Beach at plaintiff's behest was held invalid in City of Miami Beach v. State ex rel. Fontainebleau Hotel Corp., supra. It also affirmatively appears that there is no possible basis for holding that plaintiff has an easement for light and air, either express or implied, across defendants' property, nor any prescriptive right thereto—even if it be assumed, arguendo, that the common-law right of prescription as to "ancient lights" is in effect in this state. And from what we have said heretofore in this opinion, it is perhaps superfluous to add that we have no desire to dissent from the unanimous holding in this country repudiating the English doctrine of ancient lights.

　　* * *

While the chancellor did not decide the question of whether the setback ordinance had been violated, it is our view that, even if there was such a violation, the plaintiff would have no cause of action against the defendants based on such violation. The application of simple mathematics to the sun studies filed in evidence by plaintiff in support of its claim demonstrates conclusively that to move the existing structure back some 23 feet from the ocean would make no appreciable difference in the problem which is the subject of this controversy. * * * The construction of the 14-story addition is proceeding under a permit issued by the city pursuant to the mandate of this court in City of Miami Beach v. State ex rel. Fontainebleau Hotel Corp., supra, which permit authorizes completion of the 14-story addition according to a plan showing a 76-foot setback from the ocean bulkhead line. Moreover, the plaintiff's objection to the distance of the structure from the ocean appears to have been made for the first time in the instant suit, which was filed almost a year after the beginning of the construction of the addition, at a time when it was roughly eight stories in height, representing the expenditure by defendants of several million dollars. In these circumstances, it is our view that the plaintiff has stated no cause of action for equitable relief based on the violation of the ordinance—assuming, arguendo, that there has been a violation.

Since it affirmatively appears that the plaintiff has not established a cause of action against the defendants by reason of the structure here in question, the order granting a temporary injunction should be and it is hereby reversed with directions to dismiss the complaint.

Reversed with directions.

————

NOTES AND QUESTIONS

1. Courts or markets. One of the key insights of the Coase Theorem is that the market solution to conflicts such as those present in *Boomer* and *Fontainebleu* will ultimately prevail over any judicial determination of the respective rights. This can be understood as a normative commentary on the respective benefits of these two mechanisms for resolving disputes. Is this preference for markets consistent with the libertarian commitments of the law and economics school in which government actors are given a marginal role in allocating economic resources?

2. The deal. Did the court impose a deal on the parties by granting an injunction against the cement plant, conditioned on the plant paying its neighbors the amount of permanent damages determined by the court? If the court imposed a deal, is this inconsistent with the Coase Theorem? Once the court granted the conditional injunction, what would you expect the bargaining between the parties to include?

3. No transactions costs. The Coase Theorem assumes that there are no transactions costs. Imagine a scenario in which there *are* transactions costs. What might the costs include if the court had granted the permanent injunction in *Boomer*, and the plant had chosen to initiate a series of Coasian bargains with the plaintiffs, seeking to buy the right to pollute?

Might the costs include legal expenses such as the cost of retaining lawyers and drafting documents to support the agreements allowing the plant to pollute? If these costs ever exceed the value to the defendant of the right to pollute, would you expect the Coasian bargain to take place?

What if one or more of the plaintiffs has a strong moral opposition to environmental and personal injury damage caused by pollution? This plaintiff becomes a "hold out" who flatly refuses to compromise. The hold out says, "I will not sell my lungs to you for any price." What might the impact of a hold out be on the hypothetical exchange? Does the principled hold out have monopoly power in this situation? Can the hold out demand that the plant be shut down? Does it matter what motivation the hold out has to oppose the bargain? Is a mercenary who simply wants to exact an exorbitant settlement in the same position as the environmentally conscious hold out? What if the hold out demands that the defendants set up a fund for free private education and health care for as long as it operates in that community? What would expect the limit of the defendants willingness to respond to these third party directed demands?

3. The Problem of Redistribution

An especially thorny and controversial issue for law and economics theory has been the problem of economic inequality and what its response should be, if any, to the social and economic effects of the vast wealth disparities among market participants. One answer, given by the neo-classical modern economists such as Friedman, Becker, and Coase has been to regard the distribution of wealth in society as the product of market competition, and therefore not a suitable target for government intervention. In this view, as forcefully argued by Milton Friedman in the essay "Created Equal," above, central government-controlled economic equality in the distribution of wealth is antithetical to liberty. Friedman observes:

> In some intellectual circles the desirability of equality of outcome has become an article of religious faith: everyone should finish the race at the same time. As the Dodo said in *Alice in Wonderland*, 'Everybody has won, and *all* must have prizes."
>
> * * *
>
> Everywhere in the world there are gross inequities of income and wealth. They offend most of us. Few can fail to be moved by the contrast between the luxury enjoyed by some and the grinding poverty suffered by others.
>
> In the past century a myth has grown up that free market capitalism— equality of opportunity as we have interpreted that term—increases such inequalities, that it is a system under which the rich exploit the poor.
>
> Nothing could be further from the truth.

Milton Friedman & Rose Friedman, *Created Equal, in* Free to Choose 134, 146 (1980).

Libertarian aims include expanding the zone of individual autonomy and reducing the zone of governmental control. For libertarians, economic inequality, though regrettable, is unavoidable—even natural.

More recently, modern law and economics scholars have tried to grapple directly with the problem of fairness, defined as some form of redistribution, and the conflict between fairness and efficiency, defined as maximizing market forces without government intervention. Law and economics scholars Kaplow and Shavell have framed these arguments in complex detail in *Fairness Versus Welfare*, 114 Harv. L. Rev. 961 (2001) in which they argue that legal policy should be concerned with the effect of such policies on the well-being of individuals, and not with notions of fairness that extend beyond the welfare of the individual to "notions of fairness, such as corrective justice and retributive justice...." *id.* at 1381.

In what follows, law and economics scholar Mitchell Polinsky, offers a more accessible account of the tension between efficiency and equity. What solution does Polinsky ultimately identify as the acceptable avenue for attending to questions of fairness, however defined? Does this position differ markedly from the libertarian position articulated by Friedman?

———

Efficiency and Equity

AN INTRODUCTION TO LAW AND ECONOMICS 7–10 (3d ed. 2003).

■ A. MITCHELL POLINSKY

For the purposes of this book, the term *efficiency* will refer to the relationship between the aggregate benefits of a situation and the aggregate costs of the situation; the term *equity* will refer to the distribution of income among individuals. In other words, efficiency corresponds to "the size of the pie," while equity has to do with how it is sliced. Economists traditionally concentrate on how to maximize the size of the pie, leaving to others—such as legislators—the decision how to divide it. The attractiveness of efficiency as a goal is that, under some circumstances described below, everyone can be made better off if society is organized in an efficient manner.

IS THERE A CONFLICT?

An important question is whether there is a conflict between the pursuit of efficiency and the pursuit of equity. If the pie can be sliced in any way desired, then clearly there is no conflict—with a bigger pie, everyone can get a bigger piece. If, however, in order to create a bigger pie, its division must be quite unequal, then, depending on what constitutes an equitable division of the pie, there may well be a conflict between efficiency and equity. It may be preferable to accept a smaller pie (less efficiency) in return for a fairer division (more equity).

The potential conflict between efficiency and equity can be illustrated by a simple example. Suppose that the government must decide whether to build a dam and that the Dean of Stanford Law School and I are the only two individuals affected by it. Currently, without the dam, the Dean has $65 and I have $35, so total income is $100. The dam would cost $30 to build, consisting of $30 worth of my labor but none of the Dean's. The dam would create benefits worth $40, all of which would go to the Dean because the only feasible location for building the dam happens to be on her property. Should the dam be built?

On efficiency grounds, the dam clearly should be built because it creates benefits of $40 and costs only $30, thereby creating net benefits of $10. But the equity effects need to be considered as well. Before the dam is built, the Dean has $65 and I have $35. After the dam is built, the Dean will have $105 (including the $40 benefit) and I will have $5 (after subtracting my $30 cost). Whether these distributional consequences are desirable depends on what constitutes a fair distribution of income. Suppose that the most equitable distribution of income involves the Dean receiving 60 percent of income and my receiving 40 percent. If the dam is not built, then the Dean should have $60 and I should have $40. If the dam is built and total income rises by $10, the Dean should have $66 and I should have $44.

But suppose, regardless of whether the dam is built, it is impossible to redistribute income between the two of us. Therefore, the choice is between the Dean's having $65 and my having $35 if the dam is not built, and the Dean's having $105 and my having $5 if the dam is built. Building the dam is more efficient but less equitable. How this conflict between efficiency and equity should be resolved depends on how important efficiency is relative to equity. If promoting equity is very important, it might be more desirable to sacrifice some efficiency for more equity by not building the dam (in other words, "damn" the Dean).

Alternatively, suppose it is possible to costlessly redistribute income between the Dean and me. Then, given the preferred distribution of income, if the dam is not built, $5 would be transferred from the Dean to me, so that she would end up with $60 and I would have $40. If the dam is built, $39 would be transferred from the Dean to me, so that she would end up with $66 and I would have $44. Clearly, since total income is distributed according to the percentages desired and we both are better off with the dam, the dam should be built. There is no conflict between efficiency and equity.

Note that, if it is possible to redistribute income at no cost, the dam should be built regardless of what constitutes an equitable distribution of income. If, for example, an egalitarian income distribution is desired, then without the dam the Dean and I each have $50 and with the dam we each could have $55. If, alternatively, equity required that everything should go to the Dean, the dam should be built because she then could have $110 rather than $100.

The dam example illustrates two important general observations. If income cannot be costlessly redistributed, there may be a conflict between efficiency and equity. Whether there is in fact a conflict depends on the specific distributional consequences of pursuing efficiency and on what constitutes an equitable distribution of income. However, if income can be costlessly redistributed, there is no conflict between efficiency and equity. This is true regardless of the specific distributional consequences of pursuing efficiency and regardless of what constitutes an equitable distribution of income. In other words, if income can be costlessly redistributed, it is always preferable to maximize the size of the pie because the pie can be sliced in any way desired.

Whether income can be costlessly distributed is discussed [below]. Although the conclusion there is that income redistribution is generally costly, it is argued nonetheless that efficiency should be the principal criterion for evaluating the legal system. This argument rests on the observations, explained at length [below], that it is often impossible to redistribute income through the choice of legal rules and that, even when it is possible, redistribution through the government's tax and transfer system may be cheaper and is likely to be more precise. In other words, the potential conflict between efficiency and equity when income redistribution is costly should be considered in the design of the government's tax and transfer system, but not generally in the choice of legal rules. Thus, *for purposes of discussing the legal system*, a reasonable simplifying assumption is that income can be costlessly redistributed.

* * *

Before proceeding, it is worth mentioning several other standard assumptions of economic analysis that will be made in analyzing the efficiency of legal rules. First, all benefits and costs can be measured in terms of a common denominator—dollars. It is important to emphasize that this assumption is made for expositional simplicity. It is not essential to economic analysis and does not exclude considerations that might be thought of as noneconomic—such as the protection of life and limb. Second, individuals themselves determine the dollar values to place on their benefits and costs. This is known as the assumption of *consumer sovereignty*. It is an acceptable assumption if one believes that individuals generally know what is best for themselves. Third, the values that individuals place on their benefits and costs are "stable" in the sense that these values are not affected by changes in public policy. For example, an individual's evaluation of the desirability of cleaner air is assumed not to depend on whether the legal system establishes a right to clean air. This is known as the assumption of *exogenous preferences*. Finally, individuals (and, when relevant, firms) maximize their benefits less their costs. This is known as the assumption of *utility maximization* (or, when firms are involved, profit maximization).

———

Efficiency and Equity Reconsidered

INTRODUCTION TO LAW AND ECONOMICS 147–156 (3d ed. 2003).

■ A.   MITCHELL POLINSKY

The discussion of efficiency and equity [above] showed that there is no conflict between these goals if income can be redistributed costlessly. In essence, this is because any inequity in the distribution of income caused by the pursuit of efficiency could be corrected at no cost. The assumption that redistribution was costless was made at the end of that chapter. We now consider this assumption, first with respect to the redistribution of income by means of government's tax and transfer system and then with respect to redistribution by the choice of legal rules.

REDISTRIBUTION BY TAXES AND TRANSFERS

In general, the redistribution of income by taxes and transfers is costly in the following sense. * * * If the price of a good equals its cost of production, only those individuals who value the good more than its cost will purchase it. This was seen to be efficient. The good used to illustrate this point * * * was a lawnmower that cost $100 to produce. Suppose that rich people are more likely to purchase lawnmowers than poor people because they are more likely to live in houses than in apartment buildings. Then, by imposing an excise tax on purchases of lawnmowers, the government would raise more tax revenue from the rich than from the poor. Assuming that the revenue is spent in a way that does not disproportionately favor the rich—say it benefits everyone equally—then the net effect of the tax would be to redistribute income from the rich to the poor. However, an inevitable byproduct of this redistribution is that the price of lawnmowers will be "distorted"—that is, the effective price of lawnmowers, including the tax, will exceed their cost of production. As a consequence, too few lawnmowers will be bought. For example, if the excise tax is $10 per lawnmower, then everyone who values a lawnmower more than the production cost of $100 but less than $110 will not purchase one, an inefficient outcome given that they value the good more than its cost of production. In general, to redistribute income by excise tax it is necessary to sacrifice some efficiency with respect to consumption decisions. This loss of efficiency is a cost of redistributing income.

The same kind of problem applies to income taxes, although not in as obvious a way. To see the distortion from income taxes, first note that leisure is commodity desired by consumers just like any other commodity. The "price" of an hour of leisure is the income forgone by not working that hour. For example, suppose that the wage rate in the widget industry is $25 per hour. * * * If widget workers did not have to pay income taxes, then they would give up $25 to consume an hour of leisure. Thus, those individuals who valued another hour of leisure more than $25 would "buy" more leisure by working an hour less. But suppose widget workers faced a 20 percent income tax. Then for every hour worked, they would pay $5 to the government and retain $20. The "price" of leisure therefore would fall to $20 per hour. Now individuals who value leisure more than $20 per hour will work less. Assuming that the $25 per hour wage reflects a worker's contribution to the value of the widgets produced, the income tax will cause an inefficient consumption decision regarding leisure. For example, a worker who values leisure at $21 per hour will work less even though the value of the worker's time in terms of widget production is $25 per hour. As in the case of the excise tax, the income tax distorts the price of some commodity—in this case leisure—and causes inefficient consumption decisions. Thus, it too imposes a cost in order to redistribute income.

Redistributing income by transfers rather than by taxes does not avoid the problem of distorting consumption decisions. For instance, suppose the government subsidizes the price of electricity for low-income individuals. Then the individuals who receive the subsidy will face an effective price of electricity that is below the cost of producing electricity and they therefore will buy too much of it relative to what is efficient. In general, any kind of tax or transfer used to redistribute income will distort the price of some commodity and will have this kind of efficiency cost.

CAN LEGAL RULES REDISTRIBUTE INCOME?

Given the cost of redistributing income by taxes and transfers, the question naturally arises whether the legal system should be used to redistribute income. That legal rules *can* be used to redistribute income was suggested by the discussion * * * of the distributional aspects of the Coase Theorem. In the example in that chapter—of the factory polluting the residents—recall, for example, that when there were no transaction costs, the choice between the right to pollute and the right to clean air redistributed income by the $150 cost of the smokescreen (the least-cost solution to the conflict). It does not follow from that discussion, however, that legal rules always affect the distribution of income. To understand why, it will be useful to distinguish between legal disputes in which the parties are in some kind of contractual relationship, including a market relationship, and disputes in which the parties are, in effect, "strangers" prior to the dispute. The breach of contract and products liability examples would be characterized as *contractual disputes*, while the nuisance law, automobile accident, and pollution control examples would be described as *disputes between strangers*. (The products liability example is one of the first type because the victim is a consumer; it would be of the second type if the victim were a third party). It will be shown below that legal rules often cannot redistribute income in contractual disputes, whereas legal rules always can redistribute income in disputes between strangers.

To see why it is frequently difficult, if not impossible, to use legal rules to redistribute income in contractual disputes, consider * * * breach of contract. * * * [T]he seller of widgets might want to breach the contract with the initial buyer if an offer from a third party materialized. Suppose it is desirable for equity reasons to redistribute income from the seller to the buyer. Giving the buyer the remedy of expectation damages makes the buyer as well off if the contract is breached as he would have been had it been performed. Giving the buyer the remedy of reliance damages or restitution damages makes the buyer worse off if the contract is breached. However, because the contract price the buyer and seller negotiate depends on what the remedy is, it does not follow that the buyer is better off with the expectation remedy. Clearly, the seller will demand a higher price and the buyer will be willing to pay more if the buyer receives a larger payment in the event of a breach, the buyer may not be any better off with the expectation remedy. In general, the parties will take any distributional effects of breach of contract remedies into account when they negotiate the contract price; thus, how the joint benefits of entering into the contract are shared between the parties depends primarily, if not exclusively, on their relative bargaining strengths, not on the remedies available to them.

An analogous observation can be made about the products liability application when the victim of the product accident is a consumer of the good. Suppose, for example, that it is desirable for equity reasons to redistribute income from producers to consumers. * * * [U]nder the rule of negligence, producers will meet the standard of care, and, therefore, consumers will bear their own losses. But under the rule of strict liability, consumers will be fully compensated for their losses (assuming, if there is a defense of contributory negligence, they meet the standard of care applicable to them). Consumers will not, however, be better off as a class under strict liability because, in a competitive long-run equilibrium, the price of the good will rise by an amount equal to the producers' expected liability. In general, then, whenever the parties to a dispute are in some kind of contractual or market relationship, it may be difficult, if not impossible, to use the legal system to redistribute income.

To see why legal rules can be used to redistribute income in disputes between strangers, reconsider the discussion of automobile accidents * * *. In the simplest version of the example employed there, the pedestrian's expected accident losses depended solely on whether the driver chose to drive slowly, moderately, or rapidly. Under a negligence rule, the pedestrian will bear her own losses because the driver will choose to meet the standard of care—to drive moderately—whereas under a strict liability rule the driver will have to compensate the pedestrian for her losses. Because there is no contractual or market relationship between the parties, there is no contract price or market price that can be adjusted when legal rules change. Thus, shifting from one liability rule to the other will redistribute income by the amount of the expected losses.

Analogous observations can be made with respect to the nuisance law and pollution control applications. In the nuisance example * * *—of a polluting factory next to a single resident—the choices of the entitlement and the remedy for protecting the entitlement have distributional consequences. Given the entitlement, a party generally is better off if it is protected by an injunctive remedy rather than by a damage remedy (with liability equal to actual damages); although the damage remedy guarantees that the protected party will be fully compensated for damages, the injunctive remedy gives that party the right to hold out for more. And under either remedy, a party obviously is better off if the entitlement is more favorable to the party.

In the pollution control example * * * in which the pollution victims are third parties, the distributional effects of choosing between strict liability and negligence to control the polluting industry are similar to those discussed in the automobile accident context. Under negligence, the victims bear their own losses, whereas under strict liability, the producers—and ultimately consumers of the product—bear these losses. In general then, whenever the parties to a dispute are "strangers"—that is, not in a contractual or market relationship—the choice of legal rules will have distributional consequences.

Should Legal Rules Be Used to Redistribute Income?

Having now identified the types of situations in which the legal system is most likely to have distributional effects, we can return to the question of whether legal rules *should* be used in these situations to promote distributional equity. The answer to this question depends in part on the "cost" of using legal rules to redistribute income relative to the cost of using taxes or transfers.

There are two senses in which redistribution through the legal system may be costly. The first relates to the administration costs of using the legal system. Suppose, for example, that the consumers of the goods produced by some polluting industry are high-income individuals, while the victims living near the polluting factories are low-income individuals. By making the firms strictly liable for the pollution damages, income will be transferred from rich people to poor people. A similar transfer could be accomplished by taxing high-income individuals and transferring the proceeds to low-income persons. The tax and transfer system is a *much* less expensive way to redistribute income than is the legal system. Roughly speaking, to transfer a dollar through a private lawsuit from a defendant to a plaintiff costs on average about a dollar in administrative costs of both parties and costs of the court system. To transfer a dollar through the tax and transfer system costs only a fraction of this amount.

Legal redistribution also may be costly in a second sense: Inefficient rules may have to be chosen in order to achieve the desired result. For example, * * * of driver-pedestrian accidents in which both parties are risk averse and the pedestrian cannot affect expected losses. It was seen that negligence is efficient because the driver will meet the standard of care and the pedestrian will be able to buy a first-party accident insurance policy with full coverage; strict liability may not be efficient because of the moral hazard problem (which could result in the driver not being able to buy a liability insurance policy with full coverage and/or in the driver not taking appropriate care). But if drivers are wealthier than pedestrians, strict liability may be preferable to negligence on equity grounds. The loss of efficiency from using strict liability rather than negligence is a "cost" of redistributing income from drivers as a class to pedestrians as a class.

There may be instances in which redistribution through the legal system is not costly in this sense. For example, suppose that in some types of nuisance disputes the parties can be expected to bargain in a cooperative way. Then, * * * any entitlement will lead to the efficient outcome, whether protected by an injunctive remedy or a damage remedy. Thus, the choices of the entitlement and the remedy can be used to redistribute income without causing an inefficient resolution of the nuisance dispute. In general, however, not all legal rules will be efficient, so it often may be necessary to choose an inefficient legal rule in order to promote equity.

An additional consideration in deciding whether to use the legal system to promote distributional equity is the "precision" of legal redistribution. Legal rules will not be able to redistribute income systematically unless the status of the parties in a certain type of dispute corresponds closely to the groups between which redistribution is desired. For example, in automobile accidents involving drivers and pedestrians, there probably is not a close correspondence between the income of a party and whether that party is a driver or a pedestrian. It may be that higher income persons are more likely to be drivers than pedestrians, but certainly there are many low-income drivers and high-income pedestrians. Thus, liability rules regarding driver-pedestrian accidents are not very precise instruments for accomplishing income redistribution. In nuisance and pollution control disputes, there may be a closer correspondence between the income of a party and whether that party is victim or an injurer. The purchasers of the goods produced by some polluting industry may be mainly higher-income people, while the victims of the pollution may be primarily lower-income persons. Thus, in some kinds of disputes, the choice of a legal rule might contribute towards the implementation of distributional goals.

Even where there is a close correspondence between the status of the parties in a certain kind of dispute and the groups between which redistribution is desired, legal rules still might not be able to achieve redistribution as systematically as an income tax system. This is because redistribution through the legal system only may occur when a dispute arises, and not all members of a given income class will be involved in a dispute. For instance, even if the goods produced by a polluting industry were consumed exclusively by rich persons and the pollution victims were all poor people, not every rich person necessarily purchases this commodity and not every poor person lives near a factory in this industry. Thus, the legal rule used to control the pollution dispute will, as best, redistribute income from a subset of one income class to a subset of another. In sum, the legal system is not nearly as precise as the tax system in redistributing income.

The initial discussion of efficiency and equity * * * showed that, if it is costly to redistribute income, there may be a tradeoff between efficiency and equity. In other words, it may be desirable to choose an inefficient policy in order to promote the desired distribution of income. [This discussion] has shown that income redistribution generally *is* costly, whether it is accomplished by the tax and transfer system or by the legal system. Nonetheless, several reasons have been suggested * * * why the choice of legal rules should be based primarily on efficiency considerations. In some circumstances—contractual dispute—legal rule often will have little or no effect on the distribution of income. In situations in which the legal system does have distributional consequences—disputes between strangers—legal rules still should be based primarily on efficiency considerations because legal rules generally are more costly than taxes and transfers as means of redistributing income and less precise. Thus, the justification for the assumption made * * * that income could be redistributed without cost * * * is not only that this simplified the subsequent exposition by allowing us to focus on the efficiency analysis of legal rules. As this chapter has shown, the justification also is that, even when the cost of redistributing income is taken into account, there are reasons why the efficiency analysis should be of principal importance.

4. Politics

Public Choice and the Future of Public-Choice-Influenced Legal Scholarship

50 Vand. L. Rev. 647 (1997) (reviewing Maxwell L. Stearns, Public Choice and Public Law: Readings and Commentary (1997)).

■ David A. Skeel, Jr.

* * *

At a general level, the distinctive characteristic of public choice is its "use of economic tools to deal with the traditional problems of political science." Perhaps the most basic of these tools is the assumption of individual rationality. In contrast to much traditional political analysis, public choice assumes that all of the relevant players tend to act in their own self-interest, and explores the implications of self-interest for the legislative and other institutional decisionmaking processes.

The public choice literature thus can, and in my view should, be seen as including any analysis that incorporates or explicitly challenges the self-interestedness premise in addressing institutional decisionmaking processes. The literature that fits within this definition consists of two principal branches. The first can be described as interest group analysis, and the second is social choice.

The central insight of interest group analysis is that concentrated interest groups often benefit at the expense of more widely scattered groups, even if the diffuse group has much more at stake overall. Although this insight is now so familiar that it seems obvious to many, it was far from obvious when it emerged in the public choice literature. Whereas many theorists assumed that interest group competition tends to produce public-regarding legislation, public choice suggested that self-interested behavior by each of the relevant actors could lead to strikingly different outcomes.

The reasoning is as follows. For a self-interested voter, taking the time to inform herself and to vote intelligently is an unattractive proposition, since the likelihood that her vote will affect the outcome of an election is minuscule. Although voters as a group would benefit if each took the time to vote intelligently, ordinary voters simply do not have an incentive to do so. By contrast, because the members of a concentrated interest group have more at stake with respect to the issues that concern them, they tend both to inform themselves and to participate actively in the political process.

The interest group branch of public choice suggests that the distinction between ordinary voters and concentrated interest groups is not lost on legislators. Self-interested legislators are likely to focus principally on getting reelected, since legislators who fail to do so quickly become ex-legislators. Because interest groups are better informed than ordinary voters, and serve as an important source of political funding, legislators have a tremendous incentive to be responsive to interest group perspectives.

Like the interest group literature itself, I have focused principally on the advantages interest groups have in the legislative process. But this analysis, and in particular its self-interest assumption, also has generated important insights into related areas such as the incentives of agency bureaucrats and * * * the nature of the judicial process.

The second branch of public choice is social choice. At the heart of much of the recent social choice literature is Kenneth Arrow's famous impossibility theorem. Arrow's Theorem demonstrates that it is impossible to design a system that will always both aggregate the preferences of a group of decisionmakers in a rational fashion, and satisfy a short list of fairness requirements. If there is a particular kind of inconsistency, referred to as multipeakedness, across the preferences of a group of decisionmakers (each of whose individual preferences is wholly consistent), the voting procedure will cycle endlessly among the possible outcomes unless one or more of the fairness requirements is relaxed.

To see this, assume that Voter 1 prefers outcome A to B, and B to C; Voter 2's preferences are B, C, A; and Voter 3's ranking is C, A, B. In a pairwise vote between A and B, outcome A would prevail (with Voter 1 and Voter 3 voting for A). Outcome C would prevail over A in a similar vote (on the strength of votes from Voter 2 and Voter 3). But, in a third vote between C and B, B would prevail, despite the fact that it loses to outcome A, which C defeats. On closer consideration, it quickly becomes clear that none of the three options can defeat the other two in pairwise voting, and that any voting outcome is thus unstable. This cycling occurs because the preferences are "multipeaked." Preferences are multipeaked only if the decisionmakers not only disagree about which choice is best (or second best or worst), but also disagree about the relationship among the choices. If their preferences were arrayed from smallest to largest, or conservative to liberal, the problem would disappear. Cycling would not occur even if the decisionmakers each chose a different first choice.

Much of the recent literature has focused on the trade-off posed by the possibility of multipeaked preferences. A voting institution that adheres to Arrow's fairness criteria will cycle endlessly in these circumstances, but relaxing one or more of the requirements introduces the possibility of path dependence and path manipulation. To give a familiar example, Congress's prohibition against reconsidering an outcome that has been defeated in an earlier vote counteracts the risk of cycling. In the illustration above, for instance, outcome C would prevail under this rule, since outcome B could not be reintroduced after it lost to outcome A. Yet the cost of eliminating cycling is that the order of voting determines the outcome-the result is path dependent. The rule, therefore, vests significant power in anyone who has the ability to manipulate the order of the voting.

The discussion thus far suggests a rough rule of thumb for distinguishing between the interest group and social choice branches of public choice. Many of the important contributions of interest group theory stem from the insight that not all voters are equal due to the organizational advantages enjoyed by members of a concentrated group. Social choice, on the other hand, explores the dynamics of voting under conditions where voters are at least initially assumed to have an equal voice. In fact, the literature on cycling shows that voting pathologies can emerge even if each voter participates fully.

Despite this distinction, it is important to emphasize that the line between interest group theory and social choice is a rough one, and it quickly blurs in both directions. The two branches of public choice analysis share a common history, and commentators often employ both in their efforts to understand a particular voting institution. Consider the extensive literature on logrolling. From a social choice perspective, logrolling may act as a solution to cycling concerns, since legislators avoid cycling by trading votes on matters they are relatively indifferent about for votes on matters about which they care deeply. Interest group theory raises questions as to whether the "solution" is an attractive one, however, given that logrolling could enhance interest groups' ability to obtain private benefits from the legislative process.

An additional source of confusion is that the term public choice is used in two ways. I have characterized public choice as a general term comprising both interest group theory and social choice, and many commentators do likewise. But other commentators use public choice more narrowly, as a synonym for interest group analysis. When a commentator indicates that she will tell a "public choice story" about a given issue, it is often this narrower definition that she has in mind.

B. Related Concepts

Having explored in some detail what we mean when we talk about public choice, we still must consider how several related modes of analysis interact with public choice. Two of the most important are game theory and collective action theory. I will focus on these, then conclude with a brief description of the emerging literature employing "positive political theory."

Game theory refers to the economic analysis of strategic interaction—the choices that individuals make when they recognize the outcome depends in part on the decisions made by others. The "game" in game theory, then, is the interaction between two or more independent decisionmakers, each of whom attempts to account for the actions of the others. Game theoretic analysis formalizes this interaction by precisely specifying the players involved, the information available to each at any given point, and the different outcomes that would result from each set of "moves" the players might make.

The most familiar game theory insight is the prisoners' dilemma. In the prisoners' dilemma, two prisoners who have committed a crime and cannot communicate with one another must each decide whether to confess. Although the prisoners would be better off if neither confessed than if both confessed, the best outcome results from confessing when the other prisoner refuses to do so. As a result, both have an incentive to confess and the game often results in the least desireable outcome—two confessions.

The irony of the prisoners' dilemma—that the actions of individuals behaving in their own best interests can produce outcomes that are undesirable for all of them—has led to valuable insights in a wide range of areas. One of the most important is in public choice. Recall the interest group insight that diffuse groups tend to fare poorly in the legislative process. The principal reason for this is that while the members of a diffuse group might be better off if each participated in an informed fashion, each member has little incentive to do so. In other words, diffuse groups tend to face a debilitating prisoners' dilemma problem. Interest group analysis thus depends in important respects on a concept taken straight from game theory.

In contrast, the central insight in social choice theory, Arrow's Theorem, does not involve game theory in its initial formulation. The principled voting requirement precludes voters from considering the preferences and likely actions of other voters, thus ruling game theoretic interactions out of bounds. Yet once we move beyond the initial formulation—as we must, given that *no* institution can both satisfy the fairness requirements and guarantee rational outcomes—strategic interaction quickly reenters the picture. The agenda control and strategic voting concerns that have animated much of the social choice literature are classic examples of strategic interaction, and are particularly amenable to game theoretic analysis.

As should be clear by now, game theory is a useful tool in any context where we wish to consider the nature of strategic interaction between two or more decisionmakers. Because strategic interaction is integral to much of public choice, it is not surprising that we find so much game theoretic analysis in the public choice literature. The second term we need to fit into our picture is collective action—not to be confused with the misleadingly similar term "collective choice." As with game theory, we can see the relevance of collective action theory most easily by focusing on the interest group branch of public choice. Recall that the prisoners' dilemma from game theory is a useful tool for explaining the barriers that often prevent large groups from acting in concert. The collective action literature starts from precisely the same insight, that free riding prevents many groups from acting collectively.

Collective action theorists take the obstacles to collective action as their starting point, and ask how it is that some groups do succeed in acting collectively. These theorists have identified two factors that seem particularly important to successful group action. First, smaller groups have a significant advantage as compared to large ones, both because members may have a larger individual stake in successful action and because members can more easily police one another against free riding. Second, groups that have access to "selective incentives"—that is, mechanisms for rewarding or punishing members for contributing or failing to contribute to the collective action—are more likely to prove effective.

A moment's reflection will make clear that collective action analysis is central to the distinction between concentrated and diffuse groups in interest group analysis, and to any effort to predict which groups will prove successful in legislative and other decisionmaking processes. The collective action literature is less immediately relevant to social choice, since social choice tends to focus on the voting decisions made by isolated individuals within a decisionmaking process. Yet as soon as we move beyond stylized assumptions about the voting process, and integrate interest group questions such as why some voters vote and others don't into our social choice analysis, collective action concerns come back into play.

In attempting to relate game theory and collective action to public choice, it is tempting to suggest that the former apply broadly to aspects of legislative, market, and judicial behavior, whereas public choice is uniquely concerned with the legislative process. Yet this would be a mistake. Although public choice has focused primarily on legislative behavior, it increasingly has been employed to explore courts and markets as well * * *.

Before we turn to the applications of public choice, however, we should briefly consider one final term: positive political theory. Positive political theory uses game theory to explore relationships among decisionmaking institutions such as Congress, administrative agencies, and the courts. It differs from public choice in that it focuses on the strategic interactions among political decisionmaking institutions, and on institutional structures, rather than on the individuals who comprise the institutions. Positive political theory does take account of the problems of multi-individual decisionmaking that preoccupy collective action theory and the two branches of public choice. But it does so indirectly. Positive political theory incorporates these considerations into its characterization of an institution. It then takes intra-institution concerns as a given, in a sense, in order to emphasizes strategic interactions between and among institutions.

In short, this new perspective makes direct use of game theoretic analysis; though it has a different focus than either branch of public choice, it is closely connected to both.

III.   PUBLIC CHOICE AND THE LEGAL LITERATURE

As is usually the case when legal academics draw on nonlegal insights, public choice did not enter legal discourse until well after it had captured the attention of economists and political scientists. It was not until the mid–1970s that legal scholars first explored the implications of public choice, even though many of the seminal insights of both interest group theory and social choice had been in place for over a decade. Since then, public choice has taken the legal literature by storm. In this Part, I will briefly describe the diffusion of public choice into the legal literature. I then will speculate as to the future of public-choice-influenced legal scholarship.

A.   *Law and Public Choice: The First Wave*

The first wave of public choice inquiry in the legal literature can be seen as a classic illustration of legal academics sticking to their area of comparative advantage. Whereas much of the extant economic and political science public choice literature focused on the legislative process, legal academics asked what the implications of public choice are for the legal system.

The first wave took as its starting point the social choice and interest group insights that the legislative process cannot guaranty outcomes that are both fair and rational, and that concentrated interest groups will exert disproportionate influence over the process. The obvious issue raised by the prospect of legislative dysfunction was the proper role for judges to play. How should public choice affect our view of the nature of statutory interpretation and, more generally, of judicial review?

Three commentators prompted a vigorous debate on this question by offering distinct visions of statutory interpretation in a post-public choice world. The starkest proposal was that of Judge Frank Easterbrook. Judge Easterbrook suggested that courts not only should recognize the role of interest groups in the political process, but that they also should enforce any interest group bargains reflected in the legislative product. Rather than trying to "correct" the process in some way, judges should interpret statutes in accordance with the realities of how they were enacted. Judge Richard Posner initially staked out a position similar to Judge Easterbrook's, though he subsequently shifted his focus to a perspective less obviously tied to the insights of public choice.

Professor Jonathan Macey responded to Judge Easterbrook and to Judge Posner's initial position by proposing a more independent, and more aggressive, role for courts. While agreeing that courts should enforce clear interest group bargains, Professor Macey contended that courts should refuse to enforce "implicit" bargains-that is, interest group deals that legislators disguise by defending the provision in question in public-regarding terms. Professor Macey contended that by refusing to enforce implicit bargains, courts could raise the costs to interest groups of obtaining private interest legislation, and in doing so moderate the influence of interest groups.

In addition to their political conservatism, each of the commentators shared a view that the pessimistic insights of public choice do, in fact, accurately describe the legislative process. Not surprisingly, this perspective prompted a backlash of sorts. Most prominently, Daniel Farber and Philip Frickey acknowledged that the public choice account of legislation is accurate in important respects, but contended that many of the dire conclusions of public choice are overstated. In their view, judges should simply police the political process for obvious defects, and should otherwise let the political process run its course.

Although generally sympathetic to public choice, William Eskridge shared some of Professors Farber and Frickey's concerns as to its limitations. Professor Eskridge's model of statutory interpretation called for judges to show solicitude for underrepresented minorities when they exercise judicial review. Cass Sunstein has used public choice insights in somewhat similar fashion, and has argued that courts should interpret statutes and the Constitution so as to curb interest group excesses.

Despite the sophistication of the debate, nearly all of the proposals suffered from a single, obvious weakness: in striking contrast to their sober portrayal of legislators, the proposals tended to assume that judges are somehow above the fray and can be wholly objective in interpreting the statutes that come before them. Yet there is no reason to believe that the judicial process is immune from interest group activity and the other kinds of distortions that characterize legislation. Once we subject judges to the same public choice scrutiny previously reserved for legislators, it becomes much more difficult to blithely assume that statutory interpretation can counteract the problems of legislative decisionmaking.

Interestingly, the literature on the evolution of the common law has proceeded on a somewhat analogous track, with overly optimistic early accounts giving way to more realistic assessments of the judicial process. Starting in the early 1970s, Judge Posner contended that common law rules tend to become efficient over time, due in large part to judges' unarticulated preference for efficient, rather than inefficient, rules. Other commentators argued for the efficiency of the common law on other grounds. Yet the differential interests of different kinds of litigants, and other biases in the cases that go to trial, suggest that any tendency toward common law efficiency is likely to be, at most, a weak one.

The first wave of public choice scholarship has thus complicated, rather than simply clarified, our understanding of the roles of legislators and judges. The extent to which interest group influence and the distortions identified by social choice undermine the legislative process remains unclear. In addition, the ability of the judiciary to counteract these influences on legislative decisions is open to question. The obvious next step is to engage in a more nuanced comparison of decisionmaking institutions. As we shall see, this raises intriguing questions as to the future of public-choice-influenced legal scholarship.

B.   *Catching the Next Wave*

It seems safe to say, as I have just noted, that the next wave of public choice scholarship will reflect an increasing interest in comparative institutional analysis. Rather than simply identifying the flaws of a particular institution, public-choice-influenced legal scholars will consider the comparative attributes of each of the relevant institutions.

Evidence of just such a trend already exists. A recent book by Neil Komesar contends that there is an urgent need for comparative institutional analysis in order to counteract the distortions of single institution analysis in law-and-economics scholarship. Professor Komesar's transaction costs model emphasizes the interests that affected individuals or groups have, their costs of participation, and how these factors change as we shift our focus among markets, the legislative process, and the judicial system.

With the enhanced sensitivity to comparative institutional analysis, we can expect to see increasingly sophisticated applications of public choice insights in the legal literature. Ironically, however, existing comparative analysis has tended to fall into precisely the same trap that its advocates criticize: the assumption that there exists an objective, unbiased context where institutional distortions can be corrected. Thus, comparative analysis often begins with a nuanced assessment of the respective institutions, then shifts to a prescriptive mode whose proposals depend on implementation by an unbiased decisionmaker. Most frequently, the analysis awards this status to courts, whose limitations are ignored when it comes time to act on the insights of the comparative analysis.

It is easy enough to see the reason for this oversight. Because legal scholarship is at its heart prescriptive, comparative analysts feel a natural urge to progress from descriptive analysis to proposals for change. In doing so, however, they face a strong temptation to forget the real world limitations of the institutions with which they are concerned.

The obvious antidote to this problem is to pursue the analysis all the way down—that is, to resist the temptation to address correctives to a hypothetically unbiased decisionmaker. Yet this poses an intriguing dilemma for future public choice scholarship. Given the typically prescriptive nature of legal scholarship, what role can the next wave of public choice literature, with its enhanced sensitivity to institutional limitations, play? What can so relentlessly descriptive an analysis aspire to?

CHAPTER 3

BEYOND CLASSIC MARKET THEORY–INTERNAL CRITIQUES

In recent years, developments in the field of law and economics have proliferated rapidly. Many of these developments call into question various aspects of the classic market theory introduced in the previous chapter. This chapter presents examples of three kinds of challenges to classic market theory that have been raised by scholars working within the tradition of economic analysis.

First, price theory has been subject to increasing critique as scholars recognize the differences between the functioning of markets in the imaginary world of perfect competition assumed by neoclassical economics and the functioning of markets in the real world. One direction the literature on the economic analysis of law has taken concerns the question of when markets "fail" and the role that law and government should play in responding to "market failure." The fields of antitrust law, consumer protection law, and environmental law (among others) are built on the assumption of such market failures, and the concomitant necessity of government intervention to address them. The concept of "market failure" itself, however, has been challenged by economists. Price theory has also been challenged by "transaction cost economics," which relaxes traditional neoclassical economics' assumption that economic interaction is costless, and by "institutional economics," which recognizes that markets function differently depending on the organizational context in which bargaining takes place.

Second, the "rational choice" theory of human behavior on which neoclassical economics relies has been challenged from a number of different directions. "Social norms" scholars argue that people respond not only to prices and their own idiosyncratic preferences, but to the preferences of their reference group—preferences that are malleable. In the other direction, behavioral economists and evolutionary economists argue, respectively, that biologically-driven cognitive limitations of human beings and biologically-influenced preferences of human beings shape market behavior.

Finally, traditional neoclassical economics assumes that natural resources are costless and infinite, and that capitalist economies are capable of growing forever. The field of environmental economics, or ecological economics, attempts in various ways to account for finite resources, the "services" that the biosphere produces for human endeavor, and the value of present resources and goods for future generations.

A.   Beyond Price Theory

Consumer Sovereignty: A Unified Theory of Antitrust and Consumer Protection Law

65 Antitrust L.J. 713, 723–28 (1997).

■ Neil W. Averitt & Robert H. Lande

It is axiomatic that perfect competition, the perfect functioning of a competitive market, will maximize the welfare of consumers. Markets that diverge significantly from perfect competition may not do so. If a market's characteristics differ dramatically from those required for perfect competition, a condition termed "market failure" can exist. The overall level of consumer welfare may then be far below what it otherwise would be, and wealth that Congress assigned to consumers may be "unfairly" acquired by firms with market power.

Although economists generally agree on the fundamental concept of perfect competition, there is no universally agreed upon list of factors that define perfect competition or whose absence may lead to market failure. But the disagreements generally arise only over taxonomic matters—views of which concepts are implicit in others, which are assumed as necessary predicates or subsets of one another and are caused by other factors that themselves prevent markets from functioning optimally.

A leading scholar of the subject, Edwin Mansfield, believes that perfect competition requires four conditions: product homogeneity,[42] relatively small buyers and sellers,[43] mobile resources,[44] and perfect information.[45]

---

42. Mansfield describes product homogeneity as follows:

[P]erfect competition requires that the product of any one seller be the same as the product of any other seller. This is an important condition because it makes sure that buyers do not care whether they purchase the product from one seller or another, as long as the price is the same. Note that the product may be defined by a great deal more than the physical characteristics of the good.

Edwin Mansfield, Microeconomics: Theory & Applications 232 (5th ed. 1985).

43. According to Mansfield:

[P]erfect competition requires each participant in the market, whether buyer or seller, to be so small, in relation to the entire market, that he or she cannot affect the product's price.... Of course, if all producers act together, changes in output will certainly affect price, but any producer acting alone cannot do so.

Id.

44. In this regard, Mansfield states:

[P]erfect competition requires that all resources be completely mobile. In other words, each resource must be able to enter or leave the market, and switch from one use to another, very readily. More specifically, it means that labor must be able to move from region to region and from job to job; it means that raw materials must not be monopolized; and it means that new firms can enter and leave an industry.

id. at 233 (footnote omitted). "Sunk costs," a key feature of barriers to entry, are best included within this category.

45. Mansfield describes perfect information as follows:

Jack Hirshleifer has considered the converse situation and provided a list of three possible imperfections that can prevent a market from functioning perfectly: imperfect information, time lags,[47] and transaction [costs].[48] Significant problems in any of these areas can cause competition to be suboptimal.

Additional market failures are added to some other lists. These further potential problems include coerced decisionmaking, barriers to the entry of new firms, circumstances of natural monopoly, positive or negative externalities,[49] and situations involving "public goods,"[50] "free riders,"[51] "pris-

[P]erfect competition requires that consumers, firms, and resource owners have perfect knowledge of the relevant economic and technological data. Consumers must be aware of all prices. Laborers and owners of capital must be aware of how much their resources will bring in all possible uses. Firms must know the prices of all inputs and the characteristics of all relevant technologies. Moreover, in its purest sense, perfect competition requires that all of these economic decision-making units have an accurate knowledge of the future together with the past and present.

id.

47. According to Hirshleifer:

A perfect market would instantaneously digest the inputs and proclaim the correct market-clearing price. But no such magic machine exists in the real world. So a farmer bringing vegetables to a city produce market may by cleverness or chance realize a sale at a price higher than the (unknown) true equilibrium. Or, unluckily, the farmer may accept a price lower than might have been obtained.

id. at 418–19.

48. On the subject of transaction costs, Hirshleifer states:

Markets that are perfect would also be costless. In the real world, market "middlemen" such as wholesalers and retailers, brokers, dealers, and jobbers exist, and obviously must be paid for their services. While these middlemen improve the perfection of the market in other respects, the fees and payments they receive constitute a burden on the process of exchange. Transaction taxes, in which *government* collects "middleman" payments (possibly reflecting actual services

to taxpayers, but possibly not), are another important factor.

id. at 419.

49. Robert Cooter and Thomas Ulen have defined the problem of externalities as follows:

Exchange inside a market is voluntary and mutually beneficial; in contrast, an economic effect external to a market exchange may be involuntary and harmful. So, a harmful externality is defined as a cost or benefit that the voluntary actions of one or more people imposes or confers on a third party or parties without their consent. An example of an external cost is pollution.... The reason the market fails in the presence of external costs is that the generator of the externality does not have to pay for harming others, and so exercises too little self-restraint.... We would like the firm to take into account all the costs of production, including the costs imposed on others, in choosing its profit-maximizing output.... When this is accomplished, the externality is said to have been "internalized" in the sense that the private firm now takes it into consideration.

ROBERT COOTER & THOMAS ULEN, LAW AND ECONOMICS 45–46 (1988) (emphasis added).

50. According to Cooter and Ulen:

A public good is a commodity with two very closely related characteristics: first, consumption of the good by one person does not leave less for any other consumer ... and second, the costs of excluding non-paying beneficiaries who consume the good are so high that no private profit-maximizing firm is willing to supply the good. Consider the conventional example of a public good: national defense. The fact that one citizen is secure from the threat of invasion by a foreign

oner's dilemmas,"[52] "lemons,"[53] and adverse selection.[a] Despite disputes

army does not leave any less security for other citizens. Furthermore, it is difficult to exclude any citizen from enjoying the security provided to others. Because of these two characteristics, public goods are not likely to be provided at all by the market, or if they are privately provided, provided in less than socially optimal amounts.

id. at 46.

51. Cooter and Ulen provide a classic example of the free-rider problem:

[T]here is a strong inducement for consumers of the privately-provided public good to try to be "free riders": they hope to benefit at no cost to themselves from the payment of others. The related problem for the private supplier of a public good like national defense is that it is very costly to exclude nonpaying beneficiaries of the service. The attempt to distinguish those who have from those who have not subscribed to the private defense company is almost certain to fail.... As a result ..., it is not likely that the private company will be able to induce many people to purchase defense services. If private profit-maximizing firms are the only providers of national defense, too little of that good will be provided.

id. at 47–48. For a different type of "free rider" problem, see Jerry Green & Jean–Jacques Laffont, *Characterization of Satisfactory Mechanisms for the Revelation of Preferences for Public Goods*, 45 ECONOMETRICA 427 (1977). These authors are concerned with "free riders" who are willing to pay something, but less than others. This situation might arise, for example, if many people would wish to use a bridge, but would be willing to pay significantly different prices for this service. If those deciding whether to construct the bridge could not price discriminate among potential users, they might not be able to collect enough revenue to make the project profitable. Thus, it is possible that the relevant decision makers will decide not to build the bridge, even though it would be socially desirable to do so.

52. Cooter and Ulen explain how a prisoner's dilemma situation, in which the two participants seek to coordinate their actions, while at the same time being uncertain and

to some degree distrustful of the other's course of action, can result in a suboptimal outcome for each affected party.

In this two person, non-cooperative game two suspects in a crime are taken into custody, put in separate cells, and not allowed to communicate. The authorities offer each prisoner the opportunity to confess to the crime. Suppose that if either prisoner confesses and his partner does not, the confessor will receive half a year in prison and the non-confessor will receive 10 years. If they both confess, they will each receive 5 years in prison. And if neither confesses, they will each receive 1 year in prison. The prisoners will be best off if neither of them confesses. But if either prisoner adopts the strategy of not confessing, he might be left open to a long prison sentence if his partner confesses. In these circumstances, the best strategy is for each prisoner to confess. Thus, each will spend 5 years in prison. Note how different the solution to this game would have been if the participants could have communicated. Presumably, they would have coordinated their strategies so that each would have refused to confess, with the result that each would have spent only 1 year in prison.

COOTER & ULEN, *supra* note 52, at 93 n. 3.

53. George Akerlof identified an interesting market failure that might be caused by imperfect consumer information. In certain markets, consumers might not be able to easily obtain sufficient information regarding the quality of specific goods and might confuse the quality of particular goods with the quality of most goods on the market. Over time, competition from inferior goods (which can sell at a lower price due to their lower cost) could drive goods of higher quality (which have higher costs and, therefore, higher prices) from the market. Eventually, only low quality "lemons" might be left on the market. *See* George A. Akerlof, *The Market for "Lemons": Quality Uncertainty and the Market Mechanism*, 84 Q.J.ECON. 488 (1970).

a. Robert Cooter and Thomas Ulen describe adverse selection in this way:

[Adverse selection] arises because of the high cost to [insurance companies] of over taxonomy, this basic list of factors that can plausibly cause competition to become suboptimal is relatively noncontroversial.

Far more controversial is the question of just how often market failures occur and, therefore, how often remedial action under the antitrust or consumer protection statutes might be appropriate. This controversy may be illustrated by the role of imperfect information, perhaps the most important single market failure. Even Chicago School adherents concede that information often is imperfect. Much of what separates "post-Chicago" antitrust from Chicago School antitrust, however, are differing beliefs concerning the frequency and degree to which information is imperfect, the implications this has for competition, and whether government intervention is likely to correct the situation more optimally or more rapidly than the market.

Proponents of post-Chicago views are perhaps more inclined than the Chicago School to believe that important informational and other market failures may exist because they have come to believe that there are a number of ways in which such failures, perhaps small in themselves, can interact with and reinforce each other. In the final analysis, there is no substitute for close study of the facts of individual cases.

Everything for Sale

EVERYTHING FOR SALE 16–19, 24–28 (1996).

■ ROBERT KUTTNER

* * * The theory of markets posits several interrelated assumptions.

Three have to do with competition. In a stylized free market, consumers are said to possess "perfect information." This is almost never literally true, but is often close enough to be a reasonable approximation. Second, there is said to be "perfect competition"—many suppliers and freedom to

accurately distinguishing between high- and low-risk insurees. Although the law of large numbers helps the company in assessing probabilities, what it calculates from the large sample are average probabilities. The insurance premium must be set using this average probability of a particular loss. For example, insurance companies have determined that unmarried males between the ages of 16 and, say, 25, have a much higher likelihood of being in an automobile accident than do other identifiable groups of drivers. As a result, the insurance premium charged to members of this group is higher than that charged to other groups whose likelihood of accident is much lower.

But even though unmarried males between the ages of 16 and 25 are, on average, much more likely to be involved in an accident, there are some young men within the group who are even more reckless than average and some who are much less reckless than the group's average. If it is difficult for the insurer to distinguish these groups from the larger group of unmarried males aged 16 to 25, then the premium that is set equal to the average likelihood of harm within the group will seem like a bargain to those who know they are reckless and too high to those who know that they are safer from their peers.

ROBERT COOTER & THOMAS ULEN, LAW AND ECONOMICS 50 (2d ed. 1997).

shop around. Barriers to entry are necessarily low—anybody must be free to open a supermarket. This, in turn, means that producers are not monopolists, and don't have the market power to dictate prices. (Supermarkets do engage in opportunistic price hikes, but prices that are wildly out of line with competitors do not stick for very long, because word spreads and shoppers are driven away.) Prices are thus set by the interplay of supply and demand. Though there may be other forms of regulation, such as food inspection and labeling, there is little direct price regulation from third parties such as government. Third, free markets must have "mobility of factors": capital and labor, as well as consumers, are free to go elsewhere if they don't like their compensation.

A second set of assumptions is behavioral. Firms, by definition, have the single-minded goal of maximizing profits; consumers pursue the goal of rationally maximizing their well-being ("utility") by pursuing the most satisfying products at the best available price. Preferences are said to be set "exogenously"—they reflect the consumer's own tastes. * * * A perfect market also presumes the absence of significant "externalities"—social costs or benefits, such as pollution or public health, not fully captured in the price of the immediate market transaction. * * *

What describes supermarkets pretty well describes the production and sale of most consumer goods. It describes the setting of prices for many, but not all, raw materials used by producers. A relatively free market also characterizes many, if not most, services bought by consumers and producers alike. If you don't like your barber, there is likely to be another one down the block. There is no shortage of restaurants, hotels, tax preparers, photocopiers, dry cleaners from which to choose. Likewise, if your business is dissatisfied with the computer-repair service, management consultant, ad agency, office-cleaning company, office space itself, there are many more to choose from, all competing on the basis of quality and price, all—remarkably—earning a roughly normal profit. In all of these realms, the market mechanism mostly works.

This brief description of how the marketplace operates * * * allows us to appreciate why most economists are so enraptured with markets. Students of economics often hear their teachers compare markets to self-regulating systems in nature. Listening to an economist rhapsodize on how marvelously markets continuously adjust, how they deliver a humble cornflake from stalk to table through several chains of production and distribution without help from a commissar, is a bit like hearing a physicist marveling at the equipoise of the physical universe, or a doctor explaining the wonder of the self-regulating systems of the human body.

When a particular market does not work like a supermarket or a textbook one, the question is what to do about it. Free-market economists, almost intuitively, think market failure is limited to a fairly narrow set of special cases, and that the solution to market failure is more market. But is it? And when is it? And by what criteria do we know? * * *

Consider a market profoundly different from the market for retail groceries—the market for health care. This is no small, special case, since it consumes 15 percent of the entire economy, roughly as much as food does. * * * Health care is anything but a textbook free market, yet market forces and profit motives in the health industry are rife.

On the supply side, the health industry violates several conditions of a free market. Unlike the supermarket business, there is not "free entry." You cannot simply open a hospital, or hang out your shingle as a doctor. This gives health-care providers a degree of market power that compromises the competitive model—and raises prices. On the demand side, consumers lack the special knowledge to shop for a doctor the way they buy a car, and lack a perfectly free choice of health-insurer. Since society has decided that nobody shall perish for lack of medical care, we partly de-link effective demand from private purchasing power, which is also inflationary.

Health care also offers substantial "positive externalities"—diffused benefits not calculated in the instant transaction. The value to society of mass vaccinations far exceeds the profits that can be captured by the doctor or drug company. If vaccinations and other public-health measures were left to private supply-and-demand, society would seriously underinvest. The health system also depends heavily on extra-market norms. Physicians and nurses are guided by ethical constraints and professional values that limit the opportunism that their specialized knowledge and power might otherwise invite.

The fact that health care is a far cry from a perfect market sets up a chain of perverse incentives. In ordinary markets, sellers maximize profits by minimizing costs. But in health care, the profit maximizer's object is to maximize insurance reimbursement. The more complex the procedure and the more inflated the cost base, the more money can be billed to the insurance company. In recent years, private and government insurers have tried to crack down—by intensively reviewing what doctors and hospitals do, publishing book-length schedules or permissible procedures and reimbursements. Providers have fought back, by further complicating their own billing. All this inflates the cost of the whole system.

Worse, the insurance industry's efforts to reduce inflation (in a highly imperfect market) have created a second-order set of inefficiencies. Increasingly, consumers lack the ability to shop around for doctors or insurance plans. Often, they are locked in either because they get health insurance through their jobs, or because a "pre-existing condition" makes them unattractive to other insurers. They then become easy prey for insurance plans that seek to save costs by denying them care that they need, and to which they are ostensibly entitled.

Increasingly, too, insurance companies seek to minimize costs simply by refusing to insure people likely to become sick. This process of risk selection and segmentation, known as medical underwriting, is itself very expensive. So is the endless point-counterpoint of complex preapprovals and reviews of treatments. And so is the proliferation of paperwork. The providers and the insurers are each behaving "rationally" as profit maximizers, but their behavior does not yield a general good; the result is irrational for the system as a whole.

Thus, health care violates all the premises of an efficient free market—perfect competition, perfect information, mobility of factors, and so on. Yet, unless we want people dying from preventable diseases for lack of private purchasing power, the cure does not lie in liberation of the health "market." * * *

Here is the nub of the issue. Are most markets like supermarkets—or like health markets? And when a market exhibits resistance to market forms of discipline, what is the remedy? The conundrum of the market for health care is a signal example of a concept that will recur throughout this book: The General Theory of the Second Best. The theory, propounded by the economists Richard Lipsey and Kelvin Lancaster in 1956, and largely ignored today, holds that, when a particular market departs significantly from a pure market and yields an outcome that is not "optimal" in market terms, attempts to make it more marketlike in some, but not all, respects will have indeterminate results for economic efficiency—and sometimes perverse ones.

The Second Best theorem suggests that when there are multiple "distortions" in the price and supply disciplines of a given market, the removal of one distortion in the attempt to create a purer market will not necessarily improve the overall outcome. A second-best market typically has second-best forms of accountability—professional norms, government supervision, regulation, and subsidy—to which market forces have adapted. For example, if the health-care system is already a far cry from a free market on both the demand side and the supply side, removing one regulation, and thereby making the health system more superficially marketlike, may simply increase opportunism and inefficiency. In many economic realms, the "second-best" outcome of some price distortion offset by regulation and extra-market norms may be the best outcome practically available. The hapless attempt to get incrementally closer to the "first-best" state of a pure free market—in an arena like health care, where price signals are necessarily distorted—may lead to third-best outcomes. * * *

THE THREE EFFICIENCIES

* * * A review of both economic history and economic theory suggests that there are three very different concepts of efficiency in economic life. We might call them Smithian, Keynesian, and Schumpeterian. For the most part, the study of markets is dominated by issues of allocation—the efficiency of Adam Smith. Keynesian efficiency, by contrast, addresses the potential output that is lost when the economy is stuck in recession, performing well below its full-employment potential. Increasing allocative efficiency in such circumstances doesn't help. It may even hurt—to the extent that intensified competition in a depressed economy may throw more people out of work, reduce overall purchasing power, and deepen the shortfall of aggregate demand. The economy of the 1990s has offered the paradox of escalating gains to productivity via Smithian efficiency, coexisting with declining purchasing power and declining job security for most ordinary people. Resources are allocated in a more marketlike manner, but

overall performance is nonetheless mediocre and living standards are mostly stagnant.

By contrast, World War II is history's great example of an event that grossly violated allocative efficiency yet stimulated broad improvements in living standards. During the war, the United States had wage and price controls, rationing, coerced savings, monopolistic military contracts, and a variety of other affronts to free-market pricing. There was massive state intervention throughout the economy. During the peak of the war effort, nearly 50 percent of production was in response to government procurement contracts, most of which entailed monopoly pricing.

All of this violated ordinary supply and demand; it was profoundly inefficient in an allocative sense. Yet in a Keynesian sense the war was stunningly efficient. In 1941, the economy had still not fully recovered from the Great Depression. Unemployment remained at over 11 percent, and growth from June 1940 to June 1941 was less than 2 percent. But by June 1942, the economy was at full employment. Industry, which had resisted making investments because demand was slack, suddenly poured billions of dollars into war-production plants. Industry was recapitalized, at state-of-the-art technology. A generation of skilled workers was trained to operate it. Although nearly half of what was produced during the war was literally manufactured only to be blown up, the stimulus of war production rekindled economic growth. GNP increased by about 50 percent in just four years, a rate that has never been equaled before or since. By war's end, civilian purchasing power was one-third higher than it had been before Pearl Harbor. Although private-savings rates rose, much of the money that paid for the war was borrowed, through war bonds. But despite a record debt/GDP ratio of 119.8 percent at the war's end—more than double the "dangerous" ratio of the mid-1990s—this high debt was perfectly compatible with the two decades of record growth that followed.

Standard free-market economics simply does not know how to treat these two very different kinds of efficiency in the same analytical frame. * * * If a Keynesian intervention reduces allocative efficiency by distorting market prices, but appropriately stimulates demand, standard market economics is literally unable to calculate *a priori* whether the trade-off is worth the candle.

The postwar boom was also built on what I am terming "Schumpeterian" efficiencies. Joseph Schumpeter was the great prophet of technical progress as the engine of growth, and the defender of imperfect competition as the necessary agent of technical progress. Large, oligopolistic firms often turn out to have the deepest pockets. They keep on innovating, to defend their privileged market position and to fend off encroachment. Innovation within a structure of stable oligopoly may be more reliable than innovation in a context of fierce and mutually ruinous price competition. Casual readers (or nonreaders) of Schumpeter may remember him as the prophet of "creative destruction," a phrase that he indeed coined to describe the onrushing turbulence of capitalism. But the usual cartoon of Schumpeter gets his meaning backward. Schumpeter's concern was how a market system could endure *despite* its many propensities toward ruinous competition. He was no advocate of creative destruction.

The modern economy offers many examples of Schumpeterian efficiency. The old regulated Bell telephone monopoly generated excess profits, many of which were plowed back into Bell Labs. A regulated rate structure also created pricing incentives for investing in ever more advanced switching technology, since profits grew with the rate base, and the rate base grew with the base of installed capital. * * *

James Kurth, a political economist at Swarthmore, has coined the useful phrase "Military Schumpeterianism." This is an ingenious twist on the oft-repeated observation that the postwar boom was built on "Military Keynesianism," by which commentators meant the reliable stimulus of defense spending; this substituted for a more explicit and aggressive Keynesianism of large deficit spending for civilian purposes, socialized savings, public-works investment, and so on. Kurth's point is that, though large and persistent military outlays may have indeed had macroeconomic benefits, defense contracts also had immense benefits for technical innovation, industrial stabilization, and market leadership—the efficiency of Schumpeter.

A series of long-term military contracts to a prime vendor produced assaults against allocative efficiency—the hundred-dollar hammers, thousand-dollar toilet seats, cost-plus windfalls regularly exposed in congressional investigations—yet also produced stunning technical advances and market leadership. Who thinks that Boeing would be the world's leader in aircraft sales absent World War II and the Cold War? * * *

As a matter of technical economics, there is a Schumpeter/Smith disjuncture that parallels the Keynes/Smith disjuncture. An economy that is performing according to the precepts of allocative efficiency is likely to have both avoidable unemployment and collective underinvestment in technological advance. A perfectly competitive market will spend too little on innovation both because profits will be too low, and because of well-known "externality" dilemmas.

An externality, please recall, is a cost or benefit to the economy as a whole that is not captured by a party to an immediate transaction. A negative externality is a cost, such as pollution, that is imposed on others. A positive externality, such as the broad gain from a new invention or from training an employee, is a benefit to society whose economic return is not fully realized by the innovator. Because investments in innovation are risky and because they often benefit competitors, market forces tend to underinvest in innovation. Indeed, the more "perfect" the competition, the less money is left over to invest in innovations that have broadly diffused benefits but that may not pay off to the investor for decades, if ever. The greater the rate of creative destruction, the less available are the monopoly "rents" that are the innovator's reward and necessary shelter. (In economic terminology, a "rent" is a super-normal profit that would be competed away in a perfect market.)

The more the economy relies on casino-like capital markets, the less the availability of patient capital. But when is oligopoly relatively "efficient," and when is competition mutually ruinous? From a purely Smithian perspective, the question is nonsensical *ex hypothesis*. Oligopoly is never efficient, because more competition is always better. However, as Douglass North, the first economic historian to win the Nobel Prize in economics, observed in his 1993 Nobel Lecture, "It is adaptive rather than allocative efficiency which is the key to long run growth." This is, of course, the efficiency of technical progress—of Schumpeter. * * *

Another problem with allocative efficiency: the market's allocation of resources is only "efficient" based on a given distribution of income—one that reflects not only the verdicts of prior efficient markets, but also historical accidents. "Property is not theft," wrote R.H. Tawney, rebutting the anarchist Proudhon, "but a good deal of theft becomes property." Remarkably, the set of goods purchased by the existing income distribution is deemed simultaneously "efficient"—and substantially arbitrary.

In principle, we could have a wide range of possible income distributions and start the economic game again, and the usual supply-and-demand discipline would efficiently resume. Though this happens occasionally (as in the case of land reforms, or social revolutions), for the most part the allocative efficiency of the market presumes the actual income distribution bequeathed to us by recent history. By market criteria, therefore, it is allocatively efficient for a millionaire to spend an extra fifty dollars on a fine after-dinner cigar, and for a pauper to starve in the streets for lack of money to eat. The price system doesn't care about that: its job is simply to match willing buyers with available sellers, and to be a buyer you need money.

Conventional economics usually replies that it is still more efficient to let market-determined supply and demand determine prices and prizes; if we don't like the social consequences, we can always redistribute income after the fact. Fine—but who are "we"? This rather airy conclusion innocently overlooks how wealth buys, among other things, power—and how power resists income redistribution.

The usual construct of purely allocative efficiency also begs the question of "Efficiency for what?" Market pricing is an arguably efficient means, not an end. The goals, values, habits, and institutions of a good society may include an essentially market economy, but must be set by extra-market processes and forces. In their enthusiasm for the market mechanism, many theorists insist market values are an end, not a means, and that whatever society results from market forces is by definition the best available, as well as one that has delivered just rewards.

Milton Friedman and his disciples have made valiant but ultimately unconvincing efforts to infer extra-market values from the functioning of the market mechanism. If markets thrive on well-informed consumers, then a market society requires free expression. If markets express voluntary exchange and free choice, then they are the natural handmaiden of liberal democracy. This sounds plausible in the abstract, until we remember that Nazism, fascism, Latin American military dictatorships, East Asian autocracies, and a wide range of other authoritarian regimes coexisted all too well with a basically capitalist form of production and exchange. Liberal democratic values, not to mention social ones, must be found elsewhere. Taken to an extreme, markets tend to destroy them.

———

NOTES AND QUESTIONS

1. Price theory, imperfect markets, and "rents." While the concept of supply and demand is widely known and frequently discussed, non-economists may not understand the precise meaning of the terms. Jeffery L. Harrison, Law and Economics in a Nutshell 7 (2d ed. 2000). Demand is the range of prices and the amount of a good or service consumers are willing and able to purchase in a given market at a given time, not including those potential consumers who cannot or will not pay for the good or service. *id.* Supply is the range of prices and the amount of the good or service available for sale at each price in a given market at a given time. *id.* at 11. The equilibrium price combines supply and demand to establish the price and quantity toward which the market tends to gravitate. *id.* at 14.

This model assumes perfect market competition in which the sellers are price takers, passively reacting to the market-determined price. A perfect market depends on such factors as multiple suppliers with homogenous products, availability of information about prices and other relevant considerations, easiness for suppliers to enter the industry, and no single supplier large enough to affect prices by increasing or decreasing its output. An imperfect market exists if such a factor is absent and therefore a seller is able to raise prices above those of a competitive market. *Id.* at 20–22. Under perfect conditions, competitors will make a normal profit, or the minimum profit necessary to stay in business. If competition is imperfect, however, the seller may be able to make an economic profit (or "rent"), which is profit in excess of a normal profit. Competition is therefore important in determining prices. *Id.* at 24–26.

2. Market failures and "government intervention." The concept of market failure is popularly used by scholars and policymakers to explain when government mechanisms, rather than market mechanisms, should allocate a resource. As the excerpts above indicate, there may be many situations in which markets can be said to fail. In the legal literature, market failures are popularly pointed to as a reason for antitrust law, consumer protection law, and environmental law. Antitrust law responds to the market failures represented by oligopoly and monopoly power; consumer protection law responds to the market failures traceable to asymmetrical information between consumers and firms; and environmental law responds to the market failures caused by the negative externalities of pollution and the positive externalities of clean air and water.

But, assuming that government action is necessary, what should the government do? Debates have raged in the legal and economic literature for some time about whether market failures are better addressed by "command and control" government regulation, or whether government should seek to create more "marketlike" structures for bargaining. For example, rather than telling factory owners how much of which toxic substances they may emit into the environment, governments could create a system of tradeable emission permits, allowing firms to bargain with one another for the right to pollute. For a discussion of the more fundamental problems environmental pollution poses to traditional economic analysis, see section C below.

3. New theories of market failure: informational economics. Market failures have long been assumed to exist with respect to certain "public goods" such as environmental cleanliness and police and fire protection. More recently, economists such as Joseph Stiglitz and George Akerlof have argued that "market failure" is not limited to these kinds of goods, but is pervasive throughout all kinds of markets. These economists identify asymmetric information as a source of market failure. Consider the excerpt by Joseph Stiglitz (who won a Nobel Prize for his work) below.

————

Keynesian Economics and Critique of First Fundamental Theorem of Welfare Economics

MARKET FAILURE OR SUCCESS: THE NEW DEBATE 41, 48–57, 58 (Tyler Cowen & Eric Crampton eds.).

■ JOSEPH E. STIGLITZ

[Stiglitz begins by arguing that traditional neoclassical economics assumes that there is perfect information and that there is a complete set of markets for everything that can be exchanged.]

The assumption that there is a complete set of markets, including a complete set of risk and futures markets is important in the standard competitive paradigm but unrealistic. * * *

The incompleteness of markets can itself be explained by transaction costs, an important component of which is information costs. There are costs associated with establishing a market. If there were markets for each of the millions of commodities, each of the billions of contingencies, each of the infinity of future dates, then so much of societies' resources would be absorbed in organizing these transactions that there would be little left over to be bought and sold on each of these markets!

Once we recognize the myriad events that affect us, we recognize the impossibility of having even a complete set of risk markets (insurance against all contingencies). Each firm is affected not only by the events that affect the industry but by idiosyncratic events—the illness of its president, a breakdown in one of its machines, the departure of a key salesperson. The firm itself can buy insurance for many of the risks it faces, such as that its trucks get into accidents or that its factories burn down, but most of the risks it faces cannot be insured against. The notion that there be markets for each of these risks is mind-boggling. * * *

Consider * * * the market for labor. Each individual is different, in myriad ways. A complete set of markets would entail there being a different market for each type of labor—a market for Joe Stiglitz's labor, which is different from the market for Paul Samuelson's labor, which in turn is different from the market for plumbers, which in turn is different from the market for unskilled labor, and so on. If we are careful in defining markets for homogenous commodities (Joe Stiglitz's labor delivered at a particular date, in a particular state, at a particular location), then there is only one trader on one side of the market (Joe Stiglitz). If we expand the markets to embrace all theoretical economists, then it is obviously more competitive. But we have had to drop the assumptions that commodities are homogenous and that the set of markets is incomplete; there is not a separate market for each homogenous commodity. * * *

[B]eyond that, asymmetries of information greatly limit the opportunities to trade, a notion captured in the familiar maxim: I wouldn't want to buy something from someone who is willing to sell it to me. Of course the old principles concerning differences in preferences and comparative advantage providing motives for trade still remain valid, but there is another motive for trading, which can be put baldly as "cheating." While in traditional exchanges both parties are winners, I can get you to pay more for something than it is worth—to buy a used car that is a lemon—I win and you lose. Farmers have a strong incentive to sell their crops on futures markets, but most do not avail themselves much of this opportunity, and for good reason. Those markets are dominated by five large trading companies, who have every incentive to be more informed by the small farmer. The differential information means the farmer is at a disadvantage; the trading companies can make a profit off the farmer's relative ignorance. Knowing this, a choice is made to bear the risk rather than pay the price.

Asymmetries of information give rise to market imperfections in many markets, other than the insurance market, futures markets, and the market for used cars. Consider, for instance, the market for "used labor," workers who already have a job. Their present employer normally has more information concerning their abilities than do prospective employers. A prospective employer knows that if it makes an offer to attract an employee from another firm, the other firm will match it, if the worker is worth it, and will not if the worker is not. Thus, again, the prospective employer is in a heads you win, tails I lose situation: it is only successful in hiring the new employee if it has offered higher wages than the current (well-informed) employer thinks the worker is worth. To be sure, there are instances when the prospective employee's productivity at the new firm will be higher than at the old job—the employee is better matched for the job— or where there are other (nonpecuniary) reasons why the individual may wish to move (to be near relatives, or get away from them). As a result there is *some* trade in the used labor market, but apart from younger workers who are trying to get well matched with a firm, these markets tend to be thin. * * *

Asymmetries of information give rise to two problems, referred to as the (adverse) selection and the incentive or moral hazard problems. Both are seen most clearly in the context of insurance markets, but they arise in a variety of other contexts as well. The first problem results in firms being unable to obtain insurance on their profits: clearly the firm is more informed about its prospects than any insurance firm could be, and the insurance firm worries that if the firm is willing to pay the premium, it is getting too good of a deal. That is, there is a high probability that the insurance firm will have to pay off on the policy.

Moral hazard also leads to limited insurance. The more complete the insurance coverage, the less incentive individuals or firms have to take actions that ensure that the insured-against event does not occur. Because the actions that would be required to reduce the likelihood of the insured-against event occurring are often not observable (and/or it cannot be verified that the insured took the requisite actions), the payment of the insurance cannot be made contingent on the individual or firm taking those actions. Thus health insurance firms would like those they insure not to smoke or to be in places where they suffer the consequences of "second-hand smoke," that is, smoking by others. But insurance firms cannot observe these actions, and hence cannot require those they insure not to smoke.

The provision of *complete* insurance would greatly attenuate incentives, so much so in many cases that for the insurance firm to break even would require charging such a high premium that the policy would be unattractive. Thus, in general, whenever there is moral hazard, there will be incomplete insurance. * * *

It should be clear of course that for traders to have incentives to gather information required that information not be perfectly disseminated in the market. If, simply by looking at market prices, those who do not spend money to acquire information can glean all the information that the informed traders who have spent money to acquire information have, then the informed traders will not have any informational advantage; they will not be able to obtain any return to their expenditures on information acquisition. Accordingly, *if there were a complete set of markets, information would be so well conveyed that investors would have no incentives to gather information.* (Of course with all participants having the same [zero] information, incentives to trade would be greatly reduced.) To put the matter differently, the assumptions of "informed" markets and "a complete set of markets" may be mutually exclusive. * * *

The problems with the assumption of a complete set of markets run deeper. [Elsewhere] I emphasize the importance of innovations, but it is hard to conceive of there being markets for contingencies (states) that have not yet been conceived of: surely an event such as the discovery of the principles underlying atomic energy and the subsequent development of commercial atomic power is an event of immense economic importance, in particular for owners of other energy resources. Yet how could markets in these risks—or in the risks associated with lasers or transistors—have existed before the underlying concepts had been developed? This is a fundamental incoherence between the ideas of a complete set of markets and notions of innovation. * * *

Another critique of the fundamental theorem of welfare economics is that it *assumes* that there is perfect competition, that every firm is a price taker. Most markets are in fact not perfectly competitive. One reason is that when information is imperfect and costly, markets will normally not be perfectly competitive. Imperfect information confers on firms a degree of market power. Though there is competition, it is not the perfect competition of textbook economics, * * * it is *more* akin to monopolistic competition. * * * Because of imperfect information, if a firm raises its price, not all the firm's customers will immediately be able to find a firm that charges a lower price for the same commodity: indeed customers may well infer that other firms have raised their prices as well. By the same token, if it lowers its price, it does not instantly garner for itself all the customers from the higher-priced stores. Search is costly, and so those in the market rarely know the prices being charged by all the firms selling every good in which they are interested.

The imperfections of competition arise not only, however, from imperfect information but also from fixed costs, many of which are information-related costs. There are fixed costs that arise directly in production—the overhead costs of running a firm—and fixed costs associated with acquiring information about how to produce. This means that there is unlikely to be a very large number of firms producing every quality of every good at every location at every date in every state of nature. As we have noted before, with even small fixed costs, many of these "markets" will have relatively few suppliers. * * *

Finally, we think of one of the great virtues of market economies is its ability to "solve" information problems efficiently. Yet when information is costly, firms act to take advantage of that. In doing so, they may *create* noise—they create, some times deliberately, information problems for consumers.

Temporary price reductions ("sales"), though we normally do not view them from this perspective, create price dispersion. Costly search gives firms good reason to charge different prices, or to temporarily reduce prices. Low-priced firms can gather themselves a larger customer base, but the high-priced firms can still survive, serving only those who have high search costs and who have not had the good fortune to find a low-priced firm. The high-priced firms compensate for the smaller scale of their sales with a higher profit (price) per sale. * * *

Thus, while price dispersion gives rise to search and other activities directed at reducing the "noise" of the market, and search limits the extent to which prices may differ in the market, the fact of the matter is that the existence of imperfect information—costly search—is what creates the price dispersion in the first place. The price dispersion itself arises, in part, not in response to exogenous changes in economic circumstances, or the differences in economic circumstances facing different firms, but endogenously, as part of the market equilibrium where each firm recognizes the consequences of the fact that search is costly. * * *

These results * * * reduce the confidence we have in the presumption that markets are efficient. There are two important differences between the new market failures, based on imperfect and costly information and incomplete markets, and the older market failures associated with, for instance, public goods and pollution externalities: the older market failure were, for the most part, easily identified and limited in scope, requiring well-defined government interventions. Because virtually all markets are incomplete and information is always imperfect—moral hazard and adverse selection problems are endemic to all market situations—the market failures are pervasive in the economy. * * *

The new information paradigm has revealed that "market failures" are indeed pervasive in the economy. They appear in virtually every transaction among private parties in the economy, and while they may be small in each case, cumulatively they are important. Moreover the market failures are not like those concerning air pollution, for which a well-defined and effective government policy can often easily be designed. This pervasiveness of failures, while it reduces our confidence in the efficiency of market solutions, also reduces our confidence in the ability of the government to correct them. Most important from our perspective, neither the theory nor the practice of socialism paid any attention to these problems.

———

The Failure of Market Failure

18 J. POL'Y ANAL. & MGT. 558–64, 571, 572 (1999).

■ RICHARD O. ZERBE JR. & HOWARD E. MCCURDY

The question of the proper role of government in the marketplace is an old and fundamental one. Public officials throughout the world grapple with this issue, deciding which public services to provide or how to regulate the activities of individuals and firms, a task made more urgent by recent efforts to privatize public responsibilities and "reinvent" government. In the search for objective standards by which such decisions can be made, public officials have increasingly turned to the concept of market failure. Use of the market failure concept is widespread, both in teaching curricula and in practicing government circles.

* * *

The concept of market failure initially appeared as a means of explaining in economic terms why the need for government expenditures should arise. It constituted, according to its presenters, "a normative judgment about the role of government and the ability of markets to establish mutually beneficial exchanges."

* * *

* * * In one leading textbook on the new science of policy analysis, David Weimer and Aidan Vining reach a conclusion that appears frequently in the literature: "When is it legitimate for government to intervene in private affairs? In the United States, the normative answer to this question has usually been based on the concept of *market failure*—a circumstance where the pursuit of private interest does not lead to an efficient use of society's resources or a fair distribution of society's goods." Textbooks on microeconomics and public finance commonly present the concept of market failure as a general justification for government intervention.

As it matured, the market failure concept took on an additional characteristic—that of a diagnostic tool by which policymakers learned how to objectively determine the exact scope and type of intervention. Expansion of this normative concept into a diagnostic tool appeared in conjunction with the growth of policy analysis as a field of study and university training. One scholar argues: "The welfare theorem lets [us] classify inefficiencies as due to monopoly externalities, and so on. This helps us to understand and perhaps to solve such inefficiencies just as a doctor's diagnosis . . . is part of treatment."

* * *

What began as a simple attempt to provide a normative explanation for the existence of government expenditures has developed into a quasi-scientific full-scale diagnostic test with the prescription of cures. Some textbooks even present tables that allow students to identify appropriate interventions for different types of market and government failures. This appears to be a powerful and attractive model. It looks scientific. It seems to provide an objective test for governmental intervention. It appears to be something that can be usefully taught in schools.

Inevitably, such concepts and teachings find their way into public policy. Recently the U.S. government issued Executive Order 12866 [1993], which requires federal officials to conduct an economic analysis as a means of determining the need for proposed regulations. Guidelines for carrying out this order require officials to make a finding of "whether the problem constitutes a significant market failure" as a prerequisite for recommending government intervention. The guidelines further provide instructions for identifying types of failures, comparing potential interventions, and guarding against "unintentional harmful effects on the efficiency of market outcomes." The resulting regulatory impact analyses make reference to a variety of market failure concepts. * * *

An extensive flowering of the market failure concept has occurred in the field of law. The number of law review articles and court decisions using the concept run into the thousands, with 239 references turned up by a search of law reviews for the 12 months between June 1995 and June 1996 alone. These references occur not just in monopoly, antitrust, and environmental issues, but appear to span virtually the entire corpus of law. References are found, for example, in family law articles, in connection with setting product standards, in references to the plight of refugees, in connection with health care, and with regard to problems of creating markets in less developed countries, as well as in securities law, the creation of financial derivatives, moral legal theory, contracts, occupational injuries, controls on credit card interest rates, intellectual property, discrimination in insurance markets, the information superhighway, and zoning. Similarly, court decisions that refer to market failure and to externalities are made with great frequency.

Long before social scientists applied diagnostic skills to public affairs, doctors of medicine guessed that diseases of the body could be traced to imbalances in bodily "humors." By the 18th century, this fit of deductive reasoning had been elevated to the level of a diagnostic procedure. The approach led doctors to prescribe a variety of ineffective and often dangerous remedies, such as bleeding or purging. It eventually was replaced by more scientifically valid approaches, such as the discovery of antibiotics and the theory of germs. The theory of market failures, this paper will show, is little better grounded than the outdated belief in bodily humors.

A fundamental problem with the concept of market failure, as economists occasionally recognize, is that it describes a situation that exists everywhere. While the ubiquity of market failures seems well accepted, the consequences of this observation are not. * * *

Market failures are thought to occur when the market fails to produce public goods, or inadvertently produces externalities, or gives rise to natural monopolies, or disenfranchises parties through information asymmetries, or creates undesirable income distributions. All of these forms are types of externalities, since each consists of nonmonetary effects not taken into account in the decisionmaking process, which is the classic definition of externalities. Hence, when we charge that the market failure concept has certain shortcomings, we mean to apply this statement to all forms of externalities including nonmarket failures by government institutions.

The core argument against market failure analysis is derived from the study of transactions. Externalities arise when parties engage in transactions. The effect of transactions on market behavior was first analyzed in the 1930s, beginning with an examination of brokerage charges and other costs of exchange. This quickly expanded into an analysis of the relationship between property rights and the cost of transactions. The property rights approach began with an article by R.H. Coase, now well known in the discipline of economics. Coase argued that individuals form firms because use of the price system is not costless. In other words, entrepreneurs create firms in an effort to reduce the transaction costs associated with using the price system. This approach developed mainly after Coase's 1960 article on "The Problem of Social Cost" * * *.

The property rights approach is important because it defines the condition under which externalities entirely disappear. Transaction costs in this respect are defined as *the resources necessary to transfer, establish, and maintain property rights.* As property rights become more extensive and complete, transaction costs approach zero. In a similar fashion, as transaction costs decline, property rights become more complete as it is cheaper to defend them or transfer property.

Only when property rights are perfect do transaction costs vanish. In a zero transaction cost world, with well-specified rights, there would be markets for everything and all markets would clear, producing efficient outcomes for any collective problem that parties chose to resolve. This condition is expressed by the so-called "weak form" of the Coase Theorem.[3]
* * *

No such world, of course, can ever exist. This realization is critical to understanding why the market failure model fails. * * *

* * *

Market failures may be defined as departures from the optimum with respect to an operating price system that is costless. The existence of unpriced but nonzero transaction costs means that some trades are not created—trades that would be undertaken if the cost of the unpriced transactions were zero (or less than the net monetary impact to be gained). Failure to undertake these trades creates a market failure.

Market failures disappear only when the cost of operating the price system is zero. In the real world, however, this never occurs. People incur costs resolving, transferring, and maintaining property rights. This occurs wherever transactions take place. Unpriced transaction costs, as a consequence, appear everywhere. Since unpriced transaction costs are ubiquitous, this gives rise to a situation in which externalities and hence market failures can be found wherever transactions occur.

How then does an analyst distinguish between externalities that require government attention and those that do not? The market failure approach owes much of its success to the fact that sophisticated users have focused on the provision of goods with large net benefits where government has an advantage with respect to transaction costs. For example, market failure analysts have focused on goods with high exclusion costs, such as clean air. These are goods for which the government can better exploit its advantage in coercion to effect substantial per unit reductions in transaction costs and in which the potential markets—clean air and water, police and fire services, and the like—are large. The choice of these markets, however, is essentially ad hoc (aside from their transaction cost features).

---

3. The first formal statement of the Coase Theorem did not appear until 1966, when George Stigler offered that "the Coase Theorem ... asserts that under perfect competition private and social costs will be equal." Since this original formulation, the theorem has been stated in numerous ways, including: "if one assumes rationality, no transaction costs, and no legal impediments to bargaining, *all* misallocations of resources would be fully cured in the market by bargains" and "if transaction costs are zero the structure of the law does not matter because efficiency will result in any case." Paradoxically, the Coase Theorem has spawned a huge literature dealing with the artificial world of zero transaction costs, but Coase meant to emphasize real world analysis.

Going beyond these obvious cases, the market failure concept can also be applied to situations that most analysts would consider trivial and not worthy of government attention, which analysts recognize and tend to avoid. When a neighbor fails to plant more flowers even though this would increase property values in the neighborhood by more than the cost of planning, an externality and a market failure exist. The highway driver who drives too slowly fails to consider the time costs he or she imposes on other drivers, thereby creating an externality. (Since the government owns the highway we should probably say that a nonmarket failure exists.) Wherever moral hazard or adverse selection may be found, externalities arise. Companies providing fire insurance worry that policyholders will ignore efficient fire prevention measures; flood insurance may induce people to build in flood plains; government insurance for savings and loan companies may induce investments that are too risky; and * * * colleges granting tenure to professors may find they work too little thereafter.

Externalities exist anytime there is inefficiency in the law affecting markets. A law that encourages inefficient breach of contract produces an externality, as does a tort law that sets the penalty for reckless driving so low that too much reckless driving occurs. A person who inadvertently issues a fraudulent check may not take into account the burden he or she imposes on other users of checks. Suppose that buying a car involves title transfer fees imposed by the state. If these fees are set too high, some trades will not be made. The car manufacturer will produce too few cars, just as a monopolist would.

As these situations suggest, analysts in search of externalities and market failures can find them anywhere they look, providing a universal justification for any sort of government intervention that one might want to undertake. Supporters of the market failure concept avoid this problem by focusing on failures that are "big." In its worst form, this amounts to little more than the substitution of the ideological biases of the analyst. * * *

       * * *

The issue of government intervention is largely an empirical and not a theoretical one. As Nelson says, "there is no satisfactory normative theory regarding the appropriate roles of government in a mixed economy." No theory captures the variety of institutional arrangements that people have developed to resolve collective problems. The market failure concept is not inherently empirical and as such cannot provide answers to empirical questions.

The most important empirical question is this: What are the net benefits (if any) of any particular institutional arrangement? The only general statement that can be made about government intervention on Kaldor–Hicks efficiency grounds is that government should intervene where the costs of intervention are less than the benefits. No simple diagnostic scheme can indicate whether the costs of intervention will be less than the benefits for any general class of cases. Empirical analysis invites the analyst to consider the particular costs that govern each case.

* * *

For thinking about intervention decisions, the transaction cost concept provides analysts with insights into the relationship between government and the marketplace not otherwise apparent. It provides insights into the accumulation of institutional arrangements that exist in practice and it avoids the endless quest for "failures" either in the private or public sector that provide a basis for government intervention. The transaction cost concept is correct in principle, we believe, although not all of its facets have been worked out.

The transaction cost concept invites the analysis to answer a key question: What are the transaction costs that affect the search for collective solutions, and in each case how are those costs affected by government laws and actions?

The transaction cost approach does tend to restore law to a more central role in the study of government. The strengthening of private property rights often lowers transaction costs and thereby permits private parties to achieve collective solutions in situations where the costs of litigation and bargaining would otherwise be prohibitive. In such cases, government intervention through the strengthening of private property rights may improve the market. Such markets are inefficient not because of any inherent "failures," but because the government has neglected to provide the appropriate institutional framework.

* * *

Transaction cost analysis calls attention to the characteristics of government that give it an advantage relative to other institutions in its ability to lower transaction costs. There is one such advantage: the power of coercion. A classic definition of government is that of an institution that monopolizes the use of force or coercive powers over a given territory. The government may change laws and use force to compel compliance with them; it may force payment for goods through taxation and it may use police powers to forbid or compel actions. The most general statement about government intervention is that it should perform those functions for which its powers of coercion give it an absolute advantage. This is also a positive prediction about what government will do, since in failing to perform these functions government sacrifices both wealth and power. What are the important market failures to which its advocates refer? They are simply instances in which government action can lower transaction costs sufficiently to produce significant welfare gains.

* * *

Better empirical analysis, more attention to net benefits, and a deeper understanding of transaction costs would all help to improve the process of policy analysis. Continued reliance on the market failure concept will not.

* * *

NOTES AND QUESTIONS

1. Transaction cost economics, the theory of the firm, and the economic analysis of law. Recently, legal scholars have begun to abandon traditional price theory and take up transaction cost economics, or TCE, as a way of thinking about the economic analysis of law. One use to which TCE has been put, as the preceding excerpt suggests, is to provide a different way of thinking about the question of what mix of facilitative ("market") mechanisms and coercive ("government") mechanisms for the allocation of resources and production of goods will best further social welfare. Another use to which TCE has been put is in thinking about why corporate actors, or "firms," exist in markets, and what the possibilities and limitations of firms are vis-à-vis economic production and distribution. *See, e.g.,* Alan J. Meese, *Intrabrand Restraints and the Theory of the Firm,* 83 N. C. L. Rev. 5 (2004) (using TCE to justify antitrust law); Reuven S. Avi–Yonah, *Corporations, Society, and the State: A Defense of the Corporate Tax,* 90 Va. L. Rev. 1193 (2004) (using TCE to justify corporate taxation).

2. Beyond the market and the firm. Are there ways to organize economically productive activity outside markets and firms? What prospects does the "information economy" and technology such as the Internet offer to projects of democracy and economic justice? In the excerpt below, Yochai Benkler offers one perspective.

Freedom in the Commons: Towards a Political Economy of Information

52 Duke L.J. 1245, 1250–58, 1259–61, 1262, 1265–66, 1267–69, 1272, 1273–74, 1276 (2003).

■ Yochai Benkler

A. How We Got Here

For over 150 years, new communications technologies have tended to concentrate and commercialize the production and exchange of information, while extending the geographic and social reach of information distribution networks. When large-volume mechanical presses and the telegraph were introduced, newspapers changed from small-circulation, local efforts, into mass media—intended to reach ever larger and more dispersed audiences. Of practical necessity, as the size of the audience and its geographic and social dispersion increased, public discourse adapted to an increasingly one-way model. Information and opinion flowed from ever more capital-intensive commercial and professional producers to consumers who, over time, became passive and undifferentiated. This model was easily adopted and amplified by radio, television, and later, cable and satellite communications.

The Internet presents the possibility of a radical reversal of this long trend. It is the first modern communications medium that expands its reach by decentralizing the distribution function. Much of the physical capital that embeds the intelligence in the network is diffused and owned by end users. Network routers and servers are not qualitatively different from the computers that end users use, unlike broadcast stations or cable systems that are vastly different from the televisions to which they transmit. What I hope to persuade you of today is that this basic change in the material conditions of information and cultural production and distribution can have quite substantial effects on how we perceive and pursue core values in modern liberal societies.

In the wake of the hype-economy of the late 1990s, it is all too easy to treat any such claim about an Internet "revolution" as a figment of an overstimulated imagination. The dazed economy makes it seem as though the major leap—if there ever was one—has already happened, and that "normal"—gradual, predictable, nondisruptive—technological progression has set in. But to think so would be a mistake. It would be a mistake not, primarily, in the domain of technological prognostication. It would be a mistake of paying too much attention to e-commerce and stock values, which are reflections of the utility of the new medium to old modes of production and exchange. What we need instead is a focus on the basic characteristics of the medium around which information and cultural production can now be organized, and on how this medium interacts with an economy that has advanced to the stage where information and cultural production form its core.

For the moment, I will suggest that we call the combination of these two trends—the radical decentralization of intelligence in our communications network and the centrality of information, knowledge, culture, and ideas to advanced economic activity—the *networked information economy*. By "networked information economy," I mean to describe an emerging *stage* of what in the past has been called more generally "the information economy" or "the information society." I would use the term in contradistinction to the earlier stage of the information economy, which one could call the *"industrial* information economy."

The "information economy," conjuring up the Big Five (accounting firms or recording companies, your choice), began as a response to the dramatic increase in the importance of usable information as a means of controlling our economy. James Beniger's study of what he called *The Control Revolution* showed how the dramatic increase in physical production and distribution capabilities in the nineteenth century created a series of crises of control over the material world—crises resolved through the introduction of more efficient modes of producing and using information to control physical processes and the human behavior that relates to them. Ranging from the introduction of telegraph to control the rolling stock of railroads, which, as Chandler has shown, made Western Union the first nationwide prototype for modern corporate organization, to the invention of double-entry bookkeeping, scientific management, and brand advertising, that economy was largely driven by a concern with control of material flows into, through, and out of the new, unmanageably productive factories. The "cultural" offshoots of that moment—Hollywood, the broadcast networks, and the recording industry—were also built around maintaining control over the use and transmission paths of their products. For the first time, music or performance could be captured in a thing, a thing that could be replicated millions of times, and which therefore had to be made to capture the attention and imagination of millions. This first stage might best be thought of as the "industrial information economy."

"The networked information economy" denotes a new stage of the information economy, to succeed this older industrial stage. It is a stage in which we can harness many more of the richly diverse paths and mechanisms for cultural transmission that were muted by the capital structure of communications, a capital structure that had led to the rise of the concentrated, controlled form, whether commercial or state-run. The most important aspect of this new stage is the possibility it opens for reversing the control focus of the information economy. In particular, it permits the reversal of two trends in cultural production, trends central to the project of control: concentration and commercialization. Although the claim that the Internet leads to some form or another of "decentralization" is not new, the fundamental role played in this transformation by the emergence of nonmarket, nonproprietary production and distribution is often overlooked, if not willfully ignored.

I imagine you sitting there, managing a bemused nod at my utopianism as you contemplate AOL Time Warner, or Microsoft's share in Comcast's purchase of AT&T Broadband. Decentralization and nonmarket production indeed! But bear with me. That the dinosaurs are growing bigger in response to ecological changes does not mean that, in the end, it will not be these warm-blooded furry things that will emerge as winners.

What, then, would make one think that sustaining productivity and growth are consistent with a shift towards decentralized and nonmarket-based modes of production? And how would these organizational characteristics affect the economic parameters within which practical political imagination and fulfillment must operate in the digitally networked environment?

Certain characteristics of information and culture lead us to understand them as "public goods" in the technical economic meaning of the term, rather than as pure "private goods" or standard "economic goods." Economists usually describe "information" as "nonrival." The analytic content of the term applies to all cultural forms, and it means that the marginal cost of producing information, knowledge, or culture is zero. Once a scientist has established a fact, or once Tolstoy has written *War and Peace*, neither the scientist nor Tolstoy need spend a single second on producing additional *War and Peace* manuscripts or studies for the one-hundredth, one-thousandth, or one-millionth user. Economists call such goods "public," because a market will never produce them if priced at their marginal cost—zero. Given that welfare economics claims that a market is producing a good efficiently only when it is pricing the good at its marginal cost, a good that can *never* be sold both at a positive price and at its marginal cost is fundamentally a candidate for substantial nonmarket production.

Information has another quirky characteristic in the framework of mainstream welfare economics—it is both the input and the output of its own production process. This has important implications that make property rights and market-based production even less appealing as the exclusive mechanisms for information and cultural production than they would have been if the sole quirky characteristic of information were the public goods problem. These characteristics form the standard economic justification for the substantial role of government funding, nonprofit research, and other nonproprietary production in our information production system, and have been understood as such at least since Nobel Laureate Kenneth Arrow identified them in this context four decades ago.

The standard problems that economics reveals with purely market-based production of information and culture have now been coupled with a drastic decline in the physical capital costs associated with production and distribution of this public good. As I mentioned, one primary input into information or cultural production is pre-existing information, which is itself a public good. The other inputs are human creativity and the physical capital necessary to generate, fix, and communicate transmissible units of information and culture—like a recording studio or a television network. Ubiquitously available cheap processors have radically reduced the necessary capital input costs. What can be done now with a desktop computer would once have required a professional studio. This leaves individual human beings closer to the economic center of our information production system than they have been for over a century and a half. And what places human beings at the center is not something that is homogeneous and largely fungible among people—like their physical capacity to work or the number of hours they can stay awake. Those fungible attributes of labor were at the center of the industrial model that Fredrick Taylor's scientific management and Henry Ford's assembly line typified. Their centrality to industrial production in the physical economy was an important basis for concentration and the organization of production in managed firms. In contrast, human beings are central in the networked information economy because of attributes in which they differ widely—creativity, wisdom, taste, social experience—as well as their effort and attention. And human beings use these personal attributes not only in markets, but also in nonmarket relations. From our homes to our communities, from our friendships to our play, we live life and exchange knowledge and ideas in many more diverse relations than those mediated by the market. In the physical economy, these relationships were largely relegated to spaces outside of our production system. The promise of the networked information economy and the digitally networked environment is to bring this rich diversity of living smack into the middle of our economy and our productive lives.

In the physical economy, we settled more or less on two modes of making production decisions. The first was the market. The second was corporate hierarchy. Markets best coordinated some economic activities, while managers were better at organizing others. The result was that most individuals lived their productive life as part of corporate organizations, with relatively limited control over how, what, or when they produced; and these organizations, in turn, interacted with each other largely through markets. We came to live much of the rest of our lives selecting from menus of goods, heavily advertised to us to try to fit our consumption habits to the decisions that managers had made about investment in product lines.

B. Examples of Change

What is emerging in the networked information economy is a wider scope for two very different phenomena. The first is a much-expanded role for nonmarket enterprises familiar to us from the real world—both professional, like National Public Radio, nonprofit academic research, philharmonic orchestras, or public libraries, and nonprofessional, like reading groups or fan clubs. The second phenomenon is radical decentralization, which can be seen at the simplest level in the information available on the World Wide Web from an amazing variety of individuals and networks of individuals. The most radically new and unfamiliar element in this category is *commons-based peer production* of information, knowledge, and culture, whose most visible instance has been free software. Here, digital networks seem to be permitting the emergence of radically new relationships between individuals and their information environment, and, more dramatically, radically new roles that individuals play in the production process.

The role of nonmarket enterprises in information and cultural production has always been great, though appreciation for its centrality has waned over the past two decades. Think, most obviously, of science and news. In science, perhaps more than in any other cultural form, the nonprofit academic enterprise, funded by government grants, philanthropy, and teaching, has been the center of basic science, while market-based research was at the periphery. In most fields, the best scientists make the most fundamental advances in academic settings. Firms then take this science, refine it, and then apply it. They do very valuable and important work, but the core of the scientific enterprise has been people who forgo monetary rewards and work instead for glory, immortality, or the pure pleasure of learning something new. If you think of news, the story is more mixed, with commercial providers like the *New York Times* or CNN playing a tremendously important role. Still, public professional producers—like NPR or PBS in the United States, or the BBC in the United Kingdom—play a crucial role, far beyond what we usually see in, for example, automobile or wheat production.

The difference that the digitally networked environment makes is its capacity to increase the efficacy, and therefore the importance, of many more, and more diverse, nonmarket producers. A Google search for "presidential debates," for example, shows CNN as the first commercial site to show up, but it is tenth on the list, while C-SPAN, a nonprofit funded by commercial cable providers shows up fifth. Both are preceded and surrounded by nonmarket organizations, like the Commission on Presidential Debates, a museum, an academic site, and a few political action sites. If you search for "democracy" in Google, PBS is the first media organization to show up, at ninth place, and no commercial entity shows up until a story in *The Atlantic* magazine some ninety-five links into the search. A number of the most highly ranked sites are nonprofit sites devoted to disseminating information about candidates. Consider for example what DemocracyNet, the League of Women Voters website, created for the city-council elections in Raleigh, North Carolina in 2001. What one sees as compared to, say, the local television news broadcasts—is a facility that allows individuals to post questions in writing to the candidates and that allows the candidates to respond directly. For example, we see each candidate's response to the question of whether or not there should be a living-wage ordinance. The site does not provide pages on pages of analysis—one might see a line or two, although some candidates may have written more in response to questions that are more central to their agenda. But you actually see the difference between the candidates on this particular question. It is worth going to the site and looking around. The point here is that because of the low capital costs, a nonprofit organization is capable of providing information down to the level of city council elections that is richer than anything we have gotten from the commercial broadcast media. There is, then, both an increase in the number of nonmarket producers and an increase in their effectiveness.

The networked information economy departs more dramatically from the industrial information economy in the possibilities it opens for radically decentralized collaborative production, a phenomenon I call "peer production." Peer production describes a process by which many individuals, whose actions are coordinated neither by managers nor by price signals in the market, contribute to a joint effort that effectively produces a unit of information or culture. Now this is not completely new. Science is built by many people contributing incrementally—not operating on market signals, not being handed their research marching orders by their dean—but independently deciding what to research, bringing their collaboration together, and creating science. The *Oxford English Dictionary* was created in roughly the same way in the nineteenth century—laboriously and over many years. But what we see in the networked information economy is a dramatic increase in the importance and the centrality of information produced in this way.

Free software has become the quintessential instance of peer production in the past few years. Over 85 percent of emails are routed using the sendmail software that was produced and updated in this way. Over the past six years the Apache web server software has risen from being nonexistent to capturing over 60 percent of the market in server software. Choosing the server software that runs one's site is not a situation in which a few hundred or a few thousand dollars will cause a company to adopt a particular application, but superior performance will, and it is in such a market that we see tremendous adoption of software produced by peer production. Similarly, Windows NT and Sun's Solaris are steadily losing ground to the GNU/Linux operating system, which is produced in this way and already runs on some 30 percent of servers connected to the Web.

While free software is the most visible instance of peer production, in fact, peer production is ubiquitous in the digitally networked environment. We see it happening all around. Think of the web itself. Go to Google, and plug in any search request. The particular collection of information you see did not exist before you actually ran the search, and now it exists on your search page. How was it produced? One nonprofit, another person who is a hobbyist, a third company that has as part of its business model to provide certain information for free—all sorts of individuals and groups, small and large, combine on your Google results page to provide you the information you wanted.

But we also see this phenomenon occur less diffusely as well. The Mars "clickworkers" project was an experiment run by NASA that allowed 85,000 people to collaborate on mapping Mars craters. People looked at images of Mars's surface online and mapped craters, and after six months, when NASA did an analysis comparing the results from the Internet to the mapping done by the trained Ph.D.s they had used previously, they described the outcomes as "practically indistinguishable." Massive multi-player online games, like EverQuest or Ultima Online, are another example. There, thousands or tens of thousands of people play a game whose effect is to tell a story together, instead of going to the movies and receiving the story as a finished good.

Or compare "Wikipedia" (www.wikipedia.com), an online encyclopedia produced by distributed contributors, to encyclopedia.com, produced by Columbia Encyclopedia. Look up the term "copyright" on encyclopedia.com and you see "right granted by statute to the author," etc., and there is a bit of analysis, and some discussion of the Berne Convention, for example, and so on. Now we go to Wikipedia, enter the same search term, and we see a similar copyright discussion. One might agree or disagree with it, as one might, as a professional, agree or disagree with any short encyclopedia definition. But it is there, it is plausible, it may even be better than the definition offered in encyclopedia.com, and it is collaboratively produced by about 2000 volunteers.

But how are we supposed to know whether any of this is any good? What creates relevance and accreditation? The Internet also provides instances of relevance and accreditation happening through distributed peer production. * * *

How do * * * decentralized relevance-and accreditation-production enterprises compare to market mechanisms for ascertaining relevance? Perhaps most interesting in this regard is the competition between Google and Overture. Google ranks search results based on counting "votes," as it were, that is, based on how many other websites point to a given site. The more people who think your site is sufficiently valuable to link to it, the higher you are ranked by Google's algorithm. Again, accreditation occurs on a widely distributed model, in this case produced as a byproduct of people building their own websites and linking to others. Overture is a website that has exactly the opposite approach. It ranks sites based on how much the site pays the search engine. So we have a little experiment, the market vs. distributed voting. How do these compare?

Here is what Google produces when we search for "Barbie": We see barbie.com, with "Activities and Games for Girls Online!", and we see barbiebazaar.com, with "Barbie, Barbie dolls, Barbie doll magazine, etc.," but then very quickly we start seeing sites like adiosbarbie.com, "A Body Image Site for Every Body." We see more Barbie collectibles, but then we see "Armed and Dangerous, Extra Abrasive: Hacking Barbie with the Barbie Liberation Organization." Further down we see "The Distorted Barbie," and all sorts of other sites trying to play with Barbie.

What happens when we run the same search on Overture, the search engine used by Go.com, which is the Internet portal produced by Disney? We get "Barbies, New and Preowned" at Internetdoll.com, BarbieTaker wholesale Barbie store, "Toys for All Ages" at Amazon.com, and so on. The Barbie Liberation Organization is nowhere to be found. Whether Overture is better than Google's list depends on whether you are shopping for Barbie dolls or interested in understanding Barbie as a cultural phenomenon, but it certainly is not normatively neutral, and it certainly offers a narrower range of information sources. Unsurprisingly, different things emerge when the market determines relevance than when people vote on what is most important to them. For those who find the choices of market actors a persuasive source of insight, it is at least interesting to note that AOL replaced Overture with Google as its search engine in 2002, and uses the Open Directory Project database for its directory.

C. THE IMPACT OF THE CHANGE

In all these communities of production, individuals band together, contributing small or large increments of their time and effort to produce things they care about. They do so for a wide range of reasons—from pleasure, through socially and psychologically rewarding experiences, to economic calculation aimed at receiving consulting contracts or similar monetary rewards. At this point, what is important to see is that these efforts mark the emergence of a new mode of production, one that was mostly unavailable to people in either the physical economy (barring barn raising and similar traditional collective efforts in tightly knit communities) or in the industrial information economy. In the physical world, capital costs and physical distance—with its attendant costs of communication and transportation—mean that most people cannot exercise much control over their productive capacities, at least to the extent that to be effective they must collaborate with others. The digitally networked environment enables more people to exercise a greater degree of control over their work and productive relationships. In doing so, they increase the productivity of our information and cultural production system beyond what an information production system based solely on the proprietary industrial model could produce.

* * *

So let me speak about the relationship between democracy, autonomy, and social justice and the choice between a more concentrated and commercial information and cultural production system and one that is more decentralized and includes more nonmarket production.

A. DEMOCRACY

The industrial model of mass media communications that dominated the twentieth century suffers from two types of democratic deficits that could be alleviated by a greater role for commons-based production. The first deficit concerns effective political participation, the second deficit concerns cultural politics, or the question of who gets to decide the cultural meaning of social choices and conditions. Both deficits, and the potential role of emerging trends in information production in redressing them, are already present in the examples I gave of the emergence of nonmarket and radically decentralized production. DemocracyNet and Adios Barbie are the most obvious.

The primary thrust of the first deficit is the observation that in the mass-mediated environment only a tiny minority of players gets to participate in political public discourse and to affect decisionmaking directly. As Howard Jonas, chairman of a growing telecommunications company, incautiously described his ambitions, "Sure I want to be the biggest telecom company in the world, but it's just a commodity.... I want to be able to form opinion. By controlling the pipe, you can eventually get control of the content." The high cost of mass media communications translates into a high cost of a seat at the table of public political debate, a cost that renders individual participation all but impossible. The digitally networked environment makes it possible for many individuals and groups of similar beliefs to band together, express their views, organize, and gain much wider recognition than they could at a time when gaining recognition required acceptance by the editors of the mass media.

     * * *

What radical decentralization of information production promises is the correction of some of the main maladies of the electronic mass media—the centralization of power to make meaning, the increased power of corporate interest in influencing the agenda, and the inescapable sound-bite character of the discussion.

The second democratic deficit of the mass-mediated communications environment concerns what some, like Niva Elkin Koren and William Fisher, have called "semiotic democracy," a term originally developed by John Fiske to describe the extent to which a medium permits its users to participate in structuring its message. In the mass media model, a small group of actors, focused on maintaining and shaping consumer demand, has tremendous sway over the definition of meaning in society—what symbols are used and what they signify. The democracy implicated by this aspect is not political participation in formal governance, but rather the extent to which a society's constituents participate in making sense of their society and their lives. In the mass media environment, meaning is made centrally.

Commercial mass media owners, and other professional makers of meaning who can buy time from them, largely define the terms with which we think about life and develop our values. Television sitcoms, Barbie dolls, and movies define the basic set of symbols with which most of us can work to understand our lives and our society. In the pervasively networked environment, to the contrary, meaning can be produced collaboratively, by anyone, for anyone. Again, as with public political discourse, this will result in a more complicated and variegated, perhaps less coherent, story about how we should live together as constituents of society. But it will be a picture that we made, not one largely made for us and given to us finished, prepackaged, and massively advertised as "way cool."

B. Autonomy

Autonomy, or individual freedom, is the second value that I suggest can be substantially served by increasing the portion of our information environment that is a commons and by facilitating nonmarket production. Autonomy means many things to many people, and some of these conceptions are quite significantly opposed to others. Nonetheless, from an autonomy perspective the role of the individual in commons-based production is superior to property-based production almost regardless of the conception one has of that value.

First, the mass media model, and its core of an owned and controlled communications infrastructure, provides substantial opportunities for individuals to be manipulated by the owners of the media. That is, for any number of business reasons, media owners can decide to disclose or reveal information to their consumers, or change the efficacy with which certain information is available to certain users. When they do so, they can, if they choose to, shape the options that individuals know about.

* * *

Second, decentralization of information production and distribution has the capacity qualitatively to increase both the range and diversity of information individuals can access. In particular, the commercial mass media model has generally presented a relatively narrow range of options about how to live, and these options have been mostly variations on the mainstream. This is so largely because the economies of that model require large audiences to pay attention to anything distributed, constraining the content to that which would fit and attract large audiences. Decentralization of information production, and in particular expansion of the role of nonmarket production, makes information available from sources not similarly constrained by the necessity of capturing economies of scale. This will not necessarily increase the number of different ways people will actually live, but it will increase the number of different ways of living that each one knows about, and thereby enhance their capacity to choose knowledgeably.

A different type of effect of commons-based nonmarket production, in particular peer production, on autonomy is relevant only within a narrower set of conceptions of autonomy—those usually called "substantive." These are conceptions of autonomy that recognize that individuals are always significantly constrained—by genes, environment, and social and economic constraints—and consider the institutions of a society in terms of their effect on the relative role that individuals can play in planning and pursuing their own life plan. The networked information economy promises the possibility of an expansion of elements of autonomous choice into domains previously more regimented by the decisions of firm managers in the market. In particular, the shift can alter two central organizational constraints on how our lives are shaped—the organization of production and the organization of consumption. Much of our day-to-day time is occupied with, and much of our well being shaped by, production and consumption, work and play. In the twentieth century, the economics of mass production led to a fairly regimented workday for most people, at the end of which most people went into a fairly regimented pattern of consumption and play at the mall or in front of the television set. Autonomy in these domains was largely limited to consumer sovereignty—that is, the ability to select finished goods from a range of products available in usefully reachable distribution channels.

Peer production and otherwise decentralized nonmarket production can fundamentally alter the producer/consumer relationship with regard to culture, entertainment, and information. We are seeing the emergence of a new category of relationship to information production and exchange—that of "users." Users are individuals who are sometimes consumers, sometimes producers, and who are substantially more engaged participants, both in defining the terms of their productive activity and in defining what they consume and how they consume it. To the extent that people spend more of their production and consumption time in this ambiguous category of "user," they can have a greater autonomy in self-defining their productive activity, and in making their own consumption goods. The substantive capacity of individuals to control how their life goes—day to day, week to week—would increase to cover aspects of life previously unavailable for self-governance by individuals seeking to put together an autonomously conceived and lived life.

C. Justice

Finally, as we think about the relationship between the structure of information and cultural production and liberal society, there is the question of how the transition to more commons-based production will affect social justice, or equality. Here in particular it is important to retain a cautious perspective as to how much can be changed by reorganizing our information production system. Raw poverty and social or racial stratification will not be substantially affected by these changes. Education will do much more than a laptop and a high speed Internet connection in every home, though these might contribute in some measure to avoiding increasing inequality in the advanced economies, where opportunities for both production and consumption may increasingly be known only to those connected.

For some individuals and societies, where access to capital, not education, is a primary barrier to development, however, there is some promise that a substantial commons in the information economy will provide valuable opportunities.

* * *

Building * * * a commons would * * * add a more competitive layer of goods and services from market-based sources, as well as nonmarket sources, thereby providing a wider range of information and cultural goods at lower cost. On the consumption side this has an unusual flavor as an argument within a social-democratic framework. Proposing a mechanism that will increase competition and decrease the role of government-granted and regulated monopolies is not exactly the traditional social-democratic way. But lower prices are a mechanism for increasing the welfare of those at the bottom of the economic ladder, and in particular, competition in the provision of a zero-marginal-cost good, to the extent it eventually drives the direct price of access and use to zero, will have this effect. More importantly, access to such resources, free of the usual capital constraints, will permit easier access to production opportunities for some in populations traditionally outside the core of the global economy—particularly in developing nations. Such access could provide, over the long term, somewhat greater equity in the distribution of wealth globally, as producers in peripheral economies take these opportunities to compete through a globally connected distribution medium, access to which is relatively unaided by wealth endowments.

D. THE BATTLE OVER THE INSTITUTIONAL ECOLOGY

* * *

What decentralized and nonmarket information production generally, and peer production in particular, need, is a space free of the laws developed to support market-and hierarchy-based production. In the late eighteenth and early nineteenth centuries, market-based production was replacing artisan and guild-based production, and law developed the framework that that transition needed—modern property and contract law. In the late nineteenth and early twentieth centuries, larger-scale production in corporate hierarchies was necessary to coordinate the complex production decisions that technology had made possible. Law developed to accommodate these properties by developing corporate law, antitrust law, labor law, securities laws, and later, consumer protection law. Some of the newer laws had to conflict with, and partly displace, contract and property law. One example is the power that corporate law gives managers to make decisions independent of the wishes of those traditionally seen as "the owners" of the corporation, its shareholders. Similarly, labor law and consumer protection law partially displaced contract law. National policy too was harnessed to advance railroad construction, electrification, and eventually the highway system that this new, larger-scale system of production and distribution of material goods required.

As we enter the twenty-first century, law and policy must once again develop to accommodate newly emerging modes of production. The primary need is to develop a *core common infrastructure*—a set of resources necessary to the production and exchange of information, which will be available as commons—unowned and free for all to use in pursuit of their productive enterprises, whether or not market-based. Building the core common infrastructure will require a combination of both legal and policy moves to develop a series of sustainable commons in the information environment, stretching from the very physical layer upon which it rests—the radio frequency spectrum—to its logical and content layers. The idea is not to replace the owned infrastructure, but rather to build alongside it an open alternative. Just as roads do not replace railroads or airport landing slots, the core common infrastructure will be open to be used by all, and biased in favor of none.

At the physical layer, we should focus on two primary policy objectives. The first is to permit the free utilization of radio frequencies, so as to develop a market in end-user-owned equipment that will create an ownerless network. The dramatic emergence of WiFi over the past year or so points in the general direction, but metaphorically, think of this option as one that replaces railroads—owned and managed infrastructure—with sidewalks, roads, and highways—infrastructure that is open for all who have the necessary equipment—a car, bike, or legs. The main difference is that the infrastructure in spectrum will be built by individual and private equipment owners, more like the Internet than like the public highway system, and will have an even more decentralized capital investment structure than the Internet because physical connectivity itself will be provided cooperatively, by individuals.

The second policy in the physical-layer objective is to begin to move towards public investment in open infrastructure, alongside the private infrastructure. A variety of municipalities, frustrated with the slow rate of broadband deployment, in particular in the last mile, have begun to work on deploying fiber to the home networks. Chicago CityNet is probably the most ambitious effort, in terms of scope, hoping to use the city's own purchasing power to drive investment in fiber, which would then be available on a nondiscriminatory basis for all to use.

* * *

Conclusion

We are at a moment in our history at which the terms of freedom and justice are up for grabs. We have an opportunity to improve the way we govern ourselves—both as members of communities and as autonomous individuals. We have an opportunity to be more just at the very core of our economic system. The practical steps we must take to reshape the boundaries of the possible in political morality and to improve the pattern of liberal society will likely improve productivity and growth through greater innovation and creativity. Instead of seizing these opportunities, however, we are sleepwalking. We shuffle along, taking small steps in the wrong direction, guided by large political contributions, lobbyists, and well-financed legal arguments stretching laws written for a different time, policy arguments fashioned for a different economy. The stakes are too high, however, for us to take our cues from those who are well adapted to be winners in the economic system of the previous century. The patterns of press culture became settled for five hundred years within fifty years of Gutenberg's invention; radio had settled on the broadcast model within twenty-five years of Marconi's invention. Most of the major decisions that put the twentieth century broadcast culture in place were made in the span of six years between 1920 and 1926. The time to wake up and shape the pattern of freedom and justice in the new century is now.

NOTES AND QUESTIONS

1. Institutional economics. Another offshoot of Coase's work, related to transaction cost economics, has been the development of "institutional economics," also referred to as "new institutional economics" or NIE to distinguish it from the turn of the century movement inspired by Thorstein Veblen. The distinctive feature of institutional economics is its interest in the "rules of the game" that structure market behavior. As Alan Meese explains:

> [A]ll economic cooperation takes place against a backdrop of numerous "rules of the game" produced and enforced by the State. The law of contract empowers individuals and firms to make enforceable promises to each other, and such promises are the basis of cooperation. The law of property, including that of intellectual property, vests exclusive control of most resources in particular persons or entities and thus facilitates cooperative bargaining between potential users. Property law also facilitates the enforcement of bargains, by making self-help possible. (A franchisor can "terminate" a franchisee because trademark law allows the franchisor to exclude others from use of its trademark.) Finally, the law of tort facilitates bargains by, for instance, deterring fraudulent statements and thus ensuring that parties need not take wasteful precautions to verify a trading partner's representations.
>
> These "rules of the game" include more than just generally-applicable common law rules of contract, property, and tort. They also include statutory provisions and common law rules that facilitate the creation and operation of various types of business organizations such as partnerships, limited liability companies, and corporations. Each such business code, backed up by common law rules of agency and fiduciary duties, creates a distinctive series of presumptive or "default" rules that enable individuals to select and tailor that form of organization that best suits the particular enterprise they have chosen. Thus, when a firm acts, either alone or in concert, it does so because the State has recognized its authority to do so. When combined with other back-

ground "rules of the game," such rules (hopefully) minimize the cost of creating and running a business organization.

Taken together, these various rules—contract, property, tort, and the law of business entities—all create what economists call the "institutional framework." When they construct such frameworks, states recognize and facilitate the innumerable forms of cooperation that characterize the modern economy. As noted at the outset, some such cooperation takes place between firms, other cooperation occurs within them. By changing this framework, states can in turn alter the cost of entering and preserving relationships, thus affecting the allocation of resources and the nature and amount of social output. Indeed, what economists and others call a "private" market is in fact a social institution, constructed by innumerable background rules, created or enforced by the State.

Of course, cooperation between economic actors is not always a good thing. Society in general and consumers in particular should not rejoice if Ford and General Motors cooperate when setting prices or if Microsoft and Dell cooperate to exclude Netscape from its most efficient channel of distribution. As a result, an institutional framework that simply enforces all commercial contracts will not suffice to maximize social welfare. A society that wishes to reap the most possible gains from economic activity must therefore construct an institutional framework that minimizes the cost of beneficial cooperation while deterring that cooperation which injures society.

Alan J. Meese, *Intrabrand Restraints and the Theory of the Firm*, 83 N.C. L. REV. 5, 11–14 (2004).

2. Peer production, freedom, and democracy. Benkler argues that the "networked information economy" makes possible important transformations in the American (and perhaps the global) political economy, including advances for democracy, autonomy, and social justice. Is his argument persuasive? What kinds of changes would be necessary to get there? Are those changes likely?

B. BEYOND THE "RATIONAL ACTOR"

In addition to identifying the limits of price theory, contemporary economists and scholars of the economic analysis of law have begun to question another fundamental assumption of neoclassical market theory: the "rational actor." The literature on "social norms" evolved to explain the puzzle that people often engage in behavior that is from a neoclassical perspective "irrational": for example, people vote even though the likelihood of their vote making a difference is very small, and drivers stop at stoplights in the middle of the night even when their chances of being caught by the police are very low. Legal scholars became interested in social norms as an alternative to legal rules: Are legal rules really necessary in some situations? Can, and should, the state change "norms" to prevent unwanted behavior ex ante rather than simply punishing that behavior ex post? The social norms literature does not directly dispute the notion that people act rationally, but it makes accounts of the "inputs" spurring market behavior—"preferences"—more complex.

More recently, a literature in "behavioral economics" has emerged, drawing on cognitive psychology to suggest that economic behavior is influenced not only by social norms, but also by inherent quirks of human cognition. Legal scholars have put behavioral economics to use in a number of fields to explain why rules intended to cause certain kinds of behavior may fail to work properly, or may have unintended consequences.

Social Norms and Social Roles

96 COLUM. L. REV. 903, 904–14, 959–61, 967–68 (1996).

■ CASS R. SUNSTEIN

I. TALES OF RATIONALITY AND CHOICE

A. Ultimatums and Fairness

Economists have invented a game: the ultimatum game. The people who run the game give some money, on a provisional basis, to the first of two players. The first player is told to offer some part of the money to the second player. If the second player accepts that amount, he can keep what is offered, and the first player gets to keep the rest. But if the second player rejects the offer, neither player gets anything. Both players are informed that these are the rules. No bargaining is allowed. Using standard assumptions about rationality, self-interest, and choice, economists predict that the first player should offer a penny and the second player should accept.

This is not what happens. Offers usually average between 30% and 40% of the total. Offers of less than 20% are often rejected. Often there is a 50-50 division. These results cut across the level of the stakes and across diverse cultures.

B. Littering

Why do people litter? Why don't they throw things out instead? Social psychologist Robert Cialdini tried to find out. He placed flyers under the windshield wipers of cars and waited to see what drivers would do with them. Cialdini made arrangements so that before reaching their cars, some people would see someone (a Cialdini associate) walk past them, pick up from the street a bag from a fast-food restaurant, and throw it in the trash can. Of the group who both saw the responsible behavior and noticed the flyers, almost none threw them on the street. In the control experiment, with no one showing responsible behavior, over 1/3 of the drivers threw the flyers on the street.

C. Smoking, Rationality, and Race

About 400,000 Americans die each year from smoking-related causes. Government has tried to reduce smoking through educational campaigns designed to inform people of the risks. Indeed the government has now initiated a large-scale program to reduce smoking, especially among teenagers. Despite this fact, about one million Americans begin smoking each year, many of them teenagers, and people worry that educational campaigns will succeed, if at all, only with well-educated people.

But consider this. Nationally, 22.9% of white teenagers smoked in 1993, a number that basically has been unchanged in the last decade. But in the same year, only about 4.4% of African-American teenagers smoked, a number that is four times smaller than the number a decade before. What accounts for this difference? Part of the explanation appears to lie in differing understandings of what is fashionable. And part of that difference may lie in a private antismoking campaign in the African-American community, symbolized most dramatically by posters in Harlem subways showing a skeleton resembling the Marlboro man and lighting a cigarette for a black child. The caption reads: "They used to make us pick it. Now they want us to smoke it."

D. Recycling in the Hamptons

In East Hampton, New York—part of the famous and wealthy "Hamptons"—what used to be called the East Hampton Dump is now the East Hampton Recycling and Disposal Center. At the East Hampton Recycling and Disposal Center, there are separate bins for green glass, clear glass, newspapers, tin cans, paper other than newspaper, and more.

Almost every day in August (the most popular period in the Hamptons), residents can be found patiently separating their garbage for placement in the relevant bins. Sometimes this takes a long time. The people at the Center tend to own expensive cars—Mercedes Benzes, BMWs—that are parked near the bins. As they separate their garbage, they look happy.

E. John Jones

John Jones lives in California. Here is a description of some aspects of his behavior.

1. He buys smoke alarms and installs them in three rooms in his house.

2. He loves chocolate and ice cream, and eats a lot of both. He also eats a fair amount of frozen foods; he makes sure that they are "lean" whenever he has a choice. According to his doctor, he is slightly over his ideal weight.

3. On warm days, he likes to ride his bicycle to and from work, and he enjoys riding his bicycle on busy city streets, even though he has heard about a number of collisions there.

4. He is happily married. He tries to share the work around the house, but he doesn't much like domestic labor. He does less than his share. He acknowledges that this is both true and unfair, and he supports many policies that are conventionally described as "feminist."

5. He buckles his seat belt whenever he is in a car. His own car is a Volvo, and he bought it partly because it is said to be an especially safe car.

6. He is not worried about the risk of an earthquake in California. On some days, he says that he doesn't think that an earthquake is very likely; on other days, he claims to be "fatalistic about earthquakes."

7. He does not recycle. He considers recycling a personal "irritation." He is mildly embarrassed about this, but he has not changed his behavior.

8. He considers himself an environmentalist; his votes reflect his enthusiasm for environmentalism. He supports aggressive regulation designed to encourage conservation and to protect people from risks to their life and health. In fact he is in favor of mandatory recycling, notwithstanding his own failure to recycle.

9. In his own mind, his resources fall in various mental "compartments." Some money is reserved for retirement. Some money is saved for charitable donations. Some money is kept for vacation. Some money is for monthly bills. His forms of mental accounting are very diverse. He is fully aware of this.

Is Jones inconsistent or irrational? Is Jones risk-averse or risk-inclined? What is Jones's dollar valuation of a human life, or of his own life?

F.   The Point of this Article

My goal in this article is to challenge some widely held understandings of rationality, choice, and freedom, and to use that challenge to develop some conclusions about human behavior and the appropriate uses and domain of law. I particularly seek to understand and defend the place of law in "norm management."

I urge that behavior is pervasively a function of norms; that norms account for many apparent oddities or anomalies in human behavior; that changes in norms might be the best way to improve social well-being; and that government deserves to have, and in any case inevitably does have, a large role in norm management. As I will suggest, norm management is an important strategy for accomplishing the objectives of law, whatever those objectives may be. One of my goals is to show how this is so.

Part of my motivation is therefore practical. Consider the following table:

Deaths from Preventable Risks in the United States			
Risk	Percent of Total Deaths	(Range)	Total Deaths /yr
Tobacco	19	14–19	400,000
Diet/activity	14	14–27	300,000
Alcohol	5	3–10	100,000
Microbial	4	—	90,000
Toxic agents	3	3–6	60,000
Firearms	2	—	35,000
Sexual behavior	1	—	30,000
Motor vehicles	1	—	25,000
Illicit drugs	<1	—	20,000

Existing social norms encourage much risk-taking behavior; and almost all of these risks of death could be much reduced with different norms. Consider smoking, diet/activity, alcohol, firearms, sexual behavior, motor vehicles, and illicit drugs as causes of death. In all these cases, new norms could save lives. A regulatory policy that targets social norms may well be the cheapest and most effective strategy available to a government seeking to discourage risky behavior. It may complement or work more efficiently than existing regulatory approaches.

Social norms are also part and parcel of systems of race and sex equality. If norms changed, existing inequalities would be greatly reduced. It is thus transparently important to see whether shifts in social norms, brought about through law, might operate to save lives and otherwise improve human well-being.

But part of my motivation is theoretical. It involves a conceptual puzzle. In the last decade there has been an intense debate about whether and to what extent law should try to change people's "preferences." But the term "preferences" is highly ambiguous, and it is not clear what the participants in this debate are actually disputing when they say that "preferences" should or should not be respected by law. I attempt to clarify possible meanings of the term. I also suggest that when the idea of a "preference" is unpacked, it becomes plain that the term is often too abstract and coarse-grained to be a reliable foundation for either normative or positive work. We will thus find reason to doubt the elaborate edifice of social science based on the notion of "preference." The ultimate task is to separate positive, descriptive, and normative inquiries more sharply and, in the process, to try to untangle different motivational states and their influences on choices.

More particularly, I aim to make a set of conceptual or descriptive points:

1. Existing social conditions are often more fragile than might be supposed, because they depend on social norms to which—and this is the key point—people may not have much allegiance. What I will call norm entrepreneurs—people interested in changing social norms—can exploit this fact. If successful, they produce what I will call norm bandwagons and

norm cascades. Norm bandwagons occur when small shifts lead to large ones, as people join the "bandwagon"; norm cascades occur when there are rapid shifts in norms. Successful law and policy try to take advantage of learning about norms and norm change.

2.   Sometimes people do not behave as economists predict. Many important and well-known anomalies in human behavior are best explained by reference to social norms and to the fact that people feel shame when they violate those norms. Thus when people deviate from economic predictions—when they appear not to maximize their "expected utility"—it is often because of norms.

3.   There is no simple contrast between "rationality" or "rational self-interest" and social norms. Individual rationality is a function of social norms. The costs and benefits of action, from the standpoint of individual agents, include the consequences of acting inconsistently with social norms. Many efforts to drive a wedge between rationality and social norms rest on obscure "state of nature" thinking, that is, on efforts to discern what people would like or prefer if social norms did not exist. Those efforts are doomed to failure.

4.   For many purposes, it would be best to dispense with the idea of "preferences," despite the pervasiveness of that idea in positive social science and in arguments about the appropriate domains of law and the state. In normative work, the idea of "preferences" elides morally important distinctions among the motivations and mental states of human agents. In positive work, the idea is too coarse-grained, in the sense that it disregards contextual factors that produce diverse choices in diverse settings. People's choices are a function of norms, which operate as "taxes" or "subsidies"; and the content of norms depends on the context. Instead of speaking of "preferences," we might assess choice in terms of (1) intrinsic value, (2) reputational effects, and (3) effects on self-conception.

I also aim to make two normative claims involving the appropriate domain of law. These claims have a great deal to do with law's expressive function, by which I mean the function of law in expressing social values with the particular goal of shifting social norms.

1.   There can be a serious obstacle to freedom in the fact that individual choices are a function of social norms, social meanings, and social roles, which individual agents may deplore, and over which individual agents have little or no control. Norms can tax or subsidize choice. Collective action—in the form of information campaigns, persuasion, economic incentives, or legal coercion—may be necessary to enable people to change norms that they do not like.

2.   Some norms are obstacles to human well-being and autonomy. It is appropriate for law to alter norms if they diminish well-being by, for example, encouraging people to shorten their lives by driving very fast, using firearms, or taking dangerous drugs. It is appropriate for law to alter norms if they diminish autonomy by, for example, discouraging people from becoming educated or exposed to diverse conceptions of the good.

G. An Insufficiently Charted Domain

Libertarians, some economic analysts of law, and many liberals give inadequate attention to the pervasive functions of social norms, social meanings, and social roles. Often it is said that in a free society, governments should respect both choices and preferences. But the case for respecting these things depends partly on their consequences and genesis, and as I have indicated, the determinants of choices (indeed the very meaning of the term "preference") remain obscure. We should agree that social norms play a part in determining choices; that people's choices are a function of their particular social role; and that the social or expressive meaning of acts is an ingredient in choice. Of course norms vary a great deal across cultures, and sometimes even within cultures. We should try to see when social norms, social roles, and social meanings are obstacles to human well-being, and whether something might be done to change them, even if people are making "choices," even if there is neither force nor fraud, and whether or not there is "harm to others."

One of my central points here is that individual agents have little control over social norms, social meanings, and social roles, even when they wish these to be very different from what they are. This is not an argument against norms, meanings, and roles. Human beings can live, and human liberty can exist, only within a system of norms, meanings, and roles; but in any particular form, these things can impose severe restrictions on well-being and autonomy.

As I have suggested, agents who seek to make changes in norms face a collective action problem. For example, it is impossible for an individual to alter norms determining whether the act of smoking seems daring, or the act of recycling seems exotic, or the act of opposing sexual harassment seems humorless. This is so even though the relevant norms greatly influence behavior. If, for example, smokers seem like pitiful dupes rather than exciting daredevils, the incidence of smoking will go down. If people who fail to recycle are seen as oddballs, more people will recycle. If the role of secretary is not associated with susceptibility to unwanted sexual attention, there will be less unwanted sexual attention. The point bears very much on current public disputes. If single parenthood is stigmatized, social practices will change accordingly; if homosexual marriages are consistent with social norms, social practices will be much altered. In all of these cases, individual actors need to act together in order to produce the relevant shifts.

More particularly, I hope to draw attention to the fact that people's conception of appropriate action and even of their "interest" is very much a function of the particular social role in which they find themselves. This is true of (for example) judges, lawyers, doctors, parents, children, waiters, wives, husbands, colleagues, friends, and law school deans. Attention to the place of social role shows that for many purposes, the contrast between "rationality" and social norms is unhelpful. What is rational for an agent is a function of, and mediated by, social roles and associated norms. And when social norms appear not to be present, it is only because they are so taken for granted that they seem invisible.

At the same time, norms and roles—operating as taxes on or subsidies to action—can create a division between the judgments and desires that are displayed publicly and the judgments and desires that would be displayed without current norms and roles. People's private judgments and desires diverge greatly from public appearances. For this reason current social states can be far more fragile than is generally thought—small shocks to publicly endorsed norms and roles decrease the cost of displaying deviant norms and rapidly bring about large-scale changes in publicly displayed judgments and desires. Hence societies experience norm bandwagons and norm cascades. Norm bandwagons occur when the lowered cost of expressing new norms encourages an ever-increasing number of people to reject previously popular norms, to a "tipping point" where it is adherence to the old norms that produces social disapproval. Norm cascades occur when societies experience rapid shifts toward new norms. Something of this kind happened with the attack on apartheid in South Africa, the fall of Communism, the election of Ronald Reagan, the use of the term "liberal" as one of opprobrium, the rise of the feminist movement, and the current assault on affirmative action.

To spell out the most general point emerging from the discussion: The notion of a "preference" can be deeply confusing, and in many of its uses, it impairs both positive and normative analysis of law. In its standard form, a preference is supposed to be something that lies behind choices and that is more abstract and general than choices are. But what lies behind choices is not a thing but an unruly amalgam of things—aspirations, tastes, physical states, responses to existing roles and norms, values, judgments, emotions, drives, beliefs, whims. The interaction of these forces will produce outcomes of a particular sort in accordance with the particular context. Hence we might say that preferences are constructed, rather than elicited, by social situations, in the sense that they are very much a function of the setting and the prevailing norms.

This point bears on the role of government, which cannot avoid affecting social norms. A market economy will, for example, have predictable effects on norms, and historically it has been justified on just this ground, as a way of softening social divisions by allowing people to interact with one another on a mutually beneficial basis. A good deal of governmental action is self-consciously designed to change norms, meanings, or roles, and in that way to increase the individual benefits or decrease the individual costs associated with certain acts. Thus government might try to inculcate or to remove shame, fear of which can be a powerful deterrent to behavior. The inculcation of shame operates as a kind of tax; the removal of shame might be seen as the elimination of a tax or even as a kind of subsidy.

There is a thin line between education and provision of information on the one hand and attempted norm-change on the other. In fact we will see that in the process of norm management, government has a number of tools. In a democratic society, it ought to be willing to use them.

* * *

John Jones, the protagonist of the fifth tale, is in one way quite usual: There is an evident and pervasive difference between people's choices as consumers and their choices as citizens. This is because people are choosing quite different things. In their private capacity, people may watch silly situation comedies; but they may also support, as citizens, the use of government resources to assist public broadcasting. Some people seek stringent laws protecting the environment or endangered species even though they do not use the public parks or derive material benefits from protection of endangered species—and even though in their private behavior, they are unwilling to do much to protect environmental amenities. The mere existence of certain environmental goods seems to be highly valued by political participants, even if they are not willing to back up the valuation with dollars in private markets. Of course many people give to organizations that support environmental protection. But what people favor as political participants can be different from what they favor as consumers. It is in part for this reason that democratic outcomes are distinct from those that emerge from markets.

In fact a good deal of empirical work shows that people's judgments about politics are not a product of their self-interest, narrowly understood. People without health care are not more likely to support laws creating a right to health care; people recently victimized by crime are not more likely to support aggressive policies against crime. Norms and values are instead the principal determinant of political judgment.

The disjunction between political and consumption choices presents a puzzle. Would it make sense to say that consumer behavior is a better or more realistic reflection of "actual" preferences than is political behavior? In light of the fact that choices depend on context, and do not exist in the abstract, the very notion of a "better reflection" of "actual" preferences is a confusing one; there is no such thing as an "actual" (in the sense of unitary or acontextual) preference in these settings. The difference might be explained by the fact that political behavior reflects judgments made for a collectivity. For this reason it reflects a variety of social norms that are distinctive to the context of politics.

Because of the governing norms, citizens may seek to implement individual and collective aspirations in political behavior but not in private consumption. As citizens, people may seek the aid of the law to bring about a social state that they consider to be higher than what emerges from market ordering. People may, in their capacity as political actors, attempt to promote altruistic or other-regarding goals, which diverge from the self-interested preferences sometimes characteristic of markets. Political decisions might also vindicate metapreferences or second-order preferences. People have wishes about their wishes, and sometimes they try to vindicate those second-order wishes, including considered judgments about what is best, through law. And norms with respect to public discussion may impose "taxes" on public statements of various sorts—perhaps requiring them to be "laundered," perhaps inducing conformity by punishing certain dissident views that might be reflected in other spheres.

In all of these ways, the norms at work in democratic arenas can produce different choices from those produced by markets. It would be wrong to say that the market choices are more "real" or "true." The question of which choices should govern for purposes of law and policy depends on a range of contextual issues that cannot be resolved by reference to notions of "choice" and "preference" alone. * * *

  * * *

Many claims about the appropriate limits of law are insufficiently appreciative of the pervasive effects of social norms, social meanings, and social roles. In fact these effects have yet to receive much attention. But—to say the least—the impact of law on human behavior is an important matter for lawmakers to understand, and that impact has everything to do with social norms. An understanding of norms will therefore help illuminate effective regulatory policy. Many of the most dramatic gains in health and safety policy are a product of changes in norms, meanings, and roles. Many of the most severe problems in current societies are a product of unfortunate norms, meanings, and roles.

Norms relate to some broader issues as well. Often it is said that the common law, and a liberal regime dedicated to freedom, take "preferences" as they are and do not seek to change them. But the term "preferences" is highly ambiguous. If the term is meant to refer to "choices," it should be understood that choices are very much a function of context, including governing norms, meanings, and roles. Certainly the particular choices made by people in markets—in their capacity as consumers or laborers—do not suggest global or acontextual valuations of relevant goods. If the term "preferences" is meant to refer not to choices but to the motivational and mental states behind choices, it is important to recognize that those mental states include assessments of social norms, the expressive meaning of acts, and the expectations associated with a dazzling variety of social roles. Norms and roles affect both public action and public talk, in ways that can much disguise how people think privately. This point has large implications. In many settings, it would be best to dispense with the idea of "preferences," and to shift instead to more concrete ideas, including intrinsic value, reputational effects, and effects on self-conception.

We have also seen that norms can be far more fragile than they appear. Hence "norm entrepreneurs" can help solve collective action problems, and hence "norm bandwagons" and cascades are common. Sometimes law interacts with the efforts of norm entrepreneurs, facilitating or blunting their efforts, and sometimes law ratifies or accelerates—or halts—norm bandwagons and cascades.

While social life would be impossible without norms, meanings, and roles, individual people have little control over these things. The result can be severe limits on human well-being and autonomy. Certainly there is a problem with existing norms when all or almost all people would seek a change. There may well be a problem when reputational incentives lead people to do what they would otherwise refuse to do, at least if the relevant norms deny people the preconditions for autonomy or otherwise undermine well-being. In fact lives are shortened and unjustified inequalities are perpetuated by the existence of many current norms.

People need collective help if they want to change norms, meanings, or roles. Collective help may be futile or counterproductive; it may be illegitimately motivated. But these matters require an inquiry into the particular context. The issue should not be foreclosed by resort to confusing claims about the need to respect private choice.

Law and Behavioral Science: Removing the Rationality Assumption From Law and Economics

88 CAL. L. REV. 1051, 1053–56, 1057–58, 1060–75 (2000).

■ RUSSELL B. KOROBKIN & THOMAS S. ULEN

INTRODUCTION

The law-and-economics movement has suffered from the truthfulness of one of its most important postulates: the law of diminishing marginal returns. Although law and economics was once viewed as a revolutionary approach to legal scholarship that applied the principles of microeconomics price theory to the analysis of legal rules, the value of its new insights is gradually diminishing. The movement's vast initial successes were so sweeping that the current pliers of the trade have been forced to search for more narrow niches to fill. As a result, the discipline often seems to be devolving into a subdiscipline of applied economics that happens to focus substantively on legal matters. What began as a form of legal analysis that employed economics as a tool is now too often economic analysis that uses law as a target. Mathematical elegance often becomes the primary goal, with usefulness in the realm of law, that combines logic with human experience, a mere afterthought.

The seminal insight that economics provides to the analysis of law is that people respond to incentives—a generalized statement of price theory. From this insight, two important corollaries follow. First, the law can serve as a powerful tool to encourage socially desirable conduct and discourage undesirable conduct. In the hands of skillful policymakers, the law can be used to subsidize some behaviors and to tax others. Second, the law has efficiency consequences as well as distributive consequences. Intentionally or unintentionally, legal rules can encourage or discourage the production of social resources and the efficient allocation of those resources. Although efficiency need not be the sole or primary goal of legal policy, economic analysis of law teaches that policymakers ignore the efficiency implications of their actions at society's peril. Legal rights that are unobjectionable in the abstract are not free but rather must be measured against their opportunity costs.

Law and economics is, at root, a behavioral theory, and therein lies its true power. The concern of law and economics with how actors in and subject to the legal system respond to legal directives (and would respond to hypothesized changes in those directives) now permeates the mainstream of legal academic thought, far beyond the boundaries of scholarship that is self-consciously part of the law-and-economics tradition. This concern was by no means "invented" by the law-and-economics movement but certainly universalized by it. Indeed, it is so widely acknowledged and accepted that it hardly bears mentioning in the modern legal academy that law does not exist in a vacuum; rather, it has real effects on private behavior, and those effects should be considered and accounted for when examining alternative legal regimes.

To speak coherently of the legal implications of viewing law as a series of incentives, analysts have to make assumptions about the consequences of those incentives to the people subject to the legal system. To satisfy this need, early law-and-economics scholars imported from economics a series of assumptions about how people respond to incentives, known generally as "rational choice theory." There is considerable debate within both the economics and law-and-economics communities about precisely what rational choice theory is and is not. As it is applied implicitly or explicitly in the law-and-economics literature, however, it is understood alternatively as a relatively weak, or "thin," presumption that individuals act to maximize their expected utility, however they define this, or as a relatively strong, or "thick," presumption that individuals act to maximize their self-interest.

Rational choice theory provided what was, no doubt, the best series of assumptions upon which to begin to develop the application of price theory to legal rules. The use of rational choice theory enabled the law-and-economics movement, in its early days, to achieve significant advances in understanding the interaction between legal rules and society. But now that the movement has reached intellectual maturity, the rationality assumption severely limits its continued scholarly development. There is simply too much credible experimental evidence that individuals frequently act in ways that are incompatible with the assumptions of rational choice theory. It follows that the analysis of the incentive effects of legal rules based on such implausible behavioral assumptions cannot possibly result in efficacious legal policy, at least not in all circumstances.

* * *

In response to these trends, a new movement is emerging in the legal academy that builds on the core insights of law-and-economics scholarship but takes seriously the shortcomings of rational choice theory. This movement, which we call "law and behavioral science," lacks a single, coherent theory of behavior. Although such a general theory may someday develop and would be welcome, the movement's current lack of concern about this shortcoming identifies law and behavioral science as a species of legal pragmatism. As we argue in this Article, one can analyze the appropriate legal command in any given circumstance without a grand, overarching theory of behavior so long as one has a due regard for the relevant decision-making capabilities of the actors in that specific setting. By borrowing from psychological and sociocultural theories in addition to economics, the law-and-behavioral-science approach consciously chooses to emphasize its external usefulness in analyzing legal problems rather than either its internal elegance or universal applicability. Its ultimate goal, quite simply, is to understand the incentive effects of law better than modern law and economics is able to do by enlisting more sophisticated understandings of both the ends of those governed by law and the means by which they attempt to achieve their ends.

* * *

I.   THE USES AND SHORTCOMINGS OF RATIONAL CHOICE THEORY

Rational choice theory is the heart of modern microeconomic theory. It is such a powerful, straightforward, compelling, and useful construct that scholars in a wide range of disciplines contiguous to economics, such as political science, history, international relations, sociology, finance and accountancy, and, of course, law, have adopted rational choice theory as their central account of human decision making. Unfortunately for the purposes of precise analysis, there is no single, widely accepted definition of rational choice theory. Although the use of the assumption that actors behave rationally is pervasive among law-and-economics scholars, the assumption is most often implicit. As a result, there is rarely a discussion in the legal literature about what, exactly, constitutes rational behavior. In actuality, there are probably nearly as many different conceptions of rational choice theory as there are scholars who implicitly employ it in their work.

The variety of conceptions of rational choice theory makes critiquing the theory something akin to shooting at a moving target. We will simplify the task somewhat by positing that versions of the theory can be aligned along a spectrum and then addressing four specific points along the spectrum representing the most common conceptions of the theory, as it is employed in legal scholarship.

A.   Conceptions of Rational Choice Theory

The different conceptions of rational choice theory can be understood as points along a continuum of how specific and precise the predictions of the theory are. On the left side of the spectrum are "thin" conceptions of rational choice theory—that is, conceptions in which the theory is relatively undemanding and in which it is relatively easy for the behavior of actors to be consistent with the theory. On the right side of the spectrum are "thick" conceptions of the theory—that is, conceptions with more robust behavioral predictions that are more easily falsifiable by empirical evidence. Figure 1 illustrates the construct, with the dominant conceptions of the theory in bold:

Rational Choice Theory Spectrum

"Thin" Conceptions --------------------------------- "Thick" Conceptions

Definitional Version	Expected Utility Version	Self–Interest Version	Wealth Maximizing Version

1.   The Definitional Version

In its thinnest version, rational choice theory is definitional in nature. This conception postulates only that, as Richard Posner has written, "man is a rational maximizer of his ends," without providing any predictions regarding what ends an individual might attempt to maximize or what means he might employ in such an effort. On this account, rationality is understood as suiting means to ends, but no normative theory of either means or ends is assumed.

One can conceive of a situation in which the prediction of this thin theory (that economic decision makers choose means well suited to achieving their ends) would not hold—namely, when an individual chooses an action contrary to his goals. But in practice the definitional version of rational choice theory is nonfalsifiable, because both the means and the ends of behavior are defined by observing the behavior itself. Put another way, rational behavior is understood as "the way people act." Because we assume a priori that people "rationally maximize their ends" (or their "utility"), we characterize as rational any behavior that we see and any behavior that can be justified as "rational" merely by noting its existence. Even behavior that seems anomalous, such as clucking like a chicken whenever a bell sounds, is presumed to be well suited to achieving the ends of the clucker.

On this thin understanding, everything confirms the rationality of behavior, and nothing refutes it. As Arthur Leff noted in an early critique of the law-and-economics movement, this use of rational choice theory substitutes a definition for a normative or empirical proposition.

2.   The Expected Utility Version

The next conception of rational choice theory, and the one most dominant in modern microeconomics, is often termed "expected utility theory." This conception, like the definitional version, is "thin" in the sense that it does not specify what preferences or goals decision makers will pursue. As before, the particular preferences or tastes contained in the actors' utility functions are exogenous, that is, given from outside the maximization problem. The expected utility version is, however, "thicker" than the definitional version because it does specify the means (or at least some of the means) by which actors will seek to satisfy their goals and preferences.

The assumption that economic decision making can be shown to be the result of the maximization of expected utility, subject to constraints, is a thicker model of human behavior in that it posits a more formal model of individual decision making than does the version of rational choice theory considered in the previous Section. Consider expected utility theory's account of decision making under uncertainty. Suppose that an individual must choose between a certain and an uncertain course of action—for example, between a certain return on an investment and an uncertain return on a more speculative investment. Suppose, further, that outcome O^1 occurs with certainty but that outcomes O^2, ..., O^n are probabilistic: only one of them will eventuate, but they are all possible. How would the rational choice theorist predict that the actor will decide which investment to choose? The actor will presumably attach a utility to each possible outcome—$U(O^1)$, $U(O^2)$, and so forth, along with a probability of each outcome's occurring—p^1, p^2, and so on. Calculating the value of the certain course of action is straightforward. Because O^1 is certain to occur, $p^1 = 1$, so that the expected utility to the actor of O^1 equals $U(O^1)$. The uncertain investment presents more of a challenge to evaluate because the uncertain outcomes are mutually exclusive, $p^2 \ldots p^n = 1$. The decision maker can reduce the multiple possibilities to a single expected utility by solving:

$$EU(uncertain\ action) = p^2U(O^2) \ldots p^nU(O^n).$$

The rational consumer then compares the expected utility of the certain course of action with the expected utility of the uncertain course of action, and selects the one with the higher value.

Stripped of its mathematical adornments, the basic requirement of expected utility theory is that decision makers conduct an explicit or implicit cost-benefit analysis of competing options and select the optimal method of achieving their goals (that is, the method that maximizes expected benefits and minimizes expected costs, or maximizes net expected benefits), subject to external constraints.

If an actor makes a decision that does not maximize net expected benefits to him, then he violates the behavioral predictions of the expected utility version of rational choice theory. But because it is impossible to know what choices are optimal for a particular decision maker without knowing the contours of his utility function, and because utility functions are difficult to elicit, the behavioral predictions of expected utility theory often are not directly verifiable or falsifiable. Fortunately, there are some necessary (but not sufficient) conditions of rational behavior under the expected utility model that analysts can observe. These are usually understood to include the following:

(1) *Commensurability*: actors should be able to compare the utility consequences of all alternatives to each other;

(2) *Transitivity*: if an actor prefers choice A to choice B and choice B to choice C, he should then prefer choice A to choice C;

(3) *Invariance*: the preference between two or more choices should not depend on how the choice is presented or structured, so long as the outcome possibilities are constant;

(4) *Cancellation*: a choice between options should not depend on features of the options that are identical; and

(5) *Dominance*: an actor should never choose an option in which every feature is only as good as the features of a competing option, and at least one feature is not as good.

If an actor fails to follow one or more of these principles, he cannot be making decisions consistent with the expected utility model. Consequently, the predictions of the model are testable, at least at some minimum level.

3.   The Self–Interest Version

Still thicker versions of rational choice theory start from expected utility theory's predictions about the manner in which actors will attempt to achieve their utility, and add predictions about the actors' goals and preferences—that is, about the content of the actor's utility function. Perhaps the most common assumption about ends, that actors will seek to maximize what is in their self-interest, can be traced to Adam Smith's famous statement:

> It is not from the benevolence of the butcher, the brewer, or the baker that we expect our dinner, but from their regard to their own interest. We address ourselves, not to their humanity but to their self-love, and never talk to them of our necessities but of their advantages.

The implication is that if we can figure out what course of action will most profit the decision maker, we will be able to predict his course of action. This is an advance over the thin conceptions of rational choice in that it suggests falsifiable predictions about substantive behaviors, not just predictions about decision-making procedures.

Such thick versions of rational choice theory dominate the law-and-economics literature, although the assumption is almost always implicit rather than explicit. Consider, for example, the simple prediction that if there is no punishment for littering, people will litter (the cost to an individual of disposing of his litter in a lawful manner exceeds the cost to him of observing his individual litter on the ground). This prediction implicitly relies on the assumption that individuals are concerned with punishments they might receive, the disutility that they will suffer from looking at their own litter, and the time and energy it takes to dispose of litter, but not with the disutility others will suffer from looking at their litter. Or consider the prediction that if punitive damages were to be abolished or capped, more defective products would be produced. This prediction relies on the assumption that product manufacturers are concerned with their own bottom line, and are concerned with the health and safety of their customers only to the extent that those issues demonstrably affect that bottom line. Unlike the thin versions of rational choice theory, the self-interested version can lead to the creation of directly falsifiable behavioral predictions.

Suspecting an ambush, defenders of rational choice theory might at this point observe that it is plausible to hypothesize that a decision maker's "self-interest" might be served by taking account of the well-being of others, not just his or her own wants and desires. Unfortunately, expanding the conception of "self-interest" to include other-regarding preferences in addition to selfish ones would rob the notion of "self-interest" of all of its predictive value. We would no longer be able to predict that people would litter if doing so risks no punishment, or that products would be more dangerous without products liability law, because people walking in the park may or may not gain utility from keeping the park tidy for their neighbors, and manufacturers may or may not gain utility from preventing harm to their customers. Adam Smith's prediction would have to be rewritten to read:

> It is from *either* the benevolence of the butcher, the brewer, or the baker that we expect our dinner, *or* from their regard to their own interest. We address ourselves, to their humanity *and/or* their self-love, and talk to them of our necessities *and/or* of their advantages.

The point is not that we believe actors seek to fulfill only selfish preferences—in fact, we argue quite the opposite below. But if "self-interest" is defined to include anything that produces satisfaction for the decision maker, then the self-interest version of rational choice theory is no different from the thin expected utility version.

4. The Wealth Maximization Version

The thickest conceptions of rational choice theory provide even more specific predictions about the ends of decision makers than does the self-interest version. The most common of these very thick conceptions is "wealth maximization": the prediction that actors will attempt to maximize their financial well-being or monetary situation. Nearly all law-and-economics literature on business organizations, following the neoclassical economic theory of firms, is built on the explicit or implicit assumption that firms seek to maximize profits. And much law-and-economics literature on individual behavior makes an analogous assumption (usually implicitly), at least in circumstances in which money is at stake.

B. Limitations of Rational Choice Theory in Legal Analysis

None of the conceptions of rational choice theory discussed above is optimal for the purpose of understanding how actors will respond to the incentives that the law creates. The deficiencies of the different conceptions arise from one or both of two shortcomings: their inadequacy in predicting future behavior and the implausibility of their predictions. * * *

1. The Inadequacy of Thin Versions of Rational Choice Theory

Thin conceptions of rational choice theory can serve as a useful tool for social scientists attempting to explain, classify, or label human behavior from an ex post perspective. By positing that actors will seek to maximize their utility, scholars can observe behavior and then reason backwards to an understanding of preferences (ends) and strategies (means). Thin versions of rational choice theory thus can be viewed as useful for recognizing that people usually act the way they do for a reason and, consequently, that observable actions provide clues for understanding these unobservable "reasons." However, these advantages are of little use to the makers of legal policy, who need to choose among competing legal rules. Policymakers need to predict future behavior under various legal scenarios, not merely understand past actions in hindsight.

The inadequacy of rational choice theory is most obvious in its thinnest, definitional version, which offers no behavioral predictions at all. Consider, as an example, the parable of Buridan's ass, who faced a choice between two equidistant haystacks as a source of nourishment. The definitional version of rational choice theory could offer no prediction as to which haystack the ass would choose, or whether he would choose neither. Because this version of the theory interprets all acts as rational, it would conclude, *ex post*, that it was rational for the ass to stand still and die of starvation. Because he believed this version of rational choice theory to be the behavioral premise underlying the law-and-economics movement, Leff disparagingly referred to law and economics as "American legal nominalism."

The expected utility version of rational choice theory, although it rises above mere tautology, is scarcely more adequate for generating behavioral predictions *ex ante*. In virtually any imaginable situation of importance to legal policy, expected utility theory alone yields indeterminate predictions; not only does the theory fail to yield a single, unique behavioral prediction (the result that would be of most use to a policymaker), but it also fails to eliminate many conceivable possible actions. This version of rational choice theory, like the definitional version, is helpless in predicting the action of Buridan's ass, because it provides no theory or account of the content of the ass's utility function. If we knew, for example, that survival was the ass's sole preference, then expected utility theory would lead to the prediction that the ass would choose one of the two haystacks. On the other hand, if we knew that the ass placed a higher value on avoiding difficult decisions than on remaining alive, expected utility theory would predict that the ass would stand still and perish. But without some theory about the content of the ass's preferences, either standing still or choosing a haystack could be rational. Expected utility theory can yield only the prediction that the ass will not violate one of the observable necessary conditions of expected utility theory. For example, it would lead to a prediction that the ass will not announce that he cannot compare the value of choosing a haystack with the value of standing still and dying, because to do so would violate the principle of commensurability.

To use an example of direct relevance to legal policy, consider the following question: if society wishes to reduce crime, assuming all other policy decisions are held constant, should it increase or decrease the length of prison sentences? Note that, although the former appears to be the obvious answer, it is only correct if we assume that most people prefer to live outside of prison than to be incarcerated. But recall that thin versions of rational choice theory cannot aid us in creating this assumption. Virtually no predictions can be made about decisions or behaviors without thickening the conception of rational choice theory to include some predictions about the content of preferences.

2.   The Implausibility of Thin and Thick Versions

Thin conceptions of rational choice theory, such as expected utility theory, are not only inadequately specified to be valuable to policymakers concerned with the incentive effects of law, but the behavioral predictions that they do make are also implausible as predictions of general applicability: that is, they have been demonstrated, as an empirical matter, to be substantially incorrect, at least under some conditions.

Thick conceptions of rational choice theory substantially avoid the inadequacy problem. They can be used to generate predictions about how actors will respond to alternative legal regimes and, thus, can serve as a useful tool for policymakers. A thick conception of rational choice theory, for example, could enable us to predict that Buridan's ass would value life sufficiently that it would be utility-maximizing to choose one of the haystacks, even if that meant suffering the pain of making a difficult choice. Thick conceptions, however, trade the inadequacy problem of thin conceptions for even more pronounced implausibility problems than those that plague thin conceptions. The predictions that they make about the preferences of actors (in addition to predictions about the means actors will use to satisfy their preferences) are demonstrably incorrect, at least in many circumstances. Buridan's ass, of course, did not choose either of the haystacks, thus falsifying the prediction that would be produced by any thick conception of rational choice theory.

Thin and thick conceptions of rational choice theory share two types of implausibility problems. First, actors often fail to maximize their expected utility, but instead make suboptimal choices among competing options given a set of preferences and use a range of heuristics—rules of thumb rather than complex cost-benefit analysis. This "bounded rationality" results from the high cost of processing information, the cognitive limitations of human beings, or a combination of the two. * * *

Second, while all but the thinnest versions of rational choice theory assume that decision makers conduct a cost-benefit analysis that is invariant to factors external to their choice, context is quite important to behavior. How individuals will respond to legal rules depends on what reference points individuals recognize when making decisions. Decisions and behaviors are often affected by such factors as how an actor perceives choices relative to the status quo, whether choices are consistent or inconsistent with an actor's habits or traditions, and the temporal distance of the rule's effects. * * *

Thick versions of rational choice theory face yet an additional implausibility problem. There is substantial evidence that decision makers often behave in ways that are inconsistent with their direct self-interest. Individuals form preferences not merely according to their subjective conceptions of well-being, but also in accordance with norms that are often socially constructed and sometimes evolutionarily adaptive. Some preferences well established in the behavioral sciences, such as a commitment to notions of fairness or social justice even at a cost to the self, might be ingrained by social or genetic forces, or by both. * * *

C. The Responses of Rational Choice Theory to Criticisms

Defenders of rational choice theory, when confronted with the sorts of criticisms that we have voiced, generally respond in one of three ways, none of which is satisfying.

The first defense is an evolutionary account of decision making, which asserts that actors who fail to make rational decisions cannot survive in a competitive world. In the competition for resources, utility maximizing behavior will drive out nonmaximizing behavior. The argument is most compelling in the context of business enterprises. Organizations will seek to maximize profits, and those that fail to do so will be put out of business by a lack of customers, capital, or both. Even when complexity or ambiguity would appear to make optimization impossible or unduly costly, those that manage to optimize, even by chance, will survive, and their strategies will be emulated by competitors.

We find this account unconvincing as it pertains to individuals. With rare exception, individuals who fail to maximize their utility are not "driven out of the market." They might (although not necessarily) enjoy less happiness than their more rational counterparts, but they will live to make decisions another day.

Even with regard to business enterprises, for which the evolutionary force of economic rationality might be most forceful, the account is unlikely to be true in most circumstances. Certainly, firms that make clearly suboptimal decisions routinely or in extremely important circumstances may be driven out of business, but competition in product or capital markets is rarely so perfect that a firm that occasionally makes decisions that fail to maximize profits will face bankruptcy or be taken over by firms that do maximize. In any event, if it were true that competition drives imperfectly rational behavior out of business markets, such results would not occur instantaneously, and at any given moment in time a substantial number of participants in markets would likely be imperfectly rational actors who have not yet learned their lessons.

A weaker version of this defense concedes that many individual and even some firm mistakes are not fatal, but stresses that actors learn from experience and correct failures of rationality. This argument doubtlessly has validity, in the sense that there are circumstances in which correctives are possible within the rational choice theory. But we do not think that this point merits the weight that defenders place on it. First, many * * * behaviors * * * are persistent, even when experimenters bring them to the attention of their subjects. Second, learning from experience is a long-term strategy, and there will always be a substantial number of imperfectly rational actors who have not yet learned their lessons.

The second argument offered by defenders of rational choice theory when confronted with criticism is that rational choice theory, while not perfect, is the best single available behavioral theory. The theory's defenders contend that, even if the criticisms are accurate, they do not amount to a coherent theory of decision making that does a better job of predicting a wide range of human behavior than does rational choice theory. As we shall see, imperfectly rational actors undoubtedly utilize many different decision-making strategies, no single one of which provides a general behavioral description more realistic than rational choice theory. In a commonly heard phrase around the academy, "It takes a theory to beat a theory," and these criticisms, even if correct, do not amount to a theory.

This rejoinder to the criticisms is sound, as far as it goes, but not particularly relevant to the project of developing a more nuanced understanding of behavior for use by legal policymakers. Rational choice theory is descriptively and prescriptively accurate more often than any other single theory of behavior, or so even its critics generally believe. But the elegance and parsimony that a single, universal theory of behavior such as rational choice can provide is of far less importance, if it is of any importance at all, to legal policymakers than to economists. The reason is that most laws are geared toward specific portions of the populations or to people who play specific roles.

To be useful for legal policy, behavioral theories need to predict (with reasonable success) the likely responses to legal rules of the particular classes of actors to whom the rules are geared, whether or not the responses of other classes of actors would likely be identical. For instance, if policymakers are considering revising products liability law, they need a prediction of how product manufacturers, on one hand, and product consumers, on the other, will likely respond to competing proposals. The predicted responses of these two groups need not be identical, nor need they be the same as they would be for other groups operating in different contexts. Of course, it is possible that the predicted responses of the consumers of heavy machinery to a given phenomenon would be different from the predicted responses of consumers of toasters to that same phenomenon. If this is in fact the case, rather than default to a reliance on rational choice theory, policymakers should consider whether it would be efficacious for the law to approach products liability for industrial goods, which have a more limited, sophisticated market, differently than for mass consumer goods.

There is no doubt that a single, universally applicable theory of behavior is convenient and highly desirable. But if universality is inconsistent with sophistication and realism, legal policymakers are better off foregoing universality and, instead, creating a collection of situation-specific minitheories useful in the analysis of discrete legal problems. Moreover, there is a great deal to be said for an incremental approach to theorybuilding—that is, grafting on just enough theory to deal with the matter at hand rather than attempting to construct a universal theory. * * *

The third defense is to respond to evidence of a purported failing of rational choice theory by explaining how the anomaly in question could possibly be consistent with the theory if viewed from a different angle. This strategy avoids the problem of directly refuting or proving rational choice theory wrong, but in doing so the defender implicitly retreats to a conception of rational choice theory that is so thin that it can have no predictive value.

Consider, as an example, the contention that rational individuals will not pay attention to sunk costs when choosing between options because such costs cannot affect the marginal utility to be derived from future activities. This leads to the prediction that an individual who has bought an expensive ticket to the symphony will be no more likely to attend than an individual who has been given a free ticket, assuming the two have an equal appreciation for classical music and that all other things are also equal. There is ample evidence that many people would in fact be more likely to attend the performance if they have paid for the ticket, reasoning that "the money would be wasted if I don't go."

A clever proponent of rational choice theory might respond to this apparent violation of the theory by asserting that rational people are fully aware of the fact that they may be reluctant later to attend a particular concert, and, knowing that they will both enjoy the concert if they attend and that they will feel guilty if they allow an expensive ticket to go unused, they purchase a ticket in advance as a precommitment strategy to ensure their attendance. In other words, pre-purchase is used as a means to control one's tendency not to do things that may appear to be painful but are really desirable in the long run.

Responses like this provide a useful way to understand behavior ex post (although the ex post account might well be inaccurate), but they also demonstrate the problem with relying on rational choice theory to inform future-oriented policymaking. The response makes it impossible to use rational choice theory to predict whether a person will be more likely to attend the symphony if he has purchased a ticket in advance (and has, therefore, "sunk" money into a symphony ticket) than if he were given the ticket for free. This defense of rational choice theory, in fact, demonstrates our basic contention that the theory can provide a plausible description of behavior only when the theory is adopted in such a thin form that it has little prescriptive value.

D. Modifying the Behavioral Predictions of Rational Choice Theory

To claim that rational choice theory is an insufficient behavioral model on which to base legal policy is not to argue that individuals behave irrationally (although they certainly do in some circumstances). Rather, it is to assert that legal scholars seeking to understand the incentive effects of law in order to propose efficacious legal policy should not be limited to rational choice theory. The goal of the law-and-behavioral-science movement is not, at least at this stage, to replace rational choice theory with an inconsistent paradigm but to modify the implausible elements of rational choice theory and supplement the inadequate elements in order to create a tool with more predictive power in specific situations.

* * *

———

NOTES AND QUESTIONS

1.   Bounded rationality: data. Theorists of bounded rationality have identified a host of cognitive quirks of human beings that, Korobkin and Ulen argue, undermine the concept of the neoclassical "rational actor." These include the following:

(1) Complex decisions and "satisficing." Traditional economic theory would suggest that the more information that should be provided to people, the better they will be able to satisfy their preferences. But in fact people have limited abilities to process information and limited time in which to do so. Thus, when faced with very complex consumer decisions (Which cell phone plan should I adopt? Which health care insurance plan should I adopt?), people adopt decision-making shortcuts, and they look for a "good enough" outcome, rather than the "optimal" outcome.

(2) People tend systematically to make mistakes about probabilities relating to representativeness and risk. People assume that memorable events are more common than they are. For example, most people believe that homicides and car accidents kill more Americans than diabetes and stomach cancer, presumably because of the greater media coverage provided to the former two, although the two diseases kill far more people.

(3) People tend to interpret the world in self-serving ways. That is, even if they intellectually recognize the probabilities of certain events, they predict that good things will disproportionately happen to them and bad things will disproportionately happen to other people. For example, newlyweds are likely to represent the odds of their divorce as zero or close to zero, even though it is common knowledge that half of all marriages end in divorce.

(4) People employ "hindsight bias" to interpret events in the past as having been inevitable.

(5) People exhibit the "endowment effect": they place a higher monetary value on items they own than on those that they do not own. Thus, people tend to demand more money to have an item taken away from them than they would pay to acquire the same item.

2.   Bounded rationality: reliability of the theory. The theory of bounded rationality rests on experimental findings, usually involving students and other test subjects paid to participate in a research study. Should these findings be extrapolated to the real world?

Are these findings culture-specific, or might they vary cross-culturally? Consider, for example, Robin Paul Malloy's attempt to demonstrate the famous "prisoner's dilemma" to a group of Chinese legal scholars, lawyers, and officials:

> Using the classic scenario, I informed all players that they had just committed a serious criminal offense, such as a robbery. I told them they and their partner had both been arrested and that the police would deal with each of them individually. Then I separated the teams and isolated each player from the other member of his or her team.
> * * *
>
> In this classic arrangement, self-interest is supposed to lead each player to snitch on the other so that we end up with a less than optimal strategy being selected. Clearly both players are best off when they each remain silent, but the incentive structure of the game motivates the rational self-interested player to cooperate with the police. This is because neither player wants to be left "holding the bag," so to speak, in the event that the other player uses a cooperation strategy in order to pin the crime on his or her accomplice.
>
> In all six teams, each composed of players who did not know each other prior to attending this training program, every single player opted to remain silent. Thus, not one of the twelve players was convicted and no one acted in the way that traditional law and economic approaches would predict. When we took class time to discuss the outcome I explained how the pay-off matrix was supposed to encourage them to snitch on each other. Participants in the exercise responded that they understood the costs and the incentives presented by the matrix. They said that they understood that the incentive structure encouraged them to cooperate with the police but none of them gave credence to the incentives. They interpreted the incentive structure from within a community understanding in which no one in China trusts the police. Any incentive structure offered by the police would, therefore, not be expected to be honored. The best course of action when dealing with the police, I was told, was to say nothing.

ROBIN PAUL MALLOY, LAW AND MARKET ECONOMY: REINTERPRETING THE VALUES OF LAW AND ECONOMICS 12–13 (2000).

3. Bounded rationality: implications. Does the idea of bounded rationality destroy the foundations of neoclassical economics, as Korobkin and Ulen claim? Or might neoclassical economics find a way to mathematically model bounded rationality in a way that preserves the basic theory?

4. Bounded rationality and public policy. How should law and public policy respond to the fluidity of people's preferences, and the theory of bounded rationality? In the excerpt that follows, updating his earlier work on social norms, Cass Sunstein (writing with Richard Thaler) concludes that some form of government paternalism is both inevitable and desirable.

Libertarian Paternalism Is Not an Oxymoron

70 U. CHI. L. REV. 1159, 1159–66, 1184–86, 1188–90, 1199–1201, 1202 (2003).

■ CASS R. SUNSTEIN & RICHARD H. THALER

      * * *

Consider two studies of savings behavior:

- Hoping to increase savings by workers, several employers have adopted a simple strategy. Instead of asking workers to elect to participate in a 401(k) plan, workers will be assumed to want to participate in such a plan, and hence they will be enrolled automatically unless they specifically choose otherwise. This simple change in the default rule has produced dramatic increases in enrollment.

- Rather than changing the default rule, some employers have provided their employees with a novel option: *Allocate a portion of future wage increases to savings.* Employees who choose this plan are free to opt out at any time. A large number of employees have agreed to try the plan, and only a few have opted out. The result has been significant increases in savings rates.

Libertarians embrace freedom of choice, and so they deplore paternalism. Paternalists are thought to be skeptical of unfettered freedom of choice and to deplore libertarianism. According to the conventional wisdom, libertarians cannot possibly embrace paternalism, and paternalists abhor libertarianism. The idea of libertarian paternalism seems to be a contradiction in terms.

Generalizing from the two studies just described, we intend to unsettle the conventional wisdom here. We propose a form of paternalism, libertarian in spirit, that should be acceptable to those who are firmly committed to freedom of choice on grounds of either autonomy or welfare. Indeed, we urge that libertarian paternalism provides a basis for both understanding and rethinking a number of areas of contemporary law, including those aspects that deal with worker welfare, consumer protection, and the family. In the process of defending these claims, we intend to make some objections to widely held beliefs about both freedom of choice and paternalism. Our emphasis is on the fact that in many domains, people lack clear, stable, or well-ordered preferences. What they choose is strongly influenced by details of the context in which they make their choice, for example default rules, framing effects (that is, the wording of possible options), and starting points. These contextual influences render the very meaning of the term "preferences" unclear.

Consider the question whether to undergo a risky medical procedure. When people are told, "Of those who undergo this procedure, 90 percent are still alive after five years," they are far more likely to agree to the procedure than when they are told, "Of those who undergo this procedure, 10 percent are dead after five years." What, then, are the patient's "preferences" with respect to this procedure? Repeated experiences with such problems might be expected to eliminate this framing effect, but doctors too are vulnerable to it. Or return to the question of savings for retirement. It is now clear that if an employer requires employees to make an affirmative election in favor of savings, with the default rule devoting 100 percent of wages to current income, the level of savings will be far lower than if the employer adopts an automatic enrollment program from which employees are freely permitted to opt out. Can workers then be said to have well-defined preferences about how much to save? This simple example can be extended to many situations involving the behavior of workers and consumers.

As the savings problem illustrates, the design features of both legal and organizational rules have surprisingly powerful influences on people's choices. We urge that such rules should be chosen with the explicit goal of improving the welfare of the people affected by them. The libertarian aspect of our strategies lies in the straightforward insistence that, in general, people should be free to opt out of specified arrangements if they choose to do so. To borrow a phrase, libertarian paternalists urge that people should be "free to choose." Hence we do not aim to defend any approach that blocks individual choices.

The paternalistic aspect consists in the claim that it is legitimate for private and public institutions to attempt to influence people's behavior even when third-party effects are absent. In other words, we argue for self-conscious efforts, by private and public institutions, to steer people's choices in directions that will improve the choosers' own welfare. In our understanding, a policy therefore counts as "paternalistic" if it attempts to influence the choices of affected parties in a way that will make choosers better off. Drawing on some well-established findings in behavioral economics and cognitive psychology, we emphasize the possibility that in some cases individuals make inferior decisions in terms of their own welfare—decisions that they would change if they had complete information, unlimited cognitive abilities, and no lack of self-control. In addition, the notion of libertarian paternalism can be complemented by that of *libertarian benevolence*, by which plan design features such as default rules, framing effects, and starting points are enlisted in the interest of vulnerable third parties. We shall devote some discussion to this possibility.

Libertarian paternalism is a relatively weak and nonintrusive type of paternalism, because choices are not blocked or fenced off. In its most cautious forms, libertarian paternalism imposes trivial costs on those who seek to depart from the planner's preferred option. But the approach we recommend nonetheless counts as paternalistic, because private and public planners are not trying to track people's anticipated choices, but are self-consciously attempting to move people in welfare-promoting directions. Some libertarians are likely to have little or no trouble with our endorsement of paternalism for private institutions; their chief objection is to paternalistic law and government. But as we shall show, the same points that support welfare-promoting private paternalism apply to government as well. It follows that one of our principal targets is the dogmatic anti-paternalism of numerous analysts of law, including many economists and economically oriented lawyers. We believe that this dogmatism is based on a combination of a false assumption and two misconceptions.

The false assumption is that almost all people, almost all of the time, make choices that are in their best interest or at the very least are better, by their own lights, than the choices that would be made by third parties. This claim is either tautological, and therefore uninteresting, or testable. We claim that it is testable and false, indeed obviously false. In fact, we do not think that anyone believes it on reflection. Suppose that a chess novice were to play against an experienced player. Predictably the novice would lose precisely because he made inferior choices—choices that could easily be improved by some helpful hints. More generally, how well people choose is an empirical question, one whose answer is likely to vary across domains. As a first approximation, it seems reasonable to say that people make better choices in contexts in which they have experience and good information (say, choosing ice cream flavors) than in contexts in which they are inexperienced and poorly informed (say, choosing among medical treatments or investment options). So long as people are not choosing perfectly, it is at least possible that some policy could make them better off by improving their decisions.

The first misconception is that there are viable alternatives to paternalism. In many situations, some organization or agent must make a choice that will affect the behavior of some other people. There is, in those situations, no alternative to a kind of paternalism—at least in the form of an intervention that affects what people choose. We are emphasizing, then, the possibility that people's preferences, in certain domains and across a certain range, are influenced by the choices made by planners. The point applies to both private and public actors, and hence to those who design legal rules as well as to those who serve consumers. As a simple example, consider the cafeteria at some organization. The cafeteria must make a multitude of decisions, including which foods to serve, which ingredients to use, and in what order to arrange the choices. Suppose that the director of the cafeteria notices that customers have a tendency to choose more of the items that are presented earlier in the line. How should the director decide in what order to present the items? To simplify, consider some alternative strategies that the director might adopt in deciding which items to place early in the line:

1. She could make choices that she thinks would make the customers best off, all things considered.

2. She could make choices at random.

3. She could choose those items that she thinks would make the customers as obese as possible.

4. She could give customers what she thinks they would choose on their own.

Option 1 appears to be paternalistic, but would anyone advocate options 2 or 3? Option 4 is what many anti-paternalists would favor, but it is much harder to implement than it might seem. Across a certain domain of possibilities, consumers will often lack well-formed preferences, in the sense of preferences that are firmly held and preexist the director's own choices about how to order the relevant items. If the arrangement of the alternatives has a significant effect on the selections the customers make, then their true "preferences" do not formally exist.

Of course, market pressures will impose a discipline on the self-interested choices of those cafeteria directors who face competition. To that extent, those directors must indeed provide people with options they are willing to buy. A cafeteria that faces competition and offers healthy but terrible-tasting food is unlikely to do well. Market-oriented libertarians might urge that the cafeteria should attempt to maximize profits, selecting menus in a way that will increase net revenues. But profit maximization is not the appropriate goal for cafeterias granted a degree of monopoly power—for example, those in schools, dormitories, or some companies. Furthermore, even those cafeterias that face competition will find that some of the time, market success will come not from tracking people's ex ante preferences, but from providing goods and services that turn out, in practice, to promote their welfare, all things considered. Consumers might be surprised by what they end up liking; indeed, their preferences might change as a result of consumption. And in some cases, the discipline imposed by market pressures will nonetheless allow the director a great deal of room to maneuver, because people's preferences are not well-formed across the relevant domains.

While some libertarians will happily accept this point for private institutions, they will object to government efforts to influence choice in the name of welfare. Skepticism about government might be based on the fact that governments are disciplined less or perhaps not at all by market pressures. Or such skepticism might be based on the fear that parochial interests will drive government planners in their own preferred directions (the public choice problem). We agree that for government, the risks of mistake and overreaching are real and sometimes serious. But governments, no less than cafeterias (which governments frequently run), have to provide starting points of one or another kind; this is not avoidable. As we shall emphasize, they do so every day through the rules of contract and tort, in a way that inevitably affects some preferences and choices. In this respect, the anti-paternalist position is unhelpful—a literal nonstarter.

The second misconception is that paternalism always involves coercion. As the cafeteria example illustrates, the choice of the order in which to present food items does not coerce anyone to do anything, yet one might prefer some orders to others on grounds that are paternalistic in the sense that we use the term. Would anyone object to putting the fruit and salad before the desserts at an elementary school cafeteria if the result were to increase the consumption ratio of apples to Twinkies? Is this question fundamentally different if the customers are adults? Since no coercion is involved, we think that some types of paternalism should be acceptable to even the most ardent libertarian. In the important domain of savings behavior, we shall offer a number of illustrations. To those anti-libertarians who are suspicious of freedom of choice and would prefer to embrace welfare instead, we urge that it is often possible for paternalistic planners to make common cause with their libertarian adversaries by adopting policies that promise to promote welfare but that also make room for freedom of choice. To confident planners, we suggest that the risks of confused or ill-motivated plans are reduced if people are given the opportunity to reject the planner's preferred solutions.

The thrust of our argument is that the term "paternalistic" should not be considered pejorative, just descriptive. Once it is understood that some organizational decisions are inevitable, that a form of paternalism cannot be avoided, and that the alternatives to paternalism (such as choosing options to make people worse off) are unattractive, we can abandon the less interesting question of whether to be paternalistic or not, and turn to the more constructive question of how to choose among the possible choice-influencing options. To this end we make two general suggestions. First, programs should be designed using a type of welfare analysis, one in which a serious attempt is made to measure the costs and benefits of outcomes (rather than relying on estimates of willingness to pay). Choosers should be given more choices if the welfare benefits exceed the welfare costs. Second, some results from the psychology of decisionmaking should be used to provide ex ante guidelines to support reasonable judgments about when consumers and workers will gain most by increasing options. We argue that those who are generally inclined to oppose paternalism should consider these suggestions uncontroversial.

* * *

The inevitability of paternalism is most clear when the planner has to choose starting points or default rules. But if the focus is on welfare, it is reasonable to ask whether the planner should go beyond the inevitable, and whether such a planner can also claim to be libertarian. To illustrate the problem, return to the simple cafeteria example discussed above. Putting the fruit before the desserts is a fairly mild intervention. A more intrusive step would be to place the desserts in another location altogether, so that diners have to get up and get a dessert after they have finished the rest of their meal. This step raises the transaction costs of eating dessert, and according to a standard economic analysis the proposal is quite unattractive—it seems to make dessert eaters worse off and no one better off. But many people face problems of self-control, and the results include illness and disease, small and large. Once the costs of self-control are incorporated into the analysis, we can see that some diners would prefer this arrangement, namely those who would eat a dessert if it were put in front of them but would resist temptation if given a little help. To fit with libertarian principles, the planner could arrange two lines in the cafeteria: the tempting line and the non-tempting line. The tempting line would include everything, whereas the non-tempting line would make unhealthy foods less available. Since people could choose either line, this passes the libertarian test. (As a solution to the self-control problem, it might not be entirely adequate, because people would be tempted to join the tempting line.)

Hence it is possible to preserve freedom of choice, and to allow opt-outs, but also to favor self-conscious efforts to promote welfare by helping people to solve problems of bounded rationality and bounded self-control. Efforts of this kind need not attempt to give people what they would choose ex ante, even in cases in which preferences exist; but such efforts would nonetheless allow people to move in their preferred directions.

In the domain of employee behavior, there are many imaginable illustrations. Employees might be automatically enrolled in a 401(k) plan, with a right to opt out, but employers might require a waiting period, and perhaps a consultation with an adviser, before the opt-out could be effective. Thaler and Benartzi have proposed a method of increasing contributions to 401(k) plans that also meets the libertarian test. Under the Save More Tomorrow plan, * * * employees are invited to sign up for a program in which their contributions to the savings plan are increased annually whenever they get a raise. Once employees join the plan, they stay in until they opt out or reach the maximum savings rate. In the first company to use this plan, the employees who joined increased their savings rates from 3.5 percent to 11.6 percent in a little over two years (three raises). Very few of the employees who join the plan drop out. We believe that this is successful libertarian paternalism in action. In fact, the ideas of automatic enrollment and Save More Tomorrow provide quite promising models for increasing saving; they might well be more effective than imaginable economic incentives, as for example through decreased taxes on savings.

The same sort of strategy might be used in many domains. Moving from paternalism to protection of third parties, employers (or the state) might seek to increase charitable giving from workers. Is it possible to produce a form of libertarian benevolence, and if so, how might this be done? Moral suasion may or may not succeed, but compare a system of Give More Tomorrow. Because workers appear quite willing to part with a fraction of their future raises, such a system, like Save More Tomorrow, would be highly appealing to many people. In fact the ideas explored here might well be used to produce significant increases in charitable donations (of course, there are obvious complexities about institutional design and appropriate default beneficiaries).

It should now be clear that the difference between libertarian and non-libertarian paternalism is not simple and rigid. The libertarian paternalist insists on preserving choice, whereas the non-libertarian paternalist is willing to foreclose choice. But in all cases, a real question is the cost of exercising choice, and here there is a continuum rather than a sharp dichotomy. A libertarian paternalist who is especially enthusiastic about free choice would be inclined to make it relatively costless for people to obtain their preferred outcomes. (Call this a *libertarian* paternalist.) By contrast, a libertarian paternalist who is especially confident of his welfare judgments would be willing to impose real costs on workers and consumers who seek to do what, in the paternalist's view, would not be in their best interests. (Call this a libertarian *paternalist*.)

Rejecting both routes, a non-libertarian paternalist would attempt to block certain choices. But notice that almost any such attempt will amount, in practice, to an effort to impose high costs on those who try to make those choices. Consider a law requiring drivers to wear seat belts. If the law is enforced, and a large fine is imposed, the law is non-libertarian even though determined violators can exercise their freedom of choice—at the expense of the fine. But as the expected fine approaches zero, the law approaches libertarianism. The libertarian paternalism that we are describing and defending here attempts to ensure, as a general rule, that people can easily avoid the paternalist's suggested option.

* * *

We are now in a position to categorize a diverse set of paternalistic interventions: minimal paternalism, required active choices, procedural constraints, and substantive constraints.

a) Minimal paternalism. Minimal paternalism is the form of paternalism that occurs whenever a planner (private or public) constructs a default rule or starting point with the goal of influencing behavior. So long as it is costless or nearly costless to depart from the default plan, minimal paternalism is maximally libertarian. This is the form of paternalism that we have described as inevitable.

b) Required active choices. Unsure of what choices will promote welfare, a planner might reject default plans or starting points entirely and force people to choose explicitly (what we have described as the strategy of required active choices). This approach finds an analogue in information-eliciting default rules in contract law, designed to give contracting parties a strong incentive to say what they want. To the extent that planners force people to choose whether or not people would like to choose, there is a paternalistic dimension to their actions. ("Choosing is good for both freedom and welfare," some appear to think, whether or not people agree with them!) We think that the argument for requiring choices stands or falls largely on the welfare consequences.

c) Procedural constraints. A slightly more aggressive form of paternalism occurs when the default plan is accompanied by procedural constraints designed to ensure that any departure is fully voluntary and entirely rational. When procedural constraints are in place, it is not costless to depart from the default plan. The extent of the cost, and the aggressiveness of the paternalism, will of course vary with the extent of the constraints. The justification for the constraints will depend on whether there are serious problems of bounded rationality and bounded self-control; if so, the constraints are justified not on the ground that the planner disagrees with people's choices, but because identifiable features of the situation make it likely that choices will be defective. Such features may include an unfamiliar setting, a lack of experience, and a risk of impulsiveness. The Age Discrimination in Employment Act is our principal example here.

d) Substantive constraints. Alternatively, a planner might impose substantive constraints, allowing people to reject the default arrangement, but not on whatever terms they choose. On this approach, the planner selects the terms along which the parties will be permitted to move in their preferred directions. The Model Termination Act and the Fair Labor Standards Act are illustrations. The extent of the departure from libertarianism will be a function of the gap between the legally specified terms and the terms that parties would otherwise reach. Here too the justification for the constraint depends on bounded rationality and bounded self-control.

e) A thin line. A planner might reject freedom of choice on the ground that those who reject the default plan will err all or almost all of the time. Such a planner will impose significant costs on those who depart from the plan. As we have said, there is a thin line between non-libertarian paternalists and libertarian paternalists who impose high costs, procedural or substantive, on those who reject the plan. Almost all of the time, even the non-libertarian paternalist will allow choosers, at some cost, to reject the proposed course of action. Those who are required to wear motorcycle helmets can decide to risk the relevant penalty, and to pay it if need be. Employers and employees might agree to sub-minimum wage work and risk the penalties if they are caught. In this particular sense, penalties are always prices.

III.   How to Choose: The Toolbox of the Libertarian Paternalist

How should sensible planners choose among possible systems, given that some choice is necessary? We suggest two approaches to this problem. If feasible, a comparison of possible rules should be done using a form of cost-benefit analysis, one that pays serious attention to welfare effects. In many cases, however, such analyses will be both difficult and expensive. As an alternative, we offer some rules of thumb that might be adopted to choose among various options. In general, it makes sense to experiment with possible approaches to identify their results for both choices and outcomes. We have emphasized automatic enrollment plans and Save More Tomorrow because studies have suggested that both of these have a great deal of potential. In other domains, plans are likely to be proposed in the face of highly imperfect information; more data will reveal a great deal. Large-scale programs are most justified if repeated experiments have shown that they actually work.

* * *

The argument for libertarian paternalism seems compelling to us, even obvious, but we suspect that hard-line anti-paternalists, and possibly others, will have objections. We respond to three possible objections here.

The first objection is that by advocating libertarian paternalism, we are starting down a very slippery slope. Once one grants the possibility that default rules for savings or cafeteria lines should be designed paternalistically, it might seem impossible to resist highly non-libertarian interventions. Critics might envisage an onslaught of what seem, to them, to be unacceptably intrusive forms of paternalism, from requiring motorcycle riders to wear helmets, to mandatory waiting periods before consumer purchases, to bans on cigarette smoking, to intrusive health care reforms of many imaginable kinds. In the face of the risk of overreaching, might it not be better to avoid starting down the slope at all?

There are three responses. First, in many cases there is simply no viable alternative to paternalism in the weak sense, and hence planners are forced to take at least a few tiny steps down that slope. Recall that paternalism, in the form of effects on behavior, is frequently inevitable. In such cases, the slope cannot be avoided. Second, the libertarian condition, requiring opt-out rights, sharply limits the steepness of the slope. So long as paternalistic interventions can be easily avoided by those who seek to adopt a course of their own, the risks emphasized by anti-paternalists are minimal. Third, those who make the slippery slope argument are acknowledging the existence of a self-control problem, at least for planners. But if planners, including bureaucrats and human resource managers, suffer from self-control problems, then it is highly likely that other people do too.

A second and different sort of objection is based on a deep mistrust of the ability of the planner (especially the planner working for the government) to make sensible choices. Even those who normally believe that everyone chooses rationally treat with deep skepticism any proposal that seems to hinge on rational choices by bureaucrats. Part of the skepticism is based on a belief that bureaucrats lack the discipline imposed by market pressures; part of it is rooted in the fact that individuals have the welfare-promoting incentives that are thought to come from self-interest; part of it is rooted in the fear that well-organized private groups will move bureaucrats in their preferred directions. We happily grant that planners are human, and thus are both boundedly rational and subject to the influence of objectionable pressures. Nevertheless, as we have stressed, these human planners are sometimes forced to make choices, and it is surely better to have them trying to improve people's welfare rather than the opposite. In emphasizing the important effect of plan design on choice (a point under-appreciated by economists, lawyers, and planners), we hope to encourage plan designers to become more informed. And by arguing for a libertarian check on bad plans, we hope to create a strong safeguard against ill-considered or ill-motivated plans. To the extent that individual self-interest is a healthy check on planners, freedom of choice is an important corrective.

A third objection would come from the opposite direction. Enthusiastic paternalists, emboldened by evidence of bounded rationality and self-control problems, might urge that in many domains, the instruction to engage in only libertarian paternalism is too limiting. At least if the focus is entirely or mostly on welfare, it might seem clear that in certain circumstances, people should not be given freedom of choice for the simple reason that they will choose poorly. In those circumstances, why should anyone insist on libertarian paternalism, as opposed to unqualified or non-libertarian paternalism?

This objection raises complex issues of both value and fact, and we do not intend to venture into difficult philosophical territory here. Our basic response is threefold. First, we reiterate our understanding that planners are human, and so the real comparison is between boundedly rational choosers with self-control problems and boundedly rational planners facing self-control problems of their own. It is doubtful that the comparison can sensibly be made in the abstract. Second, an opt-out right operates as a safeguard against confused or improperly motivated planners, and in many contexts, that safeguard is crucial even if it potentially creates harm as well. Third, nothing we have said denies the possibility that in some circumstances it can be advisable to impose significant costs on those who reject the proposed course of action, or even to deny freedom of choice altogether. * * * Our only qualification is that when third-party effects are not present, the general presumption should be in favor of freedom of choice, and that presumption should be rebutted only when individual choice is demonstrably inconsistent with individual welfare.

* * *

In our view, libertarian paternalism is not only a conceptual possibility; it also provides a foundation for rethinking many areas of private and public law. We believe that policies rooted in libertarian paternalism will often be a big improvement on the most likely alternative: inept neglect.

C. BEYOND TRADITIONAL MACROECONOMICS: "ECOLOGICAL ECONOMICS"

The problem of pollution has long been recognized to pose a problem of market failure, because clean air and water is not a good that can be restricted to those who can pay for it. Proposals to address this market failure have often focused on creating markets for pollution, through, for example, tradable emissions permits. A deeper criticism of neoclassical economics is that such economic analysis treats the earth's resources as infinite, when in fact the depletion of nonrenewable resources should be counted as a cost. As Douglas Kysar explains:

> Conventional economists often state that growth of human economic production is not checked by restrictions imposed by nature. In other words, they treat the human economic process as an open system that draws resources and emits wastes through a relatively undefined and unexamined relationship with nature. In contrast, ecological economists view the means of production and nature as components of the same closed system. On this account, the human economic process faces hard constraints imposed by the absolute or temporal scarcity of nonrenewable resources and renewable resources, as well as by the limited capacity of ecological mechanisms to absorb the pollution produced by exploitation of those resources. As a consequence of such constraints, society must remain cognizant of the extent and quality of existing resource stocks, as well as the capacity for natural systems to absorb waste outputs created during the transformation of those stocks into human goods.

Douglas Kysar, *Law, Environment, and Vision*, 97 Nw. U. L. Rev. 675, 680 (2003).

One effect of taking the finite resources of the planet seriously is the effort to catalog and quantify the "services" provided by the natural world in order to internalize their costs. Another effect has been the recognition that questions of sustainability and scale should play a role in macroeconomic analysis. Drawing on the pioneering work of Herman Daly, Kysar argues:

> Markets, through their twin devices of price information and economic incentives, are unparalleled in their effectiveness at allocating resources efficiently. They do not, however, resolve the altogether separate problems of achieving distributive justice and ecological sustainability. Put differently, economists recognize that a Pareto-optimal allocation of resources can be achieved with respect to any given distribution of income, including ones that might be described as unjust. Similarly, a Pareto-optimal allocation of resources can be achieved with respect to any given scale of the human economy, including ones that might lead to ecological peril. "Ecological criteria of sustainability, like ethical criteria of justice, are not served by markets." Thus, Daly argues that "[o]ptimal scale, like distributive justice, full employment, or price level stability, is a macroeconomic goal," requiring unique macroeconomic policy instruments.

id. at 683–84.

In the following excerpt, Kysar introduces to a legal audience the emerging field of ecological economics. In what ways does ecological economics echo the internal critiques of microeconomics? In what ways does it undermine the neoclassical vision altogether?

———

Sustainability, Distribution, and the Macroeconomic Analysis of Law

43 B.C. L. Rev. 1, 4–7, 17–18, 19, 20–26, 28–34, 35–38, 39–44, 63–71 (2001).

■ Douglas A. Kysar

Since its inception, law and economics has attracted criticism from scholars who find its assumptions unrealistic. For a long time, this response was purely critical in form, exposing as flawed the behavioral assumptions of law and economics without proposing corresponding changes to increase its veracity. In recent years, however, a group of scholars has devoted considerable insight and energy to the project of behavioral law and economics. This emerging subdiscipline fuses traditional neoclassical economic analysis with lessons drawn from cognitive psychology and decision theory research. The result is a law and economics grounded in assumptions that comport better with observed real-world behavior than the stylized rational actor model featured in conventional law and economics. The fruits of this effort are now dominating new research in law journals, such that it is no overstatement to conclude, "The future of economic analysis of law lies in new and better understandings of decision and choice."

With a few notable exceptions, this project to improve the veracity of law and economics assumptions has focused exclusively on the foundational principles of microeconomics. A group of dedicated scholars within economics, biology, and ecology departments have undertaken a parallel project to reform the assumptions of *macro*economics. These scholars—who have banded together under the moniker, *ecological economists*—adopt the same methodology as legal behavioral economists. They examine the most robust findings from disciplines outside of economics and utilize those findings to steer economic analysis toward what they believe is greater real-world relevance. As behavioralists instill microeconomic analysis with the teachings of cognitive psychology and decision theory, ecological economists bring the findings of ecology, biology, and environmental science to macroeconomics.

This Article introduces the field of ecological economics and analyzes its potential use as a macroeconomics for legal analysis. * * *

Ecological economics * * * is built around a more complex understanding of human economic goals than traditional economic analysis. Economists recognize two primary functions served by the market: the allocation of resources among competing uses (allocation) and the distribution of wealth among market participants (distribution). In grossly simplified terms, economists believe that the first function suggests market policies designed to maximize allocative efficiency, while the second function requires a social decision best left to the political process. Ecological economists argue that a third function served by the market has been overlooked by conventional analysis: moderation of the scale of human economic activity vis-à-vis the ecological superstructure upon which all life and activity depends (scale). While allocation determines the purposes for which resources are used, scale determines the rate and amounts of resources that are used.

Like their orthodox counterparts, ecological economists offer a norm to accompany this concept. Just as economists almost instinctively believe that allocative efficiency should be maximized, ecological economists tend to believe that the scale of the economy should be sustainable, that is, capable of reproduction in perpetuity (or its practical equivalent). Readers who are uncomfortable with some of the more dramatic implications of sustainability should bear in mind that the fundamental insight of ecological economics is a recognition of the concept of scale, not necessarily the norm of sustainability. Whether or not one accepts all of the implications of sustainability as a norm, ecological economists seek acknowledgment that human economic activity impacts the environment and that the size and rate of that impact is a legitimate subject of social and legal influence.

* * *

B. Some Fundamentals

Although the field is still relatively new and ill-formed, several fundamental concepts have gained sufficient acceptance to be called "standard" ecological economics. This Section examines those concepts in detail.

1. The Relationship Between Ecological and Economic Systems

"The vision of modern economics in general, and especially of macroeconomics, is the familiar circular flow diagram." The economy is viewed as a self-contained system within which exchange value circulates between producers and consumers. The macroeconomic loop makes no accounting of the actual resource materials from which goods are produced, or the waste matter into which goods are transformed during consumption. Physical dimensions of economic activity simply do not exist in the textbook circular flow diagram. Thus, resource depletion, environmental pollution, impairment of necessary environmental services such as water filtration or carbon absorption, or indeed any other relationship between economic activity and factors outside of the narrow universe of value exchange are ignored by standard macroeconomics. As [pioneering ecological economist Herman] Daly put it, "It is exactly as if a biology textbook proposed to study an animal only in terms of its circulatory system, without ever mentioning its digestive tract...."

Ecological economists believe that this conception is misguided. Human economic activity impacts the ecological sphere in all phases of production and consumption, in ways both patently obvious, such as the clear-cutting that has occurred in the majority of the forested areas of the globe, and deceptively subtle, such as the rise of greenhouse gases in the atmosphere from 277 ppmv (parts per million by volume) to 367 ppmv since pre-Industrial times. * * *

    * * *

Humans are setting in motion complex feedback loops whose little-understood mechanisms could become self-perpetuating. Melting of polar ice caps through global warming could cause the release of billions of tons of methane gas trapped beneath crystal structures on the edges of continental shelves. One cubic meter of this methane gas has the same ultraviolet radiation trapping effect as twenty cubic meters of carbon dioxide, the most voluminous greenhouse gas produced by human activity.

    * * *

Nevertheless, even international institutions such as the World Bank continue to rely on the rarefied macroeconomic conception of exchange found at the beginning of standard texts. As Daly notes, "Things are no better when [one] turn[s] to the advanced chapters at the end of most macroeconomic texts, where the topic is growth theory." For years the theory was stated as a simple function involving K and L, capital and labor. Resource flows and waste output flows were not even a factor in the equation. Thus, the only constraints on economic growth appeared to be the availability of man-made capital and human labor. * * *

* * *

As an example of the orthodox view, many economic forecasters view China, with its 1.2 billion people, as an untapped market for goods associated with the affluent Western lifestyle. In other words, forecasters see the glimmer of economic growth in the development of China. Other commentators, however, argue that if the entire Chinese population were to adopt the lifestyle of consumers in a nation like the United States, the consequent ecological footprint would be catastrophic. Indeed, it does not appear that the Chinese could even eat like Americans, let alone buy, build, drive, and discard like Americans: "If the current world grain harvest, averaging 1.75 billion tons thus far during the 1990s, were boosted by roughly 15 percent to 2 billion tons, that harvest—if equitably distributed—could support [only] 2.5 billion people at the American level of consumption." To be sure, growth in consumption levels in China will be accompanied by growth in the nation's own productive capacity. It is far from clear, however, that arable land and agricultural productivity can be multiplied in the way that factories can.

2. The Laws of Thermodynamics

Assuming that environmental frontiers are not limitless, economics as the science of scarcity therefore must confront the scarcity of natural as well as man-made resources. While mainstream economists believe that they have found a theoretical avenue around this challenge, ecological economists confront it directly, incorporating the laws of thermodynamics into their analysis in order to better understand the quality of physical exchanges that occur between the ecological system and the economic subsystem. As [Vanderbilt economist Nicholas] Georgescu–Roegen demonstrated, such application reveals a disturbing truth about human economic activity (and indeed, about all activity within the material universe). The fixed quantum of matter-energy with which the universe is endowed must necessarily move from a state of high-availability to low-availability, of low-entropy to high-entropy, and of order to chaos. Thus, physical throughput in the human economy must always be conceived of as at least a partial liquidation of capital, rather than a mere expenditure of income.

For ecological economists, such cold fatalism is not cause for despair; it is cause for reform. Humanity is somewhat in control of the rate with which it advances entropic activity. A solar heated house only utilizes an infinitesimal fraction of the sun's several billion years of activity. A house heated by coal-fired electricity, on the other hand, transforms millions of years of condensed solar energy into greenhouse gases that persist in the atmosphere for decades. The economic argument for refusing to adopt the use of renewable energy sources immediately, on a widespread basis, is no longer as strong as it once was. The cost of solar cells has declined from more than $70 per watt in the 1970s to $4 per watt today (in 1994 dollars), while the world market has grown from 34 megawatts in 1988 to an estimated 125 megawatts in 1997. The fastest growing energy market in the past decade has not been oil, coal, or natural gas, but wind power, growing from 2000 megawatts in 1990 to 7600 megawatts in 1997, and remarkably achieving cost-competitiveness with its heavily subsidized, arguably unsustainable counterparts. But most of this development is occurring outside of the United States. Nations such as China, Mexico, Kenya, and Vietnam all currently use solar electrification to provide power to remote rural villages. In the view of ecological economists, nothing prevents industrialized nations such as the United States from doing the same besides entrenched political power and a failure to perceive the true costs of current practices. In light of this situation, * * * [i]t is not that Cadillacs prevent future spades and plows; it is that sport-utility vehicles prevent future wind turbines and solar cells.

3.   Optimal Scale and Sustainability

The foregoing discussion establishes another of the foundational principles of ecological economics: "The macroeconomy is an open subsystem of the ecosystem and is totally dependent upon it, both as a source for inputs of low-entropy matter-energy and as a sink for outputs of high-entropy matter-energy." Given such a conception, an inescapable question arises regarding how much the economic subsystem can grow before it places an unsustainable burden on the natural ecosystem. Conventional economists fail to address this issue because the macroeconomy is conceived of as the superstructure—conceptually, nothing exists "around" the macroeconomy. Thus, there is no reason to suspect that it cannot grow ad infinitum.

As Daly has noted, this failing is surprising given that every other economic concept involves a limit or point at which marginal benefits do not exceed marginal costs. More than one commentator has speculated that the disappearance of limits in macroeconomics serves as a theoretical expedient to avoid difficult questions of distribution. Instead of adopting such an approach, Daly argues that the logic of marginal analysis must apply with equal force to macroeconomics—that is, there must be a point at which the benefits from an increase in the scale of the economy are outweighed by the environmental and social costs entailed by such an increase. Economists and other thinkers interested in the welfare of humanity must therefore confront the issue of determining the optimal scale of the economy.

The most widely cited attempt to articulate a principle for limiting the scale of economic activity comes from the 1987 report of the United Nations World Commission on Environment and Development, popularly known as the *Brundtland Report*. This report urged nations to undergo only *sustainable development*, which it defined as development that "meets the needs of the present without compromising the ability of future generations to meet their own needs." As Susan Smith has explained, two principles underlie this notion of sustainable development: "[T]he Earth's finite capacity to accommodate people and industrial development, and a moral imperative not to deprive future generations of natural resources essential to well-being and quality of environment." Following the release of the *Brundtland Report*, several international agreements and statements of principles have further developed this goal of keeping human activity within the carrying capacity of the earth, including the Framework Convention on Climate Change, the Convention on Biological Diversity, the Rio Declaration, Agenda 21, and the Statement of Forest Principles.

While these developments were initially viewed as an important step toward reaching a consensus to restrict the scale of the global economy, they have come under fire more recently for lacking the conceptual clarity needed to avoid unsustainable growth. Among ecological economists, Daly has been especially critical of the *Brundtland Report*'s ambiguity: "Sustainable development is a term that everyone likes, but nobody is sure of what it means." Although the international community has agreed that it should not compromise the "needs" of future generations, it has not attempted to define what those "needs" will be. Should future generations be afforded only the natural resources necessary to maintain a basic level of subsistence? Should the "aesthetic" needs of the unborn be considered within the sustainable development rubric? What assumptions should be made about the ability of technological advancements to alleviate resource scarcities in the future? What type of allowance should be made for the limit of science's ability to recognize and assess the impact of economic activity on ecosystem viability?

 * * *

* * * Daly has advocated the necessity of a "steady-state economy" in which the scale of human economic activity—that is, "the physical scale or size of the human presence in the ecosystem as measured by population times per capita resource use"—does not exceed the point at which marginal macroeconomic benefits equal macroeconomic costs. Economists have typically ignored this type of marginal analysis at the macroeconomic level, opting to believe that micro-level consumption choices generally reflect Pareto improvements, and that therefore the aggregate of such choices must also reflect enhancements in social welfare. In Daly's view, however, prices only measure the scarcity of resources relative to each other. Micro-level choices may result in an efficient allocation of resources in relation to everything else, but they cannot determine an efficient *absolute* level of resource use. Therefore, just as full employment and fair distribution are macroeconomic goals that are not fully resolved by unfettered microeconomic activity, Daly believes that optimal scale is an issue that must be addressed by policy instruments operating on a macroeconomic level.

"A necessary requirement for this optimal scale is that the economy's *throughput*—the flow beginning with raw material inputs, followed by their conversion into commodities, and finally into waste outputs—be within the regenerative and absorptive capacities of the ecosystem." In other words, in order to be truly sustainable, the material scale of the economy must be within the carrying capacity of the earth. Giving flesh to the concept of "carrying capacity" is a challenging task that needs to be addressed before Daly's sustainable development can become a fully operable concept. Daly provides two fundamental principles toward that end: "Renewable resources should be exploited in a manner such that: (1) harvesting rates do not exceed regeneration rates; and (2) waste emissions do not exceed the renewable assimilative capacity of the local environment." Non-renewable resources should be depleted at a rate equal to the rate of creation of renewable substitutes.

These principles of resource use, however, are only the first step in what is an essentially scientific exercise. Determining whether a given level of population and per capita resource use is sustainable requires the expertise of ecologists, biologists, and environmental scientists, as well as economists. In Daly's view, the practitioners of economics should continue to practice their bread and butter of maximizing the market's allocative efficiency, but only after the optimal scale of that market has been determined by social consensus with input from both economic and noneconomic experts.

A second task that is not exclusively economic involves determining the desirable mix of population size and resource intensity that will be used to consume society's annual quota of natural capital and services. As noted above, the scale or level of physical throughput in the economy can be thought of as the product of population times per capita resource use. This definition implies that a smaller population could lead a more resource-intensive lifestyle than a larger one, while staying within ecologically-imposed constraints of sustainability. Conversely, a larger population must reduce its per capita resource use in order to maintain the ecological footprint of a smaller one. Because the level of throughput must not be allowed to exceed the point at which ecosystem losses exceed economic gains, society must make a conscious tradeoff between these two determinant factors of the scale of its economy. Obviously, such a tradeoff entails a moral, not merely an economic, choice. * * *

> * * *

4.   Measuring the Human Economy

Economics is fundamentally a quantitative discipline. As Samuelson puts it in his renowned textbook, "economics focuses on concepts that can actually be measured." Following the lead of John Maynard Keynes and Simon Kuznets, macroeconomists have focused exclusively on quantifying the productive capacity of the human economy. However, as seen in the last Section, a second constraint on economic growth exists—the carrying capacity of the ecosystem. Moreover, even ignoring ecological limits to growth, there is little reason to suppose that increases in the sheer magnitude of the human economy are always desirable from the perspective of social welfare. Recognizing the practical worth of quantification (and the need to confront conventional economists in their own language), ecological economists have begun to focus attention on the task of measuring the intersection of economic and ecological spheres. This Section addresses the response of ecological economists to traditional indexes of social welfare such as the gross national product (GNP), while the next Section outlines efforts to quantify the value of the ecological sphere.

Current national accounting measures produce a variety of results that would strike noneconomists as odd. For instance, when the Exxon Valdez oil spill necessitated $2.1 billion in clean-up costs, the U.S. GNP rose by that same amount, despite the fact that ten years later only two of the twenty-three most damaged wildlife species have recovered and 40% of area fishermen suffer depression over their destroyed livelihoods. Similarly, as Superfund contributors muster the $31 billion needed to clean the 1355 worst locations on the EPA's list of nearly 40,000 hazardous waste sites, GNP views the expenditure as an increase in economic welfare, rather than just a restoration. GNP also ignores basic accounting principles by treating the unsustainable exploitation of natural capital as pure income. Centuries of logging and construction have resulted in the loss of all but 1% to 5% of the original forest cover of the United States, yet GNP has made no allowance along the way for the depreciation of scarce natural capital.

Social as well as ecological costs frequently appear as gains under GNP accounting. When the estimated one third of American adults who are obese spent $39 billion in one year on health care costs for obesity-related diseases, the macroeconomic indicators recorded an unmitigated credit. When the position of the United States as home to 1.7 million prisoners and the largest incarceration system in the world necessitated a doubling of state spending on prisons in the last decade, GNP rose to reflect the social "progress" of unprecedented prison construction. And when the American divorce rate doubled between 1970 and the present, GNP recorded an increase from the real estate transactions, attorney bills, and other expenditures necessitated by the higher number of family fractures.

Such arguably counterintuitive results are an outgrowth of the "cowboy economy" in which more of anything is simply better, regardless of what it is. Standard national accounting measures such as GNP, and more recently gross domestic product (GDP), seek only to quantify the value of monetary transactions that occur in a given economy, with no distinction among purposes and no recognition of adverse consequences that result from such transactions. No allowance is made for the irreversible depletion of natural resource inputs, or the externalized costs of waste outputs. Indeed, such environmental costs are frequently treated as economic gains, leading to a perverse national incentive structure: A policy of maximizing GNP is "practically equivalent to a policy of maximizing depletion and pollution."

Nor is any accounting attempted of other "noneconomic" spheres such as the livelihood of communities, the stability of families, or the safety of schools. Unexamined pursuit of increases in GNP can lead to parasitic growth. Commercialization of social functions traditionally performed outside the economic sphere—such as the replacement of stay-at-home parenting by child care, prepared meals by convenience food, social networks by self-help tapes, and community activities by commercial entertainment—is a consequence encouraged by any national agenda that seeks to maximize GNP.

Nobel Prize-winning economist Simon Kuznets, one of the chief architects of the concept of GNP, warned that the measurement of GNP should never be mistaken for true national progress: "Distinctions must be kept in mind between quantity and quality of growth, between its costs and return, and between the short and the long run. Goals for 'more' growth should specify more growth of what and for what." Many policymakers, however, have largely ignored this advice, seeking continual, indiscriminate growth in GNP as the ready salve for all manner of national problems. Ecological economists, on the other hand, have criticized GNP as a concept that fosters unsustainable economic practices while failing to achieve its aim of approximating human welfare. In its stead, Daly and theologian John Cobb, Jr., have offered a substitute national wealth accounting measure that corrects for many of the GNP's failings.

Called the Index of Sustainable Economic Welfare (ISEW), Daly and Cobb's measure begins with total consumption expenditure data gathered by the U.S. Bureau of Economic Analysis and then proceeds to make a series of adjustments to arrive at a best estimate of sustainable economic welfare. The first adjustment, for income inequality, attempts to account for the fact that "an additional thousand dollars in income adds more to the welfare of a poor family than it does to a rich family." This notion, which many accept as a consequence of the principle of diminishing marginal utility of income, has important implications for the calculation of economic welfare. If income distribution becomes more uneven over a period of time, unadjusted dollar flows for that period will overstate welfare. To correct for this distortion, Daly and Cobb alter consumption expenditure data to reflect the degree of income inequality in the economy.

Next, Daly and Cobb add factors representing positive income streams from four sources that are currently absent from official consumption data—household labor, existing consumer durables, public streets and highways, and public spending on health and education. Conversely, deductions are made for expenditures that arguably do not contribute to improvement in economic welfare. For example, a portion of private spending on education is deducted to represent the "competitive" nature of such spending. Similarly, the authors disallow some private expenditures on health care because they view them as attributable to "growing health risks due to urbanization and industrialization." Other costs deducted from total expenditures because of their "defensive" nature include the costs of commuting, purchases of personal pollution control equipment such as air and water filters, and damages due to vehicular accidents.

Having attempted to refine the calculation of economic welfare in accord with certain social realities, Daly and Cobb then turn to the realities of the environment in relation to the economic subsystem. They first deduct amounts relating to the current environmental damage imposed by economic activity, including the annual cost of water pollution, air pollution, noise pollution, loss of wetlands, and loss of farmland. These costs are the least controversial of Daly and Cobb's estimates of environmental damage, as they represent tangible, present costs with little scientific dispute as to their existence. Moreover, the authors adopt a purposefully conservative approach to valuation of these costs. For instance, they do not include the costs of water pollution from nonpoint sources or the health-related costs of air pollution.

The authors also attempt to account for the long-term environmental costs associated with economic activity. First, Daly and Cobb recognize that the consumption of nonrenewable resources constitutes in part "a cost borne by future generations that should be subtracted from (debited to) the capital account of the current generation." To price this cost, the authors rely on the marginal cost of producing a renewable substitute: "For each unit of nonrenewable resource depleted, we have estimated the amount of money that would have to be invested in a process to create a perpetual stream of output of a renewable substitute for it." Second, Daly and Cobb undertake the daunting task of estimating the economic impact of long-term build-up of thermal waste in the environment. Such accounting is of course destined to be inexact, but Daly and Cobb's rough approximation seems at least preferable to the alternative of measuring the costs of global warming and ozone depletion at precisely zero. In a final set of adjustments, Daly and Cobb alter ISEW to account for changes in the domestic and international capital position of the national economy. These adjustments reflect the fact that current economic welfare can be maintained only if growth in the domestic capital stock keeps pace with population growth.

     * * *

* * * [W]hile the first subtotal of ISEW showed a consumer gain of $1737 billion for 1990, the end result revealed only $818 billion in net economic welfare created during the year. One can think of the $919 billion differential as a very rough estimate of the total cost of environmental and social externalities created by economic activity in 1990. Given that this amount is actually greater than the net value created that year, it is arguably an analytical strain to continue to refer to environmental and social costs as mere "externalities," a term suggesting only minor effects of limited interest. To the contrary, under Daly and Cobb's calculations, externalities appear to be a dominant effect of market transactions, suggesting that "it is time to restructure basic concepts and start with a different set of abstractions that can embrace what was previously external."

Contrasting the ISEW with GNP over a time series is also revealing. According to Daly and Cobb, GNP and ISEW both rose from 1951 until the 1970s (although the rate of growth in ISEW decreased from 1.57% to 0.21% between the 1960s and 1970s). In the 1980s, however, GNP continued to rise while ISEW actually declined by 0.43% per year. This decline suggests that continued increases in the scale of the human economy (as approximately signaled by increases in GNP) are anti-economic; that is, they impose more welfare costs than benefits (as signaled by decreases in

ISEW). Thus, beginning in the late 1970s and early 1980s, the United States may well have shifted from the cowboy to the spaceman economy, with all its attendant problems.

Of course, Daly and Cobb's figures are easily contestable, as would be any attempt to track and price the total social and environmental costs of human economic activity. Nevertheless, even without deducting for resource depletion and long-term environmental costs—the two most controversial and difficult to quantify aspects of ISEW—the pattern of change in ISEW remains largely the same. This suggests, at an absolute minimum, that undifferentiated growth in GNP is not necessarily consonant with economic welfare and that reliance on GNP as a measure of national success should be reevaluated.

5.   Valuing Ecosystem Services

In addition to reforming the measurement of national accounts, ecological economists have also devoted significant attention to quantifying the worth of ecosystem services. The attempt to place a monetary value on the elements of nature has long been controversial. Many view such attempts as an almost heretical failure to appreciate that nature is "priceless." Rutgers University biologist David Ehrenfeld provides a representative, if charged, example of this view: "I am afraid that I don't see much hope for a civilization so stupid that it demands a quantitative estimate of the value of its own umbilical cord." Others attack the practice from the opposite extreme, believing that the survey methods frequently used to price natural resources are fraught with complexities that render valuations wildly overstated. Nevertheless, economists, policymakers, and courts continue to place economic values on natural resources through the use of such techniques as restoration or replacement cost valuations, travel cost valuations, hedonic pricing, and contingent or willingness-to-pay valuations.

Commonly, the practice of commodifying nature occurs in the context of calculating after-the-fact damages awards for contamination of natural resources. Ecological economists have recently adopted a different approach, seeking to quantify the value of services provided by ecosystems *before* irreversible human disruption. The significance of focusing on ecosystem services, rather than natural resources, is that they are seen by researchers as largely irreplaceable and therefore more fundamental to human survival. Moreover, while the economy may be able to signal and adjust to specific resource scarcities, the services provided by the earth are generally not subject to economic signaling. Thus, in order to ensure the long-term sustainability of human economic activity, ecological economists believe that natural services which lack practical man-made substitutes should be given a quantified presence within economic decisionmaking. By generating even approximate figures for the value of these services, ecological economists hope to impress upon private and public decisionmakers the environmental costs of contemplated development schemes.

A celebrated example of such thinking can be seen in the City of New York's decision to reclaim watershed areas in the Catskills mountains rather than build a capital-intensive water treatment facility. The Catskills have long been the primary source of purified water for New York City, but in recent years the water failed EPA standards for drinking water due to development in the mountains as well as increased sewage, pesticide, and fertilizer contamination. The city estimated that a purification plant would cost $4 billion to build plus annual operating costs, while restoring the natural integrity of the Catskills through land acquisition and restoration would cost only around $660 million. Thus, the City decided to invest in "natural capital" as a more efficient and aesthetically desirable alternative to the traditional industrial solution.

The City of New York's choice was easy to make because the treatment plant option provided a clear and reliable measure of the worth of the Catskills watershed services. As James Salzman has noted, "Replacement cost provides an effective method for valuing services because one can compare dollar investments in natural capital and physical capital to determine payback periods and overall costs." Ecological economists believe that if valuations of ecosystem services are available to policymakers at crucial decision times in that manner, economic development will become much more consonant with sustainable use patterns. For instance, researchers studying alternative management strategies for mangrove forests in Indonesia have found that when nontimber uses, including fish, locally used products, and erosion control, are included in cost-benefit calculations, sustainable timber practices are significantly more economic than traditional ones, yielding $4,800 per hectare rather than merely $3,600.

* * *

Of course, in their totality, ecosystem services consist of the very ability to support human life, rendering their aggregate value equivalent to the very value one places on human existence. Economic tools are simply not designed to measure such concepts. By attempting to price the various subcomponents of ecosystems, however, ecological economists have begun to speak in a language that economists and policymakers can fathom and operationalize. As the Catskills watershed and Indonesian mangrove examples point out, the resulting dialogue can yield surprising agreement between environmental and economic interests. *The Economists' Statement on Climate Change*, signed by over 2500 economists, including eight Nobel Laureates, offers an unqualified endorsement of such collaborative exercises in the context of reducing greenhouse emissions: "[S]ound economic analysis shows that there are policy options that would slow climate change without harming American living standards, and these measures may in fact improve U.S. productivity in the longer run." Ecological economists believe that such "sound economic analysis" can become commonplace in the debate over competing business and environmental concerns.

6. Discount Rates and Intergenerational Equity

A final issue of concern to ecological economists is the use of discount rates in regulatory and investment decisionmaking. When evaluating a particular investment decision, economists typically reduce expected costs and benefits to present value using a discount rate, or a percentage factor that adjusts the amount of a value over time. For instance, using a discount rate of 10%, an investment yielding $110 in year two is worth only $100 in year one. If the investment costs $105 to make in year one, it is not an economic choice. Such reasoning holds well in the context of paper investment decisions. However, when the expected yield consists of saved lives, preserved ecosystem services, and other nontangible benefits to present and future generations, it is not altogether obvious that the same analysis should apply. Nevertheless, economists have long taken discounting to be the appropriate response to questions of environmental importance. As early as 1913, economists noted that "[t]he primary problem of conservation, . . . expressed in economic language, is the determination of the proper rate of discount on the future with respect to the utilization of our natural resources."

Frequently, discount rates are determined based on the prevailing real rate of interest charged in capital markets. However, positive interest rates, which can be said to represent the growth potential of man-made capital, are a poor indicator of the growth potential of natural capital. The fact that capital may grow in a bank at 10% per year does not necessarily imply that an old growth forest will regenerate at an equal rate. A timber company adopting a 10% discount rate to determine harvesting schedules will "rationally" clear forests faster than they can regrow, essentially liquidating the natural capital of the forest rather than consuming only its annual income. In this manner, use of positive discount rates in development strategy can lead to an "optimal" choice that is unsustainable—"the impoverishment of future generations as a result of the profligacy of present generations in such cases is not just an incidental, but a desirable outcome of the decision making process."

Besides encouraging unsustainable investment strategies, discounting can also discourage ecologically desirable government regulations. Because society must often pay the costs of environmental regulation long before the benefits accrue, discounting of future costs and benefits frequently counsels against the adoption of environmentally-protective measures. Daniel Farber and Paul Hemmersbaugh provide an extreme illustration by positing the case of two alternative designs for a nuclear waste repository. The designs will cost the same amount and will both be paid for entirely in the first year. If the first design is adopted, no workers will be killed during construction but one billion people will be killed in five hundred years due to a radiation leak from the repository. If the second design is adopted, between one and two workers will likely be killed during construction but no leaks and therefore no deaths will occur in five hundred years. Using a discount rate of 5%, the regulator selecting between designs "will choose the first option because one billion lives 500 years hence have a lower present value than one life today." Similar reasoning applies in less extreme, more common settings. Preventing greenhouse gas emissions, water contamination, species extinction, resource depletion, and many other environmental harms imposes current costs while offering mainly future benefits. As such, the measures routinely fail cost-benefit analyses that use a high positive discount rate.

Still, though, the impact of discounting on the environment is difficult to generalize. As Daly has pointed out, high positive discount rates can have two competing effects on natural resource exploitation. Although a high rate will shift the allocation of capital and labor to projects that exploit resources more quickly, the rate will also limit the total number of projects that are undertaken given that expected project benefits must overcome a higher opportunity cost value. Conversely, a low discount rate may slow the rate of resource extraction, but it may also increase the total number of extractive projects undertaken by making the projects appear more economic. Thus, the total effect of discounting on the environment is ambiguous, leading to what Richard Norgaard and Richard Howarth have called "the conservationist's dilemma."

Norgaard and Howarth have attempted to solve this dilemma by separating the questions of intragenerational resource allocation, for which discounting is an appropriate policy tool, and intergenerational resource distribution, for which discounting is not. Economists frequently recognize that unfettered market outcomes will not necessarily result in a just distribution of resources between generations, just as they do not necessarily result in distributive justice within generations. Stiglitz, for instance, noted that "[t]here is ... no presumption that the intertemporal distribution of income which emerges from the market solution will be 'socially optimal....'" Most economists, however, believe that the use of a discount rate is sufficient to solve the problem of intergenerational equity. As Stiglitz put it, "if the government correctly controls the rate of interest ... then there would be no objection to the competitive determination of the rate of utilization of our natural resources."

However, as Norgaard and Howarth point out, the discount rate cannot simultaneously serve the purpose of intragenerational allocative efficiency and intergenerational distributive equity. As noted above, governments often look to market rates of interest in setting discount rates for policy proposals, yet interest rates, like prices, quantities, and other market outcomes, are dependent upon the initial distribution of resources, including intergenerational distributions. "Since all of the variables that go into the calculation of net present value of a project or policy proposal depend on the intergenerational distribution of income, what might appear to be a good social investment under one income distribution may be marginal or worse under another." In other words, relying upon market rates of interest to guide social policies affecting intergenerational resource distribution presupposes the very judgment to be made.

Because he recognizes that discounting acts as a subtle proxy for important decisions of intergenerational equity in this manner, famed economist Robert Solow has suggested that the discount rate should be determined directly by society rather than by reference to market interest rates. Selection of a social discount rate, however, must be determined in large part by society's view of the initial intergenerational distribution of resources. Following selection of the rate, a new equilibrium will emerge in which resources are distributed differently among generations. That new equilibrium will cause the current generation to reconsider its choice of the appropriate discount rate, which will result in still another equilibrium, and so on.

Thus, relying upon use of a discount rate to automatically "correct" the problem of intergenerational distribution is problematic, no matter how the rate is determined. Intergenerational distributive questions are rate-determining, not rate-determined. In other words, the decision whether to curtail greenhouse emissions should depend directly on whether society wishes to risk depriving future generations of climate stability, not on whether the discount rate will permit it to happen. As Norgaard and Howarth put it, "Questions which are fundamentally matters of equity should be treated as such."

Returning to Farber and Hemmersbaugh's example helps to illustrate these considerations. On the standard approach, if a proposed regulation would save the lives of one billion people five hundred years from now, the value of those lives is discounted to a present value. In essence, economists attempt to measure what it is worth to society *now* to save the lives of a billion people in the future. As Farber and Hemmersbaugh demonstrate, it turns out not to be worth very much. However, the use of the present generation's valuation of the worth of a future generation's lives is a normative judgment that should not be obscured by arithmetic. As Lisa Heinzerling powerfully put it, "Generating numbers that are ultimately irrelevant to the questions to be resolved does more than waste precious regulatory resources. It changes the apparent nature of the decision itself, and permits politics and ideology to hide behind a mask of technical expertise."

* * *

III.   LAW AND ECOLOGICAL ECONOMICS

Although few in number, there have been significant efforts to incorporate macroeconomic concepts into legal economic analysis. Moreover, certain specific subject areas have benefited greatly from scholarly application of macroeconomic insights, including international trade regulation, foreign and domestic monetary policy, as well as immigration, administrative, employment, taxation, environmental, and criminal law. Despite these efforts, however, the law and economics movement remains primarily restricted to the application of microeconomic concepts to legal theory. This traditional exclusion of macroeconomic subject matter from law and economics raises an obvious question: Do we really need a macroeconomics for legal analysis?

The answer to this question requires a clear exposition of the subjects with which economics is concerned. As Daly has pointed out, there are three general dimensions to the economic problem: optimal allocation of inputs among uses, equitable distribution of wealth, and maintenance of economic scale within sustainable limits. The first dimension is the domain of microeconomics, while the latter two belong to macroeconomics. In both economic and legal economic analyses, attention has focused almost exclusively on the first of these dimensions. Traditionally, economists have argued that the best way to solve the distribution problem is to provide an effective answer to the allocation problem. By ensuring that resources are allocated to their most efficient uses, one maximizes the amount of wealth created, and hence, the amount of wealth available for distribution throughout society. Increases in economic productivity, therefore, can result, at least theoretically, in higher absolute levels of income for everyone and the possibility of significant upward mobility for some. In addition to providing an explicit laissez-faire response to the question of distribution, this growth-oriented policy also provides an implicit laissez-faire answer to the scale problem: by relying on economic growth as a response to the problem of inequitable distribution, economists necessarily believe that the optimal scale of the economy is always "bigger."

Law and economics scholars have adopted a similar, albeit far more refined, position. Most law and economics thinkers accept Steven Shavell and Louis Kaplow's forceful argument that legal rules should be constructed to achieve optimal allocation of resources among competing uses, without concern for the distributional effects of such rules. As they argue, for every inefficient but desirably redistributive legal rule, one can imagine an alternate legal rule coupled with a redistributive tax scheme that would achieve the same desired wealth transfer without the efficiency loss. For that reason (along with its comparative administrative advantage at transferring wealth), the tax and transfer system should be the exclusive means for the government to address distributional concerns. Of course, because redistribution of income through the tax and transfer system is simply a matter of setting politically-determined levels of redistribution, its interest to legal economists has been somewhat negligible. Despite a recent provocative attempt to reconsider Shavell and Kaplow's argument on empirical and theoretical grounds, its hold over the discipline remains. Consequently, the question of equitable distribution, and with it the field of macroeconomics, has been largely removed from the domain of law and economics.

Thus, both economists and legal economists have found theoretical grounds for ignoring the problem of wealth distribution and the lesser-recognized problem of sustainable scale. Meanwhile, wealth disparities have risen to record levels, a fact that might reflect contemporary America's lack of political resolve to use the tax and transfer system in the manner hypothesized by Shavell and Kaplow. This failure cannot be considered a direct or intended consequence of Shavell and Kaplow's reasoning, of course. Their argument contemplates removing distributional issues from analysis of legal rules; it does not advise ignoring such issues in all aspects of political discussion.

Yet the *effect* of their analysis might be to do just that—economics, and in particular growth economics, has become the dominant language of political speech, to the point of largely drowning out other dialects. As one scholar put it, "the increasing domination of homo economicus is evidenced by the fact that public discourse has become hostage to economics and has begun to dance to, instead of call, the economic tune: it is thoroughly infiltrated by the economic mindset and attuned to its interests." Before such economics occupied the bulk of the political landscape, it may have been appropriate to ignore distributional concerns on the assumption that they would be dealt with by the moral and political will of the people. Now it has become arguably tantamount to assigning a zero value to the goal of equitable distribution. In other words, when economists and legal economists exclude certain issues from their discussion on the assumption that some other discipline or some *other* mechanism will address the excluded concern, they may in effect be relegating that concern to the dustbin of politics.

In the terms of Shavell and Kaplow's argument, while it may be true that "any regime with an inefficient [but redistributive] legal rule [can be replaced with an] efficient legal rule and a modified income tax system in which all individuals are better off," the modified income tax system necessary to ensure that such a Pareto improvement actually eventuates may not be possible within a given political climate, including perhaps the current one. As a practical matter, therefore, Shavell and Kaplow's argument may demonstrate only that *potential* Pareto improvements may be gained by excluding distributive effects from the selection of legal rules. Whether legal decisionmakers should continue to ignore distributional effects when it is confidently known that the necessary "modified income tax system" will not be adopted—that is, when it is known that the redistribution necessary to achieve the Pareto improvement will not occur—is a question not directly addressed by Shavell and Kaplow's argument, as they themselves acknowledge.

Precisely the same analysis applies to the goal of sustainable scale. Although it has not appeared within the legal economic literature, one could make an argument against the consideration of scale effects of legal rules that tracks Shavell and Kaplow's reasoning. The same response, however, would apply: whether ignorance of scale effects is justified in the face of legislative recalcitrance is a separate, and more difficult, question. Indeed, with respect to scale, the problem is worse because no mechanism analogous to the tax and transfer system exists to regulate the scale of the economy, even if economic discourse does not crowd the issue out of political attention. The problem of achieving a sustainable scale of the human economy is left as a macroeconomic goal better addressed through unique, macro-economic policy instruments—yet no such instruments are in place. And to compound the problem, the current accepted wisdom regarding the distribution problem—that growth in the scale of the economy will raise absolute wealth levels for all market participants—directly conflicts with the goal of maintaining society's ecological footprint within sustainable parameters.

In short, current economic wisdom attempts to "solve" two of society's most urgent problems by trading them off against each other, and current legal economic wisdom appears to have found reasons for ignoring both.

The inconsistency is not recognized because mainstream macroeconomics does not acknowledge the problem of regulating scale. Perpetual growth is considered a viable response to the distribution problem because no adverse consequences to such growth are recognized. In effect, economists believe that they have found the global free lunch. Critics of this economic policy are at a decided disadvantage in popular and scholarly debates because they cannot point to any harmful effects of growth. Instead, they can only argue that economic growth has not achieved the goal of reducing wealth inequality. But that failure is not enough to overcome the compelling force of Pareto improvement: if a few people are better off because of economic growth, and no one is worse off, how can growth be opposed?

Ecological economists reveal the fallacy of this position by making the problem of sustainable scale an issue of explicit concern. Through the lens of ecological economics, growth economics becomes assailable not only because wealth increases might not "trickle down" in the predicted fashion, but also because the biophysical demands entailed by economic growth may have pushed the human economy toward unsustainable levels. Once one accepts the foundational principle of ecological economics—that the level of material throughout in the economy is subject to ecological constraints—the macroeconomic concerns of distribution and scale can no longer be pushed to the side in the ever-intensifying pursuit of allocative efficiency. Indeed, as noted above, there is some reason to believe that economic growth in America in the latter decades of the twentieth century has become harmful to society on net, once one considers the environmental and social externalities that are not ordinarily accounted for by macroeconomic indicators. Under such conditions, scale and distribution can no longer remain the neglected stepsiblings of allocation within the family of economic aspirations.

For at least two reasons, then, law and economics may be incomplete without some form of macroeconomics to inform its analysis. First, because no political mechanism analogous to the tax and transfer system exists to regulate the scale of the macroeconomy, legal economic scholars cannot safely ignore the scale effects of alternative legal rules in the way that they have ignored distributive effects. Second, because the traditional response of economists to the distribution problem is in direct conflict with the goal of sustainable scale, law and economics' continued ignorance of both problems may result in the discipline's long-term marginalization. In other words, if natural limits turn out to constrain the scale of the human economy in the manner hypothesized by ecological economists, then the economist's practice of postponing the problem of distribution by punting on the problem of scale will not be viable in the long run. In light of this possibility, legal economic scholars may be wise to address both problems now by allowing ecological economic insights to inform their analysis.

This methodological approach would have two obvious but important effects. First, it would force legal scholars to confront the problem of maintaining a sustainable economy in their relevant analyses. By incorporating ecological economic insights into legal policy discussion, legal scholars could essentially leapfrog mainstream economic thought to provide both the theoretical impetus for and the practical construction of policy tools that ensure long-term sustainability. The practical benefit of confronting the problem of scale is potentially enormous. Recently, 1586 scientists from 63 countries, including 104 of the 178 living Nobel Prize winners in the sciences, signed the World Scientists' Call for Action at the Kyoto Climate Summit which stated that "the scientific community ha[s] reached a consensus that grave threats imperil the future of humanity and the global environment." The United States' failure to heed this call to action from many of the world's most learned scientific experts demonstrates the stranglehold that mainstream economic ideology has on the political minds-cape. By incorporating ecological economic insights into their policy analysis, however, legal economic scholars could take an important step toward harmonizing economic and scientific concerns.

A secondary effect of such an effort likely would be to revitalize the debate over distributional equity. If it is accepted that sustainability requires limits to the physical strain placed by humans on the ecosphere, absolute growth in the scale of the human economy would no longer be available as an answer to the problem of inequitable distribution. Instead, society would have to address the problem directly as a necessary subissue to the problem of determining a permissible level of resource throughout that does not jeopardize the viability of future generations. Of course, Shavell and Kaplow's argument that distributional concerns are more efficiently addressed through the tax and transfer system than through legal rulemaking would still apply under such a worldview. However, legal scholars and legal decisionmakers would have renewed interest in making certain that the goal of equitable distribution is actually being served, or at least examined, by other political mechanisms. The difficult question of political philosophy not addressed by Shavell and Kaplow's argument might then become an issue of some urgency.

* * *

CONCLUSION

At the time Adam Smith developed the image of rational market behavior, science in general was captivated by Enlightenment notions of limitless human intellectual ability. That microeconomists have clung to these notions longer than practitioners of any other discipline reflects what Alfred North Whitehead called the fallacy of misplaced concreteness—a failure to recognize that one's abstract theories continually must be informed by the reality from which they were abstracted. Indeed, it has only been in recent years that scholars of behavioral law and economics have made progress in upsetting the presumption of rationality in legal economic analysis by incorporating the decidedly nonrational findings of cognitive psychologists.

A similar historical analysis applies to macroeconomics. *When the core concepts of macroeconomics developed, the world contained four billion less people than it does today.* The preanalytic vision which informed the development of neoclassical thought was that of a world in which human activity was but a tiny fraction of global activity. Human use of resources and production of wastes was considered costless because the regenerative and absorptive capacities of the earth appeared to have no limits. Today, evidence to the contrary arrives with regularity, to the point that the Royal Society of London and the United States National Academy of Sciences issued an unprecedented joint action statement, warning: "The future of our planet is in the balance. Sustainable development can be achieved, but only if irreversible degradation of the environment can be halted in time. The next 30 years may be crucial." The continued dominance within economics of a view of nature as limitless demonstrates that macroeconomic theorists also may have committed Whitehead's anti-rationalist fallacy: "an arbitrary halt at a particular set of abstractions."

Yet surprisingly little recognition has been given to the fact that macroeconomics rests on what is arguably now a discredited world-view. Among economists, increasing divergence between theory and reality is accounted for by increasing recognition of "externalities," much like the Ptolemaic astronomers who attempted to save their model of circular planetary motion through desperate addition of epicycles. However, lest society is to risk growing beyond the biophysical limits of the earth (not to mention the point at which marginal costs of macroeconomic growth exceed marginal benefits), it seems appropriate to develop an alternative economics, one grounded in scientifically plausible visions of the relationship between economic and ecological spheres. What seems needed is a body of market principles built on the assumptions that natural resources are limited, that ecosystem services have value, and that the size of the human economy is a legitimate subject for social control. Because ecological economists have provided just that, their teachings may be of great use to legal scholars in the years to come.

NOTES AND QUESTIONS

1. Bounded rationality, self-interest, and ecological economics. Does economic theory explain why ecological economics remains at present a marginal rather than a central stream within the discipline of economics? That is, are politicians and policymakers concerned with their own short-term self-interest over an altruistic concern for the earth or for future generations? Are politicians and policymakers afflicted with problems relating to bounded rationality when it comes to environmental issues?

2. The fall of neoclassical theory? Based on the critiques outlined in this chapter, what useful insights, if any, remain from classical market theory? Do the critiques outlined in this chapter challenge Adam Smith's original insights, or only the reduction of his work in neoclassical economics?

CHAPTER 4

BEYOND CLASSIC MARKET THEORY: EXTERNAL CRITIQUES

As the influence of law and economics scholarship grew in the legal academy, so did the depth and breadth of criticism directed to its organizing concepts. In this chapter, we explore the challenges to price theory, rational choice, and wealth maximization premises that have come from those who do not share the law and economics faith in markets and private ordering. Within law, the criticisms spanned a broad range of perspectives. There were doctrinalists who were unconvinced by the positive claim that the common law converges on efficiency, to critical legal scholars who rejected the normative premise that wealth maximization is a coherent value for evaluating the legal rules that govern the distribution of material goods in a democracy. The dialogue has, at times, been heated and deeply engaged. As Anita Bernstein's review of the thirty-five-year period of development of the law and economics school shows, the outside challengers have often used colorful language to report their findings that: the central tenets of law and economics were "incoherent," "dubious in the extreme," "garbage in and garbage out," and a "cult."

Ironically, critical race theorists, one group of scholars with perhaps the most incompatible world view, have largely ignored law and economics, even as their narrative methodology became the target of direct criticism from leaders of law and economics. For scholars who believe that the problem of racial subordination is a central conundrum of modern and post-modern legal thought, the law and economics model of rational choice must surely be an unpersuasively thin account of how racial identity and cultural difference works in the markets. This casebook is our contribution to engaging law and economic reasoning and identifying alternative constructions of identity, law, culture, and markets.

In this chapter we explore several of the most powerful challenges to law and economics. First, we take up the most important and central claim of law and economics, that people make economic choices on the basis of a rational assessment of their own self-interest. Second, we examine the commodification challenge to markets. In this view of markets, price theory and the wealth maximization premises impose prices on aspects of human interaction that cannot and should not be reduced to a pecuniary value. This argument insists that some "aspects of social life are inappropriate for the market." Arguing for recognition of the personal aspects of some monetary transactions, Margaret Radin urges acceptance of commodification in some spheres, while refusing to try to completely separate the two value systems. She urges us to accept her view that "[i]ncomplete commodification" allows the human impulses of altruism, social justice, community, and individuality to thrive alongside markets in which commodities with pecuniary values are exchanged. We extend this discussion to include the modifying arguments of some legal feminists who have worried that the commodification idea undercuts women's economic autonomy when they work overtime in the unpaid roles of caregivers at home.

The idea that market participants assert their preferences based upon a reasoned appraisal of their own self-interest is a major point of criticism for both internal and external critics. Much of the external criticism has been concerned with the failure of rational choice theory to account for differences in identity and cultural context. Unlike the internal critics, who rely primarily upon the insights of psychology, external critics turn to several of the other social sciences such as sociology, anthropology, and linguistics to construct a view of the economic actor that reveals the race, gender, and other identity variables that contribute to market decisions. More importantly, some scholars have based their objections on the so far underdeveloped, but promising, exploration of the role of systematic subordination in markets.

Law and economics scholarship, like neoclassical economics, is actively hostile to the idea of using government intervention to equalize the vast disparities in wealth that form the predicate to market participation. Ironically, this hostility to government intervention disappears when government policy increases the wealth of the already wealthy. In the policy realm, this contradictory approach to redistribution can be seen in the enthusiasm for tax cuts that increase the amount of wealth the upper income brackets retain, while reducing the size of government expenditures to provide subsistence for those left behind by market competition. Kevin Phillips, a popular writer on economic history and policy, writes: "Laissez-faire is a pretense. Government power and preferment have been used by the rich, not shunned." Wealth and Democracy xiv (2002).

In this chapter, we will explore the major arguments that legal scholars who do not share the economic premises of neoclassical economics have made to highlight the shortcomings of that perspective.

A. An Overview

Whatever Happened to Law and Economics?

64 Md. L. Rev. 101 (2005).

■ Anita Bernstein

* * * "Every fresh contribution to the economic analysis of tort law," wrote Ernest Weinrib in 1989, "adds a new storey to an edifice whose bottom has long since disappeared into the sand."

* * * Then came Leonard Jaffee * * *: "So, I have two big gripes against Law and Economics. One is that it's sick and spreads sickness. The other's that it doesn't work in ways it claims, or do what it pretends." * * * According to David Gray Carlson, "[t]here are two types of law-and-economics: one that is dubious and another that is dubious in the extreme." In her 2004 book, *The Triumph of Venus*, Jeanne Schroeder, who'd majored in economics in college, declared that "most law-and-economic proposals are classic cases of GIGO (garbage in—garbage out): nonfalsified theories are applied to untested assumptions in order to produce nonverifiable conclusions. Law-and-economics has all the characteristics of a cult."

These attacks arrayed in the background, I make here a somewhat different claim: that law and economics is no longer amenable to critique. This movement, in my view, is not an edifice whose bottom has disappeared into the sand. Instead it is not an edifice at all. In past decades, it did take shape as a unique structure; the Chicago school bore distinctive characteristics. A scholar generating new work in law and economics during this "edifice" era would borrow precepts from neoclassical economics and apply them to the law, in an effort either to describe, in material terms, how law affects and responds to aggregations of human beings ("positive" law and economics) or to propose measures designed to improve these consequences ("normative" or "prescriptive" law and economics). Many practitioners, Richard Posner foremost among them, dealt in both description and prescription. The combination brought to law the most philosophical strand in microeconomic theory, welfare economics.

Today the Chicago edifice shares attention with other types of law and economics. Anyone reading this far has undoubtedly heard that law and economics contains multitudes—an array of literatures, sub-movements, and schools of thought. Perhaps it does. Certainly a scholar trained in both economics and law has the vocabulary to combine the two disciplines in ways that would not hew to the descriptions of Chicago-style welfare economics, or to any other fraction of the genre. But observers with no stake in the cliché about diversity can see how well it serves insiders, who get from it a basis to say that their movement is big *and* a ready retort to semi-disavow anything in it that provokes criticism: "Well, that's one of the other schools." Law and economics can claim pluralism when pluralism suits, monolithic unity when pluralism threatens to splinter its power.

This inclination within the movement to have it both ways impels me to take a second look at its premise that law and economics is distinct from all other disciplines yet eclectic and pluralistic, the academy's big tent. The two postures are not only in tension with each other but perhaps also, I start to suspect, questionable in isolation. For law and economics to be valid, two conditions must obtain: law and economics needs a foundation of meaningful concepts and a boundary to fence out what it rejects or does not believe. If these two elements are missing, then its distinctive aspects may be unsound and its variations, offshoots, and alliances may be incoherent. In this Article I explore this question of foundations under, and boundaries around, the movement.

* * * [M]y rhetorical question, *Whatever happened . . . ?* broaches an argument that although a generation ago law and economics stood—as an edifice, if you like—it no longer endures. The movement was done in by a blend of some claims that were wrong with other claims that came across in legal circles as too right—and also too trivial to reject. Law and economics combined too little accuracy with too much: While ill founded, dubious, or tautological premises were eroding its credibility, other notions from the movement, consistent with what diverse thinkers and audiences believed, blurred the line between law and economics on one hand and everything else in jurisprudence on the other. Withdraw the mistakes and exaggerations from law and economics and what you get is either positive scholarship declaring 5 to be the sum of 3 and 2, or some indistinguishable share of the centrist, forward-looking quasi-utilitarian mélange of advice to policy-minded lawyers that now dominates the legal academy, unconfined to any sector.

During the last decade, members of the movement labored to stop the fall. Unable to do much about errors, they worked on the second front, the crisis of too much acceptance, mainly by trying to claim successful outsider movements as their own, rather than reacting to them as threats or challenges. When psychology dealt blows to the ideal of a rational actor, for instance, economic analysts invoked the label of "behavioral economics" to describe claims that were directly contrary to neoclassical dogma. Led by Robert Ellickson, they used the word "norms" to summarize phenomena inconvenient to the edifice. This capacious label not only could obscure what did not fit the neoclassical model, but also aid a contention that human behaviors deviating from the paradigm—behaviors that reveal altruism, expenditures that appear to waste rather than accrete money, refusals to cheat or defect in games, and the like are consistent with law and economics, rather than refutations of its core premises. This cooptation strategy reached a height in 2002 with the publication of *Fairness Versus Welfare*, a book from two scholars identified with the law and economics movement who declared victory by asserting that Welfare accounted for everything that jurisprudence pursues, except for a handful of silly vestigial claims which the authors disparaged as Fairness. This putative victory, however, would be better described as submergence into a larger whole. Part of the law and economics edifice has disappeared into the sand; part has joined the sand itself.

So much for Weinrib's edifice; Jeanne Schroeder had a different one-word critique. Schroeder called law and economics a "cult" in order to rebuke it for falling short of scientific standards. Yet cults are characterized by more than just clinging to a dogma that gets reality wrong. They are social groups. They contain members who disdain nonmembers, and who have been known to enjoy thinking that outsiders feel hostility towards them. I quote Schroeder's insult with approval even though one might debate her charges of falsity—as a concise description of a movement done in by the twin stabbings of excessive inaccuracy and trivial accuracy. Stripped of its distinctive intellectual features, no longer able to give descriptions or policy recommendations that could not have come from sources outside the movement, law and economics now functions mainly as a faculty club with opaque, arbitrary criteria for membership.

Where do *The Costs of Accidents* and Guido Calabresi fit in this picture? Away from the missteps. Calabresi's book, in contrast to the one by Kaplow and Shavell, focuses on Welfare without perceiving it as a prizefighter that has beaten or should beat a straw man, hapless Fairness. It draws readers in with its clarity and reason, never trying to exclude or intimidate anyone. It is a model, indeed, of what law and economics scholarship can contribute in the eras following refutation of its core tenets: a wide social science that invites participants to consider the common good.

I. Errors: What Has Crumbled, What Has Never Been

Consider how the tenets and distinguishing features of law and economics are faring at the thirty-fifth anniversary of *The Costs of Accidents*.

A. Three Precepts

1. Rational Choice.—On the first page of *Economic Analysis of Law*, Richard Posner declared a first axiom: "man is a rational maximizer of his ends in life." This individual knows what he wants and chooses means to reach his goals. The world through economists' eyes begins here, at the point where an individual makes a choice among alternatives. Rational choice is the "first and most basic" of "the critical early moves" in law and economics. Only if individuals can know what they want and act instrumentally on their desires can the other central precepts of the discipline—among them preferences, opportunities, and a consciousness of scarcity—make sense.

Moreover, Posner continues,

> the concept of rationality used by the economist is objective rather than subjective, so that it would not be a solecism to speak of a rational frog. Rationality means little more to an economist than a disposition to choose, consciously or unconsciously, an apt means to whatever ends the chooser happens to have.

According to this construction of rationality, the chooser will not lose the designation of "rational" just because her choices are self-destructive, perverse, opaque, inconsistent, unstable over time, resistant to Arrovian ordinal ranking, or dependent on the unpredictable choices that others make. Her choices can even defy the downward-sloping demand curve. As Arthur Leff noted decades ago, when

> a society dentist raises his prices and thereby increases his gross volume of business, it is no violation of the principle of the inverse relation between price and quantity. It only proves that buyers now perceive that they are buying something else which they now value more highly, "society dentistry" say, rather than "mere" dentistry.

Because "whatever ends the chooser happens to have" emerge from her behavior rather than from her own testimony or other expression, any means in this "objective" sense can be "apt."

One critique of Chicago-style law and economics argues that rational choice according to this school remains vulnerable to challenges that philosophy has long been expressing, perhaps "since the fourth century B.C." For openers, explains philosopher and classics scholar Martha Nussbaum, law and economics regards preferences as "exogenous, i.e., not significantly shaped by laws and institutions," whereas "the endogeneity of preferences has been recognized by almost all the major writers on emotion and desire in the history of Western philosophy." To speak of choice as if it originated entirely inside the actor is simply wrong. Furthermore, individuals do not simply make choices: they value their power to do so. People "do not typically view as equivalent two states of the world, one produced by their own agency and the other not." Ends, which law and economics sees as fixed, actually vary over time and through discourse; human beings deliberate about them. The concept of "preferences" sloppily throws together what philosophers have kept separated as five distinct phenomena: "belief, desire, perception, appetite, and emotion."

Along with old writings that cast the economists' version of rational choice into question, newer ones have refuted this concept through experimentation and revision. The neoclassical conception of rationality had fancied that human beings make choices within a preference ordering that is complete and transitive, subject to perfect and costlessly acquired information. Reality began to sully the premise. In the mid-twentieth century Herbert Simon established a beachhead for empiricism in economics with his identification of "bounded rationality," whereby a subject makes the best choices she can, given her limited "knowledge and computational capacities and skills." Simon's work brought about behavioral economics, the branch of microeconomics that focuses on the choices individuals make rather than the processes of their decisionmaking. "Choice," manifested in behaviors rather than the trail of conscious strategy that precedes them, came to subsume "rational": if some actor did it, then we'll say she made a choice in pursuit of her own ends.

* * * [T]his outcome cannot sit well in law and economics because of how much it gives away. * * * Posner "assumes that adding an account of 'nonrationality' in market relations would be tantamount to abandoning theory entirely in favor of a mere all-inclusive description of empirical behavior lacking any explanatory or predictive power." He concludes that "behavioral economics merely describes human actions [and does a poor job of doing so] but has no theory of action." * * *

* * * [T]he dilemma for law and economics is clear. Neoclassical assertions of rationality—abstract, laboratory-crystalline, severed from ordinary experience—stray too far from empirical fact to explain or predict much. Posner's "rational frog" expresses this limitation succinctly: we believe the frog pursues her own ends, but we have nothing but her behavior to look at when we seek support for that belief. To the extent that

economic analysts accept variety in human behavior, especially behavior that defies well-ordered pursuit of transparent ends, they became less able to explain and predict because they have conceded that human behavior is either random or, alternatively, obedient to some logic alien to the rational actor model, and thus beyond their ken.

Economic analysts regret this defeat and hope they can undo it. "Deviations from the rational-actor assumption can and should be incorporated into economic analysis," declares the Harvard law and economics website. The cooptation strategy cannot, however, readily accommodate material so contrary to a first principle of economic analysis.

 2. Efficiency vs. Wealth Maximization vs. Welfare.—What do, or should, individuals or societies or legal systems choose to pursue? Economic analysts have shuttled between terms to describe the goal. Two leading contenders have been "efficiency" (or sometimes allocative "efficiency") and "wealth maximization." A third term, "welfare," has arisen more recently. None is stable. * * *

If "efficiency" stands in for utilitarianism, Posner argued, then efficiency is inferior to wealth maximization as a description of what individuals and societies pursue, or should be understood as pursuing. Utilitarianism, in Posner's rendering, seeks a "surplus of pleasure over pain," but gives its followers no guidance as to whose pleasure counts (are animals included?), no distinction between average and total happiness, and no metric to evaluate success and failure. Wealth maximization as an alternative ideal avoids these difficulties by insisting on "value in dollars or dollar equivalents." In Posner's summation: The only kind of preference that counts in a system of wealth maximization is thus one that is backed up by money—in other words, that is registered in a market. * * *

The reliance on prices adds other complications to the wealth maximization criterion. * * * Price is a function of demand, and demand will vary in response to preexisting distributions of wealth. It is thus idle—or instead politically significant, ... —to contemplate wealth maximization without attention to how much wealth each maximizer already has. With a dollar the only metric and with the marginal utility of money a sure fact, wealth maximization "has the result of weighting the preferences of wealthy persons more heavily than the preferences of poorer persons"—that is, the rich get extra ballots in the form of dollars they don't need to save. *Tant pis* for wealth maximization.

Following this critique of the wealth-maximization criterion, "welfare" has arisen as a kind of successor to the old precursor of wealth maximization, "efficiency." Louis Kaplow and Steven Shavell have led the charge among economic analysts to promote this word as summation of what societies and individuals pursue. To many, welfare seems more capacious, perhaps more humanistic, than "efficiency" or any other word standing in for utilitarianism. Yet because it does not repair what "wealth maximization" once purported to fix—that is, vagueness, indeterminacy, disagreements about measurement—"welfare" carries economic analysts back to their old condition of not being able to describe what they seek.

We see here a dilemma similar to that which haunts the economist's view of rational choice. The movement can cling to "efficiency" and remain vulnerable to criticisms about tautology, circularity, vagueness, and evasion of pertinent political questions. Alternatively, it can focus on "wealth maximization," a path that adds misdescription to the mix and cannot escape similar perils of tautology. Or try "welfare," which in application cannot be distinguished from efficiency and its perils.

3. *Faith in Markets.*—Following *The Problem of Social Cost*, both descriptive and normative strands of law and economics evinced some enthusiasm for what they called "the market." Coase had recharacterized costs. Whereas earlier thinking, following Pigou, had seen costs as detriments that one entity imposes on another, to Coase costs were instead phenomena that obstructed market functions. The market, always central in all of microeconomics, took on after Coase even more fundamental importance to its cousin law and economics. Efficiency, for instance, could be defined as the outcome that a free market would produce. In this normative sense, the existence of a market makes efficiency (or wealth maximization) possible.

The normative truism about markets making wealth has not much occupied law and economics. In an alternative, descriptive sense, however, law and economics has seen markets wherever human beings deal with one another, including venues far from commercial transactions. Marriage and family formation take place in markets, according to Gary Becker and others. Individuals negotiate their sexual relations as trades. Scarce body parts like kidneys, say economists, could profitably become the objects of regulated exchange. The adoption of infants takes place within a market whether we like it or not, said Posner in the famously career-thwarting paper he wrote with Elisabeth Landes. Gestational surrogacy for pay is a service that American law has long been condoning. * * * In a recent essay, Claire Hill defends the faith-in-markets perspective within law and economics, and urges "skeptics" who don't want to see markets applied to "the personal sphere" to reconsider their position.

Yet even if "the market" can shed light on "the personal sphere," the law and economics project of identifying unseen markets—in human bodies and intimate associations and the like—seems to have run its course. At the risk of signing a death certificate before the patient has died, and thus compelling myself to lie next to Morton Horwitz and Owen Fiss, I will venture to say that today "the market" does not account for much novelty or centrality in this field, neither its normative nor its more recent descriptive versions. Coase's masterpiece, always amenable to divergent readings, now sounds like a warning that markets always fail, rather than a promise that exchange will work perfectly after the friction of transaction costs has been removed.

Accompanying this decline of the market in law and economics scholarship, a generation of writings skeptical of this institution has taken critical hold. The most important external criticism of the market appears in literature on "incommensurability" and "commodification." Work in this genre rejects the market insofar as this artifact assigns a cash value to anything capable of being transferred from one possessor to another. The leading scholar in this field identifies her thesis, first expressed in her title *Market-Inalienability*, as directly hostile to law and economics, whose "methodological archetype" she calls "universal commodification."

* * *

* * * "[M]arket failure" has become almost as familiar a phrase in law and economics as "the market" itself. Same recipe as the one that cooked up "behavioral economics": When truisms fail, or get refuted, reassert ownership of all material under question by adding a layer of counter-jargon. * * *

II.   WHAT LITTLE REMAINS OF LAW AND ECONOMICS

Now that rational choice, utilitarianism, efficiency, wealth maximization, markets, predictive power, and coherence have been questioned, abandoned, or smudged beyond recognition, the list of essential features defining law and economics gets shorter. I offer here all I could come up with: only three items, and even that small total contains some redundancy.

A.   The Policymaker Ascendant

The insightful critic Jeanne Schroeder has noticed something central to law and economics that seems to have escaped members of the movement and other observers: "Law and economics is a policy science," whereas some other sectors of jurisprudence have no desire to form policy or, as Schroder puts it, "give advice to the government." Not everyone writing scholarship about the law takes the perspective of the legislator or a judge. One important contributor, the "speculative theorist or critical legal scholar," instead focuses on "the position of the governed—those who are subjected to the law." * * *

* * *

Here, then, we see a piece of what remains in law and economics: an inclination to address governing entities more than governed individuals as ends of inquiry in themselves. Desires or resistances of human beings enter policymaking only in the aggregate. While the critical legal scholar works to "free the legal subject from manipulation by the law," the policymaker works to articulate the best manipulation.

* * *

* * * [A]s soon as law and economics lost its distinctive character (thanks to too much refutation and too much acceptance), its adherents lost their basis for dividing the legal academy into members and nonmembers. Nevertheless their inclination to sort people into two piles without transparent criteria for division—the kind of dichotomous sorting that a Jeanne Schroder-style "cult" would do—remains. Unconstrained by genuine criteria for membership, decisionmakers in the academy and beyond—to the extent that law and economics extends beyond law schools—are now free to substitute prejudices for standards.

The most widely suspected prejudice is of political conservatism. Consider the possibility that

> facile assumptions have been carefully chosen to push forward a politically conservative agenda. Viewed in this light, the choreography is unsurpassed. First, equate utility with ability to pay, but assume away the issue of initial wealth distribution and bargaining inequalities. Next, combine with the inevitability of common-law efficiency. The result is a bias away from government regulation toward a nineteenth-century, almost Lochneresque, laissez-faire conception of the primacy of private law. The ability of good rhetoric to make this all appear natural is remarkable.

* * *

IV. CONCLUSION: WHERE NOW?

* * * Writers frequently depict law and economics as an aging giant. Their metaphors of decline and old age perhaps rush too fast to judgment: In addition to premature proclamations of death, and wishful thinking that the movement had "peaked," the literature on law and economics includes a 1991 claim about a "mid-life crisis." I have already fretted about hurrying to entomb law and economics. That said, this birthday of a great book, marking indeed "a generation of influence," does invite thought about the state of the movement it helped inaugurate.

Conceding that dichotomous thinkers within the law and economics movement might be inclined to classify the reflections in this Article as hostile to their cause, I maintain that the Article has depicted law and economics as evolving, rather than entirely refuted or spent. This Article has indeed argued that the core tenets of the movement are refuted and spent. It has also contended that law and economics has failed to rescue itself by its tactic of trying to claim for itself various refutations of these tenets. But my reflections find a paradox in law and economics: the movement while deteriorating has been thriving. It reached heights scaled by no other jurisprudential school. Its success has consisted mainly of telling lawyers, lawmakers, and legal scholars how and why they must keep their eye on the welfare ball when making policy—but it has also fostered other triumphs: the importation of interdisciplinary findings into law and across campuses; the insistence on (if not quite the achievement of) empirical research as integral to legal policy; and the touch of science—whose perils and pretensions I have noted but that also can spur lawyers to reach for more rigorous work.

* * *

NOTES AND QUESTIONS

1. **Rational choice.** Rational choice is the central claim of law and economics. As Bernstein notes, only if rational choice obtains can the "central precepts of the discipline—among them preferences, opportunities, and a consciousness of scarcity—make sense." Bernstein, *supra* at 106. As we have explored in the previous chapter, chapter 4 at 269, behavioral economics, while sharing law and economics' faith in the market mechanism, has seriously eroded the viability of this central claim of rigid rationality. Daniel Kahneman, an experimental psychologist and a Nobel prize winner in economics, is a celebrated founder of behavioral economics and a leader in challenging the rationality assumptions of neoclassical economics. His website summarizes his influence as follows:

> Although he never took an economics course, Princeton psychologist Daniel Kahneman received the Nobel Prize in economic sciences in 2002. The award recognized Kahneman's life-long work in integrating psychological research and economic science. His work showed economists how people don't always make reasoned choices, over-turning long held views and opening up a new field of research.

> Kahneman has studied the importance of context in decision-making and the shortcuts people take ever since the 1970s, when he began publishing his groundbreaking work with the late Amos Tversky. His findings on the psychological motives that determine decisions have implications for economists, especially in areas such as individual savings behavior or participation in the stock market.

> Kahneman and Tversky's landmark paper on decision-making under circumstances where there is uncertainty was published in *Econometrica* in 1979. Prior to this publication, economists assumed humans made rational decisions. Economics was also a non-experimental science that relied on real-world observations. Today, largely because of Kahneman's work, experimental economics is burgeoning.

> Kahneman notes that his research has had a wide impact because his paper was published in an economics rather than a psychology journal. "It legitimized a certain approach to thinking about decision-making, which eventually, through the work of other economists, became influential in economics itself," he says.

Daniel Kahneman, *Case Study: Can I Trust My Intuitions*, available at http://webscript.princeton.edu/~psych/psychology/research/kahneman/case.php. Daniel Kahneman & Amostversky, *Prospect Theory: An Analysis of Decision Under Risk*, 47 ECONOMETRICA 263 (1979).

2. **What are the sources of preferences?** Bernstein endorses Nussbaum's argument that "law and economics regards preferences as 'exogenous, i.e., not significantly shaped by laws and institutions,' whereas 'the endogeneity of preferences has been recognized by almost all the major writers on emotion and desire in the history of Western philosophy.' To speak of choice as if it originated entirely inside the actor is simply wrong."

Bernstein, *supra* at 328 (quoting Martha C. Nussbaum, *Flawed Foundations: The Philosophical Critique of (a Particular Type of) Economics*, 64 U. Chi. L. Rev. 1197, 1197–98 (1997)).

Can you identify the primary "laws and institutions" that shape preferences for race and gender discrimination?

3. Blurring the line between law and economics and everything else.

> Law and economics combined too little accuracy with too much: While ill founded, dubious, or tautological premises were eroding its credibility, other notions from the movement, consistent with what diverse thinkers and audiences believed, blurred the line between law and economics on one hand and everything else in jurisprudence on the other.

Bernestein, *supra* at 104.

How persuasive is Bernstein's observation that law and economics is a "faculty club" of like-minded scholars who are seeking to preserve their influence in the academy by infinite adaptability and inclusiveness? Is the problem of porous conceptual borders a weakness or a strength in intellectual discourse? *See* Richard H. Gaskins, Burdens of Proof in Modern Discourse (1993).

4. Scientific discipline or cult? Bernstein makes two distinct, but related arguments: First, that law and economics cannot sustain its claim to scientific rigor. Second, that its adherents maintain their influence through policing membership in the genre according to prospective members' willingness to advance a politically conservative agenda. This, she concludes, is a cult—a secular belief system rooted in libertarianism.

> **a. Scientific Discipline?** As we discussed in chapter 1 at pp. 1–2, 17–23, 33–34, law and economics distinguishes itself from other genres of legal thought by claiming to be objective and scientific. Posner asserts that: "the concept of rationality used by the economist is objective rather than subjective ..." If, as Bernstein argues, the scientific foundations of law and economics have "disappeared into the sand," what is left of its contribution to modern legal thought?

> **b. Cult.** Is Bernstein's argument on this point internally contradictory? On one hand, she argues that law and economics has preserved itself by inclusion: "Unable to do much about errors, [law and economics scholars] worked on the second front, the crisis of too much acceptance, mainly by trying to claim successful outsider movements as their own, rather than reacting to them as threats or challenges. When psychology dealt blows to the ideal of a rational actor, for instance, economic analysts invoked the label of 'behavioral economics' to describe claims that were directly contrary to neoclassical dogma." Bernstein, *supra* at 104. On the other hand, she claims that they have preserved their intellectual identity by exclusion.

"Yet cults ... are social groups. They contain members who disdain nonmembers, and who have been known to enjoy thinking that outsiders feel hostility towards them.... [L]aw and economics now functions mainly as a faculty club with opaque, arbitrary criteria for membership....

Unconstrained by genuine criteria for membership, decisionmakers in the academy ... are now free to substitute prejudices for standards.

The most widely suspected prejudice is of political conservatism."

Id. at 105, 129.

Can both criticisms be true?

5. Policy science? Legal scholar Jeanne Schroder suggests that "law and economics is policy science ... [that] seeks to give advice to the government." Jeanne L. Schroder, *Rationality in Law and Economics Scholarship*, 79 Or. L. Rev. 147, 151 (2000). If this observation is convincing, would this make law and economics an oxymoron, a movement to reduce the sphere of government power, whose primary function now is giving advice to the government?

B.   Normative Critiques of Economic Analysis

The normative challenges to law and economics span a broad range of contentions. The views collected in what follows include some of the most powerful claims of scholars who are unconvinced that law and economics provides a persuasive framework through which to evaluate individual and collective decision making about allocation of the basic material goods and services required for modern life.

The challenges include skepticism about the reliability of virtually all of the central premises of modern law and economics. Among the criticized premises are: rational choice, efficiency, cost benefit analysis, wealth maximization, and the relationship between preferences expressed as monetary units and democratic participation in markets and governance. Some have challenged the gendered impacts of separating household tasks from the market economy. Finally, justice is a major theme of external criticism of law and economics. This chord has focused on law and economics' aggressive refusal to consider preexisting economic distributions. The justice critics question whether law and economics' valorization of markets over fairness for those left out, or pushed out of opportunities for work and wealth accumulation is just in a society, such as ours, with a large material surplus.

We turn to two outside scholars, Rachel Moran and James Boyd White, who each in turn survey the landscape of the major normative criticisms of law and economics. Moran presents a direct comparison between law and economics and critical race theory. White argues that economics is not a science, but is rather an alternative system of values posing as a scientific enterprise. White's alternative is a humanistic value system.

1. BEYOND: RATIONAL CHOICE

THE ELUSIVE NATURE OF DISCRIMINATION: BY VALDES, CULP, AND HARRIS

55 STAN. L. REV. 2365, 2367, 2375, 2377, 2378, 2379, 2380, 2382–83, 2385–88, 2390, 2395, 2396–97, 2401–03, 2412–14, 2416, 2417–18 (2003) (reviewing IAN AYRES, PERVASIVE PREJUDICE? UNCONVENTIONAL EVIDENCE OF RACE AND GENDER DISCRIMINATION (2001) and CROSSROADS, DIRECTIONS AND A NEW CRITICAL RACE THEORY (Francisco Valdes et al. eds., 2002)).

■ RACHEL F. MORAN

* * *

In contrast to law and economics, critical race theory has concerned itself with how race is constructed through unconscious bias and institutional structures. Race scholars do not presume that rational choice is the sine qua non of human behavior. Instead, they try to unpack the reflexive habits and hidden assumptions that guide racial judgments. Rather than worry about whether statistical discrimination is rational, critical race theorists question whether it is just. In analyzing how privilege is perpetuated, race scholars see social networks as only one example of the patterns and practices that entrench inequality. As a result, race theory has moved well beyond the marketplace to explore how everything from public bureaucracies to family life can make racial difference seem both natural and inevitable.

* * *

II. CRITICAL RACE THEORY: AN UNRULY DISCIPLINE AT THE CROSSROADS

* * *

* * * [Kevin] Johnson, for instance, argues that "during its first full decade, Critical Race Theory has failed to explore fully the relationship between race and immigration law," in part because of "the longstanding assumption that race relations in the United States exclusively concern African Americans and whites." * * *

* * *

* * * This is a crucial crossroad because the ideal "postsubordination" world, to use Valdes's term, remains a contested and uncertain destination.

* * *

Another crossroad for critical race theory is determining whether it shares a unifying methodology. * * *

* * *

Still another crossroad for critical race theorists is determining the appropriate relationship between theory and praxis. At the outset of the volume, Charles R. Lawrence comments that "we cannot teach about liberation without actively engaging in its politics." * * *

Even so, the relationship between theory and praxis remains among the least developed areas in race scholarship. Undoubtedly, this inattention can be explained in part by the relatively small number of critical race theorists working in the academy. * * *

* * *

* * * As a quantitative researcher, Ayres devotes himself to examining the aggregate consequences of discrimination. He measures price differentials in the retail car market, disparate delays in obtaining a kidney, and unequal levels of bail. Because Ayres is measuring tangible effects of discrimination, he focuses on average differences and their statistical significance. Never does he attempt to explore what it might feel like to be the victim of discrimination. In marked contrast, critical race theorists are strongly committed to exploring the victim's perspective. Compare, for example, Ayres's treatment of retail car sales with Devon Carbado's discussion of what might be termed "shopping while black." * * *

* * *

As *Pervasive Prejudice?* and the *Crossroads* reader make clear, there are divergent schools of thought about the nature and incidence of discrimination and inequality. Ayres draws heavily on rational choice theory, and his studies are situated in particular markets like car sales or bail bonds. The challenge for theorists like Ayres is to understand why discrimination persists under competitive conditions. By contrast, the anthology by Valdes, Culp, and Harris rejects the characterization of the world as presumptively rational, and it refuses to focus primarily on market transactions as the relevant site for studying racism. Critical race theorists are working to redefine the relevance of rationality in analyzing discrimination and to reconceptualize the role of institutions, both private and public, in perpetuating inequality.

A. Rational Choice and Irrational Animus

Kenneth J. Arrow has pointed out that "rational choice theory" is broader than "economic theory." As he explains:

> Rational choice theory means that the individual actors act rationally (that is, by maximizing according to a complete ordering) within the constraints imposed by preferences, technology, and beliefs, and by the institutions which determine how individual actions interact to determine outcomes. Further, the beliefs are themselves formed by some kind of rational process. By economic theory, we mean that in some sense, markets are the central institution in which individual actions interact and that other institutions are of negligible importance.

Ayres's work falls squarely within both traditions and assesses whether discrimination persists today. When he finds that it does, its resilience becomes a puzzle. After all, the ideal market is one of competitive, impersonal exchange. If discrimination is a costly, inefficient practice, it should disappear as those who irrationally engage in prejudiced behavior go out of business.

To address the robustness of discrimination, Gary Becker early on posited a taste for discrimination, a special disutility that whites attach to interaction with nonwhites. Becker's analysis treated rational behavior as the norm, and discrimination reflected an individual preference that endured even after being labeled antisocial. So long as the taste remained widespread, discrimination could persist in a competitive market. Becker's work continues to be highly influential among market theorists today. It is no accident, for example, that in his study of retail car sales, Ayres juxtaposes rational behavior with an irrational preference, or animus.

There are several problems with Becker's approach. It salvages the image of individuals as profit-maximizers by simply creating a new trait, the taste for discrimination. As Arrow notes, "introducing new variables easily risks turning the 'explanation' into a tautology" in much the same way that concepts like phlogiston have been used to save scientific theories once their explanatory value is lost. The taste for discrimination is unique in Becker's theory of market behavior. Why is it, after all, that this trait so singularly overrides a pure commitment to the pursuit of profit? The salience of a taste for discrimination seems especially surprising if market transactions are impersonal. The arm's-length quality of bargaining ought to reduce the significance of individual traits like race. Assuming that Becker's approach was a useful snapshot of market behavior when he wrote in the mid-1950s, most scholars would agree that racial animus has since declined, though not disappeared, as a result of civil rights reforms. So, why does widespread discrimination persist? Market theorists have proposed two key responses, each of which complicates the notion of discrimination.

1. Statistical discrimination.

Some scholars have focused on statistical discrimination, the practice of using race as a proxy for other traits, such as productivity, skills, and training, when individualized information is limited and expensive to obtain. The scarcity of information leads markets to work imperfectly, even when racial animus is not a factor. Race can function as a statistical proxy when rational actors believe that the performance of one racial group is on average different from that of another, based on previous statistical experience or prevailing social beliefs. For example, in Ayres's study of the retail car market, salespeople rationally seek to maximize revenues by using race and gender as proxies for the ability to bargain effectively for a lower price. Somewhat more subtly, race and gender can be statistical proxies when the variability of performance within a group varies by race. George Akerlof has described how uncertainty about quality can drive down prices for used cars, so that even those in good condition must be priced like "lemons." Akerlof argues that the "Lemons Principle" can explain an employer's refusal to hire members of racially disadvantaged groups based on concerns about the consistency and reliability of their skills, particularly if credentials are not trustworthy signals of merit.

The line between statistical discrimination and racial animus, while theoretically clear, can be hard to draw in practice. In one recent study, participants were asked to evaluate a taxi driver's decision not to pick up a black passenger. In the scenario, the cabdriver slows down to pick a person up one night in Chicago, but when he discovers that the fare is a young black man, he speeds by without stopping. As the scenario explains: "Even though [the driver] knows that he can be fined for not stopping, he fears that he might have to drive to a dangerous neighborhood and thinks: 'I'd rather be fined than have my wife a widow.' " Based on the scenario, participants must determine whether the cab driver's decision is rational or whether he is prejudiced against blacks. This assessment turns heavily on the observer's own commitment to rationality and racial attitudes. In particular, those who emphasize cognitive solutions and have negative views of blacks are most apt to describe the driver's behavior as motivated by statistical estimates rather than animus.

Although described as rational behavior unrelated to prejudice, statistical discrimination can reflect and reinforce patterns of racial exclusion and inequality. When employers use race as a proxy for productivity or reliability, their actuarial guesses may depend on incomplete information tainted by patterns of segregation. By refraining from hiring nonwhites, employers never encounter evidence that disconfirms their predictions. Perhaps most disturbingly, rational nonwhites who are aware of patterns of statistical discrimination should reduce investment in their human capital, knowing that their efforts will be neither recognized nor rewarded by the market. A statistical estimate sadly becomes a self-fulfilling prophecy.

If discrimination persists as a rational strategy for dealing with imperfect information, economists face some awkward dilemmas. In contrast to socially undesirable animus, statistical discrimination appears to be precisely the kind of rational, interest-maximizing behavior that is normatively appropriate under market theory. For those who nonetheless wish to eliminate racial disparities, it becomes necessary to step outside the economic model. As Edmund S. Phelps writes:

> A sensitive person, I have been warned, might read this paper [on statistical discrimination] as expressing an impression on the part of the author that most or all discrimination is the result of beliefs that blacks and women deliver on the average an inferior performance. Actually, I do not know (nor claim to know) whether in fact most discrimination is of the statistical kind studied here. But what if it were? Discrimination is no less damaging to its victims for being statistical. And it is no less important for social policy to counter.

By shifting to the victim's perspective and demanding that government officials address the problem, a classic economist like Phelps begins to sound a bit like a critical race theorist. Indeed, Patricia J. Williams has written eloquently about the individual pain of being rendered nothing but a second-class statistical estimate:

> I am one, I am many.

I am amiable, orderly, extremely honest, and a very good neighbor indeed. I am suspect profile, market cluster, actuarial monster, statistical being.

My particulars battle the generals.

'Typecasting!' I protest.

'Predictive indicator,' assert the keepers of the gate.

'Prejudice!' I say.

'Precaution,' they reply.

Hundreds, even thousands, of me hover in the breach.

* * *

B. *Critical Race Theory: Beyond Rationality and Animus*

Critical race theory rejects the centrality of individual animus in the market and insists on a richer picture of personal psychology, social relations, and institutional life than economic models can provide. Like economists, critical race theorists worry about the role of individual psychology in discrimination. Unlike economists, however, race scholars do not presume that conscious rational choice governs everyday judgments. Largely rejecting accounts of statistical discrimination as efficient behavior, critical race theory treats stereotypes as harmful and misleading vestiges of past discrimination. Because the social construction of race is a pervasive feature of American life, race scholars must struggle with the problem of institutional racism in a range of settings that transcend social networks and the marketplace.

* * *

Market theories of racial animus and statistical discrimination largely ignore the victim's perspective. Occasionally, economists point out that pervasive discrimination may undermine incentives for people of color to develop their human capital, so that the perception that nonwhites are less capable than whites becomes a self-fulfilling prophecy. Critical race theorists go much further in exploring the impact of being sorted, stigmatized, and stereotyped on the basis of race. Indeed, one of critical race theory's central missions has been an exploration of the victim's perspective. Stereotyping not only limits the capacity to perceive others as individuals because of their race, but it also limits the capacity of the stigmatized to imagine and develop their fullest potential. Patricia J. Williams goes so far as to label racism "spirit murder," the death of possibility that comes with "disregard for others whose lives qualitatively depend on our regard" through "a system of formalized distortions of thought" and "social structures centered on fear and hate, a tumorous outlet for feelings elsewhere unexpressed."

* * *

In focusing on the victim's perspective, critical race theory sets itself the task of listening to the disadvantaged, not just to document their harm but to "persuade, outrage, and stir to action." Race scholars use a variety of techniques to "look to the bottom," but storytelling has occupied an especially prominent place. In contrast to psychological studies that keep victims at a safe and objective distance, narrative has the power to make unique human connections. Stories can transport white readers across the color line momentarily, so that they begin to appreciate the individual experiences of nonwhites. As Angela Harris explains, "The shock of being addressed suddenly not as disembodied rational consciousness, but as a particular person caught in complex and idiosyncratic webs of emotion and intuition, is itself discomfiting and sometimes disarming." At the same time, narrative creates a sense of inclusion among those who share a common racial identity, and when artfully deployed, it can enable whites and nonwhites alike to reimagine the boundaries of human possibility. With this power comes new perils. Unlike conventional psychological studies, narrative must struggle to avoid essentializing racial experience by creating the impression that one person's account is emblematic of an entire group's experience. Paradoxically, the very stories that are designed to be individuating and idiosyncratic can, when imbued with larger symbolic significance, become a new source of stereotypes.

* * *

For economic theorists, the key puzzle has been why discrimination persists in competitive markets. So far, two important answers have emerged: statistical discrimination and social networks. Each of these approaches has important implications for law and policy. Those who focus on statistical discrimination must grapple with how to police the use of racial proxies. Should policymakers continue to punish only intentional misconduct? Should inaccurate racial generalizations also be penalized? Is the rational use of race as a proxy ever a basis for legal intervention? Economists exploring the role of social networks must consider the extent to which the law can counteract what are often largely private, informal associations. Should affirmative action programs be used to break down barriers imposed by exclusionary networks? If so, can the programs generate or redistribute social capital by setting the stage for interracial contact?

* * *

Because statistical discrimination supplements rather than supplants Becker's theory of racial distaste, the law should continue to recognize claims for disparate treatment, that is, conscious discrimination born of racial animus. In addition, statistical discrimination should be eradicated when it reflects inaccurate generalizations about race, regardless of whether the motive is benign. An economic theorist might expect distorted racial thinking to disappear naturally through competition, but if markets fail to correct these inefficiencies, state intervention could be appropriate. The real dilemma for the economic theorist is whether the government should ever ban the rational use of race as a proxy for other traits because it entrenches inequality.

* * *

In other cases, courts have been reluctant to disrupt the market's rational pricing mechanisms to redress allegedly inequitable results. So, litigators have had little success in pressing comparable worth claims, which argue that women receive less pay than men for the same type of work. Judges have found that employees are free to bargain for wages, and if women get bad deals, they should use market remedies, such as searching for better jobs, organizing for better pay, and seeking raises and promotions. Here, market theorists would likely applaud the courts' reticence to monitor wages on a broad scale in pursuit of gender equity. Pervasive wage regulation could make it hard to distinguish between remedies for sexism and penalties for otherwise rational pricing decisions.

* * *

Richard McAdams has made an important contribution to bridging the gap between critical race theory and law and economics by analyzing racial discrimination as a form of status production. Although he embraces rational choice theory, McAdams rejects Becker's reliance on animus as an explanation for racial discrimination. Instead, McAdams turns to critical race theory to identify status as a factor of critical relevance to racial subordination. McAdams posits that self-esteem is a basic interest that individuals pursue as a form of pleasure. Because an individual's regard is affected by group membership, people have a stake in whether their group's status is enhanced or diminished. Group members can pursue an indirect strategy of raising their standing by lowering the status of other group traits, a practice that McAdams defines as "discrimination." * * * McAdams believes that "affirmative action is an investment in which we bear certain costs today for the hope of a greater return tomorrow," a return that has so far proven uncertain.

* * * Status-based theories that emphasize symbolic politics must be supplemented by analyses of material inequality. Only by examining the practices of particular institutions can scholars avoid reifying status in ways that obscure the contingencies of racial discrimination. Haney Lopez also refuses to link status to rational choice theory, for he believes that unconscious racism is a significant source of status production. Indeed, Haney Lopez defines institutional racism as "racial status-enforcement influenced in an unrecognized manner by racial institutions." Though he criticizes some elements of status theory, Haney Lopez rightly infers that critical race theorists can fruitfully draw on rich and sometimes conflicting theories of status and power to explore race and racism.

2.   The limits of law reform: beyond the market.

Efforts to explain group subordination through theories of status and power are closely linked to another important development in critical race theory. Race scholars increasingly are shifting their attention from individual psychology to organizational structures that reflect and replicate racial inequality. Here, the key challenge is to move from the phrase "institutional racism" to comprehensive accounts of the patterns and practices that generate racial disadvantage in public institutions, market settings, and private life. Here, I will describe some promising examples in each area.

Public institutions. As previously mentioned, Haney Lopez's historical account of the grand jury selection process in Los Angeles demonstrates how high-level officials with substantial formal discretion actually made decisions tightly bound by informal institutional norms. In truth, these informal constraints proved more powerful than explicit formal mandates. For example, even when the judges received official memoranda advising them to diversify the jury pool, they persisted in selection practices that largely excluded Mexican Americans. Based on these findings, Haney Lopez argues that focusing on animus fundamentally misconceives the nature of racism. The intent requirement under equal protection law has become a constitutional straightjacket, one that paralyzes efforts to reach policies and practices that, though not consciously biased, entrench racial inequality. Haney Lopez concludes:

> Courts and commentators must answer why the Equal Protection Clause curtails some racism—for example, that resulting from the conscious desire to harm minorities—while other forms remain lawful—for instance, institutional racism in taxation, welfare, public services, and so on. They should not presume to resolve this issue, however, by supposing the racial neutrality of government actions that disproportionately harm minorities but do not evince a racial purpose. Institutional analysis cautions that racial status-enforcing government action is likely to reflect institutional racism.

Haney Lopez's work is an intriguing start, but critical race theorists have much work left to do in evaluating other public institutions. Courts, agencies, and legislatures differ dramatically in the ways that they allocate discretion and hold officials accountable. Judges have considerable leeway to make decisions, but this deference reflects their professional training and socialization, personal integrity and accomplishment, and collegial consultation and cooperation. Outside the courts, bureaucracies often constrain official power through centralized rules and hierarchical oversight. Differences in organizational structure undoubtedly have important implications for defining institutional racism and evaluating racial remedies. As a result, Haney Lopez's conclusions are not necessarily generalizable, and only further research will reveal the robustness of his analysis in other public settings.

* * *

Private life. Outside the marketplace, critical race theorists increasingly have turned their attention to the role of sex, marriage, and family in the reproduction of inequality. Building on the insights of feminist legal theorists, race scholars acknowledge that there is no bright-line boundary between public and private life. Even in the realm of feeling, seemingly the most interior aspect of personal life, people are trapped within a sociopolitical economy of emotion, one that replicates boundaries of race and gender.

* * *

Although critical race theorists have devoted considerable energy to imagining a world free of subordination, perhaps some of their greatest contributions will come in documenting the day-to-day policies and practices that make inequality a seemingly inevitable feature of everyday life. This work promises to be deeply interdisciplinary, drawing on such fields as anthropology, history, political science, psychology, and sociology. Race scholars will apply a range of methods in doing these case studies, but the results can unify the field by offering a coherent and compelling portrait of how racism transcends individual animus and invades the innermost reaches of our lives.

* * * [T]he concept of discrimination has grown diffuse and fragmented. To counter images of discrimination as conscious animus, critical race theorists have described unconscious racism. In response to a framework of individual transgressions, race scholars have insisted that institutional racism is at least equally if not more significant in perpetuating inequality. Although individual discrimination might be corrected through consciousness-raising or incremental legislation, subordination is so deeply entrenched that it can be eliminated only through profound transformations of the body politic. The simple truth is that once Bull Connor and Lester Maddox are gone, once angry parents are not screaming, "Two, four, six, eight, we don't want to integrate," and once spittle isn't running down the faces of civil rights protesters, it is hard to say precisely what discrimination means. * * *

NOTES AND QUESTIONS

1. Can law and economics and critical race theory be combined? In the mid 1990s, legal scholar, Edward L. Rubin urged the combination of critical race theory and law and economics. Rubin perceived enough common ground between these two, often antagonistic, schools of legal reasoning to suggest that they could be combined:

> [C]ontemporary law and economics and outsider scholarship share a common ground—the effort to locate law, social policy, and social change in a closely analyzed institutional context. What is particularly promising about the effort is that institutional analysis has also become a major theme in the academic fields that gave rise to both these schools. To develop a new synthesis of discourse for legal scholarship, ideas from all these fields must be incorporated, for most scholars agree that law can no longer sustain itself as an autonomous discipline. Whether these complex and disparate elements can actually be integrated is an open question—there is nothing inevitable about the process—but synthesis seems like an appealing alternative to the currently fragmented state of legal scholarship.

Edward L. Rubin, *The New Legal Process, the Synthesis of Discourse, and the Microanalysis of Institutions*, 109 HARV. L. REV. 1393, 1394 (1996).

Two critical race theorists, Devon Carbado and Mitu Gulati, endorse Rubin's proposal for collaboration and synthesis between the two schools, noting that:

> The argument for a collaboration between economics and [critical race theory ('CRT')] (and feminist theory and gay and lesbian legal studies) was made with force in a 1996 essay by Ed Rubin. Rubin argued that the common critical approach to institutional analysis shared by law and economics ('L&E') and CRT—both fields reject claims about the neutrality and objectivity of legal rules, albeit for different reasons would, if combined, produce not only an exciting new methodology for legal inquiry, but one with potential to succeed the Legal Process school as a unifying discourse in legal academia. In the six years since the piece was published, however, there has been little collaborative work between CRT and L&E. If anything there has been increased antagonism.

This makes little sense. Like Rubin, we believe that L&E and CRT should engage each other and that the results of this engagement would be fruitful.

> Devon W. Carbado *The Law and Economics of Critical Race Theory* 112 YALE L.J. 1757, 1761 (2003) (book review).

2.   Is statistical discrimination rational but unjust? Statistical discrimination occurs when unequal treatment is the result of cognitive short cuts that rely on the decision maker's experience with the average member of the disfavored group, or decisions based upon statistical portraits of the behavior of members of the group that may be accurate for the aggregate, but that are not accurate for any one individual in the group.

In the excerpt above, Moran has identified a central problem of rationality analysis:

> Although described as rational behavior unrelated to prejudice, statistical discrimination can reflect and reinforce patterns of racial exclusion and inequality. When employers use race as a proxy for productivity or reliability, their actuarial guesses may depend on incomplete information tainted by patterns of segregation.

Moran, *supra* at 2387.

Moran agrees with Cass Sunstein, infra at 384, 391, 393, that:

> [S]ometimes discrimination is caused by employer practices that result precisely from economic self-interest, rather than from the employer's noneconomic goals.
>
> * * *
>
> If race or sex can be a good signaling device, an employer might discriminate not because he hates or devalues blacks or women, or has a general desire not to associate with them, or is "prejudiced" in the ordinary sense, but because he believes (on the basis either of plausible assumptions or actual experience) that the relevant stereotypes have sufficient truth to be a basis for employment decisions.

CASS R. SUNSTEIN, FREE MARKETS AND SOCIAL JUSTICE 153, 156 (1997).

The Moran and Sunstein passages raise the following issues:

1. Since statistical discrimination relies on mental shortcuts, they reduce the cost of individual evaluation. Therefore, does this form of decision making provide a competitive advantage?

2. Are the portraits of average behavior of the disfavored group themselves the product of past discrimination? Statistical discrimination therefore locks in the disadvantages of the past. In this way, invidious discrimination can morph into "benign" statistical discrimination, if it is not sanctioned.

3. Is the very accuracy of statistical discrimination-based exclusions a symptom of the persistence of societal disadvantages placed upon the subordinated group?

4. The greater wealth and market power advantage of the majority will be further multiplied by reliance on statistical discrimination. In this instance, rational choices are morally offensive because they are a link in the chain of extending historic subordination.

---

2. BEYOND: WEALTH MAXIMIZATION AND PRICE THEORY

a. Humanism vs. Materialism

Economics and Law: Two Cultures in Tension

54 TENN. L. REV. 161, 166–67, 172–73, 174–75, 178, 182–83, 184–85, 191–93 (1986).

■ JAMES BOYD WHITE

* * *

Many people think of economics solely as a scientific, conceptual, and cognitive system, apparently unaware that there are any other dimensions of meaning in economic talk. But all expression is loaded with values, ethical and otherwise; all expression defines a self and another and proposes a relation between them; all expression remakes its language; in these senses all expression proposes the creation of a community and a culture. All expression, in short, is ethical, cultural, and political, and it can be analyzed and judged as such. To claim that economics is a science is perhaps to claim that it cannot be judged in such terms. But "sciences" are cultures too, with their own created worlds and values. One way to describe my aim * * *, then, is to say that it reverses the usual flow: we are used to economic analyses of this or that aspect of our common life—voting, the family, war, etc. I propose here to begin what I would call a rhetorical or cultural analysis of a certain kind of economics.

* * *

IV.   ECONOMICS AS A SYSTEM OF VALUES

We can start with the question of value. In its purest form economics claims to be a value-free social science. But as I suggested earlier I think it in fact enacts a set of values, including political ones, values to which the speaker of the language cannot avoid finding himself at least in part committed.

A.   *In the World*

Think, for example, of the way in which economics defines the economic actor and the processes by which he functions. He is for the most part assumed to be an individual of indeterminate age, sex, race and cultural background, but of adequate competence at manipulating economic relations. He acts as one who is both perfectly aware of his own wishes and wholly rational—in the special sense in which that term is used, to mean "calculating"—in his pursuit of them. He exists as an individual, not as part of a community, except insofar as he establishes contractual or exchange relations with others. He is assumed to be motivated by self-interest, which in turn is defined in terms of competition, acquisition, and dominion, at least in relation to resources and other actors, for in the process of exchange the self is reduced to those desires.

Of course a particular individual may have other values—indeed the economist insists that he must, calling them "tastes" or "preferences"—perhaps including a "taste" for altruism, for peace and quiet, for heavy metal music, for appreciating nature unspoiled, for beautiful or ugly art, and so forth. These values will drive his participation in the exchange process, or his decision to withdraw from it. But in either case they are themselves valued by the method of exchange: either by an actual exchange that takes place or by a hypothetical or imagined exchange that is forgone (or in a more complicated case by a combination of exchanges made and forgone). In both cases these external values are converted by the discourse into the acquisitive or instrumental values—the desire to extend the dominion of the will—that all economic actors are assumed to have, for this is the only kind of value about which economics can directly talk.

With respect to the external values in their original form, the system is purportedly "value neutral." That is, it regards individual values as simply exogenous to the system itself. Economics of course recognizes that these values exist, but it demeans them by calling them "tastes" or "preferences," names that imply that no serious conversation can proceed on such subjects and economics itself is by definition not about those values, but about the process by which they are reflected in the activity of exchange. This means that economics cannot, in principle, talk about any value other than the acquisitive or instrumental one that it universalizes. (Indeed it does not talk about this value either, but merely assumes and acts upon it.) This is not to be "value free," as its apologists claim, but to make self-interest the central, indeed almost the only, value, for it is the only one that can be talked about in these terms. To come at it the other way, it is to claim that all values can be talked about, at least for some purposes, as if they were selfish, quantifiable, and interchangeable.

* * *

Yet economics is troubling not only for the self-interested values it directly asserts, but also for the very neutrality, the "value freedom," that it claims. It is in principle neutral on all questions of value that are external to the acquisitive and competitive ones enacted in the exchange game, which it lumps together as "tastes" or "preferences" among which no distinctions can be drawn. But this is to be silent on all the great questions of human life: questions of beauty and ugliness in art and music, sincerity and falsity in human relations, wisdom and folly in conduct and judgment, and the greatest of all questions, which is how we ought to lead our lives. Economic analysis assumes as a given the existence of "tastes" or "preferences" which drive the system, but economics as a language can provide no way of talking about these values, whether in oneself or another, no way of thinking about which to prefer and which not. To the extent that economics does reach out for these questions it may be worse than silent, for silence after all can be a mode of controlling a discourse. When economics tries to speak about these matters it does so in the only way it knows how to speak, in purely quantitative terms and on the assumption that all human transactions can be reduced to the model of exchange.

* * *

For the purposes of economic analysis all human wishes and desires are thus reduced to the same level, as though no principled choices could be made among them, as though it didn't matter what choices one made. This in turn means that it is impossible to talk in these terms about our most important choices as individuals and communities, or about the education of mind or heart, for any impulse that we or others may happen to have is as good, valid, and entitled to respect as any other.

* * * We must and do have preferences, as the economist knows; and these necessarily commit those who have them to the inquiry of better and worse, as well as to that of greater and less. To refuse to engage in this inquiry—to privatize it—as economics in its neutral phase necessarily does, is to deny an essential and necessary aspect of human life. To reduce all value to self-interest, as it does the rest of the time, is intellectually and ethically intolerable. How could one educate one's children or oneself to live in a world that was neutral on all the great questions of life, except that it reduced them to acquisition, competition, and calculation?

* * *

The second ground upon which the market is justified is that not of its gross effects but of its fairness. In one version this justification rests upon the ethical standing of voluntary action and holds that the results of the market process are justified with respect to every actor because the choices by which the market works are voluntary. In another version, it becomes the affirmative celebration of autonomy or liberty: whether or not it is efficient, the market is good because it gives the widest possible range to freedom of choice and action. Here the claim moves beyond justifying market results by the voluntary character of the choices upon which they rest to the point of asserting autonomy as the central social and political value. The obvious trouble with this line of defense, in both of its forms, is that it assumes that all exchanges are for all actors equally voluntary and equally expressive of autonomy, a position that common sense denies.

* * *

The market purports to rest upon an assumption of the equality of all the actors in the system. In fact, it rests upon a different assumption, namely, the equality of every dollar in the system. Since some players have many more dollars, and through this fact are at a competitive advantage, it is a system that actively supports inequality among its actors.

It is not too much to say, I think, that the modern celebration of the market as the central social institution—the most fair, the most respecting of autonomy, and the most efficient—threatens to destroy the single greatest achievement of Western political culture: the discovery that a community can govern itself through a rule of law that attempts to create a fundamental moral and political equality among human beings. The great phrase in the Declaration of Independence—"all men are created equal"— is partly a theological statement about the conditions under which we are created and partly a political statement about the obligation of the government to acknowledge, indeed to create or recreate, that equality. This value is the heart of what is meant both by equality under law and by our democratic institutions more generally, resting as they do on the premise that each person's vote is worth exactly what everyone else's is. The ideology of the market, if it prevailed in its desire to convert all institutions into markets, would destroy this set of political relations and would create another in its stead, based upon the dollar.

* * *

The market ideology claims to be radically democratic and egalitarian because it leaves every person free to do with her own what she will. But this freedom of choice is not equally distributed among all people. The market is democratic not on the principle of one person one vote, but on the far different principle of one dollar, one vote. One could hardly make a greater mistake than to equate, as so much modern public talk carelessly does, the "free market" with democracy.

There are two distinct points here. First, the exchange transactions that the market celebrates are not entitled to the special respect claimed for them as free and voluntary, and hence fair, unless each person has roughly the same amount of money and the same competence and freedom in its use, which is demonstrably not the case. The accumulations of wealth it permits thus cannot be justified by the fairness of the transactions by which the accumulation occurs. Second, if the advocates of the market succeeded in converting other institutions into markets, the result would be to transfer to those who have wealth not only the economic power that inescapably follows it but also the political power that in our democratic tradition the people have claimed for themselves and have exercised through the institutions of self-government. This would validate and institutionalize private economic power held by one person over another, of the rich over the poor. If we were to yield entirely to its claims, we would gradually find our traditional government, which operates by collective deliberation on a premise of fundamental equality of citizens, replaced by a private-sector government of the few over the many, wholly unregulated by collective judgment.

* * *

VI. ECONOMICS AS A SYSTEM OF ECONOMIC ANALYSIS

D. Erasing Community

For similar reasons this kind of economics has the greatest difficulty in reflecting the reality of human community and the value of communal institutions. Its necessary tendency seems to be to destroy the idea of public action, indeed the idea of community itself. This is partly because this methodology tends to resolve all communities and organizations into the individual human actors who constitute them, partly because commitment to the market system leads one to think that everything that can be made the subject of the market should be. The idea is that every economic actor should pay for what he wants, and should not have to pay for what he doesn't want. But this tends to destroy our public institutions, all of which extend benefits far beyond those who would pay (if they were reduced to markets) or who do pay (when they are supported by taxes). Such institutions reflect a communal judgment that we need to educate ourselves and each other, that our "tastes" are not all of equal value but need to be formed, and formed well rather than badly. Public universities, libraries, orchestras, museums, parks—all these would fall before the ideology that denies the existence and reality of community and reduces all institutions, all human production, to the language of the market.

Think here of the way economists explain why people who will probably never visit, say, the Everglades or an art museum are happy to have their taxes used to maintain them. The economist says it is because the actor wants to maintain the option of visiting them some day, and calls this an "option demand." But may it not be that the voter simply takes pleasure in what other people have and in what other people can do, in belonging to a community that is good for all its members? Or that he respects their desires and wants a community based on that kind of mutual respect? This possibility is systematically denied by the assumption of economic talk, that individuals and communities are in principle incapable of generosity, or more precisely, that "altruism" can adequately be talked about as a species of selfishness.

The language of self and self-interest not only fails to reflect the reality of community and of shared interests, it draws attention away from those aspects of life and devalues them. To continue to talk on these assumptions, even hypothetically, is to encourage "self-interest" in an ethical sense and to erode the commitments we have to each other that underlie such essential practices of citizenship as the willingness to pay taxes, to work for the local school, or to serve in the army, upon which everything depends. To adopt the economic view would in fact threaten the very existence of community, for on these premises no one would conceivably die or seriously risk his life for his community: at the point of danger one's self-interest in survival would outweigh all other self-interests. And to speak of all "tastes" as if they were equivalent is to invite oneself and others to think that they are, and to confirm the premises of our culture, already drummed into the mind by the consumer economy, that the consumer is king, that whatever you happen to want is a good that you should seek to satisfy, that no distinction can be drawn between the beautiful and ugly, the wise and foolish, and so on. It is to confirm a vulgar view of democracy that makes the preference or will supreme, as if we functioned by instant referendum. It erases the sense that a democracy is a mode of communal self-constitution and self-education that may have higher ends than the satisfaction of wants, namely the creation of a community of a certain sort, at once based upon a set of responsibilities and offering us a set of opportunities for civic and social action.

* * *

NOTES AND QUESTIONS

1. When rational is wrong. White argues that the central defect of law and economics is that it is a scholarly discipline that masks its commitment to materialism with scientific precepts that do not withstand close scrutiny of their value-laden premises that elevate materialism over fairness.

The challenge for scholars working with both economics and the injuries of subordination is to create an alternative to the economic vocabulary for understanding how humans accumulate the resources to fulfill their basic needs. Since Adam Smith, the vocabulary of rationality has been dominant. In the following, Charles Pouncy argues for a "robust expression" of the "concept of economic justice" as an alternative to the neoclassical lexicon:

> The concept of economic justice finds no robust expression in the law of the United States.

> Economic justice is not a concern of neoclassical theory. Neoclassical theory is not designed to achieve economic justice, and in fact intervenes to prevent it.

> *Id.* at 23.

> Neoclassical theory intervenes in consensus reality to support the notion of colorblind economics, an economic system in which markets negate the impact of irrational criteria, such as race, in economic decision-making.

Id. at 28.

Neoclassical theory works in concert with the preservative nature of law to prevent the development of a jurisprudence of economic justice.

Id.

Racism and classism are insulated from approbation by . . . economic rationality.

Id. at 17.

When we combine the belief that the individual is the proper unit of economic analysis and that individuals base their decisions on their perception of their own best interests, then discrimination and racism are transformed from indicia of hatred or irrational hatred to good business decisions.

Id. at 20.

Charles R.P. Pouncy, *Economic Justice and Economic Theory: Limiting the Reach of Neoclassical Ideology*, 14 U. FLA. J. L. & PUB. POL'Y 11, 11 (2002).

2. Effect of terminology on White's critique. White states that "all systems of discourse commit their users to values . . . [and that] economics is [not] wrong to do what it does." James Boyd White, *Economics and Law: Two Cultures in Tension*, 54 TENN. L. REV. 161, 176 (1986). If all White wishes is for economics to acknowledge that it is no different from other systems of discourse, does his critique of law and economics have any value? Would the problems White identifies with law and economics be solved by acknowledging that law and economics has values without making any substantive changes to the discipline? Would White be satisfied with such a solution?

3. The pernicious nature of law and economics. At the close of his article, White states that "to continue to talk on . . . [law and economics'] assumptions, even hypothetically, is to encourage 'self interest' in an ethical sense and to erode the commitments we have to each other that underlie such essential practices of citizenship as the willingness to pay taxes, to work for the local school, or to serve in the army, upon which everything depends. To adopt the economic view would in fact threaten the very existence of community . . ." *Id.* at 192. If White is correct about the dire consequences of even hypothesizing in an economic framework, how can he assert that economics is not wrong to "do what it does?" *Id.* at 176.

b. The Commodification Critique

Justice and the Market Domain

MARKETS AND JUSTICE 165–89 (John W. Chapman & J. Roland Pennock eds., 1989).

■ MARGARET JANE RADIN

I. INTRODUCTION: THE METAPHOR OF THE WALL

It has been traditional to view some aspects of social life as inappropriate for the market. We speak of a metaphorical wall between the market and other realms of social life, much as we speak of a wall between church and state. There is a traditional understanding that important political activities, like voting, are on the nonmarket side of the wall. There is also an understanding that certain special kinds of interactions between persons are on the nonmarket side of the wall—that is, are morally required to be kept there—even if some people desire to "marketize" them. It is this latter understanding that I wish to explore and question here. Does justice require that we delineate and protect a nonmarket domain? In general, how might a theory of social justice take into account the question of the domain of the market?

A traditional liberal view is that the market appropriately encompasses most desired transactions between people, with a few special exceptions. Those few exceptions—for example, the way we acquire a spouse or a child—are morally and legally protected from the market. I want to suggest that the traditional view is wrong in granting too much ground to the market. The metaphor of a wall between a market and nonmarket realm is inapposite because it wrongly suggests a large realm of pure free-market transactions to which special kinds of personal interactions form a special exception. It wrongly suggests that a laissez-faire market regime is prima facie just.

* * *

In order to frame this discussion it is necessary to notice that there is another way to deny the appositeness of the wall metaphor, and that is to say that in principle there is no limit to the market. Someone who holds this view thinks of the market as encompassing the social world. She thinks not only that social justice does not require us to protect a nonmarket domain, but also that social justice requires a universal market structure. This is the approach taken by some of the contemporary theorists who bring economics to bear on political and legal theory. Hence, it is possible to see an imaginary battle being waged. The traditional liberal view, asserting that there must be a realm of personal interactions walled off from the market, is striving to hold some territory against the oncoming forces of economics and the notion that everything is grist for the market mill.

In my view, both sides are wrong, and so is the battle. Instead of trying to defend the small piece of ground representing the list of special non-market personal interactions, it would be better to try to reclaim for peaceful co-existence some of the territory the traditional liberal view concedes to the market. The traditional liberal view is wrong because it assumes that not much is on the nonmarket side of the wall, and the battle lines prevent us from appreciating the nonmarket aspects of many of our market relations. They prevent us from seeing fragments of a nonmarket social order embedded or latent in the market society. They prevent us from thinking about social justice in terms of fostering this latent co-existent nonmarket order.

II. Universal Commodification vs. the Wall

A. The Market as Methodological Archetype

Let us first consider a sketch of an archetype representing the economic view, and then consider the reasons given by its opponents for walling off a few special things from the market. Some law-and-economics theorists can be understood to endorse a methodological archetype that is sometimes referred to as market-imperialism, but which I prefer to call universal commodification. Under universal commodification, all things desired or valued—from personal attributes to good government—are goods or commodities. Commodities are usually pictured as objects separate from the self and social relations. Hence, universal commodification is a form of objectification. It assimilates personal attributes, relations, and desired states of affairs to the realm of objects. Universal commodification implies that all things can and should be separable from persons and exchanged through the free market, whenever some people are willing to sell and others are willing to buy. All human attributes are conceived of as possessions bearing a value characterizable in money terms, and all human interactions are conceived as exchanges understandable in terms of gains from trade.

The language in which this conceptual scheme is couched is the rhetoric of the market. Under universal commodification, the human universe of social interaction—from government to love and sexuality—is conceived and described in the rhetoric of trading objects for money. Hobbes conceived of the value of a person in market rhetoric: "the *Value* or WORTH of a man, is as of all other things, his Price; that is to say, so much as would be given for the use of his Power." In Hobbes's conception, everything about a person that others need, desire, or value is a possession that is priced. The Hobbesian person fits into the archetype of universal commodification. The Hobbesian conception of the political order likewise conceives of politics in market rhetoric. Modern Hobbesians view political activity as fully describable in terms of "rent seeking" by those who can achieve monetary gain from the capture of portions of Leviathan's power.

* * *

For one who is willing to conceive of everything (corneas for transplant, sexuality, babies for adoption) in market rhetoric, the only explanation for why some things might be held out of the market is market failure: free riders and holdouts, administrative costs, information costs, and so on. Judge Richard Posner, for example, apparently views a ban on selling oneself into slavery as justified by information costs. Finding no apparent market failures that would suggest noncommodification of children, he suggests that a free market in babies would be a good idea.

B.   Three Attempts to Maintain the Wall

Those who advocate the traditional wall to claim a few things for a domain that is in principle off limits to the market rely on reasons other than market failure. Three prevalent kinds of arguments are deployed in trying to keep something—babies, blood, kidneys—on the nonmarket side of a metaphorical wall. The first is an argument based upon the degradation and invasion of personhood occasioned by allowing sales. The second is an argument based upon creating or preserving opportunities for altruism. The third is a slippery slope argument that I call a domino theory, claiming that to allow sales for some people who choose them will foreclose nonmarket sharing for those who don't choose the market regime. As we shall see, the second and third arguments are related, because the argument based upon opportunities for altruism assumes the domino theory is true. But the two arguments are not coextensive, for, as we shall see, the domino theory is also applied to cases that do not fit the argument about altruism.

I shall argue that these arguments are too general for the task they have been put to, that is, to show that universal commodification is wrong because there must remain certain specific pockets of nonmarket social interactions. Instead, they seem to point toward a more generalized nonmarket perspective. That is, these arguments have been aimed at shoring up a wall between the market and nonmarket domains, but in fact they undermine the wall metaphor. These arguments fail to capture what is wrong about universal commodification.

Personhood prophylaxis. The first strand of argument is often thought of in connection with organ transplants, especially from living people. The argument holds that we must prevent poor people from being forced to sell their kidneys and corneas. The general idea is that it is somehow degrading to be selling off one's body parts, and that this is an injury to personhood that society should prevent. Thus I characterize the argument as aimed at personhood prophylaxis. In this strand of argument it is also thought that in some sense such sales are the result of coercion and do not represent a voluntary act on the seller's part.

Of course, it is problematic whether this kind of action that results from poverty should count as coerced. Does poverty "coerce" someone into selling a kidney, or does someone, because she is poor, choose to sell a kidney? A hard choice is not a non-choice. But the main problem with the personhood prophylaxis form of argument is that it seems cruelly smug. Under what circumstances do people need money badly enough to sell a kidney? Perhaps to feed, clothe, and house their children, or to support elderly or handicapped relatives. It may appear to observers that selling a kidney is degrading, but if these are the circumstances, it seems more degrading instead to have to endure the state of affairs that the sale was supposed to ameliorate.

* * *

Preserving opportunities for altruism. According to the second strand of argument, something should be held off the market when permitting sales would foreclose, or fail to create, opportunities for altruism that ought to be open. With regard to human blood, for example, Richard Titmuss claimed that altruism is encouraged if society permits only donation, and discouraged if society permits both gifts and sales. In the Titmuss style of argument, altruism is encouraged by donation rather than sale because giving is thought to be communitarian and to emphasize interdependence, whereas market transactions are thought to be individualistic and to emphasize isolation. A donor's experience in being responsible for saving a stranger's life is said to bring us closer together, cement our community, in a way that buying and selling cannot. Interdependence is also emphasized by the possibility of reciprocity. A donor's sense of obligation today could be partially founded on the recognition that she might well need to become a recipient tomorrow. A recipient's sense of gratitude and acknowledgment of dependence upon others' altruism rather than upon her own wealth creates solidarity and interdependence.

According to this argument, altruism is foreclosed if both donations and sales are permitted. If sales are not allowed, donations have no market value and remain unmonetized. If sales are allowed, then even gifts have a market equivalent. My giving a pint of blood is like giving $50 of my money. According to this argument, such monetization discourages giving. We are more willing to give health, perhaps life itself, to strangers than we are to give them $50 of our money.

    * * *

Even accepting a need to find gift objects that must remain completely unmonetized, it still seems that the argument about opportunities for altruism is more general than its proponents have thought. Many kinds of gift objects or volunteer services that can be given on a one-shot basis and do not require much special training might still fit the argument: gifts of old clothes or books; services like reading to blind people, being a subject for experimentation, driving voters to the polls, census-taking, and so on. Why do we not think of keeping these things completely unmonetized? Maybe those who make the argument about opportunities for altruism would further try to cabin it by suggesting that, in addition to being things that can be given on a one-shot basis, the things that must be kept unmonetized are extremely important, perhaps meaning the difference between life or death, to the recipient. But such an attempt to cabin the argument must fail, because it is unclear why the level of importance should matter in this way. There seems to be no reason why we must make altruism dramatic in order to preserve it.

The domino theory. The third strand of argument, the domino theory, holds that there is a slippery-slope leading from toleration of any sales (of something) to an exclusive market regime (for that thing). Although it is a necessary supposition of the argument about opportunities for altruism, the domino theory is more often brought up in connection with prostitution and sale of babies. The domino theory implicitly makes two claims: first, as a background normative premise, that it is important for a nonmarket regime to exist; and second, as an empirical premise, that a nonmarket regime cannot co-exist with a market regime. The market drives out the nonmarket version, hence the market regime must be banned.

The domino theory covers more than just the territory supposedly conducive to altruism, since those who argue that sexuality must remain nonmonetized do not argue that the reason is so that it may be altruistically given. Indeed, as I suggested earlier, it seems that the concept of altruism already presupposes more distance, remoteness, or impersonality between people than we wish to countenance in our ideals of sexuality. Those who are against monetized sex are probably against altruistic sex also.

Preserving opportunities for altruism does not, then, seem to be the main reason for asserting that noncommercial sex must remain possible. Nor does it seem to be the main reason at work in the inclination to ban baby selling, although it can play a part, as my earlier discussion indicated. Rather, it appears that the uncommodified version must remain possible because commodification somehow destroys or deeply disfigures the possible value of sex itself or the value of the baby itself.

With babies this does not seem difficult to understand. Superficially, at least, it seems to fail to treat children as persons to make them all realize that they have a definite commercial value, and that this is all their value amounts to, even if their parents did not choose to sell them or did not obtain them by purchase; the domino theory asserts that this will be the result of permitting sales for those who choose them. Is it similarly an injury to personhood to commercialize sex? If noncommercial sex becomes impossible, as we are here assuming, the argument that the answer is yes asserts that we shall all be deprived of a significant form of human bonding and interrelation. If disrespect for personhood has an individualistic flavor, perhaps this would be better put as disrespect for humanity or human relations. Under this analysis, noncommercial sex is a component of human flourishing, like the need for opportunities to express altruism. Commercial friendship is a contradiction in terms, as is commercial love. If opportunities for noncommercial friendship and love were not available, we would not be human. The argument we are reviewing asks us to see sexuality analogously.

But let us finally focus on the domino part of the theory. Is it the case that if some people are allowed to sell babies or sexual services, those things will be thereby commercialized for everyone? The argument that the answer is yes assumes that once the fact of market value enters our discourse, it must be present in, and dominate, every transaction. The fact of pricing brings with it the conceptual scheme of commodification. We cannot know the price of something and know at the same time that it is priceless. Once something has a price, money must be a part of the interaction, and the reason or explanation for the interaction, when that something changes hands. A sale cannot simultaneously be a gift. If our children know that the going rate of babies is $10,000, they will know that they are worth $10,000. They will know that they are worth as much as an economy car, but not as much as a house. Worse, if they know that the market price of "good" babies is $10,000, whereas the price of "medium-grade" babies is only $8,000, they will be anxiously comparing themselves with the "good" grade of child in hopes that they measure up. One can fill in the analogous argument regarding sexuality.

III. Incomplete Commodification:

The Metaphor of Coexistence

A. Coexistence of Market and Nonmarket Interaction

The domino theory assumes that we cannot both know the price of something and know that it is priceless. We cannot have a sale that is also, and "really," a gift. Is this assumption correct? Or does it grant too much to universal commodification at the outset, by assuming that thinking in money terms is what comes most "naturally" to us? Perhaps it is not true that an interaction cannot be both a sale and a gift at the same time; that we cannot both know the price of something, and know that it is unmonetizable or priceless. This kind of critique of the domino theory would see a nonmarket aspect to much of the market. I shall elaborate it somewhat by considering work and our ideals about work.

Because this is a market society, most people must be paid for their work if they are to live, yet the kind of work we all hope to have—I think—is that which we would do anyway, without money, if somehow by other means our necessities of life were taken care of. Our ideals about work—at least for many of us—do not turn on capitalist rationality. What we hope to get out of working is not all money, nor understandable in money terms (unless the archetype of universal commodification describes our conceptual scheme).

Inspired by Hannah Arendt, I think it is helpful here to introduce a distinction between work and labor, though it is not the same one she had in mind. It is possible to think of work as always containing a noncommodified human element; and to think of the fully commodified version as labor. I think we can understand the difference between working and laboring the way we understand the difference between playing notes and playing music. Laborers play notes, workers play the music. * * *

Many people have the sense, however, that these ideals about work are declining. As market rationality takes over, there is less and less room for working with care. Many kinds of work are becoming impersonal, some say. (Health care is a primary example.) What does it mean to say they are becoming impersonal? That seems to be simply to say that market rhetoric fully characterizes the process of interaction between seller and buyer. This is to say that to the participants in the interaction the services or things are completely commodified. The relation between health-care provider and patient, for example, is no different from that between the proverbial seller and buyer of widgets.

Putting it this way suggests that complete noncommodification—complete removal from the market—is not the only alternative to complete commodification. Incomplete commodification is also possible. Incomplete commodification describes a situation in which things are sold but the interaction between the participants in the transaction cannot be fully or perspicuously described as the sale of things. If many kinds of sales retain a personal aspect even though money changes hands, those interactions are not fully described as sales of commodities. There is an irreducibly non-market or nonmonetized aspect of human interaction going on between seller and recipient; to them the things sold are incompletely commodified. That there should be the opportunity for work to be personal in this sense does seem to be part of our conception of human flourishing—which is why those who see increasing depersonalization deplore it. Complete commodification of work—pure labor—does violence to our notion of what it is to be a well-developed person.

B. Incomplete Commodification and the Ideals of Personhood and Community

Now it may be clear why I think it gives up the ball game to argue that certain specific items (for example, blood) must remain completely noncommodified so as to keep open opportunities for altruism, especially if those who argue this way hope that these sporadic opportunities may lead the way to a less commodified society. The way to a less commodified society is to see and foster the nonmarket aspect of much of what we buy and sell, rather than to erect a wall to keep a certain few things completely off the market and abandon everything else to market rationality.

If social justice would be improved by a less commodified society, then, rather than walling off a few transactions from the pure free market, we should seek to deepen and consolidate the nonmarket countercurrents that cut across the market. One way that we already do this to some extent is, of course, with regulation. At least, that is one way of interpreting what regulation means. Such an interpretation would be consistent with prevalent critiques of liberal notions of the individual and society.

Liberal conceptions of personhood and community (individuality and sociality) have been criticized for expressing and creating an alienated, crassly commercial form of life. Liberal personhood has seemed to postulate an abstract, isolated subject radically separate from a world of objects (and other subjects). * * *

Incomplete commodification as an expression of a nonmarket order co-existent with a market order can be related to this shift in conception of the ideals of personhood and community. The kinds of goods that deviate most from laissez-faire are those related to human beings' homes, work, food, environment, education, communication, health, bodily integrity, sexuality, family life, and political life. For these goods it is easiest to see that preservation and fostering of the nonmarket aspect of their provision and use is related to human flourishing and social justice—to personhood and community as reconceived to meet the critique of liberalism. Once we accept that pervasive incomplete commodification is related to appropriate ideals of personhood and community, it is clear why the arguments for piecemeal noncommodification of specific items are unsatisfactory. It seems that the values of personhood and community require not that certain specific exceptional things be insulated by a wall while everything else is governed by market forces; rather, it seems that the values of personhood and community pervasively interact with the market and alter many goods from their pure free-market form.

* * *

IV.   Some Ramifications for a Theory of S.C. Justice

* * *

B.   *Incomplete Commodification and the Form of a Theory of Justice*

Now I wish to explore whether we can think more satisfactorily about social justice and the market if we abandon the metaphor of walls (and spheres). Before proceeding, it will be useful to take note of prevalent forms of theorizing about social justice. In one kind of theorizing, we concentrate on justice for the community as a whole. This is often conceptualized in terms of distribution of goods or wealth. A theory of justice in this form can (though of course it need not) cohere with a universal commodifying view of the social order. For example, Robert Nozick's unpatterned entitlement theory replicates the market in its global reliance on entitlement (private property) and just transfer (free contract). Hobbesian theories likewise conceive distributive justice to be the outcomes of unfettered market trades, with adjustments for market failures that mimic what a free market would have achieved.

In another kind of theorizing, we concentrate on social justice as just deserts for individuals, or respect for personhood. This kind of theory too can be captured by universal commodification; for example, when the person's deserts are conceived of as negative freedom to buy and sell all things in markets. Although it would oversimplify matters to attribute such a conception to Rawls, it is possible to see Rawls's theory as tending in this direction. For Rawls, a version of negative liberty is the primary requirement of social justice. All the bases of self-respect necessary to respect persons are conceived of as primary "goods," which at least perpetuates the rhetoric of fungible possessions and objectification.

Whether we are theorizing about justice for the community or for individuals, the still-prevalent liberal metaphor of social contract seems itself to perpetuate market rhetoric. Modern contractualists do not always mean the language of contract to imply monetary exchange or implicit monetizability of all individual and social value. Yet contract is a linchpin of universal commodification, and in the liberal tradition the contract metaphor must draw its power from the normative power of promises to exchange commodities. It is hence possible to see theories of justice that are couched in contract rhetoric as tending toward universal commodification—reduction to monetary terms of the broader normative ideas of social commitment, agreement, and consensus.

Positing the propriety of pervasive coexistence of market and non-market aspects to human interactions is an alternative both to theories that imply or can be understood to countenance universal commodification and to "wall" theories of social justice like Walzer's. Incomplete commodification would be reflected both in a theory of overall distributive fairness and a theory of proper treatment of individuals. Key principles for both these aspects of justice in such an alternative theory are that who should get what things of value depends upon the appropriate relation between persons and things, and between persons and other people.

For example, if we accept as appropriate a close connection between persons and their housing, then housing should be socially provided in such a way not only that everyone may have the shelter necessary for physical survival, but also that everyone may have the continuity of residence (often) necessary for proper self-development. Housing, both rented and owned, is appropriately incompletely commodified: it has special nonmarket significance to participants in market interactions regarding it, and it is appropriately socially regulated in recognition of the propriety of this self-investment. This is not because, as Walzer might have it, housing belongs to the "sphere" of security and welfare, in which distribution should be according to the principle of need, rather than to the "sphere" of money and commodities, in which distribution is appropriately according to the principle of free exchange. Rather it is because, although we value the efficiency of the market, at the same time housing must be incompletely commodified in recognition of its connection with personhood.

Who gets what depends upon appropriate relations between persons and other people, and not just between persons and things. People engaged in market interactions are not just acquiring things, they are relating to each other. A theory of social justice should recognize that these interactions often are (and ought to be able to be) valued for themselves and specifically, and not merely instrumentally and fungibly. As critics of Rawls (for example) have often noted, many kinds of solidarity and interrelations between people are central to our conception of human flourishing and hence must not be excluded from a theory of social justice.

* * *

D. Further Implication for Justice as Respect for Personhood

Pursuing a bit further the idea that both the overall distribution pattern and individual desert depend upon appropriate connections between persons and their contexts of things and other people, I shall comment on three kinds of connections between what I have said about the considerations counseling rejection of the wall metaphor, and the notion of justice as respect for personhood. Here I mean to discuss, first, the significance for social justice of the dilemma created when it seems we cannot respect personhood by choosing either the market or the nonmarket solution to a problem. Second, I want to note the significance of incomplete commodification, based on respect for personhood and the fostering of community, for the justification of regulation. Finally, I want to bring up the ultimate question of market rhetoric: Is it possible that it is unjust to think and talk about some things in the discourse of commodification?

The dilemma of commodification. First, there is the observation that the prophylactic personhood argument—that people should not be allowed to sell their organs, etc., because that is degrading to personhood—calls attention to a more pervasive problem of social justice. If people are so desperate for money that they are trying to sell things we think cannot be separated from them without significant injury to personhood, we do not cure the desperation by banning sales. Nor do we avoid the injury to personhood. Perhaps the desperation is the social problem we should be looking at, rather than the market ban. Perhaps worse injury to personhood is suffered from the desperation that caused the attempt to sell a kidney or cornea than would be suffered from actually selling it. The would-be sellers apparently think so. Then justice is not served by a ban on "desperate exchanges."

These considerations change the arena of argument from considerations of appropriateness to the market to explicit considerations of social justice. If neither commodification nor non-commodification can put to rest our disquiet about harm to personhood in conjunction with certain specific kinds of transactions—if neither commodification nor non-commodification can satisfy our aspirations for a society exhibiting equal respect for persons—then we must rethink the larger social context in which this dilemma is embedded. We must think about wealth and power redistribution.

* * *

One's body is bound up with one's personhood, which is why when organs are donated it is a significant expression of human interrelation. But to preserve organ donation as an opportunity for altruism is also one way of keeping from our view the desperation of poor people. Hence, one who thinks social progress can be brought about by forcing unjust conditions upon our attention might agree with the universal commodifier that sales should be permitted. The progressive thinks, in other words, that fellow feeling is better served by permitting sales so that the spectacle will awaken fellow feeling in the rest of us, to eliminate poverty. The universal commodifier, on the other hand, thinks that even altruism is monetizable, and, in cases where there are willing buyers and willing sellers, it must be worth less than sales. This type of alliance between the far right and the far left is a sure sign that something is incoherent about the middle way.

If it appears that we cannot respect personhood either with commodification or non-commodification, given the surrounding social circumstances, for example with organ-selling, and if we agree that this means we ought to change the surrounding circumstances, we are still faced with the question of whether or not we should permit commodification while we try to do that. If we opt to permit sales for those who choose, as the libertarian and radical might both recommend, we risk complete commodification—if the domino theory correctly predicts the resulting social consciousness, given the level of commodification already present. Complete commodification makes the supposed goal of greater respect for persons in a less commodified future even less imaginable. But perhaps this risk is not as bad as the degradation of personhood and reinforcement of powerlessness brought about by the regime of enforced non-commodification. Obviously, I have no handy algorithm for making this decision.

Regulation and community. A second connection between justice and my discussion of the arguments surrounding the wall metaphor is the question of nonefficiency justification for regulation—that is, socially mandated deviations from the laissez-faire market regime for many things that are bought and sold. If everything is appropriately fully commodified unless efficiency dictates otherwise, then exceptions from the laissez-faire regime are justified only where the market for some reason cannot achieve efficient outcomes. This in fact is the position of many economists on regulation. It makes many types of regulation (for example, residential rent control) difficult to justify; when these types of regulation are frequently imposed anyway by the political order, they are seen as obvious examples of selfish rent-seeking by powerful interest groups. But as I have argued above, there is another way to view regulation of many things that are important to human personhood and community, and that is as incomplete commodification. If we stubbornly intuit that these things that are very important to human life, health, and self and community development ought not to be completely monetized, then regulation that does not (theoretically) meet an efficiency test is in principle justified. Then the response of the political order in imposing the constraints on commodification may be seen as a good-faith working out of community values, so that persons and the community may properly flourish, rather than interest-group rent-seeking.

Can market rhetoric be unjust? The third question that I would like to raise here has to do with whether social justice (as respect for persons) and the rhetoric of universal commodification are connected. I think that conceiving of politics as mere rent-seeking, and essential human attributes as mere scarce commodities, expresses and fosters a conception of human flourishing inferior to that expressed and fostered by a discourse that recognizes personhood and community as essentially unmonetized and not fungible. But is it unjust to think of these aspects of human life in terms of commodities? Does Richard Posner act unjustly in trying to convince us that the right way to think of children is as commodities, and that the right way to think of much that legislatures do is in terms of rent-seeking?

NOTE ON MARKET COMMODIFICATION

Stanford Law Professor Margaret Jane Radin has written extensively on topics covering the limits of private property and freedom of contract. Her work on justice and the market domain has been highly influential in shaping debates about theories of economic justice. A discussion of her work follows:

In her piece on universal commodification in the marketplace, Radin rejects two premises: (1) the traditional economic view that universal commodification is the best vehicle to ensure social justice, and (2) the traditional liberal view that some "nonmarket" goods and services, such as sex and reproduction, should be excluded from the market. Opposing complete commodification in the market, Radin endorses incomplete commodification: rather than building a barrier to exclude certain items from the market and reserving everything else to "market rationality," individuals must recognize and promote the nonmarket aspect of the goods and services they purchase. In order to achieve social justice, Radin encourages advancing the individuality of personhood against the mass forces of commercial interest, elevating individual preference (as opposed to majority preference), and reducing the zones of commodification.

In order to translate Radin's rhetoric into practice, individuals could embark on several tasks. First, rather than abuse certain services, individuals should humanize services. People must realize that their personal behavior may have damaging implications on individuals who provide them with services, such as restaurant servers and blue-collar workers. Accordingly, when associating with workers in the service sector, customers should respect service providers with just compensation and reverence. Second, individuals need to abandon the notion of "human hierarchy" and respect all life, regardless of a person's background. The commodification of human beings lends to the notion that an American life is worth more than another life. This idea is prevalent in news broadcasts; when reporting major disasters, the media often stresses the loss of or injury to an American life, rather than covering the tragedies of peoples of other nationalities. Rather than placing one life before another, all lives should be treated with a similar amount of deference. A third way to instill nonmarket values to promote justice is to scrutinize work conditions. Rather than examining the labor environment from a macro perspective, if market actors examine conditions at the margin, individuals may have a more accurate view of how labor policies affect workers. With this knowledge, individuals can work to change the workplace to ameliorate conditions and improve labor life.

NOTES AND QUESTIONS

1. **Market inalienability.** Proponents of universal commodification say that as long as there are willing buyers and sellers and an item is separable from a human being, actors should be able to exchange that item in the market. Radin opposes this premise and argues that some items are inalienable, making them exempt from market transactions. Unless some items are excluded from the market domain, people may begin to think of themselves as commodities and life will no longer have the same value. In a law journal note, Khiara M. Bridges distinguishes those scholars who endorse market alienability from those who oppose it:

> Those in this school of thought believe that if the body were made alienable in the market, people would begin to conceptualize themselves in market terms. A liver, the potential to produce and carry

another life within the womb, or the remains of a terminated pregnancy (and all the emotions associated with it) is then a commodity or good whose price is determined by the intersection of supply and demand. Once this conceptualization has occurred, the theory continues, the damage is done: The individuals in society no longer think of themselves as incorporeal persons housed within physical temples. Thus, humanity is irreparably damaged. In contrast, these theorists believe that those activities that do not cause individuals to "price" their incorporeal persons or the physical manifestation of such do not need to be shielded from market rhetoric.

Khiara M. Bridges, Note, *On the Commodification of the Black Female Body: The Critical Implications of the Alienability of Fetal Tissue*, 102 COLUM. L. REV. 123, 130 (2002).

Though some products may serve as contributions for altruistic purposes, certain goods cannot be sold. The items that are essential to "personhood" should be inalienable. Paul Littlepage, who holds a master of sciences in microbiology from the University of California, Davis, and undergraduate degrees in both microbiology and physiology from Southern Illinois University, elaborates on Radin's theory of market inalienability:

> Radin defines items that are market-inalienable as those which should not be sold or traded in the market. According to Radin, an item that is market inalienable is not necessarily inseparable from a person. Instead, Radin's theory posits that market trading should not be used as the social mechanism for separating that item from the person. In other words, Radin allows that people may give certain resources away, but they cannot sell them.

> Radin's theory of market-inalienability is designed to promote the concept of "human flourishing." Thus she maintains that the resources that qualify as non-alienable are those that are important to personhood. Under her theory, in an ideal world, markets would not necessarily be abolished, but all things important to personhood would be protected by market-inalienability.

Paul Littlepage, *Compensated Siting Proposals and Environmental Justice: Should Communities Be Allowed to Sell Their Health Rights?*, 21–JUN ENVIRONS ENVTL. L. & POL'Y J. 3, 10 (1998). Radin differentiates market inalienability from other forms of alienability:

> Market-inalienability negates a central element of traditional property rights, which are conceived of as fully alienable. But market-inalienability differs from the nontransferability that characterizes many nontraditional property rights—entitlements of the regulatory and welfare state—that are both nongiveable and nonsalable. Market-inalienability also differs from the inalienability of other things, like voting rights, that seem to be moral or political duties related to a community's normative life; they are subject to broader inalienabilities that preclude loss as well as transfer. Unlike the inalienabilities attaching to welfare entitlements or political duties, market-inalienability does not render

something inseparable from the person, but rather specifies that market trading may not be used as a social mechanism of separation. Finally, market-inalienability differs from the inalienability of things, like heroin, that are made nontransferable in order to implement a prohibition, because it does not signify that something is social anathema. Indeed, preclusion of sales often coexists with encouragement of gifts. For example, the market-inalienability of human organs does not preclude—and, indeed, may seek to foster—transfer from one individual to another by gift.

Margaret Jane Radin, *Market-Inalienability*, 100 HARV. L. REV. 1849, 1854–55 (1987).

The means by which to make certain goods inalienable is to change legal rules governing property and its transfer. Is it possible to change laws to make certain products inalienable? What problems may ensue if certain rules are changed to disallow the commodification of some products?

> While commodification has something to do with market transfers, it is a mistake to *equate* commodification with the legality of such transfers. First, a focus on legal rules is unlikely to devote adequate attention to the many ways in which people are commodified independently of the direct power of the law. Second, equating commodification with the legal rules governing market transfers wrongly ignores the possibility of resistance to power, undermining from the outset any effort to look beyond particular issues to broader social change.

Stephen J. Schnably, *Property and Pragmatism: A Critique of Radin's Theory of Property and Personhood*, 45 STAN. L. REV. 347, 385 (1993).

If Radin's goal—the aim of making some products inalienable—becomes a reality, people may lose the legal right to make a market transfer of an item or a body part. Does making certain products market-inalienable strip an individual of a valuable legal right? University of Miami professor of law Stephen J. Schnably argues that differentiating products in an alienable/inalienable dichotomy assumes that people are passive and do not want to engage in certain market transactions:

> In Radin's conception, commodification utterly disempowers people; the only solution is for the state to counter commodification by imposing rules of market-inalienability. This conception of commodification ignores the potential for resistance. For all Radin's concern for personhood, her theory views individuals as the passive beneficiaries of a personhood-respecting state.

> The problem with such an account is that it depicts an essentially static society—a society in which the sources of change remain hidden and obscure. Radin's failure to examine consensus critically or to address the effects of power in the shaping of consensus gives her theory an implicit conservative bias.

> The problem can be restated in Radin's terminology. Treating people as passive objects renders the double bind pervasive and unresolvable. If commodification leaves people as utterly disempowered as Radin's

treatment implies, then the only way to promote decommodification is for the state to disable people by stripping them of the right to sell some relevant attribute. Alternatively, the state could partially decommodify them by partially disabling them—that is, by limiting the terms under which they may sell that attribute. Any measure that advances partial or complete decommodification will be vulnerable to the charge that it disrespects the very objects of its protection by prohibiting them from entering into a market transaction to which they would otherwise agree.

Schnably, *supra* at 379–80.

2. Personhood. Radin argues that some items, which are "personal," should not be bought or sold because the exchange of such items can damage the personhood of individuals. Because some items are instinctively tied to our humanity, they should be excluded from the market. Timothy S. Hall, *Bargaining with Hippocrates: Managed Care and the Doctor–Patient Relationship*, 54 S.C. L. Rev. 689, 727–28 (2003). Radin deems that certain aspects of life are integral to human beings, and to attach a dollar value to these life aspects would dehumanize them:

> I believe that a better view of personhood should understand many kinds of particulars—one's politics, work, religion, family, love, sexuality, friendships, altruism, experiences, wisdom, moral commitments, character, and personal attributes—as integral to the self. To understand any of these as monetizable or completely detached from the person * * * is to do violence to our deepest understanding of what it is to be human.

Margaret Jane Radin, Contested Commodities 56 (1996).

What items would Radin consider to be essential to "human flourishing" or "personhood"? Is human body tissue an item too personal to be part of the market? In *Moore v. Regents of the University of California,* 271 Cal.Rptr. 146, 793 P.2d 479 (Cal. 1990), the California Supreme Court encountered this issue. There, the court rejected a patient's claim that his property rights had been violated when his physician and other medical employees made commercial use of the patient's surgically removed spleen without first requesting his permission or sharing the profits. At first thought, it is probable that Radin would disagree with the decision because such a case may provide an incentive for destitute people to sell their organs, thereby injuring their personhood. However, Radin asserts that banning sales of organs fails to cure individuals' desperation for resources; instead, legislators should look at the poverty problem itself rather than the market for organs in determining whether some items are essential to personhood.

Based on the *Moore* decision, should the sale of human organs be regulated on the free market? An alternative to the complete commodification of items essential to one's "personhood" is allowing the government to regulate such transactions. Such a plan would not completely dehumanize products pertinent for "human flourishing," would make certain products market-inalienable, and would aid in increasing the supply of needed human organs:

> First, the removal of tissue should be both consensual and limited to circumstances that are consistent with the contributor's dignity and bodily integrity. Second, the use of such excised tissue for research and commercial purposes should be consensual. Third, the proceeds from such use should be shared with tissue sources in a manner likely to best accommodate the host of ethical and practical considerations that have surfaced in debates between the regimes of inalienability and private property.

> Requirements of informed consent and other rules of inalienability could address the first two objectives. For example, tissue could be deemed inalienable if its possessor did not give informed consent and if its removal were not medically necessary or would substantially impair the contributor's essential bodily functions. The third objective, the focus here, would be handled as described below, by a combination of market inalienability rules and a liability rule pertaining to tissues of exceptional value.

> * * *

> Private sales of tissue from its original source would be banned. If people chose to contribute their tissue, researchers could use it without up-front cost, but commercial users would be required to compensate the sample source after the fact if the commercial utility of the tissue met statutory eligibility criteria. A statutorily-established compensation tribunal would interpret and apply these criteria. The tribunal would also use statutory standards to calculate the measure of compensation to be paid.

> * * *

> Guidelines and precedents developed by the tribunal would enhance the fairness and predictability of the process. Prices would be determined according to the characteristics and uses of the tissue, not the personal circumstances of the contributors.

> * * *

Although tissue itself could not be sold, there could still be a role, and remuneration, for patient groups, physician networks or other organizations that might assemble large pools of tissue samples pertaining to a particular disease or condition. These parties could charge researchers or companies for their collection services, even though any compensation for the materials themselves would be governed by the tribunal and owed to the original source. Sources could designate the collecting organization as the beneficiary of any compensation, although this would have to be handled carefully in the clinical context so as not to raise the specter of conflict of interest or undue influence. Collecting organizations might also negotiate for non- financial terms, such as commitments regarding the use of their samples to address problems of special interest to their group.

Charlotte H. Harrison, *Neither* Moore *nor the Market: Alternative Models for Compensating Contributors of Human Tissue*, 28 Am. J.L. & Med. 77, 96–98 (2002). (Arguing for banning private sales and imposing government regulation on the transfer of needed human tissue).

For more on notions of personhood, please see Sarah E. Waldeck, *Encouraging a Market in Human Milk*, 11 Colum. J. Gender & L. 361 (2002); Zachary M. Garsek, *Napster Through the Scope of Property and Personhood: Leaving Artists Incomplete People*, 19–SPG Ent. & SPORTS LAW. 1 (2002); Radhika Rao, *Property, Privacy and the Human Body*, 80 B.U. L. Rev. 359 (2000).

3. Altruism. Some scholars suggest that making ~~all products market alienable discourages individuals from making donations,~~ for example, the market for blood samples. Price incentives offered by markets would ~~decrease opportunities for philanthropy~~ and cause the supply of blood donations to diminish. Could a market for blood and a blood donation be mutually exclusive? Would the existence of a market take away individuals' "right to give?" *See* Richard M. Titmuss, The Gift Relationship: From Human Blood to Social Policy 198, 237 (1971).

4. Incomplete commofidication. Rather than monetizing all goods and services, Radin advances ~~partial commodification, where items are exchanged but the relations between the buyer and seller remain personal and nonmonetized.~~ By retaining personal interactions with others, individuals advance the ideals of personhood and human flourishing and change many items from their standard market form. Examples of partial commodification include labor and housing. In these two domains, money is exchanged, but "[t]here is an irreducibly nonmarket or nonmonetized aspect of human interaction going on between seller and recipient."

Why is commodification so unappealing? How could monetizing all goods have a damaging impact on personhood? One consequence of attaching a dollar value to personal health rights is that it might exploit the poor.

Radin has explored commodification in the markets in babies or in sexual services. Any buying and selling in these markets is "commodified," meaning such sales dehumanize women and drain women's private power. Therefore, when sexual and reproductive activities are "commodified," there is a "threat to the personhood of women, who are the 'owners of these commodities.'" However, noncommofidication of reproductive and sexual services can also hurt women's personhood. Radin calls this dilemma faced by women the "double bind":

> The threat to personhood from commodification arises because essential attributes are treated as severable fungible objects, and this denies the integrity and uniqueness of the self. But if the social regime prohibits this kind of commodification, it denies women the choice to market their sexual or reproductive services, and given the current feminization of poverty and lack of avenues for free choice for women, this also poses a threat to the personhood of women. The threat from enforced noncommodification arises because narrowing women's

choices is a threat to liberation, and because their choices to market sexual or reproductive services, even if nonideal, may represent the best alternatives available to those who would choose them.

Thus the double bind: both commodification and noncommodification may be harmful.

Margaret Jane Radin, *The Pragmatist and the Feminist*, 63 S. CAL. L. REV. 1699, 1699–1700 (1990). Incomplete commodification can serve as a remedy for the damage caused to women's personhood. Government regulatory restriction of particular exchanges in these markets can serve to mitigate the damage to women's personhood without impairing women's financial stability. *See* Margaret Jane Radin, *Market-Inalienability*, 100 HARV. L. REV. 1849 (1987).

What are some possible policies that would put incomplete commofidication into practice?

For more on commodification, please see Margaret J. Radin, *Rent Control and Incomplete Commodification: A Rejoinder*, 17 PHIL. & PUB. AFF. 80 (1988); Michelle B. Bray, Note, *Personalizing Personality: Toward a Property Right in Human Bodies*, 69 TEX. L. REV. 209, 241 (1990); Barbara Rothman, *Reproductive Technology and the Commofidication of Life*, in EMBRYOS, ETHICS AND WOMEN'S RIGHTS 95 (Elaine Baruch et al. eds., 1988); Elizabeth Anderson, *Is Women's Labor a Commodity?*, 19 PHIL. & PUB. AFF. 71 (1990).

c. A Feminist Critique of Both Commodification Theory and Law and Economics

Commodification and Women's Household Labor
9 YALE J.L. & FEMINISM 81 (1997).

■ KATHARINE SILBAUGH

I. INTRODUCTION

A woman washes a kitchen floor. She puts the mop away and drives to the corner market. She consults a shopping list, and purchases groceries from it, carefully choosing the least expensive options. A four-year-old child is tugging at her leg while she does this, and she tries to entertain him, talking to him about the mopped floor, the grocery items. When she returns from the store, she prepares lunch from what she has brought home with her. She and the child both eat lunch. After lunch, she and the child collect laundry and she runs a load. She takes the garbage out to the curb. Then she reads him a story. They play a game where she comes up with a word, and he tries to name its opposite. Sometimes there is no opposite, and that is particularly funny to both of them. She has done housework.

There is no way to tell from this description whether these activities were market or non-market, whether her work is a commodity or not. Would it help to categorize her work if you knew the location? Is this her home? Suppose that she is a paid domestic worker, and this housework is a commodity. She leaves her employer's home. She goes home and does exactly the same thing there, but this time she is preparing dinner. The second child is her own. Whether these activities are viewed as a commodity is contextual, not activity-based.

Should we think and talk about unpaid domestic labor—housework—using market, or economic, language? What follows is a defense of economic discourse on the subject of law and housework. It is written in response to the common criticism aimed at scholars who have examined domestic labor through an economic lens. It is a response to what is commonly called a "commodification critique," and particularly as that critique is formulated within feminist discourse.

In *Turning Labor into Love: Housework and the Law*, I examined the treatment of household labor in tax law, torts, family law, social security, welfare, contracts and labor law. I argued that characterizations of domestic labor by legal actors almost never include an emphasis on its economic productivity, instead focusing on housework as an expression of the affectionate emotions associated with the family setting where housework occurs. By setting up a dichotomy between the language of economic productivity and the language of emotions, I argued that legal actors have used the language of emotions to deny material security to those who perform domestic labor. From this I concluded that a more clearly articulated understanding of the economically productive aspects of home labor would, on balance, benefit those who perform the labor, who are still primarily women. I did not, however, address commodification problems with that conclusion. The most explicit writing on commodification in legal discourse has addressed the commodification of other aspects of women's experience: sexuality and reproduction. This critique has been raised in response to some recent work on domestic labor, including my own.

I want to reject current categorical thinking about women's home activity. I argue that economic understandings are very useful, and that they do not and need not supply a complete understanding of human activities. I will make the case that economic understandings are representations of a given activity, as are sentimental or emotional understandings, and that they can and should co-exist. Margaret Jane Radin, the foremost legal scholar who has addressed commodification concerns, has also argued that multiple understandings can co-exist. Her goal, however, is to bring non-market understandings to market activities, in search of a less commodified society.

This Article questions that goal. My central argument is that the entirely emotional understanding of home labor is itself an impoverished one. If one conceded that the use of economic rhetoric could habituate people to thinking about a topic differently, as critics of economic language assert, that would not necessarily make the case *against* the use of such rhetoric in all contexts. I make the uncommon case here for the value of bringing market understandings to non-market activities where they can co-exist with non-economic conceptions. The broader implication of the thesis is that we should not assume that analyses that can remake relations are always doing a disservice, especially where those relations are already fraught with problematic analyses. In certain contexts it may be a very conservative claim that economic analysis is bad *because* it has the power to change the way we view something.

My claim is that gender equality requires us to take the economics of home labor seriously. This argument turns on a comparison between wage labor and home labor, which are similar both in content and in many of the motivations that drive workers. I argue that the difference in the treatment between them may be difference based on gender. I discuss the tendency to raise commodification concerns when women's interests are at stake, and question whether resistance to market reasoning in these contexts is a form of resistance to women's economic power. I then examine some legal doctrines touching on home labor that could benefit from economic analysis. If importing economic reasoning into these areas transforms our understanding of them, I posit that women would *benefit* from that transformation. I conclude that as long as so many of women's activities remain non-market and as long as women's economic welfare is a concern of feminists, economic analysis of non-market activities is affirmatively desirable. My objective is to show what can be gained by allowing economics to inform, without dominating, the discourse on policy and doctrine surrounding home labor. Concern over women's lives becoming entirely commodified seems by comparison an abstract worry.

II. The Commodification Objection: Setting Out the Case Against Economics

A. *The Basic Problem with Commodification*

The standard argument against commodification, often referred to as the "commodification critique," is that certain human attributes or certain resources should lie wholly or partially beyond exchange, because to allow exchange would be inconsistent with a vision of personhood or human flourishing. Prohibiting exchange may not be enough; it may be necessary to discourage economic analysis and discourse about these attributes. "[M]any kinds of particulars—one's politics, work, religion, family, love, sexuality, friendships, altruism, experiences, wisdom, moral commitments, character, and personal attributes [are] ... integral to the self. To understand any of these as monetizable ... is to do violence to our deepest understanding of what it is to be human."

Elizabeth Anderson has reviewed commodification concerns and applied them to women's reproductive labor in a piece interestingly titled, "Is Women's Labor a Commodity?" She defines a commodity as something to which "the norms of the market are appropriate for regulating its production, exchange and enjoyment." The application of market norms is inappropriate where they "fail to value *the thing* in an appropriate way." If it is appropriate to apply "use" as the proper mode of valuation, then market norms are acceptable and we may treat something as a commodity. If instead, a mode of valuation such as respect, "love, admiration, honor and appreciation," are more appropriate, then we should not treat something as a commodity. To value something differently than as a commodity is, according to Anderson, to recognize a "special intrinsic worth" to that item. This essentialist notion that things have an intrinsic worth turns out to be important to anti-commodification arguments. Anderson argues, "When women's labor is treated as a commodity, the women who perform it are degraded." Degradation means that "something is treated in accordance with a lower mode of valuation than is proper to it." Finally Anderson believes that commodifying women's labor leads to exploitation of women. This is so because women's noncommercial motivations are taken advantage of without offering anything but commercial responses.

Anderson's work draws on a notion of incommensurability of value that is seen in the work of Martha Nussbaum. As applied to the domestic labor context, the problem of incommensurability would arise with the need to give the labor a market value when it is not commensurable to market goods or services. They may not be commensurable where, for example, one is measured on a valuation scale that can translate into dollars, where another is measured on one that cannot, such as love, admiration, wonder, or respect. While these scholars have not applied their critiques directly to housework, it can be argued that there is no perfectly accurate market replacement for unpaid work, for example child-care, that a family member performs.

The commodification critique applies to an *analysis* of the economy of the home and the family labor that occurs there, as well as to the actual purchase and sale of that labor. To Anderson, market norms have an "expressive significance" as well as a practical one, and can thus infect non-market conceptions of women's labor. The argument posits that talk matters: you can pervert the personalness of something by talking about it as if it were fungible. Identifying an "economy," meaning a set of implicit valuations and exchanges, is possible even where "real markets" are either prohibited or practically impossible to imagine: organs for transplantation, sexual contacts, candidates for marriage partnerships, religious convictions, love, or a person's politics. Although in many cases this is just talk, to a commodification skeptic, that talk itself does damage to the integrity of the attribute in question: sexuality, love, marriage, health.

James Boyd White has made this case most powerfully, arguing that expression is never transparent, but instead constitutes and transforms the reality it describes. Says White: "the languages we speak, and the cultural practices they at once reflect and make possible, form our minds by habituating them to certain modes of attention, certain ways of seeing and conceiving of oneself and of the world." White concludes that economic language should be "vigorously resist[ed]" because "[t]he conventions of this discourse necessarily habituate its user[s] to thinking in terms of self-interest as a central principle." In passing, he applies this critique to an economic understanding of home labor, noting that:

> The segmentation of the exchange model tends to misvalue the work we do for ourselves, which is most of the traditional work of women. . . . This is especially true of people who raise their own children.

Such work cannot be segmented into functions and then made the material of the market process, actual or hypothetical, for what the child requires is the sustained presence of, and interaction with, a loving and respectful person, something no alternative can supply. Similarly, housework has a different meaning when one is maintaining one's own home rather than acting as a servant for others.

To those who see a difference between real and rhetorical markets, the difference tends to be treated as one of degree. Under this view, it might not hurt personhood as much to talk about markets in certain attributes as it does to create such markets, but talk certainly doesn't *help*. By condemning talk as well as trades, skeptics take away the opportunity to make the affirmative case for the benefits of an economic perspective. For legal analysts, this conflation of actual buying and selling and market analysis proves problematic * * *.

* * *

C.   *Feminism and Economic Skepticism*

Feminists rank high among those who are skeptical of economists. This skepticism proceeds on two fronts in the domestic labor context. The two parts are a negative reaction to economics as a way to describe home activities, and an affirmatively positive response to love and affections as a descriptively accurate way of understanding and explaining productivity in the home.

1.   *Offense at Economics*

Some feminists have a visceral dislike for economic analysis. While there are many reasons for this, I believe two are most strongly at play. The first is situational: Many feminists don't trust the current practitioners of economic analysis. The second is more substantive: Many feminists do not accept the implicit notion of fungibility at play in economic analysis.

The problem of distrust may come from two characteristics of economic discourse. The first is a driving, relentless essentialism among economists. Much economic literature reads like much more than a useful tool with which to explain certain phenomenon. It instead reads like the *raison d'être* of that phenomenon, its beginning and end. Everyone has her favorite example of a social phenomenon being mercilessly pushed into an economic model producing logically clean but absurd explanations: adoption, marriage, heroic rescues, voting, altruism, religion, childbirth, sexuality. This kind of relentless essentialism among economists leaves reasonable people with what appears to be a decision to either embrace the whole absurd end of the spectrum or jump ship entirely. I will argue that it is fully possible and desirable to use economics to assist in understanding a social phenomenon without turning away from other possible explanations or understandings. But this does not describe much of the dominant economic analysis practiced in the *legal* academic community. The idea of extending this sort of essentialism into the social relations surrounding family labor seems to carry the risk of damaging the complex context of dependencies and moral and emotional commitments made there.

The second reason many feminists distrust practitioners of economic analysis is that they often employ assumptions with suspect origins. Moreover, although these are almost always identified at the outset as assumptions, by the end of the equation they seem to have assumed the status of fact. In legal discourse, when an assumption is used in an economic model, we usually see the burden of proof implicitly shifted to critics of the model to disprove the factual assumption despite the frequent lack of evidence in favor of the assumption from the outset. There is the well-known joke about the economists on a desert island with a case of food in tin cans. They begin their plan for opening the cans by saying, "First, let's assume a can opener." It's funny when it's a can opener. It is not so funny, or at least it shouldn't be, when the empirically unsupported assumption is that women want children more than men do, that women have higher inherent value when they are young and men are worth more when they are older, that husbands and wives in most cases have the perfect trust and agency necessary to treat them as a single economic unit (individuals are selfish and self-interested but family heads are altruistic), or that rapists would pay for sex somehow if they had the necessary wealth of money, power, or looks themselves. Having those assumptions implicitly raised to the level of facts over the course of an economic analysis is particularly problematic.

I think of the implicit elevation of assumption to fact as "assumption slippage." It must be noted that this slippage is a dynamic process: Readers of economic texts, particularly in the legal community, are participants in its occurrence as much if not sometimes more than economic authors. Much of the most prominent economic analysis of family and gender relations, particularly that associated with Gary Becker, relies on very questionable assumptions that appear to come right out of the pages of *The Total Woman* and from there they help to build economic rationalizations for very conventional mid-twentieth century middle class suburban gender relations. In the words of Barbara Bergmann, "to say that New Home Economists [Becker et al.] are not feminists in their orientation would be as much of an understatement as to say that Bengal tigers are not vegetarians." Isabel Y. Sawhill has offered a critique of the lack of empirical basis for some of the basic assumptions of the New Home Economists who are prominent in the field. As economists know from their training but their legal readers quickly forget, an economic model is only as good as its assumptions. Hence, the implicit standard in economic scholarship is that unproved assumptions must be plausible before a model based on them is acceptable, even with caveats. In the context of home labor, those assumptions are very important. Assuming altruistic heads of households reduces the need to worry about disparate human capital investments made within the family. The assumption that women desire children more than men do provides an explanation for what otherwise might be tricky distributional results that occur within families. If these are to be the assumptions on which an economic analysis of home labor is to proceed, many people do not want any part of it.

I cannot join the routine conclusion that the problems with Gary Becker's work are so far-reaching as to make his work as a whole of limited use. We are indebted to Becker for raising extraordinarily important economic questions about the functioning of the family. Becker has brought us many ideas that are extremely helpful in thinking about family relations, including the very notion that in economic terms the home is a place of production and not just a place of consumption. If he has proceeded from unsupportable or incomplete assumptions, those can be corrected and the analysis and its outcomes adjusted accordingly. Indeed, examining and critiquing these assumptions has been a large implicit part of the feminist response to law and economics already, and should continue to be so. However, critiquing assumptions does not inflict a fatal blow to methodology. It would be a mistake to hold these questionable assumptions out as an indictment of an entire mode of analysis. This is a standard to which most scholars would not wish to be held, and feminists are no exception.

There is, however, an extremely important lesson about the scope of the usefulness of economic analysis to be learned from assumption slippage and the response to it: empiricism counts. Empirical research and data need to drive any real search for policy solutions to basic problems, or even to clear understandings of the problems themselves. Law professors are not in a great position at this time to do empirical research and must rely on fields outside of law or economics, such as sociology, to inform economic understandings. Doing so is not without its own difficulties for lawyers untrained in understanding and sorting sociological research. The most that economic understandings can do is to highlight some empirical questions that need to be answered. Even answers to empirical questions do not close debates over facts. If we are confident that a resource is scarce as a matter of empirical fact, we can either treat that as a given or instead ask *why* it is scarce. That which has an empirical basis is not thereby natural or inevitable, and so even provable assumptions should be open for well-framed criticisms. But once again, economics can assist in the framing task itself.

I do not wish to be understood as overstating the ease of remembering that we are dealing with hypothetical models when we use economic analysis. I think the risk of forgetting is more serious when we *cannot* verify the empirical assumption. We move quickly on from it, sensing that the unavailability of data threatens to make an *otherwise* elegant model useless. Perversely, the less supportable an assumption, the less contestable it is, and the more it acquires the status of fact. It may be that James Boyd White's concern with the culture of economic discourse is played out most seriously when data is least available.

The next level of concern over economic analysis does not center solely on the supposed "priors" of its practitioners. It is a more substantive criticism: A rejection of the suggestion that many attributes of family life and work are fungible, and thus that the study of value can proceed by observing choices people make. Fungibility is the idea that goods, services, or attributes can be placed on a single metric of value and then traded off against one another on that metric. Fungible things can be replaced by something else that falls in the same place on the metric, such as similar services by a different person, or simply money measured in the right amount, without regret. On this account, economics is entirely concerned with theoretically measurable maximized choice among alternatives, rather than being concerned with the personal experience of choice, methods of provisioning in general (whether by voluntary exchange, gift-giving, or coercion), or with the process of developing what economists call preferences. Radin concedes that whether we think the fact of choice between alternatives proves fungibility, as many economists believe, or instead prove nothing about fungibility, is largely a matter of intuition. Joseph Raz argues that the meaning we give to a choice is its conventional understanding, and if that does not include a trade along a single metric, then no such fungibility can be inferred. Raz taps into many people's response to the talk of fungibility when thinking about marriage, romantic partners, and family work choices that are implicit in an economic analysis of home labor.

There is a similar negative response to the notion of bargaining within marriage or within family relations, which is an important element of an economic understanding of home labor. Though a bargaining model is often thought of as an improvement on Becker's notion of an altruistic head of household which can justify a failure to examine interspousal conflict, the bargaining model itself draws a negative response from many. While many would acknowledge much day-to-day bargaining within the family, it is also thought that a bargaining analysis fails to capture the altruistic behavior layered alongside self-interested behavior in family relations. It is difficult to predict much about behavior if one can rely neither on complete self-interest nor on complete altruism, and a bargaining analysis of family labor puts forward assumptions about family behavior to which many respond negatively.

2. *The Aptness of the Emotional Understanding*

The former critique, that family labor is not fungible and not always strategic, is also frequently stated in the affirmative: Family labor is uniquely emotional. In *Turning Labor into Love*, I bring an operative mode of analysis to the surface—home labor is viewed as an expression of familial emotions. In discussing this argument with others, I would routinely hear that this is the mode of analysis at play in law because it is an accurate characterization of family behavior. What is wrong with the affections characterization? Family care *is* all about affections. Should courts ignore the emotional motivations behind caring for a child or preparing a meal for a partner or spouse? While I will argue below that this idea can co-exist with an economic understanding of home labor, many feel that an economic understanding demotes or denigrates the emotional significance of home labor: this is the essence of the domino theory at play. These criticisms of the commodification of home labor through the use of economic rhetoric and analysis, in many general respects, represent a subset of criticisms of all commodification and economic rhetoric. The family context, however, raises the concerns discussed above in a particularly bright light.

I believe that feminist skepticism of economics is understandable but should be avoided. * * * [K]eeping economic understandings away from women's activities represents a particularly gendered understanding of those activities that is itself costly. * * *

2. *Women as Non-commodifiable: Questioning the Origins of an Idea*

Does concern about the comparison between wage labor and home labor commodification grow out of an implicit assumption that there is something intrinsically different about home labor? We might want to ask whether it is coincidental, or instead highly relevant, that that intrinsic difference at play in analysis also cuts along gender lines: women's work, hereby, would be essentially non-marketable. Consider the problems with assuming that women are inclined to make gifts of attributes of their personalities. Women serve, men sell. It is a familiar notion about which many feminists have been skeptical.

a. The Gender Line: Cashless Women

At a practical level, women should at least be wary of anti-commodification arguments, because these arguments arise when women receive money for something, not when women are paying money for something. The argument is used most frequently in legal discourse when talking about women receiving money for surrogate parenting and sexual contact, and herein for household labor. While Radin extends the argument into gender neutral territories, such as housing, most of the commodification red flags are raised by her and by others when discussing *women's* commodification.

One might respond that the emphasis of the anticommodification argument is that some aspect of women's personhood is going to be sold, not that women are about to receive money. It is the sale that is objectionable, not that women may end up with cash. Consider, though, that it is not uncommon to find people who approve of altruistic transfer in these same areas, for example, human egg donation and surrogacy. In fact, the current fee caps in both of these fields reflect that ideal in practice: donors are not supposed to be *too* motivated by money, so fees are held down to ensure that there is a partially altruistic motivation for donating. In these cases, it seems arguable that the difference that a woman *experiences* may simply be whether money comes to her, and how much, as compared to other wage labor that she might similarly perform from partially altruistic motivation. This difference occurs in the name of non-commodification. It is worth asking whether Anderson's concern about exploitation due to the commodification of women's reproductive capacity might just as easily turn into exploitation from non-commodification, not just in a "nonideal" world. Here the mixed motivations of women are exploited by highlighting the altruistic aspects of those motives in a discriminatory fashion. Only *women's* mixed motives relating to feminine activities are highlighted and offered as justification for leaving women without cash. Mixed motivations in the labor force at large do not require regulatory practices aimed at keeping wages down.

Social practices also exist where the characterization of the problem as "withholding money from women" seems even more apt at the practical level than "preventing the sale of women," given the particular form that current decommodification takes. Prostitutes and pimps have a relationship that results where prohibition on sale ensures that although a female attribute is being sold, a woman is not getting most of the money. The "transitional balancing" questions raised by commodification and prostitution have been widely debated elsewhere. I raise it to illustrate that protecting women from sale does not necessarily go hand in hand with preventing women from receiving cash. Women can be sold and remain relatively cashless. Few would argue that the current form of the criminalization of prostitution is intended or designed for the protection of prostitutes, and so the lack of connection between non-commodification (and its female cashlessness) and sale is hardly remarkable. But in the reproductive areas of surrogacy and egg donation, non-commodification ideals drive the policy of leaving women relatively cashless despite their (partial?) sale.

We do not usually see the anticommodification argument raised as forcefully when things typically associated with male personhood are being sold. While it may be that women's personhood is more at risk for being inappropriately objectified and commercialized, we should at least consider an alternative understanding of why commodification concerns focus on women's issues. It may have as much to do with notions of femininity and a desire to elevate a romantic essentialism about femininity as it does with a desire to protect women's integrity. Consider Anderson's argument that women's reproductive labor is inappropriately alienated by surrogacy because a surrogate mother must "divert [her labor] from the end which the social practices of pregnancy rightly promote—an emotional bond with her child." It is not clear why the end which Anderson prefers for women's labor must be extinguished by money, but it is clear that her argument leaves women without money for their labor. If a reinscription of the public-private spheres ideology on which market rhetoric thrives occurs around women's home labor, it may depend on a particular notion of femininity that has as one of its characteristics cashless women. Perhaps Anderson recognizes this, but sees it as a necessary trade-off for the preservation of familial bonds. She does not explain though, why it is a trade-off; why markets and monetary exchange cannot coexist with expressions of affection in a realistic reflection of women's mixed motivations. We have the example of wage labor as an area where monetary exchange and mixed motivations coexist.

3. BEYOND: COST-BENEFIT ANALYSIS

Myths and Markets

PRICELESS: ON KNOWING THE PRICE OF EVERYTHING AND THE VALUE OF NOTHING 35–40 (2004).

■ FRANK ACKERMAN & LISA HEINZERLING

COSTS, BENEFITS, AND BIASES

Despite its inegalitarian premises, cost-benefit analysis presents itself as the soul of rationality, an impartial, objective standard for making good decisions. Of course some environmental programs and regulations make sense, the analysts say; it's just that we have to figure out which ones are sensible, and which are not. Who could object to a careful comparison of the pros and cons of public policies?

Yet cost-benefit analysis has become a powerful weapon in the hands of vocal opponents of regulation. This is no coincidence. There are, in fact, built-in biases in cost-benefit methods. The problem is not only that those who start from an antienvironmental perspective have often used cost-benefit analysis to support their preconceptions. Even when the methods are applied in good faith by neutral or environmentally inclined investigators, we will see that the results tilt strongly toward endorsement of business as usual, and rejection of health and environmental protection. This is not obvious from the description of the methods and objectives of cost-benefit analysis, which sounds noble and nonpartisan.

Cost-benefit analysis tries to set an economic standard for measuring the success of government projects and programs. In other words, cost-benefit analysis seeks to perform, for public policy, a calculation that happens routinely in the private sector. In evaluating a proposed new initiative, how do we know if it is worth doing or not? The answer is much simpler in business than in government.

Private businesses, striving only to make money, will produce something only if they believe that someone is willing to buy it. That is, the profit motive reliably steers firms toward producing things for which the expected benefits to consumers, measured by consumer willingness to pay for them, are greater than the costs of production. It is technologically possible to produce men's business suits in brightly colored polka dots. Successful producers suspect that few people are willing to pay for such products, and usually stick to minor variations on suits in somber, traditional hues. If some firm *did* happen to produce a polka-dot business suit, no one would be forced to buy it; the producer would bear the entire loss resulting from the unsold suits.

Government, in the view of many critics, is in constant danger of requiring the production of polka-dot suits—and making people pay for them. Policies, regulations, and public spending do not face the test of the marketplace; there are no consumers who can withhold their dollars from the government until it produces regulations dressed in navy blue and charcoal gray. There is no single quantitative objective for the public sector comparable to profit maximization for businesses. Even with the best of intentions, critics suggest, government regulations and programs can easily go astray for lack of an objective standard by which to judge whether they are meeting citizens' needs.

Cost-benefit analysis sets out to do for government what the market does for business: add up the benefits of a public policy and compare them to the costs. But there is no ledger that presents the costs and benefits of public undertakings to every member of society. Cost-benefit analyses have to create that ledger, a task that often turns into a multiyear, multimillion-dollar research effort. Calculations of costs and benefits involve challenging questions of very different varieties. We begin with the costs.

Many public policies impose measurable economic costs. For example, the government may require a certain kind of pollution-control equipment, which businesses must pay for. Even if a regulation only sets a ceiling on emissions, it results in costs that can be at least roughly estimated through research into available technologies and business strategies for compliance.

Although the calculation should be straightforward, in practice there is a tendency to overestimate the costs of regulations in advance of their implementation. Massachusetts Institute of Technology researcher Nicholas Ashford argues that compliance costs typically drop after a regulation is implemented, for three reasons: pollution-control technology gets cheaper as industry produces more of it; over time, managers learn how to comply with regulations more cost-effectively; and regulations encourage innovation, which can dramatically reduce the cost of compliance. Confirming this perspective, a study by the Office of Technology Assessment of occupational safety and health regulations found many cases in which actual compliance costs were lower than anyone had expected. For example, the Occupational Safety and Health Administration (OSHA) 1974 standard for vinyl chloride, a known human carcinogen, lowered the permissible workplace exposure from 500 parts per million (ppm) to 1 ppm. Industry predicted total economic catastrophe, and OSHA's own consultants predicted compliance costs would reach $1 billion. The actual costs were about a quarter of a billion dollars, as industry quickly developed a new control technology that improved the production process as well as lowered worker exposures.

Similar patterns show up in other regulations. One study found that costs estimated in advance of regulation were more than twice actual compliance costs in eleven out of twelve cases. Another study found that advance cost estimates were more than 25 percent higher than actual costs for fourteen out of twenty-eight regulations; advance estimates were more than 25 percent too low in only three of the twenty-eight cases. Before the 1990 Clean Air Act Amendments took effect, industry had anticipated that the cost of sulfur reduction under the amendments would be $1,500 per ton. In 2000, the actual cost was under $150 per ton.

In a related vein, many companies have begun to discover that environmental protection can actually be good for business. Increased energy efficiency, profitable products made from waste, and decreased use of raw materials are just a few of the cost-saving and profit-making results of turning more corporate attention to environmentally protective business practices. Harvard Business School analyst Michael Porter maintains that carefully crafted, moderately demanding regulations can inspire business to create profitable, environmentally friendly innovations. Cost-benefit analyses typically do not take such money-saving possibilities into account in evaluating the costs of regulation. Indeed, prominent conservative policy analysts, such as Robert Hahn of the American Enterprise Institute, have expressed great skepticism that the government could discover cost savings where the market had not—much like the old joke about the economist who refuses to pick up the twenty-dollar bill in the street on the theory that if it were real, someone else would have picked it up already.

Despite these problems, the cost side is the easy part of cost-benefit analysis. In principle, one could correct for the potential sources of bias in estimating the costs of regulations and other public policies. No such correction is possible in assessing the benefits of regulation, because the benefits are, literally, priceless. Herein lies the fatal flaw of cost-benefit analysis: to compare costs and benefits in its rigid framework, they must be expressed in common units. Cancer deaths avoided, wilderness and whales saved, illnesses and anxieties prevented—all these and many other benefits must be reduced to dollar values to ensure that we are spending just enough on them, but not too much. * * * [M]ost of what we think is important about human life, health, arid the environment is lost in this translation. By monetizing the things we hold most dear, economic analysis ends up cheapening and belittling them.

In comparing monetized benefits to monetized costs, and making this comparison the criterion for judging public policies protecting people and the environment, the analysis also stacks the deck against such policies. In practice, most cost-benefit analyses could more accurately be described as "complete cost-incomplete benefit" studies. Most or all of the costs are readily determined market prices, but many important benefits cannot be meaningfully quantified or priced, and are therefore implicitly given a value of zero. Thus, despite the common claims that cost-benefit analysis is philosophically and politically impartial, its very methodology systematically disfavors protections of goods that, like health and environmental protection, are priceless.

Perhaps recognizing the likely political unpopularity of a method that requires translation of lives, health, and nature into dollars, many policy analysts have started to take a different tack in arguing for cost-benefit analysis. They do not just say that they want to create economic efficiency—after all, few people go to the polls or pull the voting lever in pursuit of efficiency. They say, instead, that what they're after is the same as what environmentalists are after: saving more lives, protecting more health, preserving more natural resources. The government, they say, often issues rules that are insanely expensive, all out of proportion to their benefits—a problem that could be solved by the use of cost-benefit analysis to screen proposed regulations and shifting money to more efficient uses. * * *

———

NOTES AND QUESTIONS

1. Cost-benefit analysis and Kaldor–Hicks and Pareto optimality premises. Two leading scholars of the critical legal theory movement have also criticized three central ideas of law and economics: cost-benefit analysis and the Kaldor–Hicks and Pareto optimality premises. *See* MARK KEL-MAN, *Is the Kaldor–Hicks Position Coherent?, in* A GUIDE TO CRITICAL LEGAL STUDIES 141–50 (1987); Duncan Kennedy, *Cost-Benefit Analysis of Entitlement Problems: A Critique*, 33 STAN. L. REV. 387, 422–45 (1981).

2. Effect of case or controversy on entitlement background. Critical legal scholars like Kennedy would argue that accepting a pre-existing entitlement background is a political choice because it is inattentive to the possibility of redistribution. (Arguments about the validity of background entitlements are made by both Kennedy and Kelman.) However, would a doctrinalist or a formalist not argue that judges are only supposed to decide the case before them? Does a judge not have to take the world outside of his particular case or controversy as given in order to do his/her job and decide that particular case or controversy? On the other hand, how can a judge understand the dynamics of any particular case or controversy without examining the context out of which that case arises?

3. Effect of real-world politics on critical legal studies (CLS). Kelman argues that, in many cases, wealth effects stemming from the existing entitlement scheme will be great enough to determine the outcome of costless bargaining. He uses the existence of such situations, and the fact that law and economics doesn't have much to say about them, as a criticism. However, could any other theory of jurisprudence do better? Indeed, in a case involving a dispute with Native American land ownership, the Supreme Court did try to invoke the force of law in *Worcester v. Georgia*, 31 U.S. 515 (1832). The decision was ignored and the Cherokee were dispossessed of their land. Can law and economics be criticized for remaining silent in a situation where the operative premise is "might makes right?"

4. Further problems with Coase. Aside from the general indeterminacy problem noted by critical legal scholars, there is a deeper problem with analyzing legal claims based on the Coase theorem and Pareto efficiency. Specifically, if the Coase theorem is correct and the result of a transaction is the same regardless of a court's decision, why would parties go to the extra trouble and expense of going to court? Additionally, if a change is Pareto efficient, that is, if it makes no one worse off and at least one person better off, why has it not already happened?

5. Asymmetry of no-transaction-cost modeling. Some participants in the judicial system would benefit greatly from an elimination of transaction costs, while other would benefit hardly at all. For example, a large business would benefit greatly from no transaction cost bargaining because it could avoid spending money on advertising, would not need to employ focus groups, and could generally avoid all the costs which attend selling their product to the outside world. By contrast, a neighborhood would gain very little from costless bargaining. While a lack of transaction costs would allow neighbors to resolve disputes equitably, it would not significantly improve the neighborhood's relationship with the outside world because, for the most part, that relationship is an ad-hoc one between individuals which involves very low transaction costs anyway. Why then does Kennedy argue that there is no reason to expect that trying to replicate the result of costless bargaining will not necessarily benefit any one class of factors over any other?

6. CLS's endorsement of law and economics? When litigants go to court, their primary purpose is to generate substantial wealth effects such that they will be richer and, perhaps, the person or organization they sue will be poorer. For example, punitive damage awards are made to change the behavior of tortfeasors. Pain and suffering awards are made to allow victims of torts to change their consumption patterns in order to offset their losses. With this in mind, why is the observation that changing the entitlement background generates wealth effects a critique? If I sue Ford for manufacturing automobiles that explode when rear-ended, I am trying to make it too costly for Ford to continue producing such cars. I want to change the outcome of efficient bargaining. Does the CLS analysis of wealth effects not simply demonstrate the power of cost-benefit decision making concerning entitlements?

7. Additional reading. Guido Calabresi, *The Pointlessness of Pareto: Carrying Coase Further*, 100 Yale L.J. 1211 (1991); Jeffrey L. Harrison, *Piercing Pareto Superiority: Real People and the Obligations of Legal Theory*, 39 Ariz. L. Rev. 1 (1997); Jeffrey L. Harrison, *Egoism, Altruism, and Market Illusions: The Limits of Law and Economics*, 33 UCLA L. Rev. 1309 (1986); Eleanor M. Fox, *The Politics of Law and Economics in Judicial Decision Making: Antitrust as a Window*, 61 N.Y.U. L. Rev. 554 (1986); Louis B. Schwartz, *With Gun and Camera Through Darkest CLS-Land*, 36 Stan. L. Rev. 413 (1984); George C. Christie & Patrick H. Martin, Jurisprudence (2d ed. 1995).

---

4. Beyond: Market Theory

Why Markets Don't Stop Discrimination
Free Markets and Social Justice 3–9, 151–63 (1997).

■ Cass R. Sunstein

We are in the midst of a period of mounting enthusiasm for free markets. This is of course true in many of the former Communist nations. It is true for much of the West as well, prominently including England and the United States.

Free markets are often defended as an engine of economic productivity, and properly so. But they are also said to be required for social justice, and here things become far more complex. Certainly there are connections between free markets and social justice. A system aspiring to social justice aspires to liberty, and a system of free markets seems to promise liberty, because it allows people to trade goods and services as they wish. In fact, a system of free markets seems to promise not merely liberty but equality of an important sort as well, since everyone in a free market is given an equal right to transact and participate in market arrangements. This form of equality should not be trivialized or disparaged. For example, race and sex discrimination has often consisted of exclusions of certain classes of people from the market domain. In both South America and the United States, discriminatory practices frequently took the form of incursions on free markets in employment.

An appreciation of the virtues of free markets has been an important part of the economic analysis of law, perhaps the most influential development in legal education in the last quarter-century, and a development with growing effects on public policy in the United States and abroad. As it operates in law schools, economic analysis is concerned above all with the consequences of legal rules. Often its practitioners have asked whether intrusions on free markets have desirable consequences. If the minimum wage is increased, what, exactly, will happen? What are the real-world consequences of bans on discrimination, legal rules for controlling air pollution, and rent control laws? There are limits to how much economic theory can say on such issues; empirical evidence is necessary. But by looking at the effects of law on incentives, economics can point in the right direction. Often it can show that the consequences of intrusions on markets will be unfortunate or even perverse. The economic analysis of law has produced significant advances, many of which are discussed in this book. Much remains to be learned.

This * * * is not, however, a simple celebration of free markets, and it raises a number of questions about economic analysis of law in its conventional form. Free markets can produce economic inefficiency and (worse) a great deal of injustice. Even well-functioning economic markets should not be identified with freedom itself. Freedom is a complex notion, to say the least, and free markets can sharply limit freedom as that term is usually understood. In fact, free markets depend on a range of coercive legal interventions, including the law of property, which can be a serious intrusion on the freedom of people who lack ownership rights. And it should not be necessary to emphasize that important forms of equality—including race and sex equality—can be undermined, not promoted, by free markets. Race discrimination is often fueled by market forces.

Moreover, economics—at least as it is used in the conventional economic analysis of law—often works with tools that, while illuminating, may be crude or lead to important errors. Consider, for example, descriptive or "positive" economics. The economic analysis of law has been built on a certain conception of human rationality, in which people are seen as "rational profit-maximizers." For some purposes, this is a helpful foundation. Certainly it is true that most people try, most of the time, to find ways of promoting their own ends. But it is not always clear in what sense human beings can be said to be "rational" or "profit-maximizers." The motivational foundations of human behavior have enormous complexity. Sometimes people do not seem at all rational. Sometimes they are ignorant and sometimes they seem to defeat their own goals. People rely on rules of thumb, or heuristic devices, that cause them badly to misunderstand probabilities and facts; this can lead to irrationality for individuals and societies alike. Sometimes people undervalue their own futures, or suffer from weakness of will, or choose what they know, on reflection, they ought not to choose. Sometimes people care not just about social outcomes, but also about the "meaning" of such outcomes, that is, the values expressed in and by the outcomes. This point very much bears on law, in such areas as environmental protection, race and sex equality, and occupational safety and health.

Above all, social norms are an important determinant of behavior, and they have received far too little attention from those interested in free markets, economic analysis of law, and social justice. A number of puzzles and anomalies underlie human decisions. Analysis of law, economic or otherwise, would do well to incorporate an understanding of these puzzles and anomalies. * * *

Thus far, I have been discussing descriptive or positive economics. If we turn to the evaluative side—to questions about what the law should be or do—economic analysis of law encounters equally serious problems. In its usual form, economics offers an inadequate understanding of social welfare. Often it is concerned with the satisfaction of existing preferences. This is far from an unworthy goal; the frustration of peoples' preferences can lead to misery and injustice. But in any society, existing preferences should not be taken as natural or sacrosanct. They are a function of context. Sometimes they are a product of deprivation, injustice, or excessive limits in available opportunities.

Moreover, the economists' conception of social welfare is too "flat," insofar as it evaluates diverse social goods along the same metric. People care about things not just in terms of amounts, but also in different ways. Some human goods, like cash, are simply for use. But people value things for reasons other than use. They respect other people; sometimes they love each other; they see some things, like a painting or a beach, as objects of awe and wonder. A well-functioning legal system attempts to make space for people's diverse valuation of diverse human goods. This point bears on the uses and the limits of free markets.

More particularly, this book develops seven basic themes:

1. *The myth of laissez-faire.* The notion of "laissez-faire" is a grotesque misdescription of what free markets actually require and entail. Free markets depend for their existence on law. We cannot have a system of private property without legal rules, telling people who owns what, imposing penalties for trespass, and saying who can do what to whom. Without the law of contract, freedom of contract, as we know and live it, would be impossible. (People in Eastern Europe are learning this lesson all too well.) Moreover, the law that underlies free markets is coercive in the sense that in addition to facilitating individual transactions, it stops people from doing many things that they would like to do. This point is not by any means a critique of free markets. But it suggests that markets should be understood as a legal construct, to be evaluated on the basis of whether

they promote human interests, rather than as a part of nature and the natural order, or as a simple way of promoting voluntary interactions.

2. *Preference formation and social norms.* It is important not only to know what choices and preferences are, but also to know how they are formed, and whether they are really connected with human well-being. Unjust institutions can breed preferences that produce individual and collective harm. Severe deprivation—including poverty—can be an obstacle to the development of good preferences, choices, and beliefs. For example, a society in which people "prefer" to become drug addicts, or violent criminals, has a serious problem. Such preferences are likely to be an artifact of existing social norms, and those norms may disserve human freedom or well-being.

In this light a society should be concerned not simply and not entirely with satisfying the preferences that people already have, but more broadly with providing freedom in the process of preference-formation. Social practices, including law, will inevitably affect preferences. There is no way for a legal system to remain neutral with respect to preference formation. In these circumstances it is fully legitimate for government and law to try to shape preferences in the right way, not only through education, but also (for example) through laws forbidding racial discrimination, environmental degradation, and sexual harassment, and through efforts to encourage attention to public issues and to diverse points of view.

3. *The contextual character of choice.* Choices are a function of context. If someone takes a job that includes a certain danger, or chooses not to recycle on a Tuesday in March, or discriminates against a certain female job candidate, we cannot infer a great deal about what he "prefers" or "values." All of these choices might be different in a different context. Our discriminator may support a law banning discrimination; people who do not recycle in March may recycle in May or June, and they may well support laws that mandate recycling. Economists and economically oriented analysts of law sometimes think that they can derive, from particular choices, large-scale or acontextual accounts of how much people value various goods. This is a mistake, involving extravagant inferences from modest findings.

4. *The importance of fair distribution.* It is necessary to know not simply whether a society is rich in economic terms, but also how its resources are distributed. Thus a problem with gross domestic product, as a measure of social well-being, is its obliviousness to distributional concerns. Free markets can help fuel economic growth, and economic growth can improve people's lives. But many citizens are not benefited by growth, and at a minimum government should take steps to combat human deprivation and misery in the midst of growth. In any case, it is important to develop standards for measuring social well-being that allow people, in their capacity as citizens and voters, to focus on the issue of distribution.

5. *The diversity of human goods.* I have noted that human beings value things not just in different amounts, but also in different ways. They value a friend in one way; a park in another; a species in another; a spouse

in another; an heirloom in another; a large check in another; a pet in still another. The way they value a funny movie is qualitatively different from the way they value a tragedy, a mountain, a beach, or a car. Insofar as economics uses a single metric or scale of value, it flattens qualitative differences. For some purposes the flattening is very useful, but for other purposes it is harmful. Such qualitative differences can be crucial to private life, public life, and social science.

These points help show the inadequacy, in some settings, of social ordering through markets. Some goods should not be sold on markets at all; consider the right to vote or the right to be free from discrimination on the basis of sex. Markets work best when (what we rightly treat as) consumption choices are at issue. In a liberal society, some choices should be understood not to involve consumption choices at all. For example, the choice to vote, and the decision how to vote, are not best understood as involving mere consumption. How a person votes should depend not on anyone's "willingness to pay," but on the reasons offered for and against a certain candidate. The right to vote is debased if it is understood as simply a matter of "buying" something.

This claim bears on a range of issues involving the use of markets for distributing such goods as reproductive capacity, sex, endangered species, and environmental amenities in general. Some goods are best allocated on the basis of an inquiry not into economic value, but into the reasons offered for any particular allocation.

6. *Law can shape preferences.* We have seen that no market can exist without legal rules. Legal rules must also allocate entitlements. In a system of private property, it is necessary to say who owns what, at least in the first instance. It is also necessary to create rules of tort law, saying who can do what to whom, and who must pay for injuries and harms. As a great deal of empirical work has shown, these legal rules, allocating basic entitlements, have effects on choices and preferences. Someone who has been given a legal entitlement—to chocolate bars, clean air, freedom from sexual harassment, environmental goods—may well value the relevant good more than he would if the good had been allocated to someone else in the first instance. The preference-shaping effects of the initial allocation via law raise important questions for the analysis of law and free markets. They suggest that government and law may not be able to leave preferences "as they are."

7. *Puzzles of human rationality.* Are human beings rational? What criteria should we use to answer that question? These questions have become all the more urgent in light of recent work attempting to apply economic models of rationality to race and sex discrimination, family choice, pollution problems, aging, even sexual encounters (and hence to the problem of AIDS). Such work has been highly illuminating, but it is important to know in exactly what sense people might be said to be (or not to be) "rational" when they choose spouses, recycle garbage, reject employees of certain kinds, or engage in sexual or risky activity. Any views on

such matters may well depend on a controversial account of what it means to be rational.

* * *

[I] claim that the term "preference" is highly ambiguous and that people's "preferences," as they are expressed in the market domain, should not be deemed sacrosanct. On the contrary, market "preferences" are sometimes a product of background injustice or of social norms that people do not really like. Acting as citizens, people should be permitted to change those norms. I also argue that human goods are not commensurable; there is no metric by which we can assess such goods as environmental quality, employment, more leisure time, less racial discrimination, and so forth. My discussion of "measuring well-being" is designed to respond to this problem; my general treatment of incommensurability shows how the absence of a unitary metric plays a large role in both law and daily life.

[T]he basic goal is to show that markets have only a partial and instrumental role in the protection of rights. In a claim of special relevance to current disputes in the United States, I argue that free markets are not likely to stop discrimination on the basis of race and sex. On the contrary, markets often promote discrimination.

* * *

[I]t would be far too ambitious to attempt to announce a theory of justice. But debates that seem intractable at the most abstract levels may admit of solutions when the question is narrowed and sharpened, and hence an inquiry into the relation between markets and justice may be most productive when we draw close attention to the setting in which market remedies are proposed. * * * Achievement of social justice is a higher value than the protection of free markets; markets are mere instruments to be evaluated by their effects. Whether free markets promote social justice is an impossible question to answer in the abstract. Far more progress can be made by examining the contexts in which markets, adjustments of markets, and alternatives to markets are proposed as solutions.

* * *

I argue [however] that under plausible assumptions and in many settings, markets will not stop discrimination and that reliance on competitive pressures would be a grave mistake for a government intending to eliminate discriminatory practices. Indeed, markets are often the problem rather than the solution. They guarantee that discrimination will persist. Enthusiasm for markets as an anti-discrimination policy is at best wishful thinking.

I.   Why Markets Produce Discrimination: Standard Accounts

As a provisional matter, let us define discrimination as a decision by a market actor to treat one person differently from another because that person is black or female. It is irrelevant for present purposes whether the differential treatment is based on hostility, fear, taste, unconscious devaluation, selective empathy and indifference, employer self-interest, unwarranted generalizations, or an accurate perception of facts about group members. This definition has a degree of vagueness, and it is certainly disputable whether government should ban all of the conduct that it identifies. But the definition has the advantage of tracking both current law and some ordinary intuitions about the problem.

On one view, the notion that competitive markets act against discrimination, so defined, might seem odd or even idiosyncratic. In the history of the United States as well as other nations, markets and discrimination have accompanied one another at numerous points and in numerous places. Surely, governmentally imposed discrimination, because of its centralized character, has especially egregious effects; but to point to the comparative strength of collective controls is not to say that decentralized markets work in the opposite direction. Indeed, there is good empirical evidence that government programs have succeeded in reducing discrimination produced by the market. The enactment of civil rights legislation appears to have led to increases in black and female employment in various sectors. At least in general, the disputed question has to do not with the direction of change but with the degree of the improvement.

Moreover, study after study has shown that the market often devalues the products and enterprises of both blacks and women. This should not be surprising. In a system with a significant amount of race and sex prejudice, covert and overt, conscious and unconscious, the "willingness to pay" criterion—as it is reflected in the purchasing and selling decisions of employers, employees, consumers, and others—will ensure that those subject to discriminatory attitudes will be at a comparative disadvantage in the market. At least this is so when the participation of disfavored groups is highly visible, as indeed it often is. In this context, the most natural initial judgment is that if discrimination is the problem, markets are hardly the solution.

But the judgment, as stated, seems too crude. Suppose a set of companies in a competitive industry—call them "D companies"—decides not to sell to or employ an identifiable segment of the community; suppose too that the D companies must compete with nondiscriminators engaged in the same line of work ("ND companies"). In the long run, the D companies should be at a significant disadvantage. They will be unable to draw on as large a pool of workers; they will be unable to sell to as large a group of purchasers. In practice, their discriminatory behavior will place a tax on their operations. To say the least, businesses that impose on themselves a tax not faced by their competitors are unlikely to fare well.

As patrons and prospective employees drift to ND companies, the D companies will be driven out. Eventually, the consequences should be nothing short of disastrous for discrimination in general. It is this understanding that accounts for the plausible claim that an effective antidiscrimination policy consists of reliance on decentralized markets.

Notwithstanding its plausibility (and even, in some settings, its accuracy), I want in this section to make three arguments against this claim. In setting out these arguments, I make no claim to special originality. All of them can be found, at least in some form, in standard economic discussions of the problem.

Third Parties

An influential approach to the problem of discrimination, captured in the account just offered, attributes the phenomenon to employers' "taste" for discrimination. On this view, employers discriminate because they do not like to associate with blacks, women, or others. The engine that drives discrimination is employer preferences—not economic self-interest, narrowly defined. Indeed, economic self-interest is in conflict with employers' taste for discrimination. This idea has a degree of truth to it; certainly, it explains many practices by employers. But sometimes discrimination is caused by employer practices that result precisely from economic self-interest, rather than from the employer's noneconomic goals. The reason is that third parties are frequently in a position to impose financial punishments on nondiscriminatory employers. Suppose, for example, that purchasers or fellow employees refuse to buy from or work for a company that does not discriminate. Third parties can pressure employers in the direction of discrimination, even if employers would, other things being equal, choose not to discriminate or have no particular view about whether to discriminate or not. Ironically, it is the failure to discriminate that operates as a tax on the employer's business, rather than vice versa. And when this is so, reliance on competitive pressures will force employers to behave in a discriminatory manner if they wish to survive.

The phenomenon is hardly unusual. Consider, for example, a shopkeeper whose customers do not like dealing with blacks or women; a commercial airline whose patrons react unfavorably to female pilots; a university whose students and alumni prefer a primarily male or white faculty; a law firm whose clients prefer not to have black lawyers; or a hospital whose patients are uncomfortable with female doctors or black nurses. The persistence of private segregation in major league baseball is a familiar example of this phenomenon.

In all of these cases, market pressures create rather than prevent discrimination. An employer who wants to act nondiscriminatorily will be punished, not rewarded. Indeed, an employer who wants not to be a discriminator will be engaging in what is, from his point of view, a form of affirmative action. From his point of view, discrimination is in fact neutral, in the sense that it is a quite ordinary form of profit-maximization through catering to consumer demand. From his point of view, a refusal to discriminate is also economically harmful to him; if he is a nondiscriminator, it is not for the sake of profits, but in order to promote the long-range goal of race and sex equality. If discrimination is to be eliminated, it may well be as a result of legal rules forbidding discrimination from continuing.

Ideas of precisely this sort played a role in the passage of the Civil Rights Act of 1964. Many restaurants and hotels sought regulation constraining their own behavior by outlawing discrimination. Their goal was to obtain the force of the law to overcome the effects of private racism (in the form of violence as well as competitive sanctions). They sought to over-come, through law, the discrimination-producing consequences of market pressures. They sought to "hide behind the law" to do what, in a sense, they wanted to do: to behave nondiscriminatorily. Without the force of law, they would encounter third-party pressures, including social norms * * *, that would push them in the direction of discrimination.

On this account, it remains necessary to explain why third parties are not themselves hurt by their "taste." At least part of the reason lies in the fact that third parties often are not market actors in the ordinary sense—that is, they will not suffer competitive injury in markets if they indulge their discriminatory preferences. Consider, for example, ordinary people who prefer not to fly in airplanes piloted by blacks or women (or having black or male stewards). At least in many cases, the harm suffered by people who indulge their prejudice—perhaps higher prices of some form or another—will not drive them out of any "market," but instead, and more simply, will make them somewhat poorer. For a customer, a racist or sexist taste operates like any other taste, such as the taste for high-sugar cereals, luxury cars, or fancy computers; the taste may increase prices, but market pressures need not make the taste disappear.

In a competitive market that contains private racism and sexism, then, the existence of third-party pressures can create significant spheres of discrimination. To be sure, sometimes the participation of blacks or women (or the handicapped) is invisible; in any case, racism and sexism are currently not so widespread as to make it costly for all employers to act in a nondiscriminatory fashion. Because of their decentralized character, markets are usually far less effective than governmental controls in perpetuating discrimination, as the experience in South Africa has (at least sometimes) showed. Moreover, third-party effects will probably produce a degree of occupational segregation instead of, or as well as, discrimination. But discriminatory practices in many areas are likely to persist over time precisely because of the market, which by its very nature registers consumer preferences, including discriminatory ones.

There is an additional problem here. Suppose that society includes a number of traders who want to interact with blacks or women as well as a number of traders who do not. Suppose, too, that it is difficult for traders who are themselves indifferent to race and sex distinctions to tell which traders are discriminators (a frequent phenomenon in competitive markets). If these conditions are met, discrimination is likely to be a rational strategy for traders. New companies will do poorly if they refuse to discriminate. All this suggests that markets will frequently have great difficulty in breaking down discrimination, if discriminatory tastes are even somewhat widespread.

Statistical or Economically Rational Discrimination

I have referred to the common-sense understanding that employers treat blacks and women differently because of hostility or prejudice on their part—an idea that often accompanies the claim that markets are an enemy of discrimination. This form of hostility or prejudice is frequently described as "irrational." But the category of irrational prejudice is an ambiguous one. Perhaps we can understand it to include (a) a belief that members of a group have certain characteristics when in fact they do not, (b) a belief that many or most members of a group have certain characteristics when in fact only a few do, and (c) reliance on fairly accurate group-based generalizations when more accurate classifying devices are relatively inexpensive and available. In all of these cases, it is possible to say that someone is acting on the basis of irrational prejudice.

Suppose instead, however, that discriminatory behavior is a response to generalizations or stereotypes that, although quite overbroad and from one point of view invidious, provide an economically rational basis for employment decisions. Such stereotypes may be economically rational in the sense that it is cheaper to use them than it is to rely on more fine-grained approaches, which can be expensive to administer. Stereotypes and generalizations, of course, are a common ingredient of day-to-day market decisions. There are information costs in making distinctions within categories, and sometimes people make the category do the work of a more individualized and often far more costly examination of the merits of the particular employee.

Such categorical judgments are not only pervasive; they are entirely legitimate in most settings. We all depend on them every day. Employers rely on "proxies" of many sorts, even though those proxies are overbroad generalizations and far from entirely accurate. For example, test scores, employment records, level of education, and prestige of college attended are all part of rational employment decisions. Emphasis on these factors is a common form of stereotyping; at least in ordinary circumstances, it would be odd to say that such factors reflect hostility or prejudice of the sort that the law should ban. People may use stereotypes not because they are very accurate, but because they are less costly to use than any more individualized inquiry.

There can be no question that at least in some contexts, race and sex operate as similar proxies. In various ways, blacks differ from whites and women differ from men; there are "real differences" between the two groups. * * * Indeed, in light of past and present discrimination against blacks and women, it would be shocking if group-based differences were not present. Women, for example, are more likely than men to be the primary caretakers of children and more likely to leave the employment market because of that role. Along every indicator of social welfare—poverty, education, employment, vulnerability to private (or public) violence, participation in violent crime—blacks are less well-off than whites. And in light of those differences, it is fully possible that in certain settings, race- and sex-based generalizations are economically rational as proxies for relevant characteristics. Indeed, it is fully possible that race or sex is, in some contexts, every bit as accurate a signaling device as, say, test score, education, and previous employment. (Notably, the use of those proxies may itself have discriminatory consequences and indeed might be counted as a form of discrimination. But I put this point to one side for now.)

If race or sex can be a good signaling device, an employer might discriminate not because he hates or devalues blacks or women, or has a general desire not to associate with them, or is "prejudiced" in the ordinary sense, but because he believes (on the basis either of plausible assumptions or actual experience) that the relevant stereotypes have sufficient truth to be a basis for employment decisions. For example, an employer might believe that women are more likely to leave a high-pressure job than men, or that they are less suited for physically demanding employment; he might think that blacks are less likely to have the necessary training. With respect to the handicapped, the same scenario is of course readily predictable: "Real differences" call for differential treatment. As I understand it here, statistical discrimination occurs when the employer does not harbor irrational hatred or discriminatory feelings, but instead acts according to stereotypes of the sort that are typically relied on by market actors, and that are no less false than ordinary stereotypes.

It is important to be careful with this point. I do not mean to deny that ordinary, irrational prejudice accounts for a significant amount of discrimination, or even that it is hard both in practice and in principle to distinguish between ordinary prejudice and economically rational stereotyping. Sometimes employers who refuse to follow a stereotype will find employees who will move them far ahead in the marketplace. Moreover, the decision about *what kinds* of economically rational stereotypes should be adopted might itself reflect prejudice. Sometimes people refuse such stereotypes because they perceive them to be unfair. People are highly selective in their creation and selection of the very categories with which they view people—as college graduates? as children of successful parents? as nonreligious? as white males? as tall? as good-looking? People are also selective in their decisions about which categories ought to count in various sectors of social and economic life. Thus, for example, the use of sex as a proxy for flexibility with respect to overtime work may be fully rational; but other proxies may be nearly as good or better. Selectivity in the choice of the proxy may be a product of prejudice. People also tend to notice events that are consistent with previously held stereotypes and to disregard events that are inconsistent with them. This is a built-in obstacle to changes in social norms and social "knowledge," even when the governing norms increasingly fail to mirror reality.

One might agree with all this and still acknowledge what seems undoubtedly true: Discrimination sometimes persists because it is economically rational to rely on a race-or sex-based generalization. And if this is so—if discrimination of this sort is a significant part of modern practice—then markets will be the furthest thing from a corrective. If discrimination is rational, then discriminatory behavior is rewarded in the marketplace. Efforts to view people through more finely tuned (and hence more expensive) devices than stereotypes will be punished.

Moreover, if discrimination is rooted in economically rational stereotypes, it remains necessary to ask what is wrong with it. The (apparent) social consensus that prejudice is irrational tends to downplay the difficulty of finding firm moral foundations for antidiscrimination law. Contemporary American law consistently condemns discrimination even if it is fully rational—that is, if it is as accurate as other generalizations typically used in the labor market. It is no defense to a claim of race or sex discrimination that the practice under attack is reasonable stereotyping. And because contemporary law singles out one kind of rational stereotyping and bans it, the distinction between affirmative action and antidiscrimination norms is extremely thin and perhaps invisible in principle. This is because in some settings, an antidiscrimination norm itself operates to bar economically rational behavior in the interest of long-term social goals. It does so selectively; in the interest of producing a racially improved future, the law forbids rational racial stereotyping when it allows stereotyping of most other kinds. An antidiscrimination norm even requires innocent victims—for example, customers who must pay higher prices—to be sacrificed in the interest of that goal.

Indeed, the distinction between affirmative action and antidiscrimination is crisp only to those who see discrimination as always grounded in hostility and irrationality, which it clearly is not. To say this is hardly to say that there are no differences between affirmative action and an antidiscrimination principle that forbids economically rational behavior. But it is to say that a great failure of the assault on affirmative action is its failure to account for the ways in which a requirement of nondiscrimination involves very much the same considerations.

However we may think about this more adventurous claim, the central point remains. Markets will not drive out discrimination precisely to the extent that discrimination consists of economically rational stereotyping.

The Effects of Discrimination on Human Capital

Suppose that there is widespread discrimination for any number of reasons: employers have a taste for discrimination; third parties impose pressures in discriminatory directions; race or sex is used as a proxy for productivity (whether or not productivity includes the losses produced by the reactions of third parties). If any of these things is so, markets will perpetuate discrimination for yet another reason, one having to do with harmful effects on investment in human capital.

The central point here is that the productivity of blacks or whites and women or men is endogenous to, or a product of, the existence of discrimination in the labor market. Since this is so, it is a mistake to see productivity within any social group as static or independent of decisions by employers. Such decisions will have important dynamic effects on the choice of blacks and whites or women and men to invest in human capital. Decisions about education, training, drug use, trade-offs between work and leisure, and employment programs will be affected by existing patterns of discrimination. In a market that contains such discrimination, blacks and women will invest relatively less in such programs. Indeed, lower investments on their part are perfectly rational. As market actors, women should invest less than men in training to be (say) pilots, economists, politicians, or lawyers if these professions discriminate against women and thus reward their investment less than that of men.

The result can be a vicious circle or even spiral. Because of existing discrimination, the relevant groups will probably invest less in human capital; because of this lower investment, the discrimination will persist or perhaps increase because its statistical rationality itself increases; because of this effect, investments will decrease still further; and so on. Markets are the problem, not the solution.

Undoubtedly, this picture is too bleak in many settings. Proxies not rooted in sex and race have frequently evolved and employers have used them; such proxies are ordinarily far more accurate, and employers who use them sometimes prosper. More generally, the extraordinary persistence of blacks and women in attempting to enter professions dominated by whites and men is one of the most striking phenomena of the post-World War II period. Blacks and women frequently appear to invest huge amounts of human capital even in sectors that treat them inhospitably. In fact, some people respond to discrimination by increasing rather than decreasing their investments in human capital. In Western history, some racial and ethnic groups have prospered as a result of such investments, notwithstanding discriminatory tastes on the part of employers, customers, and fellow employees. But there can be little question that discrimination does have a large effect on human capital in many contexts, and that the discouraging reception, known to be accorded to blacks and women, perpetuates the exclusion of both groups from certain sectors of the economy. And when this is so, reliance on markets as an antidiscrimination policy is badly misconceived.

In General: Reinforcing Effects

The three arguments thus far—coupled with the existence of race- and sex-based hostility or devaluation on the part of employers—build on standard economic accounts of discrimination. It is notable that none of the various effects unambiguously reflects a market failure in the conventional sense. The incorporation of racist or sexist preferences is efficient, if the efficiency criterion is based on private willingness to pay; so, too, with profit-maximizing reactions to the desires of third parties and with statistical discrimination. In all of these cases, governmental interference will probably produce an efficiency loss, at least in the short term.

The only possible exception is the effect of discrimination on human capital. In that case, it is possible to conceive of discrimination as producing a serious externality, in the form of harmful effects on outsiders—prospective labor market entrants—with corresponding efficiency losses. But it is important to note that there is an optimal level of investment in human capital, and it is not entirely clear why and to what extent existing investments that are adaptive to employer behavior in the labor market should be seen as suboptimal. In fact any generalization that is used in the labor market will have a signaling effect that will shift investments in human capital, and it is not easy to develop a model revealing which signals produce suboptimal investments. In general, then, markets will perpetuate discrimination for reasons that are unrelated to the market failures that provide traditional economic grounds for legal intervention.

Moreover, and crucially, each of these effects reinforces the others in potentially powerful ways. If there is ordinary prejudice, it will interact with statistical discrimination so as to produce more of both. People tend to notice events consistent with their prejudice and disregard events that are inconsistent with them, and the result will be more in the way of both prejudice and statistical discrimination. If third parties attempt to promote discrimination, they will increase the existence of both prejudice and statistical discrimination. Employers will hire fewer blacks and women, who in turn will appear less frequently in desirable positions, with consequent reinforcing effects on both prejudice and statistical discrimination.

In addition, if there is prejudice and statistical discrimination, and if third parties promote discrimination, victims of discrimination will decrease their investments in human capital. Such decreased investments will be a perfectly reasonable response to the real world. And if there are decreased investments in human capital, then prejudice, statistical discrimination, and third-party acts will also increase. Statistical discrimination will become all the more rational; prejudice will hardly be broken down but, on the contrary, strengthened; consumers and employers will be more likely to be discriminators.

Of course, it would be necessary to compile detailed factual evidence to assess the magnitude of the relevant effects. In the abstract, it is hard to know how large they will be. But we know enough to realize that the various effects can be mutually reinforcing and might present a disaster for victims of discrimination and for society as a whole.

By this point the fact that markets often perpetuate discrimination should present no puzzle at all. Markets can be an ally of discrimination. To be sure, the precise relationship between markets and discrimination will depend on particular circumstances. The likelihood that markets will promote discrimination should increase if third-party prejudice is widespread, if stereotypes or generalizations are accurate, and if ordinary racism and sexism are pervasive. But what may be surprising is not that markets produce discrimination, but that discrimination has decreased as much as it has. And all this follows from quite conventional economic approaches to the problem.

II. Markets and Discrimination: Noneconomic Accounts

In this section, I provide two additional arguments against the view that markets will prevent discrimination. Neither of them is standard within economics, but both of them have considerable explanatory power.

Preference and Belief Formation

In economic theory, preferences and beliefs are usually taken as given—an approach that is often helpful in building models for understanding social life. But in the context of discrimination, and elsewhere as well, this approach will cause both descriptive and normative problems. The central point here is that preferences are endogenous to current laws, norms, and practices. Once those laws, norms, and practices are entrenched, there are special obstacles to bringing about change through market ordering.

In the setting at hand, the problem is that private preferences, on the part of both discriminators and their victims, tend to adapt to the status quo, and to do so in a way that makes significant change hard to achieve. The reduction of cognitive dissonance is a powerful motivating force: People attempt to bring their beliefs and perceptions in line with existing practice. The victims of inequality may well try to reduce dissonance by adapting their preferences to the available opportunities. Consider the story of the fox who concludes that he does not want unavailable grapes because he considers them sour; the reason that he considers them sour is that they are unavailable. Or people may adapt their aspirations to the persistent and often irrationally held belief that the world is just. The beneficiaries of the status quo tend to do the same, concluding that the fate of the victims is deserved, is something for which victims are responsible, or is part of an intractable, given, or natural order. All of these claims have played an enormous role in the history of discrimination on the basis of race and sex.

There is of course extremely powerful evidence in the psychological literature for the thesis that human beings try to reduce dissonance. Some work here reveals that people who engage in cruel behavior change their attitudes toward the objects of their cruelty and thus devalue them. Observers tend to do the same. The phenomenon of blaming the victim has clear motivational foundations. The notion that the world is just, and that existing inequalities are deserved or desired, plays a large role in the formation of preferences and beliefs. The reduction of cognitive dissonance thus operates as a significant obstacle to the recognition that discrimination is a problem, or even that it exists. Adaptation of beliefs to a social status quo can also affect social norms. The social norms governing women's work may be quite hard to change; the social meaning of being female, or being black, may be nearly intractable.

This problem can be tied quite tightly to the operation of a market economy, whose participants are self-consciously involved in catering to existing tastes and in perpetuating and reinforcing them. Markets, partly because of this effect, are an engine of productivity and respect for individual autonomy in most circumstances; but in this setting, they sometimes perpetuate inequality. This is especially true in the context of sex discrimination, where advertising and consumption powerfully reinforce existing stereotypes, with consequences for the development of preferences and beliefs. Consider, for example, the multiple ways in which the beauty industry, broadly understood, attempts to define and to commodify femininity, in efforts to reach men and women alike. Women as well as men have often adapted their preferences and beliefs to a system of sex inequality.

The inevitable effect of a discriminatory status quo on preferences and beliefs is related to the phenomenon, noted previously, of decreased investment in human capital. In both cases, the response to discrimination is endogenous rather than exogenous and has the consequence of perpetuating existing inequalities. But with respect to preferences and beliefs, the effect is especially pernicious. Here the consequence is not merely to shift investments in self-development but, instead, to make people believe that the existing regime, including discrimination, presents no problem at all.

Once preferences and beliefs are affected, the likelihood of social change through markets diminishes dramatically. Here, as well, there is a mutually reinforcing effect among the various sources of market discrimination. The effect of discrimination on preferences and beliefs fortifies existing prejudice, produces a decrease in investment in human capital, leads to more in the way of statistical discrimination, and increases the unwillingness of third parties to deal with blacks and women.

Baselines and Discrimination Law

Almost by definition, markets incorporate the norms and practices of advantaged groups. Conspicuous examples include the many ways in which employment settings, requirements, and expectations are structured for the able-bodied and for traditional male career patterns. Here the market, dependent as it is on the criterion of private willingness to pay, is extremely unlikely to eliminate discrimination (understood as such by reference to widespread [sic] intuitions). To say that the refusal to provide flexible time, child care, or building access for the disabled does not count as "discrimination" is to rely on an exceptionally narrow conception of what discrimination is—a conception that is repudiated in much of current American law, that is inconsistent with an approach that is alert to discriminatory purposes or effects, and that in any case will do very little about existing inequalities.

In these circumstances, a legal system committed to an antidiscrimination principle might in some cases restructure market arrangements so as to put members of disadvantaged groups on a plane of greater equality—not by allowing them to be "like" members of advantaged groups, but by changing the criteria themselves, at least when those criteria do not have a firm independent justification. Consider the conventional test of American discrimination law: Is the member of the disadvantaged group "similarly situated" to the member of the advantaged group? That is: Have women, who are otherwise the same as men, or disabled people, who are otherwise the same as the able-bodied, been treated differently from men or the able-bodied? The problem with this test is that it itself reflects inequality, since it takes the norms and practices of the advantaged groups as the baseline against which to measure equality. And here market ordering, dependent as it is on the criterion of private willingness to pay, will inevitably present a problem.

Ideas of this sort underlie recent efforts to ban discrimination on the basis of pregnancy and disability. As in the case of statistical discrimination, these forms of discrimination are perfectly rational from the standpoint of employers and others. The argument for legal controls is that, in these settings, the criteria used in private markets are hardly prepolitical or natural, have neither good moral status nor powerful independent justification, and at the least should be overridden when their predictable consequences are exclusion or second-class citizenship for certain social groups.

In the case of disability, for example, the handicapped face a wide range of obstacles to participation in both public and private spheres. These obstacles are not a function of "handicap" itself (a most ambiguous concept; what would handicap mean in an entirely different world?) but instead are the inevitable consequence of humanly created barriers, including stairs, doors, and standards in general made by and for the able-bodied. The market in these circumstances is wholly nonresponsive. In light of the humanly created barriers, the market itself may not much value the contributions of handicapped people, which are by hypothesis relatively low if measured by normal productivity standards, understood as these are through the lens of willingness to pay. Discrimination of this sort may well require a legal remedy. And though the specification of the content of that remedy is a difficult question, markets will not respond, even in the long run.

The point, then, is that the valuation of the market will be a reflection of prevailing norms and practices, and those norms and practices sometimes are what an antidiscrimination principle is designed to eliminate or reduce. When this is so, reliance on markets will be unsuccessful. The rationale for antidiscrimination laws in these cases becomes more controversial, complex, and difficult. Certainly the cost of change is highly relevant; an effort to restructure the world would not be worthwhile if it impoverished most or many people. But my basic point remains: Private markets will not stop discrimination.

III. What's Wrong with Discrimination

Thus far, the discussion has been entirely descriptive and explanatory. I have sought to show why markets are unlikely to eliminate discrimination on the basis of race, sex, and disability. But it will not have escaped notice that I have only provisionally defined discrimination—a highly protean concept, in light of the foregoing remarks—or said what is wrong with it. Indeed, one of the largest gaps in present civil rights theory consists of the absence of a full-fledged explanation of just what discrimination is and why we should eliminate it. In this highly tentative section, I want to say something about the appropriate characterization of the claim of discrimination and about how that claim should be treated.

Discrimination should, I suggest, be understood to include any decision that treats an otherwise similarly qualified black, woman, or handicapped person less favorably than a white, male, or able-bodied person, whether the reason for the decision lies in malice, taste, selective empathy and indifference, economic self-interest, or rational stereotyping. This understanding of discrimination picks up not merely overt unequal treatment, but also requirements that are neutral "on their face" but would not have been adopted if the burdened and benefited groups had been reversed. It does not pick up measures merely having discriminatory effects, unless those effects are, in the sense indicated, tied up with racial, sexual, or other bias.

It follows that the claim of discrimination, best understood, is not for prevention of certain irrational acts, or of "prejudice," but instead for the elimination, in places large and small, of something in the nature of a caste system. Hence the antidiscrimination principle is best conceived as an anticaste principle. The concept of caste is hard to define, and I will have to be tentative and somewhat vague about it. I do not mean at all to suggest that the caste-like features of current practices are precisely the same, in nature or extent, as those features of genuine caste societies. I do mean to say that the similarities are what make the current practices a reason for collective concern.

The motivating idea behind an anticaste principle is that without very good reason, legal and social structures should not turn differences that are irrelevant from the moral point of view into social disadvantages. They certainly should not be permitted to do so if the disadvantage is systemic. A systemic disadvantage is one that operates along standard and predictable lines in multiple important spheres of life and that applies in realms—such as education, freedom from private and public violence, wealth, political representation, and political influence—that are deeply implicated in basic participation as a citizen in a democratic society.

In the areas of race and sex discrimination, and of disability as well, the problem is precisely this sort of systemic disadvantage. A social or biological difference has the effect of systematically subordinating the relevant group and of doing so in multiple spheres and along multiple indices of social welfare: poverty, education, political power, employment, susceptibility to violence and crime, and so forth. That is the caste system to which the legal system is attempting to respond.

* * *

NOTE ON CIVIC REPUBLICANISM

Sunstein's work on markets is informed by his earlier constitutional and political theory that expands community participation in republican government known as "civic republicanism." Sunstein rejects traditional pluralist politics, where interest groups heavily influence government officials, and instead advocates a republican approach to politics. Largely relying on Lockean social contract theory, Sunstein stresses that a successful republican politic can be achieved if four goals are met: (1) deliberation, which involves communication among the citizenry, (2) equalizing political opportunity among all members of the community, (3) universalism, which emphasizes mediation and mutual agreement, and (4) citizenship, which stresses the need for citizens to participate in the political process and limit the influence of self-interested factions.

Consider the following themes underlying Sunstein's civic republicanism and accompanying questions.

NOTES AND QUESTIONS

1. John Locke's social contract theory. Sunstein's analysis of participatory politics is premised on the notion that American society is governed by a social contract, a theory where people agree to participate and support each other through a government mechanism. Great social thinkers of the seventeenth and eighteenth centuries, including Thomas Hobbes, John Locke and Jean–Jacques Rousseau deemed that justice flowed from the social contract, because every citizen in society consented to be governed by a lawmaking body. This premise is alluring because we as citizens are mandated to comply with the rules of justice (and the governments that implement these rules) because we have assented to do so:

> It is as if we made a contract with the state, or more properly with each other, that we would live together according to certain rules, which are also—according to our best rational calculations—in our own interest as well. In return for our obedience to the rules, everyone else will obey them too (or be threatened and forced to do so).

ROBERT C. SOLOMON, A PASSION FOR JUSTICE: EMOTIONS AND ORIGINS OF THE SOCIAL CONTRACT 55 (1990). As a Christian academic, Locke pondered how it is that human behavior follows conceptions of right represented in natural and divine law. RICHARD C. SINOPOLI, THE FOUNDATIONS OF AMERICAN CITIZENSHIP: LIBERALISM, THE CONSTITUTION AND CIVIC VIRTUE 39 (1992). In writing *True End of Civil Government*, Locke emphasized that the consent of all citizens was necessary to obey laws executed by the government and form a community. Within this community, the majority can act upon the remaining citizens to effectively manage one, unified body politic:

> Men being, as has been said, by nature all free, equal, and independent, no one can be put out of his estate and subjected to the political power of another without his own consent, which is done by agreeing with other men, to join and unite into a community for their comfortable, safe, and peaceable living, one amongst another, in a secure enjoyment of their properties, and a greater security against any that are not of it. This any number of men may do, because it injures not the freedom of the rest; they are left, as they were, in the liberty of the

state of nature. When any number of men have so consented to make one community or government, they are thereby presently incorporated, and make one body politic, wherein the majority have a right to act and conclude the rest.

* * *

And thus every man, by consenting with others to make one body politic under one government, puts himself under an obligation to everyone of that society to submit to the determination of the majority, and to be concluded by it; or else this original compact, whereby he with others incorporates into one society, would signify nothing, and be no compact if he be left free and under no other ties than he was in before in the state of nature.

SOCIAL CONTRACT: ESSAYS BY LOCKE, HUME AND ROUSSEAU 56–57 (Greenwood Press 1980) (Sie Ernest Barker ed., 1947). Locke's basic premise is that though we are influenced by the state's coercive powers, citizens share sufficient adherence to government and obedience laws for a majority of the time.

Drawing on Locke's ideals, it is evident that the objectives of social contract theory are to establish the legitimate forms of government and to decipher the justification of any given individual's duty to obey a legitimate state. A government is legitimate only if it is the outcome of a collective agreement of "free, equal and rational individuals." Elizabeth S. Anderson, *Women and Contracts: No New Deal*, 88 MICH. L. REV. 1792, 1793–94 (1990) (reviewing CAROLE PATEMAN, THE SEXUAL CONTRACT (1988)).

In his commentary on deliberation, Sunstein states that citizens and representatives should work towards a common good to promote social welfare. How does this notion relate to the Lockean social contract theory? Sunstein declares republicans should provide outlets for the exercise of citizenship. To accomplish this goal, he deems a state should be limited in size and scope. Does this idea further the notions of a social contract? Would Locke consider the size of a state significant in determining whether a social contract exists between the state and the citizens?

2. Deliberation. Sunstein argues that politics is a strength if it occurs through communication and deliberation. In this framework, political actors can advise each other to attain a degree of separation from popular preferences and subject these preferences to extensive analysis. By detaching themselves from the heavy influence of interest groups and sharing ideas with one another, government officials can reach more rational and collective decisions for the common good. Both political participation and deliberation are needed for a strong politic, but deliberation is needed to manage and mitigate the heavy pressures exerted by intermediary organizations to influence public policies. Though the two notions go hand in hand, deliberation differs from mere political participation in that it helps strengthen the political process:

If the common good is entirely a matter of an agency's decisionmaking procedure, participation and deliberation will often, but not always, be complementary, and citizens who participate in agency decisions will be afforded all of the advantages of a deliberative process. Likewise, deliberation depends upon participation because for the common good to prevail throughout the process, members of the affected community must be allowed to participate directly in its deliberations. * * * * * *

As a conceptual matter, deliberation is quite separable from participation. Participation helps to ensure that agency decisions are responsive to the will of the public, transparent, and open. Deliberation, by contrast, removes decision events from the immediate influence of the public, slowing down the political process and giving it a deeper legitimacy; it ensures that collective decisions are something more than the consensus of "mere majorities." While participation encourages breadth in the agency decisionmaking process, deliberation is more concerned with depth.

Jim Rossi, *Participation Run Amok: The Costs of Mass Participation for Deliberative Agency Decisionmaking*, 92 Nw. U. L. REV. 173, 211, 212 (1997).

Rossi is arguing that because deliberation lessens the pace of political procedures, government officials are less likely to be influenced by the clout of factions in making policy. Rather than pluralism, which Sunstein views as simply majoritarianism, with deliberation, politicians can make their own rational decisions, effectively working for a greater common good:

Deliberative democracy presumes that the public interest is more than the result of a contest between competing private interests. Politics is understood to be a process in which private interests are subordinated in "an ongoing process of collective self-determination." Because the self is understood to be "socially situated," it is only partially knowable apart from knowledge of others. As a result, a political process based merely on inputting private preferences is unsatisfactory because the political process must also shape preferences in order to permit the " 'intersubjective' constitution of individual selves."

* * *

Sunstein understands the administrative process to be deliberative. The administrator's superior technical sophistication makes it possible for agency policy to be governed by reason, not power. The expert administrator for Sunstein, though, is less Platonic guardian than informed citizen—a person whose superior knowledge facilitates deliberative democratic performance. Their technical expertise enables participants in the administrative process with "disparate views" to push past their unreflective, personal preferences and find consensus.

Note, *Civic Republican Administrative Theory: Bureaucrats as Deliberative Democrats*, 107 HARV. L. REV. 1401, 1402–03, 1406–07 (1994). Because government officials have the requisite technical knowledge to render reasonable decisions, their choices should be viewed as legitimate. Conversely, ordinary citizens may lack the civic competence to make reasonable recommendations to officials who produce policy:

Civic competence is a central preoccupation of people who want citizens to base political choices on a broad and accurate understanding of their consequences. Such desires, however, are dashed by evidence that citizens spend little time and effort engaging in politics. The finding that many Americans cannot answer common survey questions about a wide range of political phenomena, for example, dampens many observers' confidence in civic competence.

Arthur Lupia, *Deliberation Disconnected: What It Takes to Improve Civic Competence*, 65 SUM. LAW & CONTEMP. PROBS. 133, 133–34 (2002). It is arguable that Sunstein would aver that because proficient politicians engage in deliberation, they are more likely than lesser competent ordinary citizens to issue legitimate policies.

In light of Sunstein's thoughts on deliberation rather than participation, is it arguable that Sunstein and other civic republicans doubt that the common man can effectively make decisions for the greater good? Does Sunstein's criticism of political participation conflict with his ideas of political equality?

For more information on deliberation in decision-making, please refer to Morton J. Horwitz, *Republicanism and Liberalism in American Constitutional Thought,* 29 WM. & MARY L. REV. 57 (1987); Cass R. Sunstein, *Democratizing America Through Law,* 25 SUFFOLK U. L. REV. 949 (1991); Cass R. Sunstein, *Well-Being and the State,* 107 HARV. L. REV. 1303, (1994); Mark Seidenfeld, *A Civic Republican Justification for the Bureaucratic State,* 105 HARV. L. REV. 1511 (1992); Frederick Schauer, *Deliberating about Deliberation,* 90 MICH. L. REV. 1187 (1992); Robert C. Post, *The Constitutional Concept of Public Discourse: Outrageous Opinion, Democratic Deliberation and* Hustler Magazine v. Falwell, 103 HARV. L. REV. 601 (1990).

3. Political equality. According to Sunstein, political equality should develop the value and ensure the legitimacy of the deliberative process. Martin H. Redish & Gary Lippman, *Freedom of Expression and the Civic Republican Revival in Constitutional Theory: The Ominous Implications,* 79 CAL. L. REV. 267, 285 (1991). Sunstein articulates that unequal power in the polity is unfavorable because it degrades the possibility of political equality. In order to attain political equality, citizens and officials must have more access to the political process and wealth effects should be evenly distributed. Reviewing Sunstein's piece, Karan Bhatia elaborates on the civic republican position on political equality:

Political equality ensures that all individuals and groups have equal access to the political process, and thus ensures that the attainment of the public interest is not distorted by disparities in political influence. While acknowledging that political equality and economic equality are at least conceptually distinct, Sunstein strongly implies that the latter is vital for the former, pointing out that Madison and Montesquieu both envisioned economic equality as a precondition for republicanism and suggesting that "[d]ramatic differences in wealth ... are, in this view, inconsistent with the underlying premises of a republican polity."

Karan Bhatia, *Republican Reform of Government*, 93 COLUM. L. REV. 1300, 1309 (1993) (reviewing GEORGE F. WILL, RESTORATION: CONGRESS, TERM LIMITS AND THE RECOVERY OF DELIBERATIVE DEMOCRACY (1992)) (quoting Cass R. Sunstein, *Republican Revival*, 97 YALE L.J. 1539, 1552–53 (1988)). Sunstein's central premise is that a more even distribution of resources would equalize political power among government actors and individual citizens. Though this is a praiseworthy objective, without the requisite time and money, several citizens are left without political power and have no voice in decisionmaking. Society's increased stress on making financial donations has several repercussions for political equality. A 1990 study found that a family in the bottom fifth income bracket was significantly less active in politics than a family in the top tenth income bracket. In comparing these two income levels, less wealthy families are less likely to vote, they are approximately half as likely to contact a government official, they are only one-third as likely to participate in informal activity in the community, and only one-tenth as likely to make a campaign contribution. Kay Lehman Schlozman, et al. *Civic Participation and the Equality Problem, in* CIVIC ENGAGEMENT IN AMERICAN DEMOCRACY, 443 (Theda Skocpol & Morris P. Fiorina eds., 1999).

Bearing in mind Sunstein's thoughts on deliberation and the need for government actors to make rational decisions without the influence of interest groups, how can he reconcile this with the need for political equality in society? Are the two notions mutually exclusive, or can they exist in harmony?

For more on political equality, please refer to Cass R. Sunstein, *Political Equality and Unintended Consequences*, 94 COLUM. L. REV. 1390 (1994); RONALD DWORKIN, SOVEREIGN VIRTUE: THE THEORY AND PRACTICE OF EQUALITY 184–210 (2000); HOWARD GILLMAN, THE CONSTITUTION BESIEGED: THE RISE AND DEMISE OF *LOCHNER* ERA POLICE POWERS JURISPRUDENCE (1993); ANNE PHILLIPS, THE POLITICS OF PRESENCE 27–56 (1995); ROBERT A. DAHL, ON DEMOCRACY (1998).

4. Universalism. The third tenet of civic republicanism, universalism, puts forth that mediation and political truth are necessary to produce a common good for society:

> This commitment to universalism manifests itself in "a belief in the possibility of mediating different approaches to politics, or different conceptions of the public good, through discussion and dialogue." Two concepts are embedded in this commitment. The first is an emphasis on consensus. Mediation produces "substantively correct outcomes, understood as such through the ultimate criterion of agreement among political equals." The second is a notion of the common good or "political truth" discernible through deliberative dialogue.

Bhatia, *supra* at 1309–10. The roots of universalism are prevalent in Aristotle's writings, in which the great philosopher articulated that a political community is a group of citizens who share common values and believe in similar norms. In this community, the virtue of justice is prevalent and partially natural, "that which everywhere has the same force and does not exist by people's thinking this or that." 2 ARISTOTLE, NICOMA-CHEAN ETHICS, bk. V ch. 7, *in* THE COMPLETE WORKS OF ARISTOTLE 1134b18–1134b19 (W.D. Ross & J.O. Urmson trans., Jonathan Barnes ed., 1984).

With universalism, a politic can achieve justice by making decisions for the greater common good. Sunstein's universalist notions draw similarities to thoughts of liberal republicans, who deem that public policies are sound only when they protect private interests:

> Liberal republicans believe that community values emerge from a well-ordered political process, and that these values derive authority because they are supported by a consensus among political equals. * * * Liberal republicans argue that rights should be designed to protect important private interests that must be guaranteed by a legitimate government, and that judicial review is legitimate when judges enforce community values or uphold these rights.

Kenneth Ward, *The Allure and Danger of Community Values: A Criticism of Liberal Republican Constitutional Theory*, 24 HASTINGS CONST. L.Q. 171, 186 (1996). In fact, Sunstein declares that republicanism continues to protect private autonomy—but only when such independence is justified in a public context. Though citizens share distinct views regarding public policies and may fail to reach an agreement during deliberation, Sunstein relies on his "belief in the possibility of mediating ... different conceptions of the public good, through discussion and dialogue" to reach a consensus. Is Sunstein's view a little too idealistic? Florida State University professor of law Steven G. Gey asserts that Sunstein's view of universalism portrays his "blind faith" in citizens partaking in the political process. Gey argues that if even one of the civic republicans' expressions of faith is in fact false, the government runs the risk of becoming a totalitarian system:

> These statements amount to little more than assertions of blind faith: faith that there will be a dialogue in which all members of society can participate equally; faith that this dialogue will result in an agreement about the important issues of value in society; and faith that the agreement produced by the process is not a false one—no one is coerced into agreement against his or her will.
>
> The entire structure of the civic republican system rests on these expressions of faith. If the expressions of faith are well-founded, there will be little problem. Indeed, there will be cause for celebration, for society will have proceeded to the highest level of harmony imaginable to even the most optimistic political philosopher. But if even one of the civic republicans' expressions of faith proves false, the civic republican model will produce instead a governmental system that can only be called totalitarian. It will be totalitarian because civic republicanism does not incorporate the natural limitations found in pluralist systems.

Steven G. Gey, *The Unfortunate Revival of Civic Republicanism*, 141 U. PA. L. REV. 801, 841–42 (1993).What are some "natural limitations" common to a pluralistic form of government, and why are they not present in the civic republican model?

For more on universalism and the civic republican model, please refer to Martin H. Redish & Gary Lippman, *Freedom of Expression and the Civic Republican Revival in Constitutional Theory: The Ominous Implications*, 79 CAL. L. REV. 267 (1991); Linda R. Kerber, *Making Republicanism Useful*, 97 YALE L.J. 1663 (1998).

5. Citizenship. The final principle of civic republicanism, citizenship, is intended to restrict the overarching power of interest groups by encouraging citizens to scrutinize the conduct of their representatives. Sunstein deems that in current society, individuals are unfortunately isolated from the political process and that the nation has lost a sense of community values. With political participation, citizens can reach a consensus of shared virtues and collective norms could be established. Hope M. Babcock, *Democracy's Discontent in a Complex World: Can Avalanches, Sandpiles, and Finches Optimize Michael Sandel's Civic Republican Community?*, 85 GEO. L.J. 2085, 2090 (1997). Consequently, individuals should participate in making the laws that govern their lives, not only in a government contexts, but also in other circumstances:

> A civic republican conception of citizenship supposes that people must be engaged in framing the rules and administering the institutions that govern all aspects of their communal lives. These institutions include the workplace as well as governments, the fact that workers have little power over many of the decisions that immediately affect their lives is itself a serious participatory loss. Because industrial democracy can provide the foundation for active citizenship in conventionally ''public'' realms, its consequences reach beyond the workplace.

Paul Brest, *Further Beyond the Republican Revival: Toward Radical Republicanism*, 97 YALE L.J. 1623, 1626 (1988). Civic republicans emphasize the need for participation in order for citizens to have some control over policies that affect their lives. However, in order for individuals to participate in the political process, the size of the republic must be limited—a large republic runs the risk of decreasing the relationship between citizens and their representatives and reduces opportunities for participation. Karan Bhatia briefly describes the need for a small republic:

> Sunstein uses the terms ''citizenship'' and ''participation'' interchangeably. Participation in government serves several functions in the republican calculus. Obviously, it is instrumental to deliberation. Equally important, Sunstein argues, participation nurtures feelings of empathy, virtue, and community essential to a healthy republic. The importance of citizen participation makes representation at best a necessary evil in a republican scheme. This explains why republics are commonly thought of as small and decentralized.

Bhatia, *supra* at 1310. With a small republic, citizens will have a better chance to deliberate and work towards a common good; sharing similar views regarding institutions and foundations, individuals can reach agreements relatively easily. Is Sunstein correct in assuming that a small republic would encourage political participation? What are some ways in which a small republic may be an impediment to an efficient government system?

Inclusion of citizenship highlights the need for deliberation and participation. Though citizenship and discussion among community members are appealing, Sunstein may be too idealistic in assuming that all individuals will participate and reach a consensus in making policy decisions:

> Once again, the civic republicans are faced with an insoluble dilemma. On the one hand, if the community is truly organic, every citizen must have a say in the community's discussions and must participate in the process in order to develop the properly virtuous attitudes and values. On the other hand, if the community forces citizens to participate against their will, a strongly motivated minority will be able to manipulate the political process by obtaining support for their favored policies from unwilling participants in exchange for an agreement to support the unwilling participants in some later policy dispute. Unless the civic republicans make the unrealistic and utopian presumption that all citizens agree about important policy matters before political deliberation begins, their organic community dissolves into a system indistinguishable from the one whose problems civic republicanism is supposed to cure.

Gey, *supra* at 820. Gey's disagreement with Sunstein centers in on the fact that many citizens can be apathetic regarding political participation, making the possibility of every citizen taking part in the political process quite futile. However, if every citizen is forced to partake in deliberative decision-making, political bargaining and the struggle between interest groups may intensify, which is an unattractive pluralistic notion. Gey, *supra* at 820. Is Gey correct that Sunstein's impractical view of complete political participation by community members runs the risk of increasing the force of influential interest groups?

Vanderbilt University Professor of Law Suzanna Sherry would probably agree with Gey's views. She asserts that most citizens are not prepared enough to participate politically, and that unless deliberation is limited to a select few elites, Sunstein's idealized system may try to change the values of ordinary citizens:

> First, the neo-republican ideal of deliberative democracy borders on the utopian. The vast majority of Americans are neither inclined nor equipped to engage in the kind of sustained, reasoned deliberation contemplated by the republicans. Moreover, republican suggestions for promoting rational deliberation may actually have the effect of "undermining public political participation, especially among poorer groups." The republican revival will not go beyond a small corps of elite law professors if it does not face up to the citizenry's lack of interest. However, neither of the two most promising ways of coming to terms with that problem is politically acceptable to most neo-republicans: either we could acknowledge that real political participation will necessarily be limited to the few because only the few are civic minded enough to participate, or we might attempt to change the values of the

many so that they too are interested in participating in our rational political discussions. The first solution conflicts with the egalitarianism of modern republicans, and the second with their unwillingness to abandon the ethical relativism of modern liberalism.

Suzanna Sherry, *Responsible Republicanism: Educating for Citizenship*, 62 U. CHI. L. REV. 131, 137–38 (1995). Is Sherry correct in asserting that Sunstein's model may alter citizens' choices and values? What are some mechanisms by which the government can change citizens' views so they could partake in the deliberation process?

For more discussion on citizenship in the civic republican model, please refer to Kathryn Abrams, *Law's Republicanism*, 97 YALE L.J. 1591 (1988); Frank I. Michelman, *Law's Republic*, 97 YALE L.J. 1493 (1988); J. David Hoeveler, Jr., *Original Intent and the Politics of Republicanism*, 75 MARQ. L. REV. 863 (1992); G. Edward White, *Reflections on the "Republican Revival": Interdisciplinary Scholarship in the Legal Academy*, 6 YALE J.L. & HUM. 1, 13, 22 (1994); JOYCE ABBLEBY, LIBERALISM AND REPUBLICANISM IN THE HISTORICAL IMAGINATION (1992); Daniel Rodgers, *Republicanism: The Career of a Concept*, 79 J. AM. HIST. 11, 12–13 (1992); Adrian Oldfield, *Citizenship and Community: Civic Republicanism and the Modern World*, in THE CITIZENSHIP DEBATES: A READER, 75–92 (Gerson Shafir ed., 1998).

Marxism and Socialism

Marxism

The fall of the Soviet Union brought with it an intellectual disintegration of Marxist theory. However, Johns Hopkins University geographer, David Harvey writes eloquently of the history of postmodernity. Harvey argues that postmodernist culture is an extension of the "basic rules of capitalistic accumulation." In the following passage, Harvey summarizes the major insights of Marx and Engels.

The Condition of Postmodernity: An Enquiry Into the Origins of Cultural Change

Blackwell (1989) at 99–106.

■ DAVID HARVEY

In *The Communist Manifesto* Marx and Engels argue that the bourgeoisie has created a new internationalism via the world market, together with "subjection of nature's forces to man, machinery, application of chemistry to agriculture and industry, steam navigation, railways, electric telegraphs, clearing of whole continents for cultivation, canalization of rivers, whole populations conjured out of the ground." It has done this at great cost: violence, destruction of traditions, oppression, reduction of the valuation of all activity to the cold calculus of money and profit. Furthermore:

Constant revolutionizing of production, uninterrupted disturbance of all social relations, everlasting uncertainty and agitation, distinguish the bourgeois epoch from all earlier times. All fixed, fast-frozen relationships, with their train of venerable ideas and opinions, are swept away, all new-formed ones become obsolete before they can ossify. All that is solid melts into air, all that is holy is profaned, and men at last are forced to face with sober sense the real conditions of their lives and their relations with their fellow men. Karl Marx, The Communist Manifesto.

But what is special about Marx is the way he dissects the origin of this general condition.

Marx begins *Capital*, for example, with an analysis of commodities, those everyday things (food, shelter, clothing, etc.) which we daily consume in the course of reproducing ourselves. Yet the commodity is, he avers, "a mysterious thing" because it simultaneously embodies both a use value (it fulfils a particular want or need) and an exchange value (I can use it as a bargaining chip to procure other commodities). This duality always renders the commodity ambiguous for us; shall we consume it or trade it away? But as exchange relations proliferate and price-fixing markets form, so one commodity typically crystallizes out as money. With money the mystery of the commodity takes on a new twist, because the use value of money is that it represents the world of social labour and of exchange value. Money lubricates exchange but above all it becomes the means by which we typically compare and assess, both before and after the fact of exchange, the value of all commodities. * * *

The advent of a money economy, Marx argues, dissolves the bonds and relations that make up "traditional" communities so that "money becomes the real community." We move from a social condition, in which we depend directly on those we know personally, to one in which we depend on impersonal and objective relations with others. As exchange relations proliferate, so money appears more and more as "a power external to and independent of the producers," so what "originally appears as a means to promote production becomes a relation alien" to them. Money concerns dominate producers. Money and market exchange draws a veil over, "masks" social relationships between things. This condition Marx calls "the fetishism of commodities." * * *

The conditions of labour and life, the sense of joy, anger, or frustration that lie behind the production of commodities, the states of mind of the producers, are all hidden to us as we exchange one object (money) for another (the commodity). We can take our daily breakfast without a thought for the myriad people who engaged in its production. All traces of exploitation are obliterated in the object (there are no finger marks of exploitation in the daily bread). We cannot tell from contemplation of any object in the supermarket what conditions of labour lay behind its production. The concept of fetishism explains how it is that under conditions of capitalist modernization we can be so objectively dependent on "others" whose lives and aspirations remain so totally opaque to us. * * *

As commodity producers seeking money, * * * we are dependent upon the needs and capacity of others to buy. Producers consequently have a permanent interest in cultivating "excess and intemperance" in others, in feeding "imaginary appetites" to the point where ideas of what constitutes social need are replaced by "fantasy, caprice, and whim." The capitalist producer increasingly "plays the pimp" between the consumers and their sense of need, excites in them "morbid appetites, lies in wait for each of [their] weaknesses—all so that he can demand the cash for this service of live." Pleasure, leisure, seduction, and erotic life are all brought within the range of money power and commodity production. Capitalism therefore "produces sophistication of needs and of their means on the one hand, and a bestial barbarization, a complete, unrefined, and abstract simplicity of need, on the other." Advertising and commercialization destroy all traces of production in their imagery, reinforcing the fetishism that arises automatically in the course of market exchange.

Furthermore, money, as the supreme representation of social power in capitalist society, itself becomes the object of lust, greed, and desire. Yet here, too, we encounter double meanings. Money confers the privilege to exercise power over others—we can buy their labour time or the services they offer, even build systematic relations of domination over exploited classes simply through control over money power. Money, in fact, fuses the political and the economic into a genuine political economy of overwhelming power relations * * *. The common material languages of money and commodities provide a universal basis within market capitalism for linking everyone into an identical system of market valuation and so procuring the reproduction of social life through an objectively grounded system of social bonding. Yet within these broad constraints, we are "free," as it were, to develop our own personalities and relationships in our own way, our own "otherness," even to forge group language games, provided, of course, that we have enough money to live on satisfactorily. Money is a "great leveler and cynic," a powerful underminer of fixed social relations, and a great "democratizer." As a social power that can be held by individual persons it forms the basis for a wide-ranging individual liberty, a liberty that can be deployed to develop ourselves as free-thinking individuals without reference to others. Money unifies precisely *through* its capacity to accommodate individualism, otherness, and extraordinary social fragmentation. * * *

Participation in market exchange presupposes a certain division of labour as well as a capacity to separate (alienate) oneself from one's own product. The result is an estrangement from the product of one's own experience, a fragmentation of social tasks and a separation of the subjective meaning of a process of production from the objective market valuation of the product. A highly organized technical and social division of labour, though by no means unique to capitalism, is one of the founding principles of capitalist modernization. This forms a powerful lever to promote economic growth and the accumulation of capital, particularly under conditions of market exchange in which individual commodity producers (protected by private property rights) can explore the possibilities of specialization within an open economic system. This explains the power of economic (free market) liberalism as a founding doctrine for capitalism. It is precisely in such a context that possessive individualism and creative entrepreneurialism, innovation, and speculation, can flourish, even though this also means a proliferating fragmentation of tasks and responsibilities, and a necessary transformation of social relations to the point where producers are forced to view others in purely instrumental terms. * * *

Capitalists when they purchase labour power necessarily treat it in instrumental terms. The labourer is viewed as a "hand" rather than as a whole person * * *, and the labour contributed is a "factor" (notice the reification) of production. The purchase of labour power with money gives the capitalist certain rights to dispose of the labour of others without necessary regard for what the others might think, need, or feel. The omni-presence of this class relation of domination, offset only to the degree that the labourers actively struggle to assert their rights and express their feelings, suggests one of the founding principles upon which the very idea of "otherness" is produced and reproduced on a continuing basis in capitalist society. The world of the working class becomes the domain of that "other," which is necessarily rendered opaque and potentially unknowable by virtue of the fetishism of market exchange. And I should also add parenthetically that if there are already those in society (women, blacks, colonized peoples, minorities of all kinds) who can readily be conceptualized as the other, then the conflation of class exploitation with gender, race, colonialism, ethnicity, etc. can proceed apace with all manner of invidious results. Capitalism did not invent "the other" but it certainly made use of and promoted it in highly structured ways. * * *

The "coercive laws" of market competition force all capitalists to seek out technological and organizational changes that will enhance their own profitability vis-à-vis the social average, thus entraining all capitalists in leap-frogging processes of innovation that reach their limit only under conditions of massive labour surpluses. The need to keep the labourer under control in the workplace, and to undercut the bargaining power of the labourer in the market (particularly under conditions of relative labour scarcity and active class resistance), also stimulates capitalists to innovate. Capitalism is necessarily technologically dynamic, not because of the mythologized capacities of the innovative entrepreneur (as Schumpeter was later to argue) but because of the coercive laws of competition and the conditions of class struggle endemic to capitalism.

The effect of continuous innovation, however, is to devalue, if not destroy, past investments and labour skills. *Creative destruction* is embedded within the circulation of capital itself. Innovation exacerbates instability, insecurity, and in the end, becomes the prime force pushing capitalism into periodic paroxysms of crisis. Not only does the life of modern industry become a series of periods of moderate activity, prosperity, over-production, crisis, and stagnation, "but the uncertainty and instability to which machinery subjects the employment, and consequently the conditions of existence, of the operatives become normal." Furthermore:

"All means for the development of production transform themselves into means of domination over, and exploitation of, the producers' they mutilate the labourer into a fragment of a man, degrade him to the level of an appendage of a machine, destroy every remnant of charm from his work and turn it into a hated toil; they estrange from him the intellectual potentialities of the labour-process in the same proportion as science is incorporate in it as an independent power; they distort the conditions under which he works, subject him during the labour-process to a despotism the more hateful for its meanness; they transform his life-time into working-time, and drag his wife and child beneath the wheels of the Juggernaut of capital." Karl Marx, CAPITAL, vol. 1, at 604 (1955,c1952). Edited by Friedrich Engels. (Translated from the 3d German ed. by Samuel Moore and Edward Aveling. Rev., with additional translation from the 4th German ed., by Marie Sachey and Herbert Lamm) Imprint Chicago, Encyclopaedia Britannica.

Socialism

A Future for Socialism

EQUAL SHARES: MAKING MARKET SOCIALISM WORK 7–12 (Erik Olin Wright ed., 1996).

■ JOHN ROEMER

1. Introduction

The demise of the Communist system in the Soviet Union and Eastern Europe has caused many to believe that socialism cannot exist, either in the present world or as an ideal. I shall argue that it can, but that it requires some revision of standard views of what constitutes socialism. If one thought socialism were coextensive with the Soviet model, then clearly it would be dead. I shall defend the idea of market socialism.

The term "market socialism" comes to us from what has been called the socialist calculation debate of the 1930s, in which the two principal protagonists were Oscar Lange and Friederich Hayek. Lange argued that what economists now call neoclassical price theory showed the possibility of combining central planning and the market; while Hayek retorted that planning would subvert at its heart the mechanism which is the source of capitalism's vitality. Hayek's criticisms of Lange's market socialism, and more recently those of Janos Kornai, are for the most part on the mark. But the experiences of capitalism, as well as of socialism, since 1945, suggest ways of reformulating the concept of market socialism in response to the Hayekian critique of its intellectual ancestor. This reformulation is my task.

Economic theory does not yet enable us to write a complete balance sheet of the benefits and costs of the market mechanism. During the 1930s, when Lange and Hayek wrote about market socialism, the Soviet Union was undergoing rapid industrialization. There was, apparently, full employment in that country, while workers and machines were massively idle in the industrialized capitalist world. Hayek therefore wrote from a defensive position, while Lange may well have felt that his proposal was fine-tuning for a socialist system that was, inevitably, the face of the future. Today, the tables are turned. Yet both the pro-socialists of the 1930s and the pro-capitalists of today jump too quickly to conclusions, for we understand fully the effects of markets only in very special circumstances.

Economic theory can explain how, if all economic actors are small relative to the market and cannot individually affect prices, if externalities are absent, and if there is a sufficient number of insurance and financial markets, the equilibrium in a market economy will engender an allocation of resources that is Pareto efficient—that is, efficient in the sense that no other allocation of resources exists which could render everyone simultaneously better off. But this kind of static efficiency may be relatively unimportant compared to the dynamic efficiency with which markets are often credited—that they produce innovations in technology and commodities more effectively than any other economic mechanism could. Although we seem to have much evidence of market dynamism, we have no adequate economic theory of it; nor do we have a controlled experiment which would permit a skeptical scientist confidently to assert that markets are superior to planning in this dynamic sense. The real-life experiments are severely polluted, from a scientific viewpoint: the most dynamic economies of the 1960s onwards (Japan and the East Asian tigers) have used markets with a good dose of planning, and the Communist economies not only had planning and the absence of markets but also political dictatorship, a background condition an experimental designer would like to be able to alter.

The social scientist must, therefore, be more agnostic about the effects of the market than are elementary economics textbooks and the popular press. Indeed, contemporary economic theory has come to see markets as operating within the essential context of non-market institutions, most notably: firms; contract law; the interlinking institutions between economic institutions and other actors, such as between the firm and its stockholders; and the state. Large capitalist firms are centrally planned organizations (in which internal transactions are not mediated by a price system), usually run by managers hired to represent the interests of shareholders. This they do imperfectly, as their own interests do not typically coincide with the interests of shareholders. Contract law is an essential supplement to the market: long-term contracts are, indeed, instruments which render it costly for parties to them to return to the market during the life of the contract. Furthermore, in different capitalist economies different kinds of non-market institutions have evolved. We do have somewhat of a real-life experiment which can help in evaluating alternative economic mechanisms. Germany and Japan, for example, have very different institutions through which owners of firms monitor their managements from those in the United States and the United Kingdom.

In short, the market does not perform its good deeds unaided; it is supported by a myriad cast of institutional characters which have evolved painstakingly over time, and in a variety of ways, in various market economies. My central argument is that these institutional solutions to the design problems of capitalism also suggest how the design problems of socialism may be solved in a market setting.

To see why this may be so, I will first quickly, and necessarily inadequately, summarize the theory of income distribution of Hayek, more generally, of the Austrian school of economics. According to this view, the distribution of income in a market economy is, in the long run, determined by the relative scarcity of various factors of production, principally human talents, including entrepreneurial talent. Property rights should, in the long run, be viewed as themselves derivative of talent. Firms are indeed just the means through which entrepreneurs capitalize their talent; in turn, it is profits from firms which enable their owners to purchase real estate and other natural resources, so that, in the long run, natural resources, too, are owned by talented people or their descendants. Furthermore, any attempt to interfere with the operation of markets—that is, with the institution that maximizes the freedom to compete in the economic sphere—will only reduce overall welfare, as it will inevitably result in conditions which inhibit entrepreneurs from bringing their talents fully into play.

Were this "naturalistic" view correct, egalitarians would have little remedy for inequality other than education, serving to develop the talents of as many as possible, and perhaps inheritance taxes. What I believe the institutional view of capitalism that I have outlined shows, however, is that the advanced capitalist economy is in large part the product of large, complex institutions, whose operation depends upon the combined efforts of many "ordinary" people—ordinary in the sense that their talents are not of the rare variety that the Hayekian view envisions, but result from training and education. The wealth of society is not due primarily to rugged and rare individuals, but is reproducible, according to blueprints which are quite well understood. The market is necessary to implement competition and to economize on information, but not so much to cultivate the inspiration of rare geniuses.

A particular way in which the modern view of capitalism suggests a future for socialism is in its understanding of the firm as a nexus of principal-agent relationships. * * * Indeed the mechanisms that have evolved (or been designed) under capitalism that enable owners to control management can be transported to a socialist framework.

In contrast to the "thin" Hayekian and neoclassical views, which see markets as a minimal structure organizing competition among talented individuals, the modern "thick" view sees markets as operating within the context of complex, man-made institutions, through which all individual contributions become pasteurized and refined. These two views of the market are, I suggest, substantially different, and the latter "thick" view, unlike the former, is amenable to the coexistence of markets and socialism. Income distribution, in particular, is more malleable under the thick view; the door is opened to reducing inequality substantially, short of massive education, as the reallocation of profits will, if properly done, have little or no deleterious effect on economic efficiency.

In what follows, I will try to flesh out these vague claims.

2.   What Socialists Want

I believe socialists want:

1.   equality of opportunity for self-realization and welfare;

2.   equality of opportunity for political influence; and

3.   equality of social status

By self-realization, I mean the development and application of one's talents in a direction that gives meaning to one's life. This is a specifically Marxian conception of human flourishing, and is to be distinguished, for instance, from John Rawls's notion of fulfillment of a plan of life, which might consist in enjoying one's family and friends, or eating fine meals, or counting blades of grass. These activities do not count as self-realization, this being a process of self-transformation that requires struggle in a way that eating a fine meal does not. One does, however, derive welfare from enjoying one's family and eating fine meals, and so I do attribute value to these activities in the socialist's reckoning, for (1) requires equality of opportunity for self-realization and welfare.

That equality of *opportunity* for self-realization and welfare is the goal, rather than equality of self-realization and welfare, requires comment. Were equality of welfare the goal rather than equality of opportunity for welfare, then society would be mandated to provide huge resource endowments to those who adopt terribly expensive and unrealistic goals. Suppose I, a poor athlete, come to believe that my life has been worthless unless I reach the top of Mount Everest on foot. This may require a large amount of money, to hire sufficient Sherpas and other support services to make that journey possible. Equality of opportunity for welfare, on the other hand, puts some responsibility on me for choosing welfare-inducing goals that are reasonable. It is certainly tricky to decide what allocation of resources will give all people an equal opportunity for welfare or self-realization, but I hope the principle is clear from this example. What distinguishes socialists or leftists from conservatives is, in large part, the view of how deeply one must go in order to equalize opportunities. Conservatives believe in going not very deeply: if there is no discrimination in hiring and everyone has access to education through a public school system or vouchers, then the conservative standard of equality of opportunity is met. Socialists believe that those guarantees only touch the surface. Equality of opportunity requires special compensation or subsidy for children who have grown up in homes without access to privilege. Most generally, equality of opportunity requires that people be compensated for handicaps they suffer, induced by factors over which they have no control. * * *

It is, however, impossible to maximize three objectives at once. That is, the kind of social organization that maximizes the equal level of opportunity for self-realization may well induce highly unequal levels of political influence.

There are two responses to this problem. The first says: there is a form of society in which all three objectives are equalized simultaneously, when "the free development of each becomes the condition for the free development of all," or some such thing. I think this is an unsubstantiated and utopian claim. The second response says that one must admit the possibility of trade-offs among the three objectives. This, in fact, is what most of us do. For instance, a lively debate has taken place in the socialist movement on the question: "Which is primary, democracy or equality?" Is equality of opportunity for political influence more important that equality of opportunity for self-realization and welfare? Socialists have different answers to this question. For example, Western socialists assign more importance to equality of opportunity for political influence than most Soviet socialists did. Some socialists did not support the Sandinistas because of the lack of press freedom and democracy in Nicaragua.

I will not offer here any particular preference order over the three equalisanda. I shall be concerned only with investigating the possibility of equalizing income without any unacceptable loss in efficiency. Indeed, I believe raising the income of the poor is the most important single step to improving their opportunities for self-realization and welfare.

NOTE ON RADICAL THEORY

According to radical theory, which studies the socio-historic process of the political economy under capitalism, capitalism cannot meet the needs of the people collectively. Centuries of capitalism have failed to provide everyone with health care, a living wage, and a secure livelihood. Neither the conservative free market nor liberal welfare conceptions of capitalism meet the needs of society. Like Friedman, most economists identify a human capital gap, which can be overcome by increased education and technological training, as the main cause of wage and opportunity disparities. Radical theorists reject this conception. They conclude that, so long as the present capitalist economic system exists, differentials in pay, income, and employment opportunities will exist for women, minorities, and the disabled. "Neither the market nor civil rights laws can undermine the structure of inequality nor prevent its reproduction." We must return to basic questions that neoclassical economists claim the price system answered: What purposes should our economy serve? "What is work, who controls it, and what is its purpose?"

NOTES AND QUESTIONS

1.   Markets and socialism. Is Roemer's argument that the decentralized economy of private markets can be reconciled with the central planning that is characteristic of socialism? What changes would be required to make such a major conversion of the political economy of the United States?

2. Equality of opportunity. Roemer is careful to avoid making an explicit argument for equality of outcome. Would his carefully articulated definition of equal opportunity meet with approval from Milton Friedman? Reconsider Friedman's essay, *Created Equal, in* FREE TO CHOOSE: A PERSONAL STATEMENT at 153.

3. The "R" word: redistribution. Progressive philosopher and activist Cornel West argues that:

> The historic role of American progressives is to promote redistributive measures that enhance the standard of living and quality of life for the have-nots and have-too-littles. Affirmative action was one such redistributive measure that surfaced in the heat of battle in the 1960s among those fighting for racial equality.
>
> * * *
>
> In American politics, progressives must not only cling to redistributive ideals, but must also fight for those policies that—out of compromise and concession—imperfectly conform to those ideals. Liberals who give only lip service to these ideals, trash the policies in the name of *realpolitik*, or reject the policies as they perceive a shift in the racial bellwether give up precious ground too easily. And they do so even as the sand is disappearing under our feet on such issues as regressive taxation, layoffs or takebacks from workers, and cutbacks in health and child care.
>
> CORNEL WEST, RACE MATTERS 63, 65 (1993).

What are the most significant differences between affirmative action and the market socialism that Roemer advocates?

4. Does Roemer address the social, cultural, and psychological phenomena of commodification, alienation, and fetishism that Harvey conveys as the major Marxist criticisms of capitalism?

CHAPTER 5

WEALTH AND INEQUALITY

Introduction

As Deborah Malamud has observed:

Class is all but invisible in contemporary American social discourse. At most, it is a fleeting image, a rarely detected underlayer to the complex texture of race, ethnicity, and gender that captures our society's attention. For many, America stands as the model of the classless society, one in which most people think of themselves as middle class (or at least as potentially so, with hard work and a little luck) and in which middle-classness is the socioeconomic face of "American-ness." The recognized exception, the chronic poor, is seen as an aberration rather than evidence of a general system of class in the United States.

Similarly, American law does not recognize class. Constitutional equal protection doctrine and antidiscrimination statutes are the major mechanisms through which American law recognizes and redresses hierarchy in American society. Both are silent on the question of class. Welfare law advocates have utilized litigation and other mechanisms to argue that "the poor" is a legally significant group, that "poverty" is a suspect classification, and that welfare benefits are "new property" entitled to protection. Scholars have exhibited interest in addressing the question of how the law contributes both to the creation of cycles of poverty and to the social construction of poverty. But the very location of this work within poverty advocacy and theory has meant that it has drawn attention not to class as a general social phenomenon but to the aberrational nature of poverty and our social tolerance for it. Thus poverty is marked, middle-classness unmarked; poverty is figure, middle-classness ground. Poverty needs social, culture, and legal explanation. Middle-classness does not.

Deborah C. Malamud, *"Who They Are—Or Were": Middle–Class Welfare in the Early New Deal*, 151 U. PA. L. REV. 2019, 2019 (2003).

In this chapter, we will attempt to make visible the invisible category of class. Part A examines the difficulties in conceptualizing and measuring "class." Part B provides some historical perspectives on the law's role in shaping the class structure and relations we have today. Part C looks at income and wealth inequality at present and points at future trends.

A.   DEFINING "CLASS"

Martha Mahoney notes that social and political theory has been dominated by two different concepts of class. One concept of class—"status-class"—draws on the work of sociologist Max Weber, and "analyzes economic participation through a focus on distribution and the market and emphasizes status as an important aspect of structural inequality."[a] In contrast, economist and theorist Karl Marx's concept of class "emphasizes class relations in a system of production and the exploitation of labor by capital."[b] A class analysis in the Weberian tradition, then, might divide American society into upper, middle, and lower classes (looking for indicia of stratification); a class analysis in the Marxist tradition might divide American society into capitalists and workers (looking for relations of power and exploitation). Another way to distinguish the two theories of class is to note that Weberian theories take a "snapshot" of existing class relations; Marxist theories attempt to explain historically how classes emerge and evolve.

To the extent that Americans are comfortable thinking about class relations at all, they usually focus on status. The excerpt that follows points out some of the difficulties in measuring and analyzing status-class.

Class–Based Affirmative Action: Lessons and Caveats

74 TEX. L. REV. 1847, 1852–93 (1996).

■ DEBORAH C. MALAMUD

Two basic models of economic inequality compete in the American ideological marketplace, each with two major versions. * * *

One view—which I will call economic individualism—depicts the American economic order as completely open to economic mobility for those individuals with the gumption to pursue it. The economic individualist view admits (as it must) that at any given moment individuals occupy a wide range of positions on a continuum of economic attainment. But this distribution is seen as a result of, rather than a constraint on, free market forces. So long as there is sufficient mobility by individuals, the inequalities in the rewards accorded to different positions are of no theoretical or political importance.

A more moderate version of economic individualism—and the only form of economic individualism that an advocate of class-based affirmative action could embrace—is what one might call pro-interventionist economic individualism. Here, it is admitted that past economic position is a con-

a. Martha R. Mahoney, 76 S. CAL. L.   **b.** *id.*
REV. 799, 817 (2003).

straint on future economic position; for example, that lack of economic resources can interfere with an individual's capacity to make the investments in human capital necessary for advancement. It is thus perceived as necessary to make a modest level of economic assistance available on the basis of need at certain key junctures of personal economic development—financial aid for college, for example. Once modest assistance is given, previous experiences of economic disadvantage are deemed no longer relevant to future success.

The other major perspective on economic inequality posits the existence of class—a structured system of inequality (as opposed to a simple unequal distribution of economic outcomes among individuals) that is intrinsic to the economic realm and that is not fundamentally altered by the economic mobility of individuals. What distinguishes class perspectives from individualist perspectives on economic inequality is that class perspectives are inherently social (as opposed to individual) and diachronic (as opposed to synchronic). Class is social in the dual sense that the class system is inherent in and perpetuated by the structure of economic relations in the society and that shared class position has the potential for being mobilized as the basis for both group identity and political action. Class is diachronic in the triple sense that class position is (1) intergenerationally transmitted, (2) mediated through the strategic behavior of social actors over time, and (3) incapable of being understood without reference to patterns of change in the economic organization of the society.

Finally, there is an alternative version of a belief in class, which builds on the meaning of class just described, but goes beyond it. In this view, class is said to interact with race, gender, and ethnicity (and perhaps other elements of social identity, such as place of residence) in interlocking and mutually defining structures, and it is their interaction that is seen to shape both consciousness and life chances. * * *

II. MEASURING ECONOMIC INEQUALITY

A. *The Shape of Economic Inequality: Continua, Categories, and Conflicts*

On the broadest level, economic inequality can be represented in one of three ways. Under one view, relative economic advantage is represented as *gradational*, as a continuous sliding scale of relative economic position, rank ordered according to one or more specified criteria. The continuum may then be divided for convenience into categories (such as "lower class," "lower middle class," "upper middle class," etc.) by assigning labels to certain ranges on the continuum. But the validity of the gradational model does not turn on any notion that the theorist's groupings identify groups of people with similar patterns of consciousness and action.

Under the *categorical* approach, economic space is divided in a noncontinuous manner on the basis of the criterion that is, according to the relevant theory, the most significant indicator of economic status. The classic example of a categorical approach is the importance placed by some scholars on the distinction between blue-collar (manual) and white-collar (nonmanual) employment. It is generally contended that the theorists' categories capture "native" distinctions—in other words, that they describe patterns of affinity and difference that motivate social action. Thus, the fact that the values and behavior patterns of some skilled blue-collar workers appear to be closer to those of white-collar workers than to those of their unskilled blue-collar brethren is, for a categorical theorist (but not for a gradational theorist), a challenge to the theory or evidence of a flaw in methodology.

Finally, under what [Erik Olin] Wright calls the *relational* approach, the groups that matter for the analysis of economic inequality are identified not merely by patterns of affinity and difference, but also by their intrinsically antagonistic social relations with other economic groups. Just as the elements within such classic pairings as "parent and child" and "master and servant" take their meaning only in relationship to each other, relational perspectives see each economic grouping as existing only with reference to and in tension with the others. Different terms are used to describe the field in which economic groups operate (for example, "the market" or "relations of production") and the nature of the tension among them (for example, "domination," "hegemony," "exploitation," or "exclusion")—terminologies that often do a better job of identifying putative alliances with Weberian, neo-Marxist, or classical Marxist social theory than of describing different social realities. But what identifies an approach as relational is its emphasis on the structured nature of group relations and on the intrinsically antagonistic nature of group interests. * * *

B.   *Whose Economic Inequality?:* Individual Versus Household *or Family as the Relevant Unit of Analysis*

In discussing economic inequality, one cannot go far without confronting the question of whose economic position is to be measured. Many studies use the individual worker as the unit of analysis. But in any household or family with more than one worker, each worker's economic position is potentially modified by that of the others—not only as to the availability of second (or third) incomes, but in *all* the many ways in which economic position affects life chances. Indeed, the household or family is the most appropriate unit of analysis without regard to the number of income earners in the household. This is demonstrated by the work of sociologist Greg J. Duncan, who has shown on the basis of longitudinal data that changes in household composition account for much of the intragenerational economic change in the status of families.

Family and *household* are not the same concept. Family may or may not involve blood or marital ties, as work on gay and lesbian kinship demonstrates. Divorce creates families and households of numerous shapes, and decision rules must be developed to determine the economic saliency of noncustodial parents, of custodial stepparents, of the subsequent spouses of noncustodial parents, and so forth. Even in the absence of divorce (or widowhood), families may not fit the nuclear family image: family-based households often include other relatives whose economic experiences can be quite salient to all members of the household well beyond the effects of any income-sharing that may take place. Substituting the "traditional" nuclear family for the isolated individual as the unit for measuring class position is thus only a small step in the right direction, and it creates myriad problems of its own. Furthermore, class not only is shaped by family and household composition, but at times also shapes family and household composition. Measuring class position with reference to the nuclear family mirrors middle class kinship ideology, but fails both to accord validity to other classes' conceptions of family life (a flaw on the level of cultural adequacy) and to make available for measurement the wide range of relationships upon which individuals are empowered to draw for resources under these alternative conceptions (a flaw on the level of technical adequacy).

Furthermore, household or family is important in the dimension not only of space (the sharing of the space of a common household), but also in the dimension of time. For example, it is undisputed that at least to some extent, the economic characteristics of a person's family of origin shape that person's economic prospects and attainment over the life span. There is room for debate over the extent to which this is true, the length of time for which it is true, and the mechanisms that cause it to be true. But for our present purposes, what matters is the existence of "intergenerational inertia," because of which the intergenerational family is the appropriate unit for understanding a family's economic status.

The complexity of "family" as a unit existing in time and space is well demonstrated by an example used by Frank Parkin. Picture two families, in each of which the father is a blue-collar worker and the mother is a high school graduate who is not employed outside the home. In one family, the mother is the child of a blue-collar worker: she has married within her own class. In the other, the mother is the child of a white-collar worker, meaning that she has "married down." According to a study cited by Parkin, the son of the within-class marriage has a forty-two percent chance of going to college, while the son of the mother who "married down" has an eighty percent chance of going to college. In the dimension of space, it is the child's interaction with his nonworking mother that is determinative of his college prospects. In the dimension of time, the key to understanding the child's life chances lies in the grandparental generation. Without considering the economic status of the high school boys in light of their families viewed in the dimensions of time and space, the boys would appear to be similarly situated. In reality, they are not.

C. Trajectory

Sophisticated analyses of economic inequality take into consideration not merely a *snapshot* of an individual's (or household's or family's) economic circumstances, but a longer view. Jobs that require significant investments in human capital tend to have rising trajectories. In contrast, some occupations are quintessential "young man's (or woman's) games"—such as sports, dance, or physically dangerous service or industrial jobs—in which work opportunities and earnings decline over time. Furthermore,

Pierre Bourdieu correctly points out that in periods of economic change, there exists a "collective trajectory"—the mobility of an entire occupation, class fragment, or class—that does much to shape both political attitudes and the class's capacity to maintain its socioeconomic position. At the extreme, rising or falling group trajectories can destabilize basic elements of the class structure. In all of these aspects, economic position must be understood as playing out over time. There can be doubt as to whether the downwardly mobile family (intra- or inter-generational) is better or worse off than the upwardly mobile family at the point at which their trajectories cross. But it is clear that a snapshot is an oversimplification of the true position of economically mobile families.

D. Measuring Relative Economic Status: The Constituent Elements of Economic Inequality

Up to this point, I have mentioned in passing a number of factors that shape the economic situations of individuals and families: occupation, income, education, orientation toward educational attainment, and numerous extra-economic characteristics (including race and gender). When I have asked students to identify their "class," they have referred to a good number of these factors and some others. But each factor raises its own problems of definition and measurement, and their interactions are complex. I am pessimistic about the capacity of the legal system to capture enough of these complexities to achieve anything resembling a culturally adequate account; and even technical adequacy may be beyond its reach.

1. *Wealth.*—I mention wealth first precisely because it is so invisible in most studies of economic inequality: indeed, it is common to think of "socioeconomic status" as a product of earned income, occupation, and education, with no regard to wealth at all. Perhaps wealth is ignored because Americans are far more private about their wealth than about their incomes. As one working man said to Paul Fussell, classes "can't be [defined by] money, ... because nobody ever knows that about you for sure."

"Wealth" in the sense of ownership of productive assets is no longer at the core of theories of economic inequality. But that is no justification for ignoring wealth as an element of economic status. Wealth is "distributed far less equally than income" in American society. Wealth barriers are strongly resistant to intergenerational mobility, and inequalities in wealth have greatly increased in the United States since the mid–1970s.

Wealth has a major impact on life chances, in that it diminishes the dependency of an individual's economic well-being upon occupation, income, educational attainment, or any of the other conventionally measured elements of relative economic position. Even the expectation of future wealth is highly significant in assessing an individual's economic circumstances. For example, a recent college graduate who expects to inherit wealth in the near future can accept a "meaningful" low-paying job in social services, the humanities, or the arts and can even create the appearance that he is living on his salary. But he knows that if he ever wants to buy a house, he need not save in advance for a down payment (an obstacle that would be insurmountable for nonwealthy people of his income); he knows that he need not save money for retirement, limit himself to jobs that provide health benefits, or worry that his choices will render him unable to afford to raise children. Wealth is thus a source of personal economic freedom in a broader sense: it is the freedom to take risks, to make mistakes, to be cushioned from market forces. To fail to consider wealth is to understate the extent both of economic inequality in the United States and of its intergenerational transmission. * * *

2. *Occupation.*—Occupation is of central importance to the sociological study of class; indeed, it is common for studies that claim to be about "social mobility" to in fact be solely concerned with occupational mobility. For classical Marxist theory, class is largely determined by position in relations of production, and the locus of attention is therefore on occupation. Marxism is not alone in stressing occupation: so do numerous other neo-Weberian, neo-Marxist, and structuralist theories. Where these theories disagree is on why occupation is so central to class. For classical Marxists, occupation matters because the all-important exploitative relationship between capital and labor is most clearly experienced through work. For social scientists in a Weberian tradition, occupation plays an important role in shaping life chances, although it may well not be the central line of political cleavage in a society. For any number of social scientists, in contrast, there is no perceived necessity to theorize the centrality of occupation; instead, occupation is used as a convenient proxy for other important criteria (for example, income, human capital investment, or likelihood of participation in internal labor markets) or for their combined effects.

The central tool of occupation-based class analysis is some sort of scheme for grouping and ranking occupations. These scales are works of social construction on a number of different levels, in which some principled basis must be found for decisionmaking—from the level of deciding how many occupational "classes" there are, to defining and labeling them, to assigning "jobs" to them.

Occupations might be ranked according to one or more of a number of criteria, some of which are the "social prestige" or honor they command, the quantity and quality of credentials or training necessary to perform them, the degree of supervisory or managerial authority they involve, the amount of autonomy they afford, and their income-earning potential. Shortcuts might be used—such as the white-collar versus blue-collar distinction—on the theory that they capture interrelationships of a number of the important criteria. The rankings can be designed to give priority to one criterion (for example, white-collar versus blue-collar employment) and then consider other criteria for purposes of secondary fine-tuning. But unless the ranking system is to be unworkably complex, choices must be made that are bound to produce unnuanced results. Indeed, the results often seem counterintuitive or downright wrong to lay sensibilities (and perhaps to expert sensibilities as well). For example, where collar color plays a central role in the occupational hierarchy, it is considered "upward mobility" to move, via deindustrialization, from a position as a skilled machinist to one as a file clerk. * * *

The picture within categories is no more compelling. Take, for example, the category "service class"—the "top" category—in the occupational scheme of Erikson and Goldthorpe. The category is defined not in terms of the "service sector," but rather in terms of the authors' distinction between "service relationships" and relationships governed by labor contracts—with the former involving the exercise of "delegated authority or specialized knowledge and expertise" and therefore requiring the employees to be accorded a fair measure of autonomy. This means, of course, that the category is (as it should be) theory-driven, based on the view that autonomy and discretion are central to the definition of class relations. But even given the authors' theoretical approach, the category includes occupations that vary widely in respects that are theory-relevant. For example, it includes "supervisors of non-manual workers" in the same category as "large proprietors" and "higher-grade professionals"—meaning that Bill Gates of Microsoft is grouped together with the Microsoft employees who have the power to hire and fire secretaries. All professionals and high-level technicians are included in the top category as well (meaning, for example, that a high school teacher and a physician would be in the same category).

These problems of aggregation have important consequences. Frank Parkin has observed that "there is what might be called a social and cultural 'buffer zone' " between classes and that "[m]ost mobility, being of a fairly narrow social span, involves the movement into and out of th[ese] zone[s] rather than movement between the class extremes." This means that the ability to detect mobility between groups crucially depends on where the lines between the groups are drawn.

Even after "occupations" have been defined and ranked, the work of social construction continues. The "occupations" found in social scientific occupational scales are not necessarily the "jobs" that people are hired to do, which are in turn not necessarily the "jobs" that people actually do. The process of assigning a person's "job" (in either sense) to one of a restricted number of "occupational" categories is a complex process, one that produces inevitable distortions. Take the job of "secretary," routinely classified in occupational scales as "white-collar clerical." Then consider the differences between a member of a secretarial pool in a medium-sized company and a secretary for a Supreme Court Justice or for the CEO of a major corporation. Or, for another example, consider the job of "professor," likely to be classified as "professional/managerial" in most scales. Then examine the differences between a professor who strings together part-time and temporary teaching jobs and a tenured professor at a major research university. In both of these comparisons, both individuals in the pair would be classified as having the same "occupation," but there are likely to be gaps between them in prestige, autonomy, job-related social networks, job benefits, and other aspects of life and work (beyond differences in income) that would go uncaptured by their occupational classification. The latter example points, in particular, to the dangers of occupational schemes that do not reflect the important concerns of segmented labor market theory.

Finally, the problems inherent in systems of occupational classification go far deeper than mere problems of measurement. As Frank Parkin notes,

> Sociological models are almost bound to take on something of the imprint of the age in which they are put together; and the model of class recommended in a period of general affluence and economic growth is likely to look a strange and awkward thing in a period haunted by the anxieties of inflation, recession, and economic stagnation.

Many of the leading occupational frameworks have an anachronistic quality to them: they are based on theories that no longer match the realities of work. With the demise of private-sector unions, there are likely to be fewer reasons in the future to be concerned about the class placement of good blue-collar jobs. Privatization is putting pressure on the line between public and private employment. Overseas outsourcing and decreasing stability of tenure in white-collar work, including such highly trained "knowledge" work as computer programming, is increasing the commonality of job conditions across the collar color line. Cost-containment pressures are limiting the autonomy of the traditional professions. The middle classes are far from becoming an undifferentiated proletariat. But the field is wide open for social scientists to theorize the emerging economic order (or orders)—and, in particular, to theorize the elements of comparative advantage among the different segments of the middle classes. * * *

3. Income.—Many scholars focus on income rather than on occupation as the major force in determining relative economic advantage. So do many lay people. For a number of reasons, income-based measures are particularly compatible with the economic individualist perspective. A stress on income suggests that the "goodies" that constitute relative economic advantage (for example, knowledge, education, cultural refinement, residence in safe suburbs, etc.) are commodities that can be purchased with money. An income measure is (at least potentially) agnostic as to the source of income and therefore tacitly rejects the theoretical position that the labor process is at the center of economic relations. Finally, mobility studies that focus on income tend to show higher rates of intergenerational economic mobility in the United States than do occupation-based studies.

Income-based measures also have the practical advantage that the measurement of income is more straightforward than the construction and implementation of occupational hierarchies. But income measurement presents a number of methodological problems that are capable of generating troublesome inaccuracies, both in measuring individual cases and in depicting economic mobility.

First among the issues in income measurement is the question of whose income it is appropriate to measure. Many studies of income inequality look solely at the incomes of individual earners—in part because this information is easily obtained (from employers and from tax returns, for example). But households routinely pool income, so that the more accurate measure of economic position is "family" or "household" income—the measurement of which is complex. Even at the level of the individual, conventional measures of income tend to understate the economic position of high-income individuals and families by excluding the value of employee benefits (for example, pensions and health benefits). And high-income taxpayers have the greatest opportunities to shelter income from taxation, which means that relying on tax returns as the source of income data understates their economic advantage.

Once a measure of income is agreed upon, there remains the question of how (if at all) to determine which income levels correspond to meaningful "breaks"—whether for purposes of a gradational or a categorical scheme. The first question is whether the breaks are to be determined in absolute terms, in relative terms, or in terms of the purchasing power of the income. Another important question is the number of groupings to use. A fairly common approach is to divide individuals into quintiles according to income and then study mobility between quintiles. But mobility between two adjacent quintiles—the most common form of mobility—may not be much mobility at all: it may simply represent a trading of positions between those with income locations at the quintile boundaries. As is the case with occupations, aggregation is necessary for the sake of simplicity, but the data loss inherent in aggregation makes the data harder to interpret—and may well overstate the degree of income mobility in this country. * * *

* * * Education is most often quantified as the number of years studied or the highest degree attained. But to treat education as a commodity in this fashion is to miss differences that are palpably relevant in work and in life. On the college level, for example, educational attainment is routinely judged in real life by type of school (four-year college versus community college, accredited versus unaccredited, day versus night program, and so forth); quality of school (often measured by selectivity or by academic reputation); content of study (with superiority of attainment measured for different purposes along a number of potentially conflicting dimensions ranging from raw difficulty to likelihood of producing cultural literacy); grades and honors; outside enrichment activities (overseas studies, for example); and numerous other more subjective judgments about the student's "character" as reflected through her curricular choices. * * *

5. *Consumption.*—It was turn-of-the-century economist Thorstein Veblen who most colorfully pointed to patterns of consumption as definitive of class aspiration and class position. Just as inflation can be measured by the relative cost of a fixed "basket" of food items, middle class status is often described as the possession of a "basket" of middle class goods. When middle class status is so defined, mobility into the middle classes is made easier to the extent that the items in the basket are easy to identify (through advertising, popular culture, and so forth) and easy to afford (as the Levittowns democratized suburbanization for white urbanites).

At first glance, it would seem easy to create a quick material index to capture the key elements of middle class material consumption. The consumption choice that most defines ascent into the middle classes is home ownership—which is why federal tax policy subsidizes home owner- ship and why the fact that young people cannot afford homes is viewed as a breach of faith with the middle class. A conventional consumption index might include such elements as home ownership; type of home (stand-alone versus townhouse versus mobile home); location (with suburban rating highest, except for the most exclusive city homes); home size; the owner- ship of cars (divided by old and new); the purchase of private primary or secondary education; number and kind of home electronics (with class ascending as the ratio of computers and cellular phones to televisions increases); the eating of meals outside of the home; and perhaps the nature of preferred leisure activities. Such a list—reworked as required by location (for example, the lack of home ownership and cars for many affluent New Yorkers)—could provide broad brush strokes to draw a line between lower and middle classes.

But as anyone with a good ear for the culture knows, these elements of consumption are not so much measures of class unity as they are fields for the social process (and processing) of distinction. Houses can be large because they have many bedrooms (for many children) or because they offer grand spaces for entertaining. Their grounds can be groomed "just right," too poorly, or too well ("If there's no crabgrass at all, we can infer an owner who spends much of his time worrying about slipping down a class or two. . . ."). The living room can be furnished from antique markets or from Sears. Cars can be utilitarian objects or displays of wealth and taste; they can be old in order to demonstrate patrician nonconcern with material values or because the family cannot afford new. Food cooked at home can be traditional or gourmet. The gulfs in consumption within the "middle class" category are, in short, huge. The advertising industry knows this, and it markets goods not to some broad aggregate "middle class," but to very carefully defined segments within it, defined as much by class aspiration and cultural orientation as by income.

The literature on consumption-based markers of class identity always generates laughter because it so sharply points out the anxiety of our attempts to manipulate social status. But consumption is no laughing matter. The material world is a minefield for the class-mobile, and every dollar spent a potentially fatal misstep. Consumption choices shape oppor- tunities for conversation and for the formation of friendships and profes- sional networks. (If tennis is the game of choice at your office, being a top- notch bowler does you no good; and try inviting your boss to dinner if your only table is in the kitchen.) They are, at the very least, the most easily observed markers of who you are and where you fit into the social hierarchy; they may in fact be an important part of the constitution of the self.

In sum, consumption is central to our (often unarticulated) cultural understandings of class. * * *

6.   *Consciousness.*—Categorical and relational models of class are built upon the claim that the "classes" they describe have the potential for some degree of consciousness of themselves as classes. Class consciousness is important to students and practitioners of politics and for Marxist theorists, for whom the capacity of groups to organize and take action on the basis of class is all-important. It is also important to culturally oriented class theorists, for whom the system of *beliefs* about economic inequality is an important component of the system of economic inequality. And understanding the consciousness of social actors is necessary if their dignity is to be respected. * * *

7.   *Interactions Among the Elements of Economic Inequality.*—The various measures of economic inequality I have reviewed are not independent of one another, but cannot freely substitute for one another. The acquisition of credentials may have some value in and of itself, but its greatest value is in securing a job that utilizes those credentials (or purports to utilize them) and brings one into contact with coworkers who have attained similar or greater educational levels. Access to high culture is limited by lack of income, but high income alone does not guarantee the "right" kind of understanding and the entree into cultured circles that goes with it. Within prestigious occupations, status declines in relation to the relative status of one's clients. Impressive attainments of cultural capital are of little use without the income and occupation to put them to work and the education to announce their presence on the surface of a resume. Resources can be rendered far less meaningful in their impact by coming too early or too late in the lifespan. Yet there is *some* measure of tolerance for gaps in the personal economic armor, *some* capacity for substitution.

What this means is that the relationships among the elements of economic privilege are not simply additive or multiplicative. They are structural. The factors contributing to relative economic advantage exist in a delicate balance and interact in space and time, as is generally true of the elements of society and culture. Their effects are likely to be nonhomogenous—meaning that the analysis of important socioeconomic factors and their interrelationships must be "disaggregated," with an eye to spotting relevant discontinuities. No easily administered, quantitative, composite index of the elements of economic inequality can capture their complex interrelationships.

To the extent that social scientific studies can simultaneously recognize and order the complexities of class, theory allows them to do so. At some point, it is necessary to stress one element and de-emphasize the others—to decide, for example, whether class or economic inequality is or is not fundamentally grounded in the realm of work. That is the role of theory. But the corollary of the centrality of theory is that in shopping for a measurement method and in deciding which factors form the core of relative economic advantage, the legal system will be buying a social theory—whether it admits it or not, and whether it wants one or not. * * *

8.   *Outside Interactions: Race, Gender, and the Danger of False Claims of "Holding Class Constant."*—Up until this point, we have discussed class

as though it were a hermetically sealed category, impervious to other forms of inequality. But it is not. Just as economic variables interact, there are important interactions between each of those elements (and their interactions) and "outside" elements, such as race and gender.

Gender issues in class analysis are obscured (or perhaps underscored) by the fact that studies of social mobility commonly look only at the experience of men. The reason is that one of the most vexing problems in research on class and economic inequality is how to determine the economic position of women—both their individual status and their contributions as wage-earners and domestic producers to the economic status of their households and families. It should be obvious that ignoring the economic participation of women distorts the picture of household or family economic status in important ways. * * * Indeed, there is ample evidence that the interactions among economic factors differ for men and women, that women are less able than men to take personal advantage of inherited and earned economic and social capital, and that occupational schemes developed for men are less accurate for women.

Theorizing and measuring the economic status of members of racial and ethnic minority groups pose problems of equal magnitude. I will limit myself to only a few illustrations of the many ways in which strategies for the transmission of economic advantage from parents to children have historically been less successful for blacks than for whites.

Part of the problem is that black upward mobility is so recent a phenomenon for many black families. In a study of intergenerational elements of educational attainment in the black middle class, Zena Smith Blau found that when black and white families of seemingly similar socioeconomic status (measured by the occupational status of the higher ranking parent and both parents' educational attainment) were compared, black families "in fact, possess fewer resources than those white families." The key difference was that white parents' own socioeconomic status translated into a more privileged social milieu. This means, Blau concluded, that parental occupational and educational gains in white families "are more readily translated into access to middle-class influences and role models than is usually the case for black families." There is also evidence, from Coleman, that although "black parents ... show a greater interest in their child's education and greater aspirations for his success in education than do white parents of the same economic level," the interests of black, Hispanic, and Native American parents do not translate as well into improved academic performance for the child.

More generally, the past and present effects of discrimination mean that blacks and whites who appear to have the same occupation, education, or residential situation when a simple metric is used may well not occupy the same status in reality. When black families live in the suburbs, they tend to live in predominantly black suburbs that lie closer to the inner city and that are less advantaged in their public and private services. Blacks are more likely to be employed in the public sector, where civil-service employment rules diminish the ability of parents to use their influence to provide jobs for children in their community. Although patterns of segregation are breaking down, black professionals are historically more likely to serve within the black community, which means that having professionals in the family opens up a less advantaged social network for blacks than for whites. Blacks in the professions remain more likely than whites to be employed in occupations at the lower end of the category in credentials, prestige, and income. Blacks have less wealth than whites of the same income level. And skin color remains a powerful obstacle to the translation of wealth, occupation, income, education, and cultural capital into even the most basic dignity in public life. As one Jewish carpenter explained to an ethnographer in Brooklyn, New York, my hometown: "The problem is that we see blacks as a mass. It is unfortunate. We can't tell the difference between a black pimp and a black mailman. When I look at a white man, I can tell what social class he is, but if he is colored, I can't tell." There is little gain to be had from class mobility if its public indicia are overwhelmed by the more socially salient reality of race.

These examples demonstrate that if an overly simplistic measurement of class is used, systematic differences in the present and historical economic condition of blacks will be ignored, and the socioeconomic privilege of middle class blacks will be overstated. It is highly likely, given the complexity of the phenomenon, that even the most earnest efforts at designing an adequate metric will fail. And the result of failure will likely be that the law's official discourse will falsely proclaim that in the contest for economic equality, class has been "held constant"—and that if blacks still lose, their loss must be because of some postulated lack of individual or collective merit. That is a significant danger for anyone concerned with racial justice in this country.

———

NOTES AND QUESTIONS

1.   Class position. How would you describe your class position? What was your parents' class position when you were growing up? Has it changed over time? Of the factors Malamud lists as relevant to the determination of a person's "class," which do you think are the most determinative? Is class a relevant category in American life?

2.   The American Dream. A central ideology of American democracy and markets is that economic mobility is fully open to all citizens with talent and a strong work ethic. The asserted classlessness of American society remains a cherished characterization of the opportunity structure here. Americans venerate our tradition of individual achievement. Opposition to the accumulation of great wealth and the hereditary privileges associated with such concentrations of political, social and economic power have been a feature of American political rhetoric since the founding of the nation.

Political scientist Jennifer Hochschild uses a quote from former President Bill Clinton to encapsulate the "American Dream":

The American Dream that we were all raised on is a simple but powerful one—if you work hard and play by the rules you should be given a chance to go as far as your God-given ability will take you.

President Bill Clinton, Speech to Democratic Leadership Council, 1993.

In one sentence, President Clinton has captured the bundle of shared, even unconsciously presumed, tenets about achieving success that make up the ideology of the American Dream. Those tenets answer the questions: *Who* may pursue the American Dream? In *what* does the pursuit consist? *How* does one successfully pursue the dream? *Why* is the pursuit worthy of our deepest commitment?

The answer to "who" in the standard ideology is "everyone, regardless of ascriptive traits, family background, or personal history." The answer to "what" is "the reasonable anticipation, though not the promise, of success, however it is defined." The answer to "how" is "through actions and traits under one's control." The answer to "why" is "true success is associated with virtue."

Jennifer L. Hochschild, Facing Up to the American Dream: Race, Class, and the Soul of the Nation 18 (1995). How does belief in the American Dream shape attitudes toward class?

3. The immigrant story. Related to the American Dream is another central ideology in American life, one that relates to the possibility of group rather than individual class mobility. The United States is a nation of immigrants, and many Americans can tell stories of a great-grandfather or grandfather who came to this country with "nothing" and was able to "work his way up," eventually passing wealth along to his children. Nathan Glazer puts this kind of story into a larger framework:

[T]he American polity has * * * been defined by a steady expansion of the definition of those who may be included in it to the point where it now includes all humanity; * * * the United States has become the first great nation that defines itself not in terms of ethnic origin but in terms of adherence to common rules of citizenship; * * * no one is now excluded from the broadest access to what the society makes possible; and * * * this access is combined with a considerable concern for whatever is necessary to maintain group identity and loyalty.

Nathan Glazer, *The Emergence of an American Ethnic Pattern, in* From Different Shores: Perspectives on Race and Ethnicity in America 13, 14 (Ronald Tataki ed., 1987).

Is the immigrant story of individual and group social and economic mobility despite ethnic difference a story that can be told about all groups? Robert Blauner argues that there is a key historical difference between "colonized" and "immigrant" minorities. As he sets forth his argument, he identifies three assumptions on which it rests:

The first assumption is that racial groups in America are, and have been, colonized peoples; therefore their social realities cannot be understood in the framework of immigration and assimilation that is applied to European ethnic groups. The second assumption is that the racial minorities share a common situation of oppression, from which a potential political unity is inferred. The final assumption is that there is a historical connection between the third world abroad and the third world within.

Robert Blauner, *Colonized and Immigrant Minorities, in* FROM DIFFERENT SHORES: PERSPECTIVES ON RACE AND ETHNICITY IN AMERICA 149, 149 (Ronald Takaki ed., 1987).

4.   *San Antonio Independent School District v. Rodriguez.* Malamud is pessimistic about American law's ability to adequately deal with issues of class. As you read *San Antonio Independent School District v. Rodriguez,* think about how Justice Powell is trying to conceptualize wealth discrimination. Does he adequately distinguish this case from the precedents he discusses? Does "class" fit into the ways lawyers think about "discrimination"? How might Malamud conceptualize the issues faced by the litigants in the case?

B.   THE CONSTITUTION: WEALTH AND CLASS

San Antonio Independent School District v. Rodriguez
411 U.S. 1 (1973).

■ MR. JUSTICE POWELL delivered the opinion of the Court.

This suit attacking the Texas system of financing public education was initiated by Mexican–American parents whose children attend the elementary and secondary schools in the Edgewood Independent School District, an urban school district in San Antonio, Texas. They brought a class action on behalf of schoolchildren throughout the State who are members of minority groups or who are poor and reside in school districts having a low property tax base. * * *

I

The first Texas State Constitution, promulgated upon Texas' entry into the Union in 1845, provided for the establishment of a system of free schools. Early in its history, Texas adopted a dual approach to the financing of its schools, relying on mutual participation by the local school districts and the State. As early as 1883, the state constitution was amended to provide for the creation of local school districts empowered to levy ad valorem taxes with the consent of local taxpayers for the "erection ... of school buildings" and for the "further maintenance of public free schools." Such local funds as were raised were supplemented by funds distributed to each district from the State's Permanent and Available School Funds. * * *

Until recent times, Texas was a predominantly rural State and its population and property wealth were spread relatively evenly across the State. Sizable differences in the value of assessable property between local school districts became increasingly evident as the State became more industrialized and as rural-to-urban population shifts became more pronounced. The location of commercial and industrial property began to play a significant role in determining the amount of tax resources available to each school district. These growing disparities in population and taxable property between districts were responsible in part for increasingly notable differences in levels of local expenditure for education.

In due time it became apparent to those concerned with financing public education that contributions from the Available School Fund were not sufficient to ameliorate these disparities. * * *

Recognizing the need for increased state funding to help offset disparities in local spending and to meet Texas' changing educational requirements, the state legislature in the late 1940's undertook a thorough evaluation of public education with an eye toward major reform. In 1947, an 18–member committee, composed of educators and legislators, was appointed to explore alternative systems in other States and to propose a funding scheme that would guarantee a minimum or basic educational offering to each child and that would help overcome interdistrict disparities in taxable resources. The Committee's efforts led to the passage of the Gilmer–Aikin bills, named for the Committee's co-chairmen, establishing the Texas Minimum Foundation School Program. Today, this Program accounts for approximately half of the total educational expenditures in Texas.

The Program calls for state and local contributions to a fund earmarked specifically for teacher salaries, operating expenses, and transportation costs. The State, supplying funds from its general revenues, finances approximately 80% of the Program, and the school districts are responsible—as a unit—for providing the remaining 20%. The districts' share, known as the Local Fund Assignment, is apportioned among the school districts under a formula designed to reflect each district's relative taxpaying ability. * * *

In the years since this program went into operation in 1949, expenditures for education—from state as well as local sources—have increased steadily.

* * *

The school district in which appellees reside, the Edgewood Independent School District, has been compared throughout this litigation with the Alamo Heights Independent School District. This comparison between the least and most affluent districts in the San Antonio area serves to illustrate the manner in which the dual system of finance operates and to indicate the extent to which substantial disparities exist despite the State's impressive progress in recent years. Edgewood is one of seven public school districts in the metropolitan area. Approximately 22,000 students are enrolled in its 25 elementary and secondary schools. The district is situated in the core-city sector of San Antonio in a residential neighborhood that has little commercial or industrial property. The residents are predominantly of Mexican–American descent: approximately 90% of the student population is Mexican–American and over 6% is Negro. The average assessed property value per pupil is $5,960—the lowest in the metropolitan area—and the median family income ($4,686) is also the lowest. At an equalized tax rate of $1.05 per $100 of assessed property—the highest in the metropolitan area—the district contributed $26 to the education of each child for the 1967–1968 school year above its Local Fund Assignment for the Minimum Foundation Program. The Foundation Program contributed $222 per pupil for a state-local total of $248. Federal funds added another $108 for a total of $356 per pupil.

Alamo Heights is the most affluent school district in San Antonio. Its six schools, housing approximately 5,000 students, are situated in a residential community quite unlike the Edgewood District. The school population is predominantly "Anglo," having only 18% Mexican–Americans and less than 1% Negroes. The assessed property value per pupil exceeds $49,000, and the median family income is $8,001. In 1967–1968 the local tax rate of $.85 per $100 of valuation yielded $333 per pupil over and above its contribution to the Foundation Program. Coupled with the $225 provided from that Program, the district was able to supply $558 per student. Supplemented by a $36 per-pupil grant from federal sources, Alamo Heights spent $594 per pupil.

                              * * *

The District Court held that the Texas system discriminates on the basis of wealth in the manner in which education is provided for its people.[1] Finding that wealth is a "suspect" classification and that education is a "fundamental" interest, the District Court held that the Texas system could be sustained only if the State could show that it was premised upon some compelling state interest.[2] On this issue the court concluded that "[n]ot only are defendants unable to demonstrate compelling state interests ... they fail even to establish a reasonable basis for these classifications."[3]

Texas virtually concedes that its historically rooted dual system of financing education could not withstand the strict judicial scrutiny that this Court has found appropriate in reviewing legislative judgments that interfere with fundamental constitutional rights or that involve suspect classifications. If, as previous decisions have indicated, strict scrutiny means that the State's system is not entitled to the usual presumption of validity, that the State rather than the complainants must carry a "heavy burden of justification," that the State must demonstrate that its educational system has been structured with "precision," and is "tailored" narrowly to serve legitimate objectives and that it has selected the "less drastic means" for effectuating its objectives, the Texas financing system

1. 337 F. Supp., at 282.   3. *Id.*, at 284.
2. *Id.*, at 282–284.

and its counterpart in virtually every other State will not pass muster. The State candidly admits that "[n]o one familiar with the Texas system would contend that it has yet achieved perfection." Apart from its concession that educational financing in Texas has "defects" and "imperfections," the State defends the system's rationality with vigor and disputes the District Court's finding that it lacks a "reasonable basis."

This, then, establishes the framework for our analysis. We must decide, first, whether the Texas system of financing public education operates to the disadvantage of some suspect class or impinges upon a fundamental right explicitly or implicitly protected by the Constitution, thereby requiring strict judicial scrutiny. If so, the judgment of the District Court should be affirmed. If not, the Texas scheme must still be examined to determine whether it rationally furthers some legitimate, articulated state purpose and therefore does not constitute an invidious discrimination in violation of the Equal Protection Clause of the Fourteenth Amendment.

II

The District Court's opinion does not reflect the novelty and complexity of the constitutional questions posed by appellees' challenge to Texas' system of school financing. In concluding that strict judicial scrutiny was required, that court relied on decisions dealing with the rights of indigents to equal treatment in the criminal trial and appellate processes, and on cases disapproving wealth restrictions on the right to vote. Those cases, the District Court concluded, established wealth as a suspect classification. Finding that the local property tax system discriminated on the basis of wealth, it regarded those precedents as controlling. It then reasoned, based on decisions of this Court affirming the undeniable importance of education, that there is a fundamental right to education and that, absent some compelling state justification, the Texas system could not stand.

We are unable to agree that this case, which in significant aspects is *sui generis*, may be so neatly fitted into the conventional mosaic of constitutional analysis under the Equal Protection Clause. Indeed, for the several reasons that follow, we find neither the suspect-classification nor the fundamental-interest analysis persuasive.

A

The wealth discrimination discovered by the District Court in this case, and by several other courts that have recently struck down school-financing laws in other States, is quite unlike any of the forms of wealth discrimination heretofore reviewed by this Court. Rather than focusing on the unique features of the alleged discrimination, the courts in these cases have virtually assumed their findings of a suspect classification through a simplistic process of analysis: since, under the traditional systems of financing public schools, some poorer people receive less expensive educations than other more affluent people, these systems discriminate on the basis of wealth. This approach largely ignores the hard threshold questions, including whether it makes a difference for purposes of consideration under

Can you id the class?

Relative nature o. deprivation

the Constitution that the class of disadvantaged "poor" cannot be identified or defined in customary equal protection terms, and whether the relative—rather than absolute—nature of the asserted deprivation is of significant consequence.

* * *

The case comes to us with no definitive description of the classifying facts or delineation of the disfavored class. Examination of the District Court's opinion and of appellees' complaint, briefs, and contentions at oral argument suggests, however, at least three ways in which the discrimination claimed here might be described. The Texas system of school financing might be regarded as discriminating (1) against "poor" persons whose incomes fall below some identifiable level of poverty or who might be characterized as functionally "indigent," or (2) against those who are relatively poorer than others, or (3) against all those who, irrespective of their personal incomes, happen to reside in relatively poorer school districts. Our task must be to ascertain whether, in fact, the Texas system has been shown to discriminate on any of these possible bases and, if so, whether the resulting classification may be regarded as suspect.

discrimo. →
classes & suspected.

The precedents of this Court provide the proper starting point. The individuals, or groups of individuals, who constituted the class discriminated against in our prior cases shared two distinguishing characteristics: because of their impecunity they were completely unable to pay for some desired benefit, and as a consequence, they sustained an absolute deprivation of a meaningful opportunity to enjoy that benefit. In *Griffin v. Illinois*[4] and its progeny, the Court invalidated state laws that prevented an indigent criminal defendant from acquiring a transcript, or an adequate substitute for a transcript, for use at several stages of the trial and appeal process. The payment requirements in each case were found to occasion *de facto* discrimination against those who, because of their indigency, were totally unable to pay for transcripts. And the Court in each case emphasized that no constitutional violation would have been shown if the State had provided some "adequate substitute" for a full stenographic transcript.
* * *

Likewise, in *Douglas v. California*,[5] a decision establishing an indigent defendant's right to court-appointed counsel on direct appeal, the Court dealt only with defendants who could not pay for counsel from their own resources and who had no other way of gaining representation. *Douglas* provides no relief for those on whom the burdens of paying for a criminal defense are relatively speaking great but not insurmountable. Nor does it deal with relative differences in the quality of counsel acquired by the less wealthy.

Williams v. Illinois[6] and *Tate v. Short*[7] struck down criminal penalties that subjected indigents to incarceration simply because of their inability to

4. 351 U.S. 12 (1956).
5. 372 U.S. 353 (1963).
6. 399 U.S. 235 (1970).
7. 401 U.S. 395 (1971).

pay a fine. Again, the disadvantaged class was composed only of persons who were totally unable to pay the demanded sum. Those cases do not touch on the question whether equal protection is denied to persons with relatively less money on whom designated fines impose heavier burdens. The Court has not held that fines must be structured to reflect each person's ability to pay in order to avoid disproportionate burdens. Sentencing judges may, and often do, consider the defendant's ability to pay, but in such circumstances they are guided by sound judicial discretion rather than by constitutional mandate.

handwritten margin note: precedent doesn't speak to relative heavier burden but total deprivation

Finally, in *Bullock v. Carter*[8] the Court invalidated the Texas filing-fee requirement for primary elections. Both of the relevant classifying facts found in the previous cases were present there. The size of the fee, often running into the thousands of dollars and, in at least one case, as high as $8,900, effectively barred all potential candidates who were unable to pay the required fee. As the system provided "no reasonable alternative means of access to the ballot",[9] inability to pay occasioned an absolute denial of a position on the primary ballot.

handwritten margin note: only poor criteria cld meet criteria

Only appellees' first possible basis for describing the class disadvantaged by the Texas school-financing system—discrimination against a class of defineably "poor" persons—might arguably meet the criteria established in these prior cases. Even a cursory examination, however, demonstrates that neither of the two distinguishing characteristics of wealth classifications can be found here. First, in support of their charge that the system discriminates against the "poor," appellees have made no effort to demonstrate that it operates to the peculiar disadvantage of any class fairly definable as indigent, or as composed of persons whose incomes are beneath any designated poverty level. Indeed, there is reason to believe that the poorest families are not necessarily clustered in the poorest property districts. A recent and exhaustive study of school districts in Connecticut concluded that "[i]t is clearly incorrect . . . to contend that the 'poor' live in 'poor' districts. . . . Thus, the major factual assumption of *Serrano*—that the educational financing system discriminates against the 'poor'—is simply false in Connecticut." Defining "poor" families as those below the Bureau of the Census "poverty level," the Connecticut study found, not surprisingly, that the poor were clustered around commercial and industrial areas—those same areas that provide the most attractive sources of property tax income for school districts. Whether a similar pattern would be discovered in Texas is not known, but there is no basis on the record in this case for assuming that the poorest people—defined by reference to any level of absolute impecunity—are concentrated in the poorest districts.

Second, neither appellees nor the District Court addressed the fact that, unlike each of the foregoing cases, lack of personal resources has not occasioned an absolute deprivation of the desired benefit. The argument here is not that the children in districts having relatively low assessable property values are receiving no public education; rather, it is that they are

---

8. 405 U.S. 134 (1972).   **9.** *Id.*, at 149.

receiving a poorer quality education than that available to children in districts having more assessable wealth. Apart from the unsettled and disputed question whether the quality of education may be determined by the amount of money expended for it, a sufficient answer to appellees' argument is that, at least where wealth is involved, the Equal Protection Clause does not require absolute equality or precisely equal advantages. Nor indeed, in view of the infinite variables affecting the educational process, can any system assure equal quality of education except in the most relative sense. Texas asserts that the Minimum Foundation Program provides an "adequate" education for all children in the State. * * *

For these two reasons—the absence of any evidence that the financing system discriminates against any definable category of "poor" people or that it results in the absolute deprivation of education—the disadvantaged class is not susceptible of identification in traditional terms.

 As suggested above, appellees and the District Court may have embraced a second or third approach, the second of which might be characterized as a theory of relative or comparative discrimination based on family income. Appellees sought to prove that a direct correlation exists between the wealth of families within each district and the expenditures therein for education. That is, along a continuum, the poorer the family the lower the dollar amount of education received by the family's children. * * *

If, in fact, these correlations could be sustained, then it might be argued that expenditures on education—equated by appellees to the quality of education—are dependent on personal wealth. Appellees' comparative-discrimination theory would still face serious unanswered questions, including whether a bare positive correlation or some higher degree of correlation is necessary to provide a basis for concluding that the financing system is designed to operate to the peculiar disadvantage of the comparatively poor, and whether a class of this size and diversity could ever claim the special protection accorded "suspect" classes. These questions need not be addressed in this case, however, since appellees' proof fails to support their allegations or the District Court's conclusions. * * *

This brings us, then, to the third way in which the classification scheme might be defined—district wealth discrimination. Since the only correlation indicated by the evidence is between district property wealth and expenditures, it may be argued that discrimination might be found without regard to the individual income characteristics of district residents. Assuming a perfect correlation between district property wealth and expenditures from top to bottom, the disadvantaged class might be viewed as encompassing every child in every district except the district that has the most assessable wealth and spends the most on education. Alternatively, as suggested in Mr. JUSTICE MARSHALL'S dissenting opinion, * * * the class might be defined more restrictively to include children in districts with assessable property which falls below the statewide average, or median, or below some other artificially defined level.

However described, it is clear that appellees' suit asks this Court to extend its most exacting scrutiny to review a system that allegedly discriminates against a large, diverse, and amorphous class, unified only by the common factor of residence in districts that happen to have less taxable wealth than other districts. The system of alleged discrimination and the class it defines have none of the traditional indicia of suspectness: the class is not saddled with such disabilities, or subjected to such a history of purposeful unequal treatment, or relegated to such a position of political powerlessness as to command extraordinary protection from the majoritarian political process. * * *

Educ. fund Right?

[The Court turns to the question of whether education is a fundamental right protected by the Constitution.]

Lindsey v. Normet,[10] decided only last Term, firmly reiterates that social importance is not the critical determinant for subjecting state legislation to strict scrutiny. The complainants in that case, involving a challenge to the procedural limitations imposed on tenants in suits brought by landlords under Oregon's Forcible Entry and Wrongful Detainer Law, urged the Court to examine the operation of the statute under "a more stringent standard than mere rationality."[11] The tenants argued that the statutory limitations implicated "fundamental interests which are particularly important to the poor," such as the "need for decent shelter" and the "right to retain peaceful possession of one's home."[12] MR. JUSTICE WHITE'S analysis, in his opinion for the Court is instructive:

> "We do not denigrate the importance of decent, safe and sanitary housing. But the Constitution does not provide judicial remedies for every social and economic ill. We are unable to perceive in that document any constitutional guarantee of access to dwellings of a particular quality or any recognition of the right of a tenant to occupy the real property of his landlord beyond the term of his lease, without the payment of rent.... *Absent constitutional mandate*, the assurance of adequate housing and the definition of landlord-tenant relationships are legislative, not judicial, functions."[13]

Similarly, in *Dandridge v. Williams*,[14] the Court's explicit recognition of the fact that the "administration of public welfare assistance ... involves the most basic economic needs of impoverished human beings,"[15] provided no basis for departing from the settled mode of constitutional analysis of legislative classifications involving questions of economic and social policy. * * *

[The Court concludes that education is not a fundamental right and that the Texas system survives the rational basis test.]

■ MR. JUSTICE MARSHALL, with whom MR. JUSTICE DOUGLAS concurs, dissenting.

10.   405 U.S. 56 (1972).

11.   *Id.*, at 73.

12.   *Ibid.*

13.   *Id.*, at 74 (emphasis supplied).

14.   397 U.S. 471 (1970).

15.   *id.* at 485.

* * * In my view, * * * it is inequality—not some notion of gross inadequacy—of educational opportunity that raises a question of denial of equal protection of the laws. I find any other approach to the issue unintelligible and without directing principle. Here, appellees have made a substantial showing of wide variations in educational funding and the resulting educational opportunity afforded to the schoolchildren of Texas. This discrimination is, in large measure, attributable to significant disparities in the taxable wealth of local Texas school districts. This is a sufficient showing to raise a substantial question of discriminatory state action in violation of the Equal Protection Clause.

NOTES AND QUESTIONS

1. **Economic inequality.** One issue that bears both on how we measure class and on our understanding of the American Dream is the issue of economic inequality. In this section, we look at readings that investigate economic inequality along two of the dimensions of class described by Malamud—income and wealth.

2. **The right to education under state constitutions.** Forty-eight out of fifty states have education clauses in their state constitutions. *See* Michael Heise, *State Constitutions, School Finance Litigation, and the "Third Wave": From Equity to Adequacy*, 68 Temple L. Rev. 1151, 1163 (1995). *See* Paul L. Tractenberg, *Using the Law to Advance the Public Interest: Rutgers Law School and Me*, 51 Rutgers L. Rev. 1001, 1011–12 (Rutgers Law Review Symposium 1999); Susan H. Bitensky, *Theoretical Foundations for a Constitutional Right to Education Under the U.S. Constitution: A Beginning to the End of a National Education Crisis*, 86 Nw. U. L. REV. 550 (1992); Molly McUsic, *The Use of Education Clauses in School Finance Reform Litigation*, 28 HARV. J. ON LEGIS. 307 (1991); James S. Liebman, *Three Strategies for Implementing Brown Anew, in* RACE IN AMERICA: THE STRUGGLE FOR EQUALITY 112, 120–21 (Herbert Hill & James E. Jones, Jr. eds., 1993).

C.   CLASS AND INEQUALITY—HISTORICAL PERSPECTIVES

● INCOME INEQUALITY

Economic Development in Indian Country: Will Capitalism or Socialism Succeed?
80 OREG. L. REV. 757 (2001).

■ ROBERT J. MILLER

* * * European settlers and early Americans misunderstood tribal economies and property rights. Even today, there seems to be an almost universal misunderstanding that American Indian cultures had and still have little or no appreciation or understanding of private property ownership and private, free market, capitalist economic activities. This mistaken idea could not be further from the truth. It appears to be based almost exclusively on the idea that most American Indian tribes did not consider that land could be privately owned but instead thought that tribal lands were communally owned. Thus, the European and American colonists came to believe that Indians did not believe in or understand private property and capitalist principles.

In contrast, as in all societies, Indians and their governing bodies had to provide for the daily needs of their families and their tribes. Hence, Indians were continuously involved in the production of food, tools, clothing, shelter and all sorts of objects for personal use. Indians also regularly traded goods with other peoples from near and far both for survival and to make life as comfortable as possible. The majority, if not all, of this trade was conducted in free market situations where private individuals voluntarily came together to buy and sell items they had manufactured for sale and which they exchanged by barter and sometimes even sold for money. Startlingly, perhaps, it appears that the only way in which Indian principles of economics and private property differed from the European/American concepts was in the conflicting views these societies had on the private ownership of land. The actual purpose for the European and American settlers to discount or intentionally to ignore how Indians viewed and used private property may have been to provide justification for stealing Indian property rights with a clear conscience. * * *

From its inception, the United States copied the long-standing English political and economic policies towards tribes. The economic goal of the English government had been to make Indians dependent on English goods by integrating them into the colonial marketplace. Politically, England wanted to keep the peace with tribes by preventing the colonists and traders from provoking the tribes to warfare through the colonists' uncontrolled trade and land grabs. Thus, England and the American colonial governments established regulations and bonding and licensing schemes to control who traded with Indians and how the trade was conducted. * * *

* * * Government trading houses were operated at twenty-eight locations all across the frontier from 1795–1822. This process assisted in making Indians dependent on the federal government as they bought their supplies at the federal stores, and it also contributed to shutting the door to free trade and free markets in Indian country.

The federal control of free trade and economic activities in Indian country inhibited the operation of a free capitalist market and most economic development in Indian country. In essence, Congress preempted the American free market and became "a surrogate for Indian decision making in . . . economic relations with the settlers." The federal executive branch also participated in this isolation of Indian country from the American capitalist economy. Most treaties with tribes required that the tribe limit their previous trading habits or only trade with the United

States government. Many tribes later realized that they were suffering from an absence of access to trade and they negotiated in subsequent treaties to take steps to increase trade and to gain better access to goods.

One result of the Trade and Intercourse Era policy, intentional or not, was to start the process of shutting Indians, tribes, and their lands and resources out of the American capitalist economy and free trade market. Congress caused this result by refusing to allow any use of tribal assets, such as for leasing land for grazing or farming, or for mineral or timber development, by imposing strict limits on traders interacting with Indians, and by creating the federal trading houses which dominated the early American trade with Indians. The policy had the concrete impact of cutting Indian and tribal assets out of the American economy. Indians were thus severely limited if not totally prevented from participating in the American capitalist economy to whatever extent they might have wished to partici-pate. Consequently, Indians have lived in governmentally controlled, quasi-socialist economies since 1790.

* * *

For decades preceding the 1880s, liberal thinkers, politicians, "Friends of the Indians," and Christian reformers had been closely examining federal Indian policy. The predominant idea on how to deal with tribes was to civilize and christianize individual Indians and liberate them from the control and communal living of tribal life. This policy was designed to bring Indians into the American "melting pot" by assimilating them into main-stream society. This era in federal Indian policy also had the explicit goals of breaking up tribal ownership of land, ending tribal existence, and, most importantly, opening reservation lands to non-Indian settlement. In fact, the desire of non-Indians to own reservation lands and to open tribal lands and assets to the American economy may have been the prime motivation behind the allotment policy.

The allotment aspect of the policy was designed to break up the communally owned tribal lands into individual plots, or allotments, to be owned by individual Indians and operated as farms. The General Allotment Act and the tribal-specific allotment acts that followed during 1890–1910, generally provided for the division or allotment of reservations into 160 or 80 acre plots to be given to individual tribal members who could later become U.S. citizens. To protect economically unsophisticated Indians, the United States retained legal ownership of these allotments by holding the land in trust for twenty-five year periods during which the land was inalienable and not taxable by the states. The idea was that Indians over time would become astute in business affairs and farming and could eventually handle their own business matters. Significantly, reservation land not allotted to Indians was considered "surplus" and was sold for non-Indian settlement. Most tribes did not have sufficient populations to allot their entire reservation to just tribal members. Hence, the United States sold the surplus lands to non-Indians and today many reservations have much higher non-Indian than Indian populations.

In the 1890s, Congress also began opening reservation assets to the American economy, which had been closed by the Trade and Intercourse policy, by allowing the development of minerals and timber in Indian country and the leasing of reservation land to non-Indians for grazing and farming. Congress also utilized Indian lands for other purposes for the U.S. economy, such as for telephone, telegraph, and railroad rights of ways. Indian lands have also often been used for dams and reclamation and irrigation projects that benefitted non-Indians.

An important aspect of the Allotment Era policy did provide for individual Indians to gain private ownership of land free from tribal and federal governmental restraints. It appears, however, to be an exaggeration to state that the policy had the economic goal to make Indians and tribal economies capitalist in nature. Rather than having economic goals, the purpose of allotment was to turn Indians into "civilized" and "christianized" American citizens and small scale farmers based on the model of white Americans. In regard to its effect on the economy in Indian country, the Allotment policy ultimately created long-term problems that have stifled individual Indian and tribal economic activity to this very day.

Subsequent events severely limited any private benefits accruing to Indians from the allotment and ownership of ex-tribal lands. Many Indians quickly sold or lost their allotments to tax foreclosures once they received alienable patents or deeds to their land. Thus, the lands are no longer in Indian ownership to help Indians or tribal governments with economic development. Another problem, which was not foreseen, is the "fractionalization" of ownership of the individual allotments that remain in Indian ownership, which occurred because the original allottees died and their property passed intestate to ever larger numbers of heirs. Many individual allotments on reservations today have hundreds of Indian owners. This has led to a serious lack of coordinated ownership and decision making over allotments and a nightmare of record keeping and legal work to manage and utilize these lands for tribal and federal governments. In this situation, many Indians today have severe problems putting together and operating viably sized pieces of real property to make economic endeavors feasible. It is often easier for Indians passively to lease these properties than to gain consensus on projects or to consolidate enough land to develop a business or project involving allotments on reservation. * * *

The Indian Reorganization Era of Federal Indian policy ran from the early 1930s to about 1945 and was marked by passage of the Indian Reorganization Act (IRA) in 1934. Under the IRA, the United States completely reversed its allotment policy of breaking up reservations and attempting to destroy tribal governments and instead decided to support tribal governments. By the 1930s, it had become obvious that allotment of tribal lands and the attempt to assimilate Indians had led to disaster. A two-year study of Indian country showed that reservation Indians were living in far worse economic and social conditions after four decades of allotment and assimilation than they had been in 1887. Consequently, among many other goals, the IRA ended the federal policy of allotting tribal lands to individuals and placed a freeze on the sale or loss of any remaining trust allotments still held by individual Indians.

The federal government now actively encouraged and assisted tribes to organize governments and adopt constitutions and bylaws. The IRA also had a very explicit goal to increase economic activity and development in Indian country. The IRA attempted to accomplish this goal by providing for the formation of federally chartered tribal corporations to engage in economic development and business. This provision is very significant to the modern day predominant role of tribal governments in reservation economies.

The IRA allowed tribes to apply to the Secretary of the Interior for federal charters to create tribal corporations through which they could operate businesses, hire attorneys, enter contracts, and engage in litigation. The official policy of the IRA was to encourage tribal business and economic development to be undertaken by tribal governments and tribal institutions even if it worked to exclude individual Indians from the economic activity. The tribal corporations formed under section 17 of the IRA were granted the power to manage their own property, to buy and sell and manage any property, and "such further powers as may be incidental to the conduct of corporate business. . . ." Tribal corporations could also borrow money from a ten million dollar revolving loan fund authorized by Congress for tribal economic development purposes. The loan fund was created primarily to serve tribal economic enterprises although tribes could transfer loans to tribal members. The IRA arguably had a significant socialistic impact on the economic life on reservations because the federal and tribal efforts and concentration on economic development became focused on the tribal government as the entity to start and operate reservation businesses, even to the exclusion of individuals.

For this very reason, when the IRA was proposed it encountered virulent opposition by groups claiming that it promoted socialism and communism. The various opponents of the IRA thought, among other things, that assimilation of Indians should continue, that Indians were inhibited in their liberty and citizenship rights by being subject to tribal governmental control, and that reservation lands and assets should continue to be available to the American market. The charges of communism and socialism that were used to fight and later to reverse the IRA might have only been a form of "red-scare" politics in the 1930s. However, many different groups and persons described the IRA and the alleged intention to keep Indian people segregated from white society and living in a communal, tribal society as being the start of communism and socialism in America. Even Congresspersons opposed the Act and worked to amend and repeal it because of concerns about socialism.

Notwithstanding any "red scare" claims of socialism, and the serious doubts about the IRA in the 1930s, it is certain that the IRA established strong tribal governments in Indian country that today have pervasive control over the economic life and economies of reservations. Modern day observers contend that the IRA imposed tribal governments, tribally controlled economies, and artificial economies on Indian country. In fact, the IRA had such an all encompassing tribal business orientation that many of the tribal governmental entities that were formed under the IRA are today officially called the tribal business committee or tribal business council. This is no surprise since the IRA encouraged tribes "to organize along the lines of modern business corporations" and demanded that economic development proceed with a "tribal approach." Tribal governments and their role in operating tribal businesses have become so intertwined that even the federal government and others have often confused and failed to distinguish between the activities and identity of the tribal governments formed under IRA section 16 and the tribal corporations formed under IRA section 17. Commentators agree that the IRA has led to tribal governments starting and operating businesses, something they are ill-equipped to do.

The economic aspects of the IRA have led to problems for tribes and individual Indians with regard to economic development in Indian country. The primary problem beyond leading tribal governments to becoming the main economic force on reservations is that the IRA also helped create pervasive federal bureaucratic control over Indian economic activity. For example, while tribes could now hire their own attorneys, the "choice of counsel and fixing of fees [was] subject to the approval of the Secretary of the Interior." Furthermore, federal control of tribal economic activity had already been greatly increased in 1871 when Congress enacted a statute that required the Secretary of the Interior to approve all contracts tribes might sign "relative to their lands." The 1871 act and the IRA's creation of new tribal governments and businesses led to extensive federal agency oversight and direction of tribal governments in their political and business decisions. The federal control and direction of tribes became overwhelming in the IRA Era and for decades afterwards. It is universally accepted, however, that federal bureaucratic review and approval authority over tribal economic activities is a death knell to effective and efficient business decision making, yet this is the situation tribal economic development found itself in during the IRA Era and thereafter. It is no surprise, then, that tribal economies did not develop well under the IRA and the subsequent federal control over tribal decisions, assets and resources. Tribal and federal management of reservation economies and direct control over most of the reservation jobs and economic activity since the IRA Era has not created economic success. Indeed, the IRA has almost prevented the success on reservations of individual entrepreneurship and free market capitalism and instead has created governmentally controlled economies that do not function very well.

Black Wealth/White Wealth: New Perspectives on Racial Inequality

■ MELVIN L. OLIVER & THOMAS M. SHAPIRO 12–13, 13–16, 16–18 (1995).

Disparities in wealth between blacks and whites are not the product of haphazard events, inborn traits, isolated incidents or solely contemporary individual accomplishments. Rather, wealth inequality has been structured over many generations through the same systemic barriers that have hampered blacks throughout their history in American society: slavery, Jim Crow, so-called de jure discrimination, and institutionalized racism. How these factors have affected the ability of blacks to accumulate wealth, however, has often been ignored or incompletely sketched. * * *

The close of the Civil War transformed four million former slaves from chattel to freedmen. Emerging from a legacy of two and a half centuries of legalized oppression, the new freedmen entered Southern society with little or no material assets. With the north's military victory over the South freshly on the minds of Republican legislators and white abolitionists, there were rumblings in the air of how the former plantations and the property of Confederate soldiers and sympathizers would be confiscated and divided among the new freedmen to form the basis of their new status in society. The slave's often-cited demand of "forty acres and a mule" fueled great anticipation of a new beginning based on land ownership and a transfer of skills developed under slavery into the new economy of the South. Whereas slave muscle and skills had cleared the wilderness and made the land productive and profitable for plantation owners, the new vision saw the freedmen's hard work and skill generating income and resources for the former slaves themselves. W.E.B. DuBois, in his *Black Reconstruction in America*, called this prospect America's chance to be a modern democracy.

Initially it appeared that massive land redistribution from the Confederates to the freedmen would indeed become a reality. Optimism greeted Sherman's March through the South, and especially his Order 15, which confiscated plantations and redistributed them to black soldiers. Such wartime actions were eventually rescinded and some soldiers who had already started to cultivate the land and build new lives were forced to give up their claims. Real access to land for the freedman had to await the passage of the Southern Homestead Act in 1866, which provided a legal basis and mechanism to promote black landownership. In this legislation public land already designated in the 1862 Homestead Act, which applied only to non-Confederate whites but not blacks, was now opened up to settlement by former slaves in the tradition of homesteading that had helped settle the West. The amount of land involved was substantial, a total of forty-six million acres. Applicants in the first two years of the Homestead Act were limited to only eighty acres, but subsequently this amount increased to 160 acres. The Freedmen's Bureau administered the program, and there was every reason to believe that in reasonable time slaves would be transformed from farm laborers to yeomanry farmers.

This social and economic transformation never occurred. The Southern Homestead Act failed to make newly freed blacks into a landowning class or to provide what Gunnar Myrdal in *An American Dilemma* called "a basis of real democracy in the United States." Indeed, features of the legislation worked against its use as a tool to empower blacks in their quest for land.

First, instead of disqualifying former Confederate supporters as the previous act had done, the 1866 legislation allowed all persons who applied for land to swear that they had not taken up arms against the Union or given aid and comfort to the enemies. This opened the door to massive white applications for land. One estimate suggests that over three-quarters (77.1 percent) of the land applicants under the act were white. In addition, much of the land was poor swampland and it was difficult for black or white applicants to meet the necessary homesteading requirements because they could not make a decent living off the land. What is more important, blacks had to face the extra burden of racial prejudice and discrimination along with the charging of illegal fees, expressly discriminatory court challenges and court decisions, and land speculators. While these barriers faced all poor and illiterate applicants, Michael Lanza has stated in his *Agrarianism and Reconstruction Politics* that "The freedmen's badge of color and previous servitude complicated matters to almost incomprehensible proportions."

Gunnar Myrdal's *An American Dilemma* provides the most cogent explanation of the unfulfilled promise of land to the freeman in an anecdotal passage from a white Southerner. Asked, "Wouldn't it have been better for the white man and the Negro" if the land had been provided? The old man remarked emphatically:

> "No, for it would have made the Negro 'uppity.' " ... and "the real reason ... why it wouldn't do, is that we are having a hard time now keeping the nigger in his place, and if he were a landowner, he'd think he was a bigger man than old Grant, and there would be no living with him in the Black District.... Who'd work the land if the niggers had farms of their own?"

Nevertheless, the extent of black landowning was remarkable given the economically deprived backgrounds from which the slaves emerged. * * *

The suburbanization of America was principally financed and encouraged by actions of the federal government, which supported suburban growth from the 1930s through the 1960s by way of taxation, transportation, and housing policy. Taxation policy, for example, provided greater tax savings for businesses relocating to the suburbs than to those who stayed and made capital improvements to plants in central city locations. As a consequence, employment opportunities steadily rose in the suburban rings of the nation's major metropolitan areas. In addition, transportation policy encouraged freeway construction and subsidized cheap fuel and mass-produced automobiles. These factors made living on the outer edges of cities both affordable and relatively convenient. However, the most important government policies encouraging and subsidizing suburbanization focused on housing. In particular, the incentives that government programs gave for the acquisition of single-family detached housing spurred both the development and financing of the tract home, which became the hallmark of suburban living. While these governmental policies collectively enabled over thirty-five million families between 1933 and 1978 to participate in homeowner equity accumulation, they also had the adverse effect of constraining black Americans' residential opportunities to central-city ghettos of major U.S. metropolitan communities and denying them access to one of the most successful generators of wealth in American history—the suburban tract home.

This story begins with the government's initial entry into home financing. Faced with mounting foreclosures, President Roosevelt urged passage of a bill that authorized the Home Owners Loan Corporation (HOLC). According to Kenneth Jackson's *Crabgrass Frontier*, the HOLC "refinanced tens of thousands of mortgages in danger of default or foreclosure." Of more importance to this story, however, it also introduced standardized appraisals of the fitness of particular properties and communities for both individual and group loans. In creating "a formal and uniform system of appraisal, reduced to writing, structured in defined procedures, and implemented by individuals only after intensive training, government appraisals institutionalized in a rational and bureaucratic framework a racially discriminatory practice that all but eliminated black access to the suburbs and to government mortgage money." Charged with the task of determining the "useful or productive life of housing" they considered to finance, government agents methodically included in their procedures the evaluation of the racial composition or potential racial composition of the community. Communities that were changing racially or were already black were deemed undesirable and placed in the lowest category. The categories, assigned various colors on a map ranging from green for the most desirable, which included new, all-white housing that was always in demand, to red, which included already racially mixed or all-black, old, and undesirable areas, subsequently were used by Federal Housing Authority (FHA) loan officers who made loans on the basis of these designations.

Established in 1934, the FHA aimed to bolster the economy and increase employment by aiding the ailing construction industry. The FHA ushered in the modern mortgage system that enabled people to buy homes on small down payments and at reasonable interest rates, with lengthy repayment periods and full loan amortization. The FHA's success was remarkable: housing starts jumped from 332,000 in 1936 to 619,000 in 1941. The incentive for home ownership increased to the point where it became, in some cases, cheaper to buy a home than to rent one. As one former resident of New York City who moved to suburban New Jersey pointed out, "We had been paying $50 per month rent, and here we come up and live for $29.00 a month." This included taxes, principal, insurance, and interest.

This growth in access to housing was confined, however, for the most part to suburban areas. The administrative dictates outlined in the original act, while containing no antiurban bias, functioned in practice to the neglect of central cities. Three reasons can be cited: first, a bias toward the financing of single-family detached homes over multifamily projects favored open areas outside of the central city that had yet to be developed over congested central-city areas; second, a bias toward new purchases over repair of existing homes prompted people to move out of the city rather than upgrade or improve their existing residences; and third, the continued use of the "unbiased professional estimate" that made older homes and communities in which blacks or undesirables were located less likely to receive approval for loans encouraged purchases in communities where race was not an issue.

While the FHA used as its model the HOLC's appraisal system, it provided more precise guidance to its appraisers in its *Underwriting Manual*. The most basic sentiment underlying the FHA's concern was its fear that property values would decline if a rigid black and white segregation was not maintained. The *Underwriting Manual* openly stated that "if a neighborhood is to retain stability, it is necessary that properties shall continue to be occupied by the same social and racial classes" and further recommended that "subdivision regulations and suitable restrictive covenants are the best way to ensure such neighborhood stability. The FHA's recommended use of restrictive covenants continued until 1949, when, responding to the Supreme Court's outlawing of such covenants in 1948 (*Shelley v. Kraemer*), it announced that 'as of February 15, 1950, it would not insure mortgages on real estate subject to covenants.' "

Even after this date, however, the FHA's discriminatory practices continued to have an impact on the continuing suburbanization of the white population and the deepening ghettoization of the black population. While exact figures regarding the FHA's discrimination against blacks are not available, data by county show a clear pattern of "redlining" in central-city counties and abundant loan activity in suburban counties.

The FHA's actions have had a lasting impact on the wealth portfolios of black Americans. Locked out of the greatest mass-based opportunity for wealth accumulation in American history, African Americans who desired and were able to afford home ownership found themselves consigned to central-city communities where their investments were affected by the "self-fulfilling prophecies" of the FHA appraisers: cut off from sources of new investment their homes and communities deteriorated and lost value in comparison to those homes and communities that FHA appraisers deemed desirable. One infamous housing development of the period—Levittown—provides a classic illustration of the way blacks missed out on this asset-accumulating opportunity. Levittown was built on a mass scale, and housing there was eminently affordable, thanks to the FHA's and VHA's accessible financing, yet as late as 1960 "not a single one of the Long Island Levittown's 82,000 residents was black."

Race, Gender & Work: A Multicultural Economic History of Women in the United States
(1991).

■ TERESA AMOTT & JULIE MATTHEI

Chapter 4—The Soul of the *Tierra Madre*: Chicano Women

Much of the complex economic history of the Chicana/o people centers on struggles over land and national boundaries. The earliest ancestors of today's Chicanas were members of many different Indian nations who inhabited the lands now known as Mexico and the U.S. Southwest, including the Aztec, Pueblo, and Tlaxcalán. Beginning in the sixteenth century, these indigenous peoples were conquered by Spanish invaders. Sexual relations, many of them forced, between Spanish men and indigenous (and African slave) women soon produced a *mestiza/o* population. Through colonization and settlement, the Spanish extended their territories north. The vast country of Mexico was formed after independence from Spain in 1821, stretching from what we know today as Guatemala up through Texas, California, Arizona, Colorado, New Mexico, and Nevada, and even into parts of Oregon, Utah, and Idaho.

In the early nineteenth century, Anglo settlers from the deep South migrated to Texas, sowing the seeds for a war between Mexico and the United States that eventually led to the annexation of almost half of Mexico's territories in 1848. From then up until the present, Mexican citizens have migrated to the United States in search of work, and many have become U.S. citizens. * * *

As a result of this history, the economics and politics of the U.S. Chicana population are inextricably linked to those of Mexico. * * *

* * * [In Mexico, t]he period between 1834 and 1846 has been called the "Golden Age of the ranchos" because land became increasingly concentrated in the hands of a few wealthy ranchers, all of them of Spanish ancestry (or claiming to be). Next in the class hierarchy were *mestiza/o* small ranchers and farmers. Following them were *mestiza/o* artisans, skilled workers, laborers, and seasonal workers in the cattle industry. Lowest of all were the Indians, the chief source of manual labor.

The new country quickly became engaged in a bitter struggle with Anglo settlers in what we know now as Texas, culminating in the Mexican–American War of 1846. Anglo settlers began arriving in Mexico's northern territories in the early 1800s, granted land first by the Spanish government and later by Mexico, which encouraged migration to the sparsely settled area. Most anglo settlers came to farm or raise cattle, but starting in 1829, an increasing number brought slaves from the deep South to work cotton plantations. Although there were some landed Mexicans in Texas, by the 1830s, Anglo Texans outnumbered Mexicans by five to one. To discourage slavery and stem further Anglo immigration, Mexico prohibited importation of slaves in 1830. In 1835, Anglo Texans, chafing under these restrictions, began the Texas Revolt to free themselves from Mexican rule. After losses at the Alamo and Goliad, they defeated Mexican forces in 1837 and set up the Lone Star Republic. In 1845, Texas became part of the United States. One researcher documented the transfer of land ownership from Mexicans to Anglos in Nueces County, Texas in the 1800s: "at the beginning of the Texas Revolt in 1835 every foot of land in Nueces County was held under

Mexican land grants, two years prior to the Civil War all but one had passed out of Mexican hands, and by 1883 none was held by Mexicans."

* * * The [Mexican–American] war ended with the Treaty of Guadalupe Hidalgo in 1848, in which Mexico was forced to give up more than half her territory—including California, New Mexico, Utah, Nevada, Colorado, and Arizona—in exchange for $15 million. In the annexation, the United States acquired lands populated by over 80,000 Spanish-speaking people, most of them *mestiza/o* and *criolla/o*. The quarter of a million Indian peoples in these lands now faced U.S. rather than Mexican efforts to subordinate or exterminate them.

While the language of the Treaty contained protections for Mexican land titles and water rights, the United States government made no attempt to safeguard these rights. Thus the annexation of Mexican territories placed annexed Mexicans in a vulnerable position. As Anglo settlers flooded into the Southwest, they took over the lands and wealth of the Mexican inhabitants, reducing most of the Mexican population in the Southwest to a landless, politically disempowered group.

Some of the *ricos* were able to protect their landholdings by intermarrying with Anglo newcomers. In San Antonio, for instance, marriage records between 1837 and 1860 show that one daughter from almost every *rico* family had married an Anglo. Such marriages were attractive to Anglo men since daughters as well as sons inherited property in Mexican families.

But many other Mexicans, particularly those with smaller landholdings or subsistence plots, lost their lands through a variety of devices familiar to us from the history of American Indians. Anglo domination of the political and judicial systems, along with the use of force and violence, ensured Anglo economic domination. For instance, when floods, drought, or economic downturns made it difficult for Mexican ranchers to pay taxes imposed by the Anglo-controlled government, their lands were quickly sold to Anglos. California passed a law in 1851 that encouraged squatters to take over Mexican lands. Lynching was also a common tool employed by Anglos to terrorize Mexicans into leaving their lands. Some estimate that more Mexicans were lynched between 1850 and 1930 than African Americans during the same period.

* * *

During the second half of the nineteenth century, the southwestern economy expanded rapidly. Subsistence farming began to give way to huge ranches and cash crops as railroads made it possible for southwestern products to reach eastern markets. Displaced Mexicans found jobs as seasonal agricultural workers, domestic workers, or miners in isolated, company-controlled towns.

* * *

Chapter 7—Climbing Gold Mountain: Asian American Women

From 1840 through World War II, Asian immigrants—first Chinese, then Japanese, and finally Filipinas/os—were recruited as a low-wage second-class labor force by employers in the western United States and Hawaii. The U.S. legal system denied Asian immigrants the legal rights which had been accorded their European counterparts, relying on the 1790 naturalization law that restricted the privilege of citizenship to free white persons. When the law was revised after the Civil War to make African Americans eligible for citizenship, the phrase "persons of African descent" was added, and the law continued to bar Asian immigrants from naturalizing. Unable to become citizens, Asian immigrants remained permanent "aliens" (non-citizens), and whites were able to pass numerous laws which restricted their rights simply by referring to their alien status. For example, in the early twentieth century California passed laws which prevented Asian immigrants from purchasing land. However, children of immigrant Asians were allowed to become citizens and escape these restrictions if they were born in the United States.

On the West Coast, where the vast majority of Asians lived, whites bolstered their own relative economic status at the expense of Asian immigrants. White employers achieved higher profits by using Asians as low-wage replacements for white workers and as strikebreakers. White workers resented the threat Asians appeared to pose to wages and unionizing efforts. Self-employed whites felt threatened by Asian successes in small business.

To defend their economic positions, whites formed broad-based movements to restrict Asian immigration and even to send migrants back to Asia. Filipino historian Paul Valdez wrote of the anti-"Oriental" movement of the 1920s, "They used to pass out leaflets saying that the Japanese were taking the lands from the Americans, the Chinese were taking the businesses, and the Filipinos were taking the women." Under these pressures, white-controlled federal and state governments passed close to 50 laws specifically aimed at restricting and subordinating Asian immigrants between 1850 and 1950. These sentiments culminated in laws excluding further immigration. Chinese immigration was cut off in 1882 and 1892; Japanese in 1907–08 and 1924; Indian in 1917; and Filipina/o in 1934.

Whites also discriminated against second-generation Asians who, unlike white ethnics, could not disguise their ethnicity by speaking English and adopting European American ways. These barriers to upward mobility in the labor market compelled many Asian Americans to seek advancement through self-employment in family-based businesses—for the Chinese, laundries and restaurants; for the Japanese, truck farming; and for the Koreans, grocery stores.

D. Wealth, Class and Economic Mobility—The Intergenerational Effects

In what follows, three writers: two influential Princeton economists, Alan B. Krueger and Paul Krugman, as well as conservative *New York Times* columnist, David Brooks, explore the emerging problem of decreasing economic mobility and pinched opportunity structures arising from inherited economic status across all socio-economic groups. This research and argument poses a direct challenge to that part of our national story that depends on belief in the power of individual effort, merit, and achievement. If parent-child wealth correlations are as strong as these economists argue, it reveals a largely hidden force that will preserve economic inequality for a long time. This force could be described as the new "invisible hand," shaping markets and posing a threat to the democratic distribution of political power.

The Sticky Ladder

N.Y. TIMES, Jan. 25, 2005, at A19.

■ DAVID BROOKS

In his Inaugural Address President Bush embraced the grandest theme of American foreign policy—the advance of freedom around the world. Now that attention is turning to the State of the Union address, it would be nice if he would devote himself as passionately to the grandest theme of domestic policy—social mobility.

The United States is a country based on the idea that a person's birth does not determine his or her destiny. Our favorite stories involve immigrants climbing from obscurity to success. Our amazing work ethic is predicated on the assumption that enterprise and effort lead to ascent. "I hold the value of life is to improve one's condition," Lincoln declared.

The problem is that in every generation conditions emerge that threaten to close down opportunity and retard social mobility. Each generation has to reopen the pathways to success.

Today, for example, we may still believe American society is uniquely dynamic, but we're deceiving ourselves. European societies, which seem more class driven and less open, have just as much social mobility as the United States does.

And there are some indications that it is becoming harder and harder for people to climb the ladder of success. *The Economist* magazine gathered much of the recent research on social mobility in America. The magazine concluded that the meritocracy is faltering: "Would-be Horatio Algers are finding it no easier to climb from rags to riches, while the children of the privileged have a greater chance of staying at the top of the social heap."

Economists and sociologists do not all agree, but it does seem there is at least slightly less movement across income quintiles than there was a few decades ago. Sons' income levels correlate more closely to those of their fathers. The income levels of brothers also correlate more closely. That suggests that the family you were born into matters more and more to how you will fare in life. That's a problem because we are not supposed to have a hereditary class structure in this country.

But we're developing one. In the information age, education matters more. In an age in which education matters more, family matters more, because as James Coleman established decades ago, family status shapes educational achievement.

At the top end of society we have a mass upper-middle class. This is made up of highly educated people who move into highly educated neighborhoods and raise their kids in good schools with the children of other highly educated parents. These kids develop wonderful skills, get into good colleges (the median family income of a Harvard student is now $150,000), then go out and have their own children, who develop the same sorts of wonderful skills and who repeat the cycle all over again.

In this way these highly educated elites produce a paradox—a hereditary meritocratic class.

It becomes harder for middle-class kids to compete against members of the hypercharged educated class. Indeed, the middle-class areas become more socially isolated from the highly educated areas.

And this is not even to speak of the children who grow up in neighborhoods in which more boys go to jail than college, in which marriage is not the norm before child-rearing, in which homes are often unstable, in which long-range planning is absurd, in which the social skills you need to achieve are not even passed down.

In his State of the Union address, President Bush is no doubt going to talk about his vision of an ownership society. But homeownership or pension ownership is only part of a larger story. The larger story is the one Lincoln defined over a century ago, the idea that this nation should provide an open field and a fair chance so that all can compete in the race of life.

Today that's again under threat, but this time from barriers that are different than the ones defined by socialists in the industrial age. Now, the upper class doesn't so much oppress the lower class. It just outperforms it generation after generation. Now the crucial inequality is not only finance capital, it's social capital. Now it is silly to make a distinction between economic policy and social policy.

We can spend all we want on schools. But if families are disrupted, if the social environment is dysfunctional, bigger budgets won't help.

President Bush spoke grandly and about foreign policy last Thursday, borrowing from Lincoln. Lincoln's other great cause was social mobility. That's worth embracing too.

Economic Scene; The Apple Falls Close to the Tree, Even in the Land of Opportunity

N.Y. TIMES, Nov. 14, 2002, at C1.

■ ALAN B. KRUEGER

It seems increasingly apparent that the secret to success is to have a successful parent. Consider some prominent examples: George H. W. Bush and George W. Bush; Bobby Bonds and Barry Bonds; Henry Fonda and Jane Fonda; Estee Lauder and Ronald Lauder; Julio Iglesias and Enrique Iglesias; Sam Walton and Jim, John, S. Robson and Alice Walton.

As more recent and better data have become available, economists have marked up their estimate of the impact of parents' socioeconomic status on their children's likelihood of economic success.

It turns out that the famous line attributed to Andrew Carnegie— "from shirt-sleeves to shirt-sleeves in three generations"—is an understatement. Five or six generations are probably required, on average, to erase the advantages or disadvantages of one's economic origins.

This represents a marked departure from past thinking. In the 1980s, when Gary S. Becker of the University of Chicago pioneered the economic theory of intergenerational transmission of economic status, it was believed that the correlation between a father's and son's income was only around 0.15—less than half the correlation between fathers' and sons' heights.

The early studies suggested that if a father's income was twice the average, his son's expected income would be 15 percent above average, and his grandson's just 2 percent above average. This is fast "regression to the mean," a concept Sir Francis Galton used to describe the progression of offspring toward the average height.

Landmark studies published by Gary Solon of the University of Michigan and David J. Zimmerman of Williams College in The American Economic Review a decade ago, however, led economists to revise substantially upward the estimate of the similarity of fathers' and sons' incomes. They noted that income fluctuated for idiosyncratic reasons from year to year— an employee could lose a job, for example—so estimates that depended on a single year were based on "noisy" data. Also, the samples previously analyzed represented only a narrow slice of the population at different points in individual careers. These factors caused the correlation in annual incomes to understate the correlation in "lifetime" incomes.

Averaging earnings over five years produced a correlation of around 0.40 for fathers' and sons' earnings—the same as the correlation between their heights. If people's incomes were represented by their heights, the similarity in income between generations would resemble the similarity observed in the heights of fathers and sons.

New studies by Bhashkar Mazumder of the Federal Reserve Bank of Chicago suggest that the similarity in income is even greater. Using Social Security records, he averaged fathers' earnings over 16 years (1970 through 1985) and sons' earnings over four years (1995 through 1998), and found that around 65 percent of the earnings advantage of fathers was transmitted to sons. The wider window provides a better reflection of lifetime earnings.

Also, the samples previously analyzed represented only a narrow slice of the population at different points in individual careers. These factors caused the correlation in annual incomes to understate the correlation in "lifetime" incomes.

The relationship between fathers' and daughters' earnings was just as strong.

So that grandson (or granddaughter) mentioned previously could expect to earn 42 percent more than average. After five generations, the earnings advantage would still be 12 percent.

Furthermore, the degree of persistence across generations is strong for both rich and poor. Thomas Hertz of American University finds that a child born in the bottom 10 percent of families ranked by income has a 31 percent chance of ending up there as an adult and a 51 percent chance of ending up in the bottom 20 percent, while one born in the top 10 percent has a 30 percent chance of staying there and a 43 percent chance of being in the top 20 percent.

In another study, David I. Levine of Berkeley and Dr. Mazumder found that the impact of parental income on adult sons' income increased from 1980 to the early 1990s.

Why is there such a strong connection between parents' socioeconomic status and their children's? A large part of the answer involves intergenerational transmission of cognitive ability and educational level.

But these factors can "explain at most three-fifths of the intergenerational transmission of economic status," Samuel Bowles and Herbert Gintis of the University of Massachusetts wrote in the latest issue of The Journal of Economic Perspectives. They suggest that the intergenerational transmission of race, geographical location, height, beauty, health status and personality also plays a significant role.

Arthur S. Goldberger of the University of Wisconsin has long questioned whether knowledge of the "heritability" of income is of much use. Even if the father-son correlation is high because traits that affect earning power are inherited, well-designed interventions could still be cost effective and improve the lot of the disadvantaged.

To take an extreme example, the correlation in incomes between fathers and sons was high in South Africa under apartheid because race is an inherited trait. The abolition of apartheid reduced the correlation. The organization of society matters.

Perhaps the only legitimate use of the intergenerational correlation in income is to characterize economic mobility. The data challenge the notion that the United States is an exceptionally mobile society. If the United States stands out in comparison with other countries, it is in having a more static distribution of income across generations with fewer opportunities for advancement.

Anders Bjorklund of Stockholm University and Markus Jantti of the University of Tampere in Finland, for example, find more economic mobility in Sweden than in the United States. Only South Africa and Britain have as little mobility across generations as the United States.

Luke Skywalker and Darth Vader are an unusual father-son pair; in most families, the apple does not fall so far from the tree.

————

The Sons Also Rise
N.Y. TIMES, Nov. 22, 2002, at A27.

■ PAUL KRUGMAN

America, we all know, is the land of opportunity. Your success in life depends on your ability and drive, not on who your father was.

Just ask the Bush brothers. Talk to Elizabeth Cheney, who holds a specially created State Department job, or her husband, chief counsel of the Office of Management and Budget. Interview Eugene Scalia, the top lawyer at the Labor Department, and Janet Rehnquist, inspector general at the Department of Health and Human Services. And don't forget to check in with William Kristol, editor of The Weekly Standard, and the conservative commentator John Podhoretz.

What's interesting is how little comment, let alone criticism, this roll call has occasioned. It might be just another case of kid-gloves treatment by the media, but I think it's a symptom of a broader phenomenon: inherited status is making a comeback.

It has always been good to have a rich or powerful father. Last week my Princeton colleague Alan Krueger wrote a column for The Times surveying statistical studies that debunk the mythology of American social mobility. "If the United States stands out in comparison with other countries, he wrote, 'it is in having a more static distribution of income across generations with fewer opportunities for advancement.' " And Kevin Phillips, in his book "Wealth and Democracy," shows that robber-baron fortunes have been far more persistent than legend would have it.

But the past is only prologue. According to one study cited by Mr. Krueger, the heritability of status has been increasing in recent decades. And that's just the beginning. Underlying economic, social and political trends will give the children of today's wealthy a huge advantage over those who chose the wrong parents.

For one thing, there's more privilege to pass on. Thirty years ago the C.E.O. of a major company was a bureaucrat—well paid, but not truly wealthy. He couldn't give either his position or a large fortune to his heirs. Today's imperial C.E.O.'s, by contrast, will leave vast estates behind—and they are often able to give their children lucrative jobs, too. More broadly, the spectacular increase in American inequality has made the gap between the rich and the middle class wider, and hence more difficult to cross, than it was in the past.

Meanwhile, one key doorway to upward mobility—a good education system, available to all—has been closing. More and more, ambitious parents feel that a public school education is a dead end. It's telling that Jack Grubman, the former Salomon Smith Barney analyst, apparently sold his soul not for personal wealth but for two places in the right nursery school. Alas, most American souls aren't worth enough to get the kids into the 92nd Street Y.

Also, the heritability of status will be mightily reinforced by the repeal of the estate tax—a prime example of the odd way in which public policy and public opinion have shifted in favor of measures that benefit the wealthy, even as our society becomes increasingly class-ridden.

It wasn't always thus. The influential dynasties of the 20th century, like the Kennedys, the Rockefellers and, yes, the Sulzbergers, faced a public suspicious of inherited position; they overcame that suspicion by demonstrating a strong sense of noblesse oblige, justifying their existence by standing for high principles. Indeed, the Kennedy legend has a whiff of Bonnie Prince Charlie about it; the rightful heirs were also perceived as defenders of the downtrodden against the powerful.

But today's heirs feel no need to demonstrate concern for those less fortunate. On the contrary, they are often avid defenders of the powerful against the downtrodden. Mr. Scalia's principal personal claim to fame is his crusade against regulations that protect workers from ergonomic hazards, while Ms. Rehnquist has attracted controversy because of her efforts to weaken the punishment of health-care companies found to have committed fraud.

The official ideology of America's elite remains one of meritocracy, just as our political leadership pretends to be populist. But that won't last. Soon enough, our society will rediscover the importance of good breeding, and the vulgarity of talented upstarts.

 For years, opinion leaders have told us that it's all about family values. And it is—but it will take a while before most people realize that they meant the value of coming from the right family.

TABLE 2.1. "Like Parent, Like Child—Recent Studies Find That There Is Less Income Mobility from One Generation to Another than Previously Believed."

	Chance of Children Attaining Each Income Level		
Parent's Income	*Top Quintile*	*Middle Quintile*	*Bottom Quintile*
Top 20%	42.3%	16.5%	6.3%
Middle 20%	15.3%	25.0%	17.3%
Bottom 20%	7.3%	18.4%	37.3%

SOURCE: *Thomas Hertz, American University.*

For Richer

N.Y. TIMES, Oct. 20, 2002, § 6 (magazine), at 62.

■ PAUL KRUGMAN

I.   THE DISAPPEARING MIDDLE

When I was a teenager growing up on Long Island, one of my favorite excursions was a trip to see the great Gilded Age mansions of the North

Shore. Those mansions weren't just pieces of architectural history. They were monuments to a bygone social era, one in which the rich could afford the armies of servants needed to maintain a house the size of a European palace. By the time I saw them, of course, that era was long past. Almost none of the Long Island mansions were still private residences. Those that hadn't been turned into museums were occupied by nursing homes or private schools.

For the America I grew up in—the America of the 1950's and 1960's—was a middle-class society, both in reality and in feel. The vast income and wealth inequalities of the Gilded Age had disappeared. Yes, of course, there was the poverty of the underclass—but the conventional wisdom of the time viewed that as a social rather than an economic problem. Yes, of course, some wealthy businessmen and heirs to large fortunes lived far better than the average American. But they weren't rich the way the robber barons who built the mansions had been rich, and there weren't that many of them. The days when plutocrats were a force to be reckoned with in American society, economically or politically, seemed long past.

Daily experience confirmed the sense of a fairly equal society. The economic disparities you were conscious of were quite muted. Highly educated professionals—middle managers, college teachers, even lawyers—often claimed that they earned less than unionized blue-collar workers. Those considered very well off lived in split-levels, had a housecleaner come in once a week and took summer vacations in Europe. But they sent their kids to public schools and drove themselves to work, just like everyone else.

But that was long ago. The middle-class America of my youth was another country.

We are now living in a new Gilded Age, as extravagant as the original. Mansions have made a comeback. Back in 1999 this magazine profiled Thierry Despont, the "eminence of excess," an architect who specializes in designing houses for the superrich. His creations typically range from 20,000 to 60,000 square feet; houses at the upper end of his range are not much smaller than the White House. Needless to say, the armies of servants are back, too. So are the yachts. Still, even J.P. Morgan didn't have a Gulfstream.

As the story about Despont suggests, it's not fair to say that the fact of widening inequality in America has gone unreported. Yet glimpses of the lifestyles of the rich and tasteless don't necessarily add up in people's minds to a clear picture of the tectonic shifts that have taken place in the distribution of income and wealth in this country. My sense is that few people are aware of just how much the gap between the very rich and the rest has widened over a relatively short period of time. In fact, even bringing up the subject exposes you to charges of "class warfare," the "politics of envy" and so on. And very few people indeed are willing to talk about the profound effects—economic, social and political—of that widening gap.

Yet you can't understand what's happening in America today without understanding the extent, causes and consequences of the vast increase in inequality that has taken place over the last three decades, and in particular the astonishing concentration of income and wealth in just a few hands. To make sense of the current wave of corporate scandal, you need to understand how the man in the gray flannel suit has been replaced by the imperial C.E.O. The concentration of income at the top is a key reason that the United States, for all its economic achievements, has more poverty and lower life expectancy than any other major advanced nation. Above all, the growing concentration of wealth has reshaped our political system: it is at the root both of a general shift to the right and of an extreme polarization of our politics.

But before we get to all that, let's take a look at who gets what.

II.   THE NEW GILDED AGE

The Securities and Exchange Commission hath no fury like a woman scorned. The messy divorce proceedings of Jack Welch, the legendary former C.E.O. of General Electric, have had one unintended benefit: they have given us a peek at the perks of the corporate elite, which are normally hidden from public view. For it turns out that when Welch retired, he was granted for life the use of a Manhattan apartment (including food, wine and laundry), access to corporate jets and a variety of other in-kind benefits, worth at least $2 million a year. The perks were revealing: they illustrated the extent to which corporate leaders now expect to be treated like *ancien régime* royalty. In monetary terms, however, the perks must have meant little to Welch. In 2000, his last full year running G.E., Welch was paid $123 million, mainly in stock and stock options.

Is it news that C.E.O.'s of large American corporations make a lot of money? Actually, it is. They were always well paid compared with the average worker, but there is simply no comparison between what executives got a generation ago and what they are paid today.

Over the past 30 years most people have seen only modest salary increases: the average annual salary in America, expressed in 1998 dollars (that is, adjusted for inflation), rose from $32,522 in 1970 to $35,864 in 1999. That's about a 10 percent increase over 29 years—progress, but not much. Over the same period, however, according to Fortune magazine, the average real annual compensation of the top 100 C.E.O.'s went from $1.3 million—39 times the pay of an average worker—to $37.5 million, more than 1,000 times the pay of ordinary workers.

The explosion in C.E.O. pay over the past 30 years is an amazing story in its own right, and an important one. But it is only the most spectacular indicator of a broader story, the reconcentration of income and wealth in the U.S. The rich have always been different from you and me, but they are far more different now than they were not long ago—indeed, they are as different now as they were when F. Scott Fitzgerald made his famous remark.

That's a controversial statement, though it shouldn't be. For at least the past 15 years it has been hard to deny the evidence for growing inequality in the United States. Census data clearly show a rising share of income going to the top 20 percent of families, and within that top 20 percent to the top 5 percent, with a declining share going to families in the middle. Nonetheless, denial of that evidence is a sizable, well-financed industry. Conservative think tanks have produced scores of studies that try to discredit the data, the methodology and, not least, the motives of those who report the obvious. Studies that appear to refute claims of increasing inequality receive prominent endorsements on editorial pages and are eagerly cited by right-leaning government officials. Four years ago Alan Greenspan (why did anyone ever think that he was nonpartisan?) gave a keynote speech at the Federal Reserve's annual Jackson Hole conference that amounted to an attempt to deny that there has been any real increase in inequality in America.

* * * Meanwhile, politically motivated smoke screens aside, the reality of increasing inequality is not in doubt. In fact, the census data understate the case, because for technical reasons those data tend to undercount very high incomes—for example, it's unlikely that they reflect the explosion in C.E.O. compensation. And other evidence makes it clear not only that inequality is increasing but that the action gets bigger the closer you get to the top. That is, it's not simply that the top 20 percent of families have had bigger percentage gains than families near the middle: the top 5 percent have done better than the next 15, the top 1 percent better than the next 4, and so on up to Bill Gates.

Studies that try to do a better job of tracking high incomes have found startling results. For example, a recent study by the nonpartisan Congressional Budget Office used income tax data and other sources to improve on the census estimates. The C.B.O. study found that between 1979 and 1997, the after-tax incomes of the top 1 percent of families rose 157 percent, compared with only a 10 percent gain for families near the middle of the income distribution. Even more startling results come from a new study by Thomas Piketty, at the French research institute Cepremap, and Emmanuel Saez, who is now at the University of California at Berkeley. Using income tax data, Piketty and Saez have produced estimates of the incomes of the well-to-do, the rich and the very rich back to 1913.

The first point you learn from these new estimates is that the middle-class America of my youth is best thought of not as the normal state of our society, but as an interregnum between Gilded Ages. America before 1930 was a society in which a small number of very rich people controlled a large share of the nation's wealth. We became a middle-class society only after the concentration of income at the top dropped sharply during the New Deal, and especially during World War II. The economic historians Claudia Goldin and Robert Margo have dubbed the narrowing of income gaps during those years the Great Compression. Incomes then stayed fairly equally distributed until the 1970's: the rapid rise in incomes during the first postwar generation was very evenly spread across the population.

Since the 1970's, however, income gaps have been rapidly widening. Piketty and Saez confirm what I suspected: by most measures we are, in fact, back to the days of "The Great Gatsby." After 30 years in which the income shares of the top 10 percent of taxpayers, the top 1 percent and so on were far below their levels in the 1920's, all are very nearly back where they were.

And the big winners are the very, very rich. One ploy often used to play down growing inequality is to rely on rather coarse statistical break-downs—dividing the population into five "quintiles," each containing 20 percent of families, or at most 10 "deciles." * * * For example, a conservative commentator might concede, grudgingly, that there has been some increase in the share of national income going to the top 10 percent of taxpayers, but then point out that anyone with an income over $81,000 is in that top 10 percent. So we're just talking about shifts within the middle class, right?

Wrong: the top 10 percent contains a lot of people whom we would still consider middle class, but they weren't the big winners. Most of the gains in the share of the top 10 percent of taxpayers over the past 30 years were actually gains to the top 1 percent, rather than the next 9 percent. In 1998 the top 1 percent started at $230,000. In turn, 60 percent of the gains of that top 1 percent went to the top 0.1 percent, those with incomes of more than $790,000. And almost half of those gains went to a mere 13,000 taxpayers, the top 0.01 percent, who had an income of at least $3.6 million and an average income of $17 million.

A stickler for detail might point out that the Piketty–Saez estimates end in 1998 and that the C.B.O. numbers end a year earlier. Have the trends shown in the data reversed? Almost surely not. In fact, all indications are that the explosion of incomes at the top continued through 2000. Since then the plunge in stock prices must have put some crimp in high incomes—but census data show inequality continuing to increase in 2001, mainly because of the severe effects of the recession on the working poor and near poor. When the recession ends, we can be sure that we will find ourselves a society in which income inequality is even higher than it was in the late 90's.

So claims that we've entered a second Gilded Age aren't exaggerated. In America's middle-class era, the mansion-building, yacht-owning classes had pretty much disappeared. According to Piketty and Saez, in 1970 the top 0.01 percent of taxpayers had 0.7 percent of total income—that is, they earned "only" 70 times as much as the average, not enough to buy or maintain a mega-residence. But in 1998 the top 0.01 percent received more than 3 percent of all income. That meant that the 13,000 richest families in America had almost as much income as the 20 million poorest households; those 13,000 families had incomes 300 times that of average families.

And let me repeat: this transformation has happened very quickly, and it is still going on. * * *

III.   UNDOING THE NEW DEAL

In the middle of the 1980's, as economists became aware that something important was happening to the distribution of income in America, they formulated three main hypotheses about its causes.

The "globalization" hypothesis tied America's changing income distribution to the growth of world trade, and especially the growing imports of manufactured goods from the third world. Its basic message was that blue-collar workers—the sort of people who in my youth often made as much money as college-educated middle managers—were losing ground in the face of competition from low-wage workers in Asia. A result was stagnation or decline in the wages of ordinary people, with a growing share of national income going to the highly educated.

A second hypothesis, 'skill-biased technological change,' situated the cause of growing inequality not in foreign trade but in domestic innovation. The torrid pace of progress in information technology, so the story went, had increased the demand for the highly skilled and educated. And so the income distribution increasingly favored brains rather than brawn.

Finally, the "superstar" hypothesis—named by the Chicago economist Sherwin Rosen—offered a variant on the technological story. It argued that modern technologies of communication often turn competition into a tournament in which the winner is richly rewarded, while the runners-up get far less. The classic example—which gives the theory its name—is the entertainment business. As Rosen pointed out, in bygone days there were hundreds of comedians making a modest living at live shows in the borscht belt and other places. Now they are mostly gone; what is left is a handful of superstar TV comedians.

The debates among these hypotheses—particularly the debate between those who attributed growing inequality to globalization and those who attributed it to technology—were many and bitter. I was a participant in those debates myself. But I won't dwell on them, because in the last few years there has been a growing sense among economists that none of these hypotheses work.

* * *

The Great Compression—the substantial reduction in inequality during the New Deal and the Second World War—also seems hard to understand in terms of the usual theories. During World War II Franklin Roosevelt used government control over wages to compress wage gaps. But if the middle-class society that emerged from the war was an artificial creation, why did it persist for another 30 years?

Some—by no means all—economists trying to understand growing inequality have begun to take seriously a hypothesis that would have been considered irredeemably fuzzy-minded not long ago. This view stresses the role of social norms in setting limits to inequality. According to this view, the New Deal had a more profound impact on American society than even its most ardent admirers have suggested: it imposed norms of relative equality in pay that persisted for more than 30 years, creating the broadly middle-class society we came to take for granted. But those norms began to unravel in the 1970's and have done so at an accelerating pace.

Exhibit A for this view is the story of executive compensation. In the 1960's, America's great corporations behaved more like socialist republics than like cutthroat capitalist enterprises, and top executives behaved more like public-spirited bureaucrats than like captains of industry. I'm not exaggerating. Consider the description of executive behavior offered by John Kenneth Galbraith in his 1967 book, "The New Industrial State": "Management does not go out ruthlessly to reward itself—a sound management is expected to exercise restraint." Managerial self-dealing was a thing of the past: "With the power of decision goes opportunity for making money.... Were everyone to seek to do so ... the corporation would be a chaos of competitive avarice. But these are not the sort of thing that a good company man does; a remarkably effective code bans such behavior. Group decision-making insures, moreover, that almost everyone's actions and even thoughts are known to others. This acts to enforce the code and, more than incidentally, a high standard of personal honesty as well."

Thirty-five years on, a cover article in Fortune is titled "You Bought. They Sold." "All over corporate America," reads the blurb, "top execs were cashing in stocks even as their companies were tanking. Who was left holding the bag? You." As I said, we've become a different country.

Let's leave actual malfeasance on one side for a moment, and ask how the relatively modest salaries of top executives 30 years ago became the gigantic pay packages of today. * * * The key reason executives are paid so much now is that they appoint the members of the corporate board that determines their compensation and control many of the perks that board members count on. So it's not the invisible hand of the market that leads to those monumental executive incomes; it's the invisible handshake in the boardroom.

* * * That is, the explosion of executive pay represents a social change rather than the purely economic forces of supply and demand. We should think of it not as a market trend like the rising value of waterfront property, but as something more like the sexual revolution of the 1960's—a relaxation of old strictures, a new permissiveness, but in this case the permissiveness is financial rather than sexual. * * *

How did this change in corporate culture happen? Economists and management theorists are only beginning to explore that question, but it's easy to suggest a few factors. One was the changing structure of financial markets. In his new book, "Searching for a Corporate Savior," Rakesh Khurana of Harvard Business School suggests that during the 1980's and 1990's, "managerial capitalism"—the world of the man in the gray flannel suit—was replaced by "investor capitalism." Institutional investors weren't willing to let a C.E.O. choose his own successor from inside the corporation; they wanted heroic leaders, often outsiders, and were willing to pay immense sums to get them. The subtitle of Khurana's book, by the way, is "The Irrational Quest for Charismatic C.E.O.'s"

* * *

(4)

Economists also did their bit to legitimize previously unthinkable levels of executive pay. During the 1980's and 1990's a torrent of academic papers—popularized in business magazines and incorporated into consultants' recommendations—argued that Gordon Gekko was right: greed is good; greed works. In order to get the best performance out of executives, these papers argued, it was necessary to align their interests with those of stockholders. And the way to do that was with large grants of stock or stock options.

* * *

What economists like Piketty and Saez are now suggesting is that the story of executive compensation is representative of a broader story. Much more than economists and free-market advocates like to imagine, wages—particularly at the top—are determined by social norms. What happened during the 1930's and 1940's was that new norms of equality were established, largely through the political process. What happened in the 1980's and 1990's was that those norms unraveled, replaced by an ethos of "anything goes." And a result was an explosion of income at the top of the scale.

IV. THE PRICE OF INEQUALITY

It was one of those revealing moments. Responding to an e-mail message from a Canadian viewer, Robert Novak of "Crossfire" delivered a little speech: "Marg, like most Canadians, you're ill informed and wrong. The U.S. has the longest standard of living—longest life expectancy of any country in the world, including Canada. That's the truth."

But it was Novak who had his facts wrong. Canadians can expect to live about two years longer than Americans. In fact, life expectancy in the U.S. is well below that in Canada, Japan and every major nation in Western Europe. On average, we can expect lives a bit shorter than those of Greeks, a bit longer than those of Portuguese. Male life expectancy is lower in the U.S. than it is in Costa Rica.

Still, you can understand why Novak assumed that we were No. 1. After all, we really are the richest major nation, with real G.D.P. per capita about 20 percent higher than Canada's. And it has been an article of faith in this country that a rising tide lifts all boats. Doesn't our high and rising national wealth translate into a high standard of living—including good medical care for all Americans?

Well, no. Although America has higher per capita income than other advanced countries, it turns out that that's mainly because our rich are much richer. And here's a radical thought: if the rich get more, that leaves less for everyone else.

That statement—which is simply a matter of arithmetic—is guaranteed to bring accusations of "class warfare." If the accuser gets more specific, he'll probably offer two reasons that it's foolish to make a fuss over the high incomes of a few people at the top of the income distribution. First, he'll tell you that what the elite get may look like a lot of money, but it's still a small share of the total—that is, when all is said and done the rich aren't getting that big a piece of the pie. Second, he'll tell you that trying to do anything to reduce incomes at the top will hurt, not help, people further down the distribution, because attempts to redistribute income damage incentives.

These arguments for lack of concern are plausible. And they were entirely correct, once upon a time—namely, back when we had a middle-class society. But there's a lot less truth to them now.

First, the share of the rich in total income is no longer trivial. These days 1 percent of families receive about 16 percent of total pretax income, and have about 14 percent of after-tax income. That share has roughly doubled over the past 30 years, and is now about as large as the share of the bottom 40 percent of the population. That's a big shift of income to the top; as a matter of pure arithmetic, it must mean that the incomes of less well off families grew considerably more slowly than average income. And they did. Adjusting for inflation, average family income—total income divided by the number of families—grew 28 percent from 1979 to 1997. But median family income—the income of a family in the middle of the distribution, a better indicator of how typical American families are doing—grew only 10 percent. And the incomes of the bottom fifth of families actually fell slightly.

Let me belabor this point for a bit. We pride ourselves, with considerable justification, on our record of economic growth. But over the last few decades it's remarkable how little of that growth has trickled down to ordinary families. Median family income has risen only about 0.5 percent per year—and as far as we can tell from somewhat unreliable data, just about all of that increase was due to wives working longer hours, with little or no gain in real wages. * * *

Still, many people will say that while the U.S. economic system may generate a lot of inequality, it also generates much higher incomes than any alternative, so that everyone is better off. That was the moral Business Week tried to convey in its recent special issue with "25 Ideas for a Changing World." One of those ideas was "the rich get richer, and that's O.K." High incomes at the top, the conventional wisdom declares, are the result of a free-market system that provides huge incentives for performance. And the system delivers that performance, which means that wealth at the top doesn't come at the expense of the rest of us.

A skeptic might point out that the explosion in executive compensation seems at best loosely related to actual performance. Jack Welch was one of the 10 highest-paid executives in the United States in 2000, and you could argue that he earned it. But did Dennis Kozlowski of Tyco, or Gerald Levin of Time Warner, who were also in the top 10? A skeptic might also point out that even during the economic boom of the late 1990's, U.S. productivity growth was no better than it was during the great postwar expansion, which corresponds to the era when America was truly middle class and C.E.O.'s were modestly paid technocrats.

* * *

Many Americans assume that because we are the richest country in the world, with real G.D.P. per capita higher than that of other major advanced countries, Americans must be better off across the board—that it's not just our rich who are richer than their counterparts abroad, but that the typical American family is much better off than the typical family elsewhere, and that even our poor are well off by foreign standards.

But it's not true. Let me use the example of Sweden, that great conservative bete noire.

A few months ago the conservative cyberpundit Glenn Reynolds made a splash when he pointed out that Sweden's G.D.P. per capita is roughly comparable with that of Mississippi—see, those foolish believers in the welfare state have impoverished themselves! Presumably he assumed that this means that the typical Swede is as poor as the typical resident of Mississippi, and therefore much worse off than the typical American.

But life expectancy in Sweden is about three years higher than that of the U.S. Infant mortality is half the U.S. level, and less than a third the rate in Mississippi. Functional illiteracy is much less common than in the U.S.

How is this possible? One answer is that G.D.P. per capita is in some ways a misleading measure. Swedes take longer vacations than Americans, so they work fewer hours per year. That's a choice, not a failure of economic performance. Real G.D.P. per hour worked is 16 percent lower than in the United States, which makes Swedish productivity about the same as Canada's.

But the main point is that though Sweden may have lower average income than the United States, that's mainly because our rich are so much richer. The median Swedish family has a standard of living roughly comparable with that of the median U.S. family: wages are if anything higher in Sweden, and a higher tax burden is offset by public provision of health care and generally better public services. And as you move further down the income distribution, Swedish living standards are way ahead of those in the U.S. Swedish families with children that are at the 10th percentile—poorer than 90 percent of the population—have incomes 60 percent higher than their U.S. counterparts. And very few people in Sweden experience the deep poverty that is all too common in the United States. One measure: in 1994 only 6 percent of Swedes lived on less than $11 per day, compared with 14 percent in the U.S.

The moral of this comparison is that even if you think that America's high levels of inequality are the price of our high level of national income, it's not at all clear that this price is worth paying. The reason conservatives engage in bouts of Sweden-bashing is that they want to convince us that there is no tradeoff between economic efficiency and equity—that if you try to take from the rich and give to the poor, you actually make everyone worse off. But the comparison between the U.S. and other advanced countries doesn't support this conclusion at all. * * *

And we might even offer a challenge from the other side: inequality in the United States has arguably reached levels where it is counterproductive. That is, you can make a case that our society would be richer if its richest members didn't get quite so much.

I could make this argument on historical grounds. The most impressive economic growth in U.S. history coincided with the middle-class interregnum, the post-World War II generation, when incomes were most evenly distributed. But let's focus on a specific case, the extraordinary pay packages of today's top executives. Are these good for the economy?

* * *

It's easy to get boggled by the details of corporate scandal—insider loans, stock options, special-purpose entities, mark-to-market, round-tripping. But there's a simple reason that the details are so complicated. All of these schemes were designed to benefit corporate insiders—to inflate the pay of the C.E.O. and his inner circle. That is, they were all about the "chaos of competitive avarice" that, according to John Kenneth Galbraith, had been ruled out in the corporation of the 1960's. But while all restraint has vanished within the American corporation, the outside world—including stockholders—is still prudish, and open looting by executives is still not acceptable. So the looting has to be camouflaged, taking place through complicated schemes that can be rationalized to outsiders as clever corporate strategies.

Economists who study crime tell us that crime is inefficient—that is, the costs of crime to the economy are much larger than the amount stolen. Crime, and the fear of crime, divert resources away from productive uses: criminals spend their time stealing rather than producing, and potential victims spend time and money trying to protect their property. Also, the things people do to avoid becoming victims—like avoiding dangerous districts—have a cost even if they succeed in averting an actual crime.

The same holds true of corporate malfeasance, whether or not it actually involves breaking the law. Executives who devote their time to creating innovative ways to divert shareholder money into their own pockets probably aren't running the real business very well (think Enron, WorldCom, Tyco, Global Crossing, Adelphia ...). Investments chosen because they create the illusion of profitability while insiders cash in their stock options are a waste of scarce resources. And if the supply of funds from lenders and shareholders dries up because of a lack of trust, the economy as a whole suffers. Just ask Indonesia.

* * *

VI.   PLUTOCRACY?

* * *

America in the 1920's wasn't a feudal society. But it was a nation in which vast privilege—often inherited privilege—stood in contrast to vast misery. It was also a nation in which the government, more often than not, served the interests of the privileged and ignored the aspirations of ordinary people.

Those days are past—or are they? Income inequality in America has now returned to the levels of the 1920's. Inherited wealth doesn't yet play a big part in our society, but given time—and the repeal of the estate tax—we will grow ourselves a hereditary elite just as set apart from the concerns of ordinary Americans as old Horace Havemeyer. And the new elite, like the old, will have enormous political power.

Kevin Phillips concludes his book *Wealth and Democracy* with a grim warning: "Either democracy must be renewed, with politics brought back to life, or wealth is likely to cement a new and less democratic regime—plutocracy by some other name." It's a pretty extreme line, but we live in extreme times. Even if the forms of democracy remain, they may become meaningless. It's all too easy to see how we may become a country in which the big rewards are reserved for people with the right connections; in which ordinary people see little hope of advancement; in which political involvement seems pointless, because in the end the interests of the elite always get served.

Am I being too pessimistic? Even my liberal friends tell me not to worry, that our system has great resilience, that the center will hold. I hope they're right, but they may be looking in the rearview mirror. Our optimism about America, our belief that in the end our nation always finds its way, comes from the past—a past in which we were a middle-class society. But that was another country.

————

NOTES AND QUESTIONS

1.   Other factors influencing income inequality. Besides intergenerational economic position, what are other factors that could explain income inequality in America?

2.   Intergenerational economic mobility: racial implications. The above-cited study by Charles and Hurst portrays the strong correlation between individuals' parents' incomes and their own economic futures. Are such findings consistent for all demographic groups? In other words, are members of one ethnic or racial group more likely to break free of their parents' economic status than members of another demographic group?

American University professor of economics Tom Hertz encountered this question in a study of economic mobility. Using data compiled from the Panel Study of Income Dynamics, consisting of a sample of 6,723 black and white families observed over thirty two years and in two generations, Hertz found that African Americans are more likely to remain in lower income brackets than their white counterparts. The study revealed that blacks' rate of persistence at low-income levels was 42 percent, while their rate of persistence at high income levels was only 4 percent. On the other hand, for whites, the rate of persistence at the bottom was approximately half that at the top (17 percent versus 30 percent). Adjusted for age, the study revealed blacks' persistence to remain in a lower income bracket was 41 percent, while whites' persistence to remain at the bottom was 25 percent. Also, for white families, extreme upward mobility is more likely than downward mobility (14 percent versus 9 percent), but the reverse is true for blacks—blacks have a 35 percent chance of substantially sliding down the income scale, and only have a 4 percent chance of substantially moving up the scale. These findings all point to the conclusion that black families have a significantly lower rate of upward mobility from the bottom income bracket than do whites. Tom Hertz, *Rags, Riches and Race: The Intergenerational Mobility of Black and White Families in the United States*, under review for inclusion in: UNEQUAL CHANCES: FAMILY BACKGROUND AND ECONOMIC SUCCESS (Samuel Bowles, et al. eds., forthcoming).

What are the reasons for income differences among demographic groups?

———

● WEALTH INEQUALITY

Wealth and Inequality in America

BLACK WEALTH/WHITE WEALTH: A NEW PERSPECTIVE ON RACIAL INEQUALITY 53–90 (1997).

■ MELVIN L. OLIVER & THOMAS M. SHAPIRO

[A] thorough analysis of economic well-being and social and racial equality must include a wealth dimension. A lack of systematic, reliable data on wealth accumulation, however, partly explains the general absence of such an analysis until now. * * *

The bulk of our analysis and discussion of wealth is drawn from the Survey of Income and Program Participation. SIPP is a sample of the U.S. population that interviews adults in households periodically over a two-and-a-half-year period. A new panel is introduced every year. Data for this study came from the 1987 Panel. Household interviews began in June 1987, and the same households were reinterviewed every four months through 1989. The full data set of eight interviews was available for 11,257 households. * * *

What is wealth? How does one define it? What indicators of wealth are the best ones to use? Definitional and conceptual questions about wealth have produced a diverse and sometimes confusing set of approaches to the topic. Indeed, a major difficulty in analyzing wealth is that people define it in different ways with the result that wealth measures lack comparability. After working with the literature for several years, we decided to measure wealth by way of two concepts. The first, *net worth* (NW) conveys the straightforward value of all assets less any debts. The second, *net financial assets* (NFA), excludes equity accrued in a home or vehicle from the calculation of a household's available resources.

Net worth gives a comprehensive picture of all assets and debts; yet it may not be a reliable measure of *command over future resources* for one's self and family. Net worth includes equity in vehicles, for instance, and it is not likely that this equity will be converted into other resources, such as prep school for a family's children. Thus one's car is not a likely repository in which to store resources for future use. Likewise, viewing home equity as a reasonable and unambiguous source of future resources for the current generation raises many vexing problems. Most people do not sell their homes to finance a college education for their children, start a business, make other investments, buy medical care, support political candidates, or pay lobbyists to protect their special interests. Even if a family sells a home, the proceeds are typically used to lease or buy replacement housing. An exception to the general rule may involve the elderly. Mortgage payments, especially in times of high housing inflation, may be seen as a kind of "forced savings" to be cashed in at retirement or to pass along to one's children.

* * * The specific differences between net worth and net financial assets is that equity in vehicles and homes is excluded from the latter, although debts are subtracted from NFA. In contrast to net worth, net financial assets consists of more readily liquid sources of income and wealth that can be used for a family's immediate well-being. Because the distinction between net worth and net financial assets is somewhat controversial and still open to debate, we usually present both measures. Generally, in our view, however, net financial assets seem to be the best indicator of the current generation's command over future resources, while net worth provides a more accurate estimate of the wealth likely to be inherited by the next generation.

Let us now turn to the substantive questions at the heart of our study. How has wealth been distributed in American society over the twentieth century? What about the redistribution of wealth that took place in the decade of the eighties? And finally, what do the answers to these questions imply for black-white inequality?

The 1980s and Beyond Bigger Shares for the Wealthy

Available information concerning wealth in the twentieth century, until very recently, comes mainly from national estate-tax records for the very wealthy collected between 1922 and 1981, and from sporadic cross-sectional household surveys starting in 1953. Drawing from these data bases, we track trends in the distribution of wealth, paying particular attention to whether inequality is falling, remaining stable, or rising, into the late 1980s and early 1990s.

Estate-tax data show consistently high wealth concentrations through-out the early part of the twentieth century. According to Edward Wolff's "The Rich Get Increasingly Richer," the top 1 percent of American house-holds possessed over 25 percent of total wealth between 1922 and 1972. Beginning in 1972, however, the data indicate a significant decline in wealth inequality. The share of the top percentile declined from 29 percent to 19 percent between 1972 and 1976. While this decline was unexpected, it was not permanent. In fact in the next five-year period, from 1976 to 1981, a sharp renewal of wealth inequality occurred. Between 1976 and 1981 the share of the richest 1 percent expanded from 19 to 24 percent.

The standard theory explaining wealth inequality associates the phe-nomenon with the process of industrialization. Stable, low levels of inequal-ity characterize preindustrial times; the onset of modern economic growth is characterized by rapid industrialization, which ushers in a sharp increase in inequality; and then advanced, mature industrial societies experience a gradual leveling of inequality and finally long-term stability. This explana-tion highlights industrialization as a universal, master trend in the evolu-tion of market economies. The twentieth century in particular is said to represent a clear pattern, specifically from 1929 on, when, according to Jeffrey Williamson's and Peter Lindert's *American Inequality*, wealth imba-lance "seems to have undergone a permanent reduction." One must question the persistence of this reduced inequality into the 1990s, especial-ly in light of growing income inequalities.

Estimates of household wealth inequality from two relatively consis-tent sources of household survey data, the 1962 Survey of Financial Characteristics of Consumers and the Surveys of Consumer Finances conducted in the 1980s, furnish more recent information. Responses to these surveys indicate that wealth inequality remained relatively fixed between 1962 and 1983. The top 3 percent of wealth holders held 32 percent of the wealth in 1962 and 34 percent in 1983. The Gini coefficient, which measures equality over an entire distribution rather than as shares of the top percentile, rose slightly, from 0.73 in 1962 to 0.74 in 1983. The Gini ratio is a statistic that converts levels of inequality into a single number and allows easy comparisons of populations. Gini figures range from 0 to 1. A low ratio indicates low levels of inequality; a high ratio indicates high levels of inequality. Thus Ginis closer to 0 illustrate more distributional equality, while figures closer to 1 indicate more inequality. While the Gini coefficient is a very useful summary measure of inequality, it is probably most helpful and meaningful as a way of comparing distribu-tions of wealth between time periods, given its sensitivity to small changes and its clear indication of the direction of change.

What happened during the 1980s? Quite simply, the very rich in-creased their share of the nation's wealth. One leading economist dubbed the resulting wealth imbalance an "unprecedented jump in inequality to Great Gatsby levels." Notably, inequality had risen very sharply by 1989, with the wealthiest 1 percent of households owning 37.7 percent of net worth. An examination of net financial assets suggests even greater levels of inequality. In 1983 the top 1 percent held 42.8 percent of all financial assets, a figure that increased to 48.2 percent in 1989. The Gini coefficient reflects this increase in inequality, rising 0.04 during the period. Wealth inequality by the end of the 1980s closely approximated historically high levels not seen since 1922.

Our review of other wealth indicators and studies corroborates the finding that wealth is reconcentrating. It also goes a way toward revealing the relationship between trends toward wealth concentration and growing inequality and [a] lower standard of living * * *. The evidence presented by Edward Wolff in "The Rich Get Increasingly Richer" and by others using [Survey of Consumer Finances] data suggests that while the concentration of wealth decreased substantially during the mid–1970s, it increased sharply during the 1980s. In particular the *mean* net worth of families grew by over 7 percent from 1983 to 1989. However, *median* net worth grew much more slowly than mean wealth, at a rate of 0.8 percent. According to Wolff, this discrepancy "implies that the upper-wealth classes enjoyed a disproportionate share [of wealth]" between 1983 and 1989. Wolff's median net financial assets declined 3.7 percent during this period. Thus the typical family disposed of fewer liquid resources in 1989 than in 1983. In stark contrast, the wealth of the "superrich," defined as the top one-half of 1 percent of wealth-holders, increased 26 percent from 1983 to 1989. Over one-half (55 percent) of the wealth created between 1983 and 1989 accrued to the richest one-half of one percent of families, a fact that vividly illustrates the magnitude of the 1980s increase in their share of the country's wealth. Not surprisingly, the Gini coefficient increased sizably during this period, from 0.80 to 0.84. Indeed, U.S. wealth concentration in 1989 was more extreme than at any time since 1929.

SIPP as well as SCF data confirm that the wealth pie is being resliced, and that the wealthy are getting larger pieces of it. In a 1994 update on its ongoing SIPP study, the Census Bureau reports that the median net worth of the nation's households dropped 12 percent between 1988 and 1991. The drop in median wealth is associated with a sharp decline in the middle classes' largest share of net worth: home equity. The median home equity declined by 14 percent between 1988 and 1991 as real estate values fell.

The trends of increasing income and wealth inequality have disrupted long-standing post-World War II patterns. The movement toward income equality and stability expired by the mid–1970s, while the trend toward wealth equality extended into the early 1980s. By 1983 wealth inequality began to rise. The time lag in these reversals is important. Along with declining incomes, a growth in debt burden, and fluctuations in housing values and stock prices, the actions of government—and the Reagan tax cuts of the early 1980s—can only be viewed as prime causes of the increase in wealth inequality.

How has this redistribution of wealth in favor of the rich affected the middle class? Examining wealth groups by ranking all families into wealth fifths provides one way to get at this question. The average holdings of the lower-middle and bottom wealth groups (fifths) declined in real terms by 30 percent. The wealth of the middle group remained unchanged, while that of the upper-middle group increased by slightly less than 1 percent a year. The average wealth of the top group increased by over 10 percent. Combining this with previous information showing a decline in median net financial assets strengthens the argument that the economic base of middle-class life is becoming increasingly fragile and tenuous.

During the 1980s the rich got much richer, and the poor and middle classes fell further behind. One obvious culprit was the Reagan tax cuts. These cuts provided greater discretionary income for middle-and upper-class taxpayers. However, most middle-class taxpayers used this discretionary income to bolster their declining standards of living or decrease their debt burden instead of saving or investing it. Although Reagan strategists had intended to stimulate investment, the upper classes embarked on a frenzy of consumer spending on luxury items. Wolff's "The Rich Get Increasingly Richer" explains the redistribution of wealth in favor of the rich during the 1980s as resulting more from capital gains reaped on existing wealth than from increased savings and investment. He attributes 70 percent of the growth in wealth over the 1983–1989 period to the appreciation of existing financial assets and the remaining 30 percent to the creation of wealth from personal savings. Led by rapid gains in stocks, financial securities, and liquid assets, existing investments grew at an impressive rate at a time when it was difficult to convert earnings into personal savings.

One asset whose value grew dramatically during the eighties was real estate. Home ownership is central to the average American's wealth portfolio. Housing equity makes up the largest part of wealth held by the middle class, whereas the upper class and wealthy more commonly own a greater degree of their wealth in financial assets. The percentage of families owning homes peaked in the mid–1970s at 65 percent and has subsequently declined by a point or two. Forty-three percent of blacks own homes, a rate 65 percent lower than that of whites. Housing equity constitutes the most substantial portion of all wealth assets by far. SIPP results clearly demonstrate this assertion: housing equity represented 43 percent of median household assets in 1988. It is even more significant, however, in the wealth portfolios of blacks than of whites, accounting for 43.3 percent of white wealth and 62.5 percent of black assets. This initial glance at the role of housing in overall wealth carries ramifications for subsequent in-depth analysis. Thus, owning a house—a hallmark of the American Dream—is becoming harder and harder for average Americans to afford, and fewer are able to do so. The ensuing analysis of racial differences in wealth requires a thorough investigation of racial dynamics in access to housing, mortgage and housing markets, and housing values.

The eighties ushered in a new era of wealth inequality in which strong gains were made by those who already had substantial financial assets. Those who had a piece of the rock, especially those with financial assets, but also those with real estate, increased their wealth holdings and consolidated a sense of economic security for themselves and their families.

Others, a disproportionate share of them black, saw their financial status improve only slightly or decline.

In *Warm Hearts and Cold Cash* Marcia Millman notes that for most of this century, the primary legacy of middle-class parents to children has been "cultural" capital, that is, the upbringing, education, and contacts that allowed children to get a good start in life and to become financially successful and independent. Now some parents have more to bestow than cultural capital. In particular, middle-class Americans who started rearing families after World War II have amassed a huge amount of money in the value of their homes and stocks that they are now in the process of dispatching to the baby boom generation through inheritances, loans, and gifts. Millman says this money is "enormously consequential in shaping the lives of their adult children."

Much of this wealth was built by their parents between the late 1940s and the late 1960s when real wages and saving rates were higher and housing costs were considerably lower. For the elderly middle class, the escalation of real estate prices over the last twenty years has been a significant boon. * * *

Access to Assets

The potential for assets to expand or inhibit choices, horizons, and opportunities for children emerged as the most consistent and strongest common theme in our interviews. Since parents want to invest in their children, to give them whatever advantages they can, we wondered about the ability of the average American household to expend assets on their children. This section thus delves deeper into the assets households command by (1) considering the importance of home and vehicle equity in relation to other kinds of assets; (2) inspecting available financial assets for various groups of the population; and (3) looking at children growing up in resource-deficient households. We found a strong relationship between the amount of wealth and the composition of assets. Households with large amounts of total net worth control wealth portfolios composed mostly of financial assets. Financial investments make up about four-fifths of the assets of the richest households. Conversely, home and vehicle equity represents over 70 percent of the asset portfolio among the poorest one-fifth of American households, one in three of which possesses zero or negative financial assets.

Table 4.5 reports households with zero or negative net financial assets for various racial, age, education, and family groups. It shows that one-quarter of white households, 61 percent of black households, and 54 percent of Hispanic households are without financial resources. A similar absence of financial assets affects nearly one-half of young households; circumstances steadily improve with age, however, leaving only 15 percent of those households headed by seniors in a state of resource deficiency. The educational achievement of householders also connects directly with access to resources, as 40 percent of poorly educated household heads control no financial assets while over 80 percent of households headed by a college graduate control some NFA. Findings reported in this table also demonstrate deeply embedded disparities in resource command between single and married-couple parents. Resource deprivation characterizes 62 percent of single-parent households in comparison to 37 percent of married couples raising children.

TABLE 4.5 Who is on the Edge?

	Households with 0 or Negative NFA*	Households without NFA* for 3 months**	Households without NFA* for 6 months**
Sample	31.0%	44.9%	49.9%
Race			
White	25.3	38.1	43.2
Black	60.9	78.9	83.1
Hispanic	54.0	72.5	77.2
Age of Householder			
15–35	48.0	67.0	72.8
36–49	31.7	45.0	50.7
50–64	22.1	32.0	36.2
65 or older	15.1	26.4	30.6
Education			
Less than high school	40.3	55.5	60.0
High school degree	32.2	48.0	63.2
Some college	29.9	45.3	61.4
College degree	18.9	26.8	31.2
Family Type* * *			
Single parent	61.9	79.2	83.2
Married Couple	36.9	53.8	59.9

* Net financial worth
** NFA reserves to survive at the poverty line of $968 per month
*** Includes only households with children

Besides looking at resource deprivation, table 4.5 also sets criteria for "precarious-resource" circumstances. Households without enough NFA reserves to survive three months at the poverty line ($2,904) meet these criteria. Nearly 80 percent of single-parent households fit this description. Likewise 38 percent of white households and 79 percent of black households live in precarious-resource circumstances.

Among our interviewees, parents with ample assets planned to use them to create a better world for their children. Those without them strategized about acquiring some and talked about their "wish list." Parents talked about ballet lessons, camp, trips for cultural enrichment or even to Disney World, staying home more often with the children, affording full-time day care, allowing a parent to be home after day care. The parents discussed using assets to provide better educational opportunities for their children. Kevin takes great pride in paying for his son's college and being able to offer him advanced training. Stacie wants to be able to afford private school for Carrie. Ed and Alicia told us about the private school choices and dilemmas facing their children.

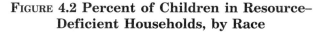

**FIGURE 4.2 Percent of Children in Resource–
Deficient Households, by Race**

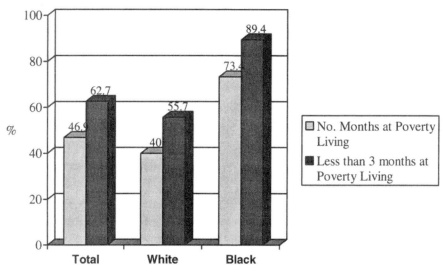

Degree of Resource Deficiency

Figure 4.2 looks at the percentage of children in resource-poor households by race. It provides information both on households with no net financial assets and on those with just enough assets to survive above the poverty line for at least three months. Close to one-half of all children live in households with no financial assets and 63 percent live in households with precarious resources, scarcely enough NFA to cushion three months of interrupted income.

A further analysis of this already disturbing data discloses imposing and powerful racial and ethnic cleavages. For example, 40 percent of all white children grow up in households without financial resources in comparison to 73 percent of all black children. Most telling of all perhaps, only 11 percent of black children grow up in households with enough net financial assets to weather three months of no income at the poverty level. Three times as many white kids live in such households.

According to Richard Steckel and Jayanthi Krishnan, cross-sectional measures of wealth acquisition and inequality may disguise underlying changes in wealth status. Analyzing surveys from 1966 and 1976, Steckel and Krishnan found that changes in marital status were associated with changes in wealth. The largest increase in wealth occurred for single women who later married. Other groups who experienced increases in wealth included households headed by the young, those with at least twelve years of schooling, and individuals who married. The greatest loss in wealth occurred among households headed by older individuals, single men, and those experiencing marital disruption.

SUMMARY

Financial wealth is the buried fault line of the American social system. The wealth distribution portrait drawn in this chapter has disclosed the existence of highly concentrated wealth at the top; a pattern of steep resource inequality; the disproportionate asset reserves held by various demographic groups; the precarious economic foundation of middle-class life; and how few financial assets most American households can call upon. This chapter has also provided documentation concerning the relationship between income inequality and wealth inequality. At one level, income makes up the largest component of potential wealth. At the same time, however, distinctive patterns of income and wealth inequality exist. Put another way, substituting what is known about income inequality for what is not known about wealth inequality limits, and even biases, our understanding of inequality. A thorough understanding of inequality must therefore pay more attention to resources than has been paid in the past.

Perhaps no single piece of information conveys the sense of fragility common to those on the lowest rungs of the economic ladder as the proportion of children who grow up in households without assets. Reducing all life's chances for success to economic circumstances no doubt overlooks much, but resources nonetheless provide an accurate measure of differential access to educational, career, health, cultural, and social opportunities. In poignantly reciting the hopes they have for their children, parents recognize the importance of resources. Our interviews show how parents use assets to bring these hopes to life, or wish they had ample assets so they could bring them to life. Nearly three-quarters of all black children, 1.8 times the rate for whites, grow up in households possessing no financial assets. Nine in ten black children come of age in households that lack sufficient financial reserves to endure three months of no income at the poverty line, about four times the rate for whites.

———

NOTES AND QUESTIONS

1. Some data on poverty rates. During the era of Gunnar Myrdal's classic study of American society, *An American Dilemma*, the majority of African Americans in the United States lived in the South; white supremacy relegated blacks to an inferior socioeconomic status; and social, political, and economic opportunity for African Americans was virtually non-existent. Ronald F. Ferguson, *Shifting Challenges: Fifty Years of Economic Change Toward Black-White Earnings Equality*, in AN AMERICAN DILEMMA REVISITED: RACE RELATIONS IN A CHANGING WORLD 76 (Obie Clayton, Jr. ed., 1996). Though almost sixty years have passed since Myrdal's commentary on the socioeconomic status of African Americans during the period between the Great Depression and World War II, grave economic inequalities continue to plague minorities, maintaining a systematic socioeconomic hierarchy in society. *Id.,* at xxiii.

Sociologists Melvin L. Oliver and Thomas M. Shapiro conclude that several variables account for wealth differences among racial and ethnic communities, including geographic region, educational attainment, the number of workers in the household, marital status, gender, and age.[16] As we have just discussed, intergenerational wealth effects are stronger than was once thought to be the case. For the poor this economic and social immobility creates brutal traps in a world of disadvantage. A study by Thomas Hertz of American University found that a child born to a family in the bottom 10 percent income bracket has a 31 percent chance of remaining in that same caste as an adult and a 51 percent chance of moving into the bottom 20 percent. However, a child born in the top 10 percent has a 30 percent chance of remaining in that income bracket and a 43 percent chance of moving into the top 20 percent.[17]

––––––––

Hidden Cost of Being African American

HIDDEN COST OF BEING AFRICAN AMERICAN 141 (2004).

■ THOMAS M. SHAPIRO

In the 20 largest metropolitan areas, where 36 percent of all African Americans live, segregation pervades basic dimensions of community life. The residential color line means that blacks have greater difficulty overcoming problems associated with poor communities, especially crime, violence, housing abandonment, unstable families, poorer health and higher mortality, environmental degradation, and failing schools. No other group experiences segregation to the extent that blacks do. In many geographical areas, two decades of rising income inequality and budget cuts have produced a concentration of poverty that further compounds problems of segregation. Poor black neighborhoods are crowded, highly concentrated, and isolated far more severely than neighborhoods where poor whites, Latinos, or Asians live.

16. MELVIN L. OLIVER & THOMAS M. SHAPIRO, *Wealth and Inequality, in* BLACK WEALTH/ WHITE WEALTH: A NEW PERSPECTIVE ON RACIAL INEQUALITY 67–90 (1997).

17. Alan B. Krueger, *Economic Scene; The Apple Falls Close to the Tree, Even in the Land of Opportunity,* N.Y. TIMES, Nov. 14, 2002, at C1.

TABLE 2.2.

1984 RESIDENCE	1994 RESIDENCE			
	PREDOMINATELY WHITE AREA	RACIALLY MIXED AREA	PREDOMINATELY BLACK AREA	TOTAL
WHITE FAMILIES				
PREDOMINATELY WHITE AREA	95.6%	4.4%	-	100.0% (456)
RACIALLY MIXED AREA	40.2%	58.8%	1.0%	100.0% (97)
PREDOMINATELY BLACK AREA	-	-	-	100.0%
TOTAL	85.9% (475)	13.9% (77)	0.2% (1)	100.0% (553)
BLACK FAMILIES				
PREDOMINATELY WHITE AREA	66.7%	33.3%	-	100.0% (21)
RACIALLY MIXED AREA	6.5%	79.0%	14.5%	100.0% (214)
PREDOMINATELY BLACK AREA	8.5%	56.4%	66.3%	100.0% (166)
TOTAL	8.5% (34)	56.4% (226)	35.2% (141)	100% (401)

SOURCE: *Id.* at 138.

Sheryll Cashin argues that "housing [is] the last plank in the civil rights revolution ... [s]egregated residential housing contributes to pervasive inequality in this country."[18]

The Price of Segregation—Unconventional Wisdom: New Facts From the Social Sciences

WASH. POST, Dec. 28, 1997, at C5.

■ RICHARD MORIN

THE PRICE OF SEGREGATION

FOR SALE: Three-bedroom, two-bath ranch-style house. Near good schools and good neighbors. Low taxes, low crime. Located in a white neighborhood.

How much would you pay for this house? If you're white, a new study of housing prices suggests that you'll pay, on average, about 13 percent more than if the same house were located in a racially integrated part of town.

That's the premium that whites appear to be willing to pay to live in the typical segregated white neighborhood, say Harvard economists David Cutler, Edward Glaeser and Jacob Vigdor.

And it's this extra cost that's now primarily either responsible for keeping America's neighborhoods predominantly black or white decades after legal segregation officially ended, Cutler argues.

18.   SHERYLL CASHIN, THE FAILURES OF INTEGRATION: HOW RACE AND CLASS ARE UNDERMINING THE AMERICAN DREAM 3 (2004) infra at 484.

To measure just how much whites will pay to live in white neighborhoods, Cutler and his colleagues collected a mountain of data on every neighborhood in three American cities: Cleveland, Atlanta and Sacramento. They selected these cities because they were "representative of the urban experience of the past century." The information they gathered included Census data, neighborhood characteristics and federal reports on housing prices back to 1940, the first year such information was collected.

They found that the whiter the neighborhood, the higher the housing prices. "We can say that the premium that a white pays in a segregated city (such as Cleveland) in 1990 is 18 percent, while the premium that a white pays in a relatively integrated city (such as Sacramento) in 1990 is 12 percent," Glaeser said.

These researchers also said [they] were able to track the shifting patterns of residential segregation, from a system enforced by laws to one sustained by market forces.

Through the 1950s, segregation was enforced by law and the "collective actions taken by whites to exclude blacks from their neighborhoods."

Real estate covenants written into deeds in some neighborhoods barred homeowners from selling or renting to blacks (or Jews or sometimes even unmarried people). When laws and covenants didn't work, Cutler said "whites took bats, broke some windows and threw things at the house to run off black families who dared to move into white neighborhoods, as well as to warn other African–Americans to stay out. You can't do that any more."

Now, Cutler said it's sticker shock that is keeping many African-Americans out.

The Failures of Integration, How Race and Class are Undermining the American Dream

Public Affairs, New York, at 4 (2004).

■ Sheryll Cashin

"Housing—where we live—is fundamental in explaining American separatism. Housing was the last plank in the civil rights revolution, it is the realm in which we have experienced the fewest integration gains. When it comes to integration, housing is also the realm in which Americans most seem to agree that separation is acceptable. We may accept, even desire, integrated workplaces and integrated public spheres. But when it come to our private life space, more visceral personal needs of comfort and security take precedence-especially for families with children. In this context, for many, integration is simply irrelevant or perceived as a threat to more fundamental concerns. . . ."

"How do you decide where to live? Eleven years ago, I bought a lovely bungalow in Shepherd Park, in integrated, albeit a majority-black, upper-middle-class neighborhood in the northwest quadrant of Washington, D.C. My goal at the time was to acquire a house in the best and safest neighborhood I could afford. The race or class of my would-be neighbors was not at the forefront of my thinking. But many communities were beyond consideration. As a committed urbanite and a hater of traffic living outside the Beltway was out of the question. As a black woman with a strong racial identity, I found the overwhelmingly white neighborhoods west of Rock Creek Park, such as Georgetown, American University Park, and Bethesda, inherently unattractive. I was not prepared, even if investment wisdom counseled otherwise, to make the profound personal sacrifice of living totally among 'others' with who I could not identify and who likely could not identify with me. Implicit in my choice about where to live was the understanding that I wanted to be among more than just a smattering of black people. If I had been forced to describe my ideal neighborhood, I suppose I would have said it was an integrated one."

NOTES AND QUESTIONS

1. Note on wealth and income inequalities. Why do parents and children have similar wealth? Availability of economic resources accounts for some of the correlation, but Charles and Hurst conclude spending patterns and comparable portfolio investment decisions between parents and their children have a considerable impact on the relationship between parents' wealth and their offspring's. They argue that when parents make investment choices, they set an example for their children to follow. For example, a mother who owns a company can advise her children on the tools necessary to succeed in running an enterprise and may pass on the company to her children. In addition, a wealthy parent may allow his children to take on investment decisions, such as stock ownership early in life. Kerwin Kofi Charles & Erik Hurst, *The Correlation of Wealth Across Generations* (National Bureau of Economic Research (NBER), Working Paper 9314, Oct. 2002), *at* http://www.nber.org/papers/w9314. *See also* DALTON CONLEY, THE PECKING ORDER: WHICH SIBLINGS SUCCEED AND WHY (2004).

Can Charles and Hurst's conclusion be extended to a large demographic group? For example, is it possible for children to learn about and mimic spending patterns and investment decisions, from not only their parents, but also from members of their own ethnic community? The Federal Reserve Board issued a Survey of Consumer Finances in 1998, reporting that the net wealth of the typical African American household was $15,500 that year; this figure is less than one-quarter that of the net wealth of the typical American household (including blacks)—$71,000. The study also revealed considerable differences in self-reported financial behavior between African American families and all families about investments, spending and income, savings tendencies, and risk aversion. Black households are much more likely than all households to have a shorter fiscal planning perspective, spend more rather than less of their earnings, not save and not save consistently, and be less willing to take monetary risks when saving or investing.

Is it possible for African Americans to persistently remain in the lower wealth brackets because members of the black community share similar ill-advised spending behaviors? Other factors influence the difference in wealth between black families and other families; for example, fewer African American households reported having received an inheritance, and black inheritors reported receiving lower bequests. Stephen Brobeck, Executive Director of the Consumer Federation of America, believes financial education is needed to aid the black community in revamping their financial behavior in order to increase wealth. However, he maintains that financial education should be shaped to meet the cultural needs of the African–American community:

> [F]inancial education needs to recognize important ethnic and cultural differences. Obviously, this education can be most effective if it uses language with which targeted populations are comfortable. But it also may be more effective if the education appeals to unique ethnic identities. For example, a Black American Saves initiative may well have more appeal to African Americans than does a more generalized America Saves initiative. Stephen Brobeck, *Black American Personal Wealth: Current Status* (Consumer Federation of America, Aug. 2002), *at* http://www.americasaves.org/back_page/BlackWealthReport 082902.-doc.

A recent study, "The Lives and Times of the Baby Boomers" by Duke sociology professors Angela M. O'Rand and Mary Elizabeth Hughes, suggests that the children of African American "baby boomers" are not doing as well as their parents. *See* Darryl Fears, *Black Baby Boomers' Income Gap Cited; Study Says That, Economically, Generation Has Not Improved Over Its Parents'*, WASH. POST, Dec. 17, 2004, at A02.

2. Wealth distribution and residential segregation. Though segregation is no longer enforced by explicitly racist laws, residential segregation is still prevalent. Due to the stark differences in wealth among racial groups, richer white families live in more affluent areas, while poorer minorities often live in meager surroundings. Though this proposition logically makes sense, it fails to consider other implications, like the dependency of housing prices on the racial makeup of the neighborhood. Harvard economists David Cutlen, Edward Glaeser, and Jacob Vigdor performed a study in 1997 and found that on average a white individual is willing to pay thirteen percent more for a house not located in a racially integrated part of town. The study intimated that because whites are willing to pay a premium to live in the typical segregated white neighborhood, housing prices are higher in white areas. In turn, residential segregation continues to prevail, standing as a clear reminder that socioeconomic inequalities based on background still exist.

3. College admissions. Educational attainment is one variable that aids in determining an individual's socioeconomic position in American society. For this reason, the prominence of one's college background plays an influential role in developing cultural capital. Parents invest tremendous amounts of time and resources in preparing their children for college by sending them to prestigious secondary schools, hoping their children's academic excellence will ensure them a prosperous lifestyle in the future.

One impressive institution, the Groton School in Massachusetts, sends countless students to prestigious colleges and universities each year. One would assume that remarkable achievement at such a school would ensure successful results in the college admissions process. However, in a society where familial status and networking are significant factors in attaining success, scholastic honors do not always guarantee a ticket to a top university. Several affluent children of universities' alumni and celebrities often have lower academic scores and still have the opportunity to study at the nation's top colleges. These students have what college admissions officers call a "hook"—criteria for preferential treatment. Henry Park, a 1998 graduate of Groton, had no "hook" to get accepted to several leading institutions. Park's parents, middleclass Korean immigrants from New Jersey, went to college in Korea and sacrificed their finances to pay Groton's $33,000 per year tuition and room and board. However, Mr. Park was ranked fourteenth in his class, earned a 1560 on his SAT, and demonstrated mathematical prowess. How do schools like those that rejected Mr. Park—Harvard, Yale, Brown, and Columbia—justify their choices in admitting less qualified students? Some assert that favoring children of alumni and prospective donors helps to ensure the growth of their institutions through the funding of scholarships, faculty salaries, and other projects by alumni parents. They further contend that children of celebrities "enhance an institution's visibility." Daniel Golden, *For Groton Grads, Academics Aren't Only Keys to Ivy Schools*, WALL ST. J., Apr. 25, 2003, at A1.

The college admissions process has serious implications for low-income and minority students. Considering most prestigious universities have relatively few minority alumni and low-income families do not have the means to contribute to colleges, many promising students are excluded from the elite academic realm. Consequently, they will attend less prestigious schools and have trouble attaining prominent occupations in the job market. In turn, these students will fail to pass to their children the capital necessary to succeed and the socioeconomic caste in society will endure through time. Economic distribution will continue to dwindle and wealth inequalities will consistently prevail.

Is it unjust for colleges to use legacy or donation criteria in deciding to offer a student admission? Some deem that the legacy preference unfairly favors wealthy applicants:

> The reason for the legacy preference appears to be primarily economic. Harvard and Yale, along with many other academic institutions, argue that the financial support provided by alumni is critical to their fiscal health. The assumption is that alumni will stop donating to fundraising campaigns if colleges reject their children. If economics were the primary basis for admission, however, why should the wealthiest applicants always not be accepted over all others? The very purpose of a need-blind admissions policy as expounded by both Harvard and Yale

is to admit students regardless of their ability to pay or their financial background. Yet by preferring legacies over other applicants based upon economic reasons, both schools are admitting that the financial resources of an applicant's family do matter. Thus, need-blind admissions are a misnomer, for economic considerations apparently are of great importance in the admissions process. John D. Lamb, *The Real Affirmative Action Babies: Legacy Preferences at Harvard and Yale,* 26 COLUM. J.L. & SOC. PROBS. 491, 517–18 (1993).

Do you agree with Lamb that admissions are not truly need-blind because admissions officers take financial issues into account when evaluating applications?

Are the legacy preferences unconstitutional? Can students like Mr. Park bring an equal protection claim against schools like Harvard and Yale for denying them admission and admitting lesser qualified students whose parents donated a gymnasium to the institution? Though no cases address the legitimacy of a private institution's admissions preference for children of alumni, a North Carolina court upheld a preference for out-of-state legacies at the University of North Carolina at Chapel Hill. There, the plaintiff asserted that she was denied equal protection when the school rejected her while accepting legacies and in-state applicants. Because the plaintiff was not part of a suspect class and no fundamental criteria were involved, the state was only required to show a rational basis for its preferential treatment. The court held that because out-of-state alumni offer considerable financial support for the school, the university's preferential treatment was a rational basis and not unconstitutional. *Rosenstock v. Governors of Univ. of N.C.,* 423 F.Supp. 1321, 1322–27 (M.D.N.C. 1976).

4.   Estate tax. The estate tax, also referred to by opponents as the death tax, is a means of limiting the impact of intergenerational transmission of wealth and redistributing wealth through government spending. Only about 2 percent of deaths result in estate tax liability due to exemptions and other provisions, and the average estate paid taxes of 17 percent. Iris J. Lay & Joel Friedman, *Estate Tax Repeal: A Costly Windfall for the Wealthiest Americans* (Center on Budget and Policy Priorities, rev. Feb. 6, 2001), *available at* http://www.cbpp.org/5-25-00tax.htm.

People in the highest 20 percent of the income distribution at the time of their death pay 99 percent of estate taxes. And 91 percent of decedents had annual incomes over $190,000. *Id.* Opponents to the estate tax claim that farms and small businesses bear the weight of the tax, but these estates in fact make up a small proportion of taxable estates and could be given additional relief without repealing the entire estate tax. *Id.* The complete repeal of the estate tax will cost the government about $60 billion annually; the wealthiest people in the country would receive windfalls, often in the millions of dollars; and income such as unrealized capital gains would never be taxed. *Id.*

Despite the potentially devastating effects, there is bipartisan political support for repealing the estate tax. The Economic Growth and Tax Relief

Reconciliation Act of 2001 phases out the estate tax between 2002 and 2009, but it includes a sunset provision that would reinstate the estate tax in 2011 unless further legislation extends the repeal. Agnes C. Powell, *Hocus-Pocus: The Federal Estate Tax—Now You See It, Now You Don't*, NAT'L BUS. ASS'N MAG. 21 (Oct. 2001).

The repeal of the estate tax would greatly increase the intergenerational transmission of wealth, further restraining economic mobility, and leading to cutbacks of government funded programs. What could prevent further legislation limiting redistribution of wealth? What alternative means of wealth redistribution could close the economic gap between rich and poor, and between black and white?

5. Race and taxes. Thomas and Mary Edsall argue in *Chain Reaction: The Impact of Race, Rights and Taxes on American Politics* that political party voting alignment with regards to tax policy is linked to issues of race. Specifically, they contend that "race has become a powerful wedge, breaking up what had been the majoritarian economic interests of the poor, working, and lower-middle classes in the traditional liberal coalition." THOMAS BYRNE EDSALL & MARY D. EDSALL, CHAIN REACTION: THE IMPACT OF RACE, RIGHTS AND TAXES ON AMERICAN POLITICS 4 (1991). The general polarization between the two parties that has taken place on issues of race has been reflected in the fashioning of a "Republican populism" in which conservative politicians have devised a strategy "to persuade working and lower-middle class voters to join an alliance with business interests and the affluent." *id.* at 13. Central to this strategy has been opposition to programs designed to benefit racial minorities, such as busing and affirmative action, along with a commitment to reduced spending and curtailed government programs, and rejection of welfare and social programs which have been portrayed as benefiting minorities to the detriment of working-class whites. *Id.* at 13–19. The Edsalls detect a new definition of taxes in which they are not understood as resources for the funding of government, but rather as a hand-out from those who work to those who do not, the latter group implicitly being racial minorities. *id.* at 214. *See also*, Woojin Lee & John Roemer, *Racism and Redistribution in the United States: A Solution to the Problem of American Exceptionalism*, Cowles Foundation for Research in Economics, Discussion Paper No. 1462 (2004).

In a progressive tax system, tax burdens rise with incomes. Dana Milbank & Jonathan Weisman, *Middle Class Tax Shares Set to Rise: Studies Say Burden of Rich to Decline*, WASH. POST, June 4, 2003, at A1. Although progressivity is evident in much of the tax system, cuts on dividends, capital gains, and estate taxes lower the burden on the wealthiest Americans, actually increasing the burden on the middle class. *Id.* How will the tax cuts affect economic equality? Will those households identified by Oliver and Shapiro as "on the edge," and therefore least equipped to handle the economic downturn, benefit from the tax cuts? Is a progressive tax system fair, or should the poor and wealthy contribute comparable portions of their income?

6.   Financial behavior. A thriving couple in *Wealth and Inequality in America* credited their financial success to the values instilled in them by their families. Could differences in financial behaviors (such as financial planning horizons, spending compared to income, saving habits, and financial risk taking in investments) explain the wealth disparities between African Americans and other Americans? Stephen Brobeck, *Black American Personal Wealth: Current Status* (Consumer Federation of America, Aug. 2002), *available at* http://www.americasaves.org/back_page/Black-WealthReport082902.doc. According to the Consumer Federation of America, differences in financial behaviors between black Americans and all other Americans "virtually disappear" when comparing similar wealth levels. *Id.* Discrepancies in financial behavior between African Americans and the nation as a whole can be attributed to the concentration of wealth-poor people—45 percent of black Americans compared with 25 percent of all Americans. While education efforts should continue to recognize ethnic and cultural differences, effective financial education should focus on the behavior of the wealth-poor. *Id.*

————

Your Stake in America

41 ARIZ. L. REV. 249 (1999).

■ BRUCE ACKERMAN & ANNE ALSTOTT

America has become a three-class society. More than twenty-five percent of its children now graduate from a four-year college and move into the ranks of the symbol-using class. Their increasing prosperity stands in sharp contrast to the grim picture of life at the bottom. The lowest twenty percent inhabit a world of low wages, dead-end jobs, and high unemployment despite the economic boom.

Then there is the vast majority. Over the past quarter century, they have endured a long period of economic stagnation. Despite optimistic rhetoric from the right, economic growth has bypassed these forgotten Americans. The richest twenty percent has captured virtually all of the growth in the nation's wealth since the early 1980s. While income trends have been somewhat less extreme, family income for the vast middle is only modestly higher than in 1973. Even treading water has been tough. Real wages for men have declined by nearly fifteen percent, and it is only the massive entry by women into the workplace that has taken up the slack.

Trickle-down economics has utterly failed and will continue to fail in the globalizing economy of the future. The past is prologue: By 1995, the top one percent owned 38.5% of the nation's disposable wealth, up from 33.8% in 1983. During the 1990s, the share of total income earned by the top twenty percent has risen to its highest point since 1947.

Our politics has not caught up with this three-class reality. On the one hand, we heap large subsidies on the college-bound. On the other, we target the underclass with diminishing amounts of assistance. However, we have done little to aid the vast middle. While the rich have been showered with tax breaks, the middle has been treated to a series of symbolic gestures signifying nothing. The 1997 "middle-class tax cut" hid a darker agenda. The average family took home a few hundred dollars in new tax credits for children and education, but the rich gained thousands of dollars from the capital gains tax cut and other goodies.

The result is simmering resentment and a ready reception of the protectionist nostrums of Ross Perot and Pat Buchanan. The current boom will hold these economic nationalists in check for a while, but it is past time to search for a more constructive response to economic inequality. How can we use the benefits of globalization to ensure that every American gets a fair start in life?

This is the question we set for ourselves in our new book The Stakeholder Society. Stakeholding seeks justice by rooting it in capitalism's preeminent value: the importance of private property. It points the way to a society that is more democratic, more productive, and more free. Bear with us, and you will see how a single innovation once proposed by Tom Paine can achieve what a thousand lesser policies have failed to accomplish.

The basic proposal is straightforward. As young Americans rise to maturity, they should claim a stake of $80,000 as part of their birthright as citizens. This stake should be financed by an annual wealth tax, equal to two percent of every individual's wealth in excess of $80,000. The tie between wealth-holding and stake-holding expresses a fundamental social responsibility. Every American has an obligation to contribute to a fair starting point for all.

Stakeholders are free. They may use their money for any purpose they see fit: to start a business or pay for higher education, to buy a house or raise a family or save for the future. But they must take responsibility for their choices. Their triumphs and blunders are their own.

At the end of their lives, stakeholders have a special responsibility. Since the $80,000 was central in starting them off in life, it is only fair for them to repay it at death if this is financially possible. The stakeholding fund, in short, will be enriched each year by the ongoing contributions of property-owners, and by a final payback at death.

There are many possible variations on the stakeholding theme, but we have said enough to suggest its broad political appeal. How many young adults start off life with $80,000? How many parents can afford to give their children the head-start that this implies?

Stakeholding liberates college graduates from the burdens of debt, often with something to spare. It offers unprecedented opportunities for the tens of millions who do not go to college and have often been short-changed by their high school educations. For the first time, they will confront the labor market with a certain sense of security. The stake will give them the independence to choose where to live, whether to marry, and how to train for economic opportunity. Some will fail, but fewer than today.

We should, of course, structure the program to maximize the successes. For starters, no stakeholder should be allowed free use of his $80,000 without completing high school and passing a state or national qualifying examination. High-school dropouts would have their stakes held in trust, and would have access only to the annually accruing interest. Since only three-quarters of American teenagers have high school degrees, this single requirement will prevent massive "stakeblowing" by those least capable of handling adult responsibilities. It will also provide a beacon of hope to kids locked in rural poverty or urban ghettos. Stay in school and graduate, and you will not be forgotten. You will get a solid chance to live out the American dream of economic independence.

Timing is also crucial. High school graduates should get immediate access to their money if they want to spend their $80,000 on college. Those choosing other paths should be obliged to learn a few lessons in the school of hard knocks before they can get their stakes—in $20,000 annual payments between the ages of twenty-one and twenty-four. The result will change the way young people think about themselves, their options, and their obligations to society.

Begin with the college-bound. Poor kids confront hardships unknown to their better-off peers—juggling schoolwork and jobs in ways that easily overwhelm self-confidence. The endless rounds of scholarship applications, and intermittent failures to pay tuition, take a toll by themselves. Statistics confirm that students in two-year colleges are even harder-pressed: a much higher percentage live at home, hold a job, and work more hours. It should be no surprise, then, that lower-class kids are much more likely to delay enrollment, and less likely to earn a degree, than their richer peers. At the end of the day, fifty-one percent of students from the top quarter earn bachelor's degrees, compared to twenty-two percent of middle-status students, and only 7.2% in the lowest socioeconomic quartile. For this large group of college-bound students, stakeholding will work a genuine revolution. It would allow all young men and women to focus their energies on academic work and compete with their peers on relatively equal terms.

Stakeholding would also inaugurate a new era of healthy competition in higher education. While colleges might try to raise tuition, they would face countervailing market pressures to keep costs low. Every student would enter the market with significant resources and an incentive to shop carefully. No longer would state universities or community colleges have a captive pool of in-state or low-income students without other options. These people could now choose a school in another community, or across the country, or even overseas.

This option will be especially valuable to people interested in a two-year college degree. At present, these colleges provide much smaller subsidies to their students than do more traditional universities. However, under the new system, students at two-year colleges will have the same buying power as their more academically inclined age-mates. To be sure, they will be utterly unwilling to spend their entire $80,000 on a couple of years of post-high school education. However, their stakes will create new incentives for serious programs directed at their distinctive concerns. Over time, two-year colleges will emerge from the shadow of their bigger brothers, and build their students' skills and self-confidence with increasing imagination and vigor.

We have left the best for last. Consider the millions of Americans who decide that college—even a two-year college—is not for them. These are today's forgotten Americans. Many of them have already been denied the decent high school education that should be every citizen's birthright. Now they are tossed unaided into the marketplace, while their upwardly mobile peers are given federal scholarships and state-subsidized tuitions.

This is just plain wrong. Joe Sixpack is every bit as much of an American as Joe College. And for the first time, his claim to equal citizenship will be treated with genuine respect. Since these high-school graduates are not going to college, they will have to wait until their early twenties to gain access to their stakes. Indeed, some may want to require young adults to wait until twenty-five or so before they get any of their money. We would be happy to compromise so long as the basic principle of universal stakeholding remains intact. The decision to go to college should not be required for an American to gain his country's support for the pursuit of happiness. All Americans have a fundamental right to start off as adults with a fair chance at making a decent life for themselves.

For all our precautions, some will fail to make good use of their stakes, and in ways they will bitterly regret. But the predictable failures of some should not deprive millions of others of *their* fair chance to pursue happiness. Each individual citizen has a right to a fair share of the patrimony left by preceding generations. This right should not be contingent on how others use or misuse their stakes.

Some poor Americans do face multiple social problems—inadequate education, drug or alcohol abuse, a propensity to violence—that leave them ill-equipped to handle financial responsibility for their stake. Despite pervasive media images, the size of the so-called "underclass" is quite tiny—less than four percent of the population. Most of these people would be excluded from full control of their stake by the requirement of high-school graduation.

In addition, we propose a cautious use of stakeholding as a sanction in the criminal law justice system. At the present time, the only way we have to punish young adults is to deprive them of their personal liberty. Stakeholding will, however, for the first time, also allow us to use financial sanctions against youth crime. For example, we would put nineteen year olds on notice that participation in the drug-trade would mean the loss of all or part of their stakes. For many people of eighteen or nineteen, such a threat might have more deterrence value than a prison term.

In any event, the important point is this: We should not allow trendy talk of "underclass" pathologies to divert our attention from the central problem posed by our emerging three-class society. Quite simply, there are tens of millions of ordinary Americans who are perfectly capable of responsible decision making in a stakeholding society, but are now becoming the forgotten citizens of our globalizing economy. We should confront this problem now before the wealth gap widens to Latin American proportions.

In our many conversations on the subject, somebody invariably suggests the wisdom of restricting the stake to a limited set of praiseworthy purposes—requiring each citizen to gain bureaucratic approval before spending down his $80,000. Would not this allow us to redistribute wealth and make sure the money is well spent?

This question bears the mark of the bureaucratic mindset that has haunted so much policymaking in the twentieth century. Our goal is to transcend the welfare state mentality, not transform stakeholding into another exercise in paternalistic social engineering. The point of stakeholding is to liberate each citizen from government, not to create an excuse for a vast new bureaucracy intervening in our lives. To be sure, the construction industry, the university sector, and the brokerage houses would prefer a plan that limited stakeholders' choices to home-buying, education, or investment. But if stakeholders want advice, they can buy it on the market. If people in their twenties can not be treated as adults, when will they be old enough?

We do not deny the need for a "social safety net" for Americans who make particularly bad choices, but this is not our primary focus. We are concerned with providing a fair opportunity for success for all Americans, and not only those lucky enough to be born to parents of the symbol-using classes. It is one thing to make a mess out of your life; quite another, never to have had a fair chance.

Indeed, the real problem with stakeholding is that it does not go far enough to redeem America's promise of an equal opportunity society. Does not the $80,000 come too late for all those who have been shortchanged as children?

Our short answer is yes. As a consequence, we certainly favor more spending on better versions of Head Start and the like. Nonetheless, we are skeptical of the egalitarian potential of enormous new investments in primary and secondary education. So long as suburbs can insulate themselves from central cities, there is only so much that money alone can accomplish. And, the upper classes have proven themselves adept in channeling federal aid for the disadvantaged into their own local school systems. Worse yet, school decentralization and privatization seem to be the order of the day—rather than a movement toward metropolitan-wide school systems and greater national efforts to provide poorer regions of the country with greater educational resources.

By contrast, it would be relatively easy to realize the goals of a stakeholder society. To a very large degree, the institutional infrastructure is already in place. We already have an Internal Revenue Service and a Social Security Administration. Although it is fashionable to denigrate these "bureaucracies," both agencies are full of competent people whose tasks might easily be broadened to encompass the jobs of identifying eligible stakeholders and paying out benefits. Unlike a comparable educational reform, stakeholding will not require a massive reorganization of the existing institutional framework. It builds on what we already have.

Americans could, in relatively short order, actually achieve the massive step toward equality of opportunity that stakeholding makes possible. This breakthrough, in turn, would give the lie to neo-conservative banalities about the inevitability of government failure. Having established that Americans *can* succeed in redeeming their fundamental ideals by inaugurating stakeholding, many other seemingly impossible initiatives may seem within our grasp.

Of course, real freedom and equal opportunity do not come cheap. Using conservative assumptions, the annual cost of stakeholding today would be about $255 billion—a little less than we spend on national defense. This is a big number, but we have made comparable commitments in the past: Would America have been a better place after the Second World War without the GI Bill of Rights? At that time, wealthy taxpayers were a lot poorer than they are today. They were paying far heavier taxes, and yet they did not seek to evade their obligation to give the rising generation a fair start in adult life.

The GI Bill represented the payment of a debt for the sacrifices that our soldiers made during the war. Today the ties that bind older to younger are less obvious—but no less important. Day after day, our society demands countless small acts of voluntary cooperation, as well as many larger personal sacrifices. If the younger generation is denied a fair start, how can the rest of us expect them to reciprocate as the need requires?

For the rest of their lives, stakeholders will endlessly consider how their $80,000 contributed to their individual pursuits of happiness—and at the same time reflect on their good fortune in enjoying this precious right of economic citizenship. Except for the most hardened cynics, this will lead to a deep and sustaining loyalty to the country that made stakeholding a concrete reality. Rather than dismissing the Declaration of Independence as boastful words on paper, stakeholders will hear in Jefferson's proud phrases a description of their own lives, and seek, as best they can, to repay their own debt by passing on their great American heritage on to the future.

We have talked enough about the potential benefits of stakeholding. Let us move to the revenue-raising side of the equation: How are we going to come up with the necessary quarter of a trillion dollars a year?

Well, there is never a good time for a tax hike, but now is the best time we will have for a long time. To be sure, we would not bet the ranch on the optimistic budgetary projections coming out of Washington right now. Since both Bill Clinton and Congressional Republicans are happy to take credit for restoring the nation to fiscal health, neither side emphasizes how much a sharp recession or two might dent their happy predictions of multi-trillion dollar surpluses over the next decade or so. More importantly, short-term surpluses will be swamped in the longer run. Depending on what we do with Medicare, the deficits looming by mid-century may well be horrific. Nevertheless, the happy numbers of the next decade should provide us a much-needed pause for reflection on our long-run fiscal responsibilities.

Stakeholding makes an initial intellectual contribution by exposing a question-begging assumption behind the emerging debate surrounding the budget surplus. Too often, the talk proceeds as if the only serious question is how much of the surplus should be used to save Social Security and Medicare. This begs the question whether our only exigent fiscal priority is aid to the elderly or whether the time has not come to emphasize the competing claim of the generation only now rising to maturity.

In raising stakeholding as a serious alternative, we do not suggest that it should automatically trump the claims of the older generation to a decent level of income and medical care. But we do believe that both social justice and social peace require America to redeem its promise of equal opportunity to the young no less than its promise of decency to the old. If we can not afford to do both, it is not obvious that we should entirely ignore stakeholding and lavish the lion's share of the surplus on the old.

America *is* rich enough to do both. Despite the fog of anti-tax rhetoric, our taxes remain far lower than those imposed by other rich Western nations, and they would remain so after we have paid the quarter-of-a-trillion-dollar annual bill for stakeholding. Obviously, there are lots of different ways of raising the money. For example, we would favor a hike in the income tax or a new national consumption tax whose revenues were dedicated to the stakeholding fund. But, so far as we are concerned, the best way to proceed is through a new comprehensive tax on wealth similar to the ones currently imposed by twelve other countries in the elite club of first-world nations called the Organization for Economic Cooperation and Development.

We have built many conservative assumptions into our economic analysis of the revenue-raising potential of such a tax. We have also allowed every American an $80,000 personal exemption, thereby eliminating the bottom sixty percent of the population from all liability. Nevertheless, our analysis reveals that an annual tax of two percent would be enough to fund the entire program.

Even when we focus on the top forty percent, this tax would have a vastly different impact on different groups. So far as the households falling between the sixtieth and eightieth percentile, the average tax would be $1100 a year, and the entire group would contribute only seven percent of the total fund. The big tax burden would be borne at the top, with thirty-nine percent of the total tax contributed by the top one percent of American households, whose median wealth in 1995 was $4.6 million.

The disproportionate impact of the tax on the rich strikes us as entirely fair. Since wealth is correlated with age, Americans over the age of fifty or sixty will bear the brunt of the burden. But it is precisely these people who have participated fully in the great post-war economic boom. The wealthy man or woman who is sixty in the year 2000 was born in

1940—just in time to avoid the agonies of the Great Depression and the Second World War, but just in time to reap the harvest. Graduating from college about 1960, the typical up-and-comer was in a perfect position to take advantage of the rich array of opportunities made possible by America's rise to world power. The best universities, the most advanced companies, the biggest pool of capital—all of these were available for Americans who seized the moment. To be sure, nobody could become wealthy without some combination of effort, insight, and luck. It would be blind for any sixty-year-old to ignore the role played by the simple fact that he was an American in an American age—and thereby gained the enormous advantages created at great sacrifice by his parents' generation. Given their existing balance of generational advantage, it is especially appropriate to ask this group of elder Americans to make a sacrifice to sustain the Republic's political and economic equilibrium.

We are calling upon older Americans to remember that they themselves were the beneficiaries of similar acts of statesmanship by earlier generations. During the New Deal and Great Society, Americans recognized the elderly as a group that was particularly threatened by the inegalitarian operation of market forces. By responding with Social Security and Medicare, our predecessors ensured a decent life for millions of elderly Americans today. Without these programs, the distribution of wealth would be even more unequal than it already is. Is it not time, then, for the elder generation to reciprocate when the market threatens to undermine the promise of economic opportunity for millions of younger Americans?

This commitment should not come at the cost of retirees who depend on their monthly Social Security checks. Rather than leading a raid on Social Security revenues, we simply urge prosperous older Americans to recognize the moral claim of younger Americans who will otherwise live out lives of quiet despair.

Or not so quiet despair. After all, the prison population has soared over the last quarter century. About 100 Americans in every 100,000 were in the nation's prisons in 1975; that number is now over 400. Young males, and increasingly females, are the prime targets for prison—men and women who might find it within themselves to take a different path in a stakeholding society. If inequality increases over the next century, are we really prepared to lock up more and more young Americans who react with rage at a system that has never delivered on its promises? If those with the greatest stake in the system do not take heed, who is supposed to?

It is time for the wealthy to accept stakeholding as part of the social compact. While wealth taxes are unfamiliar in America, they are a fixture of public finance in most other industrialized nations. Of course, every new tax generates the same old cry that it will kill the economy. Rich people are always happy to tell you the story of the goose that lays the golden eggs, but is it just a fairy tale?

Not only has our economy boomed, and busted, under very different levels of taxation, recent empirical research suggests that the link between tax rates and growth is far weaker than implied by the prevailing political rhetoric. Moreover, stakeholding will itself unleash the energies of millions of youthful entrepreneurs—while many will fail, many others will succeed in ways that will enrich the lives of us all.

Two hundred years ago, Tom Paine surveyed the revolutionary world he helped create, and sensed something missing: "A revolution in the state of civilization is the necessary companion of revolutions in the system of government." This could be accomplished, he was convinced, only through stakeholding. Every citizen, Paine insisted, had a right to a stake of fifteen pounds Sterling "when arrived at the age of twenty-one years." In a remarkable gesture for the eighteenth century, Paine argued that this expanded stake should go to every man *and* woman. Regardless of his or her claims on private wealth, each should be accorded an economic stake in the commonwealth.

Tom Paine was not alone. Our leading Founders acknowledged a deep relationship between property and citizenship. When Madison viewed "the merits alone," it was clear to him that "the freeholders of the Country would be the safest depositories of Republican liberty," and that the propertyless should be excluded from the suffrage. Standing before the Constitutional Convention, he did not conceal his anxiety as he glimpsed the dread day when the "great majority of the people will not only be without landed, but any other sort of, property."

But in 1787, this grim prospect could be deferred to the remote future. The Founders treated the problem of propertylessness in the way they dealt with the curse of slavery. They did not seek a definitive solution, leaving it to some later generation to confront the crisis when it became acute.

This seemed sensible enough. A vast frontier beckoned to generations of yeomen farmers. So long as the government sold virgin land at low prices, the link between property and citizenship could be more or less preserved. But as the nineteenth century moved on, this Jeffersonian vision of a farmer-republic became increasingly obsolete. By the time of the great Homestead Act of 1863, the statute's provision of free land on the frontier was already out of sync with the needs of the rising urban masses of the East. If the link between property and citizenship were to be sustained, provision of free land would no longer suffice. With the closing of the frontier, something like Tom Paine's vision of stakeholding was required to guarantee each citizen a property interest in America.

By then Paine's voice had become a muffled memory. The mainstream of reform was flowing in other directions: Populists, Progressives, New Dealers, and the partisans of the Great Society sought to regain control over the market economy, but none moved in the direction of citizen-stakeholding. Rather than broadening the property-owning base, their overriding aim was to regulate property more intensely in the public interest.

We think that the intellectual climate really is changing today. Nationalization of industry is on nobody's agenda anymore. People are slowly recognizing that "capitalism" is a Marxist label concealing the vast differences between economic systems built on private property and competitive markets—some bitterly unjust, and others striving for a world worthy of a free and equal citizenry. It is time to stop dreaming about the abolition of private property and get to work creating a commonwealth in which all citizens are property owners.

This intuition has been behind some major initiatives attempted by leading politicians of our age. They have gained great followings through initiatives that bear a family resemblance to our proposal. When Margaret Thatcher became Prime Minister, thirty-two percent of all housing in England was publicly owned. Though bent on sweeping privatization, Thatcher refused to sell off these vast properties to big companies. She invited residents to buy their own homes at bargain rates. With a single stroke, she created a new class of property-owning citizens, and won vast popularity in the process.

A more sweeping initiative took place in the Czech Republic in the aftermath of 1989. The Prime Minister, Vaclav Klaus, was confronting a much larger task than Thatcher's: the state sector contained 7000 medium and large-scale enterprises, 25,000 to 35,000 smaller ones. How to distribute this legacy of Communism? Klaus saw his problem as an opportunity to create a vast new property-owning class.

The mechanism was the ingenious technique of "voucher privatization." Each Czech citizen was encouraged to subscribe to a book of vouchers that he could use to bid for shares in state companies as they were put on the auction block. An overwhelming majority—8.5 out of 10.5 million—took up Klaus' offer, and claimed their fair share of the nation's wealth as they moved into the free-market system. Klaus' creative program helped cement his position as the leading politician of the Republic. More importantly, the broad involvement of citizen-stakeholders played a central role in legitimating the country's transition to liberal democracy.

Thatcher and Klaus conceived their initiatives as one-shot affairs. However, the citizens of Alaska have made stakeholding a regular part of their political economy. Once again, the occasion was the distribution of a major public asset, in this case the revenues from North Slope oil. Rather than using it all for public expenditures, the Republican leadership designed a stakeholding scheme that is now distributing about a $1000 a year to every Alaskan citizen. Once again, the system has become broadly popular, with politicians of both parties regularly pledging that they will not raid the symbolically-named Permanent Fund.

There is no good reason to limit stakeholding to physical assets like housing or factories or oil. Americans have created other assets that are less material, but have even greater value. Most notably, the free enterprise system did not drop from thin air. It has emerged only as the result of a complex and on-going scheme of social cooperation. The "free market" requires heavy public expenditures on police, courts, and much else besides. But without billions of voluntary decisions by Americans to respect the rights of property in their daily lives, the system would collapse overnight.

All Americans benefit from this cooperative activity—some much more than others. Those who benefit the most have a duty to share some of their wealth with fellow citizens whose cooperation they require to sustain the market system. This obligation is all the more exigent when the operation of the global market threatens to split the country more sharply into haves and have-nots.

This view gives our proposal a different ideological spin from those pioneered by Margaret Thatcher and Vaclav Klaus. Surely there will be some on the Right who will blanch at the implications of our proposal. But we hope that many others will come to see its justice. We expect a similar split on the Left. Some will be deeply suspicious of liberating stakeholding assets from the grip of the regulatory state, leaving each citizen free to make their own decisions. Others will be more impressed by the justice of empowering all Americans to share in the pursuit of happiness.

Stakeholding also holds out the promise of political renewal. Nobody we have met has the slightest problem grasping the idea of $80,000—or the possibility of funding the program by taxing wealth. Lots of people do not like the initiative, but at least they know what they are disagreeing with—and this is absolutely essential for a rebirth of democratic politics in this country. Unless progressives come up with projects that are transparent to the common understanding, the politics of scandal will have no real competitor. The general public has no patience for a policy debate that speaks a technocratic language accessible only to people with advanced degrees.

If Beltway babble is the alternative, ordinary Americans will turn with relief to news of the latest personal indiscretion by leading politicos. Only a program like stakeholding can focus the public mind on the prospects for real change. It raises—in a straightforward and concrete way—the leading questions of our age: Is America more than a libertarian marketplace? Can we preserve a sense of ourselves as a nation of free and equal citizens?

Stakeholding really does bring power back to the people. It marks a radical break with the elitist tradition of social engineering. We do not need a host of experts to minister to ordinary Americans. Give citizens their stakes and let them inaugurate a new age of freedom.

This call can unify a badly fractured nation. Even many Americans in the top twenty percent may recognize its power. Do they really want their own children to live in gated communities locked away from the rest of American life?

The stakeholder society is no utopia, but it does provide an alternative to our current moral drift. Perhaps we will never fully realize the American Dream of equal opportunity. But without that dream, this country will become a very ugly place.

———

NOTES AND QUESTIONS

1.   Ackerman & Alstott's proposal. Do you think the stakeholder idea effectively addresses the problems of inequality outlined in this section? Will it do what the authors think it will? Is it politically feasible?

2.   The stakeholder society and African American reparations. Does Ackerman & Alstott's proposal address racialized disparities in wealth? What can minority groups do to overcome obstacles to economic opportunity? Claud Anderson of The Harvest Institute (a think tank whose goal is to reform the social and economic aspects of African American life) offers several suggestions to African Americans to escape financial inequality, including mastering the principles of capitalism and group economics, vertically integrating industries and businesses, expanding business in minority communities, and increasing black leadership. CLAUD ANDERSON, BLACK LABOR WHITE WEALTH: THE SEARCH FOR POWER AND ECONOMIC JUSTICE 188 (1994). Another notable recommendation by Anderson is for African Americans to ask the government for reparations: "Reparation payments should be directed into black communities . . . to repair the socioeconomic damages that the dominant society and government have inflicted in 16 generations of black Americans." *Id.* at 182. Is Anderson's request too radical? If only five or six generations are needed to eradicate the indicia of slavery, why is Anderson asking for *sixteen* generations to be compensated? *See* Emma Coleman Jordan, *A History Lesson: Reparations for What?*, 58 N.Y.U. ANN. SURV. AM. L. 1,557 (2003). *See also*, ROY L. BROOKS, ATONEMENT AND FORGIVENESS: A NEW MODEL FOR BLACK REPARATIONS (2004).

3.   Stakeholding and inequality. Why do income and wealth inequality matter? After all, capitalism is premised on the notion of competition, and not everyone can be a winner. Do Ackerman and Alstott explain why we should care about rising inequality?

CHAPTER 6

LIFE IN A CLASS SOCIETY

A. DOWN AND OUT

Number of People Living in Poverty Increases in U.S.

N.Y. TIMES, Sept. 25, 2002, at A1.

■ ROBERT PEAR

The proportion of Americans living in poverty rose significantly last year, increasing for the first time in eight years, the Census Bureau reported today. At the same time, the bureau said that the income of middle-class households fell for the first time since the last recession ended, in 1991.

The Census Bureau's annual report on income and poverty provided stark evidence that the weakening economy had begun to affect large segments of the population, regardless of race, region or class. Daniel H. Weinberg, chief of income and poverty statistics at the Census Bureau, said the recession that began in March 2001 had reduced the earnings of millions of Americans.

The report also suggested that the gap between rich and poor continued to grow.

All regions except the Northeast experienced a decline in household income, the bureau reported. For blacks, it was the first significant decline in two decades; non-Hispanic whites saw a slight decline. Even the incomes of Asians and Pacific Islanders, a group that achieved high levels of prosperity in the 1990's, went down significantly last year.

"The decline was widespread," Mr. Weinberg said.

The Census Bureau said the number of poor Americans rose last year to 32.9 million, an increase of 1.3 million, while the proportion living in poverty rose to 11.7 percent, from 11.3 percent in 2000.

Median household income fell to $42,228 in 2001, a decline of $934 or 2.2 percent from the prior year. The number of households with income above the median is the same as the number below it.

A family of four was classified as poor if it had cash income less than $18,104 last year. The official poverty levels, updated each year to reflect changes in the Consumer Price Index, were $14,128 for a family of three, $11,569 for a married couple and $9,039 for an individual.

433

The bureau's report is likely to provide fodder for the Congressional campaigns. The White House said the increase in poverty resulted, in part, from an economic slowdown that began under President Bill Clinton. But Democrats said the data showed the failure of President Bush's economic policies and his tendency to neglect the economy.

Mr. Bush said today that he remained optimistic. "When you combine the productivity of the American people with low interest rates and low inflation, those are the ingredients for growth," Mr. Bush said.

But Senator Paul S. Sarbanes, Democrat of Maryland, said the administration should "start paying attention to the economic situation." Richard A. Gephardt of Missouri, the House Democratic leader, expressed amazement that Mr. Bush, after being in office for 20 months, was still blaming his predecessor.

Rudolph G. Penner, a former director of the Congressional Budget Office, said: "The increase in poverty is most certainly a result of the recession. The slow recovery, the slow rate of growth, has been very disappointing. Whether that has a political impact this fall depends on whether the election hinges on national conditions or focuses on local issues."

Although the poverty rate, the proportion of the population living in poverty, rose four-tenths of a percentage point last year, it was still lower than in most of the last two decades. The poverty rate exceeded 12 percent every year from 1980 to 1998. As the economy grew from 1993 to 2000, the rate plunged, to 11.3 percent from 15.1 percent, and the poverty rolls were reduced by 7.7 million people, to 31.6 million.

The latest recession showed an unusual pattern, seeming to raise poverty rates among whites more than among minority groups, Mr. Weinberg said.

Increases in poverty last year were concentrated in the suburbs, in the South and among non-Hispanic whites, the Census Bureau said. Indeed, non-Hispanic whites were the only racial group for whom the poverty rate showed a significant increase, to 7.8 percent in 2001, from 7.4 percent in 2000.

Poverty rates for minority groups were once much higher. But last year, the bureau said, they remained "at historic lows" for blacks (22.7 percent), Hispanics (21.4 percent) and Asian Americans (10.2 percent).

With its usual caution, the Census Bureau said the data did not conclusively show a year-to-year increase in income inequality. But the numbers showed a clear trend in that direction over the last 15 years.

The most affluent fifth of the population received half of all household income last year, up from 45 percent in 1985. The poorest fifth received 3.5 percent of total household income, down from 4 percent in 1985. Average income for the top 5 percent of households rose by $1,000 last year, to $260,464, but the average declined or stayed about the same for most other income brackets.

Robert Greenstein, executive director of the Center on Budget and Policy Priorities, a liberal research institute, said, "The census data show that income inequality either set a record in 2001 or tied for the highest level on record."

Median earnings increased 3.5 percent for women last year, but did not change for men, so women gained relative to men.

"The real median earnings of women age 15 and older who worked full time year-round increased for the fifth consecutive year, rising to $29,215— a 3.5 percent increase between 2000 and 2001," Mr. Weinberg said. The comparable figure for men was unchanged at $38,275. So the female-to-male earnings ratio reached a high of 0.76. The previous high was 0.74, first recorded in 1996.

Democrats said the data supported their contention that Congress should increase spending on social welfare programs, resisted by many Republicans. But Wade F. Horn, the administration's welfare director, said the number of poor children was much lower than in 1996, when Congress overhauled the welfare law to impose strict work requirements.

Of the 32.9 million poor people in the United States last year, 11.7 million were under 18, and 3.4 million were 65 or older. Poverty rates for children, 16.3 percent, and the elderly, 10.1 percent, were virtually unchanged from 2000. But the poverty rate for people 18 to 64 rose a half percentage point, to 10.1 percent.

Median household income for blacks fell last year by $1,025, or 3.4 percent, to $29,470. Median income of Hispanics, at $33,565, was virtually unchanged. But household income fell by 1.3 percent for non-Hispanic whites, to $46,305, and by 6.4 percent for Asian Americans, to $53,635.

The Census Bureau report also included these findings:

There were 6.8 million poor families last year, up from 6.4 million in 2000. The poverty rate for families rose to 9.2 percent, from a 26-year low of 8.7 percent in 2000.

The rate in the South rose to 13.5 percent, from 12.8 percent in 2000. The South is home to more than 40 percent of all the nation's poor, and it accounted for more than half of the national increase in the number of poor last year.

The poverty rate for the suburbs rose to 8.2 percent last year, from 7.8 percent in 2000. The number of poor people in suburban areas rose by 700,000, to 12 million. There was virtually no change in the rates in central cities (16.5 percent) and outside metropolitan areas (14.2 percent).

The bureau said the number of "severely poor" rose to 13.4 million last year, from 12.6 million in 2000. People are considered to be severely poor if their family incomes are less than half of the official poverty level.

———

Just Trying to Survive

ROSA LEE: A MOTHER AND HER FAMILY IN URBAN AMERICA 39–47 (1996).

■ LEON DASH

Rosa Lee guided her eleven-year-old grandson through the narrow aisles of a thrift shop in suburban Oxon Hill, Maryland, past the crowded racks of secondhand pants and shirts, stopping finally at the row of children's jackets and winter coats. Quickly, the boy selected a mock-leather flight jacket with a big number on the back and a price tag stapled to the collar.

"If you want it," Ross Lee said, "then you're going to have to help me get it."

"Okay, Grandmama," he said nervously. "But do it in a way that I won't get caught."

Like a skilled teacher instructing a new student, Rosa Lee told her grandson what to do. "Pretend you're trying it on. Don't look up! Don't look around! Don't laugh like it's some kind of joke! Just put it on. Let Grandma see how you look."

The boy slipped off his old, coat and put on the new one. Rosa Lee whispered, "Now put the other one back on, over it." She pushed down the new jacket's collar so that it was hidden.

"What do I do now?" he asked.

"Just walk on out the door," Rosa Lee said. "It's your coat."

Four days later, Rosa Lee is recounting this episode for me, recreating the dialogue by changing her voice to distinguish between herself and her grandson. It is January 1991. By now, I have spent enough time with Rosa Lee that her shoplifting exploits no longer surprise me.

The previous November, Rosa Lee took her eight-year-old granddaughter into the same thrift shop on a Sunday morning to steal a new winter coat for the girl one week after they were both baptized in a Pentecostal church. On the Sunday of the shoplifting lesson, Rosa Lee had decided she did not want to take her granddaughter back to the church because her winter coat was "tacky and dirty."

In the thrift shop, Rosa Lee told her granddaughter to take off her coat and hang it on the coatrack. Next, she told the grinning child to put on the attractive pink winter coat hanging on the rack.

"Are we going to take this coat, Grandma?" asked the skinny little girl.

"Yes," Rosa Lee told her. "We are exchanging coats. Now walk out the door."

A month later, a week before Christmas, Rosa Lee was searching for something in a large shopping bag in her bedroom and dumped the contents onto the bed. Out spilled dozens of bottles of expensive men's cologne and women's perfume, as well as leather gloves with their sixty-dollar price tags still attached. She leaves the tags on when she sells the goods as proof of the merchandise's newness and quality.

"Did you get all this in one trip?" I ask.

"Oh, no," she says. "This is a couple of weeks' worth."

In Rosa Lee's younger years especially, shoplifting was a major source of income, supplementing her welfare payments and the money she made during fifteen years of waitressing at various nightclubs. With eight children to feed and clothe, stealing, she says, helped her survive. Later on, when she began using heroin in the mid-1970s, her shoplifting paid for drugs.

She stole from clothing stores, drugstores, and grocery stores, stuffing items inside the torn liner of her winter coat or slipping them into one of the oversized black purses that she carries wherever she goes. When her children were young—the ages of the grandson and granddaughter—she taught them how to shoplift as well.

"Every time I went somewhere to make some money, I would take my children," she said. "I would teach them or they would watch me. 'Just watch what Mama does. I'm getting food for y'all to eat.'"

In supermarkets, she could count on her children "to distract the security guard while I hit the meat freezer. The guards would always watch groups of children before they'd watch an adult."

Her favorite targets were the department stores. One of her two older brothers, Joe Louis Wright, joked with me one day that Rosa Lee "owned a piece" of Hecht's and had put Lansburgh's out of business. "Man, she would get coats, silk dresses," he recalled. "A cloth coat with a mink collar. She got me a mohair suit. Black. Three-piece. I don't know how the hell she'd get them out of there."

Her stealing has caused divisions and hard feelings in her family, and is one reason why Rosa Lee's relationships with several of her brothers and sisters are strained. They see Rosa Lee's stealing as an extreme and unjustified reaction to their impoverished upbringing. And her sons Alvin and Eric have always refused to participate in any of their mother's illegal activities.

Rosa Lee has served eight short prison terms for various kinds of stealing during the past forty years, dating back to the early 1950s. Her longest stay was eight months for trying to steal a fur coat from a Maryland department store in 1965. She says that she went to prison rehabilitation programs each time but that none had much of an effect on her. "I attended those programs so it would look good on my record when I went before the parole board," she says. "What they were talking about didn't mean anything to me. I didn't have the education they said would get me a job. I couldn't read no matter how many programs I went to."

Nothing seems to deter her from shoplifting, not even the specter of another jail term. On the day she directed her grandson in stealing the flight jacket, she was four days away from sentencing at the city's Superior Court for stealing the bedsheets from Hecht's the previous summer.

"I'm just trying to survive," she says.

Rosa Lee had chosen her clothes carefully for her appearance before Commissioner John Treanor in November. She wanted to look as poor as possible to draw his sympathy.

She wore an ill-fitting winter coat, gray wool overalls and a white wool hat pulled back to show her graying hair. She had removed her upper dental plate to give herself a toothless look when she smiled. "My homey look," she calls it. "No lipstick. No earrings. No nothing!"

Rosa Lee did not expect to go home that day. She saw a heavyset female deputy U.S. marshal move into place behind the defense table when the courtroom clerk called her name. It was a certain sign that Treanor had already decided to "step her back" and send her to jail. She hastily handed me her purse with all her documents.

"Hold on to these papers for me, Mr. Dash," she whispered. "Looks like I'm going to get some jail time. Tell my children where I'm at. You better come see me!"

Her lawyer's statements matched her downtrodden look. Rosa Lee's life was a mess, Elmer D. Ellis told Treanor. She was addicted to heroin, a habit she had developed in 1975. She was HIV positive. She was caring for three grandchildren because their mother was in jail.

Rosa Lee told Treanor that she was trying hard to turn herself around. She was taking methadone every day to control her heroin addition and had turned again to the church. "I got baptized Sunday, me and my three grandchildren," she said, her voice breaking. "And I'm asking you from the bottom of my heart, give me a chance to prove that I'm taking my baptize seriously, 'cause I know I might not have much longer."

Tears ran down her cheeks. "I'm asking you for a chance, please," she begged Treanor. "I know I have a long record."

Rosa Lee was stretching the truth. Yes, she had been baptized, and yes, she was taking methadone. But no, she wasn't caring for her grandchildren alone. Their mother's jail term had ended in July, and she had returned to Rosa Lee's two-bedroom apartment to take care of the children, with help from Rosa Lee.

Treanor looked unimpressed with Rosa Lee's performance. He glowered at her, and Rosa Lee braced for the lecture she knew was coming. Both had played these roles before.

"Every time you pump yourself full of drugs and spend money to do it," he said, "you're stealing from your grandchildren. You're stealing food from their plates, clothes from their backs, and you're certainly jeopardizing their future. You're going to be the youngest dead grandmother in town. And you're going to have three children that will be put up for adoption or going out to some home or some junior village or someplace."

That had been Rosa Lee's opening. "Can I prove to you that my life has changed?"

"Yeah, you can prove it to me, very simply," Treanor answered. "You can stay away from dope. Now I'll make a bargain with you.... You come back here the end of January and tell me what you've been doing, and then we'll think about it. But you're looking at jail time. You're looking at the cemetery."

Rosa Lee had won. Treanor postponed the sentencing. The marshal, who had moved in closer behind Rosa Lee at the start of Treanor's lecture, moved back. Treanor, red-faced with anger, called a ten-minute recess and hurriedly left the bench. Ellis shook Rosa Lee's hand.

Rosa Lee came over to me, her cheeks still tearstained but her face aglow. "Was I good?" she asked.

"Yeah," I said, startled at her boldness.

"Thank you," she said, smiling.

The marshal walked up to Rosa Lee. She too was smiling. She had escorted Rosa Lee and her daughters to the jail several times in the not-so-distant past. "You were going to jail, honey," she said to Rosa Lee. "You stopped him with those three grandchildren. He didn't want to have to deal with making arrangements for those children if he had sent you to jail. Is their mama still over the jail?"

"Yes, she is," Rosa Lee lied, putting on a sad face.

Five days before the hearing Rosa Lee was teaching her grandchild how to shoplift. Through most of November and December, Rosa Lee stole cologne, perfume, gloves, and brightly colored silk scarves to sell to people who used them as Christmas presents. The day before her court appearance, she and a fellow drug-clinic patient, Jackie, were shoplifting in a drugstore one block from the Superior Court building shortly after they had drunk their morning meth.

When she returns for sentencing on January 22, a transformed Rosa Lee enters the courthouse. She looks good. She has a clean report from the methadone clinic. She stopped injecting heroin and cocaine in November, after her last seizure. She seems to have done everything Commissioner Treanor asked.

She always dresses well, but she has outdone herself today: she's wearing a two-piece, white-and-gray cotton knit suit with tan leather boots and a tan pocketbook. A gold-colored watch on a gold-colored chain hangs around her neck, both items she stole from the drugstore.

Before they enter Treanor's courtroom, Elmer Ellis has a word with Rosa Lee. "Please don't cry, Mrs. Cunningham," her lawyer says gently. "If you start crying again, you're only going to make Treanor angry." Rosa Lee laughs and agrees not to cry.

"What would you like to say, Mrs. Cunningham?" Treanor asks Rosa Lee when she stands in front of him.

"Well, Your Honor, I know I haven't been a good person. I know it," she begins.

Treanor cuts her off. His demeanor is softer, his words more sympathetic than in November. "Wait a minute, now. Why do you say that? ... You're taking care of those three grandchildren, isn't that right?"

"Yes, Sir," Rosa Lee says, keeping up the pretense.

"All right," he says. "Now you've raised one family, and now you have another one."

"Yes, Sir," she says.

"Which is really too much to ask of anybody, so I don't think you should sell yourself short. You're doing the Lord's work. Your daughter's in jail for drugs, right?"

"Yes, sir," Rosa Lee says.

"And you have or have had a bad drug problem yourself."

"Yes, Sir."

Then Treanor launches into another lecture about drugs. He doesn't ask Rosa Lee why she steals. "You steal to support your habit," he says. "It's as plain as the nose on your face."

But it isn't that plain. Rosa Lee began stealing long before she became a drug addict.

Finally, Treanor announces his decision: no jail. Instead, he gives her a suspended sentence and one year of probation with drug counseling. "Now, don't come back here," he says.

Rosa Lee sometimes puts on a public mask, the way she wants the world to see her. She fudges a little here, omits a little there, even when she is trying to be candid about her behavior. By her account, her stealing started when she was a teenager. It was her eldest brother, Ben Wright, who told me that Rosa Lee's stealing started when she was nine years old. Her target: the lunch money that her fourth-grade classmates at Giddings Elementary School kept in their desks.

"JESUS, BEN!" Rosa Lee shouts when I ask her about it.

"What's the matter?" I laugh. "You said I could interview Ben."

It is a late afternoon in January, not long after her court appearance. We are talking in my car, which is parked outside Rosa Lee's apartment. We watch the teenage crack dealers come and go, making the rounds of the low-rent housing complex. Two of Rosa Lee's grandchildren are playing nearby on a patch of dirt where the grass has been worn away. The sun is beginning to sink behind the buildings as she tells me about her first theft.

The year was 1946, and Giddings's imposing red-brick building at Third and G streets, S.E., was a bustling part of the District's then-segregated education system. The school served black children living in Capitol Hill neighborhoods; some, like Rosa Lee, came from poor sharecropping families who had moved to Washington during the Depression, and they did not have the new clothes and spending money that their better-off classmates did.

Rosa Lee's father, Earl Wright, never made much money. He worked for a paving contractor as a cement finisher but he was never given that title; instead, he was always classified as a "helper" and paid a lower wage. Eventually, drinking became the primary activity of his life. Rosa Lee's mother, Rosetta Lawrence Wright, brought in most of the family's money, working as a domestic on Capitol Hill during the day.

"She used to call it 'day work,'" remembers Rosa Lee. "That's what she used to do down in the country" in North Carolina. "Clean white people's houses."

Rosetta also sold dinners from the family's kitchen in the evening and on weekends, always for cash. "She wanted cash because she was getting a welfare check for us," says Rosa Lee. The welfare payments began several years before her father's death because he spent all his time drinking and did not work. After he died, Rosetta had four additional children by another man. "Back in those days, they gave you a check for each child. Seventeen dollars a check. You never want the welfare to know how much money you got. They'll cut the check."

Ben contends that his sister's memory is faulty, that the family did receive monthly deliveries of surplus government food in this period, as did all of the poorest families in Washington, but his mother did not receive a monthly welfare stipend.

Whatever the truth, Rosa Lee and Ben agree that their family—there were eleven children in all—was poor. For much of her childhood, they lived in a ramshackle wooden row house within a mile of the Capitol, since replaced with a public housing project. None of the houses they rented over the years had electricity. The toilet for each dwelling was an outhouse along the edge of the property in the back yard. Water came from a standpipe spigot in the center of the yard.

"I hated them!" says Rosa Lee of the houses, her mouth turning down in a grimace. "No privacy. People knew what you were doing when you went into" the outhouse. "No bathtub. I was always afraid of the kerosene lamps. I was scared they'd turn over and we'd all burn up in those houses."

Other girls came to school with change to buy "brownie-thins"— penny-a-piece cookies that the teachers sold to go with free milk at lunch. Rosa Lee's family was too poor to spare even a few pennies. Rosa Lee was determined to steal her classmates' money so she too could buy cookies. And she did. She knew it was wrong to steal from her classmates' desks, she says. But she couldn't stand being poor, either.

Rosa Lee soon found that she had plenty of opportunities to steal, if she were daring enough. During the summer of 1948, a sinewy Rosa Lee was the only girl among the many "roughneck" boys selling the *Baltimore-Washington Afro–American* newspaper door-to-door on Tuesday and Thursday evenings. She was eleven. The newspaper sales were timed to catch middle-class black people—low-level federal and city civil servants—when they had just come from work.

Rosa Lee was not concerned about tough neighborhood bullies taking her money or trying to force her off the blocks where an *Afro* seller was sure to be successful. "Rosa Lee would fight quick," remembers Ben. "Fight anybody! Beat up most girls and a good many boys. I don't remember ever having to stick up for her."

Selling the *Afro* also gave Rosa Lee a chance to slip into neighborhood row houses and rifle through the pocketbooks that women often left on the dining room table or the living room couch. Washington was a safer place in those days, and Rosa Lee discovered that many families would leave their front screen doors unlatched while they chatted in their back yards, trying to cool off on hot summer evenings after returning home from work.

"I would walk down Fourth Street," says Rosa Lee, in front of the row houses across from Mount Joy Baptist Church, where her family worshipped. "I would go and knock on their screen door. *'Afro!* Anybody want an *Afro?'* I would open the screen door and if no one answered, I'd go in. I could look through the house and see them out back," she remembers. "Some people would leave their pocketbooks on the chair in the front room or on their table. I would go into so many peoples' houses." * * *

Mathematics

BLACK ON BOTH SIDES (Priority Records 1999).

■ MOS DEF

* * *

Yo, it's one universal law but two sides to every story

Three strikes and you be in for life, mandatory

* * *

Young soldiers tryin' to earn they next stripe

When the average minimum wage is $5.15

You best believe you gotta find a new ground to get cream

The white unemployment rate, is nearly more than triple for black

so frontliners got they gun in your back

Bubblin' crack, jewel theft and robbery to combat poverty

and end up in the global jail economy

Stiffer stipulations attached to each sentence

Budget cutbacks but increased police presence

And even if you get out of prison still livin'

join the other five million under state supervision

This is business, no faces just lines and statistics

from your phone, your zip code, to S-S-I digits

The system break man child and women into figures

Two columns for who is, and who ain't niggaz

Numbers is hardly real and they never have feelings

but you push too hard, even numbers got limits

Why did one straw break the camel's back? Here's the secret:

the million other straws underneath it—it's all mathematics.

* * *

Homelessness and the Issue of Freedom

39 UCLA L. Rev. 295, 299–302 (1991).

■ Jeremy Waldron

Estimates of the number of homeless people in the United States range from 250,000 to three million. A person who is homeless is, obviously enough, a person who has no home. One way of describing the plight of a homeless individual might be to say that there is no place governed by a private property rule where he is allowed to be.

In fact, that is not quite correct. Any private proprietor may invite a homeless person into his house or onto his land, and if he does there *will* be some private place where the homeless person is allowed to be. A technically more accurate description of his plight is that there is no place governed by a private property rule where he is allowed to be whenever *he* chooses, no place governed by a private property rule from which he may not at any time be excluded as a result of someone else's say-so. As far as being on private property is concerned—in people's houses or gardens, on farms or in hotels, in offices or restaurants—the homeless person is utterly and at all times at the mercy of others. And we know enough about how this mercy is generally exercised to figure that the description in the previous paragraph is more or less accurate as a matter of fact, even if it is not strictly accurate as a matter of law.

For the most part the homeless are excluded from *all* of the places governed by private property rules, whereas the rest of us are, in the same sense, excluded from *all but one* (or maybe all but a few) of those places. That is another way of saying that each of us has at least one place to be in a country composed of private places, whereas the homeless person has none.

Some libertarians fantasize about the possibility that *all* the land in a society might be held as private property ("Sell the streets!") This would be catastrophic for the homeless. Since most private proprietors are already disposed to exclude him from their property, the homeless person might discover in such a libertarian paradise that there was literally *nowhere* he was allowed to be. Wherever he went he would be liable to penalties for trespass and he would be liable to eviction, to being thrown out by an owner or dragged away by the police. Moving from one place to another would involve nothing more liberating than moving from one trespass liability to another. Since land is finite in any society, there is only a limited number of places where a person can (physically) be, and such a person would find that he was legally excluded from all of them. (It would not be entirely mischievous to add that since, in order to exist, a person has to be *somewhere*, such a person would not be permitted to exist.)

Our society saves the homeless from this catastrophe only by virtue of the fact that some of its territory is held as collective property and made available for common use. The homeless are allowed to *be*—provided they are on the streets, in the parks, or under the bridges. Some of them are allowed to crowd together into publicly provided "shelters" after dark (though these are dangerous places and there are not nearly enough shelters for all of them). But in the daytime and, for many of them, all through the night, wandering in public places is their only option. When all else is privately owned, the sidewalks are their salvation. They are allowed to *be* in our society only to the extent that our society is communist.

This is one of the reasons why most defenders of private property are uncomfortable with the libertarian proposal, and why that proposal remains sheer fantasy. But there is a modified form of the libertarian catastrophe in prospect with which moderate and even liberal defenders of ownership seem much more comfortable. This is the increasing regulation of the streets, subways, parks, and other public places to restrict the activities that can be performed there. What is emerging—and it is not just a matter of fantasy—is a state of affairs in which a million or more citizens have no place to perform elementary human activities like urinating, washing, sleeping, cooking, eating, and standing around. Legislators voted for by people who own private places in which they can do all these things are increasingly deciding to make public places available only for activities other than these primal human tasks. The streets and subways, they say, are for commuting from home to office. They are not for sleeping; sleeping is something one does at home. The parks are for recreations like walking and informal ball-games, things for which one's own yard is a little too confined. Parks are not for cooking or urinating; again, these are things one does at home. Since the public and the private are complementary, the activities performed in public are to be the complement of those appropriately performed in private. This complementarity works fine for those who have the benefit of both sorts of places. However, it is disastrous for those who must live their whole lives on common land. If I am right about this, it is one of the most callous and tyrannical exercises of power in modern times by a (comparatively) rich and complacent majority against a minority of their less fortunate fellow human beings.

———

NOTES AND QUESTIONS

1. Illicit activity as means for survival. Traditionally, the majority of African American women have been obliged, by necessity, to work outside the home to support their families. LEITH MULLINGS, ON OUR OWN TERMS: RACE, CLASS, AND GENDER IN THE LIVES OF AFRICAN AMERICAN WOMEN 90 (1997). Due to severe levels of unemployment of black men, the labor force participation rate of black females has become approximately equal to that of black males. *Id.* Though black women comprise a considerable proportion of the labor force, women like Rosa Lee still face several obstacles to achieve economic stability and must therefore resort to either government assistance and/or illicit activity to support their families. In a study performed in Central Harlem in 1990, for example, 54.7 percent of women eligible to work were not in the labor force, with 28.9 percent of individuals residing in Harlem receiving Aid to Families with Dependent Children. *Id.* at 91 (citing *Persons 16 Years and Over by Labor Force Status and Sex, New York City, Boroughs and Community Districts.* (New York: Department of City Planning, no. 317, 1990)). Furthermore, that study found that more than half of all households in Harlem headed by females that include children under age eighteen have incomes below the poverty line. *Id.* (citing *Socioeconomic profiles: A Portrait of New York City's Community Districts from the 1980 and 1990 Census of Population and Housing* (New York: Department of City Planning)). Faced with poor odds of achieving economic stability, and in "just trying to survive," what can women like Rosa Lee do but break the law to support their families?

University of Pennsylvania Professor of Law Regina Austin explains that though illegal activity may be disparaged, it may be the only means for underprivileged African Americans to survive in America:

> [F]or some poor blacks, breaking the law is not only a way of life: it is the only way to survive. Thus, what is characterized as economic deviance in the eyes of a majority of people may be viewed as economic resistance by a significant number of blacks. Regina Austin, *"An Honest Living": Street Vendors, Municipal Regulation, and The Black Public Sphere*, 103 YALE L.J. 2119, 2119 (1994).

Austin reaches this conclusion based on her study of black street vendors in major cities like New York, Washington, D.C., and Philadelphia. These vendors are part of an informal economy where merchants work without a license and in violation of applicable regulations and sales tax laws. Though illegal, street vending by black workers gives people jobs, supplies African Americans with their preferred products, contributes to the maintenance of African American culture, and assists individuals in gaining the necessary capital and knowledge to operate a business in the formal sector. Because of street vending's benefits for afflicted black communities, Austin stresses that such activity should not immediately be written off, and should instead be respected:

> As blacks in America, we must not fall into the trap of automatically equating legitimacy with legality. Just because an enterprise is small,

informal, and illegal does not mean that it is not valuable or that it should be disparaged. *Id.* at 2130.

Based on her comments, how do you think Austin would react to Rosa Lee's illegal behavior? Would she disagree with Rosa Lee's actions because stealing, like street vending, does not achieve legitimate objectives such as promoting African American black entrepreneurial activity?

2. Sociology of deviance. Are lawbreakers innately inclined to transgress social norms, or are they simply reacting to society's imposed institutions? In other words, are individuals like Rosa Lee instinctively prone to deviate from societal standards, or are they simply products of their insolvent, unstable environments? Howard S. Becker addressed these questions in *Outsiders: Studies in the Sociology of Deviance*, and proposed the premise that deviant peoples violate rules because social groups establish laws whose breach constitutes deviance, and by applying those laws and penalties to an "offender." Becker defines an outsider as an individual who others deem deviant and therefore unworthy of inclusion in society's "normal" social functions.

Would Howard Becker maintain that Rosa Lee is an outsider—one who is judged by law-abiders and stands outside of conventional social groups? Is she more likely to be labeled as an outsider because she is an African American? Becker elaborates on the implications of being an outsider:

> The degree to which an act will be treated as deviant depends also on who commits the act and who feels he has been harmed by it. Rules tend to be applied more to some persons than others. Studies of juvenile delinquency make the point clearly. Boys from middleclass areas do not get as far in the legal process when they are apprehended as do boys from slum areas. The middle-class boy is less likely, when picked up by the police, to be taken to the station; less likely when taken to the station to be booked; and it is extremely unlikely that he will be convicted and sentenced. This variation occurs even though the original infraction of the rule is the same in the two cases. Similarly, the law is differentially applied to Negroes and whites. It is well known that a Negro believed to have attacked a white woman is much more likely to be punished than a white man who commits the same offense; it is only slightly less well known that a Negro who murders another Negro is much less likely to be punished than a white man who commits murder.

HOWARD S. BECKER, OUTSIDERS: STUDIES IN THE SOCIOLOGY OF DEVIANCE 12–13 (1973).

Consider Becker's proposition and Rosa Lee's case. Recall that Rosa Lee was acquitted when she returned to court for a shoplifting charge. Though she is African American and a "deviant outsider," she was able to receive approval from the judge and continue to maintain her freedom. However, was Rosa Lee not trying to portray herself as an "insider" by wearing more respectable attire and emotionally appealing to the judge?

3. "Underclass" and "culture of poverty." Since the 1970s, conservative scholars and critics have attempted to highlight the role of "culture" in maintaining poverty, arguing that poverty becomes intergenerational when poor people lack self-discipline, initiative, and "soft skills" required for success in the working world. These arguments played a large part in welfare reform from the 1970s through the turn of the twenty-first century. A similar debate has gone on about the so-called "underclass," identified as a group of people (Marx would have called them an "industrial reserve army") so chronically lacking regular employment that they can be seen as having effectively been marginalized from the economy altogether. In the late 1980s, the media spent a lot of time worrying about the "underclass," which was said to epitomize all the cultural deviance (lack of initiative, dependency, and so on) exhibited by the poor more generally, and which was thought to be a breeding ground for street crime. For scholarly discussions of the "underclass," *see, e.g.,* WILLIAM JULIUS WILSON, THE TRULY DISADVANTAGED: THE INNER CITY, THE UNDERCLASS, AND PUBLIC POLICY (1987); CHRISTOPHER JENCKS, RETHINKING SOCIAL POLICY: RACE, POVERTY, AND THE UNDERCLASS (1992).

Is it "culture" or material conditions that account for the large gaps that remain in family income, wages, and employment between African Americans and whites? For a "cultural" explanation, *see, e.g.,* STEPHEN THERNSTROM & ABIGAIL THERNSTROM, *America in Black and White* (1997); for a "material" explanation, *see, e.g.,* MICHAEL K. BROWN, ET AL., WHITEWASHING RACE: THE MYTH OF A COLOR-BLIND SOCIETY 66–103 (2003). Does a material explanation account for the behavior of people like Rosa Lee?

4. *"Underclass"* and prison industrial complex. Some might argue that to the extent that an underclass exists, it is, ironically, the effect as much as the cause of state policy. The "war on drugs" and the "war on crime" more generally have created an incarceration crisis for many poor communities. African American and Latino men are incarcerated for long periods at dramatic rates, which creates a social ripple effect of poverty: ex-felons find it difficult to get jobs when they get out of prison; the removal of these men from families and neighborhoods places extra economic and social stress on the people left behind. This social disorganization, in turn, leads to more crime in the increasingly impoverished and dangerous neighborhoods of inner cities. *See* Tracey Meares, *Social Organization and Drug Law Enforcement,* 35 AM. CRIM. L. REV. 191 (1998); Dorothy Roberts, *The Social and Moral Cost of Mass Incarceration in African American Communities,* 56 STAN. L. REV. 1271 (2004).

Some scholars argue that this vicious circle is coupled with another vicious circle: the increasing dependency of strapped towns and counties on prisons as economic engines, which leads to the increased political power of prison guards and prison officials unions, which leads in turn to a continuation of punitive criminal justice policies. *See* Stephen C. Thaman, *Is America a Systematic Violator of Human Rights in the Administration of Criminal Justice?* 44 ST. LOUIS L.J. 999 (2000). Another element in the continuing appeal of punitive policies, some scholars argue, is the declining influence of criminal justice experts: criminal justice policy today tends to be seen as a populist issue and not an issue about which experts should have any particular say. In this environment, politicians promising to be "tough on crime" and prosecutors dominate the legislative process. *See* Franklin Zimring, *Populism, Democratic Government, and the Decline of Expert Authority: Some Reflections on "Three Strikes" in California,* 28 PAC. L.J. 243 (1996); William Stuntz, *The Pathological Politics of Criminal Law,* 100 MICH. L. REV. 505 (2001).

5. **Crime, class, and race**. The United States mass incarceration policy does not seem to have been either effective at stopping crime nor economically efficient. Why, then, has it persisted? Some scholars argue that punitive criminal justice policy serves ideological functions that are more powerful than their economic or social functions. *See, e.g.,* JEFFREY REIMAN, THE RICH GET RICHER AND THE POOR GET PRISON: IDEOLOGY, CLASS, AND CRIMINAL JUSTICE (7TH ED. 2003); MICHAEL TONRY, MALIGN NEGLECT: RACE, CRIME, AND PUNISHMENT IN AMERICA (1996); DAVID COLE, NO EQUAL JUSTICE: RACE AND CLASS IN THE AMERICAN CRIMINAL JUSTICE SYSTEM (2000).

6. **Homelessness and criminal justice policy.** Like "the underclass," "the homeless" are frequently a target of fear and loathing in American culture; like the poor generally, some make an effort to distinguish the innocent or involuntary homeless from those who have "chosen" their situation; and like poverty generally, homelessness and crime are closely connected in the public mind, resulting in, ironically, more criminalization. *See* CHRISTOPHER JENCKS, THE HOMELESS (1995); PETER H. ROSSI, DOWN AND OUT IN AMERICA: THE ORIGINS OF HOMELESSNESS (1991). For a lively discussion of how not only law but architecture and urban planning are affected by the desire to make homeless people invisible in city spaces, see MIKE DAVIS, CITY OF QUARTZ: EXCAVATING THE FUTURE IN LOS ANGELES (1992).

B.   RELATIONS OF (RE)PRODUCTION

The Working Poor: Invisible in America
39–44 50, 64–67 (2004).

■ DAVID K. SHIPLER

Christie did a job that this labor-hungry economy could not do without. Every morning she drove her battered '86 Volkswagen from her apartment in public housing to the YWCA's child-care center in Akron, Ohio, where she spent the day watching over little children so their parents could go to work. Without her and thousands like her across the country, there would have been fewer people able to fill the jobs that fueled America's prosperity. Without her patience and warmth, children could have been harmed as well, for she was more than a baby-sitter. She gave the youngsters an emotionally safe place, taught and mothered them, and sometimes even rescued them from abuse at home.

For those valuable services, she received a check for about $330 every two weeks. She could not afford to put her own two children in the day-care center where she worked.

Christie was a hefty woman who laughed more readily than her predicament should have allowed. She suffered from stress and high blood pressure. She had no bank account because she could not keep enough money long enough. Try as she might to shop carefully, she always fell behind on her bills and was peppered with late fees. Her low income entitled her to food stamps and a rental subsidy, but whenever she got a little pay raise, government agencies reduced the benefits, and she felt punished for working. She was trapped on the treadmill of welfare reform, running her life according to the rules of the Personal Responsibility and Work Opportunity Reconciliation Act of 1996. The title left no doubt about what Congress and the White House saw as poverty's cause and solution.

Initially the new law combined with the good economy to send welfare caseloads plummeting. As states were granted flexibility in administering time limits and work requirements, some created innovative consortiums of government, industry, and charity to guide people into effective job training and employment. But most available jobs had three unhappy traits: They paid low wages, offered no benefits, and led nowhere. "Many who do find jobs," the Urban Institute concluded in a 2002 report, "lose other supports designed to help them, such as food stamps and health insurance, leaving them no better off—and sometimes worse off—than when they were not working."

Christie considered herself such a case. The only thing in her wallet resembling a credit card was a blue-green piece of plastic labeled "Ohio" and decorated with a drawing of a lighthouse projecting a beam into the night. Inside the "O" was a gold square—a computer chip. On the second working day of every month, she slipped the card into a special machine at Walgreen's, Save-A-Lot, or Apple's, and punched in her identification number. A credit of $136 was loaded into her chip. This was the form in which her "food stamps" were now issued—less easy to steal or to sell, and less obvious and degrading in the checkout line.

The card contained her first bit of income in every month and permitted her first expenditure. It could be used for food only, and not for cooked food or pet food. It occupied the top line in the balance sheet she kept for me during a typical October.

"2nd Spent 136.00 food stamps," she wrote. So the benefit was all gone the day she got it. Three days later she had to come up with an additional $25 in cash for groceries, another $54 on October 10, and $15 more on the twelfth. Poor families typically find that food stamps cover only one-half to three-quarters of their grocery costs.

Even the opening balance on the card was chipped away as Christie inched up in salary. It makes sense that the benefit is based on income: the less you need, the less you get. That's the economic side. On the psychological side, however, it produces hellish experiences for the beneficiaries.

Every three months Christie had to take half a day off from work (losing half a day's wages) and carry an envelope full of pay stubs, utility bills, and rent receipts to be pawed over by her ill-tempered caseworker, who applied a state-mandated formula to figure her food stamp allotment and her children's eligibility for health insurance. When Christie completed a training course and earned a raise of 10 cents an hour, her food stamps dropped by $10 a month.

That left her $6 a month ahead, which was not nothing but felt like it. Many former welfare recipients who go to work just say good riddance to the bureaucracies that would provide food stamps, medical coverage, and housing. Some think wrongly that they're no longer eligible once they're off welfare; others would rather forfeit their rights than contend with the hassle and humiliation. Quiet surrender ran against Christie's grain, however. She was smart and insistent, as anyone must be to negotiate her way through the system. She never flinched from appealing to higher authority. When she once forgot to put a utilities bill in her sheaf of papers, her caseworker withheld her food stamps. "I mailed it to her the next day," Christie said. Two weeks passed, and the card remained empty. Christie called the caseworker. "She got really snotty," Christie remembered. " 'Well, didn't I tell you you were supposed to send some documentation?' "

"I was like, 'Have you checked your mail?' " No, as it turned out, the caseworker's mail had piled up unread. "She was like, 'Well, I got people waiting up to two, three months on food stamps.' And she didn't get back with me. I had to go to her supervisor." The benefits were then restored.

It is easy to lose your balance having one foot planted tentatively in the working world and the other still entwined in this thicket of red tape. Managing relations with a boss, finding reliable child care, and coping with a tangle of unpaid bills can be daunting enough for a single mother with little such experience; add surveillance by a bureaucracy that seems more prosecutor than provider, and you have Christie's high blood pressure.

While she invoked the system's rules to get her due, she also cheated—or thought she did. Living with her surreptitiously was her boyfriend, Kevin, the father of her son. She was certain that if the Housing Authority knew, she would be evicted, either because he was a convicted felon (two years for assault) or because his earning power, meager though it was, would have lifted her beyond eligibility. So slight are the margins between government assistance and outright destitution that small lies take on large significance in the search for survival.

Kevin looked like a friendly giant—a solid 280 pounds, a shaved head, and a small earring in his right ear. His income was erratic. In decent weather he made $7.40 an hour working for a landscaper, who rewarded him with a free turkey to end the season at Thanksgiving—and then dumped him onto unemployment for the winter. He wanted to drive a truck or cut meat. He had received a butcher's certificate in a training course during imprisonment, but when he showed the document from the penitentiary, employers didn't rush to put a knife in his hand.

The arithmetic of Christie's life added up to tension, and you had to look hard through her list of expenditures to find fun or luxury. On the fifth she received her weekly child support check of $37.66 from Kevin (she got nothing from her daughter's father, who was serving a long prison sentence for assault). The same day, she put $5 worth of gas in her car, and the next day spent $6 of her own money to take the day-care kids to the zoo. The eighth was payday, and her entire $330 check disappeared in a flash. First, there was what she called a $3 "tax" to cash her check, just one of several such fees for money orders and the like—a penalty for having no checking account. Immediately, $172 went for rent, including a $10 late fee, which she was always charged because she never had enough to pay by the first of the month. Then, because it was October and she had started to plan for Christmas, she paid $31.47 at a store for presents she had put on layaway, another $10 for gasoline, $40 to buy shoes for her two kids, $5 for a pair of corduroy pants at a secondhand shop, another $5 for a shirt, $10 for bell-bottom pants, and $47 biweekly car insurance. The $330 was gone. She had no insurance on her TVs, clothes, furniture, or other household goods.

Utilities and other bills got paid out of her second check toward the end of the month. Her phone usually cost about $43 a month, gas for the apartment $34, electricity $46, and prescriptions between $8 and $15. Her monthly car payment ran $150, medical insurance $72, and cable TV $43. Cable is no longer considered a luxury by low-income families that pinch and sacrifice to have it. So much of modern American culture now comes through television that the poor would be further marginalized without the broad access that cable provides. Besides, it's relatively cheap entertainment. "I just have basic," Christie explained. "I have an antenna, but you can't see anything, you get no reception." And she needed good reception because she and Kevin loved to watch wrestling.

One reason for Christie's tight budget was the abundance of high-priced, well-advertised snacks, junk food, and prepared meals that provide an easy fallback diet for a busy working mother—or for anyone who has never learned to cook from scratch. Besides the staples of hamburgers, and chicken, "I buy sausages," Christie said, "I buy the TV dinners 'cause I might be tired some days and throw it in the oven—like Salisbury steaks and turkey and stuff like that. My kids love pizza. I get the frozen pizzas.... I buy my kids a lot of breakfast things 'cause we're up early and we're out the door. You know, those cereal bars and stuff like that, they're expensive! You know? Pop Tarts, cereal bars, Granola." The cheaper breakfasts, like hot cereal, came only on weekends, when she had time. "They eat the hot cereal, but during the week we're on the go. So I give them cereal in the bag. My son likes to eat dry cereal, so I put him some cereal in the lunch bag. Cocoa Puffs. They got Cocoa Dots." She laughed. "Lucky Charms. He's not picky. My daughter's picky." Those candylike cereals soak up dollars. At my local supermarket, Lucky Charms cost dearly: $4.39 for a box of just 14 ounces, while three times as much oatmeal goes for nearly the same price, $4.29. * * *

Her mother, "Gladys," had dropped out of high school, spent years on welfare, and nurtured the fervent dream of seeing her three children in college. The ambition propelled two of them. Christie's brother became an accountant, and her sister, a loan officer. But Christie never took to higher education. She began reluctantly at the University of Akron, lived at home, and finally got fed up with having no money. The second semester of her sophomore year, she went to work instead of to school, a choice that struck her then as less momentous than it turned out to be.

"She didn't take things as serious as they really were," Gladys complained. "Now she sees for herself how serious this is." Just how serious depended on what she wanted to do. She loved working with children but now discovered that without a college degree she would have trouble getting hired at a responsible level in the Head Start preschool program, much less as a teacher in a regular school; she was limited to a YWCA daycare center whose finances were precarious. Since 95 percent of the Y's children came from low-income families, the fees were essentially set by the center's main source of income, Ohio's Department of Human Services, which paid $99 to $114 a week for full-time care. Given the center's heavy expenses, the rates were not enough to pay teachers more than $5.30 to $5.90 an hour.

Christie's previous jobs had also imprisoned her close to the minimum wage as a hostess-cashier at a Holiday Inn, a cashier at Kmart, a waitress in a bar, a cook and waitress and cashier in various restaurants. She had become a veteran of inadequate training programs designed to turn her into a retail salesperson, a bus driver, and a correctional officer, but the courses never enabled her and her classmates to pass the tests and get hired. She had two words to explain why she had never returned to college. "Lazy. Lazy."

It was strange that she thought of herself as lazy, because her work was exhausting, and her low wage required enormous effort to stay afloat.
* * *

The new millennium arrived in a crescendo of American riches. The nation wallowed in luxury, burst with microchips, consumed with abandon, swaggered globally. Everything grew larger: homes, vehicles, stock portfolios, life expectancy. Never before in the sweep of human history had so many people been so utterly comfortable.

Caroline Payne was not one of them. A few weeks after New Year's Day, she sat at her kitchen table and reflected on her own history. Two of her three goals had been achieved: She had earned a college diploma, albeit just a two-year associate's degree. And she had gone from a homeless shelter into her own house, although it was mostly owned by a bank. The third objective, "a good-paying job," as she put it, still eluded her. Back in the mid–1970s, she earned $6 an hour in a Vermont factory that made plastic cigarette lighters and cases for Gillette razors. In 2000, she earned $6.80 an hour stocking shelves and working cash registers at a vast Wal-Mart superstore in New Hampshire. * * *

Anyone who walked all the way around the outside of the Wal-Mart superstore on Route 103 would walk a mile, Caroline said. The place was immense. It sold everything from lawn mowers to ground beef, underpricing smaller stores that were struggling to survive in the center of town. Its 300 to 330 employees, who came and went seasonally, wore Wal-Mart's uniform of blue smocks and friendly smiles, trained as they were to be surprisingly helpful to customers.

Mark Brown, the manager, could pay his people more without raising prices, he conceded. He sat at a table in the store's snack bar, watching the part of the grocery section he could see, listening to the public address system's call for help at the registers, his eyes darting around this corner of his fiefdom like a school principal waiting for the next catastrophe. He was thirty-one, but he looked as young as a college kid and spoke with the twang of his native southeast Missouri. He had come from another store in Georgia and was learning to ski here in New Hampshire.

His employees started at $6.25 an hour, earned an extra dollar at night and another 25 cents "for going to the front end," which meant working one of the twenty-four cash registers. And if he started them at $8 an hour, say, instead of $6.25, how would that change the economics of the store? "Hmmmm. I don't think it would change at all." He wouldn't have to raise prices? "No. We've got a corporate pricing structure. And the way we do things, we go out and we check our competition every single week. Every department manager in this store goes out once a week and checks competition, and that's what determines our prices. We have a core price structure that we set regionally, by areas. Definitely the base price here would be probably higher than what it is in Arkansas, where there's a cheap cost of living. So it would be higher here, but it would still be standard to this area. And then after they give us that base, then we go out and check our competition, and if we're gettin' beat, we lower our prices."

So there's enough profit to absorb an increase from $6.25 to $8? "There would be, because if we were having to raise our wages, then evidently everybody else would be too, and if we make sure we're low enough, our competitors' customers are gonna shop with us." Would wage increases have any effect at all? "We'd have to cut corners on other things like, you know, we may not be able to put all the pretty balloons up all over the store. The non-necessities we'd have to cut back on."

Three days later Wal-Mart Stores, Inc., announced a net income of $5.58 billion for 1999, up 26 percent from the previous year.

Caroline was bouncing from one department to another, from one shift to another, but her pay stayed within a narrow range, beginning at $6.25, going to $6.80, sometimes up to $7.50 if she worked at night. So unpredictable were her hours that she couldn't work a second job, which would have helped her cash flow. She kept applying to higher positions and kept hearing that she needed a bit more experience. * * *

In more depressed parts of the country and during recessions,* * * some Wal-Mart managers were accused of forcing employees to work before punching in or after punching out to avoid paying overtime as required by law. "Wal-Mart management doesn't hold itself to the same standard of rectitude it expects from its low-paid employees," wrote Barbara Ehrenreich, who worked at a Wal-Mart in Minnesota while researching her book *Nickel and Dimed*. "When I applied for a job at Wal-Mart in the spring of 2000, I was reprimanded for getting something 'wrong' on this test: I had agreed only 'strongly' to the proposition, 'All rules have to be followed to the letter at all times.' The correct answer was 'totally agree.' Apparently the one rule that need not be slavishly adhered to at Wal-Mart is the federal Fair Labor Standards Act, which requires that employees be paid time and a half if they work more than forty hours in a week." Workers were warned against "time theft," which meant "doing anything other than working during company time, anything at all," she reported. "Theft of *our* time is not, however, an issue."

Caroline never had the overtime problem in her New Hampshire store, but in six Southern states employees filed a class-action suit against the company for ordering them off the clock as their weekly time approached forty hours. Their attorney calculated the benefits to the firm: If each of 250 hourly wage "associates" in a single store worked just one hour of unpaid overtime a week, that would total 250 unpaid hours a week, 1,000 a month, 12,000 a year—and there were over 300 Wal-Mart stores in Texas, producing savings in that state alone of more than $30 million that should have been paid to employees.

Caroline did not suffer from any violations of law, as far as she could tell, but her career went nowhere. Mark Brown, the manager who liked her, got transferred to Pennsylvania, dimming her prospects for advancement. So after a year and a half at Wal-Mart, she signed up with a temp agency, which found her a $7.50–an-hour daytime job Monday through Friday assembling wallpaper sample books. And she had the pleasure of telling Wal-Mart's assistant manager that she was leaving for higher pay.

Down and Out in Discount America

The Nation, Dec. 16 2004, http://www.thenation.com/doc.mhtml?i=20050103&s=featherstone).

■ LIZA FEATHERSTONE

On the day after Thanksgiving, the biggest shopping day of the year, Wal-Mart's many progressive critics—not to mention its business competitors—finally enjoyed a bit of schadenfreude when the retailer had to admit to "disappointing" sales. The problem was quickly revealed: Wal-Mart hadn't been discounting aggressively enough. Without low prices, Wal-Mart just isn't Wal-Mart.

That's not a mistake the big-box behemoth is likely to make again. Wal-Mart knows its customers, and it knows how badly they need the discounts. Like Wal-Mart's workers, its customers are overwhelmingly female, and struggling to make ends meet. Betty Dukes, the lead plaintiff in *Dukes v. Wal-Mart*, the landmark sex-discrimination case against the company, points out that Wal-Mart takes out ads in her local paper the same day the community's poorest citizens collect their welfare checks. "They are promoting themselves to low-income people," she says. "That's who they lure. They don't lure the rich. . . . They understand the economy of America. They know the haves and have-nots. They don't put Wal-Mart in Piedmonts. They don't put Wal-Mart in those high-end parts of the community. They plant themselves right in the middle of Poorville."

Betty Dukes is right. A 2000 study by Andrew Franklin, then an economist at the University of Connecticut, showed that Wal-Mart operated primarily in poor and working-class communities, finding, in the bone-dry language of his discipline, "a significant negative relationship between median household income and Wal-Mart's presence in the market." Although fancy retailers noted with chagrin during the 2001 recession that absolutely everybody shops at Wal-Mart—"Even people with $100,000 incomes now shop at Wal-Mart," a PR flack for one upscale mall fumed— the Bloomingdale's set is not the discounter's primary market, and probably never will be. Only 6 percent of Wal-Mart shoppers have annual family incomes of more than $100,000. A 2003 study found that 23 percent of Wal-Mart Supercenter customers live on incomes of less than $25,000 a year. More than 20 percent of Wal-Mart shoppers have no bank account, long considered a sign of dire poverty. And while almost half of Wal-Mart Supercenter customers are blue-collar workers and their families, 20 percent are unemployed or elderly.

Al Zack, who until his retirement in 2004 was the United Food and Commercial Workers' vice president for strategic programs, observes that appealing to the poor was "Sam Walton's real genius. He figured out how to make money off of poverty. He located his first stores in poor rural areas and discovered a real market. The only problem with the business model is that it really needs to create more poverty to grow." That problem is cleverly solved by creating more bad jobs worldwide. In a chilling reversal of Henry Ford's strategy, which was to pay his workers amply so they could buy Ford cars, Wal-Mart's stingy compensation policies—workers make, on average, just over $8 an hour, and if they want health insurance, they must pay more than a third of the premium—contribute to an economy in which, increasingly, workers can only afford to shop at Wal-Mart.

To make this model work, Wal-Mart must keep labor costs down. It does this by making corporate crime an integral part of its business strategy. Wal-Mart routinely violates laws protecting workers' organizing rights (workers have even been fired for union activity). It is a repeat offender on overtime laws; in more than thirty states, workers have brought wage-and-hour class-action suits against the retailer. In some cases, workers say, managers encouraged them to clock out and keep working; in others, managers locked the doors and would not let employees go home at the end of their shifts. And it's often women who suffer most from Wal-Mart's labor practices. *Dukes v. Wal-Mart*, which is the largest civil rights class-action suit in history, charges the company with systematically discriminating against women in pay and promotions. * * *

SOLIDARITY ACROSS THE CHECKOUT COUNTER

Given the poverty they have in common, it makes sense that Wal-Mart's workers often express a strong feeling of solidarity with the shoppers. Wal-Mart workers tend to be aware that the customers' circumstances are similar to their own, and to identify with them. Some complain about rude customers, but most seem to genuinely enjoy the shoppers.

One longtime department manager in Ohio cheerfully recalls her successful job interview at Wal-Mart. Because of her weight, she told her interviewers, she'd be better able to help the customer. "I told them I wanted to work in the ladies department because I'm a heavy girl." She understands the frustrations of the large shopper, she told them: " 'You know, you go into Lane Bryant and some skinny girl is trying to sell you clothes.' They laughed at that and said, 'You get a second interview!' "

One plaintiff in the *Dukes* lawsuit, Cleo Page, who no longer works at Wal-Mart, says she was a great customer service manager because "I knew how people feel when they shop, so I was really empathetic."

Many Wal-Mart workers say they began working at their local Wal-Mart because they shopped there. "I was practically born in Wal-Mart," says Alyssa Warrick, a former employee now attending Truman State University in Missouri. "My mom is obsessed with shopping.... I thought it would be pretty easy since I knew where most of the stuff was." Most assumed they would love working at Wal-Mart. "I always loved shopping there," enthuses *Dukes* plaintiff Dee Gunter. "That's why I wanted to work for 'em."

Shopping is traditionally a world of intense female communication and bonding, and women have long excelled in retail sales in part because of the identification between clerk and shopper. Page, who still shops at Wal-Mart, is now a lingerie saleswoman at Mervyn's (owned by Target). "I do enjoy retail," she says. "I like feeling needed and I like helping people, especially women."

Betty Dukes says, "I strive to give Wal-Mart customers one hundred percent of my abilities." This sentiment was repeated by numerous other Wal-Mart workers, always with heartfelt sincerity. Betty Hamilton, a 61-year-old clerk in a Las Vegas Sam's Club, won her store's customer service award last year. She is very knowledgeable about jewelry, her favorite department, and proud of it. Hamilton resents her employer—she complains about sexual harassment and discrimination, and feels she has been penalized on the job for her union sympathies—but remains deeply devoted to her customers. She enjoys imparting her knowledge to shoppers so "they can walk out of there and feel like they know something." Like Page, Hamilton feels she is helping people. "It makes me so happy when I sell something that I know is an extraordinarily good buy," she says. "I feel like I've done somebody a really good favor."

The enthusiasm of these women for their jobs, despite the workplace indignities many of them have faced, should not assure anybody that the company's abuses don't matter. In fact, it should underscore the tremendous debt Wal-Mart owes women: This company has built its vast profits not only on women's drudgery but also on their joy, creativity and genuine care for the customer.

WHY BOYCOTTS DON'T ALWAYS WORK

Will consumers return that solidarity and punish Wal-Mart for discriminating against women? Do customers care about workers as much as workers care about them? Some women's groups, like the National Organization for Women and Code Pink, have been hoping that they do, and have encouraged the public not to shop at Wal-Mart. While this tactic could be fruitful in some community battles, it's unlikely to catch on nationwide. A customer saves 20–25 percent by buying groceries at Wal-Mart rather than from a competitor, according to retail analysts, and poor women need those savings more than anyone.

That's why many women welcome the new Wal-Marts in their communities. *The Winona* (Minnesota) *Post* extensively covered a controversy over whether to allow a Wal-Mart Supercenter into the small town; the letters to the editor in response offer a window into the female customer's loyalty to Wal-Mart. Though the paper devoted substantial space to the sex discrimination case, the readers who most vehemently defended the retailer were female. From the nearby town of Rollingstone, Cindy Kay wrote that she needed the new Wal-Mart because the local stores didn't carry large-enough sizes. She denounced the local anti-Wal-Mart campaign as a plot by rich and thin elites: "I'm glad those people can fit into and afford such clothes. I can barely afford Shopko and Target!"

A week later, Carolyn Goree, a preschool teacher also hoping for a Winona Wal-Mart, wrote in a letter to the *Post* editor that when she shops at most stores, $200 fills only a bag or two, but at Wal-Mart, "I come out with a cart full top and bottom. How great that feels." Lacking a local Wal-Mart, Goree drives over the Wisconsin border to get her fix. She was incensed by an earlier article's lament that some workers make only $15,000 yearly. "Come on!" Goree objected. "Is $15,000 really that bad of a yearly income? I'm a single mom and when working out of my home, I made $12,000 tops and that was with child support. I too work, pay for a mortgage, lights, food, everything to live. Everything in life is a choice.... I am for the little man/woman—I'm one of them. So I say stand up and get a Wal-Mart."

Sara Jennings, a disabled Winona reader living on a total of $8,000, heartily concurred. After paying her rent, phone, electric and cable bills, Jennings can barely afford to treat herself to McDonald's. Of a recent trip to the LaCrosse, Wisconsin, Wal-Mart, she raved, "Oh boy, what a great treat. Lower prices and a good quality of clothes to choose from. It was like heaven for me." She, too, strongly defended the workers' $15,000 yearly income: "Boy, now that is a lot of money. I could live with that." She closed with a plea to the readers: "I'm sure you all make a lot more than I. And I'm sure I speak for a lot of seniors and very-low-income people. We *need* this Wal-Mart. There's nothing downtown."

FROM CONSUMERS TO WORKERS AND CITIZENS

It is crucial that Wal-Mart's liberal and progressive critics make use of the growing public indignation at the company over sex discrimination, low pay and other workers' rights issues, but it is equally crucial to do this in ways that remind people that their power does not stop at their shopping dollars. It's admirable to drive across town and pay more for toilet paper to avoid shopping at Wal-Mart, but such a gesture is, unfortunately, not enough. As long as people identify themselves as consumers and nothing more, Wal-Mart wins.

The invention of the "consumer" identity has been an important part of a long process of eroding workers' power, and it's one reason working people now have so little power against business. According to the social historian Stuart Ewen, in the early years of mass production, the late nineteenth and early twentieth centuries, modernizing capitalism sought to turn people who thought of themselves primarily as "workers" into "consumers." Business elites wanted people to dream not of satisfying work and egalitarian societies—as many did at that time—but of the beautiful things they could buy with their paychecks.

Business was quite successful in this project, which influenced much early advertising and continued throughout the twentieth century. In addition to replacing the "worker," the "consumer" has also effectively displaced the citizen. That's why, when most Americans hear about the Wal-Mart's worker-rights abuses, their first reaction is to feel guilty about shopping at the store. A tiny minority will respond by shopping elsewhere—and only a handful will take any further action. A worker might call her union and organize a picket. A citizen might write to her congressman or local newspaper, or galvanize her church and knitting circle to visit local management. A consumer makes an isolated, politically slight decision: to shop or not to shop. Most of the time, Wal-Mart has her exactly where it wants her, because the intelligent choice for anyone thinking as a consumer is not to make a political statement but to seek the best bargain and the greatest convenience.

To effectively battle corporate criminals like Wal-Mart, the public must be engaged as citizens, not merely as shoppers. What kind of politics could encourage that? It's not clear that our present political parties are up to the job. Unlike so many horrible things, Wal-Mart cannot be blamed on George W. Bush. The Arkansas-based company prospered under the state's native son Bill Clinton when he was governor and President. Sam Walton and his wife, Helen, were close to the Clintons, and for several years Hillary Clinton, whose law firm represented Wal-Mart, served on the company's board of directors. Bill Clinton's "welfare reform" has provided Wal-Mart with a ready workforce of women who have no choice but to accept its poverty wages and discriminatory policies.

Still, a handful of Democratic politicians stood up to the retailer. California Assemblywoman Sally Lieber, who represents the 22nd Assembly District and is a former mayor of Mountain View, was outraged when she learned about the sex discrimination charges in *Dukes v. Wal-Mart*, and she smelled blood when, tipped off by dissatisfied workers, her office discovered that Wal-Mart was encouraging its workers to apply for public assistance, "in the middle of the worst state budget crisis in history!" California had a $38 billion deficit at the time, and Lieber was enraged that taxpayers would be subsidizing Wal-Mart's low wages, bringing new meaning to the term "corporate welfare."

Lieber was angry, too, that Wal-Mart's welfare dependence made it nearly impossible for responsible employers to compete with the retail giant. It was as if taxpayers were unknowingly funding a massive plunge to the bottom in wages and benefits—quite possibly their own. She held a press conference in July 2003, to expose Wal-Mart's welfare scam. The Wal-Mart documents—instructions explaining how to apply for food stamps, Medi-Cal (the state's healthcare assistance program) and other forms of welfare—were blown up on posterboard and displayed. The morning of the press conference, a Wal-Mart worker who wouldn't give her name for fear of being fired snuck into Lieber's office. "I just wanted to say, right on!" she told the assemblywoman.

Wal-Mart spokespeople have denied that the company encourages employees to collect public assistance, but the documents speak for themselves. They bear the Wal-Mart logo, and one is labeled "Wal-Mart: Instructions for Associates." Both documents instruct employees in procedures for applying to "Social Service Agencies." Most Wal-Mart workers I've interviewed had co-workers who worked full time for the company and received public assistance, and some had been in that situation themselves. Public assistance is very clearly part of the retailer's cost-cutting strategy. (It's ironic that a company so dependent on the public dole supports so many right-wing politicians who'd like to dismantle the welfare state.)

Lieber, a strong supporter of the social safety net who is now assistant speaker pro tempore of the California Assembly, last year passed a bill that would require large and mid-sized corporations that fail to provide decent, affordable health insurance to reimburse local governments for the cost of providing public assistance for those workers. When the bill passed, its opponents decided to kill it by bringing it to a statewide referendum. Wal-Mart, which just began opening Supercenters in California this year, mobilized its resources to revoke the law on election day this November, even while executives denied that any of their employees depended on public assistance.

Citizens should pressure other politicians to speak out against Wal-Mart's abuses and craft policy solutions. But the complicity of both parties in Wal-Mart's power over workers points to the need for a politics that squarely challenges corporate greed and takes the side of ordinary people. That kind of politics seems, at present, strongest at the local level.

Earlier this year, labor and community groups in Chicago prevented Wal-Mart from opening a store on the city's South Side, in part by pushing through an ordinance that would have forced the retailer to pay Chicago workers a living wage. In Hartford, Connecticut, labor and community advocates just won passage of an ordinance protecting their free speech rights on the grounds of the new Wal-Mart Supercenter, which is being built on city property. Similar battles are raging nationwide, but Wal-Mart's opponents don't usually act with as much coordination as Wal-Mart does, and they lack the retail behemoth's deep pockets.

With this in mind, SEIU president Andy Stern has recently been calling attention to the need for better coordination—and funding—of labor and community anti-Wal-Mart efforts. Stern has proposed that the AFL-CIO allocate $25 million of its royalties from purchases on its Union Plus credit card toward fighting Wal-Mart and the "Wal-Martization" of American jobs.   * * *

Such efforts are essential not just because Wal-Mart is a grave threat to unionized workers' jobs (which it is) but because it threatens all American ideals that are at odds with profit—ideals such as justice, equality and fairness. Wal-Mart would not have so much power if we had stronger labor laws, and if we required employers to pay a living wage. The company knows that, and it hires lobbyists in Washington to vigorously fight any effort at such reforms—indeed, Wal-Mart has recently beefed up this political infrastructure substantially, and it's likely that its presence in Washington will only grow more conspicuous.

The situation won't change until a movement comes together and builds the kind of social and political power for workers and citizens that can balance that of Wal-Mart. This is not impossible: In Germany, unions are powerful enough to force Wal-Mart to play by their rules. American citizens will have to ask themselves what kind of world they want to live in. That's what prompted Gretchen Adams, a former Wal-Mart manager, to join the effort to unionize Wal-Mart. She's deeply troubled by the company's effect on the economy as a whole and the example it sets for other employers. "What about our working-class people?" she asks. "I don't want to live in a Third World country." Working people, she says, should be able to afford "a new car, a house. You shouldn't have to leave the car on the lawn because you can't afford that $45 part."

NOTES AND QUESTIONS

1. **Wal-Mart as avatar of new economy.** Simon Head notes the phenomenal success of Wal-Mart:

> Within the corporate world Wal-Mart's preeminence is not simply a matter of size. In its analysis of the growth of U.S. productivity, or output per worker, between 1995 and 2000—the years of the "new economy" and the high-tech bubble on Wall Street—the McKinsey

Global Institute has found that just over half that growth took place in two sectors, retail and wholesale, where, directly or indirectly, Wal-Mart "caused the bulk of the productivity acceleration through ongoing managerial innovation that increased competition intensity and drove the diffusion of best practice." This is management-speak for Wal-Mart's aggressive use of information technology and its skill in meeting the needs of its customers.

In its own category of "general merchandise," Wal-Mart has taken a huge lead in productivity over its competitors, a lead of 44 percent in 1987, 48 percent in 1995, and still 41 percent in 1999, even as competitors began to copy Wal-Mart's strategy. Thanks to the company's superior productivity, Wal-Mart's share of total sales among all the sellers of "general merchandise" rose from 9 percent in 1987 to 27 percent in 1995, and 30 percent in 1999, an astonishing rate of growth which recalls the rise of the Ford Motor Company nearly a century ago. McKinsey lists some of the leading causes of Wal-Mart's success. For example, its huge, ugly box-shaped buildings enable Wal-Mart "to carry a wider range of goods than competitors" and to "enjoy labor economies of scale."

McKinsey mentions Wal-Mart's "efficiency in logistics," which makes it possible for the company to buy in bulk directly from producers of everything from toilet paper to refrigerators, allowing it to dispense with wholesalers. McKinsey also makes much of the company's innovative use of information technology, for example its early use of computers and scanners to track inventory, and its use of satellite communications to link corporate headquarters in Arkansas with the nationwide network of Wal-Mart stores. Setting up and fine-tuning these tracking and distribution systems has been the special achievement of founder Sam Walton's (the "Wal" of Wal-Mart) two successors as CEOs, David Glass and the incumbent Lee Scott.

Simon Head, *Inside the Leviathan,* 51 N.Y. Rev. Books 80 (2004), *available at* http://www.nybooks.com/archives. Wal-Mart's success has also, however, crucially relied on its ability to keep wages and benefits low. Like Featherstone, Head argues for stronger and better enforced labor laws, asserting that "Wal-Mart has reached back beyond the New Deal to the harsh, abrasive capitalism of the 1920s." *Id.*

2. Wal-Mart and gender discrimination. In the summer of 2004, a federal district court certified a sex discrimination class action against Wal-Mart on behalf of 1.6 million women who had worked at Wal-Mart since December 26, 1998. The plaintiffs in *Dukes v. Wal-Mart,* 222 F.R.D. 137 (N.D. Cal. 2004), the largest private civil rights case in United States history, alleged that Wal-Mart discriminated against its female employees in making promotions, job assignments, pay decisions and training, and retaliated against women who complained about such practices. *See* http://www.walmartclass.com.

3. Markets in poverty. Many services as well as goods are targeted to the poverty market. As David Shipler describes in his book, *The Working*

Poor: Invisible in America (2004), tax preparers, check-cashing outlets, credit card companies, and mortgage and other loan providers often market their services to poor people. Services to the poor, however, tend to cost more money than the same services to the middle-class or the wealthy. The "subprime" market is a lucrative one because the customers have few options, urgent need, and often little information about their rights. Shipler offers an example of how poverty costs money:

> Say you're short of cash, and the bills are piling up, along with some disconnection notices. Payday is two weeks away, and your phone and electricity will be shut off before then. The guy at the local convenience store, who has a booth for cashing checks, throws you a lifeline. If you need $100 now, you write him a check for $120, postdated by two weeks. He'll give you the $100 in cash today, hold your check until your wages are in your bank account, and then put the check through. Or you can give him the $120 in cash when you get it, and he'll return your check. Either way, 20 percent interest for two weeks equals 1.438 percent a day, or 521 percent annually. * * *

> Furthermore, the loans are not technically loans in some states, because there's a check. And if a check bounces, more severe penalties apply than those for unrepaid loans. Borrowing $300, for instance, an Indiana woman paid a $30 fee and wrote a check for $330. When the check bounced, her bank and the payday loan establishment charged $80 in fees. Then the lender took her to court, won triple damages of $990, lawyer's fees of $150, and $60 in court costs. The total charge on the $300 loan: $1,310.

SHIPLER, THE WORKING POOR, *supra* at 18–19.

4.   Health care and bankruptcy. A recent study found that about half of personal bankruptcy filers interviewed cited "medical causes" as the reason for their filing bankruptcy. Among those whose illnesses led to bankruptcy, out-of-pocket costs averaged $11,854 since the start of illness; 75.7 percent had insurance at the onset of illness. David U. Himmelstein et al., *Market Watch: Illness and Injury as Contributors to Bankruptcy*, HEALTH AFFAIRS, Feb. 2, 2005, http://content.healthaffairs.org/cgi/content/full/hlthaff.w5.63/DC1. The authors of the study concluded that "Even middle-class insured families often fall prey to financial catastrophe when sick." *Id.*

————

Nanny Diaries and Other Stories: Imagining Immigrant Women's Labor in the Social Reproduction of American Families

52 809, 813, 814–22, 832–47 (2003).

■ MARY ROMERO

> *Wanted: One young woman to take care of four-year-old boy. Must be cheerful, enthusiastic, and selfless—bordering on masochistic. Must*

relish sixteen-hour shifts with a deliberately nap-deprived preschooler. Must love getting thrown up on, literally and figuratively, by everyone in his family. Must enjoy the delicious anticipation of ridiculously erratic pay. Mostly, must love being treated like fungus found growing out of employer's Hermes bag. Those who take it personally need not apply.

INTRODUCTION

Two former nannies employed on the Upper East Side of Manhattan offer this want advertisement as an illustration of employers' expectations and working conditions awaiting potential employees. Although it is a fictionalized account of their total six-year experience as nannies while attending college, Emma McLaughlin and Nicola Kraus's *The Nanny Diaries: A Novel* has spurred significant attention from the media. * * *

  * * *

II.   *THE NANNY DIARIES*: REALITY OR FANTASY?

Given the media attention and public discourse generated by the novel, it is worth asking the question: How representative is *The Nanny Diaries?* * * *

Given the large number of undocumented immigrants and United States workers employed "off the books," workers with temporary or permanent visas, and the broad category that the Department of Labor and the Census classify as domestic service, precise numbers of domestics and nannies are difficult to obtain. Assessing the United States Bureau of Labor Statistics, Human Rights Watch estimates that 800,000 private household workers were officially recorded in 1998, of which 30% were immigrant women. Regions exporting the largest number of women to labor as domestic servants are Asia, Africa, Latin America, and Eastern Europe. Research conducted on domestics in the United States include immigrants from Latin America, the Caribbean, and the Philippines.

A distinctive characteristic of domestic service in the United States is the race and ethnic differences between employer and employee. The intersection of class, race, and ethnicity has been a prominent component to the study of African-American, Chicana and Japanese-American domestics. Racial distinctions remain a striking feature identifying caregivers from their charges and employers. Reflecting on the playground scene in Central Park depicted in *The Nanny Diaries*, one onlooker contrasted the faces of children and caretakers:

There are also adults there, but curiously, the faces of the two groups (adults and children) don't match. For every white child in a stroller, there is a black woman leaning down, to guide a juice box into their mouth. If she isn't black, she is Hispanic or Asian. The women are the children's nannies. In many cases, they are stepping in for white parents, who are working full-time.

Apparent differences between native-born and immigrant women of color employed as maids and nannies are education and previous work experience. African-American, Chicana and Japanese-American women rarely have more than a high school education. A growing number of Latina and Caribbean immigrants are high school and college graduates, and some have held white-collar positions in their homeland. Helma Lutz noted the international trend toward older and better educated third-world immigrant women in her survey of research on the globalization of domestic service. Unlike younger and single European immigrant women at the turn of the twentieth century, these women work to cope with financial crisis, to support families, and to educate their children. Thus, Nan's race, marital status, and citizenship are not characteristic of many women employed as nannies in the United States. With the exception of European women immigrating to the United States with J-1 visas to work as *au pairs* while pursuing their education, most immigrant women are not part-time college students. Nan's career trajectory is obviously destined for a professional or managerial position; whereas, older immigrant working mothers find little if any social mobility. For these women, domestic service is best described as a ghetto occupation rather than a bridging occupation.

Nan informs the reader of the existing continuum of childcare arrangements which she designates as three types of nanny gigs: (1) "a few nights a week for people who work all day and parent most nights;" (2) " 'sanity time' a few afternoons a week to a woman who mothers most days and nights;" and (3) "provide twenty-four/seven 'me time' to a woman who neither works nor mothers." Embedded in this classification are live-in positions (twenty-four hours a day, seven days a week) and day workers that might work solely for one employer full-time or for a number of employers. Employers make arrangements with agencies, franchises, collectives, or directly with the employee. Employees working on their own include some that are bonded and considered self-employed, and others working in the underground economy. However, the actual distinctions are reflected in the working conditions: hours of employment, wages, lack of benefits, and the inclusion of all household work alongside childcare.

Researchers and labor advocates reporting wages for immigrant women over the last decade point to the variability in the market. Grace A. Rosales found wages ranging from $100 to $400 a week in Los Angeles. In her study of immigrant women employed as domestics and nannies in Los Angeles, Pierrette Hondagneu-Sotelo states that many Latina live-in workers do not receive minimum wage, whereas day workers averaged a higher wage of $5.90 an hour. Doreen Mattingly interviewed current and former Latina domestics in San Diego during the same period and found the average hourly rate for day workers was $8.02 and for live-ins was $2.72. Rhacel Salazar Parreñas reports that Filipina women migrating to Los Angeles earned an average of $425 a week for providing elderly care and $350 a week for live-in housekeeping and childcare. In a survey conducted in 2000, the Center for the Childcare Workforce in Washington, D.C., found that half of childcare providers earned less than $4.82 an hour and worked 55 hours a week. Human Rights Watch reviewed 43 egregious cases among domestic workers with special visas in the United States, and found a median hourly rate of $2.14.

Variation in wages and working conditions among employees points to the hierarchical structure in domestic service reinforced by employers' preferences. Obviously the hierarchy was not completely lost by McLaughlin and Kraus. In a reading at a Barnes & Noble bookshop, Kraus acknowledged the privileged subject position she and her colleague experienced: "We were the Hermès bags of nannies.... [A]s white, middle-class and university-educated nannies they [she and McLaughlin] were able to avoid the seamier elements of the industry." Latina and Caribbean immigrants are more vulnerable in the labor market than European immigrants. Skills do appear to be taken into consideration under certain circumstances. For instance, in her study of language between nannies and children in Los Angeles, Patricia Baquedano–López concluded that speaking English and a high school education were assets that domestics used in their negotiations with employers.

McLaughlin and Kraus portray a typical day of nanny tasks as "spent schlepping Grayer to French class, music lessons, karate, swimming, school and play dates." Although consistent with the image of Maria Rainer, the governess that Captain Von Trapp hired to care for his children in the film *The Sound of Music*, most employers with a live-in nanny assign employees a wide range of household tasks. While the distinction between housekeepers and nannies is frequently used to distinguish workers employed primarily to care for children, housekeepers may occasionally be asked to assist in childcare and nannies may be expected to cook, wash dishes, "pick-up," and do other household work directly related to the care of children. A consistent complaint among nannies is the expectation that they do housework and cook, alongside caring for children. Distinctions between domestic workers or private household workers and nannies are blurred in the everyday reality of employees as they engage in a broad range of household and caregiving activities, including cleaning, cooking, laundry, nursing the sick, supervising, playing with children, and grocery shopping.

Obviously, the most lucrative and sought after positions are the ones that make a clear distinction between tasks and recognize employees' skills, expertise, and experience. Immigrant women, particularly those who are undocumented, are more likely to be hired for live-in, as well as day work, positions that do not have clearly defined job descriptions. These nannies are unlikely to have much authority over the children or in planning activities. Instead, they find themselves at the beck and call of children as they serve and wait on them. Given the number of immigrant women nannies that McLaughlin and Kraus saw in the park, it is not surprising that they wrote, "[E]very playground has at least one nanny getting the shit kicked out of her by an angry child." *San Francisco Chronicle* reporter Adair Lara differentiated job descriptions offered to non-immigrant women:

"At the other end of the spectrum, a professional nanny often works weekends, engages the child in imaginative play, knows CPR. . . . She will want her hours guaranteed, will expect a bonus, and might be persnickety about doing more than the dishes and the baby's laundry."

Nan's life implies that work as a nanny is filled with new learning opportunities and adventures, from learning to cook exotic foods for Grayer to vacationing among the rich and famous. This depiction does not capture the overwhelming sense of isolation reported by immigrant women, particularly among live-in workers. Since Lucy Salmon's sociological study at the turn of the century, extreme isolation continues to be cited among live-in workers as one of the worst aspects of the job. Isolation from relatives, friends, and other domestic workers removes them from gaining resources to find employment elsewhere. Separation from their own children is frequently identified as a major force in developing strong emotional attachment to their charges. Domestics' loneliness is not countered by stimulating tasks. In the transformation of domestic labor from the unpaid work of mothers to low-wage work, physical demands are increased and more creative aspects are eliminated. The transformation from unpaid to paid childcare results in assigning immigrant nannies to the least pleasant tasks. Childcare advocates Suzanne W. Helburn and Barbara R. Bergmann describe the division as follows: "The parents try to reserve the more interesting child-rearing tasks for themselves. They do the storytelling and reading, supervise homework, and organize outings and parties in order to spend 'quality time' with their children."

Like the public discourse generated by the Nannygate scandals over the last decade, *The Nanny Diaries* examined the impact on employers and their children rather than on the employees and their children. Editorials and book reviews focus on employer rights to privacy, poor parenting, and the suffering and deprivation of "the poor little rich boy, Grayer." Since the novel's fictionalized couple who hired the nanny was portrayed as a cheating husband and an unemployed trophy wife, the stage is set against a public debate over the needs of working parents. Labor issues are contextualized as interpersonal gender relationships between women (and their competing expectations and emotions in doing "women's work") and the difficulty of employees identifying as a servant. Reference to immigrant nannies are curtailed to discussions concerning the impact that their limited English skills and cultural differences have on children under their care.

However, when immigrant women speak for themselves, the following list of labor issues are similar to the concerns expressed by workers in the United States: low wages, unpaid hours, lack of decent standards, absence of health insurance and other employee benefits, and constant supervision. In the case of live-in domestics, employer abuses include violations of their human rights. Grievances reported in Bridget Anderson and Philzacklea's international study that are also found in the United States include:

> denial of wages in cases of dismissal following trial or probation periods, refusal by employers to arrange legal resident status (for tax

reasons, etc.); control and sexual harassment; pressure to do additional work (for friends and colleagues); excessive workloads, especially where in addition to caring for children and elderly people they are responsible for all other household chores; and finally the very intimate relationship between the domestic helpers and their employers.

Human Rights Watch cites the following additional employer abuses in the United States: "basic telephone privileges, prohibiting them from leaving employers' homes unaccompanied, and forbidding them to associate or communicate with friends and neighbors." "To prevent domestic workers from leaving exploitative employment situations, employers confiscate the workers' passports and threaten them with deportation if they flee. In the most severe cases of abuse, migrant domestic workers—both live-in and day workers—have reported instances of sexual assault, physical abuse, and rape." Health hazards posed by cleaning chemicals "causing everything from skin irritation and rashes to serious respiratory problems from inhaling toxic fumes" is another grievance reported by human rights and labor advocates.

* * *

IV.   IMMIGRANT NANNY CARE AND THE REPRODUCTION OF PRIVILEGE

Globalization of childcare is based on income inequality between women from poor countries providing low-wage care work for families in wealthier nations. Even with the low wages and variability in the market cited above, hiring a nanny is recognized as the most expensive childcare option. Researchers recognize this reality: "The grim truth is that some women's access to the high-paying, high-status professions is being facilitated through the revival of semi-indentured servitude. Put another way, one woman is exercising class and citizenship privilege to buy her easy way out of sex oppression." The largest number of domestic workers are located in areas of the country with the highest income inequality among women. In regions with minimal income inequality, the occupation is insignificant. Particular forms of domestic labor that affirm and enhance employers' status, shift the burden of sexism to low-wage women workers, and relegate the most physically difficult and dirty aspects of domestic labor. However, little attention has been given to the ways that privilege is reproduced through childcare arrangements and the significance that third-world immigrant women's labor plays in the reproduction of privilege.

Intensive and competitive mothering revolves around individuality, competition, and the future success of their children. Competition and individualism are values embedded in children's activities. Annette Lareau refers to this version of child rearing as "concerted cultivation" geared toward "deliberate and sustained effort to stimulate children's development and to cultivate ... cognitive and social skills." Concerted cultivation aims to develop children's ability to reason by negotiating with parents and placing value on children's opinions, judgments, and observations. Family leisure time is dominated by organized children activities, such as sports, clubs, and paid lessons (e.g., dance, music, tennis). Most children's time is adult-structured rather than child-initiated play. "Play is not just play anymore. It involves the honing of 'large motor skills,' 'communication skills,' 'hand-eye coordination,' and the establishment of 'developmentally appropriate behavior.' "

Qualities of intensive and competitive mothering are at odds with demanding careers. Everyday practices of intensive mothering [require] immense emotional involvement, constant self-sacrificing, exclusivity, and a completely child-centered environment. These mothering activities are financially draining and time-consuming. Mothers with disposable income use commodities to fulfill areas of intensive and competitive mothering that they find themselves falling short of. In *The Mother Puzzle*, Judith D. Schwartz argues that advertising companies use guilt as significant child leverage:

> Companies who are marketing to our guilt inevitably start marketing the guilt itself in order to keep us shopping. This toy will help your child develop motor skills (implicit message: his motor skills will suffer without it). This line of clothing is made of the softest cotton (implicit message: other, less expensive fabrics may be abrasive).

By the 1990s, "babies and children were firmly entrenched as possessions that necessitated the acquisition of other commodities (and that became more valuable with further investment in goods and services)." Advertisers targeted the new "Skippies" market (*s*chool *k*ids with *i*ncome and *p*urchasing *p*ower). Quoting *People* magazine, Schwartz characterizes parents of these "gourmet children" as "rapaciously grabbing kudos for their kids with the same enterprise applied to creating fortunes on Wall Street." She suggests that, "Teaching values to our children has been replaced by building value into them ... by preparing them to compete and giving them what we think they need to do so."

Hiring a live-in immigrant worker is the most convenient childcare option for juggling the demands of intensive mothering and a career. Purchasing the caretaking and domestic labor of an immigrant [woman] commodificates reproductive labor and reflects, reinforces, and intensifies social inequalities. The most burdensome mothering activities (such as cleaning, laundry, feeding babies and children, and chauffeuring children to their various scheduled activities) are shifted to the worker. Qualities of intensive mothering, such a sentimental value, nurturing, and intense emotional involvement, are not lost when caretaking work is shifted to an employee. Employers select immigrant caretakers on the basis of perceived "warmth," "love for children," and "naturalness in mothering." Different racial and ethnic groups are stereotyped by employers as ideal employees for housework, childcare, or for live-in positions. Stereotyping is based on a number of individual characteristics—race, ethnicity, class, caste, education, religion, and linguistic ability—and results in a degree of "otherness" for all domestic servants. However, such a formalization of difference does not always put workers in the subordinate position, and employers' preferences can vary from place to place. Janet Henshall Momsen notes that, "Professionally-trained British nannies occupy an élite niche in Britain and North America." Interviewing employers in Los Angeles and New York City, Julia Wrigley observed Spanish-speaking nannies were identified by employers for their ability to broaden the cultural experience of their children, particularly in exposing them to a second language in the home. Employers referenced the growing Latino population in their community and the long-term benefits of their children learning Spanish. However, the socialization to race and culture politics may be the most significant consequence of the current commodification of reproductive labor.

The primary mission of reproductive labor in contemporary mothering is to assure their children's place in society. This is partially accomplished through socialization into class, gender, sexual, ethnic and race hierarchies. Employment of immigrant women as caregivers contributes to this socialization. Reinforced by their parents' conceptualization of caretaking as a "labor of love," children learn a sense of entitlement to receiving affection from people of color that is detached from their own actions. Children learn to be "consumers of care" rather than providers of caregiving. Caretaking without parental authority does not teach children reciprocal respect but rather teaches that the treatment of women of color as "merely means, and not as ends in themselves." The division of labor between mother and live-in caretaker domestic stratifies components of reproductive labor and equates burdensome, manual and basic maintenance labor with immigrant women of color. This gendered division of labor serves to teach traditional patriarchal privilege. Privilege is learned as they acquire a sense of entitlement to having a domestic worker always on call to meet their needs.

Stratified reproductive labor of a live-in immigrant domestic assures "learned helplessness and class prejudice in the child," and teaches "[dependence], aggressiveness, and selfishness." Systems of class, racial, ethnic, gender and citizenship domination are taught to children by witnessing "the arbitrary and capricious interaction of parents and servants or if they are permitted to treat domestic servants in a similar manner." As children move from their homes located in class (and frequently racially) segregated neighborhoods to schools (also likely to be segregated), power relationships and the larger community's class and racial etiquette are further reinforced. "As care is made into a commodity, women with greater resources in the global economy can afford the best-quality care for their family." If mothering is directed toward assuring their child's social and economic status in society—a society that is racist, capitalist, and patriarchal—then her goals are strengthened by employing a low wage, full-time or live-in immigrant woman. Conditions under which immigrant women of color are employed in private homes is structured by systems of privilege and, consequently, employers' children are socialized into these norms and values.

V.   PROLONGATION OF IMMIGRANT WOMEN SUBORDINATION

Paid reproductive labor in the United States is structured along local, national and international inequalities, positioning third-world immigrant women as the most vulnerable workers. Careworkers are sorted by the degree of vulnerability and privilege. Consequently, paid domestic labor is not only structured around gender but is stratified by race and citizenship status, relegating the most vulnerable worker to the least favorable working conditions and placing the most privileged in the best positions. A major initiative in the American childcare movement is addressing low wages in the childcare industry. However, the plight of live-in caregivers and immigrant women as a specific group is rarely addressed. The solution of hiring a live-in domestic, used by a relatively privileged group, is a component of reproductive labor in the United States, and serves to intensify inequalities between women: first, by reinforcing childcare as a private rather than public responsibility; and second, by reaping the benefits gained by the impact of globalization and restructuring on third-world women. The globalization of domestic service contributes to the reproduction of inequality between nations in transnational capitalism and cases reported of domestic servitude is increasingly characterized as global gender apartheid.

Devaluation of immigrant women in the international division of labor begins in the home as unpaid labor; then is further devalued in the segregated labor forces within third-world countries used by wealthier nations for cheap labor. Women are relegated to low-wage factory work in textiles and electronics industries with no opportunities available for better-paid positions. Migrating and working as domestics becomes the primary strategy for sustaining households for both poor and middle-class women. The demand for low-wage migrant workers expands the pool of cheap labor that unemployment and welfare regulations are unable to maintain. Theorists have traditionally argued that women's unpaid domestic labor in the home served as a reserve labor force. Applying this qualification to immigrant domestic workers, the employment of third-world women becomes a significant source for reproducing a labor reserve, similar to the function of the unemployed and underemployed. Saskia Sassen states this proposition in the following question: "Does domestic service—at least in certain locations—become one of the few alternatives and does it, then, function, as a privatized mechanism for social reproduction and maintenance of a labor reserve?" The transnational export of women from global south to the rich industrialized countries of the north has resulted in promoting domestics as a major "export product." Transnational division of labor is determined "simultaneously by global capitalism and systems of gender inequality in both sending and receiving countries of migration."

A prominent feature of globalized reproductive labor is commodification. Parreñas argues that, "Commodified reproductive labor is not only low-paid work but declines in market value as it gets passed down the international transfer of caretaking." However, Anderson argues that the commodification process in globalization is not limited to the labor but is extended to the worker. In her work on the global politics of domestic labor, she points out that employers "openly stipulate that they want a particular type *person* justifying this demand on the grounds that they will be working in the home." Having hired the preferred racialized domestic caretaker on the basis of personal characteristics rather than former experience or skills, the emotional labor required is not recognized by the employer but the worker's caring "brings with it no mutual obligations, no entry into a community, no 'real' human relations, only money."

Employers' hiring preferences for employees who are a particular race, ethnicity, and nationality contributes to the hierarchical chain of domestic caretakers. Hondagneu-Sotelo notes that African Americans are no longer the preferred employee in Los Angeles homes because [they] are portrayed as "bossy" and with "terrifying images associated with young black men." Similar images are applied to Caribbean women in New York and are cautioned against coming "across in interviews as being in any way aggressive." Latina immigrants in Los Angeles are perceived as "responsible, trustworthy, and reliable" workers as well as "exceptionally warm, patient, and loving mothers." In the case of Filipina women, Dan Gatmaytan argues that their labor is distinctively featured in international division of labor as "docile and submissive," and thus, ideally packaged to be imported "by other countries for jobs their own citizens will not perform and for wages domestic citizens would not accept." Parreñas's findings suggest that employers view Filipinas as providing a "higher-quality" service because they speak English and generally have a higher education than Latina immigrants.

However, without state regulations of labor and immigration policies, employers' preferences are irrelevant in the racialization of reproductive labor in the United States. Joy Mutanu Zarembka, director of the Campaign for Migrant Domestic Workers' Rights, argues that the estimated four thousand special visas issued annually for third-world immigrant women contributes to commodification of these workers into a "maid to order" in the United States. Three visas perpetuating the subordination of immigrant women of color as live-in domestic workers are:

> A-3 visas to work for ambassadors, diplomats, consular officers, public ministers, and their families; G-5 visas to work for officers and employees of international organizations or of foreign missions to international organizations and their families; and B-1 visas to accompany U.S. citizens who reside abroad but are visiting the United States or assigned to the United States temporarily for no more than four years, or foreign nations with nonimmigrant status in the United States.

In contrast to special visas given primarily to third-world immigrant women, the J-1 visa is increasingly used to bring young and middle-class European immigrant women as nannies or *au pairs* with "educational and cultural exchange" their primary purpose. Under this visa, each nanny receives an orientation session and is placed in geographical locations near other nannies. After her placement, she attends an orientation session and "receives information on community resources, educational opportunities and contacts for a local support network." Counselors have monthly sessions with each employer and nanny to "report any problems and resolve disputes." "In contrast, with the G-5, A-1 and B-1 domestic worker programs, there are no official orientations, no information, no contact numbers, no counselors, and no educational programs. In practice, as well, there is often no freedom—many are systematically (though illegally) forbidden from contacting the outside world."

Human Rights Watch further asserts that special visas intensify workers' vulnerability to abuse and facilitate the violation of other human rights. Procedures, guidelines, laws, and regulations governing special domestic worker visas construct circumstances that tolerate and conceal employer abuses, and restrict workers' rights. Among the problems cited by Human Rights Watch are the lack of INS follow-up monitoring or investigations to verify employer compliance with employment contracts, and the Department of Labor's lack of involvement with administrating these visas. Consequently, no governmental agency is responsible for enforcing contracts. Zarembka asserts that the secrecy of the whereabouts of G-5, A-3 and B-1 workers makes "them some of the most vulnerable and easily exploited sectors of the American workforce" and violation of human rights is silenced by their invisibility. In addition to low wages, long hours, and the lack of both privacy and benefits that are common among live-in conditions, immigrant women experience other abuses. They include passport confiscation, limited freedom of movement and ability to communicate with others, employer threats of deportation, assault and battery, rape, servitude, torture, and trafficking. Changing employers under live-in conditions has always been difficult for workers, and for women with employment-based visas, they are faced with weighing "respect for their own human rights and maintaining their legal immigration status." For similar reasons, women are reluctant to report abuse because they fear losing their jobs, deportation, unfamiliarity with the American legal system, social and cultural isolation, and fear that "their retaliation powerful employers will retaliate against their families in their countries of origin."

Exclusion from a number of labor policies contribute to the hardships immigrant women experience as live-in domestics. They are excluded from overtime provisions provided in the Fair Labor Standard Act, from the right to organize, strike, and bargain collectively in the National Labor Relations Act, and from regulations in the Occupational Safety and Health Act. "In practice, too, live-in domestic workers are rarely covered by Title VII protections against sexual harassment in the workplace, as Title VII only applies to employers with fifteen or more workers."

Third-world immigrant domestics experience first hand the inequalities of caregiving as they provide labor for parents in rich industrialized countries while leaving their own children. Sarah Blaffer Hrdy equates mothers leaving their children with relatives in their homelands to European infants left in foundling homes or sent to wet nurses during the eighteenth century: "Solutions differ, but the tradeoffs mothers make, and the underlying emotions and mental calculations, remain the same." Anderson notes that immigrant women's care for their children is limited "in the fruits of hard labour, in remittances, rather than in the cuddles and 'quality time' that provide so much of the satisfaction of care." Transnational mothering cannot provide the "physical closeness, seen as healthy and 'normal' in the Western upbringing of a child, are not given, because most of the women are not allowed to take their children with them." These conditions reduce mothering to the basic function of economic support. In her research on Filipina women in Rome and Los Angeles, Parrenas observed the impact of economic ties rather than affective ties between mother and child departed from each over a long period of time. The use of material good, financial assistance, and school tuition result in commodifying family relationships and motherhood. Inequalities in the distribution and quality of domestic labor and caregiving is a cost borne by the children of live-in workers. The absence of retirement benefits pension assures that workers will not be able to contribute financially to their children's future, but rather will need their assistance.

VI. CONCLUSION

Before the September 11 attacks, the Federation for American Immigration Reform (FAIR), Patrick Buchanan, Pete Wilson and others vilified immigrants as the cause of all problems in the United States. Homeland security has further fanned the flames of xenophobia and support for vilifying immigrants. Yet, within the intimacy of many American homes, immigrant women (primarily Latina and Caribbean immigrants) continue to provide assisted reproductive labor that fulfills the basic tasks of maintaining families of dual career couples and contribute to middle-upper- and upper-class lifestyles. Popular culture functions to normalize the hiring of immigrant women by depicting domestic service as a bridging occupation that offers social mobility, opportunities to learn English, and other cultural skills that assist in the assimilation process. The characterization of nannies and private household workers in *The Nanny Diaries*, as well as in films and sitcoms, serves to reduce the significance of immigrant women in fulfilling childcare needs in the United States and to erase issues of employee rights from the American imagination. Instead, employers are classified as good or bad: good employers who are benevolent and provide immigrant women with a modernizing experience, or bad employers who are rich couples ignoring their children. Popular culture does not contextualize paid reproductive labor. Economic, political and legal structures surrounding the migration of Latina, Caribbean and Filipina women are ignored along with the circumstances that relegate their labor to low-wage dead-end jobs. Consequently, we can maintain our illusions of Latina domestics as sexually out of control and utterly colorful spitfire, the self-deprecating accented smart-mouthed, or the rosary-praying maid. We can continue to see these images and sing out, "Yes, that's what maids are like."

     * * *

Centering immigration on questions of "belonging" (and related concepts, e.g., assimilation, ethnic differences, and ethnic loyalty) blinds us to inquiries into the role of immigration in sustaining systems of privilege and perpetuating myths and ideologies central to national identity. Immigration and labor regulations reproduce race, class, gender and citizenship inequalities and privileges. In the case of immigrant women employed as private household workers or caregivers, the social reproduction of inequalities begins in the employer's home. Managing the contradictions of intimacy and vilification of immigrants through cultural images that falsify employee-employer relationships, allows Americans to reap the benefits of retaining a vulnerable labor force unprotected from exploitation while arguing humanitarian positions. The popular version of nannies depicted in *The Nanny Diaries* assists in normalizing privilege and erases issues of economic injustice. Our complacency in the subordination of immigrant women is once again obtained by our fascination with chatty gossip on sex, drugs, money, and family values of the wealthy on Park Avenue. Moreover, our illusion that there is no greater state of being than Americans is further enhanced by denying the privileges gained by third-world assisted social reproduction.

The Hidden Injuries of Class

79–87 (1972).

■ RICHARD SENNETT & JONATHAN COBB

Josiah Watson Grammar School is an old red-brick building with a simple but well-kept playground. It is a large school, in the midst of an urban neighborhood of mostly three-decker houses. In the community surrounding the school live groups of Irish, Italian, and old-stock New Englanders, but almost all are manual laborers. The median family income in the neighborhood is about $8000—neither poor nor affluent.

The rooms at the Watson School evoke the interiors of the children's homes: old, rather run down, and yet clean, almost austere. In each schoolroom the only decorations consist of an American flag, a bound set of maps, and a plaque with the Pledge of Allegiance. The school desks are new—tubular steel legs holding up flat wooden boxes. In them, children's supplies are neatly arranged, even for the littlest children. The teachers take a certain pride in this, but they apologize to the visitor for the tops scratched with the obscene words, drawings, and initials that children always seem to inflict on such objects.

The classes in Watson School, even as low as the second grade, jolt the outsider who has lost touch with the institutional life of children. Everything that goes on in the second-grade class, from reading preparedness to play with toys, is directed by the teacher. She takes great pains to see that the children act "good and proper." The visitor who is aware of his own presence in these classrooms at first thinks this show of discipline, this constant commanding and watching, is the teacher's response to that presence. After the teacher relaxes and forgets he is there, however, the discipline continues. It varies among the teachers from harsh to loving; but all those in charge of classrooms at the Watson School act like conductors who must bring potentially unruly mobs of musicians under their direction.

As the principal remarks, "It is by establishing authority that we make this school work."

In Watson School, teachers restrict the freedom of the children because these figures of authority have a peculiar fear of the children. It is the mass who seem to the teachers to threaten classroom order, by naughty or unruly behavior; only a few are seen as having "good habits" or the right attitude. As one teacher explained, "These children come from simple laborers' homes where the parents don't understand the value of education." Yet in the early grades the observer noticed few examples of disruptive behavior. He sensed among the six-and seven-year olds a real desire to please, to accept the teacher's control and be accepted by her. One pathetic incident, although extreme, stands out. In the middle of a reading-preparedness class, a child wet his pants because he was absorbed in his lesson. "What can you do with children like that?" the teacher later remarked in a tone of disgust.

What happens is that the teachers act on their expectations of the children in such a way as to *make* the expectations become reality. Here is how the process worked in one second-grade class at Watson School—unusual in that it was taught by a young man. In this class there were two children, Fred and Vincent, whose appearance was somewhat different from that of the others: their clothes were no fancier than the other children's, but they were pressed and seemed better kept; in a class of mostly dark Italian children, these were the fairest-skinned. From the outset the teacher singled out these two children, implying that they most closely approached his own standards for classroom performance. He never praised them openly by comparison to the other children, but a message that they were different, were better, was spontaneously conveyed. As the observer watched the children play and work over the course of the school year, he noticed these two boys becoming more serious, more solemn, as the months passed. Obedient and never unruly from the first, by the end of the year they were left alone by the other children.

By then they were also doing the best work in the class. The other children had picked up the teacher's hidden cues that their performance would not be greeted with as much enthusiasm as the work of these two little boys. "It's not true of the other children that they generally have less potential," the teacher remarked. "It's a question of not developing their ability like Fred and Vincent. I know you're right, I tend to encourage them more despite myself, but I—it's obvious to me these little boys are going to make something of themselves."

In the Watson School, by the time the children are ten or eleven the split between the many and the few who are expected to "make something of themselves" is out in the open; the aloofness developing in the second grade has become open hostility by the sixth. Among the boys, this hostility is expressed by images which fuse sex and status. Boys like Fred and Vincent are described by the "ordinary" students as effeminate and weak, as "suck-ups." The kids mean by this both that the Freds and Vincents are getting somewhere in school because they are so docile, and that only a homosexual would be so weak; the image of a "suck-up" crystallizes this self-demeaning, effeminate behavior that to them marks off a student whom the institution can respect.

What has happened, then, is that these children have directed their anger at their schoolmates who are rewarded as individuals rather than at the institution which is withholding recognition of them. Indeed, the majority of boys in the fifth and sixth grades are often not consciously in conflict with the school at all. Something more complex is happening to them.

These "ordinary" boys in class act as though they were serving time, as though schoolwork and classes had become something to wait out, a blank space in their lives they hope to survive and then leave. Their feeling, apparently, is that when they get out, get a job and some money, *then* they will be able to begin living. It is not so much that they are bored in school—many in Watson School like their classes. It is rather that they have lost any expectation that school will help them, that this experience will change them or help them grow as human beings.

One teacher in this school, an enthusiastic young woman who liked to work with "ordinary" students, said her greatest problem was convincing the students that they could trust her. The other teachers and the principal disapprove of her because she runs her class in an informal manner. They feel she lets the students "get away with anything," "that she can't keep discipline." Permissiveness is a vice, order a necessity, in the minds of the other teachers; they believe that most of their charges, due to family class background and past school performances, will resist following the rules which to an educated adult seem so logical and beneficial. It is not that these teachers are intentionally mean, but that they unwittingly set in motion in the classroom a vicious circle that produces exactly the kind of behavior they expect.

There is a counterculture of dignity that springs up among these ordinary working-class boys, a culture that seeks in male solidarity what cannot be found in the suspended time that comprises classroom experience. This solidarity also sets them off from the "suck-ups." Hanging around together, the boys share their incipient sexual exploits, real and imagined; sex becomes a way to compete within the group. What most cements them as a group, however, is the breaking of rules—smoking, drinking, or taking drugs together, cutting classes. Breaking the rules is an act "nobodies" can share with each other. This counterculture does not come to grips with the labels their teachers have imposed on these kids; it is rather an attempt to create among themselves badges of dignity that those in authority can't destroy.

A full circle: outsider observers—parents, teachers, and others—who see only the external aspects of this counterculture, are confirmed in their view that "hanging around" is destructive to a child's self-development. Dignity in these terms exacts a toll by the standards of the outer world.

The division of children, in schools like Watson, into groups with a shared sense of loyalty and individuals alone but "getting somewhere," characterizes many levels of education; it is not something unique to, say, college-bound youth as opposed to vocational school boys. Studies of trade schools show the same phenomenon occurring: boys who are good at car mechanics in school start to feel cut off from others, even though the possession of those skills might make them admired by their less-skilled peers outside of school. It is an institutional process that makes the difference, a question of mere toleration versus active approval from those in power.

The drama played out in the Watson School has as its script the assigning and the wearing of badges of ability like those described earlier, worn by adults. The teachers cast the Freds and Vincents into the role of Andrew Carnegie's virtuous man. Ability will make these children into individuals, and as individuals they will rise in social class. The mass find themselves in a role similar to that which Lipset assigns to adult workers: their class background allegedly limits their self-development, and the counterculture of compensatory respect they create reinforces, in a vicious circle, the judgments of the teachers.

The teacher has the *power* to limit the freedom of development of his or her students through this drama. But why is he or she moved to act in this repressive way? This question is really two questions: it is first a matter of a teacher legitimizing in his own mind the power he holds, and second, a matter of the students taking that power as legitimate.

The teachers are in a terrible existential dilemma. It is true that they are "prejudiced" against most of their students; it is also true that they, like all human beings, want to believe in the dignity of their own work, no matter how difficult the circumstances in which they have to work seem to them. If a teacher believed that every single student would perpetually resist him, he would have no reason to go on teaching—his power in the classroom would be empty. A teacher needs at least a responsive few in order to feel he has a *reason* to possess power. The few will confirm to him that his power to affect other people is real, that he can truly do good. To sort out two classes of ability, then, in fear of the "lower" class of students, is to create a meaningful image of himself as an authority rather than simply a boss.

It is true that an analysis at this level of teachers, or other power figures dealing with working-class people, is by itself inadequate. A teacher may be having an existential crisis, but that doesn't explain why images of social class and classes of ability have come to fuse in his mind, nor does it explain how useful, how convenient, this crisis of self-legitimacy is in keeping the present class structure going. Still, it is important to keep before ourselves the experiential reality facing a person who has power over others. The teachers at Watson did not think of themselves as tools of capitalism, or even as repressive. They felt they had to legitimize their own work's dignity in the face of working-class students; and making a moral hierarchy on the basis of ability—however artificially and unjustifiably—was the natural means they used.

The perceptions the children had of the teachers similarly concerned not their power, but their legitimacy.

The observer is playing marbles with Vinny, a third-grader, described by his teacher as an "unexceptional average student who tolerates school," and Vinny begins absentmindedly to arrange the marbles in sets by color. The observer points out to him that he is doing something like what the teacher had asked him to do in arithmetic hour and he hadn't then been able to do. Vinny replies, "I didn't want to give her no trouble"—an answer the observer notes without, at the time, understanding what Vinny meant. In a class on grammar, Stephanie gives a past participle incorrectly; the teacher asks her to try again, but while she is thinking, one of the bright children interrupts with the right answer. The teacher—the experimental and "permissive" woman already described—tells the bright child to shut up and gives Stephanie another answer to work out. Stephanie looks at her in total surprise, wondering why the teacher should still care about whether *she* can learn to do it, if the right answer has already been provided. Max, an obnoxious fifth-grade bully, has somehow formed an interest in writing doggerel rhymes. During a composition hour he reads one, but when he finishes, the teacher makes no reply, merely smiles and calls on the next pupil. Asked later how he felt, Max looks a little crestfallen and says with characteristic grace, "Lookit, shithead, she ain't got time to waste on me."

———

NOTES AND QUESTIONS

1. "Globalization" at top and bottom of economy. Saskia Sassen argues that "globalization" has produced both transnational marginalized labor classes and transnational privileged classes: while the elite of "global cities" such as New York, Hong Kong, and Paris are increasingly intertwined through networks of education and training, the "underclass" in such cities are also intertwined, through networks of migration and the demand for low-end service work. Saskia Sassen, *Toward a Feminist Analytics of the Global Economy*, 4 IND. J. GLOBAL LEGAL STUD. 7 (1996). Sassen argues that migration (legal and illegal), which is often treated as only a problem for the government sector to be solved through immigration law, should be seen as intimately connected to trade policy and economic policy more generally.

How might the increasing income and wealth inequality brought about by globalization affect women as a group? Sassen is hopeful that the globalizing economy, as it pulls more women into wage work, will empower them within their families and in the public sector. *Id.*, at 27. At the same time, she acknowledges that women are "constituted as an invisible and disempowered class of workers in the service of the strategic sectors constituting the global economy." *Id.*, at 26.

2. Modern-day slavery. The very lowest caste of contemporary workers is made up of those whose labor power is forcibly expropriated by others. Kevin Bales argues that slavery is alive and well today, although it takes different legal and social forms than the "old" slavery:

> *My best estimate of the number of slaves in the world today is 27 million.*
>
> This number is much smaller than the estimates put forward by some activists, who give a range as high as 200 million, but it is the number I feel I can trust * * *. The biggest part of that 27 million, perhaps 15 to 20 million, is represented by *bonded labor* in India, Pakistan, Bangladesh, and Nepal. Bonded labor or debt bondage happens when people give themselves into slavery as security against a loan or when they inherit a debt from a relative * * *. Otherwise slavery tends to be concentrated in Southeast Asia, northern and western Africa, and parts of South America (but there are some slaves in almost every country in the world, including the United States, Japan, and many European countries). There are more slaves alive today than all the people stolen from Africa in the time of the transatlantic slave trade. Put another way, today's slave population is greater than the population of Canada, and six times greater than the population of Israel.
>
> These slaves tend to be used in simple, nontechnological, and traditional work. The largest group work in agriculture. But slaves are used in many other kinds of labor: brickmaking, mining or quarrying, prostitution, gem working and jewelry making, cloth and carpet making, and domestic service; they clear forests, make charcoal, and work in shops. Much of this work is aimed at local sale and consumption, but slave-made goods reach into homes around the world. Carpets, fireworks, jewelry, and metal goods made by slave labor, as well as grains, sugar, and other foods harvested by slaves, are imported directly to North America and Europe. In addition, large international corporations, acting through subsidiaries in the developing world, take advantage of slave labor to improve their bottom line and increase the dividends to their shareholders.

KEVIN BALES, DISPOSABLE PEOPLE: NEW SLAVERY IN THE GLOBAL ECONOMY 8–9 (1999).

Bales argues that the new slavery differs from the old slavery in several ways. Among these differences are the following: slaveholders no longer assert legal ownership over their slaves; slaveholders do not contribute to the maintenance costs of their slaves; ethnic differences between slaveholding and slave classes are less important than they were in, for example, American slavery; slaves produce very high profits; the relationship between slaveholder and slave tends to be short-term rather than long-term; and there is a surplus rather than a shortage of potential slaves. *Id.*, at 15.

The International Labor Organization defines "forced labor" as "all work or service which is exacted from any person under the menace of any penalty and for which the said person has not offered himself voluntarily." International Labor Organization, Convention Concerning Forced Labor (No. 29). Using this definition, a team of researchers at the University of California at –Berkeley, working with a nonprofit antislavery organization, examined the nature and scope of forced labor in the United States from January 1998 to December 2003. According to their report:

> Over the past five years, forced labor operations have been reported in at least ninety U.S. cities. These operations tend to thrive in states with large populations and sizable immigrant communities, such as California, Florida, New York, and Texas—all of which are transit routes for international travelers.

> Forced labor is prevalent in five sectors of the U.S. economy: prostitution and sex services (46%), domestic service (27%), agriculture (10%), sweatshop/factory (5%), and restaurant and hotel work (4%) * * *. Forced labor persists in these sectors because of low wages, lack of regulation and monitoring of working conditions, and a high demand for cheap labor. These conditions enable unscrupulous employers and criminal networks to gain virtually complete control over workers' lives.

HUMAN RIGHTS CENTER & FREE THE SLAVES: FORCED LABOR IN THE UNITED STATES 1 (2004), *available at* http://www.hrcberkeley.org/download/hiddenslaves_ report.pdf. (posted September 2004) (last visited, Mar. 6, 2005). The researchers estimated that approximately 10,000 people are working as forced laborers in the United States at any given time. *Id.*, at 10.

In the United States, slavery and human trafficking are subject to the federal Victims of Trafficking and Violence Protection Act of 2000, § 107, 22 U.S.C. §7105 (2004). The act, among other things, establishes mandatory restitution from convicted traffickers, and an amendment allows survivors to sue their captors for civil damages for violations of the statute. *See* Trafficking Victims Protection Reauthorization Act of 2003, 18 U.S.C. §1595 (2004) (civil damages provision). The act also provides social services and immigration status to victims of a "severe form of trafficking" who cooperate with law enforcement to prosecute the traffickers.

3. Women, prostitution and sex work: abolitionists versus labor activists. Feminists have long argued over whether prostitution and other forms of sex work should be abolished as forms of violence against women, or legalized and regulated as just another kind of labor. Jane Larson argues that the dichotomy is unhelpful and that prostitution, like sweatshop labor, child labor, and various forms of bonded and indentured labor, should be examined more closely to help us think more generally about what kinds of labor are acceptable and why:

> Instead of fruitless debates about the "essential nature" of the commodity relation of prostitution, I urge instead a common project aimed at defining the material, moral, and legal differences between free and unfree labor, describing with empirical depth and range what conditions of work characterize commercial sex in its various forms and

locales, and measuring the sex industry against the free labor standard. What is force and compulsion in the sex labor setting? Is the definition of force such that the exchange of money refutes the claim of compulsion, or can the liberal concern for substantive freedom in labor relations translate into international standards? What working conditions render prostitution a per se unacceptably exploitative practice for children? Is it different for adults? Why or why not? What kinds of discrimination on the basis of sex or race are unacceptable? Does the demographic constitution of the market for sexual labor demonstrate such discrimination? If prostitution is one of women's best economic options, how does this shape other economic opportunities for women? Does female prostitution violate the equality ideal?

Jane E. Larson, *Prostitution, Labor, and Human Rights,* 37 U.C. DAVIS L. REV. 673, 698–99 (2004).

4. Public education and construction of failure. Cobb and Sennett were concerned primarily with the education and socialization of the sons of white working class "ethnic" immigrants. Other scholars have found that public education similarly sets up African American and Latino/a working class children, especially boys, to fail. For example, Theresa Glennon observes:

> First, African American boys are much more likely to be identified as disabled or delinquent than other children, including African American girls. Second, they are more likely than other children to be placed in educational, mental health, and juvenile justice programs that exert greater external control and deliver fewer services despite identified needs. Third, these negative experiences lead African American boys to stay away from or exit these institutional settings.

Theresa Glennon, *Knocking Against the Rocks: Evaluating Institutional Practices and the African American Boy,* 5 J. HEALTH CARE L. & POL'Y 10, 11 (2002). Glennon argues that these disparities are a result of racism.

Sociologist John Ogbu found another dynamic among African American children similar to that identified by Sennett and Cobb: black students both underperform and pressure one another to underperform by associating school success with "acting white." Signithia Fordham & John U. Ogbu, *Black Students' School Success: Coping with the "Burden of Acting White,"* 18 URB. REV. 176 (1986). Ogbu and Fordham's findings have been controversial in African American communities.

The Overworked American: The Unexpected Decline of Leisure

17–24 (1991).

■ JULIET B. SCHOR

Time squeeze has become big news. In summer 1990, the premiere episode of Jane Pauley's television show, "Real Life," highlighted a single father whose computer job was so demanding that he found himself at 2:00 A.M. dragging his child into the office. A Boston-area documentary featured the fourteen-to sixteen-hour workdays of a growing army of moonlighters. CBS's "Forty–Eight Hours" warned of the accelerating pace of life for everyone from high-tech business executives (for whom there are only two types of people—"the quick and the dead") to assembly workers at Japanese-owned automobile factories (where a car comes by every sixty seconds). Employees at fast-food restaurants, who serve in twelve seconds, report that the horns start honking if the food hasn't arrived in fifteen. Nineteen-year-olds work seventy-hour weeks, children are "penciled" into their parents' schedules, and second-graders are given "half an hour a day to unwind" from the pressure to get good grades so they can get into a good college. By the beginning of the 1990s, the time squeeze had become a national focus of attention, appearing in almost all the nation's major media outlets. * * *

The time squeeze surfaced with the young urban professional. These high achievers had jobs that required sixty, eighty, even a hundred hours a week. On Wall Street, they would regularly stay at the office until midnight or go months without a single day off. Work consumed their lives. And if they weren't working, they were networking. They power-lunched, power-exercised, and power-married. As the pace of life accelerated, time became an ever-scarcer commodity, so they used their money to buy more of it. Cooking was replaced by gourmet frozen foods from upscale delis. Eventually the "meal" started disappearing, in favor of "grazing." Those who could afford it bought other people's time, hiring surrogates to shop, write their checks, or even just change a light bulb. They cut back on sleep and postponed having children. ("Can you carry a baby in a briefcase?" queried one Wall Street executive when she was asked about having kids.)

High-powered people who spend long hours at their jobs are nothing new. Medical residents, top corporate management, and the self-employed have always had grueling schedules. But financiers used to keep bankers' hours, and lawyers had a leisured life. Now bankers work like doctors, and lawyers do the same. A former Bankers Trust executive remembers that "somebody would call an occasional meeting at 8 A.M. Then it became the regular 8 o'clock meeting. So there was the occasional 7 A.M. meeting.... It just kept spreading." On Wall Street, economic warfare replaced the clubhouse atmosphere—and the pressure forced the hours up. As women and new ethnic groups were admitted into the industry, competition for the plum positions heightened—and the hours went along. Twenty-two-year-olds wear beepers as they squeeze in an hour for lunch or jogging at the health club.

What happened on Wall Street was replicated throughout the country in one high-income occupation after another. Associates in law firms competed over who could log more billable hours. Workaholics set new standards of survival. Even America's sleepiest corporations started waking up; and when they did, the corporate hierarchies found themselves coming in to work a little earlier and leaving for home a little later. As many companies laid off white-collar people during the 1980s, those who remained did more for their monthly paycheck. A study of "downsizings" in auto-related companies in the Midwest found that nearly half of the two thousand managers polled said they were working harder than two years earlier.

At cutting-edge corporations, which emphasize commitment, initiative, and flexibility, the time demands are often the greatest. "People who work for me should have phones in their bathrooms," says the CEO from one aggressive American company. Recent research on managerial habits reveals that work has become positively absorbing. When a deadline approached in one corporation, "people who had been working twelve-hour days and Saturdays started to come in on Sunday, and instead of leaving at midnight, they would stay a few more hours. Some did not go home at all, and others had to look at their watches to remember what day it was." The recent growth in small businesses has also contributed to overwork. When Dolores Kordek started a dental insurance company, her strategy for survival was to work harder than the competition. So the office was open from 7 A.M. to 10 P.M. three hundred and sixty-five days a year. And she was virtually always in it.

This combination of retrenchment, economic competition, and innovative business management has raised hours substantially. One poll of senior executives found that weekly hours rose during the 1980s, and vacation time fell. Other surveys have yielded similar results. By the end of the decade, overwork at the upper echelons of the labor market had become endemic—and its scale was virtually unprecedented in living memory.

If the shortage of time had been confined to Wall Street or America's corporate boardrooms, it might have remained just a media curiosity. The number of people who work eighty hours a week and bring home—if they ever get there—a six-figure income is very small. But while the incomes of these rarefied individuals were out of reach, their schedules turned out to be downright common. As Wall Street waxed industrious, the longer schedules penetrated far down the corporate ladder, through middle management, into the secretarial pool, and even onto the factory floor itself. Millions of ordinary Americans fell victim to the shortage of time.

The most visible group has been women, who are coping with a double load—the traditional duties associated with home and children and their growing responsibility for earning a paycheck. With nearly two-thirds of adult women now employed, and a comparable fraction of mothers on the job, it's no surprise that many American women find themselves operating in overdrive. Many working mothers live a life of perpetual motion, effectively holding down two full-time jobs. They rise in the wee hours of the morning to begin the day with a few hours of laundry, cleaning, and other housework. Then they dress and feed the children and send them off to school. They themselves then travel to their jobs. The three-quarters of employed women with full-time positions then spend the next eight and a half hours in the workplace.

At the end of the official workday, it's back to the "second shift"—the duties of housewife and mother. Grocery shopping, picking up the children, and cooking dinner take up the next few hours. After dinner there's clean-up, possibly some additional housework, and, of course, more child care. Women describe themselves as "ragged," "bone-weary," "sinking in quick-sand," and "busy every waking hour." For many, the workday rivals those for which the "satanic mills" of the Industrial Revolution grew justly infamous: twelve-or fourteen-hour stretches of labor. By the end of the decade, Ann Landers pronounced herself "awestruck at the number of women who work at their jobs and go home to another full-time job ... How do you do it?" she asked. Thousands of readers responded, with tales ranging from abandoned careers to near collapse. According to sociologist Arlie Hochschild of the University of California, working mothers are exhausted, even fixated on the topic of sleep. "They talked about how much they could 'get by on': ... six and a half, seven, seven and a half, less, more ... These women talked about sleep the way a hungry person talks about food."

By my calculations, the total working time of employed mothers now averages about 65 hours a week. Of course, many do far more than the average—such as mothers with young children, women in professional positions, or those whose wages are so low that they must hold down two jobs just to scrape by. These women will be working 70 to 80 hours a week. And my figures are extremely conservative: they are the lowest among existing studies. A Boston study found that employed mothers *average* over 80 hours of housework, child care, and employment. Two nationwide studies of white, married couples are comparable: in the first, the average week was 87 hours; in the second, it ranged from 76 to 89, depending on the age of the oldest child.

One might think that as women's working hours rose, husbands would compensate by spending less time on the job. But just the opposite has occurred. Men who work are also putting in longer hours. The 5:00 Dads of the 1950s and 1960s (those who were home for dinner and an evening with the family) are becoming an "endangered species." Thirty percent of men with children under fourteen report working fifty or more hours a week. And many of these 8:00 or 9:00 Dads aren't around on the weekends either. Thirty percent of them work Saturdays and/or Sundays at their regular employment. And many others use the weekends for taking on a second job.

A twenty-eight-year-old Massachusetts factory worker explains the bind many fathers are in: "Either I can spend time with my family or support them—not both." Overtime or a second job is financially compel-ling: "I can work 8–12 hours overtime a week at time and a half, and that's when the real money just starts to kick in.... If I don't work the OT my wife would have to work much longer hours to make up the differences, and our day care bill would double.... The trouble is, the little time I'm home I'm too tired to have any fun with them or be any real help around

the house." Among white-collar employees the problem isn't paid overtime, but the regular hours. To get ahead, or even just to hold on to a position, long days may be virtually mandatory.

Overwork is also rampant among the nation's poorly paid workers. At $5, $6, or even $7 an hour, annual earnings before taxes and deductions range from $10,000 to $14,000. Soaring rents alone have been enough to put many of these low earners in financial jeopardy. For the more than one-third of all workers now earning hourly wages of $7 and below, the pressure to lengthen hours has been inexorable. Valerie Connor, a nursing-home worker in Hartford, explains that "you just can't make it on one job." She and many of her co-workers have been led to work two eight-hour shifts a day. According to an official of the Service Employees International Union in New England, nearly one-third of their nursing-home employees now hold two full-time jobs. Changes in the low end of the labor market have also played a role. Here is less full-time, stable employment. "Twenty hours here, thirty hours there, and twenty hours here. That's what it takes to get a real paycheck," says Domenic Bozzotto, president of Boston's hotel and restaurant workers union, whose members are drowning in a sea of work. Two-job families? Those were the good old days, he says. "We've got four-job families." The recent influx of immigrants has also raised hours. I.N. Yazbeck, an arrival from Lebanon, works ninety hours a week at three jobs. It's necessary, he says, for economic success.

This decline of leisure has been reported by the Harris Poll, which has received widespread attention. Harris finds that since 1973 free time has fallen nearly 40 percent—from a median figure of 26 hours a week to slightly under 17. Other surveys, such as the 1989 Decision Research Corporation Poll, also reveal a loss of leisure. Although these polls have serious methodological drawbacks, their findings are not far off the mark. A majority of working Americans—professionals, corporate management, "working" mothers, fathers, and lower-paid workers—*are* finding themselves with less and less leisure time.

———

Life.com

The Berkeley Monthly, October 1999.

■ Clive Thompson

The elevator door slides open and Jess slides in, looking slightly rumpled. Tara sizes her up.

"Didn't get much sleep last night?"

"You can tell?"

"Well, you're wearing the same clothes as yesterday."

Jess laughs. Her music show, Freq, broadcast live over the internet here at the new-media house Pseudo, went late last night and the staff wound up hanging around till dawn. Now it's 10:30 a.m. and she's back from breakfast to make some calls and set up meetings.

"At some point I'm gonna have to shower," she mutters as she wanders off to her desk.

Tara and I tour the studios, strolling through Pseudo's odd mix of high camp and high tech. The office is a study in chaos and energy, each room reflecting the peculiar pop-cultural animus of the twenty-somethings who work here. There's the room for the women's net shows, done up in late-'70s drag with a rainbow-colored bead-curtain entrance. There's a group of goateed musicians hanging out in one room, holding keyboards and a computer monitor. Who are they? "I have no idea," Tara says.

"Sorry," she apologizes at one point, yawning. "I'm a bit burnt out today."

I'm not surprised. In new media it's difficult to find anyone who can boast a full night's rest. Later in the day I visit a 23-year-old acquaintance at a website design firm across town and find him collapsed on a sofa in the staff room.

Late night? "Yeah." He's been setting up a database for a website that's set to go live in two days. The deadline looms and the client—a major corporation—is getting twitchy. Some deeply caffeinated all-nighters will be called for.

"It's intense but it's going pretty well," he says, his hair out of whack with a minor case of bed-head. "I figure I have another two days like this. But it's cool. It's a really cool project."

He pours himself a thick coffee in the well-stocked kitchen and heads back to his workstation, plopping down beside some two dozen other coders and designers clacking away at their keyboards as a stereo pumps out ambient techno in an endless loop. Most of them figure they'll be here until 4 in the morning.

Working till sunup, destroying your eyesight, playing Quake on the company lan, hanging out in a funky office with your dog: in the modern digital workplace this sort of stuff is de rigueur. Indeed, for young Turks in new media—software, website development or the amorphous zone of "content"—aggressively casual and freewheeling is the signature office style.

On the surface it has to do with making work seem a lot more fun and thus a lot less like work. It is, as it were, the master narrative of the New Work, which we could sketch out like this: young digital employees have thrown off the 9-to-5 straitjacket in which their parents so miserably toiled. No more suits, no more rigid corporate hierarchies, no more dull, repetitive tasks. Today work means getting to wear your Star Wars T-shirt, sport multiple piercings and hang out in an office with homey perks: massage-therapist visits, pets, wacky furniture, toys and lots of beer. The staff dines together and parties together. It works hard, sure, but it plays hard too, and usually at the same time. And the workers aren't chained to one job.

Instead they hop at will from company to company, forcing hapless employers to scramble after them, offering ever more perks and stock options to lure their portable, highly paid talents. These kids hold all the cards.

It's a story that has fascinated the media. Reporters covering the industry regularly marvel at the scenes of controlled chaos and pop-cultural riot. In Mountain View [California], Netscape staff members are willing to quit if they can't bring their dogs to work. *USA Today* once breathlessly noted that the office at Organic Online "has been the scene of a dance party, complete with disc jockeys, for 400 people."

Which is precisely the problem.

The studied hipness of new media is a rather devious cultural illusion. Those ultracool offices cover up a seldom-discussed truth: that the jobs themselves often demand intense work and devotion for relatively low pay and zero security. By making work more like play, employers neatly erase the division between the two, which ensures that their young employees will almost never leave the office.

High-tech employees hang out at work long after the city has gone to bed. They'll kill themselves over deadlines, putting in up to 80 hours a week. Then they'll smile and thank their lucky stars that they're part of the digital revolution, the cultural flashpoint of the '90s. For employers, of course, it's a sweet deal—you can't buy flexibility like that. As more than one worker has told me, a website design company can almost always hold a meeting at 2 o'clock on a Saturday afternoon because, well, everyone's there. Where else would they be?

New-media companies are notorious for employee burnout and nanosecond turnover. It's not surprising: given the insane hours, the payoffs are rather slim. We're hit relentlessly with media hype about digital workers' high pay, desirability and stock options. But none of these myths holds up under statistical scrutiny. The vast majority of new-media workers in New York, for example, make less than junior accountants, enjoy the job security of fast-food workers and have a laughably small chance of getting offered any stock anytime anywhere. As for programmers, most are paid surprisingly little and hurled overboard as soon as they hit their mid-30s.

Enamored of its distorted image, the digital workforce is reluctant to accept the facts. "People do not want to face reality," says Bill Lessard, a veteran of the industry who runs NetSlaves, a website that compiles true tales of new-media burnout. "Someone will tell you, 'Oh, I'm a producer.' But they're just a schmuck who's working 90 hours a week. You give these companies body and soul and you really get nothing back."

These workers are touted as the most renegade, the most entrepreneurial generation in years. Yet they are, in traditional labor terms, amazingly compliant. Chained to their keyboards, working far longer hours than they're paid for and blurring the boundaries between their jobs and their lives, digital employees paradoxically present the kind of servile workforce that would have pleased Henry Ford, Nelson Rockefeller and probably Chairman Mao.

When I visit Fred Kahl he's busy designing a computer game based on the TV cartoon "Space Ghost." I peer over his shoulder at the screen, where Fred is fiddling with a sequence: Space Ghost chasing the arch-villain Lokar, who is impersonating Santa Claus. In a few days this will air on the website of the Cartoon Network, one of the major clients of Funny Garbage, the new-media design firm that Kahl works for.

It's hard to deny that new-media workplaces are, aesthetically anyway, extremely pleasant places to be. Kahl shows me around Funny Garbage—a firm respected for its right-brained, creative web animations—and it's not unlike wandering through a gallery of '70s kitsch. Workstations are cluttered with retro-pop toys and icons. One of the company's founders, 33-year-old Peter Girardi, has three different video-game systems in his office.

This is not to suggest that everyone is horsing around. Over by the animation computers, three designers are hunkering down for a long haul, even though it's already past 5 o'clock on a Friday night. By 9, staff members will likely launch into a Quake tournament on the company lan. ("I had to stop," Kahl says. "I almost destroyed my wrists.") In this context, it's easy to see how work and life inexorably bleed into each other. It's also easy to see how new-media employers can capitalize on the confusion. For people involved in digital culture, a highly wired office—replete with digital toys and fueled by a T1 connection—can be a more inviting place to hang out than a cramped apartment or a bar or club.

In fact, sometimes work offers even better partying than a club.

One of Psuedo's longest-serving staff members, a 29-year-old programmer named Joey Fortuna, remembers arriving on his first day four years ago to find the office in a fantastic mess from a party held the night before. Pseudo CEO Josh Harris staggered in from his on-site apartment wearing nothing but boxer shorts and instantly set Fortuna to work, even though Fortuna had never written a line of code in his life.

To get up to speed on HTML, Fortuna—like most of the staff—put in months of 12-hour days. In 1996 he spent Christmas Day writing code for a video-publishing database. "It was just insane!" he says. "I was working all the time. I lived here. But I didn't mind. It was like a clubhouse."

He gestures around the loft, pointing to its kooky mix of high-and low-tech. "You know, it's ironic," he grins, "but in the last century this used to be a sweatshop."

If there's an archetypal success story in new media it's probably that of Jeff Dachis and Razorfish. In spring 1995, Dachis and his friend Craig Kanarick, both in their late 20s, founded the website design company in their living rooms. Last year they had 350 employees in eight offices and did $30 million in business.

Companies like Razorfish have built the mythos of gold-rush success in new media: start a firm in your garage, wow senior executives at Fortune 500 companies, then take occasional breaks from your PlayStation to watch the dough roll in. "The trappings of power have changed," wrote *Time* magazine in an October 1997 survey of the "cyber-elite."

But here too the hype outstrips the reality. True, there are dozens of fantastic entrepreneurial successes. But when you look at the statistics the New Work starts to look like an old story: low pay, no security and those who no longer suit the company profile pitched instantly overboard.

In 1997 the New York New Media Association did a study of the local scene. It discovered that high-tech jobs paid an average of $37,212. That's middling at best for a city as expensive as New York. It's also far outpaced by the average salaries in other media: advertising, $71,637; periodicals, $69,849; TV broadcasting, $85,938.

The churn rate in new-media jobs is amazingly high. The New York study found that almost half the work in new media is freelance or part time. More than two-thirds of all freelance contracts last fewer than six months, most are three-month stints. Part-time jobs are growing four-times faster than full-time positions.

In place of decent pay and regular work, new media offers the lure of instant wealth—the fabled stock options that turned the creators of Amazon.com or TheGlobe.com into overnight multimillionaires. It's a seductive tale, and those who have won the game have won huge. Berkeley's Adam Sah, who was in on the ground floor at Inktomi, cashed in some stocks when the company went public. The years of 400-hour months paid off. "It wasn't fun," he says, "but it did turn out all right for me."

Sah previously worked at Microsoft, which pretty much invented the stock-options trick, knowing that the lure of the market is one of the few things that will motivate coders to impale themselves upon unshippable products with unmeetable deadlines. "It's amazing what people will do for money," Sah laughs wryly.

The stock payoff, though, is about as chimerical as you can get. There are no stats on new-media stock cash-ins but high-tech hunters counsel their clients that the chance of getting lucrative options are slim.

"To cash in on stock you have to stick around for several years at a company," says Alex Santic, head of Silicon Valley Connections, one of the first headhunting firms to specialize in new media. "But few people really want to. They want to move on after a year. They get lured in by the promise of stock but rarely see it through." Indeed, as the New York new-media study found, the only folks who own substantial equity are management and founders—worker bees have a statistically insignificant slice of the pie.

Perhaps the most persistent myth of recent years, though, is that of the "programmer shortage." According to this tale, the geeks now run the show. There isn't enough programming talent to go around, so companies are fighting tooth and nail over warm bodies. Mainstream media have taken up the story like a mantra. "Business leaders say the shortage has reached near-crisis proportions," wrote the *Washington Post* in an article detailing—with a sort of horrified fascination—the incredible perks offered to lure programmers, from "signing bonuses like professional athletes" to $70-an-hour rates for temp work.

Again, the facts contradict the hype. Last year Norman Matloff, a professor of computer science at UC Davis, released one of the few studies ever done on the programmer job market. He surveyed the hiring practices of software and new-media firms and concluded that there was, in fact, no shortage of programmers. Companies were hiring only two to four percent of the people they interviewed, a rate far below that for other types of engineers.

Older programmers, meanwhile, are ruthlessly squeezed out. Age discrimination, Matloff says, is "amazingly rampant." He found that after age 35 and increasingly as they get older, programmers are ditched in favor of the fresh-scrubbed kids released each year from technical colleges. By their early 40s fewer than one-fifth of all trained programmers are still working in the field. One 47-year-old programmer Matloff talked to was fluent in C++, Perl, Unix and a host of other languages, but when he went looking for a new job he landed only two interviews in 15 months of searching. Another man had been programming since 1976. "I can't get so much as an interview," he told Matloff. "I now earn about $24,000 a year in retail sales and management."

When you look at the facts you begin to realize the incredible power of new-media workplace culture. It sells a lifestyle of liberation and autonomy that is wildly out of sync with reality. Then you begin to realize why those Quake marathons, those cappuccino machines in the staff kitchen and all those dogs at work are important. Absent decent pay and a commitment from your boss, maybe a game of Quake is the best you can get.

————

The Law and Economics of Critical Race Theory

112 YALE L.J. 1757, 1789–93, 1795–96, 1797–99, 1801–14 (2003) (reviewing CROSSROADS, DIRECTIONS, AND A NEW CRITICAL RACE THEORY (Francisco Valdes et al. eds., 2002)).

■ DEVON W. CARBADO & MITU GULATI

A starting point for thinking about workplace discrimination is to raise the question of whether today's workplace is buttressed by institutionalized racial norms. With respect to explicit racial norms, the answer is no: That would violate antidiscrimination law. But do implicit racial norms structure today's workplace culture? [Critical race theory, or CRT] answers this question affirmatively, pointing to workplace practices like English-only rules and grooming regulations (e.g., rules prohibiting employees from braiding their hair) that restrict the expression of particular identities and, in so doing, marginalize them.

There is, however, a subtle form of institutional discrimination to which CRT scholars have not paid attention. This discrimination derives from a commitment on the part of many employers, particularly employers who use teams to manage their workplace culture to achieve trust, fairness, and loyalty (TFL). Why? TFL reduces transaction costs. Empirical evidence suggests that the effectiveness of teams is enhanced when employers engender TFL among their employees. Employees who perceive that they are a part of a "TFL community" work hard, cooperate, police each other, and share valuable information. Based on this evidence, scholars have argued that law should be structured to facilitate the creation of TFL workplaces. In addition to its efficiency gains, TFL values seem normatively appealing.

TFL's normative surface appeal helps to explain why the institutional discrimination story we articulate below has not yet been told. Central to our story is not the fact that employers are invested in TFL but rather how they go about realizing that investment—by aggressively promoting homogeneity. Evidence suggests that, at least in the short term, a manager with a demographically homogeneous work team has a better chance of producing TFL than one with a diverse team. If, as is often suggested, managers focus primarily on short-term results, there is an incentive for managers to seek demographically homogeneous teams.

The relationship between the pursuit of demographic homogeneity and racial discrimination is direct. In short, workplaces organized to achieve homogeneity are likely to discriminate because homogeneity norms, by their very nature, reflect a commitment to sameness (favoring people perceived to be members of the in-group ("insiders")) and a rejection of difference (disfavoring people perceived to be members of the out-group ("outsiders")). Coupled with the fact that, within most professional settings, whites are insiders and nonwhites are outsiders, the relationship between discrimination and homogeneity becomes clear.

The foregoing suggests that race-neutral workplace norms institutionalize insider racial preference. Is this a reason for concern? The answer is not obviously yes. One might argue that, even to the extent that there are incentives for employers to create and maintain homogeneous workplaces, the threat of antidiscrimination sanctions undermines that incentive. Richard Epstein famously worried about exactly this effect of antidiscrimination law. According to Epstein, part of the problem with antidiscrimination law is that it compromises workplace efficiency by preventing employers from establishing homogeneous workplace cultures. One might conclude, then, that given the threat of legal sanctions, the institutionalized racism problem we have identified is theoretical—not real.

Moreover, there are institutional legitimacy concerns that militate against the establishment of homogenous workplaces. White-only work forces can create public relations problems. Perhaps not surprisingly, there is no employer-driven movement afoot to have antidiscrimination laws repealed because they prohibit employers from establishing demographically homogenous workplaces. To the contrary, even a cursory examination of the management and organizational behavior literature reveals (at least rhetorically) an institutional commitment to manage, and not to eliminate, heterogeneity. Thus, all seems well: Law prevents institutions from privileging homogeneity, and institutions perceive the pursuit of homogeneity to be problematic.

Our claim, however, is that all is not well. Neither antidiscrimination law nor the affirmative pursuit of diversity operates as a meaningful barrier to, or substantially undermines the incentives for employers to achieve, workplace homogeneity. Epstein need not worry. To be sure, the law prohibits blatant racial animus in hiring and promotion. But that is a minimal barrier to the managerial pursuit of racial homogeneity. To move from a phenotypic conception of race to a performative conception is to find that, to a significant extent, judges can (and, we surmise, do) apply antidiscrimination law to actually *protect* the pursuit of racial homogeneity. They do so by failing to capture employment discrimination based on *intraracial* distinctions—distinctions employers make among people within a particular racial group.

Driving these distinctions is a question about racial stereotypes and racial salience. Other things being equal, employers prefer nonwhites whose racial identity is not salient and whose identity performance is inconsistent with stereotypes about their racial group. In other words, employers screen for racial palatability. With respect to Asian Americans, for example, employers determine whether, notwithstanding phenotypic difference, a particular Asian American is (based on how she performs her identity) sufficiently like insiders to be successfully assimilated into a homogenized workplace.

To date, there are no Title VII cases that render a racial palatability discrimination claim cognizable. Thus, employers can make these kinds of intraracial distinctions with legal impunity. And to the extent employers engage in this practice, their associated institutional legitimacy remains intact because the practice anticipates and produces at least some workplace racial integration. Finally, because the racial diversity employers achieve by making intraracial distinctions is literally skin deep, it comfortably coexists with their commitment to homogeneity.

The foregoing sets forth a theory of institutional racism—that it is a function of an investment on the part of employers to realize the efficiency gains of homogeneity. Because many institutions operate under what we call a *diversity constraint*—a constraint that requires the firm to hire at least some nonwhites—employers will determine which nonwhites to hire on evidence of racial palatability. The more racially palatable employers perceive a potential employee to be, the less concerned they will be over the possibility that that potential employee will (racially) disrupt workplace homogeneity. * * *

B. *The Incentive for Employers To Pursue Homogeneity*

* * *

1. *Theories*

There are at least three theories suggesting that employers are motivated to pursue homogeneity: social identity theory, similarity-attraction theory, and statistical judgments theory.

Social identity theory suggests that people have an affinity for those they perceive to be part of their in-group. In concrete terms, people are more likely to demonstrate TFL (which, again, is shorthand for trust, fairness, and loyalty) to those they perceive to be members of their in-group. Conversely, they are more likely to discriminate against those they perceive to be members of an out-group. Race, being both socially salient and facially visible, is one of the primary categories along which people make initial in-group and out-group categorizations. One explanation is that people assume that those of a similar race are likely to share similar values and to have had similar experiences. As a result, racial outsiders are vulnerable to discrimination from their racial insider colleagues. To avoid this distrust and dislike (which will likely undermine workplace efficiency by increasing transaction costs), employers will want to hire people who are similar to insiders.

The similarity-attraction theory is largely analogous. It posits that people are attracted to those who are similar. The theory is that race is one of the primary categories used to determine similarity and that this similarity, in turn, translates into attraction. * * *

The final theory suggesting that employers are motivated to pursue homogeneity is statistical judgments theory. Most often attributed to economics (though also central to psychology), this theory claims that racial differences often activate *statistical judgments* about likely behavioral tendencies. These statistical judgments are a type of mental shortcut, a resource-saving device. For example, white workers may see a new black colleague as likely to be lazy, untrustworthy, disloyal (especially to her white colleagues), frequently angry (perhaps as a result of oversensitivity about race), and difficult to communicate with (due to her likely having different values, different interests, and different cultural and experiential points of reference). Under this theory, whether an insider-employer will hire a black person turns on the currency of the foregoing statistical judgments. The stronger the statistical judgment, the stronger the employer's perception that a prospective black employee will not fit into the institution.

These theories suggest that there is a disincentive for employers to hire outsiders and a corresponding incentive for employers to hire insiders. Difference engenders distrust, dislike, disconnection, disidentification, and disassociation. Each of these characteristics (and certainly all of them together) undermines a necessary condition for the effective operation of teams—cooperative behavior—and therefore increases the transaction costs of managing the workplace.

2. *Empirical Evidence*

a. *The Basic Story*

In addition to the theoretical literature, there is empirical evidence predicting that racially heterogeneous teams are likely to be less effective than homogenous ones. Studies consistently show what the above theories suggest: Racial heterogeneity undermines trust and cooperation. Team members in heterogeneous teams tend not to communicate as well as team members in homogeneous teams. Turnover rates in heterogeneous teams are higher. And managerial attempts to spur innovation by diversifying their teams have "met with mixed success."

b.   *The More Complicated Account*

Recent scholarship on diversity management suggests that the empirical story about workplace homogeneity may be more complicated than we have thus far described. The complication is that heterogeneity can operate as a double-edged sword. To appreciate how this is so, it is helpful to conceptualize heterogeneity/diversity as operating in a two-stage process. At stage one, superficial differences in terms of variables like race cause distrust, difficulties in communication, and a reluctance to cooperate. However, under the right conditions of intergroup contact—equal status, opportunities for self-revelation, egalitarian norms, and tasks that require cooperative interdependence—diverse team members can, at stage two, gain each other's trust, begin to see commonalities, work cooperatively, and realize the benefits of working as a diverse team. Central to this theory is the notion that there are meaningful things an employer can do at stage one—the initial contact stage—to facilitate cooperative behavior at stage two. * * *

C. *Summary*

There is theoretical and empirical evidence suggesting that employers are motivated to pursue homogeneity: Put simply, homogeneous workplaces facilitate trust, loyalty, and cooperative behavior. The story with respect to heterogeneous work teams is different. First, at an institutional level, heterogeneity is difficult and costly to manage. Second, the most cost-effective way for individual supervisors to manage heterogeneity is to "socialize away" outsider difference. Thus, it is more accurate to characterize this strategy as eliminating, rather than managing, heterogeneity. Third, even assuming that heterogeneity can be effectively managed, the benefits of a heterogeneous workplace are speculative, and they are realized primarily over the long term.

Acknowledging the homogeneity incentive is helpful to CRT in at least two ways. First, it provides critical race theorists with a different perspective on colorblindness. The homogeneity incentive exists because of the transaction costs of heterogeneity. Like colorblindness, then, the homogeneity incentive requires the submersion of racial difference. Second, the existence of the homogeneity incentive supports CRT's claim that an employer's preference for racial sameness won't always be motivated by racial animus. One of the most important ideas in CRT is that racism is not just a function of individual bad actors. From here, CRT advances one of two arguments: (1) that discrimination is unconscious and (2) that discrimination is institutional. The homogeneity incentive provides an additional base from which to theorize about the latter. It demonstrates that institutional discrimination can exist in the absence of racial animosity. * * *

IV. HOW EMPLOYERS RESPOND TO THE HOMOGENEITY INCENTIVE

Given antidiscrimination laws and social norms disfavoring racial exclusivity, institutions are unlikely to respond to the homogeneity incentive by hiring only insiders. They will hire outsiders as well. The claim we advance is that employers will use specific mechanisms to screen outsiders for evidence of racial palatability. These mechanisms select "but for outsiders"—outsiders who, but for their racial phenotype, are very similar to the insiders—and they select against "essential outsiders"—outsiders whose personal characteristics are consistent with the image of the prototypical outsider. * * *

A. *The "Race–Neutral" Response to the Homogeneity Incentive*

1. *The Basic Idea: Selection and Socialization*

Broadly speaking, there are two mechanisms employers can use to respond to the homogeneity incentive: "selection" and "socializing" mechanisms. Selection mechanisms operate at the hiring and the promotion stages. Here, an employer screens individuals for particular characteristics that function as proxies for determining whether a given individual (1) is willing to be homogenized into the workplace culture *and* (2) has the capacity to do so. Socializing mechanisms, in turn, are used to initiate and integrate the individual into the workplace. In other words, socializing mechanisms are the rites of passage that structure a new employee's experiential travels through the workplace after selection mechanisms are used to bring her into the firm. Constituting this passage are numerous rituals through which the individual is expected to demonstrate her commitment to homogeneity. More particularly, she must effectively prove that the employer made the right selection decision. Due to space constraints, we do not elaborate further on socialization mechanisms. We focus on selection, identifying four selection mechanisms employers can use to screen potential employees for evidence of performative (and not simply phenotypic) homogeneity.

2. *The Selection Mechanisms*

Four interrelated selection mechanisms that we draw out of the theory and evidence on homogeneity are: similarity, comfort, differentiation, and respectable exoticism.

a. *Similarity*

This mechanism is intuitive. The question is whether the individual exhibits personal characteristics suggesting she is similar to employees already at the firm. The more an individual appears to be similar to existing employees, the more likely an employer is to conclude that the individual has the potential to be assimilated. The potential employee's response to standard interview questions can signal her potential for assimilation to employers. Consider, for example, Johnny, who is being considered for a mid-level associate position at an elite corporate law firm. A senior partner has asked Johnny to "tell us a little bit about yourself." Johnny's response includes the following:

I enjoy tennis and golf, though I confess that both need improvement. I like a good Gore Vidal novel; in fact, I'm in the process of rereading Julian, *which, by the way, I highly recommend. I'm not a huge sports fan, but I try to make time to watch a good basketball game—usually with colleagues and friends. I wasn't always fond of theater, but two years ago my wife took me to see* The Tin Man, *and I've been sold on theater—both high and low—ever since. I enjoy Italian cinema, the old Fellini stuff as well as some of the more contemporary productions. And every so often, I truly enjoy a good B movie—not a B movie masquerading as an A movie, but a B movie that knows it's a B movie. I love going to the museum with my kids. We try to go twice a month. You'd be surprised at the interpretational skills of a six-year old.*

This response provides the employer with signals about Johnny's socialized identity, information that the employer can use to make a determination as to whether Johnny is sufficiently like the firm's existing employees. Johnny plays tennis and golf, the preferred sports of corporate America. The fact that both need improvement suggests that he is available to play both sports with his colleagues and not likely to be unduly competitive when he does so. In this way, both games can function as sites for socialization. Johnny's response also indicates that he is not an avid sports fan, but that he enjoys a good basketball game. Here, Johnny signals respectable (but not hyper-) masculinity and a willingness to participate in group-based spectator sport rituals. Johnny is married with kids, which reveals his heterosexuality and possibly a certain traditionalism. He appears to be cultured (he reads Gore Vidal, watches Italian cinema, attends the theater, and visits museums), but he is not overly elitist or pompous (he enjoys the occasional B movie and attends low-brow (and just barely high-brow) theater). Finally, the fact that Johnny's wife successfully socialized him into the theater, an experience that he was not predisposed to enjoy, suggests that he will likely not resist the firm's socialization efforts.

Not every institution will select for the foregoing qualities: Similarity selection mechanisms will vary from institution to institution. The point here is twofold: (1) Most employers will have a set of characteristics that they perceive to define their workplace, and (2) without much difficulty, employers can screen for these qualities in interviews.

b.   *Comfort*

Related to similarity is comfort. Here, employers want to know whether incumbent employees will be comfortable working with the prospective hire. Again, they can select for comfort (or at least select against discomfort) by considering a prospective employee's response to standard interview questions. Stipulate once more that Johnny is interviewing for a job with an elite corporate law firm. The partner asks Johnny: "Tell us what kind of firm you're looking for." Johnny responds:

I am looking for a firm doing high-level, sophisticated corporate work. Quite frankly, most of the firms I am interviewing with seem to fall in that category—certainly your firm does. What becomes important for me, then, is firm culture. I am looking for a firm that values and respects difference. I guess I believe that people shouldn't have to lose themselves at work. They should be permitted to be who they are. I was happy to learn that your firm recently adopted a casual Friday policy.

I am also looking for a firm within which junior associates have a voice—that is, an opportunity to comment on the institutional governance of the firm, for example, the firm's billing, hiring, and pro bono policies. That sort of participation helps to make junior associates invested in the firm.

Employers could interpret Johnny's response in a number of ways. But if they are screening for comfort, a given employer may have concerns about whether Johnny "fits." Johnny's view is that individuals should be permitted to be themselves and that a firm should value difference. However, difference can be uncomfortable or discomforting. To employ what many would consider an extreme example, the firm would likely be uncomfortable with Johnny coming to work as a cross-dresser. If Johnny does cross dress, the firm would expect him to do so (if at all) outside of the workplace.

Recall that Johnny wants a voice in institutional governance and provides an indication of the kinds of issues he hopes to engage. Johnny's representations here might send a positive signal—specifically, that he wants to become a part of the firm. To the extent the employer is selecting for comfort, however, the employer could interpret Johnny's comments to suggest that he will likely make the firm uncomfortable about its hiring, pro bono, and billing practices, among other institutional governance matters.

c. *Differentiation*

Employers are most likely to utilize the differentiation mechanism when they perceive themselves to be making a "risky hire." Here, prospective employees are in a *category* that is presumed to be incapable of homogenization (or that is disinterested in socialization). Imagine that Johnny is seeking an entry-level job with a law firm. He is a third-year law student at State Law School, which is a third-tier law school. He is on law review and has an A-grade point average. His letters of recommendation are effusive; his writing sample is strong.

The firm has never hired a law student from State Law School, in part because the school is insufficiently elite and because most of the students at State Law School are from working-class backgrounds. The firm therefore assumes that these students are likely to have difficulty fitting into an elite corporate law firm. The firm might not be right for them (read: they might not be right for the firm). Given this concern, whether the employer hires Johnny will be a function of whether Johnny can differentiate himself from the category within which he is situated—that is, State law students. Consider the following exchange between Johnny and a senior partner.

Partner: Good of you to stop by. Come in and have a seat. It seems that I've left your resume elsewhere in the office. You wouldn't happen to have an extra copy, would you?

Johnny: Yes, in fact I do.

Partner: Oh yes ... I am beginning to remember this resume. I see that you went to Harvard undergrad and that you rowed crew. How did we do this year? I graduated Harvard in '75.

Johnny: We lost to Yale, second year in a row, no pun intended. I suppose if we're going to lose to any school, it ought to be Yale. Their heavyweight eight was selected to represent the country at the World Championships in London.

Partner: So you did really well at Harvard—Magna in history, 3.7 GPA, member of the debating team. I suspect that you had a lot of options when you applied to law school.

Johnny: I was fortunate to have a few. In addition to State, NYU, Columbia, and Michigan said yes. Harvard and Stanford placed me on a waiting list. Yale said no.

Partner: I didn't get into Yale, either. What's more, I've lived to tell the tale. You will, too. But, seriously, you had all these options. I'm curious as to how you made your decision.

Johnny: Well, to a considerable extent my decision was a financial one. I couldn't afford to attend any of the other schools. And I didn't want to burden my parents anymore than I had to. Besides, I hoped that if I distinguished myself at State, I would have many of the same opportunities as if I had attended, say, Michigan.

Partner: So, Johnny, tell me about how you're thinking about law firms. Big law firms are not for everyone, and as you know, we're a pretty big law firm.

Johnny: I had the good fortune of clerking for two summers at Bronton, Stevely & Kellog in Chicago.

Partner: Yes, yes, an excellent firm.

Johnny: I had a good time there. People got along well. They had interests similar to mine. I got the sense that the attorneys there felt that they were part of a larger community. Your firm describes itself in precisely that way. Most of my classmates run away from big firms. Why go through that haze, some ask?

Partner: They consider big firms a haze?

Johnny: Some do. Most simply believe that big firms treat individuals as fungible commodities. That's not my assumption but it is the predominant assumption on campus.

Partner: What's your view, then? Let me guess: You love big firms?

Johnny: Of course. Kidding aside, I'd say that, whether it's a big firm or a small firm, the question is really twofold: whether the individual is committed to becoming a part of a team and whether the firm provides him with the opportunity to play ball.

The foregoing reflects enough differentiation on Johnny's part to effectively remove him from, or at least situate him on the periphery of, the outsider group (again, students at State Law School). Presumably, few law students at State attended Harvard. Johnny's Harvard education is significant in at least three respects. First, it signifies Johnny's intellectual capacity. Second, the fact that Johnny graduated from Harvard (and rowed crew) suggests that he has the potential for socialization. Finally, Johnny's Harvard education places Johnny and the partner in a community that has significant cultural capital—the community of Harvard alumni. That the partner recognizes this shared community is evident in his question: "How did we do this year?"

Nor would many students at State have had the opportunity to attend NYU, Michigan, and Columbia or to clerk at an elite corporate law firm. Here, too, Johnny is different. Finally, Johnny is also different in terms of his strong academic performance and the fact that he does not have a bias against big-firm practice. In short, after completing the interview with Johnny, the partner could tell himself that, although, as a formal matter, Johnny belongs to the group of State Law students, in a substantive sense, he is different. It is this kind of information that the differentiation selection mechanism is designed to ascertain.

d.   *Respectable Exoticism*

Certain differences do not threaten firm homogeneity. To the extent that a given difference is both exotic (not an awful lot of people are likely to have it) and respectable (the difference is not overdetermined by a negative social meaning), firms can commodify this difference to their advantage. Thus, while hiring too many immigrants might compromise a firm's commitment to homogeneity, hiring an immigrant of royal lineage might not produce that effect. Immigrant difference that is located in the context of royal identity can be marketed—for example, to employees who might feel special because they have a royal coworker.

Another example of respectable exoticism might be an ex-NBA player in a corporate context. Note, however, that while a firm's homogeneity might tolerate one such individual, it may not be able to tolerate several. The incentive for the employer to utilize the exotic difference selection perhaps is not as strong as the employer's incentive to utilize similarity, comfort, or differentiation. In this respect, it might be more accurate to say that a firm will not select against respectable exoticism than it would be to say that the firm will actively select for that characteristic.

B.   *Explicitly Racializing the Discussion: Combining CRT Insights*

The preceding discussion does not identify the racial effects of selection mechanisms. These effects can be demonstrated by adopting CRT's methodology of racializing the analysis. To borrow from Jerome Culp, we "raise ... the race question" and, in the process, make a number of empirical assumptions about race. While we think the assumptions are plausible, the analysis is necessarily tentative and meant only to be illustrative of the type of analysis that might be performed.

1. *How Likely Is It That Johnny Will Be a Racial Minority?*

How likely is it that "Johnny" will be a racial minority? Consider, for example, the Johnny who is a student at State Law School. Recall that this Johnny attended Harvard College and rowed crew. Rowing crew often means that one attended an elite East Coast prep school, and the number of minorities who fit in this category will be small. Further, although Johnny is at State Law School, he had the option of attending first-tier law schools. Not many students of color at a third-tier law school will have had that opportunity. In short, few minorities will have the kind of cultural capital reflected in Johnny's background.

2. *Assuming That the Johnny at State Law School Is Black, Will He Be "Selected"?*

Our hypothetical assumes that an elite corporate firm would select a person like Johnny, notwithstanding the fact that Johnny does not fit the standard profile (that is, a person who has attended a first-tier law school). But if Johnny is black, this issue is far from clear. Few elite corporate firms hire blacks from schools other than those in the first-tier—more specifically, in the top ten. This may be (at least in part) due to two assumptions. The first is an assumption about affirmative action and intellectual competence—namely, that given race-based admission preferences, "smart blacks" should end up at first-tier schools. The second is an assumption about race and class—namely, that a black person at State Law School is likely to be working class and thus may have difficulty fitting into the law firm. While both assumptions can be rebutted, doing so would require an employer to engage in more intensive (read: more costly) screening of Johnny.

3. *As a General Matter, What Kind of Person of Color Is Johnny Likely to Be?*

Except for respectable exoticism, each of the selection mechanisms described above is designed to ascertain the extent to which a prospective employee is different from firm insiders. The outsiders likely to be the least different from the firm's insiders are those on (or who perform their identity as if they are on) the periphery of their outsider group identity. These "most peripheral outsiders" are likely to have grown up in predominantly white neighborhoods and to have attended elite (and predominantly white) high schools, colleges, and law schools. Employers can use these background characteristics as proxies for whether, and to what extent, outsider candidates will fit comfortably into a predominantly white workplace.

But there is a more direct method the employer can use to determine whether an outsider has the capacity to work within a homogenized workplace. There is evidence suggesting that particular types of outsiders are, from an employer's perspective, likely to cause fewer problems in the operation of a team dominated by insiders than are other types of outsiders. Racial outsiders who are "extroverted" and effective at "self-monitoring" are more likely to succeed than those who are not. Good self-monitors assess how others perceive them and adjust their behavior accordingly; extroverts project a strong and identifiable self-identity. Presumably, the reason these types of outsiders cause minimal disruption is that they actively engage in "impression management." That is, they are constantly interacting with others, sending signals about themselves, and reacting to the impressions that others have of them. An employer's selection decision likely will take account of how well outsiders manage impressions about their racial identity (that is, at least in part, how well they disprove racial stereotypes).

4. *How Do People of Color Signal Racial Differentiation?*

The point of differentiation strategies is to convey one of three ideas—that one does not identify as an outsider, that one is a different kind of outsider, or that what others think of outsiders is wrong. To convey the first idea, that one does not identify as an outsider, an employee would engage in disidentification or disassociation strategies—strategies that signal that the employee does not really identify with his outsider group. Imagine that, in the context of an interview with an elite firm, a partner says this to Johnny: "I have to tell you, Johnny, racial diversity at our firm is not good. We do our best. But the numbers are what they are—not pretty." That statement offers Johnny an "opportunity" to articulate his relationship to his outsider identity. To disidentify and disassociate, Johnny can say: "I appreciate your telling me this, but I am more interested in learning about how your firm cultivates and trains junior associates." Johnny's response could also reflect even stronger evidence of outsider disidentification and disassociation. He might have said: "I appreciate your telling me this, but I just don't believe in identity politics. Diversity is fine and good, but people are people." The point is that the earlier response is enough differentiation to suggest to the employer that Johnny is not a "race man."

To convey the second idea of differentiation, that one is a different kind of outsider, the outsider could adopt an individualized stereotype negation strategy. Here, the outsider would attempt to convey to the employer that stereotypes about his outsider identity do not apply to him. Imagine that the employer asks Johnny what he does with his spare time and Johnny responds: "Fishing, golfing, and catching up on foreign cinema." The employer could interpret this response to suggest that Johnny is not an ordinary black man (who, based on stereotypes, would have responded: "Watching basketball, playing basketball, and listening to hip-hop."). To the extent the employer does not perceive Johnny to be a black male prototype, the employer is less likely to attribute negative stereotypes of black men to Johnny.

Johnny can convey the final idea of differentiation—that others' assumptions about outsiders are wrong—through generalized stereotype negation. Under this strategy, Johnny attempts to persuade the employer that stereotypes about the employee's outsider group are inaccurate. This strategy is difficult and risky to perform when one is interviewing for a job. For instance, after articulating what he likes to do in his spare time (fishing, golfing, and catching up on foreign cinema), Johnny could add something like: "Not all black men like basketball. Moreover, most of the stereotypes about blacks are simply inaccurate. Consider, for example, crime. . . ." It is unlikely that, in the context of an interview, Johnny would engage the employer in this way: The statement presupposes that the employer harbors stereotypes about blacks, a presupposition that could engender racial discomfort on the part of the employer ("This black guy thinks I am a racist."). Further, even if Johnny did make such a statement to the employer, it is unlikely that the employer would be persuaded by it. For generalized stereotype negation to work, there needs to be a level of trust, and sustained interaction, between the outsider and the employer.

Performing each of the foregoing differentiation strategies constitutes a form of work—identity work. Among other problems with this work, it can compromise one's sense of identity.

5. *What Are the Racial Community Costs of Differentiation Strategies?*

One of the problems with the first two differentiation strategies (disidentification/disassociation and individual stereotype negation) is that they are individually oriented. To the extent that an employee feels pressured to perform these strategies, he privileges his individual advancement over that of his group. Differentiation strategies are a response to an institutionalized problem—the employer's investment in homogeneity. So long as the homogeneity incentive drives employment decisions, there is little room for racial diversification. Society ends up with minimal (or token) outsider economic advancement into the workplace. The incentives for the outsider group, therefore, should be to engage in a collective struggle to change the system to tolerate (if not welcome) greater expression and representation of outsider identities. The first two differentiation strategies undermine that goal. They encourage outsiders to disidentify with, and disassociate from, the collective interests of the outsider group. In this sense, the problem with homogeneity is not simply that it drives employers to hire only certain kinds of outsiders, but also that the outsiders whom the employer hires are not likely to lift as they climb.

To summarize, the employer's pursuit of a homogenous workforce is likely to produce the following effects (subject to the assumptions made):

● Given the negative presumption that applies to the ability and willingness of outsiders to satisfy the homogeneity requirement (and the positive presumptions that apply to whites), the quantum of cultural capital (or the price of entry) that employers require of outsiders is likely to be higher than that for their white counterparts.

● Within the outsider community, only the elite are likely to possess the quantum of cultural capital necessary to gain entry. Employers seeking to satisfy the diversity constraint will affirmatively pursue this small subset of minorities.

● The strategies that an individual outsider employee is likely to pursue, such as differentiation, may hurt the collective cause of her minority group and compromise her sense of self. The collective cause may be better served by a struggle to reduce and remove barriers, as opposed to a competition among outsiders for a few slots (and which requires outsider homogenization).

* * *

———

NOTES AND QUESTIONS

1. **"Lean" production and new, ruthless economy.** Changes in technology have permitted a steady rise in economic productivity for the United States in recent years. These changes, however, collectively have made labor much more insecure. William Greider discusses the case of labor unions and the manufacturing sector:

> Starting in the 1970s, U.S. companies gravitated toward a different strategy in which global price pressures were offset by extracting more from labor. Corporations discarded their long postwar truce with unions and began moving jobs, first to the low-wage South and then offshore. They closed factories and demanded wage contracts that depressed wages. They mobilized both political and economic power to weaken labor's bargaining position.
>
> American corporate managers might point out that they themselves were driven to these defensive actions by the global economic forces. The "virtuous circle" of the 1950s and 1960s had also been sustained by the existence of industrial oligopolies—a few big companies that dominated major sectors like autos, steel and aircraft and were powerful enough to set prices and wages in a clubby, arbitrary fashion. The rise of foreign producers, especially from Japan, broke up that comfortable arrangement forever.
>
> As firms shifted production to lower-wage workers, organized labor lost members and became steadily less able to discipline managements. The decline in wages was not confined to union members, however, but was more general. Retail sales workers, for instance, experienced a much sharper fall than manufacturing. In 1970, wages constituted 67 percent of all personal income in the United States, a ratio that had held constant for decades. By 1994, wages were less than 58 percent of total incomes. In 1960, wages were about 26 percent of total sales. By 1994, they were about 20 percent.

WILLIAM GREIDER, ONE WORLD, READY OR NOT: THE MANIC LOGIC OF GLOBAL CAPITALISM 77 (1997). Greider argues that these trends are symptomatic of a larger phenomenon: "wage arbitrage." Wage arbitrage "moves the production and jobs from a high-wage labor market to another where the labor is much cheaper. The producers thus reduce their costs and enhance profits by arbitraging these wage differences, usually selling their finished products back into the high-wage markets." *Id.* at 57. Since labor is much less mobile than capital, wage arbitrage means the upper hand in bargaining power for capital in particular disputes. Unions, which are usually organized within national boundaries, become vulnerable to the threat of moving jobs to lower-wage countries.

2.   Law firms as internal labor markets. For an extended application of economic theory to explain the hiring and promotion practices of large law firms, see David B. Wilkins & G. Mitu Gulati, *Reconceiving the Tournament of Lawyers: Tracking, Seeding, and Information Control in the Internal Labor Markets of Elite Law Firms*, 84 Va. L. Rev. 1581 (1998).

3.   Winner-take-all markets. Some economists argue that a new feature of contemporary labor markets is the existence of the "winner take all" market. In such markets there are many competitors for a very few extremely lucrative slots. The entertainment industry provides many examples: as reality shows like *American Idol* dramatically illustrate, the possibility of fame and fortune in the entertainment world draws many more people than could possibly succeed. As the economists argue, and as *American Idol* also illustrates, winner-take-all markets are socially wasteful because the possibility of extremely high rewards (coupled with the cognitive quirks identified by bounded rationality theory) draws people who would do better for themselves and the rest of society if they put their time and energy elsewhere. Winner-take-all markets also contribute to income inequality, since a very small number of players make a huge amount of money and the rest make very little. Robert Frank and Philip Cook argue that changes in tax policy, tort reform, health care finance, educational finance, and antitrust policy, among other reforms, could promote both efficiency and equity by reducing the spread and impact of winner-take-all markets. *See* Robert H. Frank & Philip J. Cook, The Winner-Take-All Society 211–31 (1995).

4.   Women and emotional labor. Arlie Russell Hochschild, in *The Managed Heart: Commercialization of Human Feeling* (20th anniversary edition 2003), argues that women in the workplace often face demands not placed on men, that they display certain kinds of emotions, usually cheeriness and nurturance. Arlie Russell Hochschild, The Managed Heart: Commercialization of Human Feeling (20th anniv. ed. 2003). Thus, women may be asked to smile, will be expected to be peacemakers in workplace disputes, and are expected to defer to the emotional needs and desires of men. Hochschild argues that the requirement of emotional labor also tends to fall upon occupations that have been heavily feminized, such as secretaries and nurses, without regard to the sex of the people in those occupations. *See also* Arlie Russell Hochschild, Commercialization of Intimate Life: Notes From Home and Work (2003). Does Carbado and Gulati's analysis suggest a similar burden of emotional labor on racial minorities in the workplace?

5.   Impression management. Carbado and Gulati's analysis is indebted to the work of sociologist Erving Goffman, who coined the phrase "impression management" to describe how individuals attempt to control how they are seen by others, while those others in turn attempt to discern the "real" self behind the front. *See, e.g.*, Erving Goffman, *The Arts of Impression Management, in* The Presentation of Delf in Everyday Life 208–37 (1959).

Goffman emphasizes that everyone in social life is constantly engaged in impression management, both in private and in public settings, and uses the metaphor of the dramatic performance throughout his analysis:

> In this report, the individual was divided by implication into two basic parts: he was viewed as a *performer*, a harried fabricator of impressions involved in the all-too-human task of staging a performance; he was viewed as a *character*, a figure, typically a fine one, whose spirit, strength, and other sterling qualities the performance was designed to evoke. The attributes of a performer and the attributes of a character are of a different order, quite basically so, yet both sets have their meaning in terms of the show that must go on. * * *

> A correctly staged and performed scene leads the audience to impute a self to a performed character, but this imputation—this self—is a *product* of a scene that comes off, and is not a *cause* of it. The self, then, as a performed character, is not an organic thing that has a specific location, whose fundamental fate is to be born, to mature, and to die; it is a dramatic effect arising diffusely from a scene that is presented, and the characteristic issue, the crucial concern, is whether it will be credited or discredited.

Id., at 252–53.

C. CLASS AND CONSUMPTION

The Overspent American: Why We Want What We Don't Need

80–91 (1998).

■ JULIET B. SCHOR

While television has long been suspected as a promoter of consumer desire, there has been little hard evidence to support that view, at least for adult spending. After all, there's not an obvious connection. Many of the products advertised on television are everyday low-cost items such as aspirin, laundry detergent, and deodorant. Those TV ads are hardly a spur to excessive consumerism. Leaving aside other kinds of ads for the moment (for cars, diamonds, perfumes), there's another counter to the argument that television causes consumerism: TV is a *substitute* for spending. One of the few remaining free activities, TV is a popular alternative to costly recreational spending such as movies, concerts, and restaurants. If it causes us to spend, that effect must be powerful enough to overcome its propensity to save us money.

Apparently it is. My research shows that the more TV a person watches, the more he or she spends. The likely explanation for the link between television and spending is that what we see on TV inflates our sense of what's normal. The lifestyles depicted on television are far different from the average American's: with a few exceptions, TV characters are upper-middle-class, or even rich.

Studies by the consumer researchers Thomas O'Guinn and L.J. Schrum confirm this upward distortion. The more people watch television, the more they think American households have tennis courts, private planes, convertibles, car telephones, maids, and swimming pools. Heavy watchers also overestimate the portion of the population who are millionaires, have had cosmetic surgery, and belong to a private gym, as well as those suffering from dandruff, bladder control problems, gingivitis, athlete's foot, and hemorrhoids (the effect of all those ads for everyday products). What one watches also matters. Dramatic shows—both daytime soap operas and prime-time drama series—have a stronger impact on viewer perceptions than other kinds of programs (say news, sports, or weather).

Heavy watchers are not the only ones, however, who tend to overestimate standards of living. Almost everyone does. (And almost everyone watches TV.) In one study, ownership rates for twenty-two of twenty-seven consumer products were generally overstated. Your own financial position also matters. Television inflates standards for lower-, average-, and above-average-income students, but it does the reverse for really wealthy ones. (Among those raised in a financially rarefied atmosphere, TV is almost a reality check.) Social theories of consumption hold that the inflated sense of consumer norms promulgated by the media raises people's aspirations and leads them to buy more. In the words of one Los Angeles resident, commenting on this media tendency, "They try to portray that an upper-class lifestyle is normal and typical and that we should all have it."

Television also affects norms by giving us real information about how other people live and what they have. It allows us to be voyeurs, opening the door to the "private world" inside the homes and lives of others. * * *

Another piece of evidence for the TV-spending link is the apparent correlation between debt and excessive TV viewing. In the Merck Family Fund poll, the fraction responding that they "watch too much TV" rose steadily with indebtedness. More than half (56 percent) of all those who reported themselves "heavily" in debt also said they watched too much TV.

It is partly because of television that the top 20 percent of the income distribution, and even the top 5 percent within it, has become so important in setting and escalating consumption standards for more than just the people immediately below them. Television lets *everyone* see what these folks have and allows viewers to want it in concrete, product-specific ways. Let's not forget that television programming and movies are increasingly filled with product placements—the use of identifiable brands by characters. TV shows and movies are more and more like long-running ads. * * *

Part of what keeps the see-want-borrow-and-buy sequence going is lack of attention. Americans live with high levels of denial about their spending patterns. We spend more than we realize, hold more debt than we admit to, and ignore many of the moral conflicts surrounding our acquisitions. The

importance of denial for dysfunctional consumers has been well documented. We've all heard the stories about people who drive around in cars full of
unpaid credit card bills, who sneak into the guest room at 2:00 A.M. to make
a QVC purchase, or who quietly slip off at lunchtime for a quick trip to the
mall. What is not well understood is that the spending of many normal
consumers is also predicated on denial. (How many times have you heard
someone say, "Oh, I'm not materialistic, I'm just into books and CDs—and
travel"?) * * *

Nowhere is denial so evident as with credit cards. Contrary to economists' usual portrayal of credit card debtors as fully rational consumers
who use the cards to smooth out temporary shortfalls in income, the
finding of the University of Maryland economist Larry Ausubel was that
people greatly underestimate the amount of debt they hold on their cards—
1992's actual $182 billion in debt was thought to be a mere $70 billion.
Furthermore, most people do not expect to use their cards to borrow, but,
of course, they do. Eighty percent end up paying finance charges within any
given year, with just under half (47 percent) always holding unpaid
balances.

Not paying attention to what we spend is also very common. How
many of us really keep track of where the cash from the ATM goes? Most
Americans don't budget. And they don't watch. Many "fritter," as this
downshifter recalled: "All I know is at the end of the month I never had
anything left. And so I have to say I spent it all. I don't know what I
frittered away. I really don't know what I spent the money on." * * *

Finally, denial also helps us navigate the moral conflicts associated
with consumption. Most of our cherished religious and ethical teachings
condemn excessive spending, but we don't really know what that means.
We have a sense that money is dirty and a nagging feeling that there must
be something better to do with our hard-earned dollars than give them to
Bloomingdale's. As our salaries and creature comforts expand, many of us
keep alive our youthful fantasies of doing humanitarian work, continuing
the inner dialogue between God and Mammon. Not looking *too* hard helps
keep that inner conflict tolerable. Squarely facing the fact that you spent
$6,000 on your wardrobe last year and gave less than one-third of that sum
to charity is a lot harder than living with a vague sense that you need to
start spending less on clothes and giving away more money. * * *

In many places, private school is becoming a part of the upper-middle-
(and even middle-) class standard of living—a requisite element in the basic
package. Parents worry that without it their children will fall behind. Fears
about education become magnified because they tap into larger, more deep-
seated anxieties. Class position seems to be at stake. And, of course, as the
middle and upper-middle classes abandon the public schools, the class
divisions widen. Public school becomes tainted with a lower-class image. As
another mother in the Los Angeles study explained, the public schools work
well for her "housekeeper's child," who will have language problems, but
not for her children. "Our concern with the public schools is really the
safety issue. I have blond-haired, blue-eyed children who are not very

physical and not very aggressive, and I worry about interactions on playgrounds.''

At the same time, these parents have to deal with the complications of schooling alongside the super-wealthy. The same woman who is afraid of the public school playgrounds also worries about her children being at the bottom of the economic ladder in their private school. "The wealth of these kids is just mind-boggling. You put them in an environment in which we cannot compete, nor do we *want* them to compete and have those kinds of values. I don't want them to come home and say, 'Why don't we live in a ten-bedroom house?' " * * *

We have no problem acknowledging the "conspicuous consumption" of the early twentieth century that [Thorstein] Veblen wrote about. Middle class Americans shake their heads at what inner-city youths do to obtain expensive sneakers or gold chains. We can even get passionate about the dangers of status symbols in the Third World. Many Americans boycotted Nestle for promoting infant formula, the often deadly status alternative to breast milk. (Nestle and other companies had women in "modern" white uniforms doling out free supplies of formula in hospitals, leading to sickness, malnutrition, and even death among "bottle babies.") Many Americans deplore the entry of soft drinks and fast-food outlets into poor countries because they contribute to comerciogenic malnutrition: the poor spend their few pesos on soft drinks or French fries, forgoing nutritious food and becoming sick in the process. On the lighter side, we can chuckle at Peruvian Indians carrying rocks painted like transistor radios, Chinese who keep the brand tags on their designer sunglasses, Brazilian shanty-town dwellers with television antennae but no TV's, or the Papua New Guineans who substitute Pentel pens for boars' nose pieces. Third World status consumption seems straightforward, unambiguous in motive.

We have more trouble seeing the counterparts of these behaviors in the American middle class, and in ourselves.

———

No Scrubs

TLC, *on* FANMAIL, LA FACE (1999).

■ KEVIN BRIGGS, KANDI BURRUSS, TAMEKA COTTLE

A scrub is a guy that thinks he's fly
And is also known as a buster
Always talkin' about what he wants
And just sits on his broke ass
So (no)

I don't want your number (no)
I don't want to give you mine and (no)
I don't want to meet you nowhere (no)
I don't want none of your time and (no)

Chorus:
I don't want no scrub
A scrub is a guy that can't get no love from me
Hanging out the passenger side
Of his best friend's ride
Trying to holler at me
I don't want no scrub
A scrub is a guy that can't get no love from me
Hanging out the passenger side
Of his best friend's ride
Trying to holler at me

But a scrub is checkin' me
But his game is kinda weak
And I know that he cannot approach me
Cuz I'm lookin' like class and he's lookin' like trash
Can't get wit' no deadbeat ass
So (no)

I don't want your number (no)
I don't want to give you mine and (no)
I don't want to meet you nowhere (no)
I don't want none of your time (no)

Chorus
If you don't have a car and you're walking
Oh yes son I'm talking to you
If you live at home wit' your momma
Oh yes son I'm talking to you (baby)
If you have a shorty but you don't show love
Oh yes son I'm talking to you
Wanna get with me with no money
Oh no I don't want no (oh)

No scrub
No scrub (no no)
No scrub (no no no no no)
No scrub (no no)
No

* * *

Dress As Success
BEAUTY SECRETS: WOMEN AND THE POLITICS OF APPEARANCE 79–80, 83–85, 88–93 (1986).

■ WENDY CHAPKIS

Appearance talks, making statements about gender, sexuality, ethnicity and class. In a sexually, racially and economically divided society all those visual statements add up to an evaluation of power. Economic power, or class position, is easily suggested by a man's use of the standard business suit. An expensive tailored three-piece suit says authority and privilege quietly but unmistakeably. For a woman to get that kind of attention, she must speak up more loudly. Even dressed in designer everything and costly jewelry her appearance makes a less unambiguous statement than a man's $1,000 suit.

Traditionally, a woman dressed in money has been assumed to be making a statement not about herself, but about a man. Her expensive clothing was thought to signal to the world that her husband or other male provider was so wealthy he could afford a clearly useless luxury in the form of this female. In this Veblenesque* interpretation, the woman herself is relegated to the position of a passive object much like a clothes hanger in someone else's closet. While this may well explain a husband's rationale for paying the bills, conspicuous consumption has a special purpose in a wealthy woman's life, too. * * *

Not only has consuming been one of the few pursuits open to women of a certain class, but being dressed in money demonstrates to the viewing public that the woman's one all important investment—marriage—has paid off nicely. Woman to woman we know that the marriage contract is far from an agreement between peers. At least being well-dressed serves as the visual equivalent of a large pay check.

Women in the role of wife establish social position second hand. A wealthy husband provides access to power for the woman married to him. But this ascribed power has to be made visible. If he has it, you flaunt it—not merely to reflect well on him, but to protect yourself. Dressed in money, a woman looks like someone not to be trifled with despite her sex. She is clearly protected by someone with the ability to do the job.

Increasingly, though, women are finding a need to indicate *personal* financial authority through their dress. Many more women now are bread-winners than in the past. This change is due in part to the women's movement. However, perhaps even more important than feminism is rising male unemployment and inflation making a woman's paycheck indispensable. Higher divorce rates, too, have helped make female financial independence a necessity.

How a woman should indicate professional power through her appearance is still a subject of debate. But all those voices presuming to advise women on how to put together such an image seem to agree on two fundamental things. First, *looking* "successful" is more than half the battle in actually achieving professional success. And second, success is a formula not to be tinkered with—that is, women may now aspire to professional success but should not attempt to redefine it.

Both these precepts have a particular resonance for women. Haven't we always known that how we look is far more important than what we do or how we do it? And as interlopers in the man-made world of business, we

* Thorstein Veblen, author of *The Theory of the Leisure Class,* published in 1899.

tend toward gratitude if someone even takes the time to explain the rules of the game—we may feel in no position to try to change them. Success in these terms is intensely individual and conformity a useful strategy.

* * *

The carefully composed look of success is not without its fashion competition. New Wave culture and punk style are among the most radical forms of visual dissent. At a very minimum, punk is a statement about consumerism. At least initially, the fashion was put together from hand-made or second hand clothing. Jewelry was to be found or created from inexpensive materials like rubber, plastic and cheap metals.

Punk has also been an explicit message on the state of the economy. If there is a possibility of a job interview in the near future, one probably won't choose a fluorescent green hair dye or a Mohawk haircut. But when unemployment becomes a predictable long-term condition, little is put at risk by looking outrageous. Radically transforming one's personal appearance can be an exercise of personal power in a life that feels out of control. While it may not be possible for an individual to change the reality of high unemployment, housing shortages and poverty, it is possible to transform one's body into a visual shout: "No, I do not accept the goodness of your goals and expectations. No, I will not help you feel secure in your choices. Do I look frightening? Do I look angry? Do I look dangerous? Do you still feel safe in thinking that the system works just fine? Think again."

Not surprisingly, it is not the Punk but the young urban professionals—the so-called Yuppies—who have become the darlings of contemporary media. Their aerobic bodies and expensive dress speak confidently of physical and economic health. The image is above all reassuring. The system works just fine if you play by the rules. We accept the goals and the methods and we will be among the winners.

Success as it is known in the contemporary corporate world is dependent on a division between winners and losers, with a built-in guarantee that more will fail than will be rewarded. Women have always been the structural losers in the system. To be a woman was to be slotted for the position of support staff, both professionally and personally. The reality remains that even today most women will not become senior executives. In fact, most women will not even marry senior executives. The majority of working women will remain on a parallel job ladder which ends in the position of executive secretary or senior administrative assistant.

As anyone with experience in the business world knows, these are the women who run the show, without whom many organizations would come to a standstill. Yet they will never have the money or the authority to accompany the responsibility.

As long as success remains an individual characteristic, only one name will go on the by-line, while research assistants will have to be satisfied with a thank you in the acknowledgements. Secretaries will continue to receive lunch invitations or roses once a year instead of colleague-to-colleague respect and recognition of their partnership in the business endeavor. And women who do make it to a position of recognized power will have to quickly switch class and gender allegiance. Too close an identification with the secretarial crowd, too much empathy with those who come up on the short end of the unequal division of rewards will only be detrimental to one's own climb toward success.

It is arguably an improvement if women as a group are no longer automatically relegated to subordinate positions. But only those who find Jeane Kirkpatrick and Margaret Thatcher shining examples of feminism will believe that this sort of individual success is the same thing as women's liberation.

* * *

In the early days of the contemporary women's movement, women created strategies of empowerment that focused on shared experience and collective labor. However, we also longed for the individual perques of authority and prestige. But we were operating in an economic structure that insured that while our efforts might allow some of us to "make it," all of us would not. Western industrial society is based on competition and scarcity; equality not of condition but of opportunity. Taking on male bastions of power like the corporate world and opening them up to women meant collectively breaking down the barriers to women's participation. We worked for and achieved legislation that guaranteed us access. But once we succeeded in opening the door, we stepped through and realized that the stairway to the top was narrow and already crowded.

Still, now that the opportunity was there, failure became evidence of personal inadequacy not a political problem. Nor was class (known in America as one's "background") a political concern—provided one knew how to hide it. An entire literature developed teaching the common woman how to reach uncommon heights by "applying" herself and dressing for the part. * * *

Once inside and part way up the corporate ladder, the need to disguise your origins becomes imperative. In order to become executive materials, you must look as if you come from executive stock—the upper middle class. Enter John T. Molloy and *Dress for Success*:

> We can increase [a woman's] chances of success in the business world; we can increase her chances of being a top executive; we can make her more attractive to various types of men.

Molloy believes at least as firmly as [Helen Gurley Brown, founder of *Cosmopolitan* magazine] that a woman's business success lies in her own hands. Failure, too, is a personal not a structural problem: "If you have to tell your boss not to send you for coffee, you must have already told him non-verbally that you were ready to go." He quotes "Two extremely successful women" to back him up on this; these women expressed the belief that "The reason most young women wouldn't succeed was because they didn't look like they wanted to succeed."

Dressed in the proper outfit and sporting the proper attitude, the political problem of sexism can be sidestepped. The trick is learning to *accept* reality, not trying to change it. "It is a stark reality that men dominate the power structure.... I am not suggesting that women dress to impress men simply because they are men [but rather because men have power] ... It is not sexism; it is realism."

In the chapter entitled "Does Your Background Hurt You," Molloy dismisses class as a political problem as neatly as he does sex. Women who intend to move into "The power ranks of American society" first must "learn the manners and mores of the inner circle. And the inner circle is most emphatically upper middle class." Not to worry; his advice is exceedingly specific:

> My research showed that a woman wearing a black raincoat is definitely not automatically categorized as lower middle class. Raincoats are important for women, but not as important as they are for men.... The country-tweed look is very upper middle class and highly recommended.... The blazer, by its very nature, is upper middle class; every woman should have at least one.... Office sweaters ... say lower middle class and loser. Don't wear lower middle class colors such as purple and gold.

Predictably, the colors that test best are "gray, medium range blue, beige, deep maroon, deep rust." And the colors to avoid are "most pastels, particularly pink and pale yellow, most shades of green, mustard, bright anything, any shade that would be considered exotic." What we end up with as acceptable colors in the business world are those commonly associated with men and with the white upper class. This look is then defined as "serious." Serious becomes a question of conformity not creative difference, of masculinity not femininity and of the bland over the exotic, i.e. the foreign or racially "deviant."

Racial difference is indeed problematic to success and must be minimized. The process begins with learning to lose any ethnic accent and avoiding exotic fashions. But people of color serious about success are also advised to do whatever possible to transform even their bodies. In African women's magazines, advertisements promote the skin lightner Clere:

> Clere for your own special beauty. We are a successful people and have to look successful. We use Clere for a lighter, smoother skin. Now, Clere will work its magic for you, and make you more beautiful and successful.

Of course, it is not only among dress for success advisors that one finds these prejudices. They just help make them respectable. Even among articulate critics of sexism and racism in contemporary society there is evidence that these standards have been internalized. * * *

The shift from full-time homemaking to double duty (working both for wages and in the home) has helped create a need for new symbols of identity. Women are discovering that they are expected to have not one, but several conflicting images: the wholesome mother, the coolly professional businesswoman and the sexy mistress. No wonder women turn to the magic of wardrobe and makeup to provide inspiration for their multiple selves:

"Springfever by Elizabeth Arden ... New make-up. New inspiration." "I can bring home the bacon, fry it up in a pan and never let you forget you're a man ... En Jolie" "Colors that inspire ... Let L'erin do the talking." You almost can hear the poor woman sigh "gladly."

The cosmetics industry has been carefully studying how best to make use of this bewildering set of demands made upon working women. Women's wages have been a mixed blessing for the beauty trade. In 1983, *Advertising Age*, an industry trade journal, noted with some alarm an increase in the number of women working outside the home:

> Today, 49% of America's mothers with children under six years old are employed as opposed to only 18% in 1960 ... Where women in this group once spent middays at the department store, they are now in the office.... Women who formerly had the time to sample and listen and spend money are no longer shoppers. Even when they do visit the store, they do so as buyers.

The subtle distinction between "shopping" and "buying," *Advertising Age* points out, is that the former implies leisure. This distinction seems to be borne out by figures on grocery store cosmetic sales (cheap and fast). In the U.S., they increased by 35 percent from 1980 to 1982.

Without the leisure to linger and shop, a woman may buy what is handy and in the process discover that what she is buying for convenience is not substantially different than the more expensive brand she used to carefully seek out. *Advertising Age* warns: "This is a dangerous conclusion for the industry."

And indeed after decades of constant growth, the beauty trade is now faced with a leveling off of sales and, in some cases, even a slight decline. Not all product lines have felt the squeeze, though. "Customers seem to be turning away from medium price products," the vice-president for marketing of one of America's largest cosmetic companies notes. "They are buying better goods or switching to generic, low-price products." * * *

Often the expensive and cheap products are not only produced by different divisions of the same conglomerate, but they are made of nearly identical ingredients. Even when we know this to be true, we often will buy the more expensive item because the fantasy it offers is more attractive. Psychologist Erika Freeman explains,

> An item that promises a fantasy by definition must be priced fantastically.... If a cream begins to sell at 50 cents it will not sell as well nor will it be considered as miraculous as a cream that sells for $30.
> * * *

Why do women buy costly beauty products that demonstrably have little purpose other than participation in a fantasy? The purchase of a new cosmetic, the decision to change the color or style of one's hair, the start of a new diet are the female equivalent of buying a lottery ticket. Maybe *you* will be the one whose life is transformed. Despite daily experience to the contrary, we continue to hope that maybe this time, maybe this product, will make a difference in our lives. And if it doesn't, it is still a relatively inexpensive way to visit the mysterious orient of Shiseido, the elite circle of Chanel, the smouldering, sensuous world of Dior. Everything that is so difficult to attain in real life is promised for the price of a new perfume or eye shadow.

––––––

NOTES AND QUESTIONS

1.   Thorstein Veblen and social meaning of consumption. Thorstein Veblen [1857–1929] was an American economist whose work focused on the embeddedness of economic activity in a larger social world in which the desire for prestige in the eyes of others is as central as the desire for purely material gain. Two of the concepts he elaborated—"conspicuous consumption" and "pecuniary emulation"—illustrate this focus. Veblen argued that wealthy people desire to signal to others that they are wealthy, and that buying and displaying luxury goods is an important means by which this is done. Thus, "Conspicuous consumption is how the wealthy demonstrate their wealth, and thus their success in war or in business. By purchasing the finest houses, autos, suits, and shoes—all visible and public signs of financial success—they gain the respect and admiration of their peers and subordinates." Janet Knoedler, *Thorstein Veblen and the Predatory Nature of Contemporary Capitalism, in* INTRODUCTION TO POLITICAL ECONOMY 66 (Charles Sackrey & Geoffrey Schneider eds., 3d ed. 2002).

Veblen also argued that people in all economic classes make consumption decisions based not only on their rational desire for goods and services to make their life better, but out of envy of those who are more successful. This desire to be like and to be seen as like those with more money and social success he named "pecuniary emulation":

> [T]he standard of expenditure which commonly guides our efforts is not the average, ordinary expenditure already achieved; it is an ideal of consumption that lies just beyond our reach ... The motive is emulation—the stimulus of an invidious comparison which prompts us to outdo those with whom we are in the habit of classing ourselves ... [e]ach class envies and emulates the class next above it in the social scale, while it rarely compares itself with those below or with those who are considerably in advance.

THORSTEIN VEBLEN, THE THEORY OF THE LEISURE CLASS 81 (HOUGHTON MIFFLIN Co. 1973) (1899).

2.   Crisis of over-production and creation of desire. Economic historians argue that after 1890, as modern forms of industrial production began to take shape and more and more mass-produced goods began to flood American markets, American business interests began a campaign to change consumption patterns away from patterns of thrift, self-denial, and self-reliance. As William Leach argues:

From the 1890s on, American corporate business, in league with key institutions, began the transformation of American society into a society preoccupied with consumption, with comfort and bodily well-being, with luxury, spending, and acquisition, with more goods this year than last, more next year than this. American consumer capitalism produced a culture almost violently hostile to the past and to tradition, a future-oriented culture of desire that confused the good life with goods. It was a culture that first appeared as an alternative culture—or as one moving largely against the grain of earlier traditions of republicanism and Christian virtue—and then unfolded to become the reigning culture of the United States. It was the culture that many people the world over soon came to see as *the* heart of American life.

WILLIAM LEACH, LAND OF DESIRE: MERCHANTS, POWER, AND THE RISE OF A NEW AMERICAN CULTURE, xiii (1993); *see also* STUART EWEN, CAPTAINS OF CONSCIOUS-NESS: ADVERTISING AND THE SOCIAL ROOTS OF THE CONSUMER CULTURE (2001).

Consumer culture is partly a response to what Veblen identified as an incipient crisis within capitalist societies: the threat of overproduction, too many goods chasing too few buyers. As William Greider puts it:

As economist Thorstein Veblen taught several generations ago, the problem of capitalist enterprise is always the problem of supply: managing the production of goods in order to maximize profit and the return on invested capital. * * *

The great virtue of capitalism—the quality that always confounded socialist critics and defeated rival economic systems—is its ability to yield more from less. Its efficient organization of production strives to produce more goods from less input, whether the input is capital, labor or raw resources. Assuming markets are stable, the rising productivity increases the profit per unit, the yields that get distributed as returns to invested capital or as rising wages for labor or in lower product prices for consumers and, in the happiest circumstances, all three.

But this expanding potential to produce more goods also poses the enduring contradiction for capitalist enterprise: how to dispose of the surplus production. You can make more things, but can you sell them? An undisciplined expansion of productive capacity will be self-defeating, even dangerous for a firm, if all it accomplishes are continuing supply surpluses that degrade prices and undermine the rate of return. The problem of surplus capacity drives not only the competition among firms for market shares but also the imperative to discover new markets.

WILLIAM GREIDER, ONE WORLD, READY OR NOT: THE MANIC LOGIC OF GLOBAL CAPITALISM 44–45 (1997).

3. Branding and consumption. As the culture of consumption has matured, advertising strategies have changed as well. In the early 1990s, American corporations began to shift even more profoundly away from advertising what Karl Marx would have called the use-value of their products, to focus instead on using advertising to create an affective link between their products and the consumer's dreams and fantasies. This new technique relied on "branding," and the advertising of the brand rather than the product. As Naomi Klein observes:

> Overnight, "Brands, not products!" became the rallying cry for a marketing renaissance led by a new breed of companies that saw themselves as "meaning brokers" instead of product producers. What was changing was the idea of what—in both advertising and branding—was being sold. The old paradigm had it that all marketing was selling a product. In the new model, however, the product always takes a back seat to the real product, the brand, and the selling of the brand acquired an extra component that can only be described as spiritual. * * *

> On Marlboro Friday [a day in 1993 when Marlboro announced plans to dramatically reduce its prices in an attempt to compete with bargain cigarette brands], a line was drawn in the sand between the lowly price slashers and the high-concept brand builders. The brand builders conquered and a new consensus was born: the products that will flourish in the future will be the ones presented not as "commodities" but as concepts: the brand as experience, as lifestyle.

NAOMI KLEIN, NO LOGO: TAKING AIM AT THE BRAND BULLIES 21 (1999).

Does the ever-more-ephemeral link between products and the consumer's actual need for them threaten the pursuit of happiness?

———

Advertising At the Edge of the Apocalypse

Available at http://www.sutjhally.com/onlinepubs/onlinepubs_frame.html (n.d.)

■ SUT JHALLY

In this article I wish to make a simple claim: 20th century advertising is the most powerful and sustained system of propaganda in human history and its cumulative cultural effects, unless quickly checked, will be responsible for destroying the world as we know it. As it achieves this it will be responsible for the deaths of hundreds of thousands of non-western peoples and will prevent the peoples of the world from achieving true happiness. Simply stated, our survival as a species is dependent upon minimizing the threat from advertising and the commercial culture that has spawned it. I am stating my claims boldly at the outset so there can be no doubt as to what is at stake in our debates about the media and culture as we enter the new millennium.

COLONIZING CULTURE

Karl Marx, the pre-eminent analyst of 19th century industrial capitalism, wrote in 1867, in the very opening lines of *Capital* that: "The wealth of societies in which the capitalist mode of production prevails appears as an 'immense collection of commodities'". * * * In seeking to initially distinguish his object of analysis from preceding societies, Marx referred to the way the society showed itself on a surface level and highlighted a *quantitative* dimension—the number of objects that humans interacted with in everyday life.

Indeed, no other society in history has been able to match the immense productive output of industrial capitalism. This feature colors the way in which the society presents itself—the way it *appears*. Objects are everywhere in capitalism. In this sense, capitalism is truly a revolutionary society, dramatically altering the very landscape of social life, in a way no other form of social organization had been able to achieve in such a short period of time. (In *The Communist Manifesto* Marx and Engels would coin the famous phrase "all that is solid melts into air" to highlight capitalism's unique dynamism.) It is this that strikes Marx as distinctive as he observes 19th century London. The starting point of his own critique therefore is not what he believes is the dominating agent of the society, *capital*, nor is it what he believes creates the value and wealth, *labor*—instead it is the *commodity*. From this surface appearance Marx then proceeds to peel away the outer skin of the society and to penetrate to the underlying essential structure that lies in the "hidden abode" of production.

It is not enough of course to only produce the "immense collection of commodities"—they must also be sold, so that further investment in production is feasible. Once produced commodities must go through the circuit of distribution, exchange and consumption, so that profit can be returned to the owners of capital and value can be "realized" again in a money form. If the circuit is not completed the system would collapse into stagnation and depression. Capitalism therefore has to ensure the sale of commodities on *pain of death*. In that sense the problem of capitalism is not mass production (which has been solved) but is instead the *problem of consumption*. That is why from the early years of this century it is more accurate to use the label "the consumer culture" to describe the western industrial market societies.

So central is consumption to its survival and growth that at the end of the 19th century industrial capitalism invented a unique new institution— the advertising industry—to ensure that the "immense accumulation of commodities" are converted back into a money form. The function of this new industry would be to recruit the best creative talent of the society and to create a culture in which desire and identity would be fused with commodities—to make the dead world of things come alive with human and social possibilities (what Marx would prophetically call the "fetishism of commodities"). And indeed there has never been a propaganda effort to match the effort of advertising in the 20th century. More thought, effort, creativity, time, and attention to detail has gone into the selling of the immense collection of commodities that any other campaign in human history to change public consciousness. One indication of this is [simple] the amount of money that has been exponentially expended on this effort. Today, in the United States alone, over $175 billion a year is spent to sell us things. This concentration of effort is unprecedented.

It should not be surprising that something this central and with so much being expended on it should become an important presence in social life. Indeed, commercial interests intent on maximizing the consumption of the immense collection of commodities have colonized more and more of the spaces of our culture. For instance, almost the entire media system (television and print) has been developed as a delivery system for marketers—its prime function is to produce audiences for sale to advertisers. Both the advertisements it carries, as well as the editorial matter that acts as a support for it, celebrate the consumer society. The movie system, at one time outside the direct influence of the broader marketing system, is now fully integrated into it through the strategies of licensing, tie-ins and product placements. The prime function of many Hollywood films today is to aid in the selling of the immense collection of commodities. As public funds are drained from the non-commercial cultural sector, art galleries, museums and symphonies bid for corporate sponsorship. Even those institutions thought to be outside of the market are being sucked in. High schools now sell the sides of their buses, the spaces of their hallways and the classroom time of their students to hawkers of candy bars, soft drinks and jeans. In New York City, sponsors are being sought for public playgrounds. In the contemporary world everything is sponsored by someone. The latest plans of Space Marketing Inc. call for rockets to deliver mile-wide Mylar billboards to compete with the sun and the moon for the attention of the earth's population.

With advertising messages on everything from fruit on supermarket shelves, to urinals, and to literally the space beneath our feet (Bamboo lingerie conducted a spray-paint pavement campaign in Manhattan telling consumers that "from here it looks likes you could use some new underwear"), it should not be surprising that many commentators now identify the realm of culture as simply an *adjunct* to the system of production and consumption.

Indeed so overwhelming has the commercial colonization of our culture become that it has created its own problems for marketers who now worry about how to ensure that their *individual* message stands out from the "clutter" and the "noise" of this busy environment. In that sense the main competition for marketers is not simply other brands in their product type, but all the other advertisers who are competing for the attention of an increasingly cynical audience which is doing all it can to avoid ads. In a strange paradox, as advertising takes over more and more space in the culture the job of the individual advertisers becomes much more difficult. Therefore even greater care and resources are poured into the creation of commercial messages—much greater care than the surrounding editorial matter designed to capture the attention of the audience. Indeed if we wanted to compare national television commercials to something equivalent, it [would be] the biggest budget movie blockbusters. Second by second, it costs more to produce the average network ad than a movie like *Jurassic Park*.

The twin results of these developments are that advertising is everywhere and huge amounts of money and creativity are expended upon them.

If Marx were writing today I believe that not only would he be struck by the presence of even more objects, but also by the ever-present "discourse through and about objects" that permeates the spaces of our public and private domains. * * * This commercial discourse is the *ground* on which we live, the space in which we learn to think, the *lens* through which we come to understand the world that surrounds us. In seeking to understand where we are headed as a society, an adequate analysis of this commercial environment is essential.

Seeking this understanding will involve clarifying what we mean by the power and effectiveness of ads, and of being able to pose the right question. For too long debate has been concentrated around the issue of whether ad campaigns create demand for a particular product. If you are Pepsi Cola, or Ford, or Anheuser Busch, then it may be the right question for your interests. But, if you are interested in the social power of advertising—the impact of advertising on society—then that is the wrong question.

The right question would ask about the *cultural* role of advertising, not its marketing role. Culture is the place and space where a society tells stories about itself, where values are articulated and expressed, where notions of good and evil, of morality and immorality, are defined. In our culture it is the stories of advertising that dominate the spaces that mediate this function. If human beings are essentially a storytelling species, then to study advertising is to examine the central storytelling mechanism of our society. The correct question to ask from this perspective, is not whether particular ads sell the products they are hawking, but what are the consistent stories that advertising spins as a whole about what is important in the world, about how to behave, about what is good and bad. Indeed, it is to ask what values does advertising consistently push.

HAPPINESS

Every society has to tell a story about happiness, about how individuals can satisfy themselves and feel both subjectively and objectively good. The cultural system of advertising gives a very specific answer to that question for our society. *The way to happiness and satisfaction is through the consumption of objects through the marketplace.* Commodities will make us happy. * * * In one very [important sense] that is the consistent and explicit message of every single message within the system of market communication.

Neither the fact of advertising's colonization of the horizons of imagination or the pushing of a story about the centrality of goods to human satisfaction should surprise us. The immense collection of goods have to be consumed (and even more goods produced) and the story that is used to ensure this function is to equate goods with happiness. Insiders to the system have recognized this obvious fact for many years. Retail analyst Victor Liebow said, just after the second world war:

Our enormously productive economy ... demands that we make consumption our way of life, that we convert the buying and the selling of goods into rituals, that we seek our spiritual satisfaction, our ego satisfaction in commodities ... We need things consumed, burned up, worn out, replaced, and discarded at an ever increasing rate. * * *

So economic growth is justified not simply on the basis that it will provide employment (after all a host of alternative non-productive activities could also provide that) but because it will give us access to more things that will make us happy. This rationale for the existing system of ever-increasing production is told by advertising in the most compelling form possible. In fact it is this story, that human satisfaction is intimately connected to the provisions of the market, to economic growth, that is the major motivating force for social change as we start the 21st century.

The social upheavals of eastern Europe were pushed by this vision. As Gloria Steinhem described the East German transformation: "First we have a revolution then we go shopping." * * * The attractions of this vision in the Third World are not difficult to discern. When your reality is empty stomachs and empty shelves, no wonder the marketplace appears as the panacea for your problems. When your reality is hunger and despair it should not be surprising that the seductive images of desire and abundance emanating from the advertising system should be so influential in thinking about social and economic policy. Indeed not only happiness but political freedom itself is made possible by access to the immense collection of commodities. These are very powerful stories that equate happiness and freedom with consumption—and advertising is the main propaganda arm of this view.

The question that we need to pose at this stage (that is almost never asked) is, "Is it true?" Does happiness come from material things? Do we get happier as a society as we get richer, as our standard of living increases, as we have more access to the immense collection of objects? Obviously these are complex issues, but the general answer to these questions is "no."

        * * *

In a series of surveys conducted in the United States starting in 1945 (labeled "the happiness surveys") researchers sought to examine the link between material wealth and subjective happiness, and concluded that, when examined both cross-culturally as well as historically in one society, there is a very *weak* correlation. Why should this be so?

When we examine this process more closely the conclusions appear to be less surprising than our intuitive perspective might suggest. In another series of surveys (the "quality of life surveys") people were asked about the kinds of things that are important to them—about what would constitute a good quality of life. The findings of this line of research indicate that if the elements of satisfaction were [divided up] into social values (love, family, friends) and material values (economic security and success) the former outranks the latter in terms of importance. What people say they really want out of life is: autonomy and control of life; good self-esteem; warm family relationships; tension-free leisure time; close and intimate friends; as well as romance and love. This is not to say that material values are not important. They form a necessary component of a good quality of life. But above a certain level of poverty and comfort, material things stop giving us the kind of satisfaction that the magical world of advertising insists they can deliver.

These conclusion[s] point to one of the great ironies of the market system. The market is good at providing those things that can be bought and sold and it pushed us—via advertising—in that direction. But the real sources of happiness—social relationships—are outside the capability of the marketplace to provide. The marketplace cannot provide love, it cannot provide real friendships, it cannot provide sociability. It can provide other material things and services—but they are not what makes us happy.

The advertising industry has known this since at least the 1920s and in fact have stopped trying to sell us things based on their material qualities alone. If we examine the advertising of the end of the 19th and first years of the 20th century, we would see that advertising talked a lot about the properties of commodities—what they did, how well they did it, etc. But starting in the 1920s advertising shifts to talking about the relationship of objects to the social life of people. It starts to connect commodities (the things they have to sell) with the powerful images of a deeply desired social life that people say they want.

No wonder then that advertising is so attractive to us, so powerful, so seductive. What it offers us are images of the real sources of human happiness—family life, romance and love, sexuality and pleasure, friendship and sociability, leisure and relaxation, independence and control of life. That is why advertising is so powerful, that is what is real about it. The cruel illusion of advertising however is in the way that it links those qualities to a place that by definition cannot provide it—the market and the immense collection of commodities. The falsity of advertising is not in the appeals it makes (which are very real) but in the answers it provides. We want love and friendship and sexuality—and advertising points the way to it through objects.

To reject or criticize advertising as false and manipulative misses the point. Ad executive Jerry Goodis puts it this way: "Advertising doesn't mirror how people are acting but how they are dreaming." * * * It taps into our real emotions and repackages them back to us connected to the world of things. What advertising really reflects in that sense is the dreamlife of the culture. Even saying this however simplifies a deeper process because advertisers do more than mirror our dreamlife—they help to create it. They translate our desires (for love, for family, for friendship, for adventure, for sex) into our dreams. Advertising is like a fantasy factory, taking our desire for human social contact and reconceiving it, reconceptualizing it, connecting it with the world of commodities and then translating into a form that can be communicated.

The great irony is that as advertising does this it draws us further away from what really has the capacity to satisfy us (meaningful human contact and relationships) to what does not (material things). In that sense advertising reduces our capacity to become happy by pushing us, cajoling us, to carry on in the direction of things. If we really wanted to create a world that reflected our desires then the consumer culture would not be it. It would look very different—a society that stressed and built the institutions that would foster social relationships, rather than endless material accumulation.

Advertising's role in channeling us in these fruitless directions is profound. In one sense, its function is [analogous] to the drug pusher on the street corner. As we try and break our addiction to things it is there, constantly offering us another "hit." By persistently pushing the idea of the good life being connected to products, and by colonizing every nook and cranny of the culture where alternative ideas could be raised, advertising is an important part of the creation of what Tibor Scitovsky * * * calls "the joyless economy." The great political challenge that emerges from this analysis is how to connect our real desires to a truly human world, rather than the dead world of the "immense collection of commodities."

"THERE IS NO SUCH THING AS 'SOCIETY'"

A culture dominated by commercial messages that tells individuals that the way to happiness is through consuming objects bought in the marketplace gives a very particular answer to the question of "what is society?"— what is it that binds us together in some kind of collective way, what concerns or interests do we share? In fact, Margaret Thatcher, the former conservative British Prime Minister, gave the most succinct answer to this question from the viewpoint of the market. In perhaps her most (in)famous quote she announced: "There is no such thing as 'society'. There are just individuals and their families." According to Mrs. Thatcher, there is nothing solid we can call society—no group values, no collective interests— society is just a bunch of individuals acting on their own.

Indeed this is precisely how advertising talks to us. It addresses us not as members of society talking about collective issues, but as *individuals*. It talks about our individual needs and desires. It does not talk about those things we have to negotiate collectively, such as poverty, healthcare, housing and the homeless, the environment, etc.

The market appeals to the worst in us (greed, selfishness) and discourages what is the best about us (compassion, caring, and generosity).

Again this should not surprise us. In those societies where the marketplace dominates then what will be stressed is what the marketplace can deliver—and advertising is the main voice of the marketplace—so discussions of collective issues are pushed to the margins of the culture. They are not there in the center of the main system of communication that exists in the society. It is no accident that politically the market vision associated with neo-conservatives has come to dominate at exactly that time when advertising has been pushing the same values into every available space in the culture. The widespread disillusionment with "government" (and hence with thinking about issues in a collective manner) has found extremely fertile ground in the fields of commercial culture.

Unfortunately, we are now in a situation, both globally and domestically, where solutions to pressing nuclear and environmental problems will have to take a *collective* form. The marketplace cannot deal with the problems that face us at the turn of the millennium. For example it cannot deal with the threat of nuclear extermination that is still with us in the post-Cold War age. It cannot deal with global warming, the erosion of the ozone layer, or the depletion of our non-renewable resources. The effects of the way we do "business" are no longer localized, they are now global, and we will have to have international and collective ways of dealing with them. Individual action will not be enough. As the environmentalist slogan puts it "we all live downstream now."

Domestically, how do we find a way to tackle issues such as the nightmares of our inner cities, the ravages of poverty, the neglect of healthcare for the most vulnerable section of the population? How can we find a way to talk realistically and passionately of such problems within a culture where the central message is "don't worry, be happy." As Barbara Ehrenreich says:

> Television commercials offer solutions to hundreds of problems we didn't even know we had—from 'morning mouth' to shampoo build-up—but nowhere in the consumer culture do we find anyone offering us such mundane necessities as affordable health insurance, childcare, housing, or higher education. The flip side of the consumer spectacle ... is the starved and impoverished public sector. We have Teenage Mutant Ninja Turtles, but no way to feed and educate the one-fifth of American children who are growing up in poverty. We have dozens of varieties of breakfast cereal, and no help for the hungry. * * *

In that sense, advertising systematically relegates discussion of key societal issues to the peripheries of the culture and talks in powerful ways instead of individual desire, fantasy, pleasure and comfort.

Partly this is because of advertising's *monopolization* of cultural life. There is no space left for different types of discussion, no space at the center of the society where alternative values could be expressed. But it is also connected to the failure of those who care about collective issues to create alternative visions that can compete in any way with the commercial vision. The major alternatives offered to date have been a gray and dismal stateism. This occurred not only in the western societies but also in the former so called "socialist" societies of eastern Europe. These repressive societies never found a way to connect to people in any kind of pleasurable way, relegating issues of pleasure and individual expression to the non-essential and distracting aspects of social life. This indeed was the core of the failure of Communism in Eastern Europe. As Ehrenreich reminds us, not only was it unable to deliver the material goods, but it was unable to create a fully human "ideological retort to the powerful seductive messages of the capitalist consumer culture." * * * The problems are no less severe domestically:

> Everything enticing and appealing is located in the (thoroughly private) consumer spectacle. In contrast, the public sector looms as a realm devoid of erotic promise—the home of the IRS, the DMV, and other irritating, intrusive bureaucracies. Thus, though everyone wants national health insurance, and parental leave, few are moved to wage political struggles for them. 'Necessity' is not enough; we may have to find a way to glamorize the possibility of an activist public sector, and to glamorize the possibility of public activism. * * *

The imperative task for those who want to stress a different set of values is to make the struggle for social change fun and sexy. By that I do not mean that we have to use images of sexuality, but that we have to find a way of thinking about the struggle against poverty, against homelessness, for healthcare and child-care, to protect the environment, in terms of *pleasure and fun and happiness*.

To make this glamorization of collective issues possible will require that the present commercial monopoly of the channels of communication be broken in favor of a more democratic access where difficult discussion of important and relevant issues may be possible. While the situation may appear hopeless we should remind ourselves of how important capitalism deems its monopoly of the imagination to be. The campaigns of successive United States government against the Cuban revolution, and the obsession of our national security state with the Sandinista revolution in Nicaragua in the 1980s, demonstrates the importance that capitalism places on smashing the alternative model. Even as the United States government continues to support the most vicious, barbarous, brutal and murderous regimes around the world, it takes explicit aim at those governments that have tried to redistribute wealth to the most needy—who have been prioritized collective values over the values of selfishness and greed. The monopoly of the vision is vital and capitalism knows it.

THE END OF THE WORLD AS WE KNOW IT

The consumer vision that is pushed by advertising and which is conquering the world is based fundamentally, as I argued before, on a notion of *economic growth*. Growth requires resources (both raw materials and energy) and there is a broad consensus among environmental scholars that the earth cannot sustain past levels of expansion based upon resource-intensive modes of economic activity, especially as more and more nations struggle to join the feeding trough.

The environmental crisis is complex and multilayered, cutting across both production and consumption issues. For instance just in terms of resource depletion, we know that we are rapidly exhausting what the earth can offer and that if the present growth and consumption trends continued unchecked, the limits to growth on the planet will be reached sometime within the next century. Industrial production uses up resources and energy at a rate that had never before even been imagined. Since 1950 the world's population has used up more of the earth's resources than all the generations that came before. * * * In 50 years we have matched the use of thousands of years. The west and especially Americans have used the most of these resources so we have a special responsibility for the approaching crisis. In another hundred years we will have exhausted the planet.

But even more than that even, we will have done irreparable damage to the environment on which we depend for everything. As environmental activist Barry Commoner says:

> The environment makes up a huge, enormously complex living machine that forms a thin dynamic layer on the earth's surface, and every human activity depends on the integrity and proper functioning of this machine.... This machine is our biological capital, the basic apparatus on which our total productivity depends. If we destroy it, our most advanced technology will become useless and any economic and political system that depends on it will flounder. The environmental crisis is a signal of the approaching catastrophe. * * *

The clearest indication of the way in which we produce is having an effect on the eco-sphere of the planet is the depletion of the ozone layer, which has dramatically increased the amount of ultraviolet radiation that is damaging or lethal to many life forms on the planet. In 1985 scientists discovered the existence of a huge hole in the ozone layer over the South Pole that is the size of the United States illustrating how the activities of humans are changing the very make-up of the earth. In his book *The End of Nature* Bill McKibben reminds us that "we have done this ourselves.... by driving our cars, building our factories, cutting down our forests, turning on air conditioners." * * * He writes that the history of the world is full of the most incredible events that changed the way we lived, but they are all dwarfed by what we have accomplished in the last 50 years.

> Man's efforts, even at their mightiest, were tiny compared with the size of the planet—the Roman Empire meant nothing to the Artic or the Amazon. But now, the way of life of one part of the world in one half-century is altering every inch and every hour of the globe.

The situation is so bad that the scientific community is desperately trying to get the attention of the rest of us to wake up to the danger. The Union of Concerned Scientists (representing 1700 of the world's leading scientists, including a majority of Nobel laureates in the sciences) recently issued this appeal:

> Human beings and the natural world are on a collision course. Human activities inflict harsh and irreversible damage on the environment and on critical resources. If not checked, many of our current practices put at serious risk the future that we wish for human society and the plant and animal kingdoms, and may so alter the living world that it will be unable to sustain life in the manner we know. Fundamental changes are urgent if we are to avoid the collision our present course will bring.

It is important to avoid the prediction of immediate catastrophe. We have already done a lot of damage but the real environmental crisis will not hit until some time in the middle of the next century. However to avoid that catastrophe we have to take action *now*. We have to put in place the steps that will save us in 70 years time.

The metaphor that best describes the task before us is of an oil tanker heading for a crash on the shore. Because of its momentum and size, to avoid crashing the oil tanker has to start turning well before it reaches the coast, anticipating [its] own momentum. If it starts turning too late it will smash into the coast. That is where the consumer society is right now. We have to make fundamental changes in the way we organize ourselves, in what we stress in our economy, if [we] want to avoid the catastrophe in 70 years time. We have to take action *now*.

In that sense the present generation has a unique responsibility in human history. It is literally up to us to save the world, to make the changes we need to make. If we do not, we will be in barbarism and savagery towards each other in 70 years time. We have to make short-term sacrifices. We have to give up [our non-essential appliances]. We especially have to rethink our relationship to the car. We have to make *real* changes—not just recycling but fundamental changes in how we live and produce. And we cannot do this individually, we have to do it collectively. We have to find the political will somehow to do this—and we may even be dead when its real effects will be felt. The vital issue is "how do we identify with that generation in the next century?" As the political philosopher Robert Heilbroner says:

> A crucial problem for the world of the future will be a concern for generations to come. Where will such concern arise? ... Contemporary industrial man, his appetite for the present whetted by the values of a high-consumption society and his attitude toward the future influenced by the prevailing canons of self-concern, has but a limited motivation to form such bonds. There are many who would sacrifice much for their children; fewer would do so for their grandchildren. * * *

Forming such bonds will be made even more difficult within our current context that stresses individual (not social) needs and the immediate situation (not the long-term). The advertising system will form *the ground* on which we think about the future of the human race, and there is nothing there that should give us any hope for the development of such a perspective. The time-frame of advertising is very short-term. It does not encourage us to think beyond the immediacy of present sensual experience. Indeed it may well be the case that as the advertising environment gets more and more crowded, with more and more of what advertisers label as "noise" threatening to drown out individual messages, the appeal will be made to levels of experience that cut through clutter, appealing immediately and deeply to very emotional states. Striking emotional imagery that grabs the "gut" instantly leaves no room for thinking about anything. Sexual imagery, especially in the age of AIDS where sex is being connected to death, will need to become even more powerful and immediate, to overcome any possible negative associations—indeed to remove us from the world of connotation and meaning construed *cognitively*. The value of a collective social future is one that does not, and will not, find expression within our commercially dominated culture. Indeed the prevailing values provide no incentive to develop bonds with future generations and there is a real sense of nihilism and despair about the future, and a closing of ranks against the outside.

IMAGINING A DIFFERENT FUTURE

Over a 100 years ago, Marx observed that there were two directions that capitalism could take: towards a democratic "socialism" or towards a brutal "barbarism". Both long-term and recent evidence would seem to indicate that the latter is where we are headed, unless alternative values quickly come to the fore.

Many people thought that the environmental crisis would be the linchpin for the lessening of international tensions as we recognized our interdependence and our collective security and future. But as the Persian Gulf War made clear, the New World Order will be based upon a struggle for scarce resources. Before the propaganda rationale shifted to the "struggle for freedom and democracy," George Bush reminded the American people that the troops were being dispatched to the Gulf to protect the resources that make possible "our way of life." An automobile culture and commodity-based culture such as ours is reliant upon sources of cheap oil. And if the cost of that is 100,000 dead Iraquis, well so be it. In such a scenario the peoples of the Third World will be seen as enemies who are making unreasonable claims on "our" resources. The future and the Third World can wait. Our commercial dominated cultural discourse reminds us powerfully everyday, we need *ours* and we need it *now*. In that sense the Gulf War is a preview of what is to come. As the world runs out of resources, the most powerful military sources will use that might to ensure access.

The destructive aspects of capitalism (its short-term nature, its denial of collective values, its stress on the material life), are starting to be recognized by some people who have made their fortunes through the market. The billionaire turned philanthropist George Soros * * * talks about what he calls "the capitalist threat"—and culturally speaking, advertising is the main voice of that threat. To the extent that it pushes us towards material things for satisfaction and away from the construction of social relationships, it pushes us down the road to increased economic production that is driving the coming environmental catastrophe. To the extent that it talks about our individual and private needs, it pushes discussion about collective issues to the margins. To the extent that it talks about the present only, it makes thinking about the future difficult. To the extent that it does all these things, then advertising becomes one of the major obstacles to our survival as a species.

Getting out of this situation, coming up with new ways to look at the world, will require enormous work, and one response may just be to enjoy the end of the world—one last great fling, the party to end all parties. The alternative response, to change the situation, to work for humane, collective long-term values, will require an effort of the most immense kind.

And there is evidence to be hopeful about the results of such an attempt. It is important to stress that creating and maintaining the present structure of the consumer culture takes enormous work and effort. The reason consumer ways of looking at the world predominate is because there are billions of dollars being spent on it every single day. The consumer culture is not simply erected and then forgotten. It has to be held in place by the activities of the ad industry, and increasingly the activities of the public relations industry. Capitalism has to try really hard to convince us about the value of the commercial vision. In some senses consumer capitalism is a house of cards, held together in a fragile way by immense effort, and it could just as soon melt away as hold together. It will depend if there are viable alternatives that will motivate people to believe in a different future, if there are other ideas as pleasurable, as powerful, as fun, as passionate with which people can identify.

I am reminded here of the work of Antonio Gramsci who coined the famous phrase, "pessimism of the intellect, optimism of the will." "Pessimism of the intellect" means recognizing the reality of our present circumstances, analyzing the vast forces arrayed against us, but insisting on the possibilities and the moral desirability of social change—that is "the optimism of the will," believing in human values that will be the inspiration for us to struggle for our survival

I do not want to be too Pollyannaish about the possibilities of social change. It is not just collective values that need to be struggled for, but collective values that recognize individual rights and individual creativity. There are many *repressive* collective movements already in existence—from our own home-grown Christian fundamentalists to the Islamic zealots of the Taliban in Afghanistan. The task is not easy. It means balancing and integrating different views of the world. As Ehrenreich writes:

> Can we envision a society which values—not "collectivity" with its dreary implications of conformity—but what I can only think to call *conviviality*, which could, potentially, be built right into the social infrastructure with opportunities, at all levels for rewarding, democratic participation? Can we envision a society that does not dismiss individualism, but truly values individual creative expression—including dissidence, debate, nonconformity, artistic experimentation, and in the larger sense, adventure ... the project remains what it has always been: to replace the consumer culture with a genuinely *human* culture.
> * * *

The stakes are simply too high for us not to deal with the real and pressing problems that face [us as a] species—finding a progressive and humane collective solution to the global crisis and ensuring for our children and future generations a world fit for truly human habitation.

———

Uneasy Ryder! Jury Finds Winona Guilty in Shoplift Case

N.Y. Daily News, Nov. 6, 2002.

THE ASSOCIATED PRESS

BEVERLY HILLS, Calif.—Actress Winona Ryder was convicted Wednesday of stealing $5,500 worth of high-fashion merchandise from Saks Fifth Avenue last year.

The jury found the star of "Girl, Interrupted" guilty of felony grand theft and vandalism but cleared her of burglary.

She faces anywhere from probation to three years in prison. Sentencing is scheduled for Dec. 6.

Ryder showed no emotion as the verdict was announced. She kept her eyes on the jurors as they were asked whether the verdicts were accurate. They said yes.

She whispered to her attorney, Mark Geragos, took a drink of water and looked briefly toward her supporters in the audience.

The jury reached the verdict after 5 1/2 hours of deliberations over two days. The one count on which she was acquitted required a specific intent to go into the store to steal. District attorney's spokeswoman Sandi Gibbons said jurors often believe burglary is a crime of breaking and entering, but it does not require those circumstances.

"We're gratified with the verdicts," Gibbons added.

Ryder, a two-time Oscar nominee who marked her 31st birthday in the defendant's chair, was arrested Dec. 12 as she left the Beverly Hills store, her arms filled with packages.

Ryder did not testify during the two-week trial.

Prosecutors said Ryder came to Saks with larceny on her mind, bringing shopping bags, a garment bag and scissors to snip security tags off items.

"She came, she stole, she left. End of story," Deputy District Attorney Ann Rundle said. "Nowhere does it say people steal because they have to. People steal out of greed, envy, spite, because it's there or for the thrill."

Jurors were shown videotape of Ryder moving through the store laden with goods, and Saks security workers testified that after she was detained she apologetically told them a director had told her to shoplift to prepare for a movie role.

Her attorney denounced the security guards as liars even before the trial began.

At the start of her shopping trip, she paid more than $3,000 for a jacket and two blouses. The defense said Ryder believed the store would keep her account "open" while she shopped and would charge her later. But there was no evidence of an account.

In closing arguments Monday, Geragos suggested that the store, trying to avoid a lawsuit, conspired with employees to invent a story that would make Ryder appear guilty.

Geragos ridiculed the charge that Ryder vandalized merchandise by cutting holes in clothes when removing the security tags.

"This woman is known for her fashion sense," he said. "Was she going to start a new line of 'Winona wear' with holes in it?"

He carried a hair bow, which she allegedly had stolen, over to her, placed it on her head and said: "Can anyone see Ms. Ryder with this on top of her head? Does that make sense?"

Settlement talks between the defense and prosecution failed, but just before trial the district attorney's office agreed to dismiss a drug charge after a doctor said he had given her two pills found in her possession when she was arrested.

The 12-member jury included several people with Hollywood connections, including producer Peter Guber, who presided over Sony Entertainment Pictures when three successful Ryder films were made there.

Ryder has made some two-dozen films since 1986, including "Beetlejuice," "Heathers," "Mermaids," "Little Women," "The Age of Innocence," "Edward Scissorhands," "Bram Stoker's Dracula," "Reality Bites" and "Mr. Deeds."

She received her Academy Award nominations for "Little Women" (best actress) and for "The Age of Innocence" (supporting actress).

Ryder was raised by parents who were part of the counterculture revolution in the 1960s. Her godfather was LSD guru Timothy Leary.

In 1993, Ryder posted a $200,000 reward in the kidnap-murder case of a 12-year-old girl, Polly Klaas, in Petaluma, Calif., where the actress grew up. When Ryder was charged with shoplifting, Polly's father, Mark, came to legal proceedings to support her.

In recent years, Ryder has been featured frequently in fashion magazines. Her delicate beauty and waiflike persona were on display at the trial along with a wardrobe of appropriate trial clothes—dark sweaters and skirts, soft dresses and, on the climactic day of closing arguments, a cream silk suit with a pleated skirt and short jacket.

NOTES AND QUESTIONS

1. Consumerism and capitalism. Can capitalism survive without ever-expanding production and ever-expanding consumer demand? William Greider argues that a global crisis is on the way:

> The economic luxury hidden in the capitalist process is space—capitalism's ability to move on and re-create itself, abandoning the old for the new, creating and destroying production, while trailing a broad flume

of ruined natural assets in its wake. Because globalization has narrowed distances, the luxury has diminished visibly. It is now possible for people to glimpse what was always true: the wasteful nature of their own prosperity. So long as the consequences could be kept afar from the beneficiaries, no one had much incentive—neither producers nor consumers—to face the collective implications.

The brilliant possibility of "one world" is the emerging recognition that there is not going to be anyplace to hide. If Thailand becomes rich, where will it ship its toxic wastes? To Vietnam? To Africa? When every nation has industrialized, will they all dump their refuse in the ocean, as the so-called civilized societies now do? If the rain forests are shrinking, will someone invent machines to purify the air and generate rainfall? When the automobile conquers China, will the world be choking on the polluted atmosphere?

The economic dilemma embedded in these questions revolves around price: global producers are caught up in the desperate competition to reduce costs and prices to hold on to market share, yet the earth's imperative asks the economic system to achieve the opposite—to raise the price of goods so that consumers will begin paying the real production costs of their consumption. The marketplace (including most consumers) is naturally hostile to that imperative since it puts enterprises at immediate disadvantage unless all their competitors in the global system are required to accept the same pricing standards. There is at present no mechanism to achieve such harmony of purpose even if everyone agreed on its wisdom.

The social dilemma grows out of the same facts: If the collective interest requires a transformation of the industrial system's values, the poor will likely be injured more profoundly than the rich since they are the new entrants and least able to pay higher prices for consumption. The developing nations, after all, are emulating the rapacious practices they learned from the advanced economies and are understandably skeptical when high-minded reformers urge them not to repeat the same environmental mistakes—"mistakes" that have made Americans and Europeans quite wealthy. The environmental ethic proposes to alter the basic rules of capitalism at the very moment when some impoverished former colonies are at last enjoying the action.

WILLIAM GREIDER, ONE WORLD, READY OR NOT: THE MANIC LOGIC OF GLOBAL CAPITALISM 446–47 (1997).

2. Consumerism and fantasy. Can exhortations like Jhally's and Greider's stand up against the entwining of goods, the good life, fantasies, and dreams?

COPYRIGHT PERMISSIONS & FURTHER ACKNOWLEDGMENTS

Professors Jordan and Harris, along with Foundation Press, would like to gratefully acknowledge the authors and copyright holders of the following works, who permitted their inclusion in this work:

Ackerman, Bruce & Alstott, Anne, *Your Stake in America*, 41 ARIZ. L. REV. 249, 249–261 (1999). Copyright © 1999 by Bruce Ackerman, Ann Alstott and the Arizona Law Review. Reprinted with permission of the Arizona Law Review in the format Textbook via the Copyright Clearance Center.

Ackerman, Frank & Heinzerling, Lisa, *Priceless: On Knowing the Price of Everything and the Value of Nothing* 35–40 (2004). Copyright © 2003 *Priceless: On Knowing the Price of Everything and the Value of Nothing* by Frank Ackerman and Lisa Heinzerling. Reprinted by permission of The New Press. www.thenewpress.com.

Associated Press, *Uneasy Rider! Jury Finds Wynona Guilty in Shoplift Case*, N.Y. DAILY NEWS, Nov. 6, 2002. Copyright © 2002 by the Associated Press. Reprinted by permission.

Averitt, Neil W. & Lande, Robert H., *Consumer Sovereignty: A Unified Theory of Antitrust and Consumer Protection Law*, 65 ANTITRUST L.J. 713 (1997). Copyright © 1997 by the Antitrust Law Journal. Reprinted by permission.

Ayres, Ian, *Pervasive Prejudice? Unconventional Evidence of Race and Gender Discrimination* 3–7 (2001). Copyright © 2001 by Ian Ayres and the University of Chicago Press. Reprinted by permission.

Benkler, Yachai, *Coase's Penguin, Or, Linux and the Nature of the Firm*, 112 YALE L.J. 369 (2002). Reprinted by permission of The Yale Law Journal Company and William S. Hein from The Yale Law Journal, Vol. 112, pages 369–446. Copyright © 2003 by Yochai Benkler. This Article is released under the Public Library of Science Open–Access and the Creative Commons Attribution License.

Bernstein, Anita, *Whatever Happened to Law and Economics*, 64 MD. L. REV. 101 (2005) *available at* http://law.bepress.com/emorylwps/papers/art2. Copyright © 2005 Anita Bernstein and the Maryland Law Review. Reprinted by permission of Anita Bernstein.

Bernstein, Michael A., *A Perilous Progress: Economists and Public Purpose in Twentieth Century America* 45–46 (2001). Copyright © 2001 Princeton University Press. Reprinted by permission of Princeton University Press.

Carbado, Devon W. & Gulati, Mitu, *The Law and Economics of Critical Race Theory*, 112 YALE L.J. 1757, 1789–93, 1795–96, 1797–99, 1801–14 (2003) (book review). Reprinted by permission of The Yale Law Journal Company and William S. Hein from The Yale Law Journal, Vol. 112, pages

INDEX

539

†

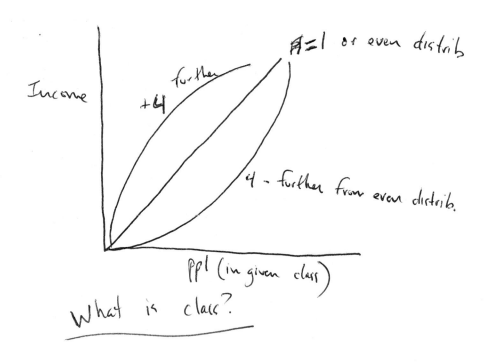

Income

+4 further

= 1 or even distrib

4 - further from even distrib.

ppl (in given class)

What is class?